Global Conceptualism: Points of Origin 1950s–1980s

Global Conceptualism: Points of Origin 1950s–1980s

Foreword by
Luis Camnitzer
Jane Farver
Rachel Weiss

Introduction by
Stephen Bann

Essays by
László Beke
Okwui Enwezor
Gao Minglu
Claude Gintz
Apinan Poshyananda
Mari Carmen Ramírez
Terry Smith
Reiko Tomii, *in cooperation with* Chiba Shigeo
Margarita Tupitsyn
Sung Wan-kyung
Peter Wollen

Queens Museum of Art, New York

This publication has been prepared to accompany the exhibition *Global Conceptualism: Points of Origin, 1950s–1980s*, organized by the Queens Museum of Art

Exhibition Tour
Queens Museum of Art, New York, April 28–August 29, 1999
Walker Art Center, Minneapolis, December 19, 1999–March 5, 2000
Miami Art Museum, Miami, September 15 – November 26, 2000

Global Conceptualism: Points of Origin, 1950s–1980s is sponsored by AT&T. Major support is also provided by the Rockefeller Foundation, the Andy Warhol Foundation for the Visual Arts, and the Lannan Foundation. Additional funding is from the Peter Norton Family Foundation, Korea Foundation, Trust for Mutual Understanding, The Japan Foundation, Asian Cultural Council, Institut für Auslandsbeziehungen, Shiseido Co., Ltd., and the British Council. The National Endowment for the Arts, New York State Council on the Arts, and New York Council for the Humanities, a state program of the National Endowment for the Humanities, provided generous support.

QMA

Queens Museum of Art
The New York City Building
Flushing Meadows Corona Park
Queens, New York 11368

The Queens Museum of Art is housed in the New York City Building which is owned by the City of New York. With the assistance of Queens Borough President Claire Shulman and the New York City Council, the Museum is supported in part by public funds from the New York City Department of Cultural Affairs. Additional funding is provided by the New York State Legislature and the New York State Council on the Arts.

Edited by Philomena Mariani
Designed by Linda Florio Design

Printed and bound in Spain by Artes Graficas Toledo
D.L.TO-122–1999
Paper: Creator silk
Typefont: Meta

Available through D.A.P./Distributed Art Publishers
155 Sixth Avenue, 2nd Floor, New York, N.Y. 10013
Tel: (212) 627-1999 Fax: (212) 627-9484.

ISBN 0-960-45149-8
Library of Congress no. 97-075938

Contents

Acknowledgments

Global Conceptualism: Points of Origin, 1950s–1980s is a bold and groundbreaking attempt to document conceptualism in art as a worldwide phenomenon originating independently in many places in response to specific local conditions. The exhibition consists of more than 240 works of art by over 135 artists from 30 countries. In keeping with its theme of presenting multiple perspectives, *Global Conceptualism* is the result of a curatorial collaboration involving many individuals.

Jane Farver, Director of Exhibitions at the Queens Museum of Art, and project directors Luis Camnitzer and Rachel Weiss conceived and directed this project together. We thank them for their leadership in assembling an international team of essayists and curators, and for their work in bringing this exhibition and accompanying catalogue to fruition. We recognize the international group of curators/essayists consisting of László Beke(Eastern Europe), Chiba Shigeo and Reiko Tomii (Japan), Okwui Enwezor (Africa), Gao Minglu (Mainland China, Taiwan, Hong Kong), Claude Gintz (Western Europe), Mari Carmen Ramírez (Latin America), Margarita Tupitsyn (Soviet Union), Terry Smith (Australia, New Zealand), Sung Wan-kyung (South Korea), and Peter Wollen (North America) for their contributions in shaping the exhibition and catalogue.

We are grateful to Stephen Bann and Apinan Poshyananda for their thoughtful catalogue essays. In its earliest stages, the project benefited from the advice of Iaroslava Boubnova, Graciela Carnevale, Michael Corris, Henry Drewal, Geeta Kapur, Anne Rorimer, Alla Rosenfeld, Stephen Snoddy, Cathy de Zegher, and others. We also appreciate assistance by Jon Hendricks, André Magnin, Susanna Singer, and Kunstverein München, as well as Randall Magro, UBS Audio Visual, University of Sydney, and BLOWUP Imaging and Max Drummond, MACRAY Specialized Services, Ltd., also of Sydney.

The works for this exhibition have come to the Museum from several continents through the generosity of many artists, lenders, and contributors. We thank AT&T for their sponsorship of this project. The Rockefeller Foundation, the Andy Warhol Foundation for the Visual Arts, and the Lannan Foundation provided major support. Additional funding was provided by the Peter Norton Family Foundation, the Korea Foundation, Trust for Mutual Understanding, The Japan Foundation, Asian Cultural Council, Institut für Auslandsbeziehungen, Shiseido Co., Ltd., and the British Council. The National Endowment for the Arts, the New York State Council on the Arts, and the New York Council for the Humanities have also been generous in their support.

The planning for *Global Conceptualism* was significantly advanced by a conference of the curatorial group held at Bard College in 1998; we appreciate the assistance and hospitality provided by Norton Batkin and his staff at Bard. Sondra Farganis, Kathy Goncharov, Jonathan Veitch, Lynne Winters, and George Calderaro of the New School University have cooperated with the Museum to bring the exhibition's curators together again for a conceptualist art symposium at their institution while the exhibition is on view at the Museum. We appreciate the participation of Lucy Lippard and others in the symposium. Linda Weintraub and Robert Thill participated in the development of the exhibition's interpretive materials. The publication was enhanced by the expertise of designer Linda Florio and editor Philomena Mariani.

It is my pleasure to thank the Board of Trustees, the staff, and volunteers of the Queens Museum of Art for making all our programs possible. This project received the wholehearted support of the Museum's former director, Carma C. Fauntleroy. We recognize Jane Farver, Director of Exhibitions, and curatorial staff members Christina Yang, Skowmon Hastanan, William Valerio, Arnold Kanarvogel, Alvin Eng, and Paola Morsiani for the expertise and dedication they contributed toward the realization of this ambitious exhibition. Special thanks are extended to Assistant Registrar/Assistant Curator Hitomi Iwasaki for her tireless devotion to this project. The curatorial staff were ably assisted by interns and volunteers Mihee Ahn, Alexander Yao Alexander, Ben Borthwick, Rick Estevez, Sooyeon Kim, Georgia Lobacheff, Young Park, Evelyn Samuel, Hyun-Jin Shin, Mako Wakasa, Susan Wolman, and Zhang Zhaohui. We also wish to acknowledge the contributions of Robyn Love, Michael Langley, and Maureen Healey. Indeed, the planning, presentation, and associated interpretive programming of every exhibition involve the professional skills and commitment of the Museum's entire staff. We thank Curator of Education Sharon Vatsky, Controller Mary Brown, Director of Development Kerry McCarthy, Public Information Officer Robert Mahoney, Facilities Manager Louis Acquavita, Manager of Museum Services/Chief of Security Anthony Kemper, and the members of the Museum's Administration, Development, Education, Facilities, and Security Departments.

Marilyn L. Simon
Interim Executive Director

Foreword

Global Conceptualism: Points of Origin, 1950s–1980s

Luis Camnitzer
Jane Farver
and
Rachel Weiss

This exhibition traces the history of a key development in 20th-century art in which art's response to both its own traditions and to its immediate milieu shifted from a consideration of the object to that of the idea. This shift, with its inevitable destabilization of artistic convention, occurred in locations around the world in two relatively distinct waves of activity: the first, from the late 1950s to around 1973, the second from the mid-1970s to the end of the '80s. The emergence of conceptualist art also coincided with broadly destabilizing sociological and technological trends propelled by large historical forces, as the political, economic, and social landscapes of large parts of the world underwent significant, often traumatic, transition.

The first period was shaped in large part by the Cold War, with its bipolar tensions between communism and capitalism, and its relative political stasis. This postwar period also saw the rise of the "Third World" and the end of most colonial empires. Both developed capitalist countries and the Eastern bloc experienced a similar set of demographic and sociopolitical shifts: a steady migration of laborers from rural to urban areas; increased food production and access to education; major gains in communication and information technologies; pharmaceutical advances that contributed to the sexual revolution; a world boom in tourism. By the 1960s, however, it was also apparent that byproducts of this growth were ecological deterioration, growing economic inequality on the national and international level, an elaborate international divison of labor, colossal expenditures on the arms race, and another U.S. war in Asia.

In response, there was also a worldwide mobilization of student radicalism that peaked in 1968. While the actions of students, intellectuals, and artists involved in rebellions in Japan, the U.S., Western Europe, Mexico, Poland, Czechoslovakia, and Yugoslavia, had more cultural than political significance, they would in time motivate larger, less combustible groups of citizens. In Czechoslovakia, political and cultural agitation during the Prague Spring of 1968 precipitated a crackdown by Moscow. Although the Soviet Union would hold the socialist bloc together for another twenty years by threat of military force, this event marked the end of the Moscow-centered international communist movement. By 1973, further events—the oil crisis, the collapse of the Bretton Woods financial system, the loss of industrial jobs to developing countries, and the U.S. defeat in Vietnam—would help to bring about the end of this period of economic expansion. The first wave of conceptual, idea-based art that developed during this time in Japan, Western and Eastern Europe, Latin America, the U.S., Canada, and Australia, responded to and participated in these massive social and political transitions by calling into question the underlying ideas of art and its institutional systems. During the second period, from the mid-1970s through the end of the '80s, the deaths of Mao Zedong and Brezhnev hastened the changes in China and the Soviet Union that would ultimately end the Cold War. Although a number of Third World countries such as South Korea and Taiwan, and the city-states of Hong Kong and Singapore, experienced "economic miracles" and rose to First World status, the gap between rich and poor countries widened. Development in the NICs (newly industrialized countries) replicated the postwar patterns of those regions that had experienced the earlier boom. Staggering changes were prompted by the abandonment of rural agricultural economies, as millions moved to urban areas seeking employment in new industries. Few Third World countries escaped the experience of revolution, military takeover, or internal armed conflict. Accelerated education programs created huge numbers of students who could be easily mobilized; and where there was an absence of real politics and a free press, students, artists, and other intellectuals were often the only citizens who spoke on behalf of the people. As before, the need for an urgent response to social and political conditions encouraged artists in the Soviet Union, South Korea, China, and parts of Africa to abandon formalist or traditional art practices for conceptualist art.

While inevitably connected by a complex system of global linkages, these conceptualist movements were also clearly spurred by urgent local conditions and histories. It is important to emphasize that the reading of "globalism" that informs this project is a highly differentiated one, in which localities are linked in crucial ways but not subsumed into a homogenized set of circumstances and responses to them. We mean to denote a multicentered map with various points of origin in which local events are crucial determinants.

During both periods, conceptualism questioned the idea of art, not in the sense of negation (as in anti-art), but in order to enlarge and deepen the scope of what art could be. Art's role as catalyst, as stand-in for forbidden speech, as exemplification of systems of thought and belief, and as vehicle for dissent became central. The artwork underwent a shift from object to subject. This represented a change in function, purpose, and capability, a recasting of the object's status and meaning. The processes that came to signify conceptualist practice—a change in emphasis from the object to the idea; a prioritization of language over visuality; a critique of the institutions of art; and, in many cases, a consequent dematerialization of the artwork—were set in motion long before the anointing of Conceptual Art, but received such added emphasis and focus as to essentially redefine the nature of the activity.

It is important to delineate a clear distinction between *conceptual art* as a term used to denote an essentially formalist practice developed in the wake of minimalism, and *conceptualism*, which broke decisively from the historical dependence of art on physical form and its visual apperception. Conceptualism was a broader attitudinal expression that summarized a wide array of works and practices which, in radically reducing the role of the art object, reimagined the possibilities of art vis-á-vis the social, political, and economic realities within which it was being made. Its informality and affinity for collectivity made conceptualism attractive to those artists who yearned for a more direct engagement with the public during these intense, transformative periods. For them, the deemphasis—or dematerialization—of the object allowed artistic focus to move from the object to the conduct of art.

Over time the history of conceptual art has been assimilated by critics and historians into postminimalism, with its focus on materials, techniques, and style. However, even in its most mainstream appearances, conceptual art, while reductionist in form, has been among the most accommodating of art movements, open to disciplines as diverse as linguistics, systems theory, philosophy, sociology, ethics, logic, theater, history, political science, music, Eastern religions, and poetry. This interdisciplinarity, along with the characteristics noted above, give conceptualism its particular character and importance.

Dematerialization of the Art Object

The phenomenon of dematerialized art built on ideas introduced by Marcel Duchamp in 1913 when he signed an ordinary mass-produced object (the "readymade"), called it a work of art, and introduced it into the art world. Duchamp catalyzed an awareness of art as a system dominated by language and context, with meanings determined by consensus and use rather than by qualities inherent in a handmade object.

Much of the art produced in the West since World War II has been informed by this awareness. The dadaists and surrealists were influenced by Duchamp, as were the neodadaists of the 1950s. Many works created by these artists set the stage for conceptual art, as did the happenings of the 1960s and the multimedia events of Fluxus. Minimalism (also indebted to Duchamp in its use of readymade industrial forms, unmanipulated materials, factory fabrication, and mathematical systems) led many artists to conclude that painting and sculpture were indeed dead. This notion pushed them to eliminate or deemphasize the object and turn to language, mathematics, and facts about the known world and themselves for subject matter.

In a broader reading of conceptualism, however, "dematerialization" did not always mean the disappearance of the object, but a redefining of the role of the object as a carrier of meaning, the reinvestment of meaning in preexisting objects, and the attempt to eliminate the erosion of information. Dematerialization became a tool to approach artmaking in a way that was more adaptable to the interests of merging art and daily life—an increasingly important concern of postwar artmaking in many countries.

While much of the impulse toward dematerialization of the art object—or the "withdrawal of visuality," as Benjamin Buchloh has termed it—arose out of a critique of the commodity status of art, dematerialization was also a strategic move adopted by artists for a variety of other reasons. In countries with repressive political regimes, dematerialization broke the stranglehold of the state in relation to the display of art. What's more, "idea art" was easier to slip by the censors. It could be made without expensive art materials, and was an affordable way for artists on the geographic margins to participate in international venues. Exhibitions of dematerialized art could be organized quickly and informally among artists, circumventing both official and market structures and orthodoxies, and could be used to criticize these structures.

Much of Latin American conceptualism retained and even relied on tangible objects and the traditions supporting them. There, according to Mari Carmen Ramírez, conceptualism entailed a process in which, given the highly politicized environment, "ideology itself became the fundamental 'material reality' for the conceptual proposition."

Institutional Critique

Another definitive aspect of conceptualism is that of institutional critique which, generally speaking, arose out of a concern about the hidden yet determining structures of power and ideology within the art system. As deployed by mainstream Western artists, institutional critique was derived from an analysis of the conditions of late capitalism and of the problematic status of material goods. Minimalism's cool, industrial facture had already been seen by some critics as a reification of capitalism. Conceptual artists found further targets for attack in galleries, formalist art criticism, the collection, the market, and the tangible product. (These attacks were often seriously weakened by the fact that the artists, in spite of their ideological stance, still defined themselves within the gallery landscape.) This critique, however, was far from homogeneous, since the institutional landscape in different settings was diverse, mirroring the development of local economic and administrative structures.

The particular institution, or set of institutions, under scrutiny varied from place to place. In North America and Western Europe, this critique was often undertaken in a "dialectical" manner, to quote Claude Gintz, in that artists often positioned themselves both inside and outside the art institution. In Japan, theoretical postulations on conceptualism identified an "internal" institution, where the idea of "art" is most stringently located. In the case of some Eastern European artists, it was not art institutions per se but rather the ubiquity of institutions overall, and their agency on behalf of state ideology, that was seen as the problem.

Art as Protagonist

While much of the work produced in the early stages of conceptualism in the market centers remained tied to questions of art and the art system, in other areas conceptualism became the means for expanding art to function as an act of political engagement or resistance. Evasion of material substance made possible a kind of political dissent that was too dangerous to formulate in more concrete form. This conceptualism can only be properly understood in its local context, where it often fulfilled a precise consciousness-raising function.

Radical forms of conceptualism's art-into-life platform, guided by local political crisis, evolved into activist projects such as Tucumán Arde in Argentina or the Catalan Grup de Treball. The group orientation of much early conceptual work in Eastern Europe, meanwhile, related to "utopian notions of social organization," and was "intrinsically critical of statist regulation," according to László Beke. Such works offered models to the underground opposition, evident in the events of 1989–90. For many Latin American conceptualists included in this exhibition, a key project was refuting the subservient role the region suffered under U.S. imperialist influence. This, and the struggle against authoritarian regimes, galvanized much conceptualist work in Latin America.

In Japan, the artist collective Bikyōtō's slogan "Dismantle the power machine of art!" linked their activities to the student radicalism of 1968–69. In the mid-1980s, conceptualists in the Korean Min Joong movement engaged with political issues such as reunification and U.S. support of the Korean military regime through the design of protest rallies. In Mainland China, conceptualism was tied to the much broader movement opposing state ideology and an intrusive bureaucracy that culminated in the events at Tiananmen Square in June 1989.

The activist role prescribed by many conceptualisms played out differently in terms of the physical site of the works, in some cases (Latin America) prompting an appropriation of the public sphere, while in others (the Soviet Union and later Eastern Europe) a decisively, even hermetically private course of action was pursued. This question of public/private space closely paralleled, and had important ramifications for, the concept of audience that was operative for these artists. Western conceptualists theorized conceptualism as a way of displacing the specialist, privileged spectator who typified the conventional art audience. In Russia, conversely, work was propelled by the virtual lack of a public audience for nonconformist art. Meanwhile, Latin American conceptualists often aspired to address and mobilize the entire populace.

Language and Linguistic Orientation

Conceptualism's affinity for language and linguistic theory was based on the relatively more "elastic" nature of language as compared with objects, and the fact that language promised an open space where art could intersect with other fields and bring art and artists into a more vital, effective conversation with society. The use of language also gave artists a means to tackle the problem of official information by appropriating the space of media or replacing official information with their own analysis.

Language could sometimes seem to be merely a "negative material," a further consequence of minimalism, characteristic of what Joseph Kosuth would term Stylistic Conceptual Art. However, the instrumentalization of language could instead be a more important strategy in developing alternate meanings for art, and for the critical investigation and subversion) of the underlying premises of art. As Peter Wollen notes, conceptualism insisted on a megalanguage that was necessary in order for the work to be understood, "and that metalanguage was intrinsic to the work."

Conceptualism frequently replaced the object with discourse. Art not only used language, it became "languagelike," implying that art is a broadly cultural, rather than personally expressive, activity. For conceptualist artists, the use of language could be a way of reconstituting the work of art into an active—interactive—circuit. Unfortunately, despite such democratizing aspirations, the particular language employed by conceptualists was often obscure, elite, or otherwise not compelling to the intended audience, causing a short circuit.

In the traditional African context, as sketched by Okwui Enwezor, the presence of a visible object invariably signals the presence of another which cannot be perceived, but which becomes manifest through linguistic and performative interactions. Additionally, language—as used in Frédéric Bruly Bouabré's taxonomic Bété alphabet project—is a means particularly well suited to the reclamation and preservation of traditional culture.

Relation to Mainstream Conceptual Art

While Western conceptualism generally was derived from the notion of the autonomy of art, in locations such as Mainland China and Africa the absence of such a legacy meant conceptualism focused less on the problematic of the art system per se, and more broadly addressed issues between art and life which were also strongly attached to traditional cultural and/or religious foundations.

Different locales represented in this exhibition had a variety of responses to conceptual art as it was consecrated in New York and London. In Western Europe, the adoption of conceptualist modes had the connotation of acknowledging the new ascendance of the U.S. as the primary center of new art, and a reorientation to that development. Australian and South African artists connected to conceptualist ideas in London, then sought to transpose those ideas into the specificities of their own countries. Some Japanese art movements, including conceptualism, have roughly paralleled events in the West stylistically, but these parallels also emerged out of distinct local concerns that included postwar tensions with the U.S., a layering that has caused what Reiko Tomii terms an "entanglement" of local and international discourses. In Mainland China, dada and the precepts of Chan Buddhism were equally important in the formulation of a conceptualist approach, while in Taiwan an art-for-art's-sake tradition, along with growing dissent against a repressive political culture, established the framework for conceptualism.

It is also important to acknowledge that, for political reasons, artists in different locales held widely differing positions about their relation to the international mainstream: in some cases (e.g., Eastern Europe) artists were eager to be associated with the West, elsewhere (e.g., Latin America) such an association was anathema. It was probably more common for such feelings to be mixed, as they were in Australia.

Latin America, as Mari Carmen Ramírez points out, has been for centuries in a "dialogical" relationship to Euro–North American culture by virtue of the colonial experience and legacy. While there are shared referents, to conflate the two situations is a major distortion—it was and is a highly contested relation. The forces that created modernism or development in Latin America produced radically different effects from those in the colonialist and imperialist centers. This resulted in an "autonomous version—or even inversion" of conceptualism, as understood in the North.

Conceptualism's Legacy

Assessments of conceptualism's importance to contemporary artmaking vary, from those who feel it failed because it was quickly absorbed into art's commodity system, to others who feel that it actually reformed if not revolutionized important aspects of the idea of art. Many of the intellectual constructs of conceptualism have been integrated into the present understanding of an artwork, as evidenced by the focus of so many contemporary artists on idea, process, and experience; on political and social contexts; as well as the ubiquity of installation, photography, language, earth art, cross-overs to science, mapping, and other systems, and a continued interest in merging art and life.

With its emphasis on identity (of, among others, art itself), conceptualism provided a framework for the identity-based art politics of subsequent decades, and its declarations against the primacy and authenticity of material goods also laid the groundwork for the appropriationist and simulationist strategies of postmodernism. However, conceptualism's revolutionary political aspirations present an uncertain legacy. In fact, it has been argued persuasively that it was conceptualism's status as an "unfinished" project that made it so influential later on. László Beke, however, credits East European conceptualism with "perform[ing] a 'linguistic' function in preparation for the political and social transformation of the 1980s—in other words, a genuinely new aesthetic language was not created in the 1990s *because this had been accomplished decades before*."

For some artists, the pressure conceptualism brought to bear on the idea of (formalist/modernist) art for art's sake led to a painful art-politics competition, in which art often lost. Examples include those in the New York Art & Language group who abandoned art to pursue revolutionary politics; Australian Ian Burn's and others' switch from art to labor organizing; members of the Tucumán Arde collective who stopped making art for many years, as some went "underground" while a few "disappeared"; the Japanese Bikyōtō group, who consciously withdrew from making or exhibiting art during 1973; and Hsieh Tehching, a conceptual artist from Taiwan (known for his collaborative projects with artist Linda Montano) who, at his request, is not included in this exhibition because he is refraining from making or exhibiting art from 1986 through December 31, 1999. This politicization of the avant-garde was, as Blake Stimson has argued, in conflict with the antipolitical ideals of 1940s and '50s bohemian culture, and inevitably reopened even older wounds as art aspired to escape the confines of its own cloister and become a truly activist force.

The Exhibition

This survey is constructed in chapters, each derived from the perspective of the region under consideration. We extend our thanks to the team of curators, who have placed the idea-based works of each of the regions in their specific sociopolitical context in order to fully appraise their impact. Still, the enormous geographical scope of the exhibition necessitated abbreviated coverage in various ways. For example, "regions" have been designated according to either geographic or historical conventions, even though these are in some cases problematic in that the grouping of nations according to geographic proximity obscures deep cultural and historical differences and implies a misleading overall consistency of activity in that area. Moreover, amassing countries into exhibition chapters attenuates the curators' ability to focus on national and even individual characteristics, and encourages a reading in terms of "movements" and concerted, widespread activity, which is not entirely accurate in all cases. However, although organized by region, curators have, in fact, located various centers and affinities within these regions where conceptualist practices first emerged.

Since comprehensive coverage is impossible, this survey seeks to identify emblematic works and movements, rather than encompass the full range of activity worldwide. An additional tension in this project has been between the impulse to revise existing histories—to "expand and decenter the canon"—and to broaden the scope of discussion overall. While this exhibition intends to revise conventional historicizations of conceptual art, it does so through the strategic addition of multiple, poorly known histories presented as equal corollaries rather than as appendages to a central axis of activity. Limitations of physical space, and of the possible scope of inquiry of a single exhibition, preclude the inclusion of the dozens or hundreds of other artists who are un- or underrecognized. Priority has been given to broadening the geographic scope of the definition of conceptualism, to open up the meaning of the term itself to include a spectrum of artistic intents and responses to reality/circumstances that goes beyond the limits of the usual (and formally derived) art world scope.

Finally, we have had to grapple with the difficulties involved in constructing a museal display out of works which often were intended to counter or undermine the institutions of the museum and the art world. We regret that, unavoidably, intentions have been blurred and the sacralization of intentionally profane acts has occurred in the interest of recovering these histories.

Given the range and complexity of its subject, *Global Conceptualism: Points of Origin, 1950s–1980s* can never be a definitive account. We sincerely hope others will take up the task and further the understanding of this important work. To that end, we have invited Dr. Apinan Poshyananda to contribute an essay to this catalogue on the activities of conceptual artists working in South and Southeast Asia today. Since the end of the Cold War, South and Southeast Asia, the Middle East, and other rapidly developing areas have seen the rise of identity politics, ethnic cleansing, nationalism, and the theocratic state. Currently, like others before them, artists in these regions are adopting conceptualist practices in their work, opening new chapters in this ongoing history.

1950s through circa 1973

Japan

Western Europe

Eastern Europe

Latin America

North America

Australia and New Zealand

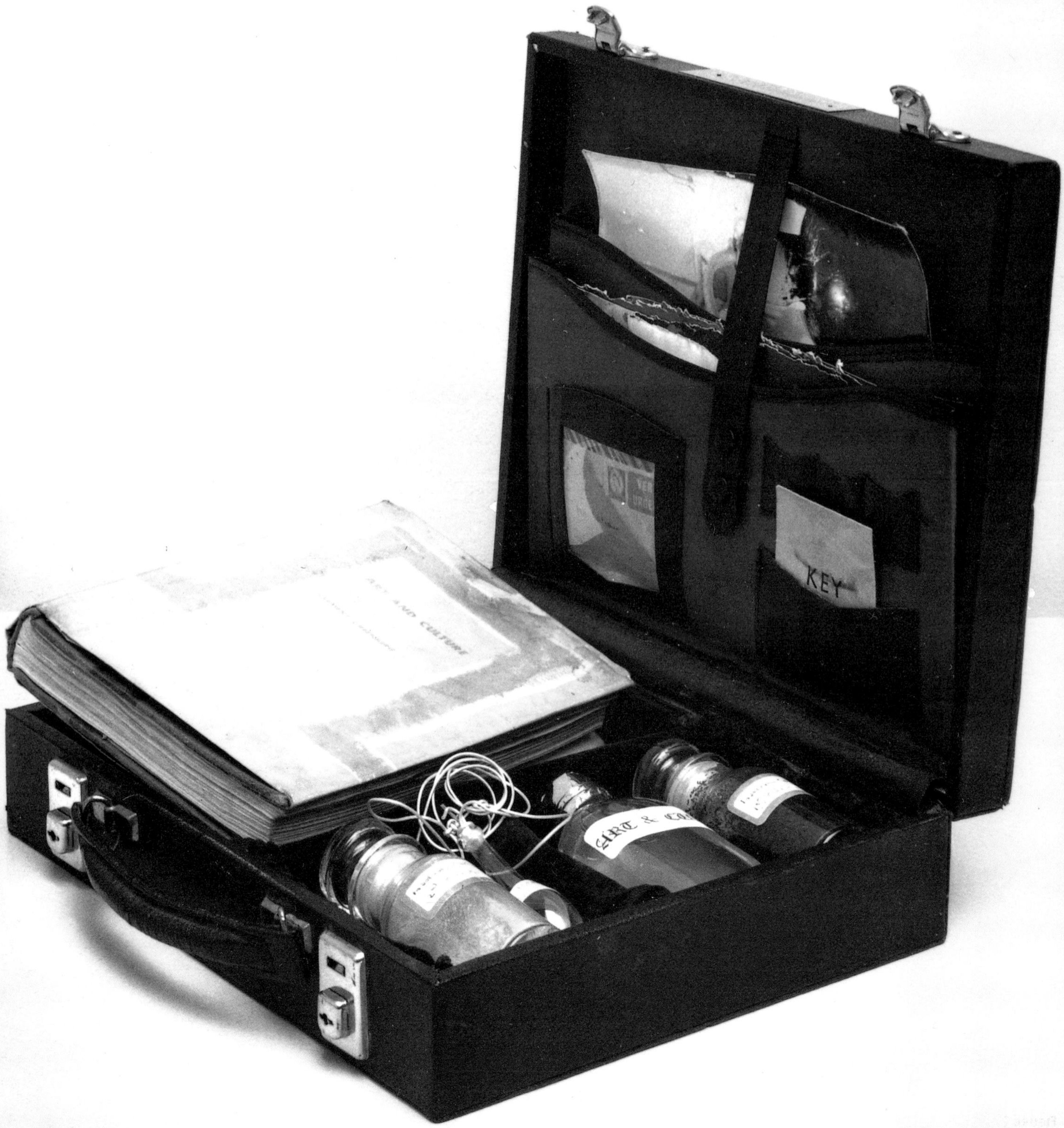
KEY

Introduction

Stephen Bann

The history of the art of our times is inevitably bound up with the historiography of the modern world in general, and with the recurrent attempts of historians to make sense of the accelerating pace of contemporary events. Contemporary art is just one aspect of the vast cultural shift that—in analyzing the societies that have come into being in the second half of the 20th century—has made imperative a full account of "global" as well as local and national dimensions. But it is fair to say that most historians are prone to regard art as offering particularly elusive testimony in this respect, or indeed providing redundant evidence to back up the harder data gleaned from economic and political trends.

Those concerned with the arts, of course, think differently. The present exhibition, with its highly ambitious global reach, puts forward a persuasive case for the historical importance of a view of contemporary art that breaks decisively with the heritage of modernism. That is to say, it explicitly rejects the customary practice of plotting out the topology of artistic connections in terms of "center" and "periphery": Paris or New York in relation to the various satellites that have come within their sphere of influence. Instead, *Global Conceptualism* offers an alternative framework of multiple "points of origin." The contention is that global conceptualism marks a radical shift, not merely in the morphology of modernist art but in the pattern of art's development and diffusion worldwide. This perspective would certainly mark out the art exhibited here as representing a decisive break with the preconditions of artistic development during the modern movement. But it might go further than that. Global conceptualism may be the visible proof that the Western hegemony in ways of seeing, ushered in by the perspectival science of the Renaissance, no longer holds sway.

I put this issue in a hypothetical form not only because it is a bold and original claim, but because it throws into relief the ways in which even the best historical interpretations of the modern world fail to come to terms with the radical potential of advanced art as a catalyst for change. Consider Geoffrey Barraclough's *Introduction to Contemporary History* (1964), which bears on the front cover of its widely circulated paperback edition that shining icon of the high modernist epoch, Epstein's *Rock Drill* (1913–14).[1] Barraclough's work is without doubt one of the first historical studies to argue systematically for the view that "contemporary history" must also be "world history," and he vigorously repudiates the view that taking a global perspective simply involves "supplementing our conventional view of the past by adding a few chapters on extra-European affairs."[2] But his treatment of modern art and literature falls into a similar trap. In the final chapter, entitled "Art and Literature in the Contemporary World," Barraclough reduces such manifestations as "cubism, dadaism, and abstract painting" to reflections of "a transition from one stage of civilization to another."[3] This might be described as the purgative view of modernism: advanced art, at best, is a rapid and effective way of "jettisoning ... the inherited baggage of European culture."[4]

Figure 1.
John Latham, *Art and Culture*, 1966–69, book, labeled vials filled with powders and liquids, letters, photostats, and other materials in a leather case. The Museum of Modern Art, New York, Blanchette Rockefeller Fund.

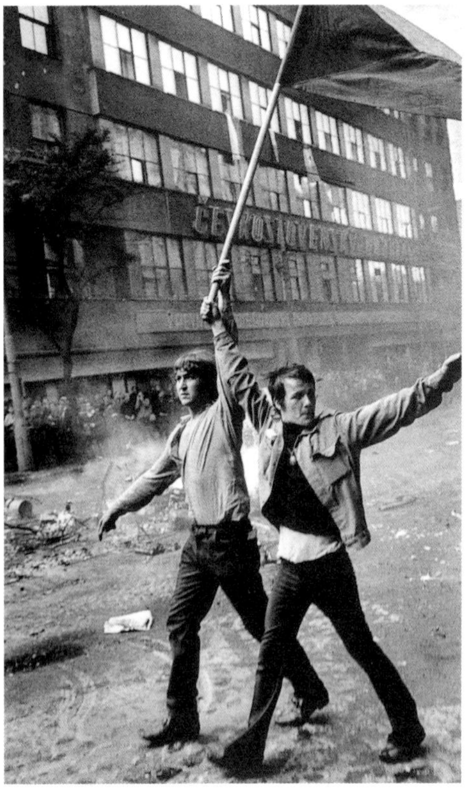

Prague, near the Radio headquarters, during the invasion of Warsaw Pact troops, August 1968. Courtesy of Magnum Photos, Inc. © 1998 Josef Koudelka.

Barraclough was writing at the height of the Cold War period, and in the very decade when conceptualism began to assume its global role. It is not surprising that his diagnosis of the state of the arts, at any rate, seems to be fixed in a blinkered, prewar mode. However, it is interesting to compare his approach to a similarly ambitious and brilliantly wide-ranging work published thirty years later, after the fall of the Berlin Wall: Eric Hobsbawm's *Age of Extremes* (1994). Hobsbawm's end-of-century perspective is necessarily quite different from that of Barraclough, and has been exceptionally helpful in setting the stage for this exhibition. Writing with verve and authority, Hobsbawm interprets 20th-century history in terms of three epochs: the Age of Catastrophe, spanning the two world wars from 1915 to 1945; the Golden Age, from 1947 to 1973, combining the political and military stand-off of the Cold War with unprecedented growth in the developed capitalist countries; and finally, the Landslide of 1973 to 1991, in which the world "lost its bearings and slid into instability and crisis."[5]

No doubt, future historians will commend Hobsbawm's insights in some domains and question his conclusions in others. For our purposes, his thesis on the relation of contemporary art to the historical process takes no more account of the catalytic role of artistic practice than does Barraclough's. For him, the achievements of postwar modernists are "usually much inferior" to those of their prewar precursors. Moreover, the closest he gets to conceptualism is through banal references to "gestures reducing the sort of art which was primarily bought for investment and its collectors *ad absurdum,* as by adding an individual's name to piles of brick or soil ('minimal art') or by preventing it from becoming such a commodity through making it too short-lived to be permanent ('performance art')."[6] Not unexpectedly, Hobsbawm says more about the origins and character of conceptualism in his discussion of the new conditions of worldwide communications in general, than when he is denouncing the economic basis of the art world. Thus he comments on the widespread student revolt of the late 1960s:

> It was global, not only because the ideology of the revolutionary tradition, from 1789 to 1917, was universal and internationalist ... but because, for the first time, the world, or at least the world in which student ideologists lived, was genuinely global. The same books appeared, almost simultaneously, in the student bookshops in Buenos Aires, Rome and Hamburg ... The same tourists of revolution crossed oceans and continents from Paris to Havana to São Paulo to Bolivia. The first generation of humanity to take rapid and cheap global air travel and telecommunications for granted, the students of the late 1960s, had no difficulty in recognizing what happened at the Sorbonne, in Berkeley, in Prague, as part of the same event in the same global village in which, according to the Canadian guru Marshall McLuhan ... we all lived.[7]

What Hobsbawm identifies as the defining feature of the late 1960s can, of course, be readily transposed into specifically artistic terms. Indeed, Peter Wollen has written an interesting essay on "the cosmopolitan ideal in the arts" which concludes with a similar insight: that the postmodern period is bound to be "cosmopolitan" insofar as it reflects the "substantive changes in the underlying structure of the world economic system."[8] The point is not to be seduced into the all-too-facile conflation of cosmopolitanism and utopian politics that was the dream of many modernists. Wollen himself notes that the French Revolution's first generous impulse in welcoming foreign nationals was quickly replaced with the practice of guillotining them. And Hobsbawm starkly observes that the 1970s—the very decade that followed the diffusion of the concept of the global village—was also "the darkest era of torture and counter-terror in the history of the West."[9] But the essential point remains unaltered. Whatever atrocious effects were triggered by the new political circumstances of Hobsbawm's "landslide," the reality of rapid communication within an increasingly interconnected world economy remained a distinctive and novel feature of the period in which conceptualism emerged. Terry Smith underlines this point in his catalogue contribution on the zone geographically furthest from the traditional centers of modernism. If artists like Ian Burn from Melbourne and Billy Apple from Auckland could produce their work in cities like London and New York—if the Australian Ian Burn could develop a working relationship with the British artist Mel Ramsden which survived the latter's visit to an Australian art school—this was because "much art of this period came out of a suitcase, or could be made on the spot by people in transit." Indeed, one could say that this new topology of locations that succeeded the metropolitan ties of modernism worked with equal efficiency in securing less dramatic but no less important connections. The Art & Language group, generated initially from the collaboration between Michael Baldwin and Terry Atkinson at the Coventry School of Art in the mid-1960s,

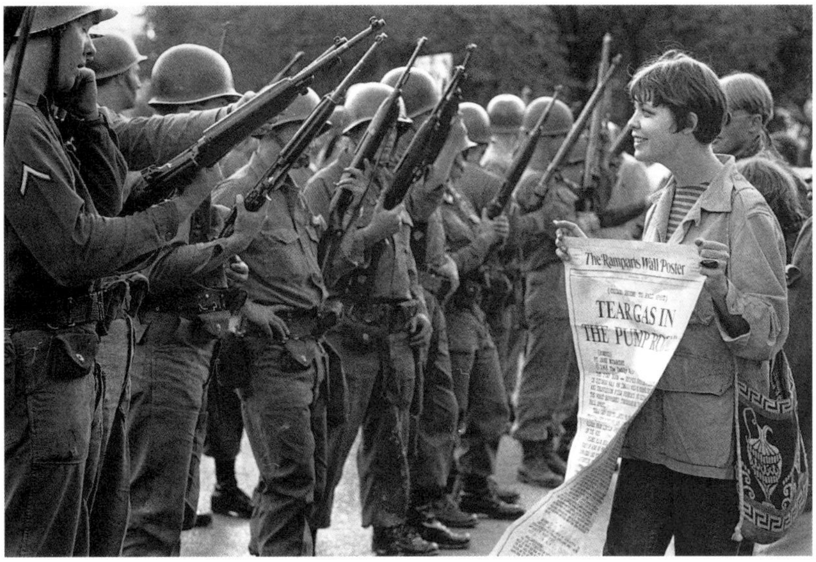

Chicago, protests outside the Democratic National Convention, August 1968. Courtesy of Magnum Photos, Inc. © 1968 Raymond Depardon.

Paris, night of May 10–11, 1968, students with Molotov cocktails. Courtesy of Magnum Photos, Inc. © 1968 Bruno Barbey.

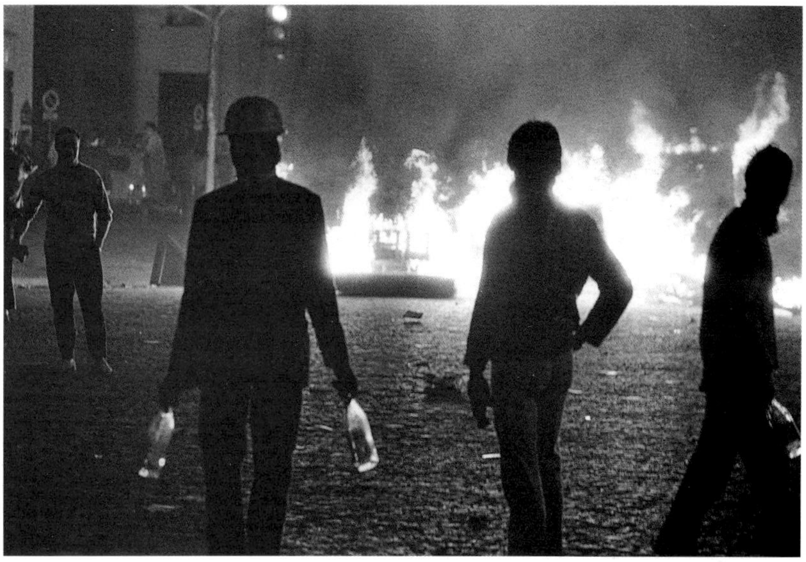

Mexico City, student demonstration, September 1968. Courtesy of Magnum Photos, Inc. © Abbas/Magnum.

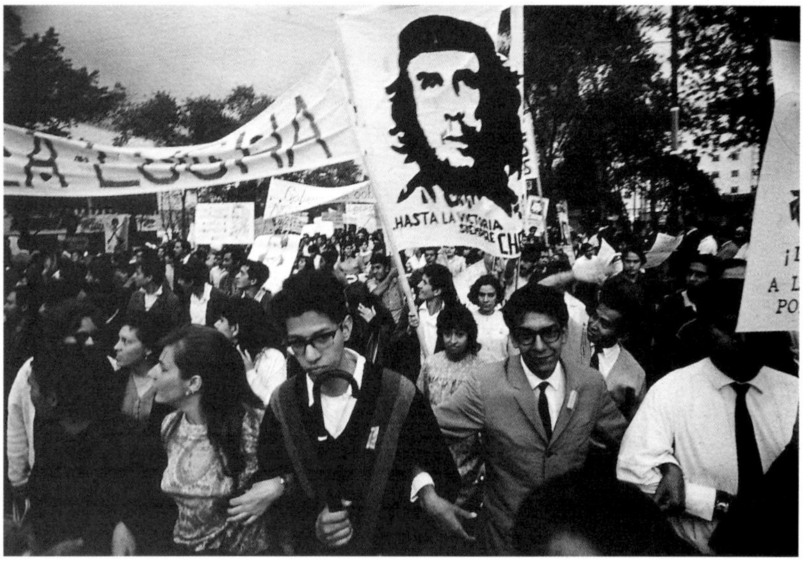

could be said to have acquired its reputation in Europe before London: a suitcase was enough to transport copies of its eponymous journal on a flight to Zurich.

There is, of course, a danger in loading too much significance onto conceptualism as the artistic movement that most fully and revealingly expresses the tendency toward globalization. Undoubtedly there is a historical problem in sorting out the complex strands of advanced art activity in the 1960s, and this is compounded by the need to look at the many different "points of origin" in which the conceptual approach defined itself against local as well as internationally shared conditions. McLuhan, whose celebrity at the time is noted by Hobsbawm, saw the cultural aspect of globalization as primarily a shift from print-dominated communication technologies to electronic media. The French one-time revolutionary and current media expert Régis Debray—whose career vividly exemplifies the chaotic sequence of events from Cold War confrontation to the end of the Landslide era—has recently written eloquently of his view that a "chronological and moral divide ... separates the cult of the book from the cult of the image."[10] There is no doubt in his mind that the momentous changes in political and social behavior which he has observed through his privileged access to Fidel Castro, at one end of his career, and François Mitterrand, at the other, can be summed up in the implications of the transition from lead type to the electronic press. And where does conceptualism belong in this broad cultural diagnosis? It is obvious that the forms taken by conceptual art reflect, at the very least, a movement in the direction of new electronic media, as opposed to the traditional artistic media largely retained by the pioneers of modernism. But conceptualism is also, no less obviously, word-based in many of its manifestations. Does this mean that as a cultural phenomenon it bypasses the kind of confident generalization made above?

The answer to this question is not an easy one to deliver. In fact, it obliges me to make a general statement bearing on the status of conceptualism and the way it might be understood, in relation to the individual statements of the guest curators contributing to this exhibition, as well as to the historiographical background sketched out above. Conceptualism is certainly not, in my view, an avant-garde concerned with jettisoning cultural baggage, as Barraclough maintains in relation to modern and contemporary art in general. Nor is it to be assimilated to the second-rate, repetitive modernism assailed by Hobsbawm, a modernism whose reason for existence is almost exclusively economic and whose cultural effect can only be described as "postmodern" in the weakest sense of the term. On the contrary, conceptualism derives its special currency and vitality from the fact that it is both a critique and a continuation of modernism: it consolidates precisely the critique of the institutions and discourses of Western post-Renaissance art commenced by modernism, while shifting its own discursive strategy from a material-based to a concept-based approach. Indeed, in this respect it was conceptualism's role to expose and pass beyond the internal inconsistency in the modernist strategy. For insofar as modern art had involved the fetishization of material—the painter's pigment and the sculptor's stone—it had focused attention on the artist's individual "touch" and thus implicitly rejected the academic and intellectual protocols of Western perspectival art. Conceptualism represents the return of this repressed element, in a form that broke open not merely the structures of modernism but also the political economy of center and periphery which modernism had inherited, ultimately, from Renaissance Europe.

To gloss this very general statement, I would like to add some more specific comments on the confrontation between end-game modernism, as one might term it, and nascent conceptualism in the 1960s. Inevitably, the different elements are difficult to sort out. Claude Gintz is certainly correct in his identification of lines of continuity from the Situationism of Guy Debord and nouveau réalisme of Yves Klein to the strategies of early conceptualism. He is also accurate in underlining the significance of John Latham's dissolution through mastication of Clement Greenberg's *Art and Culture* in 1966 (fig. 1), which dovetails with the later determination of Art & Language to "disqualify the competent spectator presupposed in the aesthetic discourse of Modernist culture."[11] But in this context it is also worth looking at the ways in which certain artists revealed the bankruptcy of modernist logic by their very determination to push it to extremes. For example, in the early 1960s the highly publicized work of the Paris-based Groupe de Recherche d'Art Visuel was modernist both in the institutional sense—here was a group of French and Latin American artists working in the traditional center of European modernism, publishing manifestos and exhibiting together—and also in their intensified perceptualism. On the one hand, they defended a policy of enhancing spectatorship by providing vivid optical and electronic stimuli, which could be seen historically as an updating of the French impressionists' assault on the senses. On the other hand, they argued (no less stringently than Art & Language at the end of the decade) for a repudiation of the "cultivated, sensitive, intellectual, aesthetic, dilettante" eye.[12] The group's enterprise came adrift through its numerous internal inconsistencies, the most significant from our point of view being their decision to exacerbate the perceptualist position and stop short of conceptualism.

Pursuing this argument further, I would suggest that two of the most indicative signs of the shift from modernism to conceptualism in this transitional period can be found in the abrupt emergence to prominence of several pioneer modernist artists whose work had peaked by the 1920s. Marcel Duchamp's pivotal significance for the late 1960s may be gauged in part from a revealing tribute published in April 1969 shortly after his death by a fellow member of the modernist avant-garde, Hans Richter (fig. 3). Summing up his contribution through some highly important distinctions, Richter declared that Duchamp "did not hail 'Anti-Art' like the Berlin Dadaists, but

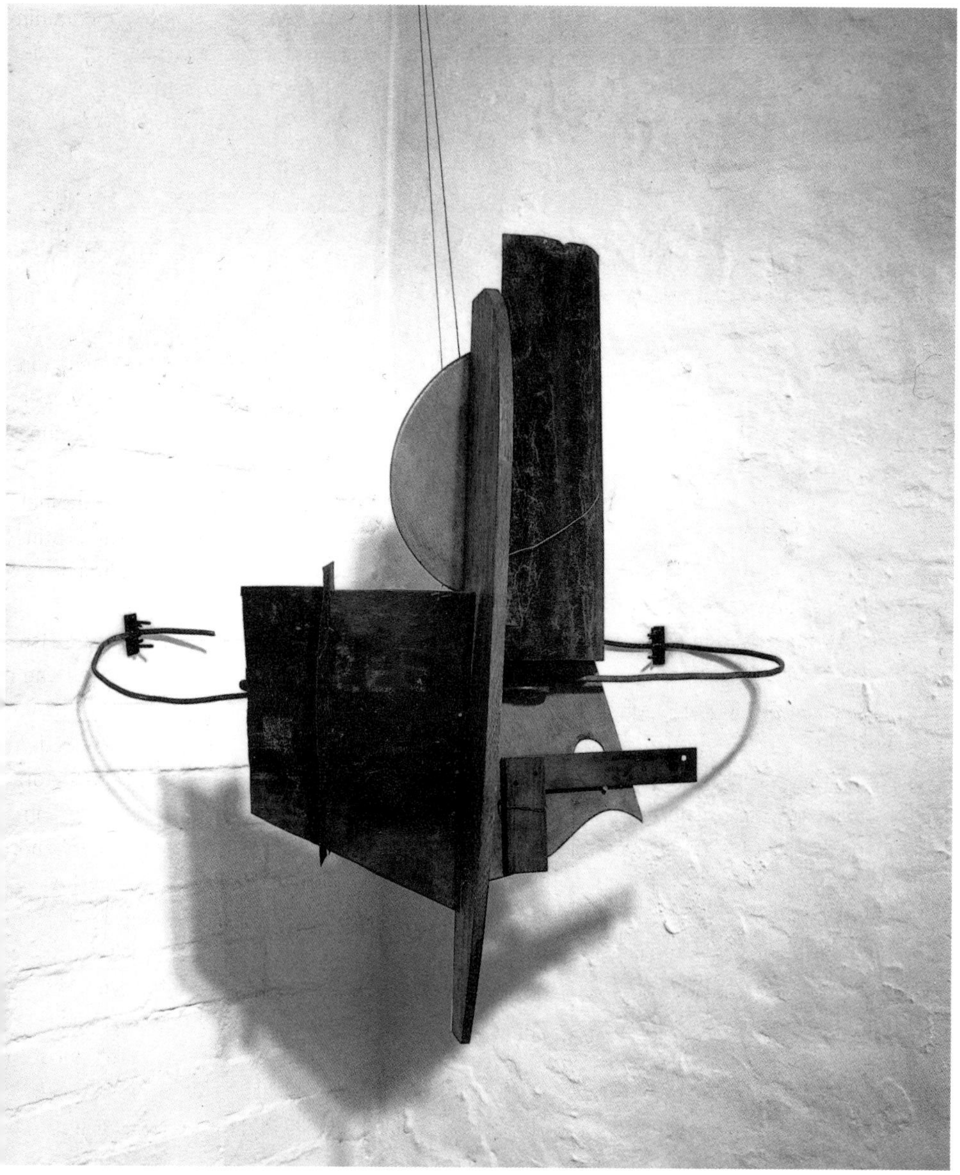

FIGURE 2.
Vladimir Tatlin, *Complex Corner Relief* (1982 reconstruction: Martyn Chalk), 1915, iron, aluminum, and zinc. Courtesy of Annely Juda Fine Art, London.

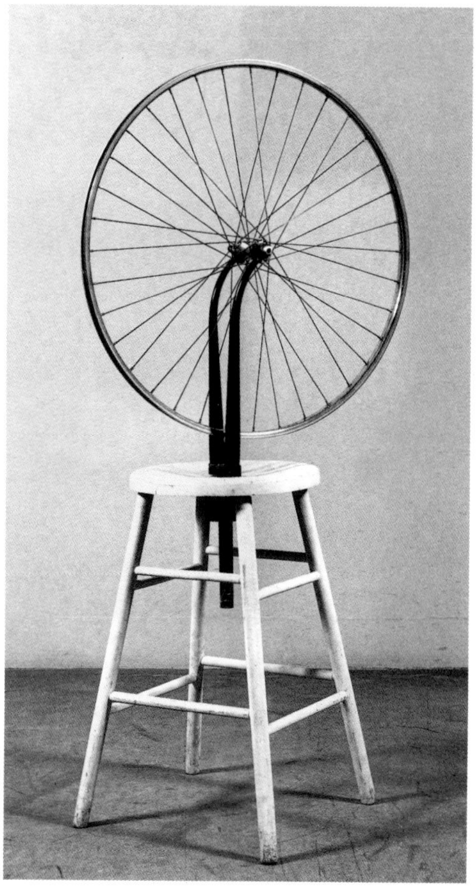

FIGURE 3.
Marcel Duchamp, *Bicycle Wheel*, 1913, 3rd version: replica from 1951, bicycle wheel mounted on painted wooden stool. The Museum of Modern Art, New York, The Sidney and Harriet Janis Collection.

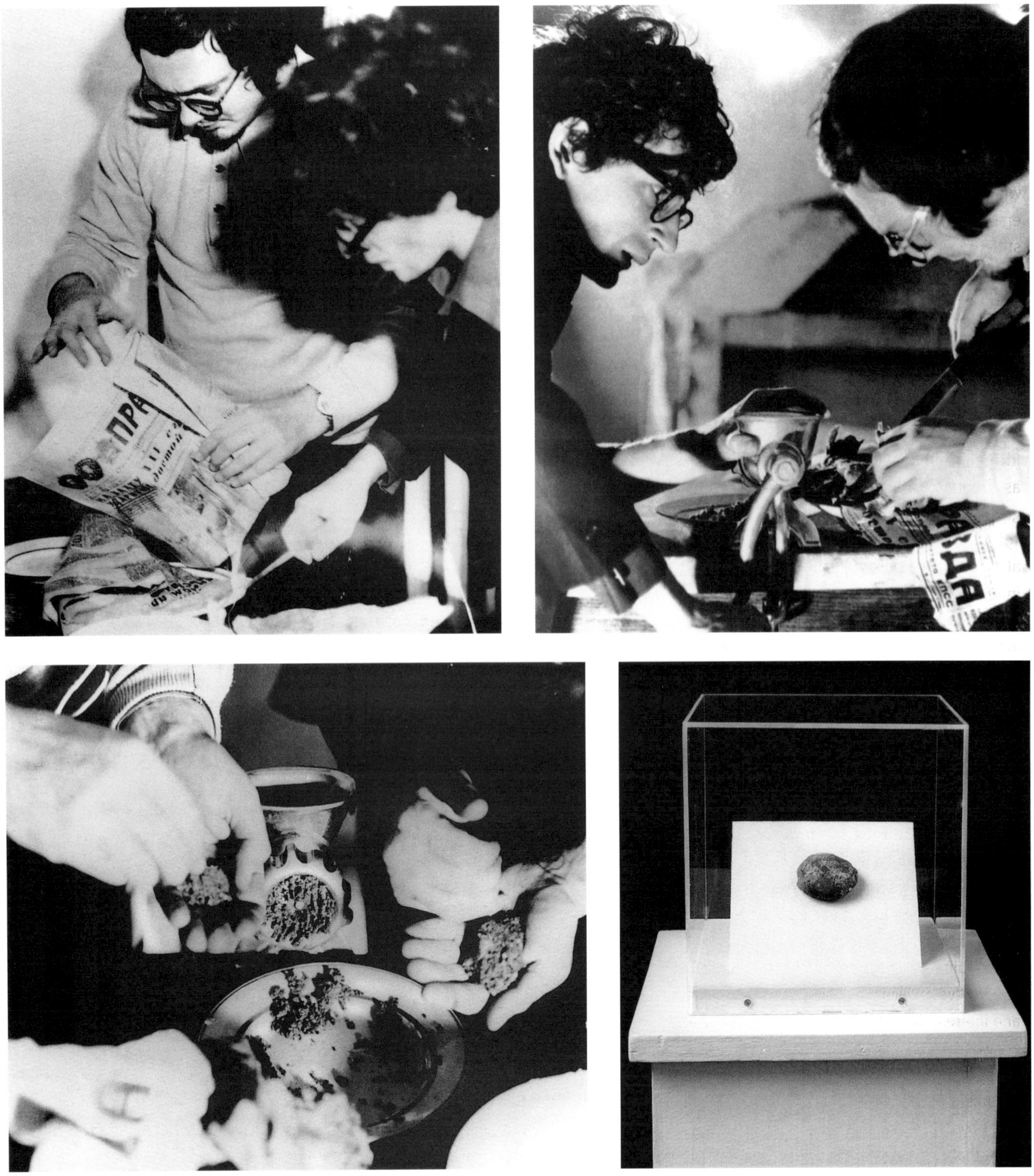

Figure 4.
Vitaly Komar and Aleksandr Melamid, *Hamburgers "Pravda"* (*Kotlety "Pravda"*), 1975, three mounted silver gelatin prints, ground newspaper in Plexiglas box mounted on painted wooden pedestal. Jane Voorhees Zimmerli Art Museum, Rutgers, the State University of New Jersey, Gift of Norton and Nancy Dodge.

rather 'Non-Art.'"[13] In this simple formula, a great deal of Duchamp's literally revolutionary significance can be contained. His stance was not oppositional, in which case he would inevitably have ended up endorsing the structures and values that he attacked. On the contrary, he aspired to the *negation* of Art, which implied a conscientious and consistent emptying out of those very values and structures. Richter is himself entirely consistent in the way he accounts for this particular quality of Duchamp's approach when he further asserts, "I find the secret of Duchamp's magical force of attraction in the vacuum he created to replace 'rejected' moral and artistic attitudes."

Richter is undoubtedly speaking here not only as a representative of the historical avant-garde, but also as a spokesperson for the 1960s. The 1968 exhibition of Vladimir Tatlin at the Moderna Museet, Stockholm, revealed in a comparable way the new importance of the historical avant-garde for a rapidly evolving audience (fig. 2). The remarkable feature of this widely acclaimed show was that it did not include any significant original work by Tatlin. Although it was certainly not the intention of the organizers to create an exhibition on this basis, and the reluctance of the Soviet Ministry of Culture to come to terms with the heritage of the avant-garde probably accounted for their tactful message that Tatlin's works were undergoing extensive restoration, the result was not entirely divorced from the organizers' original aims.[14] For Tatlin, like Duchamp but for different reasons, had become by this stage a "vacuum" into which the engagement and interest of contemporary Western onlookers was compulsively attracted, precisely because of the mythic role that each had assumed. Duchamp became a conceptual artist by virtue of his lifelong defense of the truth that the artwork was not a construct of canvas and paint, but a "brain-fact." Tatlin had defended throughout his much abbreviated career the premise that materials were more important than any representational project, yet became a conceptualist by accident, simply because of the disproportion between the fame of his work and its inaccessibility—and because the time was right.

I should emphasize here that I am writing specifically about Tatlin as he was perceived from a Western perspective, and not in any sense as he was viewed in his native Russia at the same juncture. As Peter Wollen states in his catalogue essay on North American conceptual artists, with particular reference to the period of the late 1960s and early '70s, "conceptual art sealed the fate of modernism in the visual arts, but paradoxically it also brought back into currency the avant-garde ideas of Marcel Duchamp and the Russian constructivists, particularly Rodchenko and Tatlin." The very paradox that Wollen mentions here goes to the heart of Western conceptualism, and points to its irreducible difference from non-Western varieties. Gao Minglu approaches the question from the other side when he points out that, in China, the "anti-art project did not develop from a logical historical progression of aesthetic avant-gardism. There has never existed in China a sphere of aesthetic autonomy as theorized by Peter Bürger for the West." In other words, what was unique to the Euro–North American experience, and perfectly epitomized by the stance of Duchamp himself, was the tradition of "art for art's sake" *(l'art pour l'art)* inaugurated by critics like Théophile Gautier and Baudelaire in the early 19th century, and turned into a creed by artists like Manet, Whistler, and the Pre-Raphaelites. Elaborated originally to protect the artist's freedom of expression from the encroachments of bourgeois morality, this creed was both given a new lease on life and comprehensively deconstructed by Duchamp, who recognized how intimately it depended on the very institutions it so vigorously contested: the Salon and the Academy. Victor Burgin was undoubtedly right when he identified Joseph Kosuth's concern with "the whole question of self-reflexivity" with the tradition of art for art's sake. Such an ideology, as reinforced by Duchamp, was indeed powerful when it could draw such seemingly opposed phenomena as Russian constructivism and productivism into its sphere.

Margarita Tupitsyn's account of early Soviet conceptualism indicates how very differently the tradition of the avant-garde operated within the Russian context. Whereas in the West, the Soviet avant-garde of the immediate postrevolutionary period could be reinvented as a utopian moment detached from subsequent history, the Russian conceptual movement that developed from the mid-1960s had to reckon with the overwhelming legacy of the Stalinist epoch.[15] Socialist realism could not simply be ignored, but formed the visual and ideological canon which an artist like Ilya Kabakov or the team of Vitaly Komar and Aleksandr Melamid (K/M) could incorporate in the form of appropriation and parody. It is easy to draw attention to the parallelism between the strategies of these Soviet artists and their Western contemporaries. For example, John Latham's previously mentioned reduction of *Art and Culture* to pulp has its counterpart in Komar and Melamid's performance, *Hamburgers "Pravda"* (*Kotlety "Pravda,"* 1975; fig. 4), in which pages of the *Pravda* ("Truth") newspaper were ground up and made into a grayish ball. But Tupitsyn is right to stress the inverse logic (in relation to the Western experience) that governed their actions. If, in her view, Western conceptualism developed "in reaction to the overpresence of the beholder and the critic, then Soviet conceptualism was a reaction to the absence of both."

The example of Soviet conceptualism enables us to assess, again paradoxically, the strength of the Western tradition and its capacity for "globalization." For as the experience of the last three decades suggests, the absence of any institutional basis except for the monolithic state implied not a new freedom for the artist when that state began to decline, but the atrophy even of the oppositional stances that had existed before. Tupitsyn writes of the "empty actions" or "trips in the direction of nothingness" performed by the Collective Actions Group from 1976 onward, in which the hollowness of the Brezhnev era was evoked. In a recent catalogue on contemporary art in Moscow and Saint Petersburg, the critic

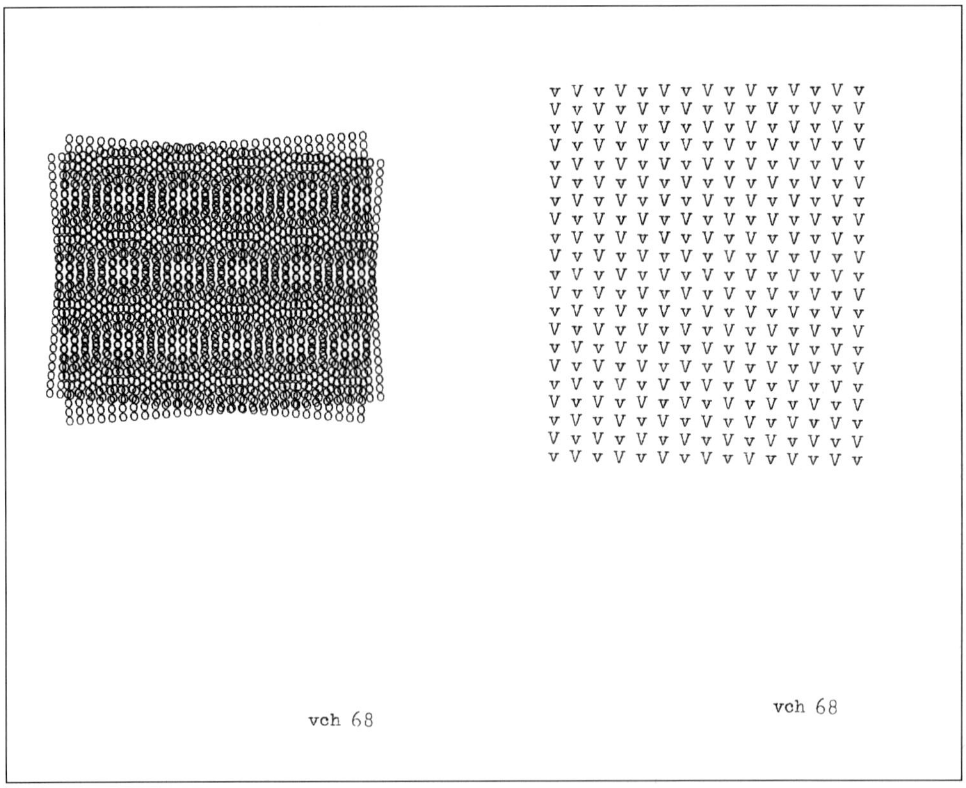

FIGURE 5.
Jiří Valoch, *Optical poem 59* and *Rhythmical poem*, 1968.

Brandon Taylor has emphasized the point that "the prevailing material base of the Russian art system has all but withered away" in the years following *perestroika*.[16] It may well be true that there is no longer a base for art, let alone conceptual art, within the new Russian society, but it is undeniable that the Russian conceptualists who devised strategies for coping with the lack of an audience in the 1960s and '70s have secured a unique position as world artists, operating precisely in the space that conceptual art has opened up. Both Kabakov and K/M have achieved an extraordinary ubiquity in the Euro–North American network of avant-garde galleries; indeed, the latter have turned the interpellation of national audiences throughout the globe into their own art form.

The logic that underwrites Russian conceptualism almost as a negative pole of its Euro–North American counterpart does not, of course, apply in the case of Eastern Europe. In his essay for this catalogue, László Beke has the formidable task of making sense of a geographical description that is derived from a Western viewpoint and bypasses the very real differences in historical traditions and identities existing throughout the region. One point, however, is quite clear. In countries within the former Soviet bloc that were once part of the Austro-Hungarian and German empires (for instance, the Czech Republic, Hungary, and Slovenia), the flowering of modernism was not terminated with the same brutal rigor as in the Soviet Union. Particularly in the case of Poland, the phase of officially sanctioned socialist realism was short-lived, and one can speak of a virtually uninterrupted stream of avant-garde art, from the interwar period when the Blok group continued the pioneering work of Malevich and the city of Lódź opened the first European museum devoted to contemporary art, to the late 1950s and '60s when artistic freedom was recognized (like Polish Catholicism) as a token of national independence vis-à-vis the communist state.

Thus it would be inappropriate to search in Eastern Europe for the radical and purist forms of conceptual art linked to the long-established tradition of aesthetic autonomy that developed in the West. Beke correctly describes conceptualism in Eastern European countries as "flexible and elastic, ironic, humorous and ambiguous, nonprofessional, communicable, always ready to become a social activity of a group of young people or even an alternative movement." Nevertheless, a very wide spectrum of activities legitimately falls under the heading of conceptualism in Eastern Europe, and not all of them operate within the activist mode evoked here. Poland produced, in the painter Roman Opalka, an almost unique example of an artist with a clearly defined life-project whose monochrome canvases, covered with successive numbers, vividly recall the plastic experiments of the Blok group. The last surviving Blok member, Henryk Stazewski, shared a studio with the conceptualist Edward Krasiński, notable for his environments defined by uniform strips of carefully aligned blue tape. At the other extreme from this conceptual mode, which prolonged and transformed the existing avant-garde tradition of modernist abstraction, one could place the Slovenian group Neue Slovenische Kunst (NSK), which deliberately adopted the presentational strategies of pop art in order to foreground a political message that became happily redundant when their country absconded from the Yugoslavian federation.

Eastern Europe thus presents the utmost diversity of avant-garde strategies over the period when conceptualism developed, and it should cause no surprise to see different modalities, different media pressed into service to meet a variety of situations. Jiří Valoch, whom Beke describes as a visual poet and theorist concerned with "'hard-core' logical-conceptual problems," was certainly still sending his vigorous concrete poems from Brno to the West in the autumn of 1968, after the Russian tanks had entered Prague (fig. 5). No doubt it is in response to a similar problem of setting the context for a plurality of national responses to an international problematic that Mari Carmen Ramírez titles her catalogue essay

"Tactics for Thriving on Adversity." By any account, the history of Latin America from 1960 to 1980 has been utterly different from that of Eastern Europe over the same two decades. But the meager points of comparison, within a global artistic perspective, are still worth recording. In particular, Latin America was (and is) a region deeply—though selectively—influenced by the diaspora of artists, architects, and designers that occurred in the heyday of the modern movement. Younger Latin American artists took a positive role in reanimating Paris as a center for avant-garde art of a broadly constructivist tendency in the early 1960s. It is against this background of a well-based participation in international modernism that we can place the manifesto slogan of the Brazilian artist Hélio Oiticica, dating from 1967: ON ADVERSITY WE THRIVE!

Ramírez is especially cogent in her assessment of the way conceptualism developed in Latin America, and she demonstrates how the reductive accounts based on the metropolitan model, and the dichotomies implied in the plotting of center and periphery, can be avoided in this group of twenty countries. It is in line with her broad interpretation that the Latin American experience in the post-1945 period should have been a progressive disillusionment with the projects of technological modernization that characterized Hobsbawm's Golden Age. But she sees the local responses to this crisis of the Enlightenment project as taking different and apparently contradictory forms. For example, she identifies as a rallying point in the avant-garde practice of Colombia and Mexico the term *no-objetualismo* (non-object-based art) coined by the Peruvian critic Juan Acha. This term—"a catchword," according to Ramírez, "for all forms of experimental art (installations, performance, conceptual)"—coexists with the *nova objetividade* (new objectivity) of Oiticica, which implies a "recovery" of the object, though in a form recognizably akin to the mass-produced readymades of Duchamp.

In Ramírez's account, there is an evident connection between the broad artistic framework within which she sees the practices of conceptualism coming into force, and the wider historical perspective in which the developments of these years require to be placed. Noting the number of Latin American countries under military rule between 1964 and 1976, and the impact of authoritarianism on the emergence of conceptual art, she then quotes Juan Acha's claim that non-object-based art was a means of "destroying in us the humanist Renaissance tradition." The conjunction is significant, if we reflect that the "humanist Renaissance tradition" was, indeed, largely a construct of the 19th century. It was Jacob Burckhardt who, in his astonishing work *The Civilization of the Renaissance in Italy* (1860), retrospectively assembled the concepts that gave the Renaissance its unique ideological force, and can be read from his chapter headings, in particular, "The State as a Work of Art" and "The Discovery of the World and of Man." Implicit in Burckhardt's historical vision is the understanding that the Renaissance invention of perspective offers a basic model for analyzing both the systematic ordering of state power in the modern world and the projection of power relations onto the rest of the world through successive waves of colonization. If Burckhardt's insight foreshadows a deconstructive approach to the link between real power relations and the symbolic power of the perspectival conquest of space, then it is especially appropriate that conceptualism should both assist and reflect the annulment of the "Renaissance tradition" in the societies that have become established at the vanishing point of the European projection of power.

Ramírez does not doubt the significance of conceptualism as a "second major shift" in the advanced art of the 20th century, which moreover replaces the ultimately Renaissance cult of the "autonomous art object" with a practice bearing on "the more elastic realm of linguistics." But in the very area of linguistics, there is an inbuilt advantage to English as a worldwide language which cannot be wholly dissociated from the question of conceptualism's Euro–North American bias. Margarita Tupitsyn recounts as an amusing anomaly the point that Kabakov—the artist without an audience—took as his program "seeing words instead of objects," whereas the Western viewers who eventually got to see his works were, in fact, seeing his words without being

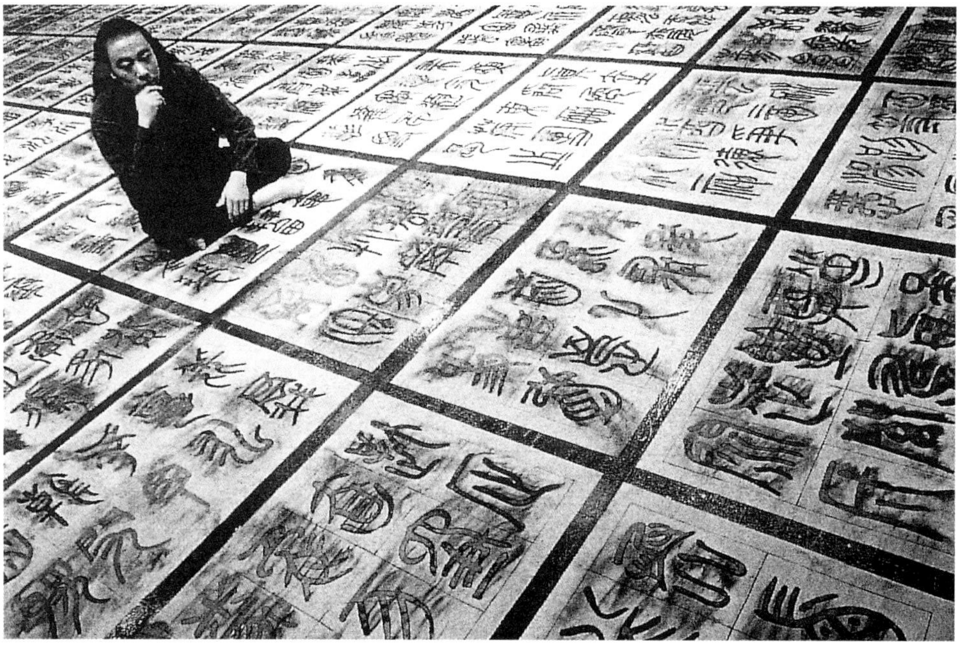

FIGURE 6.
Wenda Gu, *pseudo characters (cobiezi)*, 1985, ink on paper.

able to read them. But the issue can be extended from questions of simple vocabulary, important though these may be, to the wider issue of the systems of thought underlying linguistic behavior. Given that the different areas of the world instanced up to this point (with the exception of China) could all be placed in the orbit of Greco-Roman and predominantly Judeo-Christian culture, one might ask what the consequences are when that boundary is crossed.

In this connection, it is particularly interesting and illuminating to turn to Okwui Enwezor's essay on African conceptualism, for Enwezor traces a series of close connections and concordances that explain his strategy of "adding to" (rather than "displacing") the Euro–North American model. Africa enters the history of modernism as the acceptable "other" of metropolitan avant-garde practice, most notably with the cubist cross-reference to African tribal objects. This latter became a topic of critical and curatorial debate most recently in the highly contested *Primitivism* show mounted at the Museum of Modern Art in New York by William Rubin in 1984. It is easy to see how, in this context, the rupture with the modernist avant-garde initiated by conceptualism has offered a welcome change of orientation. Enwezor makes the crucial point that conceptualism, which places the artwork "within a fluid system of exchanges and relationships among object, artist, and audience," is faithful to the general character of traditional art practices in African societies. He shows that the object-bound nature of African art is not to be equated with the cult of the autonomous art object in Western tradition, since the meaning and intention of such art remains decisively "anti-object and antiperceptual." This is not enough to establish the existence of anything approaching a "movement" of conceptualism in postindependence Africa. But it is enough to prove, as Enwezor does, that the isolated examples of conceptual practice from the 1970s are not mere aberrations, only acquiring significance in relation to Euro–North American prototypes. Artists like Willem Boshoff and Frédéric Bruly Bouabré clearly demonstrate the fertility of language-based investigations on African soil: Boshoff prepared for his work with dictionaries by lengthy exercises in concrete poetry, and Bouabré essayed compilations based on the history of his people. Enwezor also singles out a conceptual strand of South African contemporary art beginning with Malcolm Payne, whose experience of the London art scene in the 1970s led him to consciously transplant conceptual work into the context of the apartheid state.

Most of the conceptual works from Africa in this exhibition date from the late 1970s to '90s, testifying to a second wave of conceptualism that has parallels in other parts of the world. In Mainland China, for example, the avant-garde flourished in the mid-1980s, a decade after the death of Mao and the end of the Cultural Revolution in 1976. Gao Minglu reports that over 2,000 young artists took part in this upsurge of activity, which involved both a "humanist" tendency and a "conceptualist" movement undertaking broadly deconstructionist, anti-utopian projects. In part, the latter tackled an agenda left behind by the unfinished revolutionary program of Maoism, using their art to attack the illusion of subjectivity generated by Maoist ideology. But it is also striking how, like the African artists already mentioned, the Chinese discovered in conceptualism a bridge to their own traditional cultural forms, and in particular the art of calligraphy, considered a close adjunct to painterly representation. Wenda Gu's *pseudo characters* (*cobiezi*, 1985; fig. 6), which combine the aesthetic features of traditional calligraphy with a destruction of meaning—the characters being wrongly written and hung upside down—epitomize this ironic and skeptical attitude.

Conceptualism in Mainland China appears to have had the effect of both supplying the new avant-garde with strategies for contesting the different manifestations of state power and enabling a return to non-Western mentalities embedded in the traditional culture, for instance, the spiritual discipline of Buddhism. Its effects seem at once more radical and more precarious than those obtained in societies that have been more open to Western influence in the post-1960 period, such as Taiwan and Korea. As Gao Minglu explains it, Taiwanese conceptualism developed as a generalized reaction to the hegemony of Western-oriented abstract painting and drew upon the dadaist heritage of anti-art. But it also claimed justification in the materialist view of nature implied in the Chinese philosophical tradition. Sung Wan-kyung acknowledges the stimulus to Korean conceptualism, from the mid-1970s onward, to have been the "Duchamp effect," which reached Korea via various intermediaries with its message of "concept" and "antiform." He cites several examples of the way in which this approach became a tool in the struggle against censorship imposed by the military government, such as the newspaper cutouts of Sung Neung-kyung, which consisted in the excision of all the lines of print and recalled the popular saying: "the truth is printed between the lines." Nevertheless, Sung Wan-kyung concedes that conceptual art was initially seen by many Koreans as a type of formalism, as opposed to the realist practice of the Min Joong cultural movement, which developed in the 1980s.

This brief world tour of conceptualism, which is offered as a prelude to the various more detailed studies that follow, comes full circle with Japan. This is the country that received the ingenious perspectival devices introduced by Dutch traders as no more than curiosities. It is also the country that virtually closed its frontiers against Western and European influence until the dawn of the modernist epoch, at which point Japan's distinctive traditional art was at least as much a stimulus to Western innovation as the other way around. And, as Reiko Tomii reminds us at the very beginning of her catalogue essay, Japan is a society in which, now more than ever, the technologically advanced modern, indeed postmodern world coexists with a culture deeply entrenched in nature and the material environment. "Postwar Japan," as she puts it, "is a site where the international and the local contend and conflate." Consequently, it comes as no surprise to find in Japanese art a striking parallelism with the development of conceptual art in the West, which springs not only from a common awareness of Duchamp and the dadaists but also from the Japanese fascination with modernism in all its forms after World War I. Artists like On Kawara, who formulated his theory of "printed painting" in 1958–59, and Yoko Ono, whose *Instructions for Painting* series dates from the early 1960s, occupy a significant place in any roster of the preconceptual phase. But Tomii also points out that Japan had its own patriarch of conceptualism in Matsuzawa Yutaka, whose mission statement "Vanish *objets!*" dates from 1964. Although Japanese art critics later welcomed the purist conceptual message of Joseph Kosuth, and Japan acquired its own special name for conceptualism in *gainen geijutsu,* it is possible to see in Matzusawa's position and influence an exemplary case of how Western art was met halfway by the autonomous local culture and philosophy: in this case, a primarily Buddhist blend focusing on the idea of the void.

It would certainly be an artificial exercise to try and draw the threads of this introductory survey together. The Buddhist idea of the void cannot be equated, other than in a simple-minded way, with that "vacuum" which Hans Richter saw as providing the secret explanation for the power of Duchamp's work. Yet art is concerned with representation, and not with analytic clarity. What is more, it thrives on interpretation and dissemination, which necessarily takes it outside the original conceptual framework to which it belonged. What is undoubtedly true about the international collaborators who have made this exhibition possible is that they have recognized the cross-cultural potential of conceptualist art. They have contributed in their different ways to understanding this potential in the light of recent world history. But, more importantly, they have put the public in the position of being able to experience this labyrinth of vital interconnections for themselves.

Notes

1. Geoffrey Barraclough, *An Introduction to Contemporary History* (Harmondsworth: Penguin, 1967), 10.

2. Ibid., 243–44.

3. Ibid.

4. Ibid.

5. Eric Hobsbawm, *The Age of Extremes: The Short Twentieth Century* (London: Abacus, 1994), 403.

6. Ibid., 516.

7. Ibid., 446–47.

8. Peter Wollen, "The Cosmopolitan Ideal in the Arts," in *Travellers' Tales: Narratives of Home and Displacement,* ed. George Robertson et al. (London and New York: Routledge, 1994), 195.

9. Hobsbawm, *Age of Extremes,* 446.

10 Régis Debray, *Loués soient nos seigneurs: Une éducation politique* (Paris: Gallimard, 1996), 108.

11. Charles Harrison, "Art Object and Artwork," in *L'art conceptuel, une perspective,* ed. Claude Gintz (Paris: Musée d'Art de la Ville de Paris, 1990), 630.

12. See the group's manifesto, "Assez de mystifications," published in September 1961 on the occasion of the Paris Biennal. For the group's consistent perceptualist bias, see also the manifesto "Stop Art," published in 1965 for the showing of their collective *Labyrinthe 3* in New York. Here "perception" is clearly stated to be the only "common means" by which the spectator can become involved.

13. Hans Richter, "In Memory of Marcel Duchamp," *Form* (Cambridge) 9 (April 1969): 4.

14. See Troels Andersen, *Vladimir Tatlin* (Stockholm: Moderna Museet, 1968). Pontus Hulten, the museum's director, makes it clear in the catalogue foreword that his original intention had been to exhibit Tatlin's paintings, reliefs, theater designs, flying machines, etc., but the cooperation of the Soviet authorities was not forthcoming. Consistent with the decision to show exclusively reconstructions and documentation, Hulten lays particular stress on the conceptual element of the Russian artist's work, writing of "Tatlin's ideas," and insisting that the "material of the Revolution was its basic idea" (p. 5).

15. See my foreword to Alla Efimova and Lev Manovich, *Tekstura: Russian Essays on Visual Culture* (Chicago: University of Chicago Press, 1993), vii–xvii.

16. Brandon Taylor, "Learning from the 'Luriki': Recent Photoaesthetics in Russia," in *Photo-Reclamation: New Art from Moscow and Saint Petersburg* (Southampton: University of Southampton, John Hansard Gallery, 1994), 9.

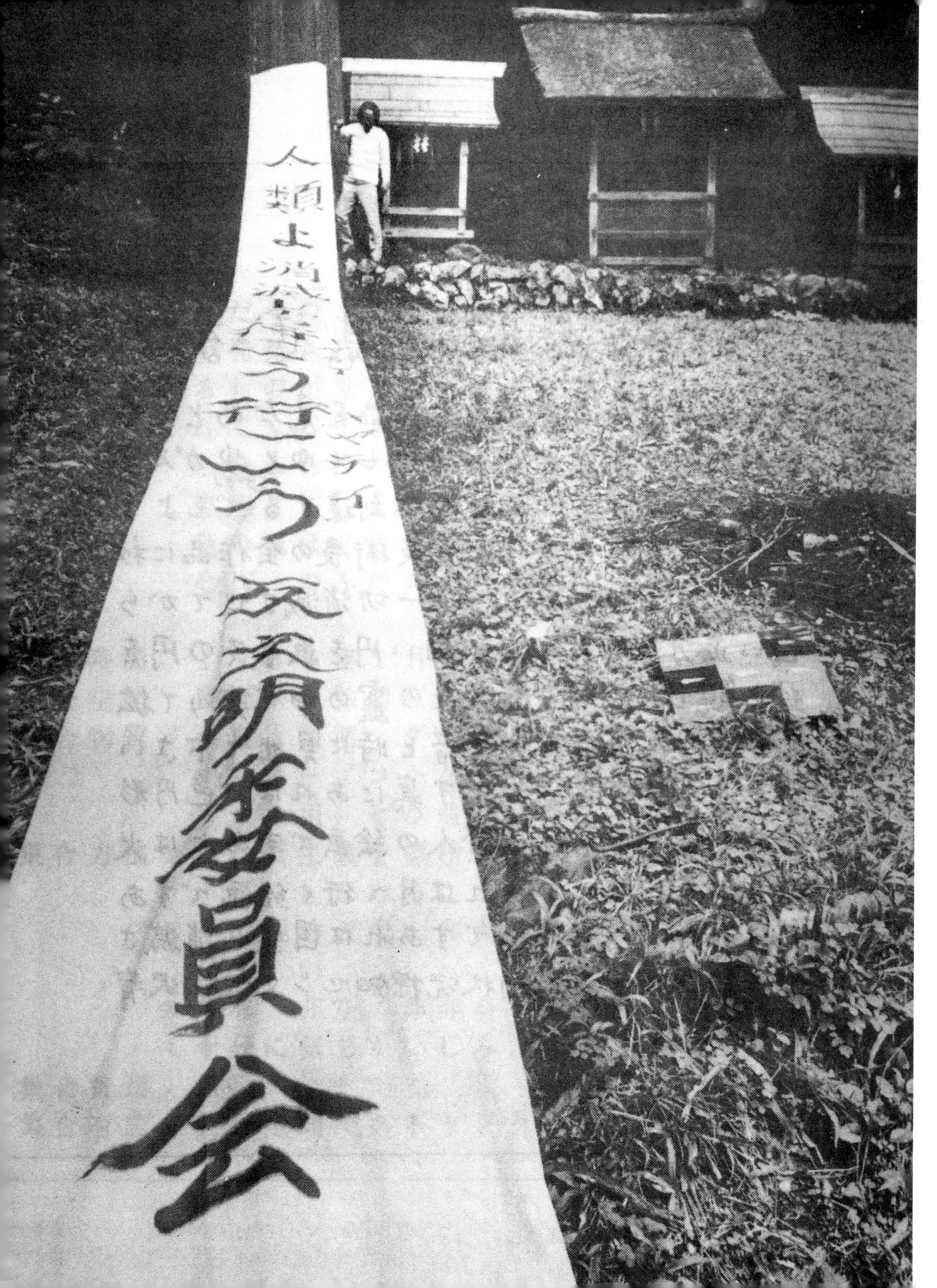

Concerning the Institution of Art: Conceptualism in Japan

Reiko Tomii

I am deeply indebted to my co-curator Chiba Shigeo. His pioneering works on postwar Japanese art, including Bikyōtō and the history of art criticism, have served as a starting point for all who have come after him, myself included; and his invaluable input has helped me draft fuller accounts on the subject in which the two of us share an abiding interest.

FIGURE 7.
Matsuzawa Yutaka, *Humans, Let's Vanish, Gate, Gate—Anticivilization Committee (Jinrui-yo, shōmetsu shiyō, gyatei, gyatei—Han-bunmei iinkai),* 1970, performance at Mt. Misa, Suwa, Japan, documentary photograph.

An Exploratory Overview

Postwar Japan is a site where the international and the local contend and conflate.

Politically, Japan's existence has been predicated on a close alliance with the United States, which also helped bring about economic recovery and growth to the nation defeated and ravaged in World War II. The Japanese people's desire that their country be a peaceful democratic member of the international community, and the reality that it served as America's front base in Asia under the shadow of the Cold War, long constituted two defining, though conflicted, facts of life. While Japan showcased its prosperity in the 1964 Tokyo Olympics, Expo '70 in Osaka, and the 1972 Sapporo Winter Olympics, the inherent contradiction erupted most tangibly in 1960, and less explosively in 1970, in the form of massive protests against renewal of the U.S.–Japan Security Treaty (Anpo), the cornerstone of the strategic arrangement that allowed American troops to be stationed in Japan. Within the leftist movement, the university conflicts that spread nationwide in 1968–69 embodied the younger generation's disillusionment with the authoritarian educational and, by extension, political system recalcitrant to change under an American-given democracy that was increasingly perceived as hollow and spurious in practice. Furthermore, in the 1970s, the fragile foundation of Japan's economic miracle was exposed by two calamities: in the "Dollar Shock" of 1971, the fixed dollar-yen exchange rate (carried over since the American Occupation) was ended; and in the "Oil Shock" of 1973, higher oil prices, precipitated by the Middle East conflict, triggered the so-called crazy prices.

In art, the phrase "international contemporaneity" *(kokusai-teki dōjisei),*[1] which gained considerable currency in the 1960s, attests to the confluence of the international and the local in a country where the legacy of modern art and civilization has often been understood as a universally shared frame of reference. A series of stylistic parallels between Japanese and Euro–North American tendencies are hard to ignore: Gutai vs. art informel/abstract expressionism and happenings; anti-Art *(han-geijutsu)* vs. nouveau réalisme, neodada, and pop; mono-ha (school of things) vs. arte povera and minimal/process/land art; and conceptualism.[2] At the same time, however, underneath—or rather, despite—these parallels, distinct local concerns were at work among artists and art critics as well, constituting yet another layer of the local context.

In this respect, the case of conceptualism is confounding, unlike Gutai, anti-Art, and mono-ha, which have been comparatively better studied in Japan and abroad as well. On the one hand, it is not difficult to compile retrospectively an inclusive list of artists and their works, based on certain widely recognized characteristics of conceptualism, both stylistic and strategic, including: the emphasis on concept/idea rather than form, the dematerialization of the object, and institutional critique.

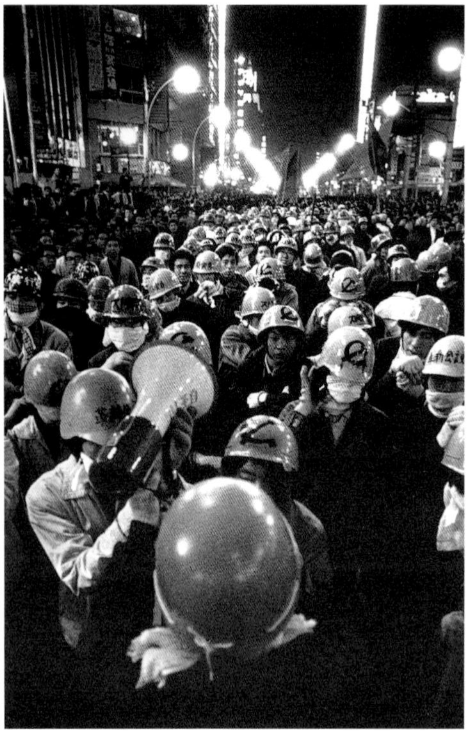

Tokyo, student demonstration, fall 1968. Courtesy of Magnum Photos, Inc. © 1968 Bruno Barbey.

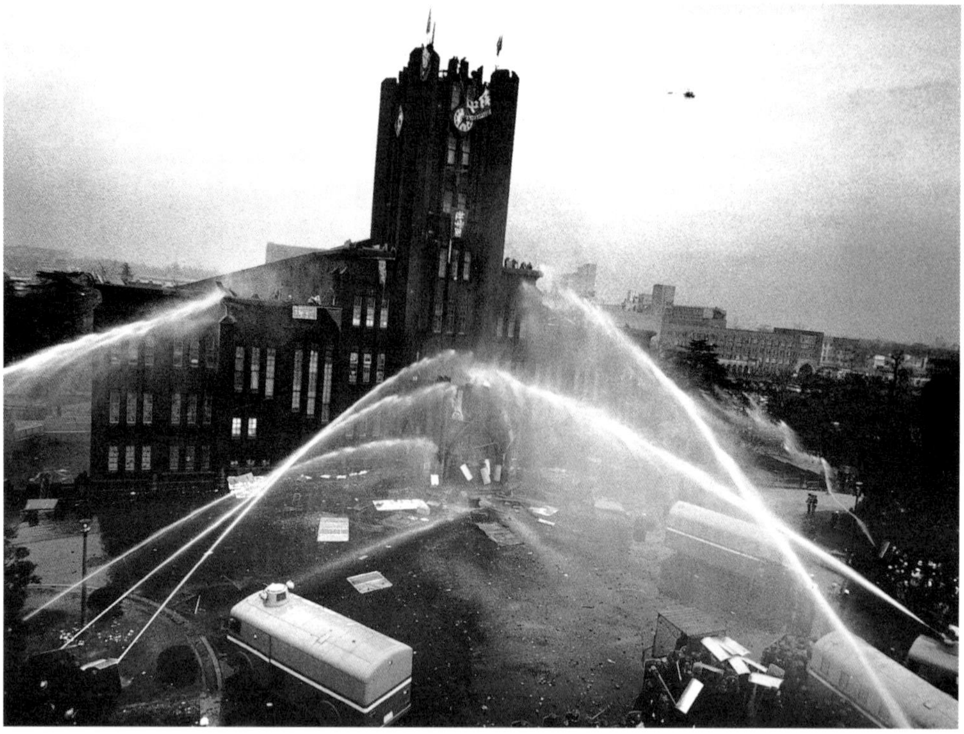

Tokyo, January 18, 1969: police use fire hoses to clear students from the auditorium of Tokyo University, where they had barricaded themselves in protest against the government. Courtesy of Magnum Photos, Inc. © 1969 Hiroshi Hamaya.

This list may be prefaced by proto-conceptualist episodes of Gutai's inventive experiments in the mid-1950s and On Kawara's theory of "printed painting" in the late '50s.[3] Entering the 1960s, the roster discretely converges with the cerebral segments of anti-Art: Yoko Ono's *Instructions for Painting* series; the intermedia explorations of Tokyo Fluxus; Matsuzawa Yutaka's art of *kannen* (literally, "idea"); and the activities of Hi Red Center and its associates, including Akasegawa Genpei's *Model 1,000-Yen Note Incident.* From the mid-1960s to the mid-'70s, diverse ideatic and/or conceptual practices emerged: the task-oriented events and exhibitions by Group "I"; *shuchi-shugi* (intellectualism), especially of Takamatsu Jirō and Kashihara Etsutomu, who investigated issues of perception and cognition;[4] the pursuit of *saishū bijutsu* (literally, "final art") by the Nirvana school gathered around Matsuzawa; systemic works by such artists as Nomura Hitoshi and Inumaki Kenji, often associated with mono-ha; the events, performances, and installations by members of Bikyōtō and its affiliates;[5] and scores of language-, mail-, performance-, and photo-based works by numerous other artists.

On the other hand, a survey of the local discourses on *gainen geijutsu* (literally, "concept Art") yields a smaller ensemble of artists and works, providing few clues to illuminate the origins of Japanese conceptualism or its development as outlined above.[6] The compiler of such a list may wonder if s/he has committed the sin of imposing the Western model of conceptualism, which is itself not free of controversy, on the reality of Japanese art. A closer scrutiny, however, reveals a crucial entanglement of the local and international discourses: ironically, it is the introduction of Euro–North American conceptual art toward 1970 that heavily and narrowly shaped Japanese art criticism.[7] Above all, the term *gainen geijutsu* itself was a translation of the English *conceptual art.*[8] Although space limitations allow no detailed historiographic inquiry,[9] suffice it to say that while Japanese critics made frequent reference to statements by, among others, Sol LeWitt, Lawrence Weiner, Daniel Buren, and Jan Dibbets, Duchamp's precedence was routinely invoked and the literal reading of Joseph Kosuth's writing (especially "Art After Philosophy") was more or less sanctioned.[10]

It should also be noted that another level of the local discourse was formed in a visually or work-derived manner, so to speak: the 1970 Tokyo Biennale, subtitled *Between Man and Matter,* which encompassed postminimalism, arte povera, conceptual art, and mono-ha, was the watershed incident in Japan confirming the generally "conceptual" *(gainen-teki)* international tendencies.[11] This type of visual collection was conducted in the graphic domain of the art magazine.[12]

By and large, in the discursive space, the label and image of conceptual art, thus delineated externally, configured what was understood to be *gainen geijutsu* in the local scenes and have provided to this day the inescapable backdrop for any further discourse or counter-discourse on conceptualism. Just as Kosuth was recognized as the quintessential conceptual artist, so Matsuzawa—who had produced text-based works since 1964—was considered the representative of *gainen geijutsu.* Not surprisingly, some artists and critics disavowed the categorization.[13] Yet others—some of whom we actually enlist in our conceptualist roster—staunchly attacked conceptual art/*gainen geijutsu.* It should also be noted that although the local discourse did not entirely evolve on its own, there has always been a strong sense that Japanese *gainen geijutsu* developed quite differently from its Euro–North American counterpart.[14]

The challenge we face today when we study "conceptualism in Japan" is daunting.[15] It must be simultaneously situated in the local context and the global arena, wherein conceptualism has become a major paradigm of art practice in the last half of the 20th century, much like abstraction has for the entire century.

Among the relevant questions that come to mind immediately is a thorny one. To what degree were works by Japanese artists influenced by Euro–North American conceptual art that developed prior to or contemporaneous with them? Although each case must be individually examined, care must be taken, because a surface similarity does not necessarily mean an influence. For example, Takamatsu Jirō's language piece from 1970, *English Word (Eigo no tango),* is a work on paper consisting of the phrase "These Three Words." The resemblance to Joseph Kosuth's 1965 work, *Five Words in Blue Neon,* is uncanny. Needless to say, it is vital from an art historical perspective to establish whether Takamatsu knew or could have known Kosuth's work. Still, it should also be noted that this kind of self-reflexivity, not limited to language, had preoccupied Takamatsu since 1964–65, as recorded in his notebook.[16] Not surprisingly, a reverse situation also occurred. In 1969, Robert Barry devised *Telepathic Piece.* This work, which reads "During the exhibition I will try to communicate telepathically a work of art ...,"[17] clearly reminds us of Matsuzawa Yutaka's *Independent '64 Exhibition in the Wilderness (Kōya ni okeru andepandan '64 ten,* 1964) (fig. 8; see Text 1), of which the New York–based artist may not have been aware.

This essay and the Japanese section of the exhibition attempt to give focused attention to those artists who, from the early 1960s through the mid-'70s, strategically confronted the issues concerning the institution of art on various levels. Since that institution is both universal and locally specific, this approach will hopefully locate a link between conceptualism's local story in Japan and its global narrative. Furthermore, the institutional critique, in a sense, can be considered a subcategory under the definition of conceptualism as "antidiscursive strategies" given by Mari Carmen Ramírez elsewhere in this volume, for the institution constitutes a hegemonic discourse to be called into question. Although the institutional critique has scarcely figured in the discussion of conceptualism per se in Japan, the "discourse on the institution" *(seido-ron)* was an integral part of Japanese art criticism during the same period. The focus on the institutional critique affords us a new perspective through which to examine the artists long accepted into the canon of *gainen geijutsu*—in this exhibition, Matsuzawa Yutaka, Kashihara Etsutomu, and Nomura Hitoshi. It also allows a fresh look at those previously overlooked or excluded from the canon: Yoko Ono, Yasunao Tone, Akasegawa Genpei, and Bikyōtō (Hikosaka Naoyoshi and Hori Kosai). Finally, we can investigate the theoretical and intellectual underpinnings of all their works within the complex web of context that surrounded them.

Moments of Rupture: The Institution of Art/art Exposed

Confrontation with the institution has been the process of self-cognition for Art.

—Tani Arata, 1973[18]

The Collapse of "Modern"

In the evolution of Japanese conceptualism, a major impetus came from anti-Art tendencies, which centered in and around the annual Yomiuri Independent Exhibition from 1958 to 1963. Or more precisely, moments of rupture were informed by a larger intellectual shift, of which anti-Art was a vital factor. Through its "descent to the mundane,"[19] anti-Art made fervent assaults on Art *(geijutsu)* as a metaphysical construct of modern times, and art *(bijutsu)* as the material means to achieve the goal that is Art. The distinction between "Art" and "art," employed throughout this essay, is especially pertinent to a discussion of postwar Japanese art, for the Japanese language has two different words that correspond to the English *art.* In general, *bijutsu* is the descriptive term that includes painting and sculpture, corresponding to "art." *Geijutsu* is an elusive word that can be translated as "the arts" when the word descriptively encompasses art, music, literature, etc.; "Art" with a capital A when there is a certain metaphysical connotation (as in anti-Art, or anti-*geijutsu*); or simply "art" when interchangeable with *bijutsu.*

The questioning of Art/art by anti-Art helped foreground the "collapse of the modern ideal of Art,"[20] which in turn pointed to the collapse of "modern" *(kindai)* as a historical paradigm, compelling a new formulation of "contemporary" *(gendai).*[21] To complicate the matter, anti-Art's failure to nullify Art in the sphere of life engendered a contradictory thesis that it was impossible for Art *not* to exist.[22]

The discourse on the institution arose in the mid-1960s as the conundrum of Art came to be recognized. Especially significant was the postulation of "Art/art as institution." Derived from sociology, this particular concept of the institution is not limited to physical entities, such as "museum" and "exhibition," but signifies a system that "governs not only the behavioral modes but also the cognitive and emotional patterns of members of a given society."[23] In this latter sense, unlike Peter Bürger who primarily equated it with the "autonomy of Art,"[24] Japanese critics interpreted "Art/art as institution" more broadly as being internal. That is, in addition to the "external conditions of Art," the institution "also exists internally within the expression, work, and act of creation."[25] This new awareness of the institution changed a key question concerning Art: "What is Art?"—no longer a viable question—was replaced by "What makes Art Art?"[26] Accordingly, faced with a novel and baffling work, one must now inquire "Why is it Art?" rather than "Is it Art?"[27]

Three Levels of Institutional Critique
If critics theorized on the institution of Art/art, artists worked and thought in their own ways, tackling the issues of the institution in their own practices. The proto-conceptualism of On Kawara, internationally known for his "date paintings" (1966–present), provides an invaluable preamble to the identification of the different levels on which the institutional critique operates. In 1958–59, prior to his departure from Japan, Kawara produced the "printed paintings" *(insatsu kaiga)*—shown at the 1958 Yomiuri Independent Exhibition—in which he extensively utilized mechanical printing processes (fig. 108). Deeply concerned with "contemporary painting's loss of the social function," he asked himself, "What is Art?," which in turn led to another obvious question: "What is communication?"[28] In his analysis, painting's fulfillment of its communicative potential as a genuine "two-way exchange" was hampered by the convention of the unique original and its method of presentation through a gallery/museum exhibition. Both conditions, according to Kawara, gravely limited painting's exposure to the masses, his target audience.[29] Equally troublesome was the fact that, due to the proliferation of print media, published reproductions became a reality of sorts. Therefore, Kawara reasoned, why not create "a work that is complete only when it is reproduced and has numerous originals" through commercial printing techniques?[30] In one instance, he published a questionnaire, together with one of his printed paintings, in an art magazine, in order to "know how my own work is understood and communicated" and to encourage a "creative production on the part of the audience."[31]

Kawara's clear-eyed cogitation engaged at least three levels of institutional critique. First, by asking what Art is, Kawara—though only rhetorically—set the stage to question "Art as institution." Second, he confronted the gallery/museum exhibition as a "physical institution of art." And third, by calling into question the idea of "unique original," he challenged the received notion and conventionalized practice of artmaking.

In a sense, emerging on the other end of the Japanese art spectrum in the late 1950s, anti-Art by and large *acted out* a dissent against the institution of Art/art. Some artists, however, crossed the gulf between a mere gesture of negation and conceptualism, each bringing the conditioning of Art/art into sharper focus and marking a moment of rupture.

Painting as Institution
Painting is the site of contention in modern art history. In *Instructions for Painting (E no tame no insutorakushon,* 1961–64), Yoko Ono revoked the self-sufficient body of the painting: not only was paint replaced by language, the structural syntax of the medium was also laid bare. Moreover, the role of the viewer was reconfigured as an active agent who completed the artwork either physically by her/his making it, or simply as a mental process. The series' evolution from instruction-based event-performances, however, was gradual. In the earliest presentation in New York in 1961 (figs. 109, 110), the instructions were delivered orally to the viewer by the artist in front of the canvases. Although the use of cards was documented in 1961, words alone, handwritten in Japanese and taped on the wall, constituted the work in Tokyo in 1962 (fig. 111).[32] Once Ono plainly demonstrated the institutionalized premise of painting (i.e., canvas hung on the wall) and reiterated the validity of language as its material, her "paintings"—together with her music, events, objects, and poetry—could be collected in a bilingual book of instructions, *Grapefruit,* in 1964 (fig. 112).

Instructions for Painting highlights overall traits of conceptualism that derived from anti-Art: the interest in intermedia that catalyzed a break with habitual modes of artmak-

Text 1
Independent '64 Exhibition in the Wilderness

Don't believe matter
Don't believe senses
Don't believe the eye

Site: Tundra Field, Nanatsushima
Yatsushima Highland, Nagano Prefecture

Period: Before daybreak, December 3 to before daybreak, December 9

Installation/deinstallation date: Past, present, future

Entry fee: None

Entry method: Please keep your entry in your hand and deliver the formless emission from it (imaginary work) to the exhibition site. Any delivery method will do. It is very likely the site will be filled with many bizarre, formless things of Nil, making the exhibition a rare merry occasion. Those who wish to enter may begin contact in material and/or immaterial ways.

Please contact: Void-Space Situation Research Center, 5370 Shimo Suwa-chō, Nagano Prefecture

—Matsuzawa Yutaka

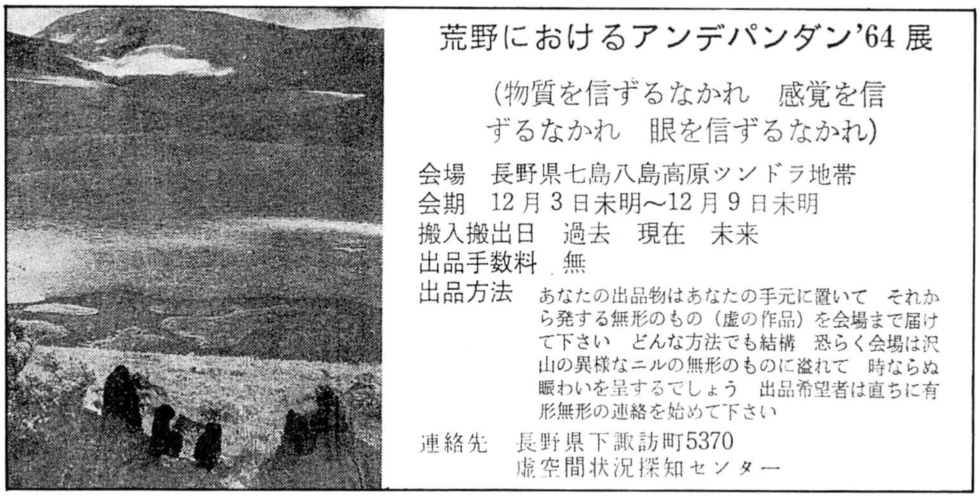

Figure 8.
Matsuzawa Yutaka, *Independent '64 Exhibition in the Wilderness (Kōya ni okeru andepandan '64 ten)*, 1964, advertisement placed in *Bijutsu Journal*, no. 15 (1964).

ing; the performative use of language to create or operate an eventlike setting;[33] and the exploitation of the viewer's participation, voluntary or otherwise. Furthermore, the series may be situated in a historical context that had haunted Japanese artists since the late 19th century: the concept, and attending institution, of "painting" as codified in the West was, and still is, a challenge of modernity that cannot be easily negotiated.[34] Whereas Ono confronted it through deconstruction, two other New York–based Japanese conceptualists, Shusaku Arakawa and On Kawara, retained the nominal body of painting in their respective diagram and date paintings.

Matsuzawa and Antimaterialism

If Ono engages the viewer through playful poetry, Matsuzawa Yutaka, once a poet himself, does so with spiritual conviction. The elder statesman of Japanese conceptualism, Matsuzawa is in a class by himself. The object of his critique is the materialism of modern civilization as a whole. In 1964, as the legend goes, he heard a voice which commanded, "Vanish *objets!*"[35] He thereupon set out to create art solely from text, as a denunciation of art's materiality and human sense-reception. Inevitably, the institutions of art were subjected to drastic reform in his noble project to propagate an art that would constitute "acts of 'anticivilization' engaged by humankind equipped with an 'omnipotence of sorts' under no restriction."[36]

The first to go was painting: *Ψ Corpse (Pusai no shitai itai,* 1964; fig. 113), a printed handbill that immediately followed his revelation, announces "nonsensory painting," which is invisible to the eye yet present, similar to the intangible subatomic reality hypothesized by quantum mechanics.[37] Neither does the exhibition need a material display. The viewer can visualize *Anticivilization Exhibition (Han-bunmei ten,* 1965) reading a flier in the midst of a cluttered group exhibition (see Text 2). Even the exhibition hall can be bypassed: in *Independent '64 Exhibition in the Wilderness* (1964), a magazine ad is all that is necessary to incite the mental movement of his fellow artists toward a faraway place (fig. 8); and in *Postcard Paintings (Hagaki kaiga,* 1967–68), postcards deliver aphoristic directives to his audience.[38] Still, the immediacy of experience is never disposed of, for recitative performances join the artist and his audience in *Humans, Let's Vanish,*

Text 2
Vanishing of Objet: Seeing Anticivilization Exhibition

This text consists of 729 characters. The number is obtained by multiplying 9 to the power of 3. I am submitting an exhibition to the exhibition. My submission is *Anticivilization Exhibition*, which is an exhibition unto itself. This *chirashi* flier ["bloody naked paper"] is a section of negative. Using this negative, you will make a print of *Anticivilization Exhibition* in your consciousness. First, completely vanish the All-Japan Independent Exhibition unfolded in front of you, with your eyes closed or open. And there! Please replace its entirety with my, no, your *Anticivilization Exhibition*. By that small action, *Anticivilization Exhibition* will be realized. This is the greatest *dépaysement* [dislocation] in the history of art. What makes such a horrifying thing possible? By the principle of "omnipotence of sorts." That is, ψ (psi) is capable of vanishing and creating an *objet*. It is an extremely dangerous truth. Too dangerous to be harmful, for now. Ah, *Anticivilization Exhibition*, held at the Yokohama Citizen's Gallery from May 18 through 31, was an extraordinarily terrifying exhibit. He made a *mudrā* [hand sign] and stood at its entrance. He boldly entered it. Therein appeared to be almost nothing, it was imperceptible whether anything or nothing was there. Thus, Nil was brimming there. In that "void" thrown over the floor were *chirashi* fliers, printed in the color of blackened blood on paper as white as a bone ...

—Excerpted from Matsuzawa Yutaka, *Anticivilization Exhibition*, 1965

Gate Gate—*Anticivilization Committee*[39] *(Jinrui-yo, shōmetsu shiyō, gyatei, gyatei—Han-bunmei iinkai,* 1966–ongoing; fig. 7).

Matsuzawa's indebtedness to Asian thought, especially Buddhism, is evident in his aspiration for the ideas of "nothingness" and "void," his use of the mandala-derived three-by-three grid that embodies the Esoteric Buddhist cosmology, and his reliance on the viewer's ideation. Yet what distinguishes Matsuzawa's contribution is not so much cultural borrowings as the fact that his injection of nonmaterialist Eastern spiritualism into avant-garde art practices generally perceived as part of Western tradition offered a viable alternative to Euro–North American conceptualism.

Unlike Ono, who left Japan in 1964, the charismatic Matsuzawa enjoyed an enthusiastic following of younger artists collectively called the Nirvana school. From around 1969, Matsuzawa's estate in Suwa, a few hours' train ride from Tokyo, became a communelike gathering place for likeminded artists and critics. In 1973 he also established in Suwa a "workshop to contemplate final art" for the Tokyo-based Bigakkō art school. The Nirvana artists exhibited their work at *Nirvana: For Final Art* in 1970 and participated, under the name Ultimate Expression Institute (Kyūkyoku Hyōgen Kenkyūjo), in the 1973 Kyoto Biennale, both held at Kyoto Municipal Museum of Art.

Exhibition as Institution

Social institutions of art—the exhibition and museum, among others—are by definition molded by the sociohistorical particulars of a given locale. And *Jury Event: Tone-Prize Exhibition (Shinsa ivento: Tone-shō sakka-ten,* 1964) is intricately embedded in the matrix of local history, with the musician-artist Yasunao Tone, a member of Tokyo Fluxus, commenting on the state of such institutions at the specific moment of 1964.[40]

In the annals of avant-garde art, the year of the Tokyo Olympics is marked by the Yomiuri newspaper company's termination of its annual Yomiuri Independent Exhibition, established in 1949 to democratize the art world. Japan's art world had evolved around the state-sponsored annual salons and other annual exhibitions organized by dozens of art associations since the late 19th century. As a rule, the larger periodic salons/exhibitions, including the Yomiuri Independent, were held at art museums *(bijutsukan),* which were not repositories of masterpieces but primarily exhibition halls for rent. The most typical example is the Tokyo Metropolitan Museum of Art.[41] Smaller group and solo exhibitions were held at galleries, which were not yet an engine of the art market—then virtually nonexistent for avant-garde art—but, which again, could be rented. For younger artists, a museum exhibition generally meant the open-entry *(kōbo)* format, whether juried (salon and association annuals) or not (independents), with prizes an essential element of juried exhibitions.

The sudden termination of the Yomiuri Independent in 1964 represented an acute loss of what had become the principle forum of anti-Art. But it also prompted discussion of the dependency of vanguard artists on the corporate-sponsored "independent."[42] There were two immediate, but diametrically opposite, responses by artists to the situation. Whereas the *Independent '64 Exhibition (Andepandan '64-ten),* held at the Tokyo Metropolitan, clung to the institutional site, the rival exhibition *Off Museum (Ofu myūzeamu),* held concurrently at a gallery, defied institutional encroachment. While Tone participated in the latter, Matsuzawa joined the former with *Ψ Corpse,* which signaled the death of his *objet*-based works and paid an inadvertent eulogy to the *objet*-flooded Yomiuri Independent. The artist-organized independent was also ostensibly referred to in Matsuzawa's *Independent '64 Exhibition in the Wilderness.*

Staged a few months later, *Tone-Prize Exhibition* was a critical commentary on the entire exhibition system. To lend his enterprise an official aura, Tone assembled an impressive panel of jurors, including Yoko Ono, the Butoh dancer Hijikata Tatsumi, and the critic Takiguchi Shūzō, who would each give a prize. He then placed an ad in a music magazine (fig. 9; see Text 3) and drafted an application form. Yet he undermined the jury framework by awarding his namesake prize to every entry, essentially turning the exhibition into an independent. (The prizes involved no monetary awards.) With a similarly subversive spirit, Hi Red Center (of which Takamatsu Jirō and Akasegawa Genpei were principle members) contributed an entry, *Cleaning Event (Chō-sōji ivento,* 1964), covertly beautifying the streets of Tokyo six days after the Tokyo Olympics opened (figs. 10, 182).

Art as Institution

Among the efforts of anti-Art, Akasegawa Genpei's *Model 1,000-Yen Note Incident (Mokei sen-en-satsu jiken,* 1963–73) is a particularly complex work that allows manifold readings (figs. 11, 114). *Incident* began in 1963 when Akasegawa ordered mechanical reproductions of the 1,000-yen note from commercial printers. The replicated notes were then used in his exhibition announcement, object-based works, and performances. However, the artist's desire to operate in society—outside the gallery and museum—backfired, resulting in a criminal investigation for currency fraud in 1964. Akasegawa's ensuing legal ordeal, which ended with a guilty verdict, was memorable chiefly for the infamous "exhibition event in the courtroom" on the trial's first day in 1966.

However, in postwar Japanese art, *Model 1,000-Yen Note Incident* is a rare instance in which the nature of Art was made an explicit issue. As such, *Incident* can be interpreted as a conceptualist work. In fact, during the entire course of *Incident,* language played a much larger role than action: already during the police investigation, Akasegawa introduced the concept of *model* to rebut the legal notions of *counterfeit* and *imitation* (see Text 4).[43] Once he was indicted for "imitation" in 1965, the 1,000-Yen Note Incident Discussion Group (Sen-en-satsu Jiken Kondankai), which included Tone, devised the courtroom strategy, issued public statements, and organized benefits (fig. 213).

Text 3
Call for Entries: 1st Tone-Prize Composition

Tone Prizes are given to all entries.

Deadline: October 1.

Certificates will be mailed in lieu of official announcement in early October.

There is no restriction on form or content. However, phenomena will not be accepted for they are impossible to present; instead, please submit texts, etc. For further details, please contact: Yasunao Tone, 11 Asakusa Shōtenchō, Taitō-ku, Tokyo.

Announcement of Prizes
Works that receive Tone Prizes automatically qualify for the following individual prizes, which will be presented at a concert at Sōgetsu Hall in late November.

Prizes include:
Kosugi Prize, Ichiyanagi Prize, Okuyama Prize, Ono Prize, Akasegawa Prize, Nakanishi Prize, Takiguchi Prize, Takeda Prize, Ishizaki Prize, Shinohara Prize, Kobayashi Prize, Hijikata Prize, etc.

Performed and juried by:
Kosugi Takehisa, Ichiyanaga Toshi, Okuyama Jūnosuke, Yoko Ono, Akasegawa Genpei, Nakanishi Natsuyuki, Takiguchi Shūzō, Takeda Akimichi, Ishizaki Kōichirō, Shinohara Ushio, Hijikata Tatsumi, etc.

Cocurrence [sic] event 1964 Tokyo
This ad was placed in Ongaku Geijutsu *22, no. 10 (September 1964). The application form, available from Tone, includes the exhibition information: "Tone-Prize Exhibition: October 12–17, at Naiqua Gallery ... will exhibit all the entries as they are accepted." It also contains restrictions concerning the Ono Prize, which, "given by Yoko Ono, will be open to works by male composers only. [Entrants] are required to present 'face and forms,' i.e., a photograph and data for weight, height, bust size, etc."*

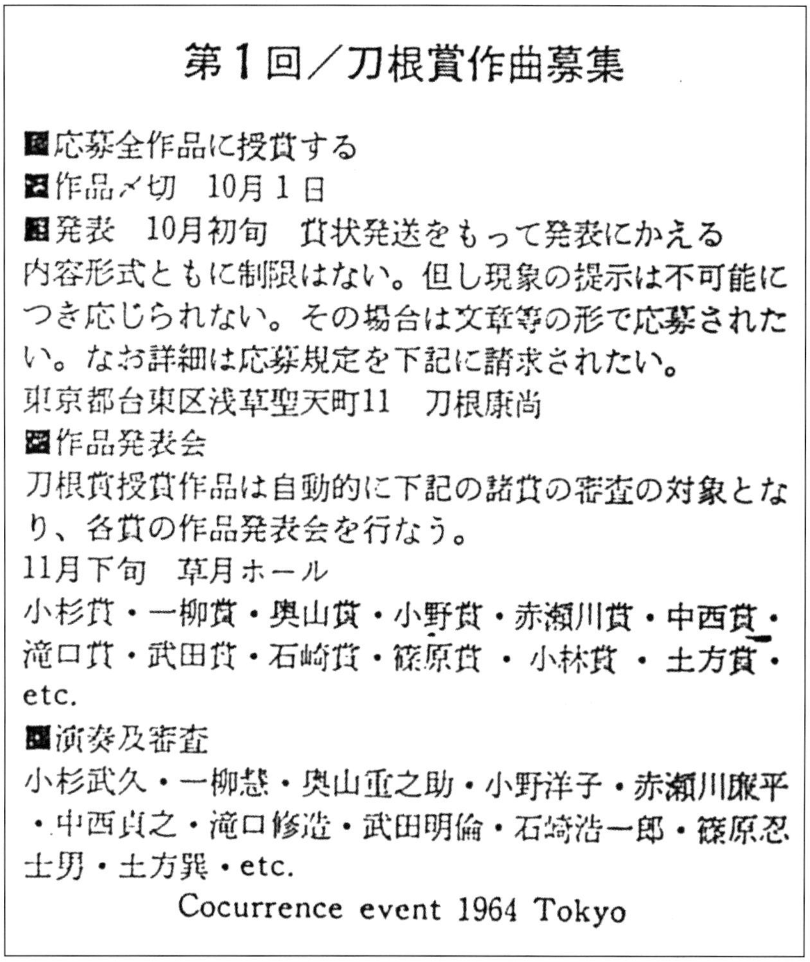

第1回／刀根賞作曲募集

■応募全作品に授賞する
■作品〆切　10月1日
■発表　10月初旬　賞状発送をもって発表にかえる
内容形式ともに制限はない。但し現象の提示は不可能につき応じられない。その場合は文章等の形で応募されたい。なお詳細は応募規定を下記に請求されたい。
東京都台東区浅草聖天町11　刀根康尚
■作品発表会
刀根賞授賞作品は自動的に下記の諸賞の審査の対象となり、各賞の作品発表会を行なう。
11月下旬　草月ホール
小杉賞・一柳賞・奥山賞・小野賞・赤瀬川賞・中西賞・滝口賞・武田賞・石崎賞・篠原賞・小林賞・土方賞・etc.
■演奏及審査
小杉武久・一柳慧・奥山重之助・小野洋子・赤瀬川原平・中西貞之・滝口修造・武田明倫・石崎浩一郎・篠原忍士男・土方巽・etc.

Cocurrence event 1964 Tokyo

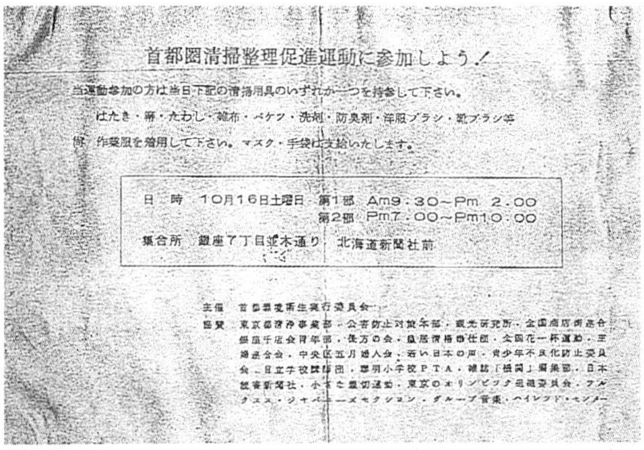

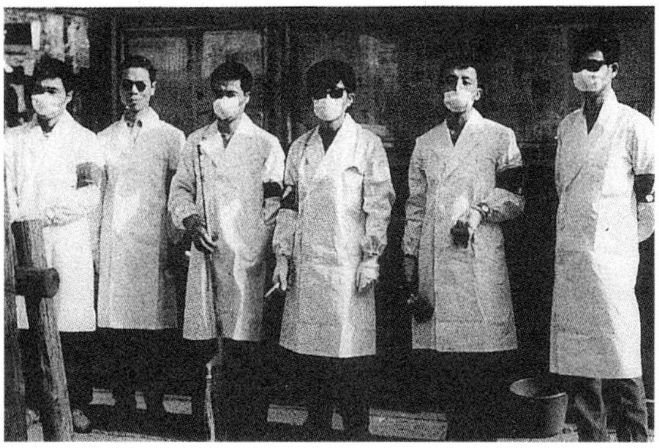

Figure 9. (above)
Yasunao Tone, *Jury Event: Tone-Prize Exhibition (Shinsa ivento: Tone-shō sakka-ten),* 1964, advertisement placed in *Ongaku Geijutsu* (September 1964).

Figure 10. (left)
Hi Red Center, *Cleaning Event* (*Chō-sōji ivento*), an entry to *Tone-Prize Exhibition,* 1964, flier (top) and documentary photograph (bottom). Collection of Akasegawa Genpei, courtesy of Nagoya City Art Museum.

Text 4
Model 1,000-Yen Note Incident: Definitions

Counterfeit *(gizō)*
Section 16: Crime of Currency Counterfeit. Article 148: 1. Those who counterfeit or forge money, paper currency, or banknotes with an express intent to use will be punished with three years to life of hard labor.

—From Criminal Codes

Imitation *(mozō)*
Article 1 (Prohibition of Imitation and Sale): It is prohibited to produce or sell that which has an appearance that could be confused with currency, government-issued notes, bank-notes, [and other official money equivalents]. Article 2 (Penalty): Those who violate the above Article 1 will be punished with one to three years of hard labor ...

—From Law to Regulate the Imitation of Currency and Bond Certificates

Model *(mokei)*
My printed matter that became a legal matter of sorts, contrary to my intention, is not a counterfeit but a model of the 1,000-yen note. It differs from a counterfeit or a real 1,000-yen note in that in my intention and in its actuality it is "unusable" and thus a model of the 1,000-yen note stripped of the function of paper currency.

—From Akasegawa Genpei, "On 'Capitalist Realism'" (February 1964)

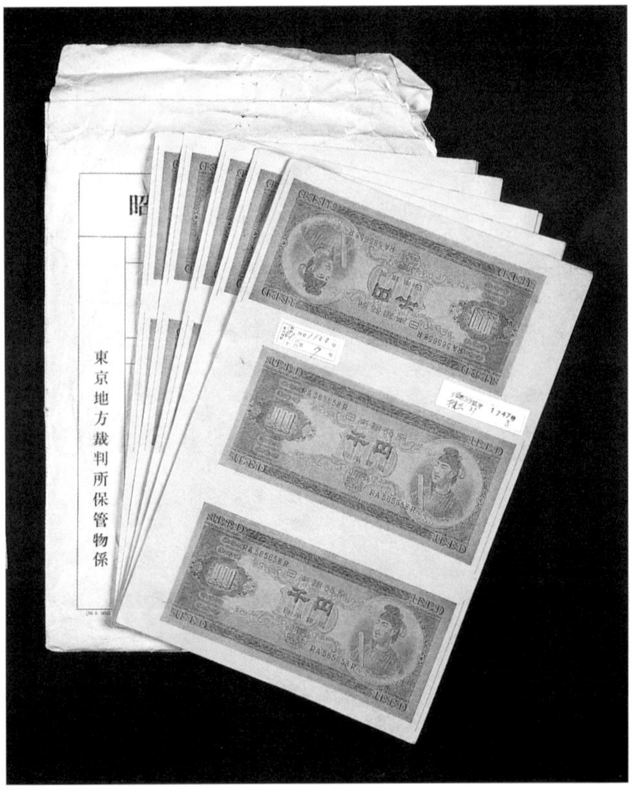

Figure 11.
Akasegawa Genpei, *Model 1000-Yen Notes: Printed Work,* 1963, printed matter with court envelope.

The most critical implication of *Incident* lies in the defense claim that Akasegawa's work—as well as other types of anti-Art—*is* Art. To make the point loud and clear, Akasegawa and the Discussion Group appropriated the courtroom first as an impromptu exhibition hall and then as a sphere of discourse that the defense monopolized by the force of tens of thousands of words. Ironically, by accepting the defense claim, the court legitimized Akasegawa as an Artist *(geijutsuka),* but still found him guilty. At stake was not so much whether Akasegawa, who defined himself as a painter, was an Artist—or whether his work was Art, for that matter—as what such labels (or "names," in Akasegawa's parlance) as Artist and Art mean and how they come to assume meaning. The bitter lesson learned by Akasegawa was that the authority to define (name) Art belonged to him, yet the name Artist defined him in society.[44] In other words, this "name" acquired its relevance when society, via the court in his case, wanted to situate him within it. In this sense, the "names" Art and Artist serve the function of social conditioning and, thus, constitute another level of institution.

After the trial, Akasegawa, now an ex-convict, explored "parody," as exemplified by *Greater Japan Zero-Yen Notes (Dai-Nihon zero-en-satsu,* 1967) and *A Course in Capitalist Realism (Shihon-shugi riarizumu kōza,* 1973; fig. 190). Meanwhile, Tone pursued "historicization." Having embarked on critical writing on Art as "reflections through language and history,"[45] Tone was especially instrumental in compiling the history of '60s art, in collaboration with critic Akatsuka Yukio and Bikyōtō member Hikosaka Naoyoshi, in the pages of *Bijutsu Techō* (Art Notebook).[46] Their project culminated in the 400-page, multicolumn *Chronology: Five Decades of Contemporary Art, 1916–1968 (Nenpyō: Gendai bijutsu no 50-nen, 1916–1968,* 1972), a "temporal tableau" framing the '60s avant-garde within the process of "institutionalization" (fig. 108).[47]

After Anti-Art: In the Ruins of Modernism

The legacy of anti-Art gradually crystallized in 1965–70. The nature of the avant-garde appeared to be changing, as signaled by Akasegawa's trial and the massive participation of vanguard artists in the technological

Text 5
An Appeal to Artists

Let us win the struggle of the '70s to destroy modern rationalism. Dismantle the power machine of art!

....

Dismantle the National Museum of Modern Art!

....

Smash the open-entry exhibition system that exists between the two opposite poles of the [annual salon] Nitten and Mainichi [Newspaper]'s [biannual] Contemporary Art Exhibition!

....

Dismantle the Tokyo Metropolitan Art Museum!

The art power that we must smash has its de facto headquarters at the Tokyo Metropolitan Art Museum. Let us begin a struggle to liberate the enemy's fortress by our own hands. ... The function has already been imposed upon our expression. In order to win and acquire our own expression, let us turn this already imposed function into our weapon. ...

Smash the Tokyo Biennale! Smash Expo '70!

Let us disavow the Tokyo Biennale and Expo '70, which confine expression in the state's framework, exist as international competitions, and help the state to demonstrate its cultural standard. ...

Let us gather under Bijutsuka Kyōtō Kaigi [Artists Joint-Struggle Council]!

... Only through the process of a struggle on which our bodies, sites of our expression, are staked, does our own expression become possible. In order to acquire our own expression through a struggle:

Let us gather under Bijutsuka Kyōtō Kaigi!

—Excerpted from the agitational flier dated July 5, 1969, as reprinted in *Bikyōtō Documents*

Text 6
Practice 3

Four artists among us founded the Bikyōtō Revolution Committee and agreed that each would organize an exhibition, with admission charged and without using a museum or a gallery over the period of one year.

Can these activities, held on a riverbank, at a home, on a university campus, and at a space laboratory, be labeled "off museum"?

No. We are dissociated from optimists who believe they can escape the institution through advocating "off museum."

The museum emerges wherever one conducts an act of artmaking.

However, it is meaningless if one artist holds an exhibition outside the museum/gallery. Our starting point is: several people encounter and discover the museum manifesting itself within the act of artmaking, of which we as individuals have been previously unaware.

Through our activities, we have aimed to concretely possess this "internal museum" as our commonality.

Produced by Bikyōtō Revolution Committee, directed by Hori Kosai, *Floor, Ceiling, Walls, Act, Water* (at space laboratory Hair [an underground theater] in Shibuya, 1971)

Produced by Bikyōtō Revolution Committee, directed by Hikosaka Naoyoshi, *Floor Event* (at Hikosaka residence, 1971)

Produced by Bikyōtō Revolution Committee, directed by Yamanaka Nobuo, *Projecting the Film of a River onto the River* (at the Tama River, 1971)

Produced by Bikyōtō Revolution Committee, directed by Tajima Renji, *Work* (at the Tama Art University campus, 1971)

—Excerpted from Shihyō Group and Hikosaka Naoyoshi, "Death of the Group: Four Practices in Pursuit of Collectivity," *Bijutsu Techō*, no. 372 (October 1973)

pageant of Expo '70. In anticipation of the 1970 Anpo renewal, the sociopolitical situation was volatile. Meanwhile, as the destabilization of Art/art became a given condition, the state of art was sobering to those artists now at the forefront who had begun their careers after 1965.

Radicalism and "Internal Institution"

If the 1960 Anpo protest was the psychopolitical landscape that informed anti-Art, the university conflicts of 1968–69 incited art students' radicalism. The issues surrounding the institution of Art/art exposed by anti-Art were brought to both militant and theoretical extremes.

Bikyōtō (short for Bijutsuka Kyōtō Kaigi, or Artists Joint-Struggle Council) was founded in July 1969 by, among others, Hori Kosai (chairman) and Hikosaka Naoyoshi of Tama Art University in Tokyo. Since the left's enemy list included the modernization programs pushed by the state, modern concepts such as "Artist" *(geijutsuka)* and "Art" were suspect by association. But, ever committed to "expression," which is more general than Art or art, Bikyōtō chose to accept the inescapable "name" *artist (bijutsuka)*. This was not merely a semantic gesture but a manifestation of their resolution: in their "battlefield" of art,[48] they sought to achieve "expression" untainted by the negative social function imposed on them by the state. Yet, eschewing the traditional subordination of art to politics, Bikyōtō politicized art by making the institution its object of attack. They thus cried out, "Dismantle the power machine of art!,"[49] which consisted of the Tokyo Metropolitan Museum of Art (*the* site of institutionalized exhibitions), the open-entry exhibition system, and the state's cultural apparatus (i.e., Expo '70 and the National Museum of Modern Art, Tokyo) (fig. 115; see Text 5). At the same time, Bikyōtō's desire to locate expression on a horizon where the social and the artistic intersect, underscored by its keen historical consciousness, enabled it to see the institution of art both externally and internally.[50]

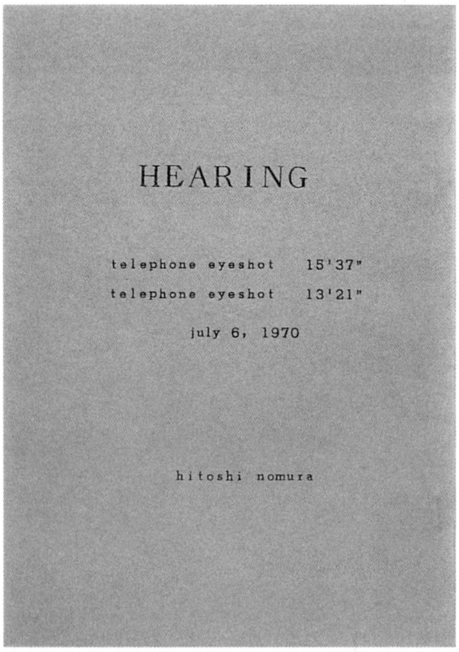

HEARING

telephone eyeshot 15'37"
telephone eyeshot 13'21"

july 6, 1970

hitoshi nomura

FIGURE 12. (LEFT AND BELOW)
Nomura Hitoshi, *Telephone Eyeshot,* 1970,
two photographs, translated transcript.
Collection of the artist.

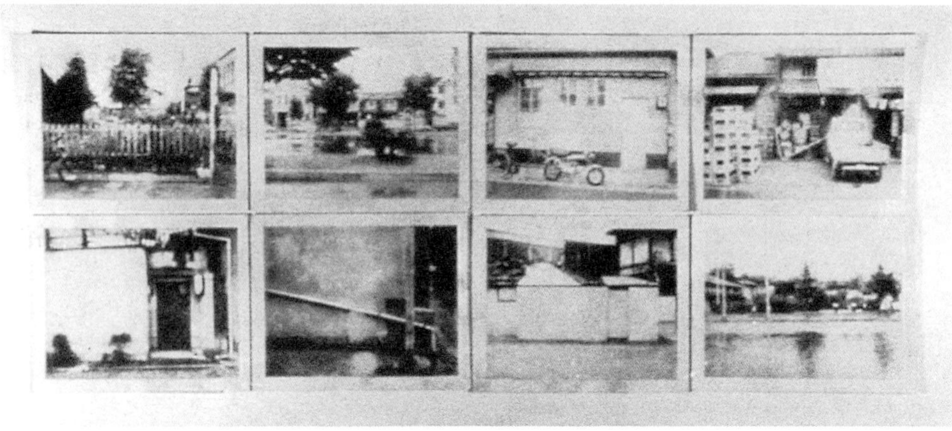

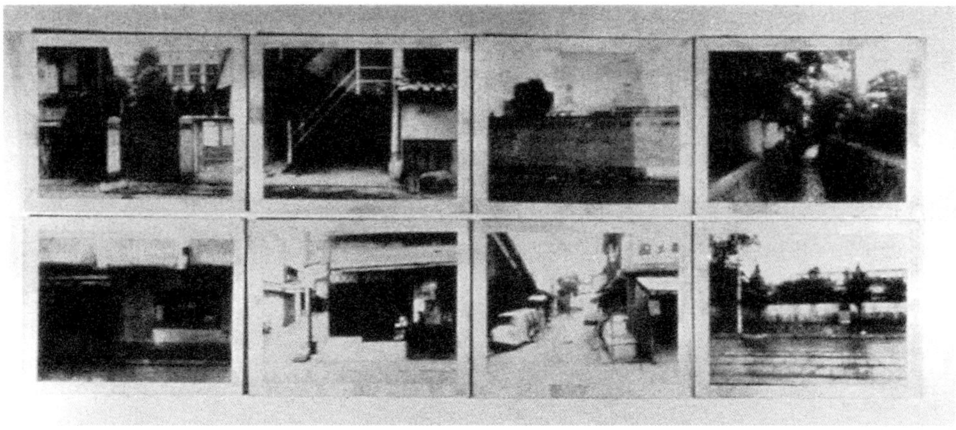

Text 7
On July 6, 1970, Nomura Hitoshi made a series of reports from public phones to 075-761-4114 (National Museum of Modern Art, Kyoto), which were recorded by the curator Ogura Tadao.

This is from the phone box 4601.
I am facing the north.
It's from the phone box.
Through the pale blue glass, I can see street trees—one, two, three, four, five, six, seven, and the rest looks like a long row.
The electric cable, running northward, extends, uh, straight.
Uh, on the sidewalk, there are bicycles—one, two, three, four, five, and a motorbike—and toy boxes are scattered, blown by the wind.
Uh, three children and, uh, a woman are picking up these boxes.
A sunshade, uh, with red-and-blue stripes, is violently fluttering in the wind.
Uh, on the second floor of that building, two bamboo shades are also fluttering violently.
Authorized monthly installment payment available for National electric appliances.
National color televisions.
National monthly installment program ...
[recording unclear]
... blue, red, yellow, blue, red ...
Yellow acrylic board is shining.
Five meters beyond that, I can see yellow-and-brown, uh, sunshades.
I can see a red-and-blue sunshade, too.
One, two, three, four billboards. A barber's.
A sushi restaurant's.
Beyond that, a row of ...
Ping pong peen, pong ping poon [sounds signaling the end of three minutes on a public phone].
A fence extends northward, twenty to thirty meters long.
Beyond the fence, trees grow densely.
Far away, 100 to 150 meters beyond that,
I can see a red-and-white billboard.
People, three people, are walking beneath the billboard.
Red ...

—Excerpted from Nomura Hitoshi, *Hearing*
(transcript of *Telephone Eyeshot,* 1970)

Text 8
Exhibition, 1971
(Pinar Galleries, Tokyo)

[Statement]
Everyday objects in the boxes are borrowed from six people based on the request on the right.

[Request]
Exhibition is an "Exhibition" of "Kashihara Etsutomu Exhibition." In an attempt to separate or isolate "Exhibition" from "Kashihara Etsutomu" as much as possible, I request your cooperation as follows:

1) I would like to borrow your private belongings as exhibits in this exhibition. By "private belongings," I mean anything that is blended into your life.

2) At an exhibition venue, there will be 20 cardboard boxes, each 70 cm high and 36 x 36 cm in section. Please place each belonging in the box that roughly corresponds to its position in your room. However, the orientation of the room can be arbitrary.

3) Please select 6 to 10 objects by yourself. When you choose objects, please avoid, as much as possible, taking into consideration features unrelated to your everyday life, such as forms and images.

4) Please do not disclose, to me or the audience, private meanings you may see in these objects.

5) Below is the placement of the boxes.

1	2	3	4	5
6	7	8	9	10
11	12	13	14	15
16	17	18	19	20

Thank you for your cooperation.

July 1971, Kashihara Etsutomu

To Mr./Ms. ________________

Before Bikyōtō could expand its campaign beyond the initial tactical targets—the commercial artists' association Nissenbi and the semi-official salon Nitten[51]—the group's political struggle as well as the nationwide student movement ended in defeat under the state's ruthless deployment of force in late 1969. By 1971, Bikyōtō's core members Hori and Hikosaka reorganized the group into a cluster of collectives, including the first Bikyōtō Revolution Committee (Bikyōtō Revolution Iinkai), and continued their struggle in the sphere of expression, wherein the notion of "internal institution" took on greater significance. According to the Committee's formulation, even when artmaking occurs outside of institutional sites (i.e., museum/gallery), "art as institution" inevitably presents itself within one's "internal museum," which is characterized by the "impossibility of dissolution."[52] If going "off museum" à la anti-Art is not even an option, what can an artist do? The answer: s/he must comprehend the "internal museum" not only theoretically but concretely through practice. Based on this premise, the Committee agreed to use no museum/gallery during 1971, and instead produced four solo exhibitions at a private home, on a riverbank, on campus, and at an underground theater, with admission charged (see Text 6). Yasunao Tone was the Committee's nominal member who contributed no solo exhibition in 1971; however, his synergetic alliance with Bikyōtō was mutually important in the development of the discourse on "Art/art as institution."

To Make or Not Make

After anti-Art, "making" in any conventional sense was in danger. In art criticism, with art reformulated as the "institution of seeing," the hand—the traditional agent of making—was superceded by the machine that fabricates and the eye that sees.[53] Among artists, the "refusal to make"[54] increasingly dominated: in addition to Matsuzawa's ideatic conceptualism, Lee U Fan postulated mono-ha (school of things) in the Eastern mode of "seeing the world as it is."[55] An open question remains: is mono-ha in fact object-based conceptualism?

The most engaging aspect of conceptualism in Japan in the 1970s can be found in the resistance to mono-ha and *gainen-ha* (school of concepts)—which categorically rejected the West but "mystified expression"[56]—by those artists who insisted on confronting the problematics of art in the very process of making. Kashihara Etsutomu and Nomura Hitoshi, who independently developed their modus operandi, shared this endeavor with Bikyōtō, occasionally collaborating with the group in exhibitions and publications.

Not unlike Bikyōtō's central members, Kashihara Etsutomu knew the importance of theoretical reflection. In his "situational analysis," he found contemporary tendencies—from anti-Art to technology art to mono-ha, from pop to minimal to conceptual art—lacking, for they failed to "develop a structure of imagination and production." For him, an escape route from the predicament of "not making" did not begin with the clever "relativization" (of Warhol, say) of such "absolute" notions as originality, which constituted the "myth of Art," but rather with an investigation of the "structure of making and seeing."[57] In fact, this direction developed from *What Is Mr. X? (Mr. X towa nanika?,* 1968–69), a collaborative experiment with two fellow artists to create a fourth identity, Mr. X, as the average of the three. Particularly vital were their numerous discussions to formulate the concept of Mr. X, who nominally issued the "orders" *(shirei)* through which he instructed the three to create his "portraits."[58] In his *Exhibition* series (*Ten,* 1970–73), Kashihara, now on his own, modified the tactic, having others perform certain functions based on his "requests" (fig. 116; see Text 8). Yet in these deceptively simple and impersonal works, one factor remained unchanged: the artist is a committed agent of making who plans and, more importantly, interprets the work, whether or not this conceptual process is rendered visible to the viewer.

Among the very first Japanese artists to adopt photography as a primary means of inquiry, Nomura Hitoshi is perhaps the most tacit

Text 9
Produced by Bikyōtō Revolution Committee II

Printing Machine
Ikeda Shōichi
Suzuki Kanji
Hikosaka Naoyoshi
Hori Kosai
Yano Naokazu
Yamanaka Nobuo

The above six have founded the Second Bikyōtō Revolution Committee and agree that during the coming year of 1974 will perform no activity related to the creation and exhibition of works.

Based on this agreement, the present exhibition is organized and the works shown here are produced.

During this year the above six will produce and exhibit as described below:

The Group of Five's Photobook Editorial Committee, founded in '71, will publish the third volume of *Group of Five's Photographs: Revolution* in December of this year and disband, as had originally been planned. Thereafter, for the next year, Ikeda, Suzuki, Hikosaka, and Yano will suspend production and exhibition of their works.

The second *Duet* series begun by Masako & Naoyoshi in May '73 will end with *Duet No. 10* to be shown at the exhibition *Artists Today '73* (at Yokohama City Museum) in November of this year. Thereafter, for the next year, Hikosaka will suspend production and exhibition of his works.

After *Inquiry Vol. 3*, to be shown at Tokiwa Gallery on October 14 of this year, and the participation in *Artists Today '73* in November, Hori Kosai will suspend production and exhibition of his works for the next year.

After the participation in *Artists Today '73* in November of this year, Yamanaka Nobuo will suspend production and exhibition of his works for the next year.

—Excerpted from the exhibition flier for *Printing Machine*, 1973

practitioner of conceptualism in Japan. Asked to explain the intention behind his work, he retorted: "My artmaking begins precisely with a desire not to talk about that."[59] Having realized the irrelevance of objects as such almost from the beginning, he exploited the camera's recording function. Nomura initially documented the changing state of things (for instance, the evaporation of a block of dry ice) and his own actions (e.g., falling down), but soon focused his camera/eye on the everyday environment. As demonstrated in *Telephone Eyeshot* (1970), which incorporates language, a collection of visual and vocal recordings of random mundane scenes deny the artist the possibility of attaching any significance to his act, while disavowing any meaning to what is recorded (fig. 12; see Text 7). In this sense, Nomura exemplifies the type of artist who locates the issue of expression in "all aspects of life, wherein an act of making is articulated in real time."[60] When his principle of repeated recording was aimed at the heavens, *'moon' score* series (1975–80) was born (fig. 118). The simple act of photographing the moon with a roll of thirty-six exposures per night over more than a decade resulted in a visuality of subtle beauty, despite the intentional emptiness.

The activist notion of "practice" was a key to Bikyōtō members' individual probe for a renewed engagement with making. For both Hikosaka and Hori, a methodological structure arose from the instruction-based event, which they learned from their mentor/ally Tone. Their experiments in this direction included Hikosaka's *Floor Event (Furoa ivento,* 1970; figs. 119, 204) and Hori's *Revolution: Ceiling, Wall, Floor (Revolution: Tenjō, kabe, yuka,* 1971; figs. 120, 205). The theory of "practice" was further elaborated through the Aristotelian concept of *praxis* (action) in contrast to *poiesis* (making): instead of claiming that "to clean the street is also Art," as did Hi Red Center, an artist may clean the street as a "practice from the perspective of art," which may never produce a work.[61] In 1974, Bikyōtō once again went to the extreme: the second Bikyōtō Revolution Committee, formed by Hikosaka and Hori among others, pledged not to produce or exhibit any work at all during 1974 (see Text 9). It is quite symbolic that "not making" was the final act of Bikyōtō as a group. Ever critical of anti-Art's gesture of negation, the members felt it necessary to scrutinize the internal conditioning that governed "making" and recover its potential, all the more because the "internal institution" implicated those who undertook any act of making.

By 1975, the cycle of the institutional critique was completed and conceptualism had run its course after two decades. Subsequently, "making" increasingly regained its status.[62] Some second-generation conceptualists, such as Hikosaka and Hori, played a major role in this new development. Perhaps an irony of history is that the institution of art thus acquired another layer when the factions once called "avant-garde," including Gutai and anti-Art, transmuted into "contemporary art" *(gendai bijutsu)*, an institution unto itself within Japan's art world today.

Notes

I thank the artists who contributed to the Japanese section of the present exhibition, as well as Jon Hendricks, Tatsuo Kondō, Nakajima Masatoshi, and Nakajima Yasuko for their generous research assistance.

All translations from Japanese material are by the author.

1. The critic Haryū Ichirō credited himself with popularizing the term in the 1960s in the roundtable discussion "Gendai Nihon bijutsu wa dō ugoitaka" (How Did Contemporary Japanese Art Evolve?), special issue on "Nihon no gendai bijutsu 30-nen" (Three Decades of Contemporary Art in Japan), *Bijutsu Techō* (Art Notebook), no. 436 (July 1978): 18.

2. For a historical overview of postwar Japanese art, see Alexandra Munroe, *Japanese Art After 1945: Scream Against the Sky* (New York: Abrams, 1994), and Chiba Shigeo, *Gendai bijutsu itsudatsu-shi, 1945–1985* (A History of Deviations in Contemporary Art) (Tokyo: Shōbunsha, 1986). Both volumes comprise the most comprehensive literature to date in English and Japanese.

3. Gutai examples include, among others, two 1956 works by Murakami Saburō: an empty frame hung beneath a tree, entitled *All Landscapes;* and a wooden box with instructions that invite the audience to sit on it. See Ashiya City Museum of Art and History, ed., *Gutai shiryō-shū/Document Gutai, 1954–1972* (Ashiya: Ashiya City Culture Foundation, 1993), 91, 376. However, rather than pursuing conceptualist possibilities, Gutai artists soon turned their attention primarily to painting under the guidance of their leader Yoshihara Jirō and the French critic Michel Tapié. Gutai's proto-conceptualism remained an unfinished project, unlike that of Kawara, which he would bring to a logical conclusion in the mid-'60s in New York.

4. Intellectualism also informed the work of such mono-ha artists as Sekine Nobuo, whose visual trickery in *Phase—Earth* (1968) was recast into the theory of things *(mono)* by Lee U Fan. Not coincidentally, Lee incorporated Takamatsu's work after "shadow paintings" into mono-ha theory.

5. Bikyōtō affiliates here refer to those artists involved with the group's publication and exhibition activities in 1971–75.

6. Two important sources are: special feature on "Gainen no geijutsu to geijutsu no gainen" (Art of Concept and Concept of Art), *Bijutsu Techō,* no. 342 (May 1971): 41–105; and special issue on "Gainen geijutsu" (Conceptual Art), *Geijutsu Kurabu* (Art Club), no. 8 (April 1974). Hereafter referred to as *BT's* special and *GK's* special.

7. Early references include Fujieda Teruo's mention of *konsepucharu āto* (a phonetic rendition of "conceptual art"), accompanied by *gainen-teki geijutsu* as a translation, in "Atarashii mono no owari" (The End of the New), special feature on "Gendai geijutsu no jōkyō" (The State of Contemporary Art), *Bijutsu Techō,* no. 307 (January 1969): 54; and Lee U Fan's use of *konsepucharizumu* (i.e., "conceptualism") in "Kannen no geijutsu wa kanō-ka? Obuje shisō no shōtai to yukue" (Is Idea Art Possible? The Fact and Future of *Objet*-Thinking), special feature on Marcel Duchamp, *Bijutsu Techō,* no. 319 (November 1969): 73. Fujieda and Lee held generally negative views of conceptual art.

8. There was much confusion about how to translate *conceptual art* into Japanese; before *gainen geijutsu* became the standard, with the phonetic rendition also favored, *kannen* (literally, "idea") and *bijutsu* ("art") were alternately employed. See below under the heading "The Collapse of 'Modern'" for the difference between *geijutsu* and *bijutsu.*

9. A useful overview is given by Hayami Takashi in "'Jikan' e—montāju-fū ni" (Toward "Time"—à la montage), special feature on "Gendai bijutsu '73" (Contemporary Art '73), *Bijutsu Techō,* no. 375 (December 1973): 187–210.

10. For example, see individual texts in *BT's* and *GK's* specials. Most typically, *GK's* special carried a Japanese translation of Kosuth's "Art After Philosophy" (pp. 42–57), followed by Minemura Toshiaki's critique of Kosuth's analytical conceptual art (pp. 58–67). Minemura noted that Kosuth alone managed to contribute ideas fundamentally different from any existing art theories (p. 60).

11. *Ningen to busshitsu: Dai 10-kai Nihon kokusai bijutsu-ten/Between Man and Matter: 10th Tokyo Biennale* (Tokyo: Mainichi Newspapers and Japan International Art Promotion Association, 1970).

12. In both *BT's* and *GK's* specials, Nakahara Yūsuke, the commissioner of the 1970 Tokyo Biennale, as well as Matsuzawa and his group, were responsible for the graphic presentations. With *BT's* special, Nakahara, as a compiler, received the cooperation of the Nirvana group. In *GK's* special, Nakahara gathered the Euro–North American works under the title "Konsepucharu ātosukēpu" (Conceptual Artscape), 5–56, and Matsuzawa's Void-Space Situation Research Center (Kokūkan Jōkyō Tanchi Sentā) organized "Sekai hōki/The World Up-Rising [sic]," 153–81, representing both Japanese and foreign artists.

13. For example, the critic Yoshida Yoshie expressed indignation with the journalistic tendency of appreciating Matsuzawa's art under the pretext of *gainen geijutsu* in "Matsuzawa Yutaka: Yami o tōshi suru kyōdōtai" (A Commune That Sees Through Darkness), *Bijutsu Techō,* no. 360 (November 1972): 26.

14. Chiba's *Gendai bijutsu itsudatsu-shi* is a seminal work on the "particularities" of postwar Japanese art.

15. In this sense, the contribution of Alexandra Munroe in *Scream Against the Sky* was to include Tokyo Fluxus in the discussion and devise the grouping "Metaphysical School" in an attempt to capture the philosophical and aesthetic characteristics of Japanese conceptualism.

16. For a translated excerpt, see Munroe, *Scream Against the Sky,* 373–74.

17. The work is documented in Lucy Lippard, ed., *Six Years: The Dematerialization of the Art Object* (Berkeley: University of California Press, 1973), 98.

18. Tani Arata, "Geijutsu ni okeru 'seido' no mondai II" (Concerning the "Institution" in Art, 2), *Bijutsu Techō,* no. 362 (January 1973): 311. For a translated excerpt, see Munroe, *Scream Against the Sky,* 386. Tani is one of a few critics who recognized the importance of conceptual tendencies in 1970s Japanese art.

19. Miyakawa Atsushi, "Han-geijutsu: Sono nichijō-sei eno kakō" (Anti-Art: Descent to the Mundane), *Bijutsu Techō,* no. 234 (April 1964), reprinted in *Miyakawa Atsushi chosakushū* (Writings by Miyakawa Atsushi), vol. 2 (Tokyo: Bijutsu Shuppan-sha, 1980), 87–96, hereafter referred to as *Chosakushū.* For a translated excerpt, see Munroe, *Scream Against the Sky,* 385. Miyakawa's criticism is insightful, especially in the context of conceptualism as institutional critique, for the critic endeavored to articulate not the "style concepts" but the "value concepts" after the collapse of the "modern."

20. Miyakawa Atsushi, "Bijutsu jihyō" (Review of Art), *Tokyo Daigaku Shinbun,* February 12, 1964, reprinted in *Chosakushū,* 80.

21. In addition to Miyakawa, who made it his mission to positively postulate the concept of *contemporary* as distinct from that of *modern,* this awareness was widely shared by Japanese critics. See, for example, Nakahara Yūsuke, "Gendai bijutsu to bijutsu ni okeru gendai" (Contemporary Art and "Contemporary" in Art), in *Gendai,* Iwanami kōza, vol. 10 (Tokyo: Iwanami Shoten, 1964), esp. 85–89; Ishiko Junzō, *Hyōgen ni okeru kindai no jubaku* (Spell of the Modern in Expression) (Tokyo: Kawashima Shoten, 1970); and Yasunao Tone, "Hi-geijutsu-ka suru geijutsu: Geijutsu ni okeru kindai no hōkai" (Art Becoming Nonart: The Collapse of "Modern" in Art), *SD* (July 1969), reprinted in *Gendai geijutsu no isō: Geijutsu wa shisō tariuruka?* (Phases of Contemporary Art: Can Art Be Thought?) (Tokyo: Tabata Shoten, 1970).

22. Miyakawa Atsushi, "Fukanōsei no bigaku" (Aesthetics of Impossibility), *Chūō Daigaku Shinbun,* January 11, 1966, reprinted in *Chosakushū,* 174–75.

23. Miyakawa Atsushi, "Kaiga to sono kage" (Painting and Its Shadow), *Me,* no. 6 (November 1965), reprinted in *Chosakushū,* 138.

24. Peter Bürger, *Theory of the Avant-Garde* (1974), trans. Michael Shaw (Minneapolis: University of Minnesota Press, 1984), lii.

25. Haryū's comment in Haryū Ichirō, Miyakawa Atsushi, and Nakahara Yūsuke, "Zadankai: Geijutsu hyōron sengo" (Roundtable Discussion: After Judging the Art Criticism Competition), *Mizue* (October 1972), reprinted in *Chosakushū,* 513. Critics engaged in the discourse of the institution include Ishiko, Miyakawa, Tani, and Tone.

26. Yasunao Tone wrote: "What makes Art Art is neither creation, nor expression, nor form, but institution." Yasunao Tone, "Seido to shiteno geijutsu to 'shigusa' to shiteno geijutsu" (Art as Institution and Art as Act), *Film,* no. 5 (1970), reprinted in *Gendai geijutsu no isō,* 39.

27. It is thus fitting that *Bijutsu Techō,* no. 329 (July 1970), featured the controversial Tokyo Biennale under the title "Naze kore ga geijutsu ka?" (Why Is It Art?).

28. On Kawara, "Genga itten eno gimon" (Question About the Unique Original Painting), *Bijutsu Techō,* no. 140 (April 1958): 24–25; On Kawara, "Insatsu kaiga" (Printed Painting), supplementary issue on "Kaiga no gihō to kaiga no yukue" (Techniques of Painting and Its Future), *Bijutsu Techō,* no. 155 (March 1959): 86, 89.

29. Kawara, "Genga itten," 24.

30. Ibid.

31. Kawara, "Insatsu kaiga," 90, and inserted questionnaire. Kawara's proto-conceptualist theory also prefigures the radical nature of his later conceptualist work: each date painting serves as a daily reproducible, subtly variable, never self-fulfilling component that either individually or collectively forces the viewer to creatively produce a meaning of the work as a whole. Which is to say that the *Today* series is, in a truly Barthesian sense, an apparatus to transform the viewer into a reader of text that is painting. For various "meanings" of the series, given both verbally (i.e., through writings) and visually (i.e., through exhibitions), see *On Kawara: Whole and Parts, 1964–95* (Villeurbanne: Nouveau Musée/ Institute d'Art Contemporain, 1997).

32. For reproductions, see Munroe, *Scream Against the Sky,* pls. 110–16.

33. The word *performative* is employed here in the spirit of J. L. Austin, *How to Do Things With Words* (Cambridge, Mass.: Harvard University Press, 1962). This is to say, a statement is not constative (i.e., used to describe) but "is, or is a part of, the doing of an action" (p. 5).

34. Studies on this subject include Chiba, *Gendai bijutsu itsudatsu-shi;* Kitazawa Noriaki, *Me no shinden* (The Pantheon of the Eye) (Tokyo: Bijutsu Shuppan-sha, 1989); Satō Dōshin, *"Nihon bijutsu" tanjō* (The Birth of "Japanese Art") (Tokyo: Kōdansha, 1996).

35. The episode, which is referred to as a "revelation" in his handwritten *Brief Report on Nonsensory Painting* (1964), appears in later accounts, i.e., "Matsuzawa Yutaka jihitsu nenpu 1922–2222" (Autochronology), special issue on the artist, *Kikan,* no. 13 (1982): 51. In the Japanese art lexicon, the French-derived term *objet* (pronounced "obuje") encompasses both "readymade or found object" and "object-based work, such as combine, assemblage, and junk art."

36. Yoshida, "Matsuzawa Yutaka," 37. Matsuzawa first used the phrase "omnipotence of sorts" in *Anticivilization Exhibition* (1965).

37. ψ, or "psi," here refers to both "psyche" and the solution to the physicist Erwin Schrödinger's equation.

38. Another notable example of Japanese mail art in the 1960s is *Spatial Poems* (1965–75) by the Fluxus musician-artist Shiomi Mieko, who communicated with people worldwide from her home, the place of her obligation as a housewife. Postcards, in particular, were a favorite conceptualist device in Japan into the 1970s, allowing artists to circumvent the exhibition system.

39. Used by Matsuzawa in the sense of "let us go," *gate* (Sk., pronounced "gah-teh") derives from the *Heart Sutra,* the last line of which is often recited as a mantra, reading: "Gate gate pāragate pārasamgate bodhi svāhā."

40. In the ad, this event is entitled *Cocurrence [sic] Event,* which probably derived from the French word *concours* (phonetically rendered as *konkūru* in Japanese and meaning "competition" in this context). It is also listed as *Investigation Event* in *Chronology: Five Decades of Contemporary Art* (1972), part 2, 126, for which Tone looked up *shinsa* (jury) in a Japanese-English dictionary and picked the first word, *investigation,* listed under the heading. Unfortunately, not much documentation remains of this work.

41. In Japan, *hakubutsukan* (museums) have played a role as repositories of artifacts and traditional art since the late 19th century. As for modern art, the history of public art museums in today's sense began with the establishment of the Museum of Modern Art, Kamakura (1951), and the National Museum of Modern Art, Tokyo (1952). For further information, see "Glossary," in Munroe, *Scream Against the Sky,* 393–98, and "Issues and Institutions," in *Nihonga: Transcending the Past,* ed. Ellen P. Conant (St. Louis: Saint Louis Art Museum, 1995), 75–112.

42. For the anti-Art debate, see Munroe, *Scream Against the Sky,* 384–86.

43. Akasegawa Genpei, "'Shihon-shugi riarizumu' ron" (On "Capitalist Realism") (February 1964), reprinted in *Obuje o motta musansha* (An Objet-Carrying Proletarian) (Tokyo: Gendai Shisōsha, 1970), 31.

44. Akasegawa Genpei, "Poketto ni haburashi o" (Having a Toothbrush in My Pocket) (May 1967) and "Kaiko sareru geijutsu genba" (The Site of Art Retrospected) (November 1967), reprinted in ibid., 50–57 and 78–82.

45. Tone, *Gendai geijutsu no isō,* 256.

46. Special features they edited include: "Shūdan no nami, undō no nami: 60-nendai bijutsu wa dō ugoita-ka" (Waves of Groups, Waves of Movements: The Development of '60s Art), no. 347 (October 1971); "Hyōgen, jōkyō: 60-nendai bijutsu wa dō ugoita-ka" (Expression, Situations: The Development of '60s Art), no. 349 (December 1971); and "Atarashii hihyō no tame ni: 60-nendai no chihei kara" (For New Criticism: From the '60s Horizon), no. 350 (January 1972).

47. Compilers' statement, *Bijutsu Techō,* no. 354 (April 1972): 2.

48. Bikyōtō, untitled and undated flier (July 20, 1969).

49. Ibid. The slogan first appeared in the July 20 flier that reported on the July 12 preliminary meeting and was added to the July 5 flier, "An Appeal to Artists," when *Bikyōtō Documents* was later compiled.

50. Hikosaka Naoyoshi and Hori Kosai, "Bijutsu ni shisu" (To Die in Art), *Bijutsu Shihyō 2,* no. 5 (May 1978): 66.

51. An attack by Bikyōtō and other student-artist groups on Nissenbi (Nihon Senden Bijutsukai, or Japan Advertisement Art Society) in August 1969 had an immediate result: the society canceled its open-entry exhibition. In November, Bikyōtō's action against Nitten (Nihon Bijutsu Tenrankai/Japan Art Exhibition), the postwar incarnation of the government-sponsored salon, was unsuccessful due to a counteraction by the organizers and the police.

52. Shihyō Group and Hikosaka Naoyoshi, "Shūdan no shi: Kyōdō-sei o tsuikyū shita 4-tsu no purakutesu" (Death of the Group: Four Practices in Pursuit of Collectivity), *Bijutsu Techō,* no. 372 (October 1973): 149; Hori Kosai, "Han-hihan: Sugaritsukitai Kyō-onna e" (Anticriticism: To a Kyoto Woman Who Wants to Cling), *Shihyō-sha Tsūshin* (Shihyō-sha News), May 1, 1973.

53. Miyakawa Atsushi, "E o mirukoto eno toi" (A Question About Seeing a Painting), *Bijutsu Techō,* no. 317 (September 1969), reprinted in *Chosakushū,* 276; "Te no shikken: Sinboru to shiteno kikai to shukō-teki-na shikō" (The Hand Lost Its Privilege: The Machine as a Symbol and Handcraft-Based Thinking), *Bijutsu Techō,* no. 309 (February 1969), reprinted in *Chosakushū,* 248–55.

54. Kashihara Etsutomu, "Tsukurukoto eno hangyakusha-tachi: *Gendai bijutsu no dōkō-ten,* Kyoto Kokuritsu Kindai Bijutsukan" (Rebels Against Making: *Trends in Contemporary Art* at the National Museum of Modern Art, Kyoto), *Sansai,* no. 249 (October 1969): 49.

55. Lee U Fan, "Sekai to kōzō" (The World and Structure), *Dezain Hihyō,* no. 9 (June 1969), reprinted in *Mono-ha to posuto mono-ha no tenkai: 1969-nen ikō no Nihon no bijutsu/Art in Japan Since 1969: Mono-ha and Post Mono-ha* (Tokyo: Seibu Museum of Art, 1987), 170.

56. The term *Nihon gainen-ha* (literally, "Japan concept school") was coined by Hikosaka à la *Nihon mono-ha,* in reference to Matsuzawa's version of mystic conceptualism. Hikosaka Naoyoshi, *Hanpuku: Shinkō geijutsu no isō* (Recapitulation: Phases of New Art) (Tokyo: Tabata Shoten, 1974), 283–84. Both Hikosaka and Hori revealed their uncompromising antagonism to mono-ha and gainen-ha in their writings.

57. Kashihara Etsutomu, "Mr. X shisaku nōto" (Thoughts on Mr. X), unpub. ms, 1969, 7–20.

58. Despite its theoretical importance, the final room-size presentation of *What Is Mr. X?,* which prominently incorporates the discussion transcripts, is too massive to include in this exhibition.

59. Quoted in EK (Kashihara Etsutomu), "Nomura Hitoshi koten," *Kirokutai,* no. 1 (1972): [10].

60. This "orientation" is cited as the common tendency among some artists who were invited to the exhibition *'73/5: Affair and Practice by 12,* organized by Bijutsu Shihyō-sha, a Bikyōtō organ. See the request for participation in *Kirokutai,* no. 3 (1973), which serves as the first of two volumes of the exhibition catalogue.

61. Hikosaka Naoyoshi, "Tojirareta enkan no kanata wa: 'Gutai' no kiseki kara nani o" (Beyond the Closed Circle: What to Learn from the Trajectory of Gutai), *Bijutsu Techō,* no. 370 (August 1973): 85. The statement by Hi Red Center's Nakanishi Natsuyuki first appeared in *Bijutsu Jānaru* (Art Journal), no. 56 (1966).

62. Hikosaka declared the revival of "making" in the panel discussion, "Ima aete 'seisaku' o" (Daring to "Make" Now), *Bijutsu Techō: Bijutsu nenkan 1978,* no. 429 (January 1978): 12–38.

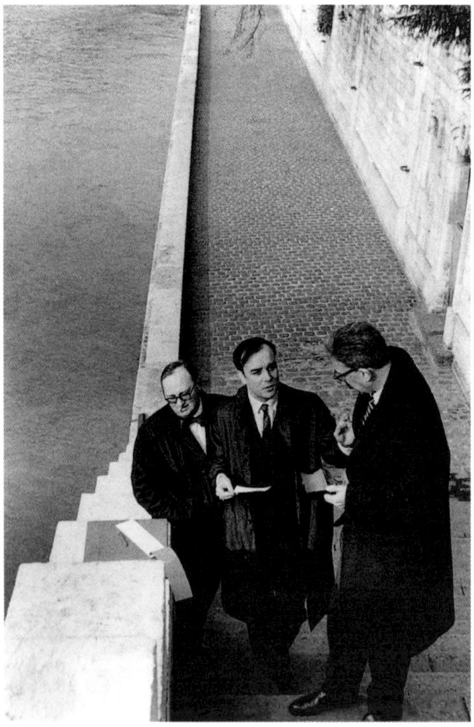
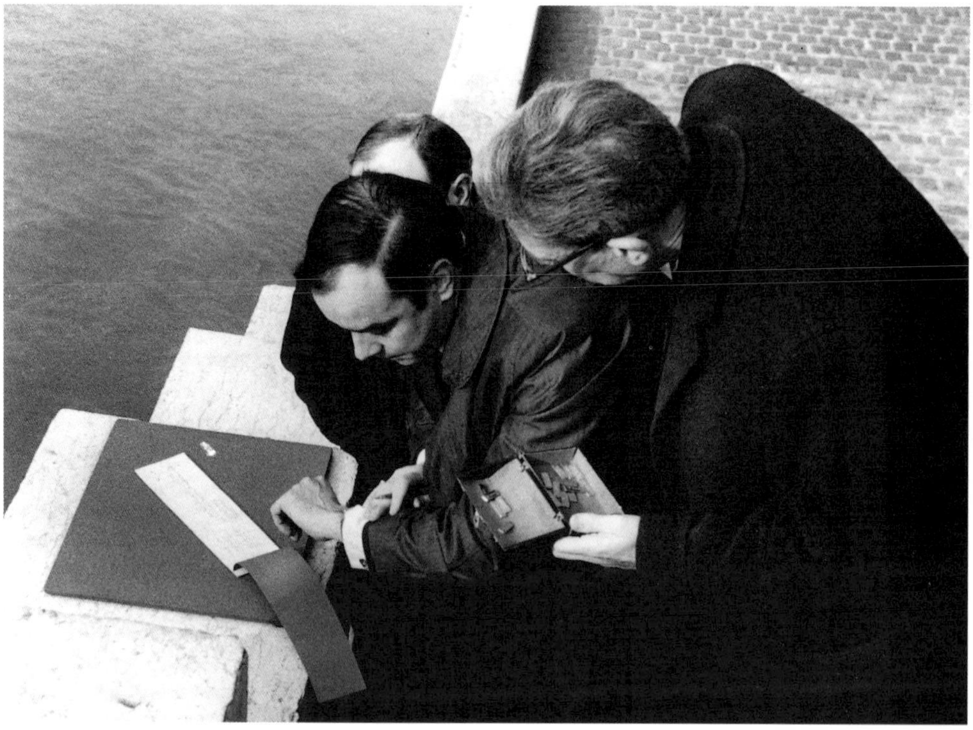
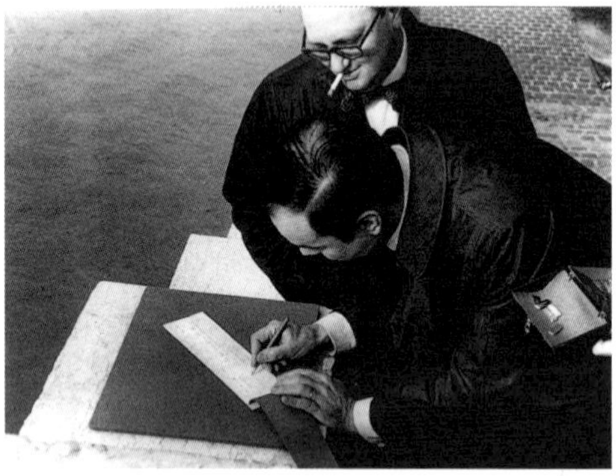
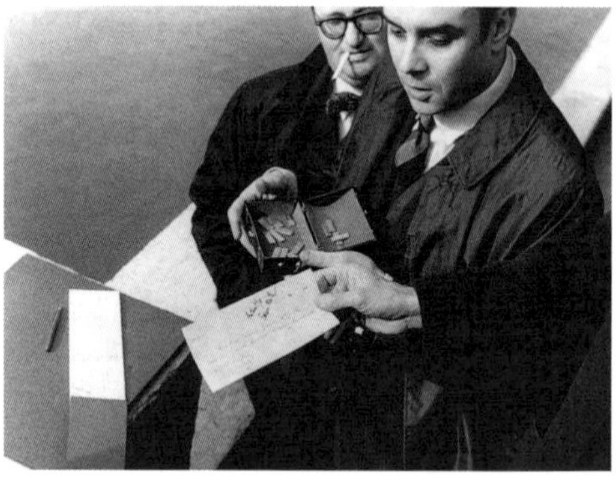
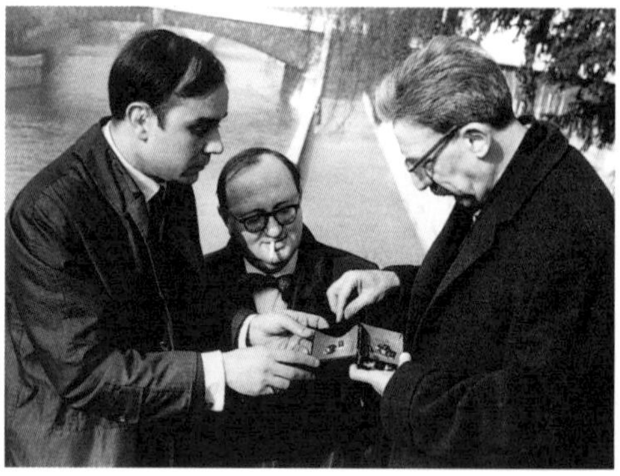
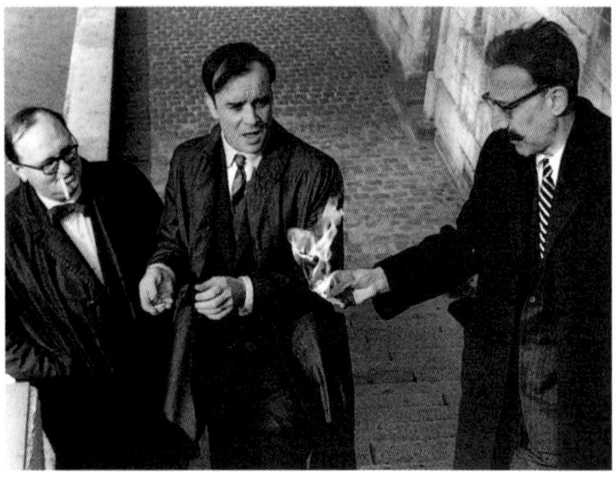
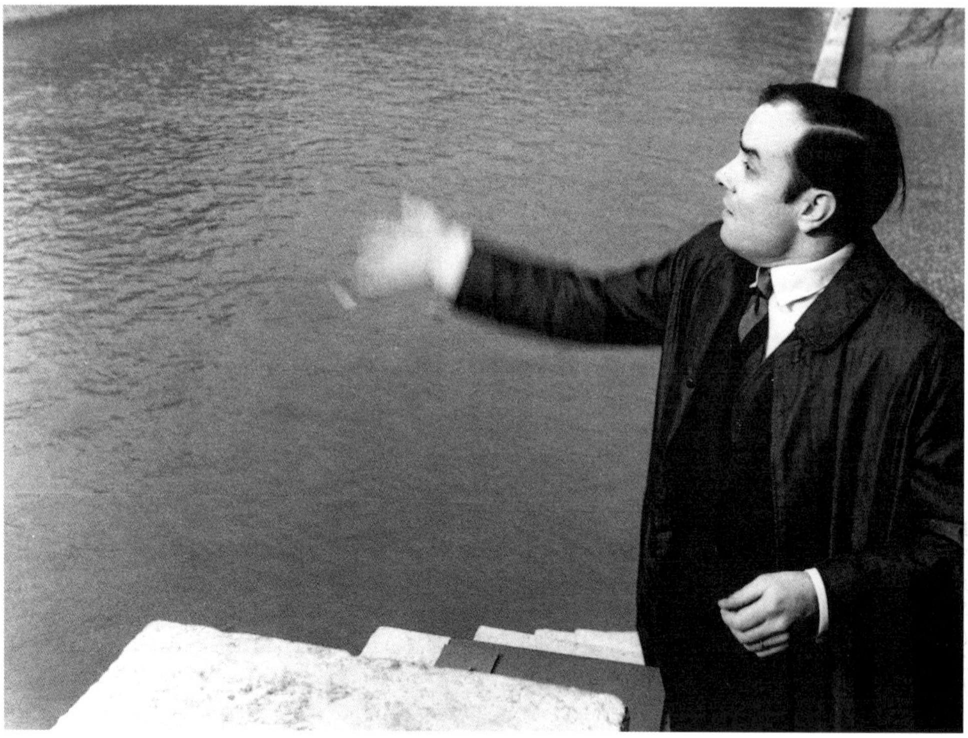

European Conceptualism in Every Situation

Claude Gintz

One never really contests an organization of existence without contesting all of that organization's forms of language.
—Guy Debord, 1959

FIGURE 13.
Yves Klein, *Cession de zone de sensibilité picturale immatérielle, cession à M. Blankfort/ Série no. 4, zone no. 01, Paris, 2 février, 1962 (Sale of a Zone of Immaterial Pictorial Sensibility, Sale to M. Blankfort/Series no. 4, Zone no. 1, Paris, February 2, 1962).*

Was there such a thing as a specifically European conceptualism—or even a "conceptual" movement, assuming the term applied first and foremost to some North American (and British) artists during the second part of the 1960s? If so, to what extent was it autonomous vis-à-vis its American counterpart, or was it simply an offspring of a mainstream international art discourse originating in New York? And if it were autonomous, what would be its own genealogy?

These are among the questions addressed in this essay, bearing in mind that as a signifier, *conceptual* necessarily refers within the art context to something that is being opposed to perceptual (i.e., visual). However, since the term is now in common usage among artists, art critics, and far beyond, there have developed many possible ways of being "conceptual." The term seems to embrace a lot.

In Western Europe, conceptualism cannot be considered an autonomous art practice without examining how it relates to Situationism, probably the last true avant-garde movement to appear in Europe in the 1950s. Indeed, in some of the early expressions of Western European conceptualism, there was already a prevalent refusal of the visual per se, an attitude akin to that found in the earlier (pre-Situationist) Lettrist films.

The movie industry was an object of both hate and love, as if the Lettrists could not decide whether film—as the contemporary entertainment mass medium *par excellence*—were too deeply entrenched in the Spectacle or if it could be diverted, if not actually redeemed. This dilemma had already been encountered by Walter Benjamin in his famous essay, "The Work of Art in the Age of Mechanical Reproduction," in which he ultimately had to acknowledge that the new technologies were first and foremost serving totalitarian ideologies (hard and soft) in the constituting of "subjects." For instance, Gil J. Wolman's film *L'anticoncept,* shown for the first time in Paris in February 1952, projects a sequence of "nonimages"—flashing lights of longer or shorter duration repeated at various intervals upon a white sphere—while the audiotape, made of fragmentary sentences, onomatopoieas, etc., free from any synchronicity with the visual, expresses its own "a-tonic" discontinuousness (fig. 14). Likewise, Guy Debord's first film, *Hurlements en faveur de Sade (Howls in Favor of Sade),* produced a few months later, deprived the audience of any visual gratification, addressing the spectator only with intermittent speech and sound. This withdrawal from the visual will later be fully developed by Western European conceptual artists. Similarly, other Situationist or even pre-Situationist strategies such as *dérive* (drift) or *détournement* (diversion) found an echo in the practice of some proto-conceptual artists (figs. 15, 21).[1]

Hurlements is an imageless, eighty-minute black-and-white film—white when the audio band reproduces the sound of a voice, black when the audio is silent. The film ends with twenty-four minutes of *blackout,* during which

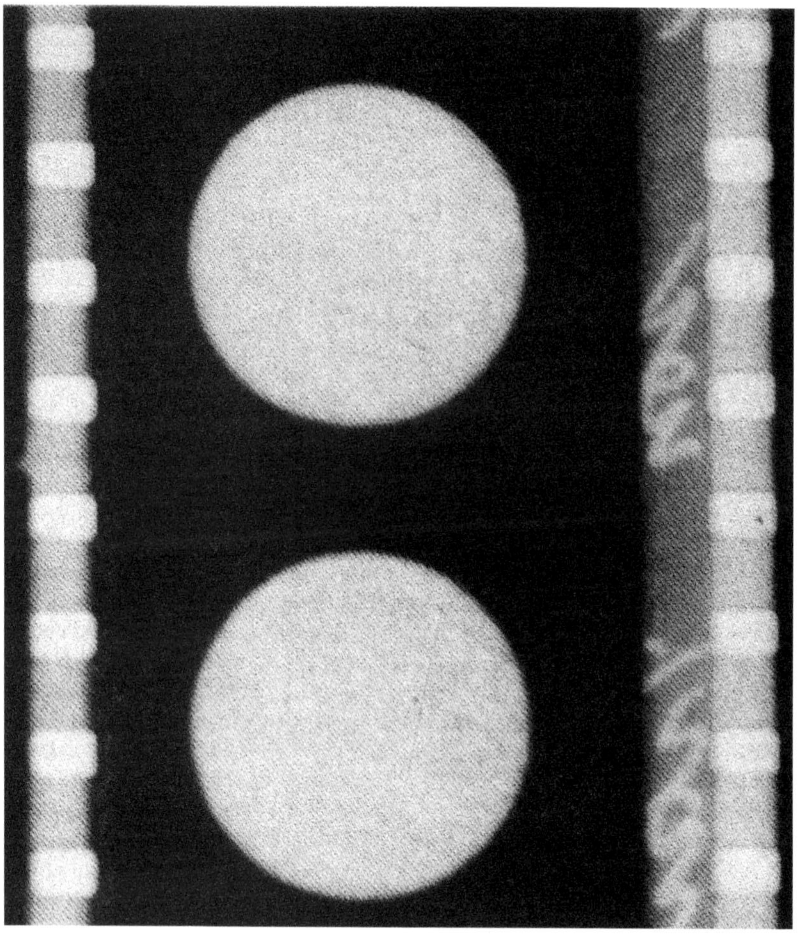

FIGURE 14.
Gil Wolman, *L'anticoncept,* September 1951, 35mm black-and-white film, approximately 70 min.

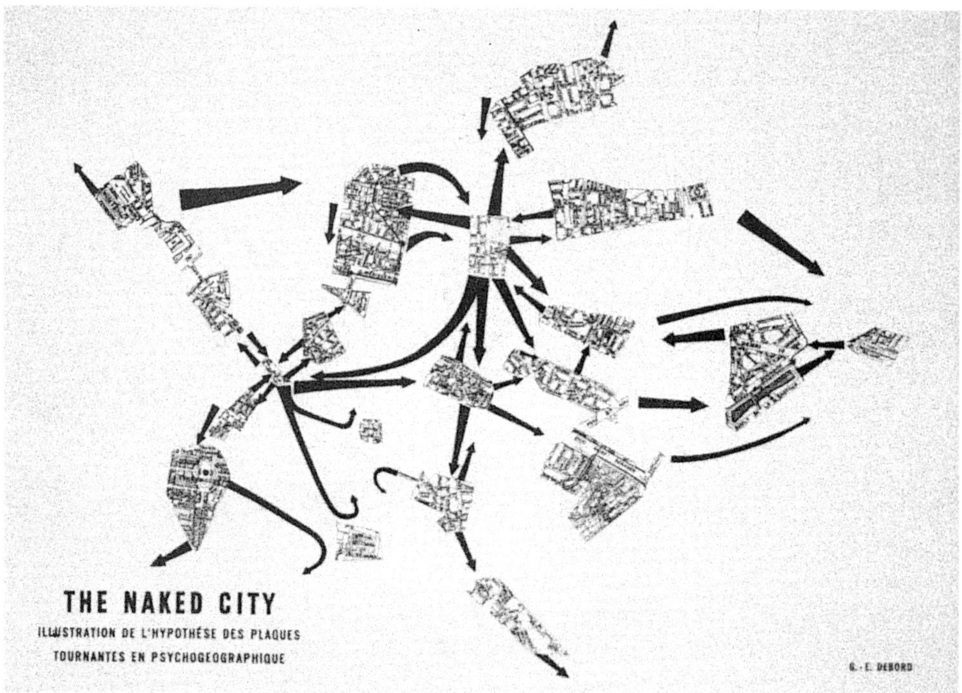

FIGURE 15.
Guy Debord, *The Naked City: Illustration de l'hypothése des plaques tournantes en psychogéographique,* 1957.

the "viewer" does not hear anything except the continuous noise of the unwinding reel. This amounts to a new *situation,* so to speak, for the frustrated audience, in which the spectacle-producing apparatus becomes the sole object of attention:

> ... the lack of images in *Hurlements* is employed as the essential ingredient in a recipe of provocation intended to "radically" transform the cinematic "situation" from a shrine of passive consumption into an arena of active discussion, a shift *away* from the spectator and *towards* critical engagement.[2]

If we accept Debord's account (and there is no reason that we should not), Yves Klein attended the first screening of *Hurlements* and experienced it with a shock. The "painter Yves Klein," Debord recounts, "whom I knew at the time and who was present at the very tumultuous projection of this film, was overwhelmed by a convincing black sequence lasting twenty-four minutes."[3]

Aside from Klein's monochrome paintings—which, incidentally, might also be related to Rauschenberg's *White Paintings,* conceived and executed at Black Mountain College in 1951 and derived from a Zen idea of passivity, or John Cage's famous silent *4'33"* in 1952, opening "the doors of the music to the sounds that happen to be in the environment" (Cage)—two other works seem to proceed more specifically from Debord's film. These are Klein's certified *Cessions de zones de sensibilité picturale immatérielle (Sales of Zones of Immaterial Pictorial Sensibility,* 1959–), which were "exchanged" with art collectors for a specified amount of fine gold (figs. 13, 122), and even more pertinent, his show *La spécialisation de la sensibilité à l'état matière première en sensibilité picturale stabilisée (The Specialization of Sensibility in the State of Raw Material into Stabilized Pictorial Sensibility),* organized in April 1958 at Galerie Iris Clert in Paris, for which he made *Le Vide (The Void).* Here, Klein painted afresh the white gallery walls, while keeping the room entirely clear of any objects for two weeks. The "event" was carefully orchestrated to attract maximum publicity (for instance, Republican Guards in full dress were stationed at the entrance), and the strategy paid off. Visitors streamed in and had to be strictly channeled until late in the evening of the opening. The fact that Klein's staging of the event managed to turn Guy Debord's own radical critique into spectacle (or farce?) is another matter.

Just as Debord chose to *détourner* (divert) the cinematographic medium precisely because it was the ultimate form of expression of an emerging market economy and its "system of illusions," some conceptual artists deprived the visual arts of visuality in order to question—by means of such a *déni d'exposition* (exhibition denial)—the objectlike quality of the artwork through which it acquires its status of hypercommodity in a society of images (eye-consumerism). The work of Piero Manzoni, in particular, exemplifies this attitude of visual withdrawal, while responding in its own subtle way to Klein's personal strategy of turning the artist himself into spectacle (fig. 183). Manzoni's conceptualism stood as a way to question the supposed immediacy of the visual art object. In *Linea m. 10, dicembre 1959 (Line 10 Meters Long, December 1959;* fig. 123), probably for the first time in the history of the visual arts, the actual "content" of an artwork (as the material result of a mechanical process controlled by the "worker"-artist, instead of being a "pure" idea as in the case of Klein's *Sales of Immaterial Pictorial Sensibility)* was ironically withdrawn from sight and became accessible (referred to) through language alone. The audience is able to apprehend the materiality of the work—marks of a line previously inked on a roll of paper by the artist himself—only through an inscription printed on the outside of a cardboard cylinder. The inscription reads:

> CONTIENT UNE LIGNE LONGUE MT. 10
> EXECUTEE PAR PIERO MANZONI 12/59
>
> IT CONTAINS A LINE 10 METRES LONG
> MADE BY PIERO MANZONI THE 12/59

Likewise, between 1958 and 1960, Manzoni produced several serigraphic works entitled *8 tavole di accertamento (8 Identification Tables),* in which he addressed the question of referentiality as a substitute for representation. Here, the referent is signified through maps, serially repeated letters, or traces (handprinted lines or fingerprints). In other words, everything but what is normally expected in the visual arts—an image of the thing itself.

Having been subjected to the constraints of socialist realism, Gerhard Richter, a German painter who moved from East to West in 1961, arrived with a background completely different from colleagues like Klein and Manzoni. In 1963, when Richter (along with Konrad Lueg, later known as Konrad Fischer, an art dealer supportive of emerging conceptual artists) displayed himself in a Düsseldorf department store among all the other commodities, he was acting as an artist compelled to adjust his artistic discourse to a new context. At the same time, he implied that *capitalist* realism—the ideological and cultural condition imposed upon the individual in the West, as emblematized by pop art—might be a dialectical counterpart to what he had experienced in the East. *Life with Pop: A Demonstration for Capitalist Realism* was, so to speak, the tribute to pay and the shift to operate to become a Western artist (figs. 124, 125). Paraphrasing Walter Benjamin, it was as if the artist now had not only to consider his own work a commodity, but also to stage *himself* as one.

In the case of such a secretive artist as Stanley Brouwn, it might be adventurous to suggest an affinity with the Situationists. Rather than staging a withdrawal of the visual, Brouwn's practice tends to reduce his own authorial activity to the benefit of the anonymous passerby (fig. 126). For instance, in 1960–61 he collected the marks left by pedestrians' shoes on sheets of white paper he had previously scattered at random during a *dérive* through the streets of Amsterdam. Then the anonymous passerby was transformed into an active participant when, standing at an intersection,

Brouwn asked people to explain how to get from there to another place in town by drawing the directions for him on a piece of paper stamped *this way brouwn*.

In the work of Klein, Manzoni, and Brouwn (each with a different kind of intentionality), it is possible to trace the extent to which those early conceptualists were indebted to Situationist ideas. And yet the Situationists themselves had decided in the meantime, no later than 1962, to abandon art per se as well as any other kind of autonomous cultural practice in favor of a direct insertion into the social arena through a devastating critique of the sociocultural state of things (the avant-garde for real change in real life):

> Thus, after the immediate practice of art had ceased to be the most eminent activity and the predicate of eminence had shifted to theory as such, it now detaches itself from theory, inasmuch as a synthetic posttheoretical practice comes into being, whose mission is to be the foundation and the truth of art as well as philosophy.[4]

With this rather emphatically Hegelian quotation of the rather obscure August von Cieszkowski in another of his films, *La société du spectacle* (1973), Debord pointed to what he thought was his own "posttheoretical practice." That same Hegelianism could qualify the "conceptual" phase of the British Art & Language group when, having ceased to produce art objects, its members were still giving the "predicate of eminence ... to theory as such." Art & Language had on its agenda a program of leaving artistic practices suspended, while conducting theoretical reflections on the hegemony of modernism in its late American period. These investigations were carried out in articles and essays published in their *Art-Language* journal, starting in 1969 (fig. 127). From its inception, the journal was open to American conceptual artists as well—Sol LeWitt, Dan Graham, Lawrence Weiner—and Joseph Kosuth was even appointed an American editor for two issues in 1970: "The artists, both in England and New York, who adopted the name Art & Language were among those who had produced or proposed various forms of exotic art objects during the period 1965–68 as a means to test or resist the habits and assumptions of modernist production and connoisseurship."[5]

John Latham expressed a similar concern in 1966. As a part-time instructor at St. Martin's School of Art in London, Latham asked his students to chew up and spit out in a flask the pages of *Art and Culture,* a collection of essays by the famous American modernist art critic Clement Greenberg. The flask contained a solution of sulphuric acid (fig. 1).

The theoretical trope taken for a few years by Art & Language and others was meant to "disqualify the competent spectator presupposed in the aesthetic discourse of Modernist culture, and to unseat him from his position as an ideal arbiter of taste."[6] Yet, unable to address the very audience the group was trying to disqualify, such a project had no real public outside those people engaged in implementing it. This was probably the main contradiction of the program as well as its weakness—not opening up to everyone, but instead remaining restricted to those who already shared its concerns.

Aside from Art & Language in Britain, other artists of the late '60s generation—in particular, Daniel Buren in France and Marcel Broodthaers in Belgium—were developing their own paradigm regarding conceptuality as a discursive strategy in the visual arts. Historically speaking, European conceptualism of the late '60s seems to be situated at a crossroads, where the collapse of the European hegemonic cultural and artistic tradition, signaled by Situationist attitudes, gives way to a reorientation of the cultural apparatus now mainly controlled from the United States. At the same time, this reorientation often appears to be idiosyncratically accommodated and integrated in the work and language of a good number of European artists from the mid-'60s to mid-'70s.

Yet conceptualism was hardly political as such. If anything, it was deliberately self-critical, as long as we understand self-criticism here to be a practice directed against European art, suddenly viewed as an institution and ideology bearing the burden of its own tradition and of past European culture and history, as in the work of Giulio Paolini (fig. 130). Understood as such, European conceptualism seems to act as the invalidation of that glorious past—seen as expressing irredeemably lost values—or as a critique of that part of the ideological state apparatus to which artists and their audience were submitted. For the Salon de Mai 1968, hosted by the Musée d'Art Moderne de la Ville de Paris, Daniel Buren pasted up unauthorized posters made of green-and-white vertically striped paper in some 200 outdoor locations throughout Paris, and used the same visual tool to cover a 5 x 18 meter wall inside the museum. Meanwhile, two unidentified men, wearing sandwich boards swathed in the striped paper, paraded around outside. Although visually constant, all these works—posters, wall, sandwich boards—represent a radical reconsideration of the boundary of the artwork, in which meaning is conveyed only through context.

Then, for his first significant gallery show in October 1968, Buren closed off access to (i.e., withdrew from sight) the entire Galleria Apollinaire in Milan by covering its transparent glass entrance with striped paper (fig. 131). This action might be thought of as a visual antithesis to Yves Klein's *Void,* since gallerygoers were left with the task of mentally reconstituting the familiar aspects of the inner space from which they were barred—a strategy reminiscent of the one implemented earlier with Manzoni's cylinder.

Buren's *Les formes: peintures (The Forms: Paintings,* 1977) offers a perfect paradigm for the withdrawal of visuality in the visual arts. The work consisted of five black-and-white striped canvases cut to exactly the same size as five paintings in the permanent collection of the Centre Georges Pompidou. The striped canvases were then installed directly under

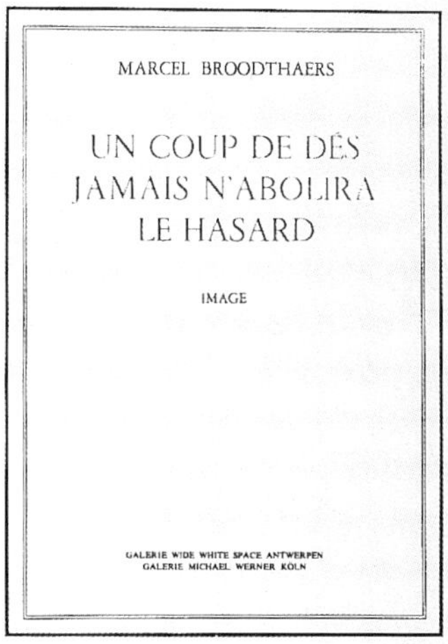

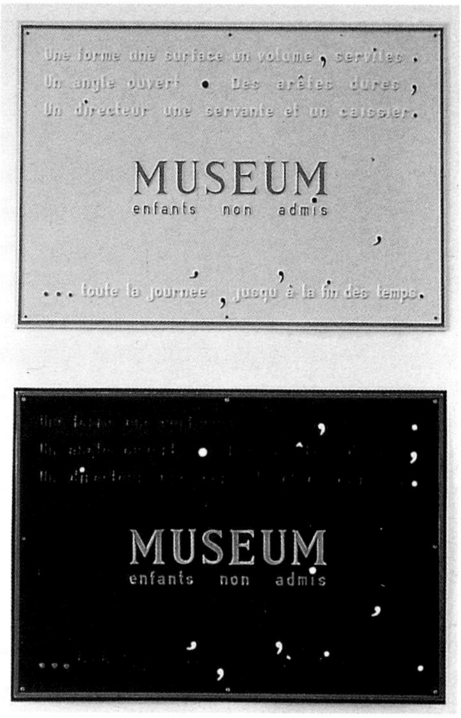

FIGURE 16. (NEAR RIGHT)
Marcel Broodthaers, *Un coup de dés jamais n'abolira le hasard (Image)*, 1969, aluminum. Private collection.

FIGURE 17. (FAR RIGHT)
Marcel Broodthaers, *Museum, enfants non admis (Museum, Children Not Admitted)*, 1968–69, two thermopressed plastic plates. Private collection.

the paintings, their physical presence made known to the viewer only through a museum label adjacent to the one referring to the visible work. For instance, the label placed beside the one referring to Theo van Doesburg's *Composition* reads:

> Daniel Buren—Boulogne-sur-Seine 1938
> *Les formes: peintures* 1977
>
> Sous "Composition" de VAN DOESBURG, un tissu de 136x86,4cm rayé blanc et noir de bandes verticales de 8,7cm et dont la première bande blanche à gauche est recouverte de peinture acrylique blanche. 4 peintures, toutes de même type, se trouvent derrière 4 autres oeuvres du Musée. (Under VAN DOESBURG's "Composition," a canvas 136 x 86.4 cm with vertical black-and-white stripes and whose first white stripe on the left is covered with white acrylic paint. 4 paintings, all of the same type, are to be found behind 4 other works belonging to the Museum.)

As a comparatively late work, it might be said that with *Les formes,* conceptualism had found its "niche" inside the very institution toward which its critique is directed.

Marcel Broodthaers's work is too complex and source-rich—surrealism, nouveau réalisme, pop—to be reduced to a single dimension, that is, conceptualist. And yet his work is central to this discussion, since its discursive strategy, sustained by a literary bias, in one way or another addresses each of the issues tackled by European conceptualism: the visual arts within the museum institution as part of the state cultural apparatus, the art object's autonomy and the validity of its traditional categories. For instance, Broodthaers may simultaneously question the museum institution and the principle art trend of the moment (at that time, minimalism). In *Museum, enfants non admis (Museum, Children Not Admitted,* 1968–69; fig. 17), his description of both collapses into a single (d)enunciation inscribed upon a pair of thermopressed plastic plates (of the type used by small contractors on their truck for publicity purposes). The inscription, set against alternating black and white backgrounds, reads:

> Une forme une surface un volume, serviles
> Un angle ouvert. Des arêtes dures.
> MUSEUM
> enfants non admis
> ... toute la journée, jusqu'à la fin des temps.
> (A shape a surface a volume, servile
> An open angle. Hard edges.
> MUSEUM
> children not admitted
> ... all day, till the end of time.)

Broodthaers also plays with the stability of artistic categories. *Un coup de dés jamais n'abolira le hasard (Image)* (1969; figs. 16, 128) is a *détournement* of Stéphane Mallarmé's famous poem. Its letterpress text is systematically blotted out, while the spatiality of its peculiar Mallarmean visual deployment (its "image," so to speak) is rigorously maintained through the wide white space of the pages. Conversely, *Rubens* (1973), a series of nine letterpress texts printed on stretched canvas, is a magnificent illustration of the linguistic shift at work in the visual arts. Within the pictorial space, all the "things" that were once depicted—represented—are now referred to through a linguistic rendering which seems to acknowledge the end of (representational) painting as such, while paying melancholic tribute to its past glory. Here, left with what seems to be nothing more than an epitaph, the contemporary (European) viewer is deprived of all that once provided him or her with sensuous visual gratification.

André Cadere approaches conceptualist issues from another direction. Cadere, the Romanian artist who came in from the cold in the early '70s, traveled the Western art world performing his own *dérive.* Going from city to city and place to place—parks, cafés, commercial galleries, museums—Cadere always carried with him a rounded bar of wood, divided into segments painted in various colors whose height equals their diameter and in which the perfectly serialist order of permutation of the given colors always includes a unique error (figs. 18, 129, 196). As Walter Benjamin would say of the *flâneur* in Zentral Park, Cadere "protests, with his ostentatious nonchalance, against the production process." Carefully recorded day after day, his actions were signaled by the bar of wood, his identity mark, much like a pilgrim's staff. His appearances—not always welcome—were meant to introduce *heterogeneity* into a seamless institution, where artists, critics, art dealers, and curators are bound to prescribed productive roles. As a perfectly portable object, Cadere's bar of wood does not depend on any supporting structures (walls or floor). Liberated from the art object's traditional function as a prop for passive contemplation, the bar acted as a *shifter* through which the people he met would engage in a dialogue, begin a discussion. Cadere's idea was to make/let something happen, expecting each intrusion of the bar—inside or outside the art world—to result in an unexpected *situation* pecular to its context or circumstance.

The institutional critique implemented at the end of the '60s and beginning of the '70s by artists such as Buren, Broodthaers, Cadere, and others could in a sense be related to Debord's own attitude when, more than ten years earlier, he had questioned the validity of the strategy of former Lettrist friends. The latter, in Debord's view, were wrong to think that traditional art categories could be revitalized, even transformed, within the same old framework. Instead, this cultural apparatus had to be bypassed or brought down, as Debord wrote in his *Rapport sur la construction des situations et sur les conditions de l'organisation et de l'action de la tendance situationniste internationale* (Report on the Construction of Situations and on the Conditions of Organization and Action of the Situationist International Movement), used in 1957 as the platform for the founding of the Situationist International. In a sense, both Debord and the conceptual artists considered here rejected the search for new aesthetic forms. But they differed in terms of strategy. Debord ignored existing structures and looked for "new ways of intervening in daily life." Conceptualists adopted a dialectical tactic, addressing critically the institution from both within and without.

Of course, European conceptualism's debt to Situationism does not apply to the work of all European artists labeled conceptual. Still, the work of these artists questions—transforms—the traditional notions and categories of the visual arts. Typically, artists like Jan Dibbets and Giovanni Anselmo (fig. 132) used both photography and language, to document an activity and to displace the traditional notions of sculpture. Dibbets and Hanne Darboven give their work a temporal dimension (a strategy employed by some American and Japanese conceptual artists at the same moment), time being taken as the generative system of the artwork (fig. 199). And if time versus presentness is one of the distinctive traits of conceptual art, the work of Roman Opalka is its perfect paradigm, even more so than Darboven's. Opalka's lifetime project began in 1965, when he inscribed a white painted figure "1" on the upper left corner of a 195 x 135 centimeter canvas with a brush no. 0 on a black background. The work represents a progression toward both infinity and

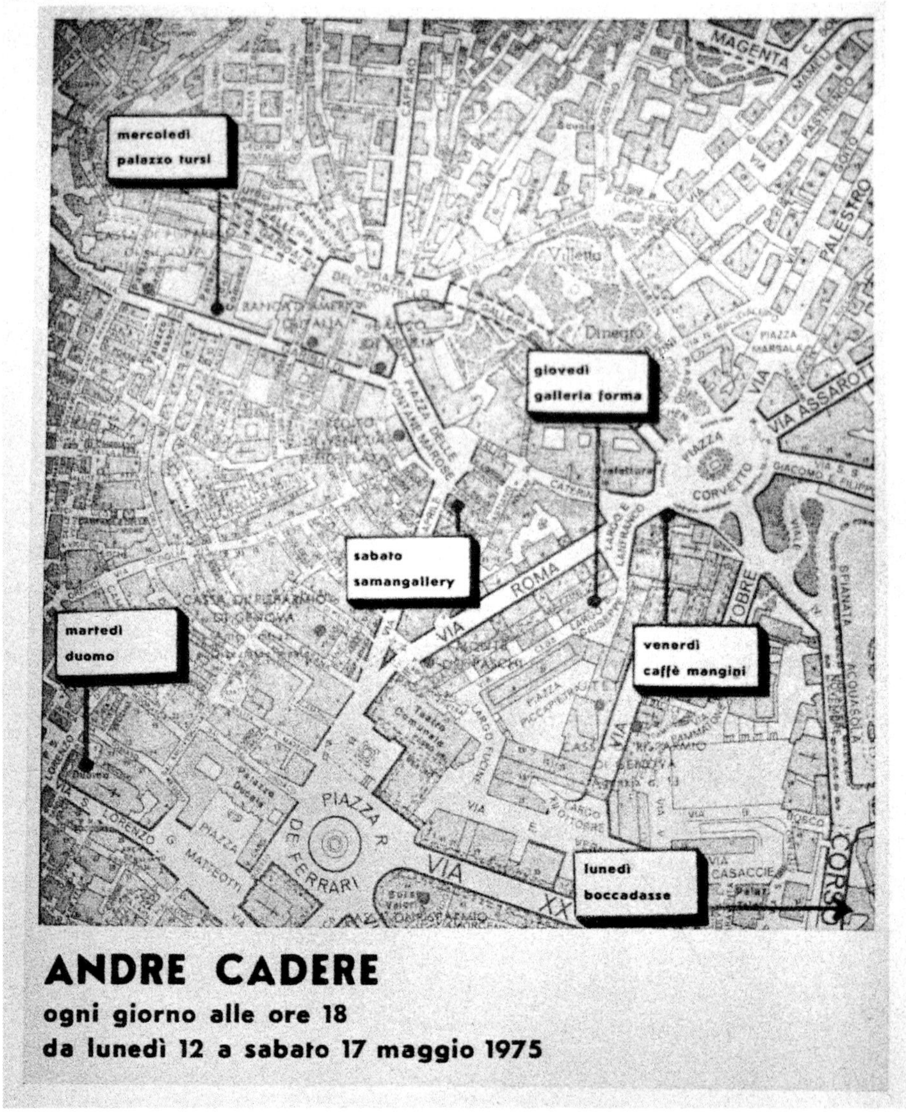

Figure 19.
Roman Opalka, *1965/1–∞*, detail *1896176–1916613*, oil on canvas. Courtesy of John Weber Gallery, New York.

Figure 18. (left)
André Cadere, *Histoire d'un travail*, 1982, book, printed matter. Private collection.

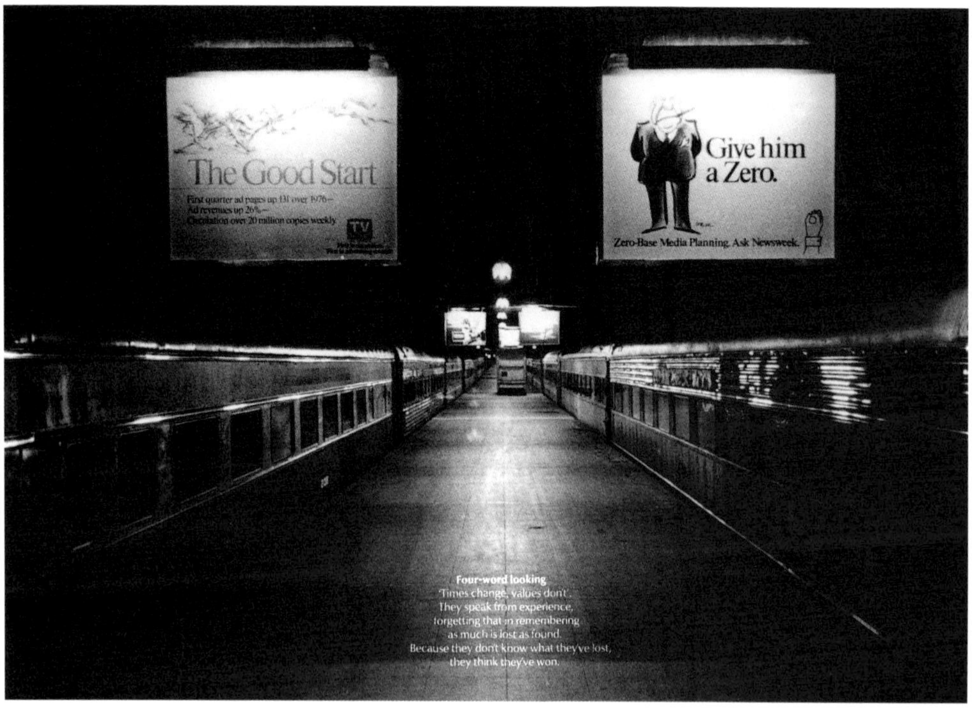

FIGURE 20.
Victor Burgin, *Series: US 77. Framed,* 1977, one of twelve panels. Courtesy of John Weber Gallery, New York.

actual disappearance, since the background of each new painting (each "detail")—covered with its succession of ever-larger figures—is one percent whiter than the previous one (fig. 19). The project will end with the author's death. But "project" is a bit of a misnomer, for Opalka's obsessive activity is a somewhat more dramatic version of a process without subject so typical of work by many European and North American conceptual artists.

In many respects, the works of some Italian artists now usually identified under the label arte povera were informed by a conceptualist trope, for instance, Luciano Fabro's *Concetto spaziale (Tautologia) (Conceptual Space [Tautology],* 1967), an environment made of two identical spaces. Access to the second space is physically denied by the back of a canvas placed across the entrance, and the viewer must read a written text to "see" the space. This tactic reveals a clear debt to Manzoni's conceptualism. Giovanni Anselmo and Alighiero e Boetti (fig. 134) should also be mentioned as artists whose work either toys with the indeterminacy of language (Anselmo)—a Wittgensteinian notion—or hybridizes the abstractness of language with the use of sensuous, exotic non-European fabrics produced by Third World craftsmen (Boetti). Hybridization is also visible in a work like Mario Merz's *Che fare? (What Is to Be Done?,* 1968; fig. 184), in which a famous Leninist motto written in neon emerges out of formless matter.

The codes deployed by conceptual artists in the market-driven economy of the Western world—inserts from the classified section of newspapers, appropriations of dictionary definitions, etc.—were also used by a group of Catalonian artists active during the final years of Franco's dictatorship (1972–75). Grup de Treball (Working Group) appropriated conceptualist tools to fight the fascist regime (fig. 203). For example, in *Recorreguts (Distances Traveled,* 1973; fig. 135) the group deals with the various ways of tracing on a map of Barcelona the route taken by 113 members of the nascent Assembly of Catalonia as they were led by authorities from the site of their arrest (a church) to prison. This is probably a unique example in the history of Western European conceptualism of overtly political commitment.

In Britain, the work of Art & Language propelled various offshoots and divergences. Victor Burgin, for instance, began his art career with a programmatic theoretical orientation close to that of Art & Language. In 1970, he proposed "a 'moratorium' on things—a temporary withdrawal from real objects during which the object analogue formed in consciousness may be examined as the origin of a new generative system."[7] His *All Criteria* (1970) fits such a proposal.[8] But he soon abandoned this withdrawal from "things" (a posture that could easily devolve into hyperabstraction achieved through linguistic propositions and photography) and moved progressively toward more psychoanalytic and sociocultural concerns related to late capitalist societies.

Such a strategic move appears in full light with series of works like *Performative/Narrative* (1971; fig. 133), and *Series: US 77* (1977; fig. 20), in which the discrepancy between image and text becomes a springboard for commenting on psychosexual difference and "a redistribution in the 'economy of desire' as mapped in the theory of psychoanalysis."[9] As is now apparent, Burgin's conceptualism pointed to a new direction along which other artists (mostly North American) such as Jeff Wall, Cindy Sherman, Richard Prince, Jenny Holzer, Barbara Kruger, and many others embarked from the late 1970s onward.

In its many different aspects, European conceptualism was first of all a questioning of the immediacy of the visual art object. This was done through a variety of strategies: the mediation of language, site-specificity, self-reflexive criticism of the "fiction" of the autonomous artwork, recording (making sensible) the passage of time in the artwork itself. Yet conceptualism was largely a "process without subject" and, for that matter, an investigation that might well have been the swan song of modernism in the visual arts. In the mid- to late '70s, new concerns with gender and ethnic difference and the social constitution of the desiring subject directed conceptual preoccupations toward a reintroduction of the subject as the return of the repressed in modernist Western artistic discourse, and as a resistance against the occurrence of a strategically organized historicist return to painting meant to counter conceptualist "nihilism."

Notes

1. Guy Debord's *Mémoires* (Paris: Situationist International, 1959), composed entirely of quotations without marks, is a good example of the technique of *détournement* applied to printed matter.

2. Thomas Leavin, "Dismantling the Spectacle: The Cinema of Guy Debord," in *The Situationist International, 1957–1972* (Cambridge, Mass.: MIT Press, 1990), 84.

3. Guy Debord, *Considérations sur l'assassinat de Gérard Lebovici* (Paris: Editions Gérard Lebovici, 1985), 45.

4. August von Cieszkowski, quoted in Guy Debord, *Oeuvres cinématographiques complètes, 1952–1978* (Paris: Champ Libre, 1978), 75.

5. Charles Harrison, "Art Object and Artwork," in *L'art conceptuel, une perspective,* ed. Claude Gintz (Paris: Musée d'Art de la Ville de Paris, 1990), 61.

6. Ibid., 63.

7. Victor Burgin, "Thanks for Memory," *Architectural Design* (August 1970).

8. Its first definition reads as follows: "All criteria by which you might decide that any series of bodily acts, directly known to you at any moment previous to the present moment, constitutes a discrete event."

9. Harrison, "Art Object and Artwork."

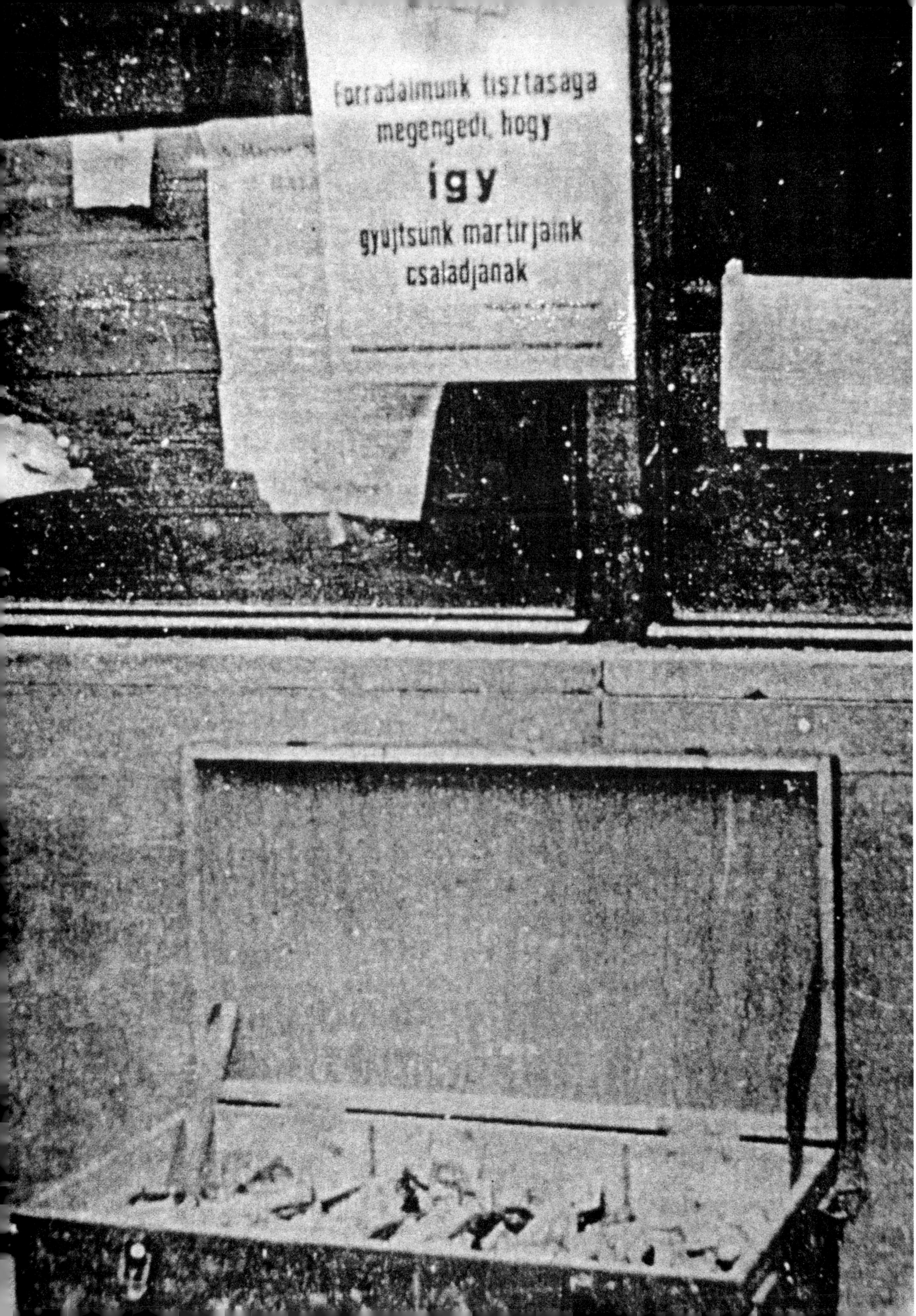
Forradalmunk tisztasága
megengedi, hogy
így
gyűjtsünk mártírjaink
családjának

Conceptual Tendencies in Eastern European Art

László Beke

Figure 21.
Miklós Erdély, *Unguarded Money (Örizetlen pénz),* October 26, 1956, photograph documenting a street action. Collection of Miklós Erdély Foundation, Budapest.

Looking back from the end of the 1990s, we may observe the extremely important historical role of conceptualist art in Eastern Europe from the mid-'60s to around 1980. What is more, conceptualism is currently experiencing a revival in the region, chiefly because of several retrospective exhibitions. During the period in question, conceptualism involved ten to sixty artists in each of these countries. Moreover, hundreds of "concepts" were born in Eastern Europe during the 1970s, produced by professional artists and amateurs, and just as quickly disappeared again. How to present these works, given that they were immaterial?

But before launching directly into a discussion of Eastern European conceptualist art, it would be useful to define precisely what is meant here by that amorphous entity "Eastern Europe." Often, different authors refer to the region by different names—for instance, Central Europe—without specifying its cultural, historical, political, even geographical context. Hungarian historians invented the term "Mid-Eastern Europe" to describe all the states of the former Austro-Hungarian empire. Quite naturally, the problem has political implications, mostly due to "the East" being seen as such from a Western point of view. That is, "Eastern Europe" is a geographical concept created by theoreticians of developed Western states as a synonym for the former "socialist bloc," which at times included the entire territory of the Soviet Union or, alternatively, the area west of the Ural Mountains. But our focus will be much narrower. Eastern Europe as defined here encompasses Poland, the former Czechoslovakia (now Czech Republic and Slovak Republic), Hungary, Romania, the former Yugoslavia (Croatia, Slovenia, Serbia, and four or five other regions), Bulgaria, as well as East Germany (now part of the united German Republic).

Together with my colleague Gábor Pataki, I was first confronted with these definitional problems in terms of postmodern theory while working on a joint project in 1989, the so-called Eastern Europe Questionnaire, which was circulated among art historians and theoreticians. We had formulated several questions which seemed to us crucial in light of the rapidly changing political and social conditions generated by the fall of the Soviet Union. For instance, did our countries have a common art history on the basis of which a new artistic cooperation could be forged under new social and political conditions? Was there any change in the relationship "center and periphery"? Would these new historical conditions produce a new kind of Ostkunst (vs. Westkunst, i.e., Eastern European vs. Western art)? Today, the framework of our questionnaire would be expanded to address the numerous problems wrought by so-called European integration.

To these questions (assuming they are still viable) should be added one about the historical role of conceptualism. Generally, all neo-avant-garde tendencies of the 1960s in the "socialist" countries, especially conceptualist art, performed a "linguistic" function in prepa-

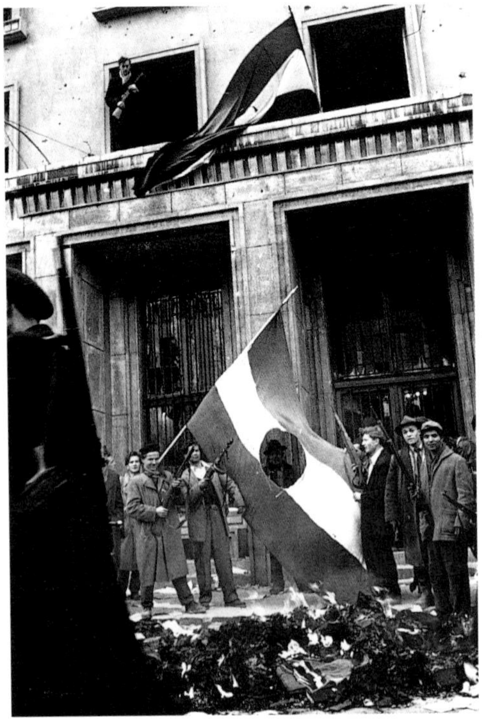

Budapest, 1956: Freedom fighters, occupying the AVO headquarters at Koeztarsasag Square, remove the Soviet emblem from the Hungarian flag. Courtesy of Magnum Photos, Inc. © 1995 Erich Lessing.

ration for the political and social transformation of the 1980s—in other words, a genuinely new aesthetic language was not created in the 1990s because this had been accomplished decades before. As used here, *linguistic* refers to the framework through which the methodologies and discourses of the human sciences, philosophy, and art were interrogated and redefined by their own practitioners. Models for this inquiry were served by linguistics, semantics, semiotics, and theories of communication. So, for example, Eastern European conceptualists considered structuralism a form of scientific research parallel to constructivist art tendencies, while linguistics—as a method used by Ferdinand de Saussure or Roman Jakobson—was aligned with different theories of conceptualism.

After World War II, Eastern European countries shared the following characteristics: dependency on Moscow in larger or smaller measure; assuming the authority of the Communist parties on the basis of Marxist-Leninist ideology; the struggle against capitalist imperialism;[1] and a violent regulation of the problems of national and ethnic minorities in the name of proletarian internationalism. This latter was always the reference point when revolutions or insurrections were brutally suppressed, as in Poland and Hungary in 1956 or Czechoslovakia in 1968.

In the cultural field, the Marxist-Leninist (-Stalinist) theory of socialist realism was predominant. Different avant-garde tendencies in art, such as abstraction (nonfigurative art), surrealism, etc., were considered formalist and thus "alien to socialist ideology." However, the response of the Communist parties to progressive artists differed from state to state, and one can perceive local characteristics in the degree of control or censorship. In Yugoslavia, which was otherwise closely linked to the Western art scene (namely through Italy, Austria, and later West Germany), communist artists constructed several partisan monuments but were still a minority in relation to avant-garde artists. In Poland there was no censorship in the visual arts and, as a consequence, artists experienced more freedom of expression, but a strong political protest art did not develop. In the 1970s, Hungarian artists elaborated a sophisticated evaluation criteria, the so-called three Ts (three Hungarian words beginning with "T"—*tűrni, tiltani, támogatni*—meaning "to support," "to tolerate," and "to prohibit"). In Czechoslovakia, even after the failure of the Prague Spring, it was still possible to exhibit pop, minimal, or conceptual works, while in Hungary this was forbidden.

From the late 1960s, new tendencies appeared in the work of Eastern European avant-garde artists. Old-fashioned abstraction was joined by op art, kinetic art, systems art, and new geometry (based partly on new research into folk art patterns). New figuration, hyperrealism, environments, and pop art influenced the younger generations. Together with happenings, Fluxus, and object art, pop also provided a sympathetic context for the development of conceptualist art et al.: process art, project art, arte povera, anti-art, mail art, stamp art, rubber stamp art, artists' books, visual and concrete poetry, land art, body art, actions, experimental photography, film, video, dance, music, and so on.

Strictly speaking—that is, according to Western precepts—conceptual art can be immaterial, made from/by concepts (Henry Flynt, 1963), can be a linguistic-philosophical-logical proposition (which changes the function of art; Joseph Kosuth, mid-1960s), but need not be exclusively immaterial, as long as the idea embodied in the process of creation is paramount (Sol LeWitt, late 1960s). (To the Hungarian reception of Kosuth's "theory of art/art as theory" belongs the slightly dubious legend of his Hungarian origins, which resulted finally in his participation in the 1993 Venice Biennale in the Hungarian pavilion.) In comparison to this Western notion of conceptual art, the Eastern European variant was never so rigorous. Rather, it was flexible and elastic, ironic, humorous and ambiguous, nonprofessional, communicable, always ready to become a social activity of a group of young people or even an alternative movement. This group orientation, most likely an expression of utopian notions of social organization, was intrinsically critical of statist regulation, which is why it was hardly acceptable to the communist authorities. On the other hand, the "immaterial" nature of conceptualist works, and the "poorness" of the media employed—"just an idea," words and concepts, paper and pencil, typewriter, postcards, a telephone call, ephemeral actions—made communication easier and censorship more difficult. This is why conceptualist art had to be invented in Eastern Europe, and its function as a strategy for evading authority should be considered a feature specific to its development in the region.

For example, prohibited from participating in international exhibitions, artists could send mail art pieces all over the world by the simple means of a postal envelope (unless, of course, the postal police caught them). In 1971, I initiated a project entitled *Imagination*—motto:

"an artwork is nothing but the documentation of an idea"—in which artists were asked to submit ideas for works that, given political constraints, were unrealizable. In 1972 Jaroslaw Kozlowski and Andrzej Kostolowski in Poznań, Poland, compiled an international mailing list of artists, putting out a call for conceptual and mail art, on the basis of which I began to build my "World Famous World Archives" in Budapest. It is worth mentioning that the common language of Eastern European conceptualists was English and rarely their own national language. Another fact to be considered in the problem of nationalism versus internationalism is that many artists emigrated to other countries (about half of the main avant-garde contingent in Hungary, for instance), returning only after 1989. Long-term exile was understandable, given the restrictions on travel. Although citizens were entitled to a tourist trip abroad once every three years, and later once a year, artists' travel applications were often rejected with a written explanation stating that "your travel abroad would be against the interests of the state."

Curiously enough, in spite of the popularity of mail art, interregional contacts among Eastern European artists were infrequent, especially in the early phase of conceptualism. A Czech avant-garde artist could meet a Serbian colleague more easily in Paris, or even through a West German publication, than in Prague or Belgrade. In the early 1970s, the Balatonboglár Chapel Gallery in the Hungarian countryside, loaned by the artist György Galántai, became a venue for several meetings among Eastern European artists, for instance, when Czech, Slovak, and Hungarian artists joined in an "anticelebration" of the 1968 military occupation of Czechoslovakia by Soviet troops. The Young Artists Club in Budapest and, later, the East Berlin apartment gallery of Jürgen Schweinebraden also became gathering places for Eastern European conceptual artists.

A strategy for eluding authorities, conceptualism also meant control of media by the artists.

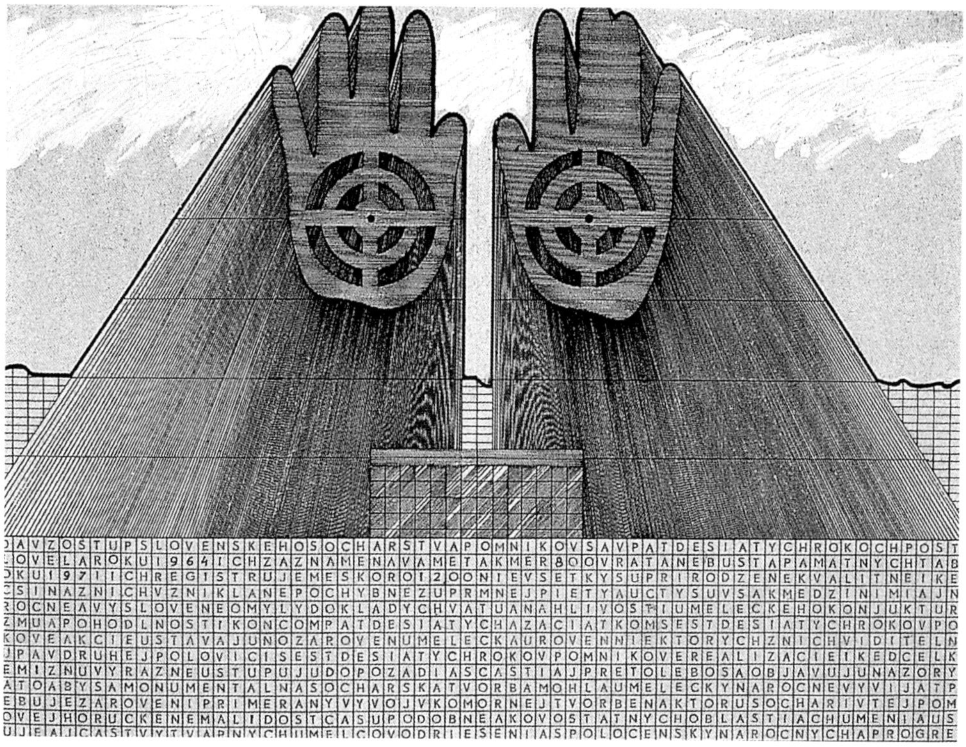

Figure 22.
Jozef Jankovič, *Project of the Monument of Slovak Sculpture (Projekt pamätníka slovenského sochárstva)*, 1976, ink and oil on paper. Collection of the artist.

If conceptualism was a tautological enterprise, researching the nature of art itself, so the experimental (conceptual) artist studied (and expanded) the expressive capacities of photography, film, video, and even traditional media, from drawing to textiles. A general avant-garde mentality framed this expansive approach: every kind of media, from the telephone, telex, laser beam, photocopy, computer, and graphic processes to the human body had to be reinterpreted and refunctionalized from the perspective of a new aesthetics.

The period of conceptualist art began in most Eastern European countries in the second half of the 1960s. In Czechoslovakia, a socialist people's republic with perhaps the most democratic liberal tradition in the region, a principal problem was the tension between the Czech and Slovak parts of the federation, and this ambiguity was resolved in the 1990s with the schism into two independent nations. A very early conceptualist piece from Bratislava, the Slovak capital, is Július Koller's 1964 "antipainting" of a single motif, the word *more* (sea), in the middle of a color field (fig. 25). A year later, within the framework of their *Happsoc* (i.e., "happenings" plus "society") activities, Stano Filko, Alex Mlynárčik, and Zita Kostrová declared the city of Bratislava, together with all its inhabitants, buildings, and objects, an artwork. In the early '70s, Filko (fig. 201) became interested in speculations about the cosmos, Mlynárčik in folk festivals resembling happenings, and other Slovak artists in natural phenomena and traditional art forms: Peter Bartoš (fig. 26) in animals; Rudolf Sikora and Michal Kern, landscapes; Vladimir Popovič, rural life; and Juraj Meliš, peasant architecture and crafts as vehicles for the representation of philosophical ideas (fig. 23). Jozef Jankovič produced architectural utopias (fig. 22) which later became "realities" to a certain extent, for instance, his separation of Czech and Slovak citizens by two tunnels in the same railway station.

In the Czech part of the country, the informel painter Vladimír Boudník had initiated a kind of mail art activity as early as the 1950s, but his contribution was rather considerable in

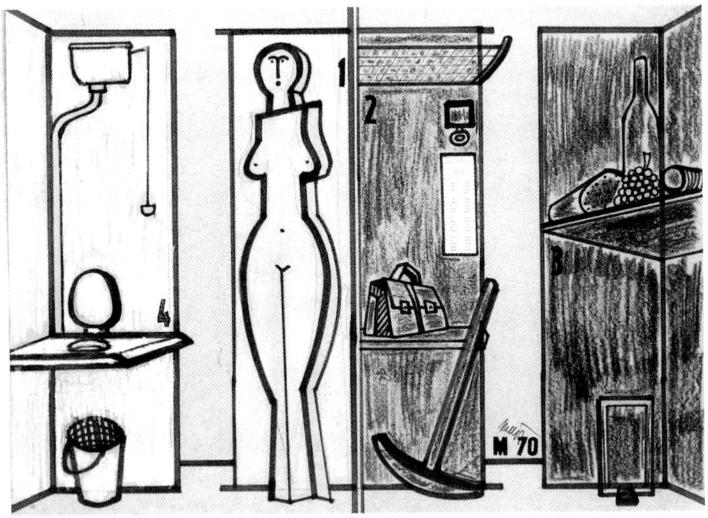

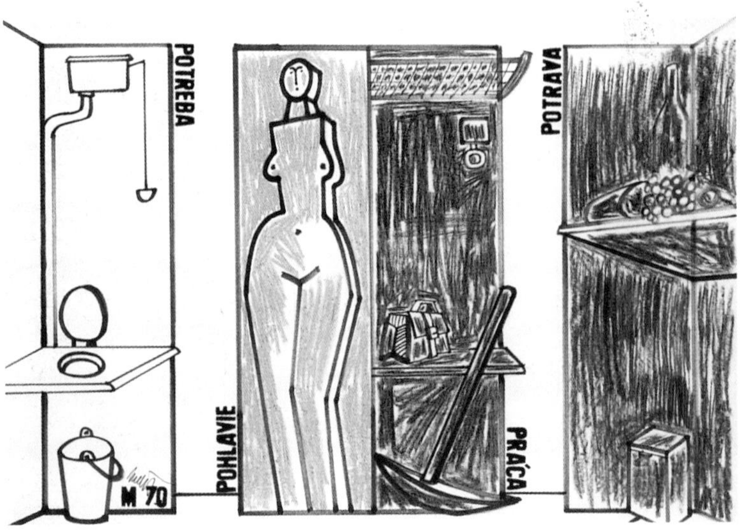

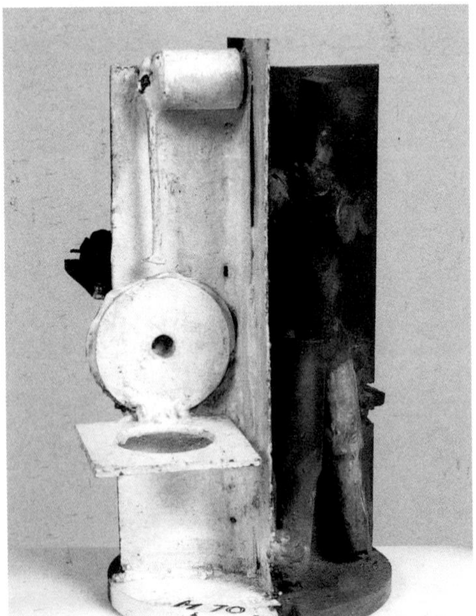

Figure 23. (ABOVE LEFT AND RIGHT; LEFT)
Juraj Meliš, *4 x P*, 1970, mixed media. Collection of the artist.

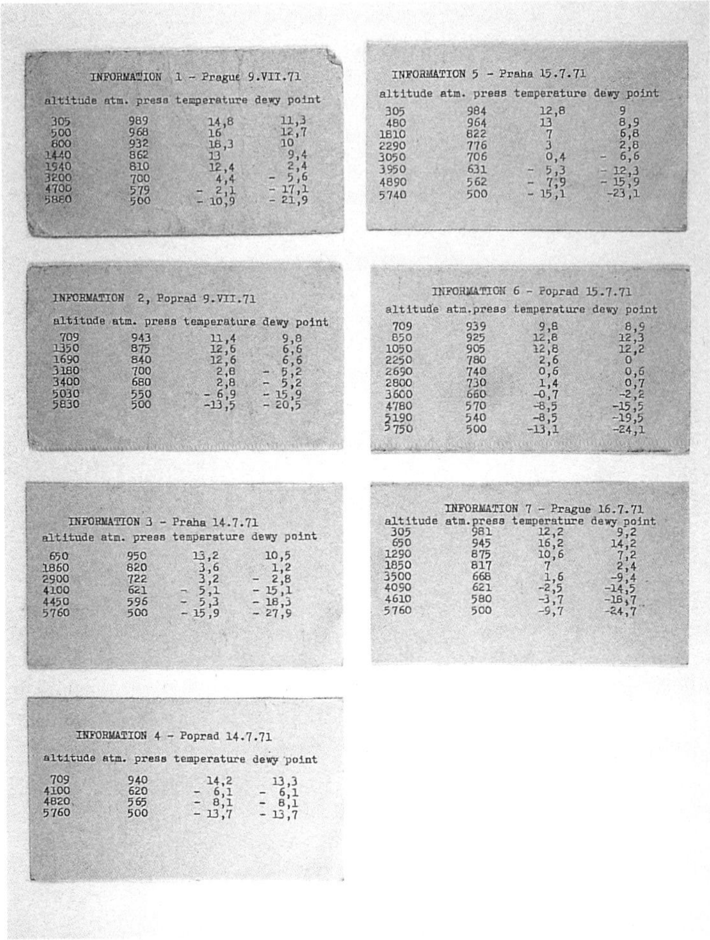

INFORMATION 1 - Pragu[e] 9.VII.71

altitude	atm. press	temperature	dewy point
305	989	14,8	11,3
500	968	16	12,7
800	932	16,3	10
1440	862	13	9,4
1940	810	12,4	2,4
3200	700	4,4	- 5,6
4700	579	- 2,1	- 17,1
5880	500	- 10,9	- 21,9

INFORMATION 2, Poprad 9.VII.71

altitude	atm. press	temperature	dewy point
709	943	11,4	9,8
1350	875	12,6	6,6
1690	840	12,6	6,6
3180	700	2,8	- 5,2
3400	680	2,8	- 5,2
5030	550	- 6,9	- 15,9
5830	500	-13,5	- 20,5

INFORMATION 3 - Praha 14.7.71

altitude	atm. press	temperature	dewy point
650	950	13,2	10,5
1860	820	3,6	1,2
2900	722	3,2	- 2,8
4100	621	- 5,1	- 15,1
4450	596	- 5,3	- 18,3
5760	500	- 15,9	- 27,9

INFORMATION 4 - Poprad 14.7.71

altitude	atm. press	temperature	dewy point
709	940	14,2	13,3
4100	620	- 6,1	- 6,1
4820	565	- 8,1	- 8,1
5760	500	- 13,7	- 13,7

INFORMATION 5 - Praha 15.7.71

altitude	atm. press	temperature	dewy point
305	984	12,8	9
480	964	13	8,9
1810	822	7	6,8
2290	776	3	2,8
3050	706	0,4	- 6,6
3950	631	- 5,3	- 12,3
4890	562	- 7,9	- 15,9
5740	500	- 15,1	-23,1

INFORMATION 6 - Poprad 15.7.71

altitude	atm.press	temperature	dewy point
709	939	9,8	8,9
850	925	12,8	12,3
1050	905	12,8	12,2
2250	780	2,6	0
2690	740	0,6	0,6
2800	730	1,4	0,7
3600	660	-0,7	-2,2
4780	570	-8,5	-15,5
5190	540	-8,5	-19,5
5750	500	-13,1	-24,1

INFORMATION 7 - Prague 16.7.71

altitude	atm.press	temperature	dewy point
305	981	12,2	9,2
650	945	16,2	14,2
1290	875	10,6	7,2
1850	817	7	2,4
3500	668	1,6	-9,4
4090	621	-2,5	-14,5
4610	580	-3,7	-18,7
5760	500	-9,7	-24,7

Figure 24.
Petr Štembera, *Weather Report (Information)*, 1971–72, ink on paper. Collection of László Beke, Budapest.

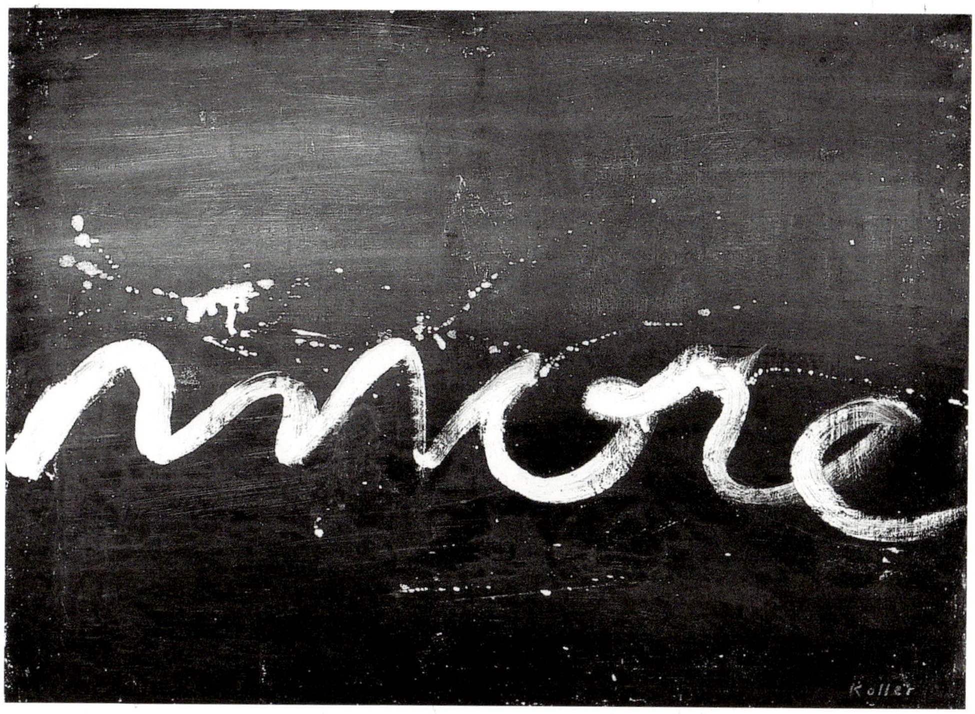

Figure 25.
Július Koller, *Sea (More),* 1964, oil on canvas. Courtesy of Auction Company SOGA, Bratislava, Slovak Republic.

Figure 26. (below)
Peter Bartoš, *Nothing, Point, Shift (Nič, Bod, Posun),* 1969, paint on cardboard. Courtesy of Slovenská Národná Galéria, Bratislava, Slovak Republic.

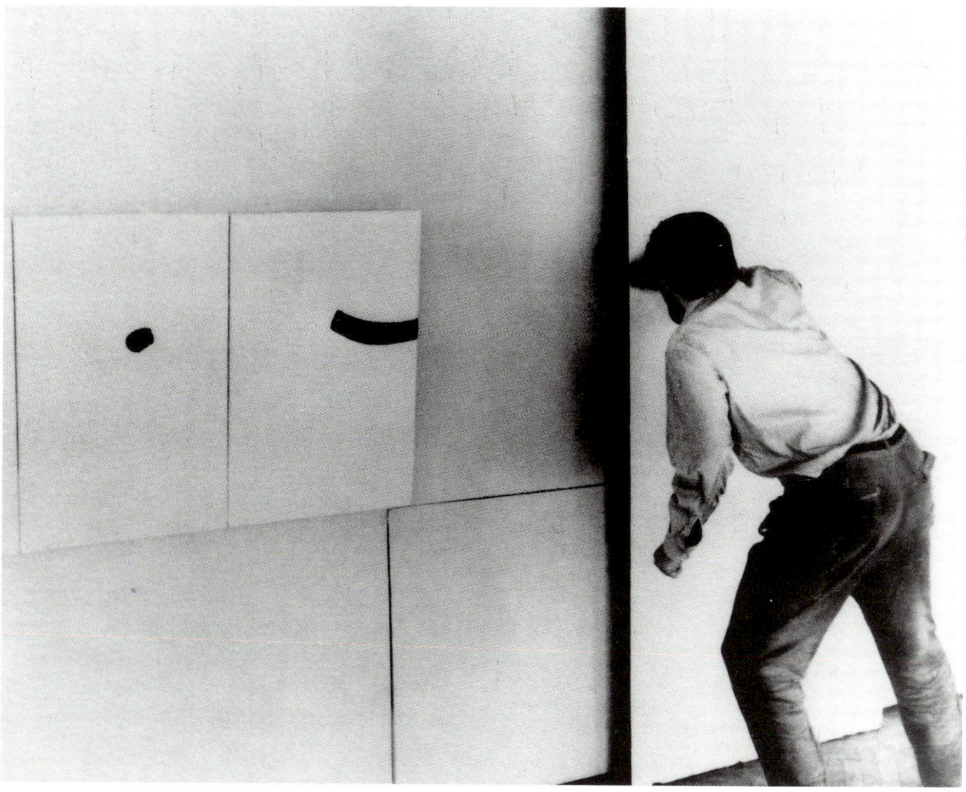

the field of painting (brilliantly described by Bohumil Hrabal in his 1973 novella *Něžný barbar*). Prague artist Milan Knížák and the Aktual Group around him played an important role in maintaining contact with the Fluxus and happening movements (Knížák was head of Fluxus East), and elaborated actions and concepts that contributed to the political events of spring '68. These included lectures in public places on "the second atomic explosion in China," the destruction of books, and walks through Prague staged as happenings. A counterpart to the "activist" Knížák was Petr Štembera, with his Prague weather broadcasts (fig. 24) and risky body works, sometimes performed with friends Karel Miler and Jan Mlčoch. Similarly, intimate and restrained "individual mythologies" were developed by Ladislav Novák in poems, drawings, and actions on the basis of his *alchimage* method (i.e., noticing figures by chance in a crumpled sheet of paper). In Brno, Milan Grygar synthesized movement, drawing, and music; the theorist Jiří Valoch combined visual poetry and "hard-core" logical-conceptual problems (fig. 5); the veterinarian J. H. Kocman produced limited-edition handmade books; and Dalibor Chatrný tackled conceptual issues in his epistemological series of photographs.

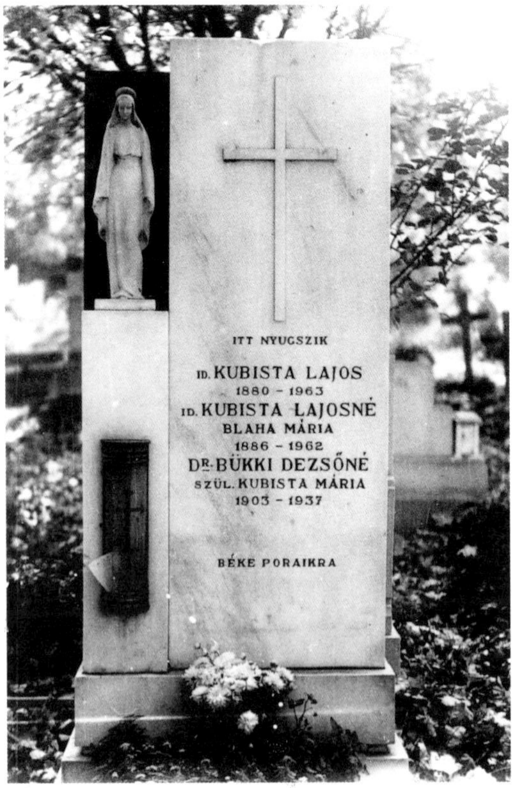

1 Kubista Lajos Budapesten a Farkasréti-temetőben lett eltemetve
2 A kubizmus nem Budapesten született
3 Budapesten még semmilyen izmus sem született
4 Victor Vasarely Magyarországon született
5 Az Op-art nem Magyarországon született
6 Nicolas Schöffer Kalocsán született
7 A Kinetik-art nem Kalocsán született
8 Herzl Tivadar Budapesten született
9 A cionizmus nem Budapesten szület_tt
10 Szilárd Leó az atombomba atyja, Magyarországon született, meghalt az USA-ban
11 A Pop-art az USA-ban született, hatása Magyarországra is kisugárzott
12 Bartók Béla Magyarországon született, meghalt New-Yorkban
13 A Koncept-art New-Yorkban született, azóta Budapesten is nem egy koncept született
14 Neumann János, a kiváló matematikus, mellesleg a kompjuter feltalálója, Magyarországon született és az Egyesült Államokban halt meg
15 A kibernetikát már több technikailag fejlett országban alkalmazták sikerrel műalkotások előállítására, Magyarországon eddig – tudomásom szerint – még nem került sor erre

- -

Ha – mint állítom – a fenti koncept minden tétele bizonyítható tény, /fact/ akkor ebben az esetben találóbb lenne a "koncept-art" helyett, a "fact-art" elnevezés.

Megszületett volna Budapesten a Fact-art ?

Ez a hipotézis csak akkor tartható fenn, ha az alapjául szolgáló tételek mindegyike valóban tény. Mikor azonban átvizsgáltam e tételek helyességét, kiderült hogy a 3. tétel téves.

A Fact-art tehát halva-született Budapesten, mert a tételek egyike, melyből létrejöttére következtettünk, – az, mely szerint Magyarországon még semmilyen izmus sem született, – téves, nem tény, /non fact/.

16 Született már Magyarországon is egy izmus, a bicsérdizmus.

17 Bicsérdy Béla Amerikában halt meg.

Figure 27.
János Major, *Fact Art*, c. 1970, photograph, typewritten text. Collection of the artist.

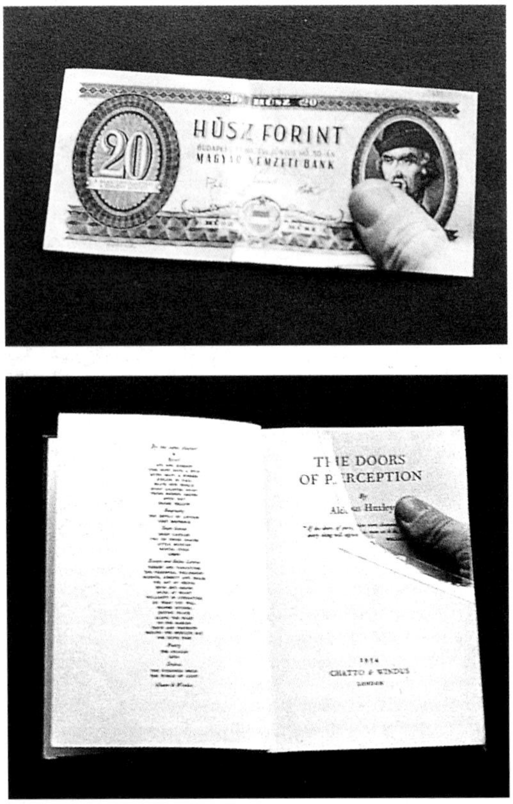

Figure 28.
Tibor Hajas, *Restoration 2 (Restored Money) (Pótlások 2 [Restaurált pénz])*, 1976, bank note and photograph. Collection of Tibor Hajas Estate, Budapest.

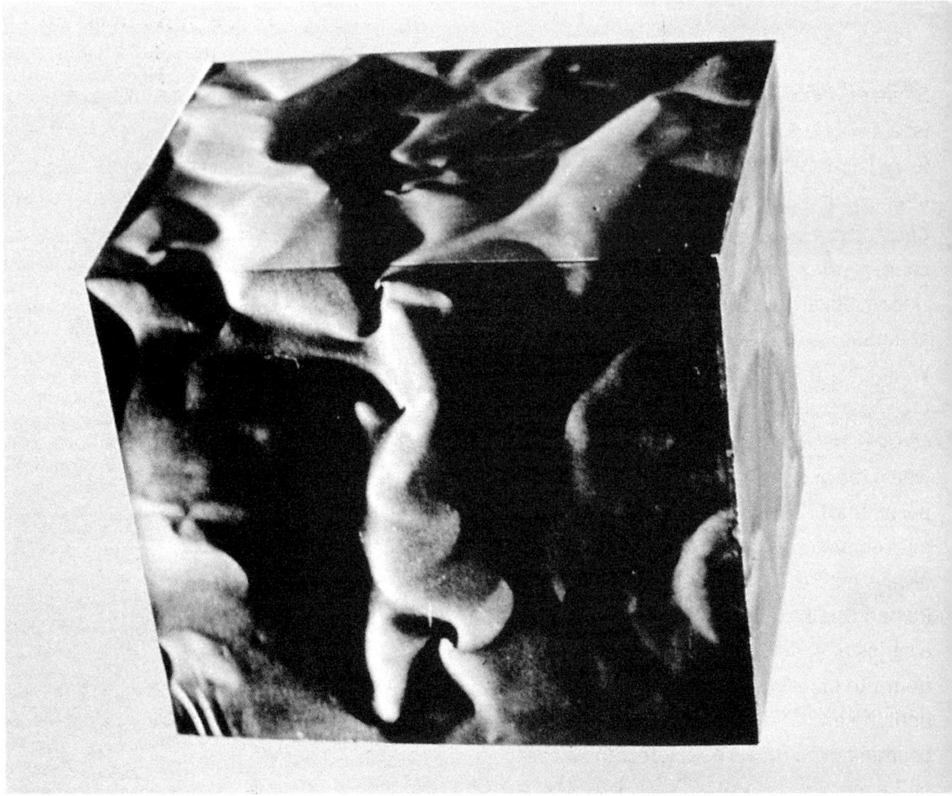

Figure 29.
Gyula Pauer, *Pseudo*, 1970, photograph, airbrush on paper. Collection of László Beke, Budapest.

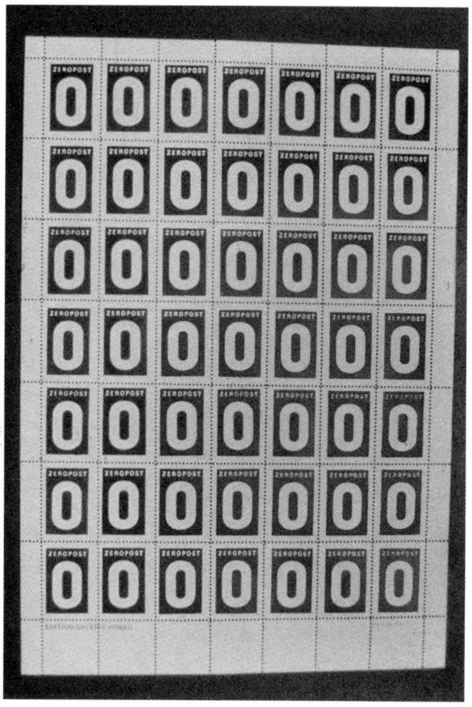

Figure 30.
Endre Tót, *Zeropost,* 1976, postal stamps on paper. Collection of László Beke, Budapest.

Similarly, in Poland the ground for conceptualist art was prepared by the happenings of Jerzy Bereś and Tadeusz Kantor (fig. 136), who later became famous with his play *The Dead Class (Umarla klasa,* 1975), as well as the very conceptual activity of abstract painters like Henryk Stazewski and—from the younger generation—Maria Stangret and Ryszard Winiarski.[2] It is significant that the history of the visual arts in Poland includes a very strong constructivist and avant-garde tradition, to which the young Stazewski belonged. (A very peculiar artist, Edward Krasiński, created environments and assemblages that were always marked with a blue strip.) In 1965 Roman Opalka (now living in France) began a series of paintings of consecutive numbers from 1 to infinity, which he intends to continue until the end of his life (fig. 19). In Opalka's counting exercise we can detect the mentality of the medieval monk patiently copying manuscripts, a kind of ascetic training, and the *principe nulla dies sine linea* as well. In Warsaw, Marek Konieczny developed his Fluxus-like "Think crazy!" activity, and Krzysztof Wodiczko (now in the U.S.) produced strange vehicles, for instance, an "automobile" powered by walking on its hood. At the Film Academy in Lódź, Józef Robakowski (fig. 188) and his friends promoted a very dynamic brand of conceptualism based in experimental film and mixed media. Poland's conceptual artists were supported by a relatively large number of alternative spaces such as the Foksal, Studio, and Remont galleries in Warsaw, the private Bureau de la Poésie of Andrzej Partum, the Permafo Gallery in Wroclaw, the Gallery Adres in Lódź, Akumulatory 2 in Poznań, Labirynt in Lublin, Krzysztofory in Cracow, and other centers in Gdańsk, Sopot, and elsewhere. These galleries featured a variety of conceptual activities, for instance, Jan Swidziński's international colloquium on "contextual art" in the late 1970s and Henryk Gajewski's performance festival *I Am* (1980), both organized at the Remont Gallery.

The experience of Hungarian artists was quite different. Hungary suffered under Communist Party dictatorship from 1948 onward, and during the 1950s even abstract art was considered a form of political opposition. The "heroic period" of conceptualism ran its course under the signs of 1968 and the slogans of the New Economic Policy, a timid reform movement toward "market socialism" begun in 1968 and halted by Moscow in 1972. The economic crackdown brought with it hard restrictions on culture and the arts. After the closing of Balatonboglár Chapel Gallery by authorities, the only alternative space for avant-garde activities in the entire country was the Young Artists Club in Budapest. The first conceptual works were made rather intuitively in the mid-1960s. Gyula Konkoly constructed a very Beuys-like installation in a grimy cave (which he himself later considered "the first Hungarian public conceptual work"), with some shovels, pails, and an inscription on the wall reading "five uniformed men apply here." Géza Perneczky, an art critic, edited exercise books with logical paradoxes (i.e., "this is not a shoe") and made drawings without any direct political content. Dóra Maurer produced her first experimental etchings in 1966. Most of the early Hungarian conceptualists were professional painters and sculptors who began to elaborate theoretical systems preliminary to their works, for instance, László Méhes in his hyperrealist paintings. Endre Tót (fig. 30) followed his reductionist Ellsworth Kelly–like paintings with pure verbal pieces marking the

Figure 31.
Tamás Szentjóby, *Czecho-Slovakian Radio 1968,* 1969, brick with sulphur paper cover. Collection of the artist.

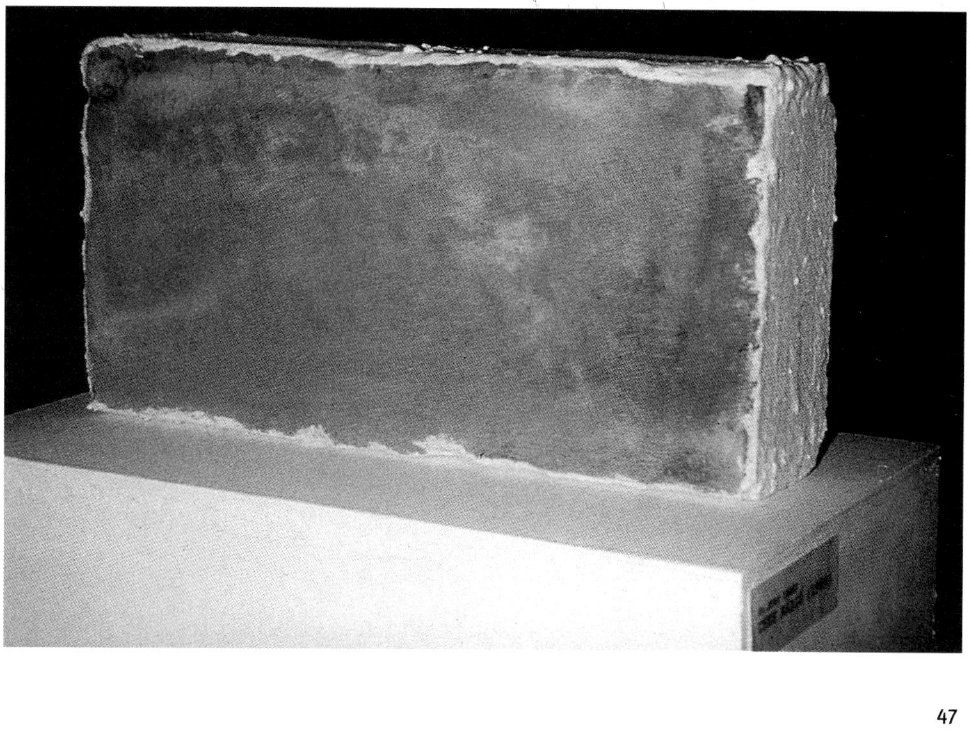

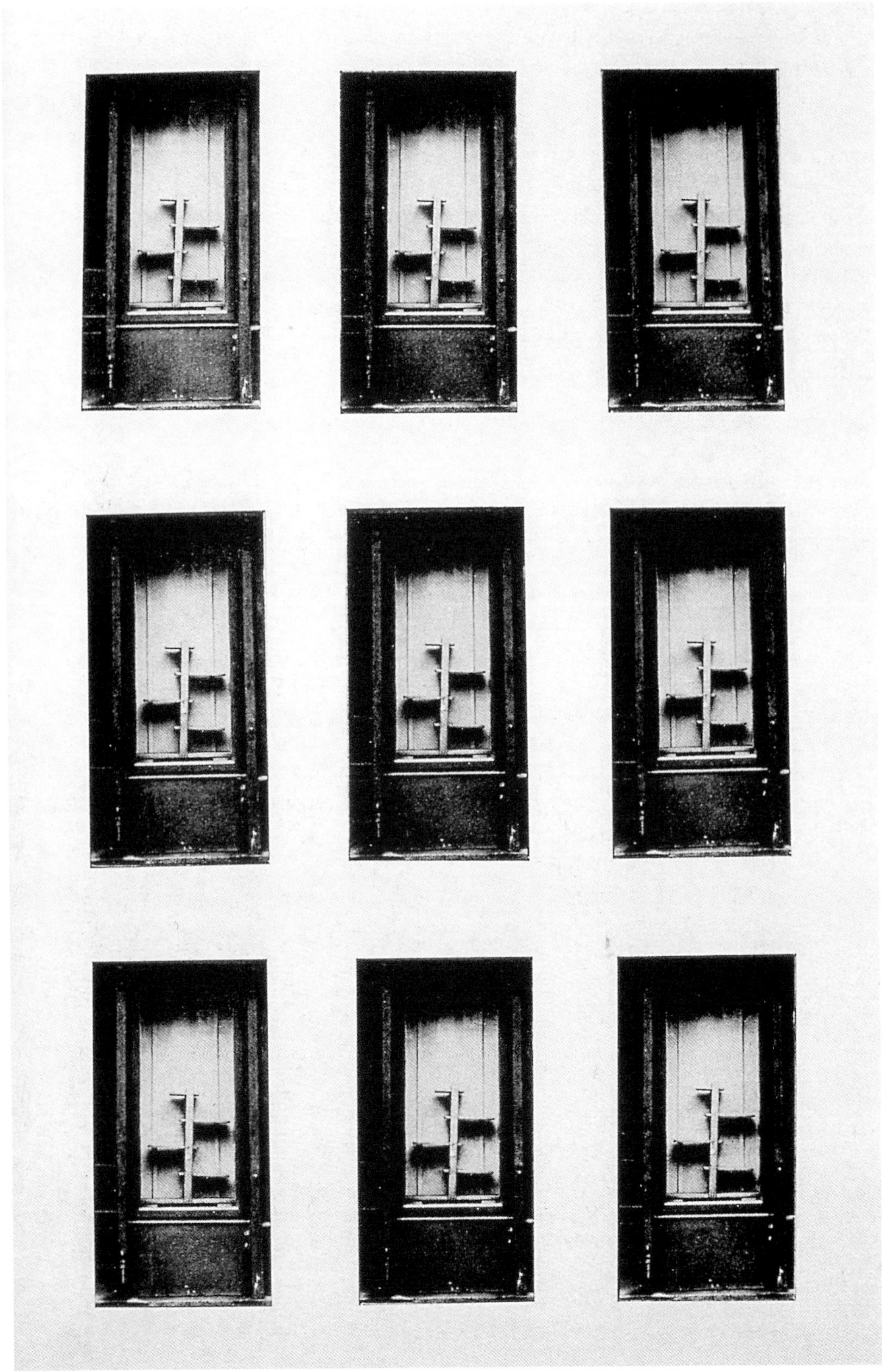

FIGURE 32.
Gorgona Group, *9 Identical Photos 9 (Gorgona,* no. 1, by Josip Vanişta,) 1961, journal. Muzej Suvremene Umjetnosti, Zagreb.

empty space of absent images, or signs of "nothing," then the *I Am Glad If...* series (*Örîlök, ha ...,* 1970–). The sculptor György Jovánovics reconstructed chess matches between, for instance, Tristan Tzara and V. I. Lenin, Zurich 1916, and took up the problem of artmaking in his photo sequence entitled *Liza Wiathruck* (1976). Graphic artist János Major (fig. 27) wrote a brilliantly ironic commentary inspired by an inscription on a tombstone (the name of the deceased was Kubista!), declaring that all *isms* came to die in Hungary. The "pseudo-art" theory of Gyula Pauer, in which he took up the ambiguities of sculpture, was embodied in his photolike creased surfaces prepared by means of an airbrush (fig. 29). Several Hungarian conceptualists routinely used photography, including the Group of Pécs (Sándor Pinczehelyi, Kálmán Szíjártó, Károly Halász, Ferenc Ficzęk, Károly Kecskeméti), Gábor Attalai, Tibor Csiky, Péter Türk, probably the most serious Hungarian conceptualist who worked with logic paradoxes, and Tibor Hajas (fig. 28), the most important Hungarian performance artist, in his *Prostheses* series (*Protézisek,* c. 1970). Hajas's activity signaled the end of the conceptual period, as he preferred risky performance works to dry conceptual constructions.

The work of Miklós Erdély and Tamás Szentjóby, the most politically radical of the Hungarian conceptual artists, derived from pop art, happenings, and Fluxus. Along with Knížák's activities in Czechoslovakia, the early works of Szentjóby and Erdély tested the limits of political protest, and the authorities' willingness to tolerate it, in their own and in all Eastern European countries. For the first ever Hungarian happening in 1966, *The Lunch: In Memoriam Batu Khan (Az ebéd: In memorian Batu kán),* Erdély found the venue, a cave where Szentjóby and Gábor Altorjay staged a Kaprow- or Oldenburg-like scenario. During the second happening, again in 1966, entitled *Sunday Before Christmas (Arany vasárhap),* Altorjay and Erdély constructed an environment in which, among other things, pieces of bread were nailed to the wall. During the Revolution of 1956, Erdély had participated in a solidarity

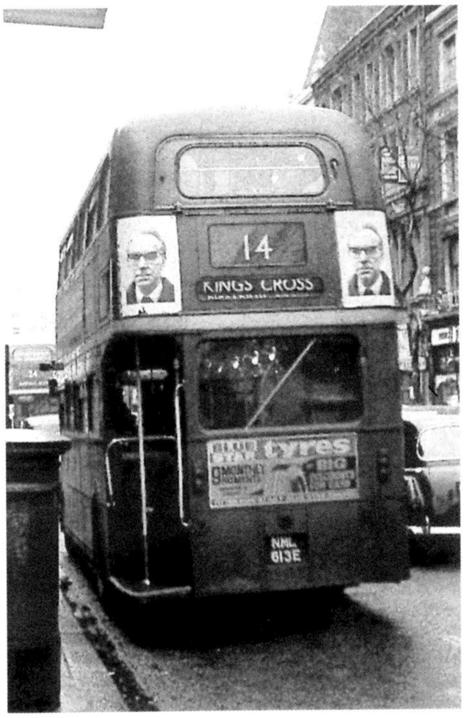

Figure 33.
Braco Dimitrijević, *Casual passerby I met at 11:28 pm, London, 1972*, 1972, documentary photograph. Collection of the artist.

action, which he later referred to as a "happening" entitled *Unguarded Money (Őrizetlen pénz*; fig. 21). With his friends, he placed boxes in the streets of Budapest to collect money for the families of martyrs. The boxes were left unguarded so as to maintain the "purity of the Revolution." Erdély went on to work with a variety of media (film, photography, text, environments, objects [fig. 137], sound), and his late paintings contained many conceptual elements as well. He incorporated film into his actions and made several experimental films, for instance, *Train Trip (Vonatút*, 1981), about the mathematical-musical structure of the film itself.

A former poet, Tamás Szentjóby started with objects and visual poems, then moved on to political protest actions and statements, such as *Portable Trench* (1969, fig. 141). In *Sit Out* (1972; fig. 185), an homage to black activist Bobby Seale, Szentjóby sat in front of the entrance to an elegant hotel tied to a chair, a black bandage over his mouth. *Czechoslovakian Radio 1968* (1969; fig. 31) consisted of a brick covered with sheets of sulphur, an alchemistic allusion to an act of resistance by the citizens of Prague: when the Soviet occupation army confiscated their portable radios, the people of Prague began to carry paper-covered bricks and stones. More recently, Szentjóby has redefined the concept of the readymade, for instance, in his installation *The Coat of János Major (Major János kabátja)*. Inspired by an ordinary coat, the project was an avant-garde gesture of "making something new which is not new at all."

Yugoslavian artists often considered themselves not eastern but southeastern European. This orientation reflects the country's cultural ties to Italy and Austria, as well as its relative independence from Moscow under the leadership of Marshall Tito. In the arts, a kind of proto-conceptualism is evident in the 1950s in *Parafluxus Objects* by Vladan Radovanovič. In Zagreb, now the Croatian capital, the Gorgona Group came together in 1961 and progressed from informel painting to conceptual projects like their "antimagazine," in which were published repetitive series of mundane photographs and signs (fig. 32). The international New Tendencies Movement, headquartered in Zagreb, organized exhibitions and meetings of kinetic, geometric, systems, and op artists from all over the world. During the late 1960s, a new generation took up the ideas of pop, actionism (Tomislav Gotovac), and conceptualism, represented by Braco Dimitrijević's oversized photos of *Casual passersby I met ...* (1971–; figs. 33, 138); Goran Trbuljak's humorous and banal actions documented with photographs (fig. 139) and his contributions to the Tenant Gallery run by himself and Ida Biard; graphic designer Boris Bučan's art posters; and the experimental film and video of Sanja Ivekovič, Dalibor Martinis, and Ladislav Galeta.

As in Zagreb, student centers were in the front ranks of alternative culture in Belgrade (today the Serbian capital). Marina Abramović (later an internationally recognized artist based in the Netherlands) and Raša Todosijević developed intermedial forms between conceptualism and action/performance art (fig. 142). A few solitary artists such as Miroljub Todorović in Belgrade, or Slavko Matković in Novi Sad specialized in "signalism" and comic strip art, respectively. Matković 's short life (1948–1994) was unique from another perspective as well: he was active in Voivodina, a bilingual (Serbian and Hungarian) region of Yugoslavia where the Hungarian minority played an important role. The latter included the group Bosch+Bosch with Bálint Szombathy, László Kerekes, and László Szalma, who created not only conceptualist works but also land art, actions, photos, and experimental poetry.

Figure 34.
Paul Neagu, *Palpable Art*, 1969, ink on paper. Courtesy of Generative Art Trust (P.N.).

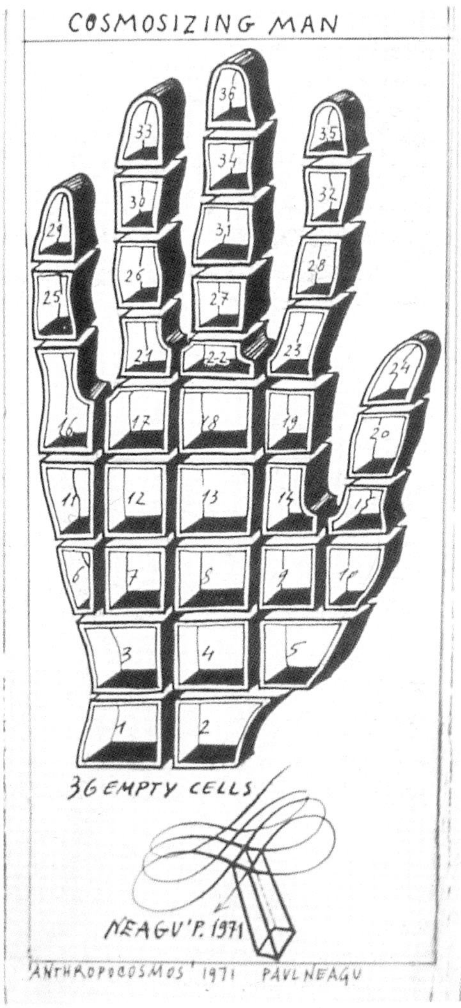

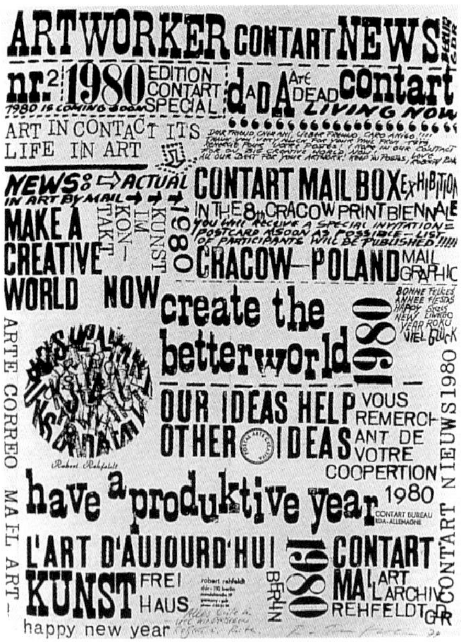

Figure 35.
Robert Rehfeldt, *Art Worker* (*Contart News 1980*), 1979, lithograph. Mail Art Archiv Rehfeldt, Berlin.

The group OHO, formed in 1966, operated in Ljubljana, now the capital of Slovenia. Its members included Marko Pogačnik, Iztok Geister Plamen, Milenko Matanović, Franci Zagoričnik, and others, and their work can be considered the most significant in the region, not only for its diverse media but also its intellectual originality (fig. 140).[3] Nuša and Srečo Dragan produced the first conceptual video works in Slovenia, and Franci Zagoričnik ran Westeast Editions, producing experimental publications. With the "parapolitical" groups Laibach, IRWIN, and NSK (Neue Slovenische Kunst), the art of Slovenia entered a new phase in the 1980s.

The most important forerunner of conceptualist art in Romania is a "peasant mystic," Constantin Brancusi, particularly his *Endless Column* (a reference for Carl Andre). Proto-conceptualist thinking can also be found in the analytic and geometric works of the Timişoara Group 111—Stefan Bertalan, Roman Cotosman, and Constantin Flondor—which, after participating in the 1969 Biennial of Constructivist Art in Nuremberg, was renamed Sygma and included the mathematician Doru Tuncan. The MaMű Group (an acronym for Studio of Marosvásárhely—Tîrgu-Mureş) launched its activities in Transylvania, home of a large Hungarian minority. Headed by Károly Elekes, MaMű moved to Budapest in the 1980s. In Bucharest, the first group of avant-garde artists included the sculptors Paul Neagu (now living in London) and Mircea Spâtâru (and from Baia Mare, Mihai Olos), and the painters Horia Bernea and Mircea Dumitrescu. The works of Neagu (fig. 34), Spâtâru, and eight other artists were featured in an important exhibition at the Richard Demarco Gallery in Edinburgh in the early 1970s, all conceptual or minimal pieces. Along with their pictorial and sculptural work, these artists also produced utopian projects and mathematical formulae, and engaged in theological speculations. Later, most of them formed close ties to the Orthodox Church. In Cluj, the earthworks and actions of Ana Lupaş influenced an entire generation of young Romanian and Hungarian artists. For example, in 1970 she invited all the women of Margau, a village in Transylvania, to create a beautiful plein-air landscape by hanging their white laundry on a green hillside (fig. 143).

Leaving aside the early work of Christo,[4] a progressive tendency in Bulgarian art appeared relatively late, in the second half of the 1980s. Guillermo Dreisler, a political emigré from Chile, started his mail art career there, but then went over to the German Democratic Republic. Luchezar Boyadjiev and Nedko Solakov, two outstanding Bulgarian artists with international reputations, took up conceptualist ideas in the 1980s. Boyadjiev made ironic drawings on traditional orthodox icons, while Solakov critiqued the contemporary international art scene in sophisticated and humorous installations.

After the construction of the Berlin Wall in 1961, the new German Democratic Republic began a schizophrenic life, in some respects maintaining close ties with West Germany, in others not. A loose network of local district cultural centers sprang up around the country in the 1960s and '70s, out of which were organized exhibitions in Dresden, Leipzig, and Berlin, as well as in private homes, for instance, Jürgen Schweinebraden's apartment gallery in East Berlin. Conceptualism, particu-

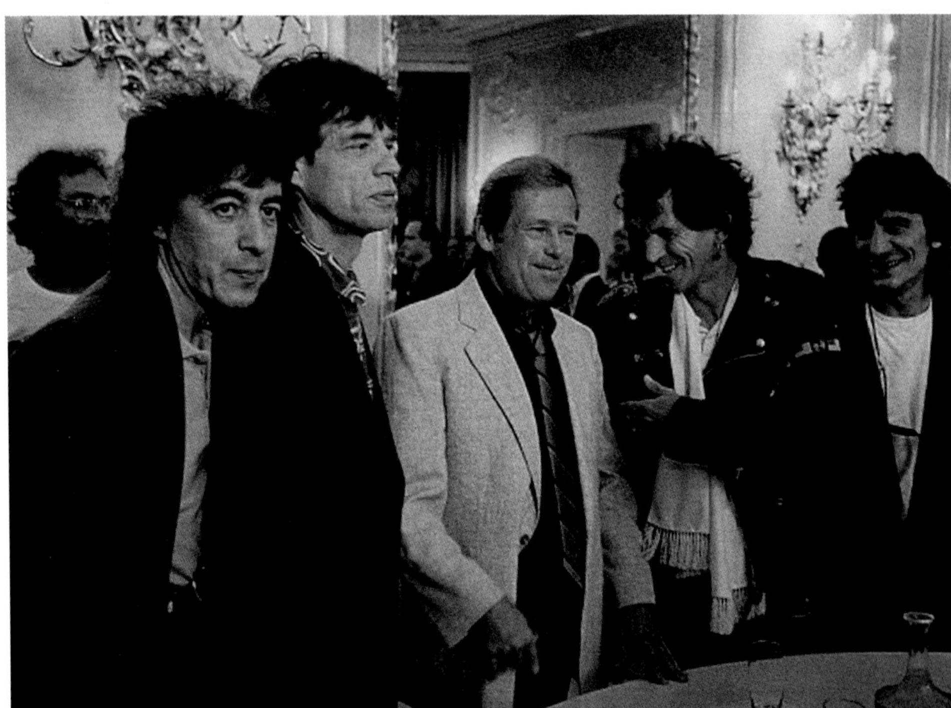

The Rolling Stones meet President Vaclav Havel, Prague, 1995. Photograph by Miroslav Zajic, courtesy of Corbis.

larly mail art, developed within this informal network. Sometimes, the occasion of a political solidarity action (e.g., with Chile), or even the social authority of the Lutheran Church, were used as a cover for conceptualist events. In 1975, Robert Rehfeldt (fig. 35), an excellent graphic artist and principal promoter (along with his wife Ruth Rehfeldt) of the German mail art movement, organized an important exhibition of mail art at the Galeria Theatru Studio in Warsaw. For the project *Nature Is Life—Save It,* East Berlin artist Joseph W. Huber sent sunflower seeds all over the world to be planted. The mail art project *Umwelt und Gesellschaft* was held in Schweinebraden's EP ("Erste Private") Gallery in 1981, and the same year Birger Jesch organized the *Targets-Projekt* at the Weinberg Church in Dresden. Independent of mail art activities, artists such as Carlfriedrich Claus developed a graphic style combining texts and visual poetry. R. A. Penck's paintings functioned as a transition from conceptualism to new expressionism. Penck invented a system of reductive graphic signs (human figures, symbols, and letters) and with this visual language communicated his views on life and death, German history, and humanity in general. Penck later became a leading figure in Germany's new painting movement.

The oppositional milieu in which avant-garde art—including conceptualism—had flourished in Eastern Europe lost its *raison d'être* with the razing of the Berlin Wall. To take one example, Hungary's last radical protest group, Inconnu, disbanded in 1990 with the declaration that there was no more power to fight against (as if capitalism did not present its own set of problems). Subsequent developments—postmodernism, transavantgardism, new painting—represent a rejection of the formal asceticism and search for the new expressed in conceptualist practices. However, significant works with conceptual overtones continue to be produced, for instance, the *Commemorative Monument to the 1956 Revolution in Budapest (Az 1956 os forradalom emlékmüve,* 1991) by György Jovánovics, in which one element, a black granite column, measures exactly 1,956 millimeters.

After a decade of social and political transition, it is now clear that although conceptualist art was short-lived, its impact was profound. In Eastern Europe, conceptualism did not so much alter the status of the object as it blurred the boundaries among the different branches of art and—following Fluxus ideas—between art and life. The commitment to the possibility that "everything can become (conceptual) art" and "anyone can become a (conceptual) artist" expressed in conceptual work liberated art (and not only art) communication, created new aesthetic forms, offered models and methods to the underground "democratic opposition," and thus contributed to the social-political-economic transformation of 1989–90. Conceptualists elaborated utopian social propositions in the framework of "project art." They initiated the ironic "refunctioning" of totalitarian symbols and those of socialist realism, from Milan Knížák's red bandage to the hammer and sickle of Hungarian Sándor Pinczehelyi and the red stars of Romanian Teodor Graur in the 1990s. The influence of conceptualism is evident in the demonstration tactics of the Czech Velvet Revolution, the political struggles of the Polish Orange Alternative, the street actions of the City of Truths in Bulgaria, the social-critical art of the ex-Soviet Baltic countries, the methods of the Romanian "media revolution" of 1989–90, the ecology movement in Hungary, and the antigovernment manifestations in Yugoslavia/Serbia.

Was the fate of Eastern European conceptualism to pave the way for social and political change, and once accomplished, disappear from the "mainstream" of contemporary art? Or, rather, to liberate itself from the ballast of politics and create a playground of pure aesthetics? Hopefully, this exhibition will promote a critical examination of these questions and, perhaps, assist a genuine revival of conceptual art.

Notes

1. As for the relationship of the Ostbloc to the United States during the Cold War vis-à-vis the arts, American "abstraction" generally was important to artists, but not its specific manifestations, i.e., abstract expressionism, art informel, action painting. The first movement to acquire such importance for Eastern European artists was pop art and, immediately after, conceptual art.

2. The two geometric painters, Stazewski and Winiarski, executed their works on the basis of theoretical systems and programs, while Maria Stangret created painted objects (for example, a huge book).

3. See the catalogue *OHO: A Retrospective* (Ljubljana and Graz: Moderna Galerija Ljubljana and Neue Galerie am Landesmuseum Joanneum, 1994), which also demonstrates how a thirty-year-old "passé" art production can be absolutely fresh and actual by means of well-done museum reconstructions.

4. The story goes that Christo, working in the Bulgarian Communist Youth Organization, was assigned the task of covering rusty agricultural machinery lying alongside international rail routes, thus preparing him for his later "packagings."

Si yo supiera pintar, si Dios en su apuro y turbado por error confuso me hubiera tocado, agarraría los vellos
de la marta en la punta de una rama de fresno, flexible, empapados sumergidos en óleo bermejo y pre-
cisamente en este lugar empezaría una librea delgada flaca ya con la intención de cubrir la des-
pués maniobrando con la trasparencia al lado un pozo absolutamente negro y definitivo
en las ramas de unos repugnantes amarillos circuncisos como hilos de seda enganchados
el cochino pájaro del Ártico que utiliza a sus mismísimos hijos para alimentar las focas
que le placen (nadie supo nunca porque y siguen naciendo) colgantes arracimados amasijados
a la tela a ver. Virgen de la Ducha. Él dejó dos cuartas cuadradas libres y en-
seguida un caballo formidable de las colas pero frustratorio por retocado blanco corriendo espumante
con las crines desplegadas un verdadero corcel del malón resuelto con
realismo fotográfico pero con cierto aire metafísico para introducir uno de los elementos de confusión y también
un sospechado sugerido significado opaco bajo el barniz, no simbólico, como para que al
verlo alguien mi siguiera se dé cuenta
nificado de ese caballo veloz que se refriega preguntándose cual es el sig-
brada magnética luego el volcán. El pincel hacia sus entrañas de Venus entre las piernas altas oscuras la gran que-
negros. Pero ese significado debe ser inexistente más afilado el estilete de pelo lacio para escribir esos pastos
bra debe ser engendrada en los ojos por verdadero y ni la más pequeña sospecha de certidum-
de la espuma ocultará los ojos que miran: un sudor gaseoso temprano parto
facción del adivinar los sagaces indicios, los signos de la pesquisa, la satis-
manzanilla despedazada los escasos temblores, los roces. Nada - Flores de
del blanco. Con
ella no me refiero estos por las herraduras para levantar la nada
si fuera una bayoneta
unas rugosidades sólo a la pintura siempre a puro óleo sino en especial al modo de tomar el pincel como
pero tres puntos de apoyo terminados al más cambiaría de técnica a las antípodas con
esquina calada en las uñas pero medio resbaladiza de modo que el aceite con sus naranjas tome
debe abstracción me servirán como la nata una vez arranciada; esas sombras de jengibre blanqueado
las quedar suspendida demasiado para apoyar una suerte de ofensiva contra el caballo pero sin caer
nacia la quebrada como un péndulo lírico que podría desbaratar mi plan pues esta batalla
pupilas y esto no sería para invadirla quieto, una plomada, nadie gana nadie pierde ignorantes del favorito veloz
oscuros tan trabajosa
ongariz de Alafia y sería una ... que empieza los
un Klein, entre ellas produció el arrepentimiento o una modificación en su futuro
pero familiar airosamente con forma que claro evidentemente me dice con los rulos o-
apretado como si me hubiera con esas huellas de recordarla con sus huellas para la eternidad, dejó
entre en este renglón. Achicado el mismo cuerpo que las dejó
miento de frutas, luego parecido entre los plácidos como si fuera un organismo desconocido
lados oncavos ... alejando lugar cordiales celestes casi tocando la línea inicial bermeja pero medio como
es cierto, pero no frutas ... estrellas ... como si fuera un error como cuando uno estruja la palabra última para que
solverlo ... que me dejé un poco de sorprendente por el peso de Alafia inmortal contra un amontona-
el corazón ... ni piedras ni pelota ... aunque ... como si Fontana hubiera roto la tela en triángulos de
impacto de la ... atrás para saber adonde va eso a tocar con la uña para saber si
adrede en lo escondido de toda la fiebre inspirante, algo absolutamente nuevo desconocido
varios metros que tiene este OBRA: cuarenta centímetros cuadrados disimulados y reser-
varte la satisfacción de un sabio estudioso futuro de este cuadro para que pueda percibir el lenguaje inaudible los huesos
en mi cajón para hacer con ellos una especie de amuleto expuesto en un museo escondida en Castelar
pro- termados felig reses res adores por mi alma no ... pintarían ... atacaría el tórax digno de un sector
estos mismos huesos que con su carne en amar ... los cascos de ... corral ... un campo de pastoreo virginal o
collage inventado por Dios. Sin descansar apenas ... un rincón ... verde ... tachar ... a imaginar
a la derecha del pantano y haría tocando ... en el mismo para respirar las hojas ... volver a la respuesta
donde el observador encuentre flores su descanso para tirarse allí a ... los ojos como si fueran los lados del valle del
crecientes de sabiduría y que tenía los pómulos bajo los ojos como si fueran lados del valle de
de nuevo aquella mujer que se extendían majestuosamente a ambos lados redonda nadar
el duplo del rebote de los montes importantes ... valles ... a soñar la siesta a la sombra rodando cayendo
esternón quedarse en el ... escamas y trepar mojado los montes en espiral con el pincel y la
en sus ríos dorado de aferrarme a la punta con el pincel ... capilarmente
sabiendo hasta aferrarme a la ... que me suben ... capilarmos
para utilizar esos jugos que me suben concluía sus senos
tela para ... las frutillas donde Alafia ... saco por el pincel de
desde las frutillas ... sin tocarla y ... frutillas apenas exprimidas
mientras ... Alafia ... los jugos de la ... trasparente de un nuevo cuadro encima del otro como
rulos de Alafia para hacer la superficie la piel con algunas palabras que al azar coinciden y se refuerzan en re-
de Alafia para ... explicación ... en combinaciones estupefactas transformadas
si no existiera siendo sólo una nueva ... jadas ... de una casa consumida
sonancia. pero el resto casi todas entremez ... los revoques ... la evidente confusión de la
en dibujos, enredaderas secas contra los revoques para alcanzar
o borrándose las unas a las otras para ... Pero Dios no lo quiso así:
verdad. y así terminaría mi cuadro capital - Pero Dios ... con el alma exten-
cuando yo en mi turno pasé a su lado con el alma exten-
dida en una limosna Dios no quiso tocarme: tenía su mano entretenida
haciendo los montes valles y nalgas de Alafia y no quiso sacarla ensimismado
en Alafia aunque era mi turno y no quiso sacarla y no quiso tocarme.

"Cuadro Escrito" 17/11/64 León Ferrari

Tactics for Thriving on Adversity: Conceptualism in Latin America, 1960–1980

Mari Carmen Ramírez

Figure 36.
León Ferrari, *Cuadro escrito, 17/12/64 (Written Painting, 17/12/64)*, 1964, ink on paper. Collection of the artist.

Shooting Tactics

What is art, then, if only a way of thinking. Social phenomena are also works of art and they concern everyone.
—Roberto Jacoby, Buenos Aires, c. 1966–67

At least three questions should be raised from the start.[1] How can we retrospectively reference a movement under the globalizing term *conceptualism* when, originally, its authors never conceived of it in such terms? Is it possible to postulate regional, autonomous versions of what has generally been perceived as a mainstream phenomenon? And if so, what particular features would constitute the specificity of Latin American versions? The fact that in this region the highly divergent manifestations comprised by this category never assumed the conceptual label further confounds the attempt to locate them within the general history of the term.[2] Such a task will only prove relevant if the authority of hindsight clarifies the heterogeneous, even contradictory, gamut of individual and collective practices that embraced the conceptual paradigm in this region.[3] Furthermore, investigating the objectives of these practices in their local and ideological specificity may well prove to be much more than an academic exercise. It may, indeed, illuminate a crucial aspect of an underestimated project whose aims not only opposed art itself, but transcended it—that is, the project to straddle in a culture "not subordinated" to central, metropolitan canons. It is from the shifting boundaries of this utopian search that the eclectic practices constituting conceptualism in Latin America should be approached.

Before proceeding further, however, I must clarify the meaning of the term *conceptualism,* both in itself and in the context of this essay. My argument stresses that after the initial artistic revolution undertaken by the historical avant-garde movements (particularly cubism, futurism, and dada), conceptualism can be considered the second major 20th-century shift in the understanding and production of art. By canceling the status and preciousness of the autonomous art object inherited from the Renaissance, and transferring artistic practice from aesthetics to the more elastic realm of linguistics, conceptualism paved the way for radically new forms of art. For this reason, conceptualism cannot be seen as a style or movement. It is, rather, a strategy of antidiscourses whose evasive tactics call into question both the fetishization of art and its systems of production and distribution in late capitalist society. As such, conceptualism is not limited to a particular medium but can appear in a variety of (in)formal, (im)material, or even object-based "manifestations." Furthermore, in every case, the emphasis is not on "the artistic" but rather on specific "structural" or "ideatic" processes that extend beyond mere perceptual and/or formal considerations. Thus, in its most radical form conceptualism can be read as a "way of thinking" (to recall Jacoby) about art and its relationship to society.

Recasting conceptualism in such broad terms will allow me to approach the specificities of Latin American conceptual practices in ways that go beyond the crass reductionism of metropolitan accounts, as well as the commonplace dichotomies of the center/periphery model. That is, it will enable me to engage the work of these artists not as reflections, derivations, or even replicas of center-based conceptual art but, instead, as local responses to the contradictions posed by the failure of post–World War II modernization projects and the artistic models they fostered in the region. Within this framework, the present essay is not intended as a definitive or even a partial history of conceptualism in Latin America, but is largely circumscribed to the development of conceptual practices in the urban centers of Buenos Aires, Rosario, and Rio de Janeiro, with references to similar developments in Bogotá, Mexico City, and the community of Latin American artists in New York. Through these paradigmatic cases, I will attempt to characterize certain general aspects of the conceptual shift in the Latin American context. This objective, in turn, entails stepping beyond the (synchronic) naive claims for truth of historicist accounts in order to (diachronically) apprehend the nature of Latin American contributions to the overall achievements of global conceptualism.

The continuing relevance of this task is supported by two overriding biases. On the one hand, there is the prevalence of an extremely reductive and self-serving art historical framework that, despite a decade of critical reevaluation, continues to privilege a small, iconoclastic group of North American and British artists whose work, in the form of linguistic or ideatic propositions, first attracted public attention in the late 1960s. On the other hand, there are the misunderstandings generated within our own countries by the Cold War legacy, of which critic Marta Traba's biased "thesis of resistance" is representative. From the very beginning, Traba zealously denounced conceptual practices as "imported fads" whose emergence revealed the degree to which a sector of our artists had "surrendered" to North American cultural imperialism.[4] The end of the Cold War era, together with the perspective of the last three decades, requires that we also bring such passionate claims for continental autonomy under critical scrutiny.

Contesting both views, I will argue, first, that the processes leading to the emergence of conceptualism were not exclusive to North American or British artists, but also involved cultural producers for whom the ontological crisis of European art after 1945 provided a frame of reference. This has been the position of Latin American artists who, by reason of their colonial legacy, have for centuries been situated in a dialogic relationship with various artistic traditions of Europe and the United States. As with any other tendency originating in nonhegemonic areas, however, the work of these artists engaged in a pattern of assimilation/conversion largely guided by the internal dynamics and contradictions of the local context. This dialectical exchange resulted in an autonomous version—or even inversion—of important tenets of European and North American modernism. From this perspective, the emergence of conceptualism in Latin America not only closely paralleled but, in many key instances, even anticipated important developments of center-based conceptual art.[5] The inversion model proposed throughout this essay is thus a theoretical stratagem that allows me to dialectically illustrate such an autonomy. Secondly, I argue that in making politics and ideology the starting point for their radical questioning of art-as-institution, Latin American conceptualists produced some of the most creative responses of our century to the question of art's function first raised by Marcel Duchamp. Understanding the origins of Latin American conceptualism in these terms will thus entail apprehending the complex articulations between local "ex-centric needs" and center trends, a rough interplay whose dialectic implies a reciprocal circuit of artistic and cultural exchange.

It must be stressed, however, that conceptualism in Latin America was neither a continentally broad nor homogeneous phenomenon. The complexity and heterogeneity of the region—consisting of twenty countries with diverse social, political, economic, and racial makeups even within their own borders—precludes consideration of uniform regional or national artistic developments. Such conditions necessarily encompassed not one, but distinctly separate histories and modes of conceptualism that correspond not only to individual countries but to specific urban centers within those countries. In the case of Argentina, we must distinguish between conceptual manifestations that developed in Rosario and Buenos Aires. A similar distinction must be established between the Rio de Janeiro and São Paulo groups in Brazil, while in Colombia, although conceptualism was largely restricted to Bogotá, important manifestations appeared later in Cali and Medellín. In most other Latin American countries, conceptualism flourished primarily in the capitals: Caracas, Mexico City, Santiago.

The fact that none of the artists or groups considered in this essay overtly subscribed to the term *conceptual* serves to underscore the authenticity of the local impulses that gave birth to and nurtured their manifestations. In Rio de Janeiro, for instance, artists' questioning of the nature and function of the art object, as well as its reformulation into forms of idea-based art, led Hélio Oiticica to coin the term *nova objetividade* (new objectivity).[6] In Buenos Aires and Rosario, the appropriation early on of structuralist, semiotic, and communicational theories as subjects/objects of conceptual propositions led to the popularization of the term *arte de los medios* (mass-mediatic art). Meanwhile, in Colombia and Mexico the term *no-objetualismo* (non-object-based art), coined by Peruvian critic Juan Acha, became a catchword for all forms of experimental art (installation, performance, conceptual) that sought to do away with the fetishistic status of art.[7] In every case, however, the specificity of the local was placed at the service of the broader objective of producing radical forms of idea-based art. As an inevitable counterpoint to the spontaneity of the phenomenon I have accentuated thus far, there were, additionally, derivative reactions to the dissemination of the figure of Joseph Kosuth in the international press after 1969.

The degree of concentration of conceptual activities throughout the continent allows me

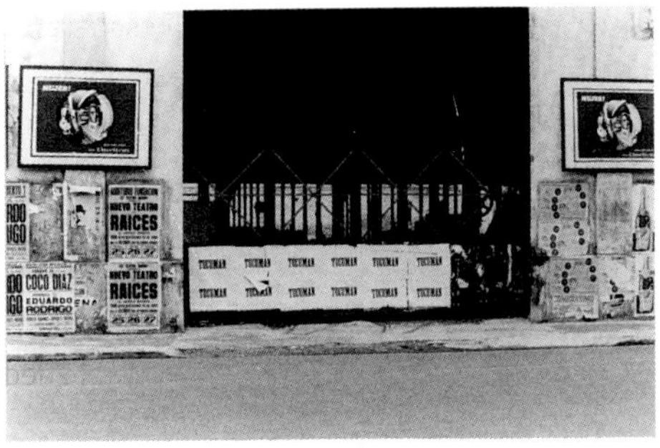

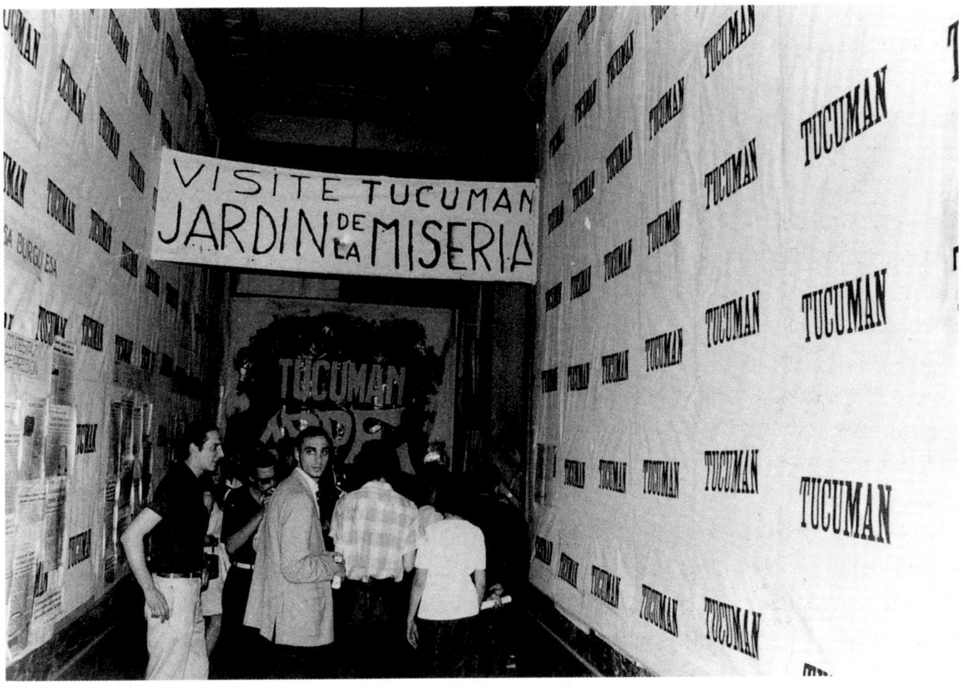

Figure 37. (above)
Tucumán Arde, *Campaña publicitaria, 1º parte, Rosario, noviembre 1968* (*Publicity Campaign, First Part, Rosario, November 1968*), documentary photograph. Collection of Graciela Carnevale.

Figure 38. (right)
Tucumán Arde, *C.G.T. de los Argentinos—Rosario, noviembre 1968: Entrada a la muestra* (*Argentinean Workers' Central Union [CGT]—Rosario, November 1968: Entrance to the Room*), documentary photograph. Collection of Graciela Carnevale.

to broadly distinguish three chronological moments. The first, roughly covering the years 1960 to 1974, is largely restricted to Brazil (Rio de Janeiro),[8] Argentina (Rosario and Buenos Aires),[9] and the New York–based community of South American artists.[10] This first moment, which closely parallels the emergence of conceptual art in Europe, Japan, and the United States, produced several dense conceptual nuclei. The latter were, for the most part, ideologically and theoretically grounded in the elaboration of radical avant-garde movements for societies struggling against authoritarian rule. In the next stage, from roughly 1975 to 1980, a similarly dense concentration of conceptual groups appeared in Chile,[11] Colombia, Venezuela, and Mexico. This second moment, which coincides with the worldwide explosion of conceptualism, was characterized by a broad rearticulation of conceptual practices in terms of both artists' appropriation of urban spaces and their attempts to involve popular audiences in their idea-based proposals. This tendency was best exemplified by the belated phenomenon of Los Grupos in Mexico City.[12] Anticipating each one of these moments is the work of iconoclastic figures such as Alberto Greco (Argentina/Spain/Italy), Alejandro Jodorowsky (Chile/Mexico), Rogelio Vicuña (named Juan Pablo Langlois; Chile), and Bernardo Salcedo and Antonio Caro (Colombia), all of whom generally worked in isolation. Still a third moment of Latin American conceptualism (not covered by the chronological framework of this exhibition) was the emergence of neoconceptual practices in the late 1980s and '90s. With notable exceptions, this last stage corresponds to the institutionalization of conceptualism as both a high-priced commodity and lingua franca of global artistic circuits.[13]

Despite the heterogeneity of Latin American conceptual practices, however, it is possible to detect in the work of many artists from this region at least three common features that clearly distinguish them from their Anglo-American counterparts. First is the strong ideological and ethical profile of this body of production. From its earliest manifestations, conceptualism in our countries extended the self-referential principle of North American conceptual art to a reinterpretation of the social and political structures in which it was inscribed. For these producers, the search for antidiscursive strategies of making art "was no longer the concern of a group coming from an isolated elite, but a far-reaching cultural issue, of great amplitude, tending toward collective solutions."[14] Thus, while North American artists—echoing Kosuth's dictum, "the absence of reality in art is, precisely, the reality of art"—addressed their criticism to the institutionalized world of art, Latin American artists, for the most part, made the public sphere their target. Thus, not only was the work intended to operate at the ideological level, but ideology itself became the fundamental "material identity" for the conceptual proposition.[15] In such terms, "ideological conceptualism," as Simón Marchán Fiz observed in 1972, is not "a pure productive force, but a social one," in other words, one that is not satisfied with an investigation of its own recurrent conditions (tautology) but seeks to actively transform the world through the specificity of art.[16] The substitution of the discursive nature of art with its cognitive function is implicit in this transformation, which allowed such artist groups as Tucumán Arde "to posit the aesthetic phenomenon as a real and positive action, with the potential to modify the context which generated it." Translated into the political arena of 1968, the notion of conceptual art as a vehicle for understanding and problematizing "the real" led Tucumán Arde to reject aesthetics in favor of "violent collective action." In their view, violence had become "the generating force of new contents."[17] A similar position is implicit in Luis Camnitzer's comparison of the means and strategies of the new anti-art with those of urban guerrilla tactics. For him, both shared a common goal: "to communicate a message and at the same time to change through the process the conditions in which the public finds itself."[18] It is timely to point out that the initial work of these artists clearly anticipated forms of political conceptualism developed in the 1970s and '80s by feminist, multicultural, and other politically engaged movements in central countries.

The active engagement with "the real" which characterizes conceptual practices in Latin America is also responsible for their second salient feature, that is, their paradoxical and conflictive relation to a fundamental principle of North American/British conceptual art: the idea of the "dematerialization" of the art object and its replacement by a linguistic or analytical proposition. Latin American artists inverted this principle through several interrelated shooting tactics.

The most antagonistic of these tactics consisted of the "recovery" of the object, in the form of the mass-produced or "assisted readymade," as a vehicle of the conceptual program (Bony, Barrio [figs. 145, 193], Caldas, Camnitzer, Dias, Grippo [fig. 146], Meireles, Oiticica, Manuel). This type of conceptualism—more akin to the "impure" model of Robert Morris, Dan Graham, and Daniel Buren than to that of Kosuth or Lawrence Weiner—was grounded in an interpretation of Duchamp's legacy that went beyond issues of intentionality (artist) or productivity (readymade). As an integral element of more encompassing, frequently ephemeral, antidiscursive strategies of signification, the notion of the readymade as a "package [in which] to communicate ideas"[19] involved a significant questioning of the object's visual and semiotic functions in order to produce meanings related to its structural position within a larger social circuit or context. By means of this dialectical interplay with elements from "the real," artists sought to provoke a "participatory proximity" with the spectator.

Another tactic consisted of a perceptual-cognitive approach applied to both individuals and society as a whole, for the purpose of exposing and contesting conformist attitudes. This type of proposal (Clark, Barrio, Oiticica) displaces the emphasis from the object itself onto the spectator's participation (bodily, tactile, visual, etc.) in the action. Such an approach presupposes that the human senses are social organs through which the individual apprehends and relates to the world.[20] The conceptual proposal, then, seeks to transform the way in which the "participant/receptor" reacts to specific situations that re-create his/her place in the social and political structure.

A third tactic concerns Latin American artists' use of communication and information theories to investigate the mechanisms through which meanings are conveyed to audiences.

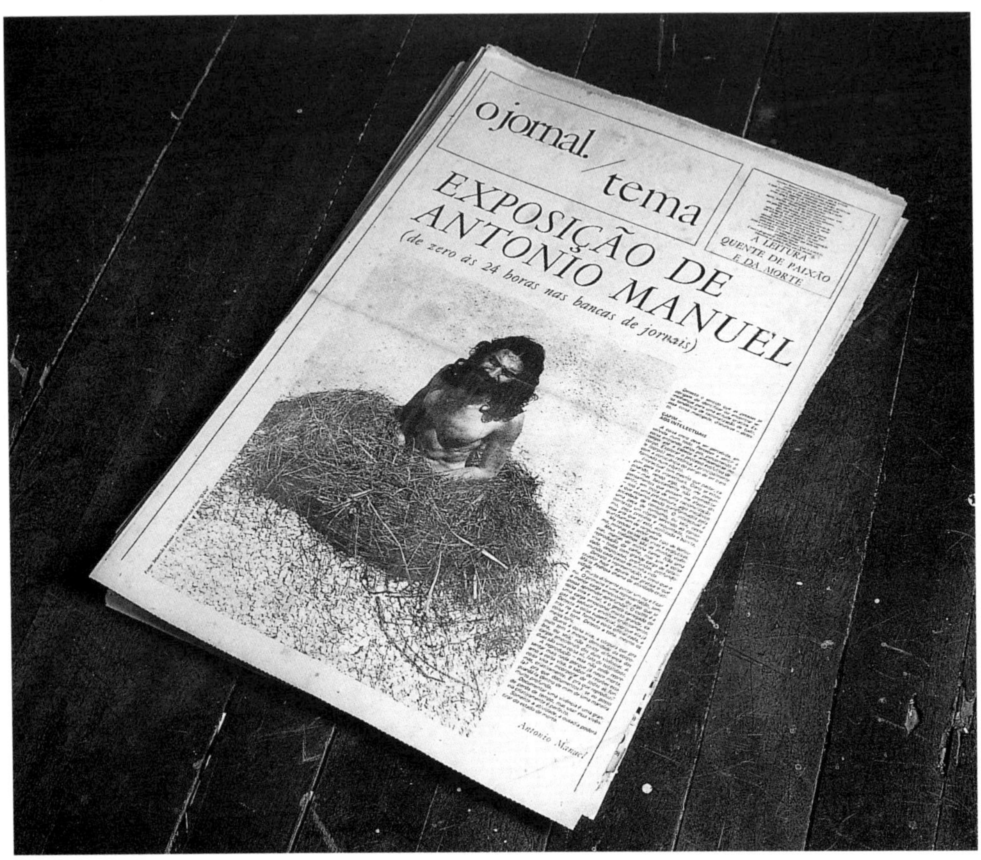

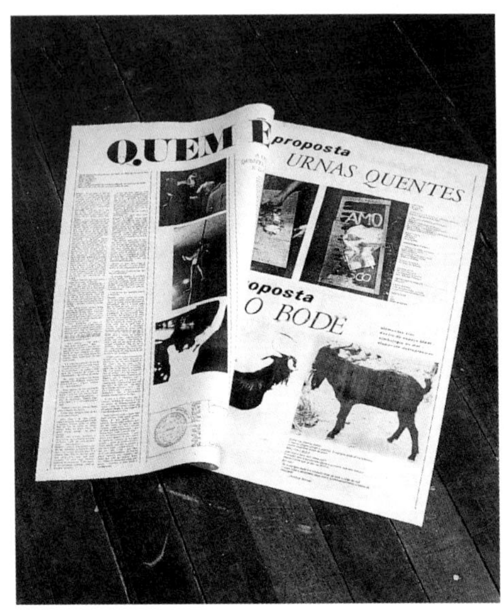

Figure 39.
Antonio Manuel, *Exposição de 0 a 24 horas (Exhibition from 0:00 to 24:00 Hours)*, 1973, newspapers. Collection of the artist.

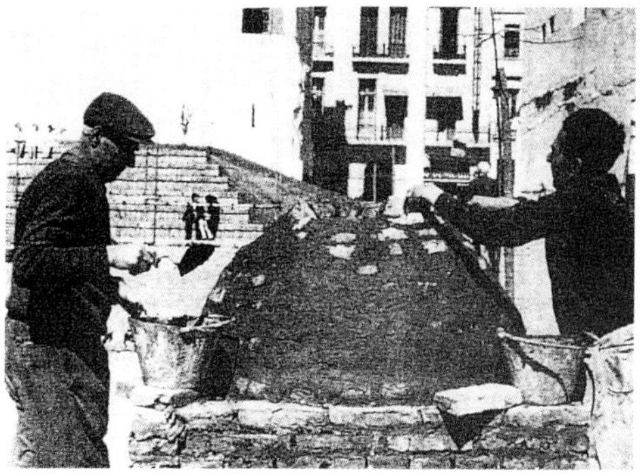
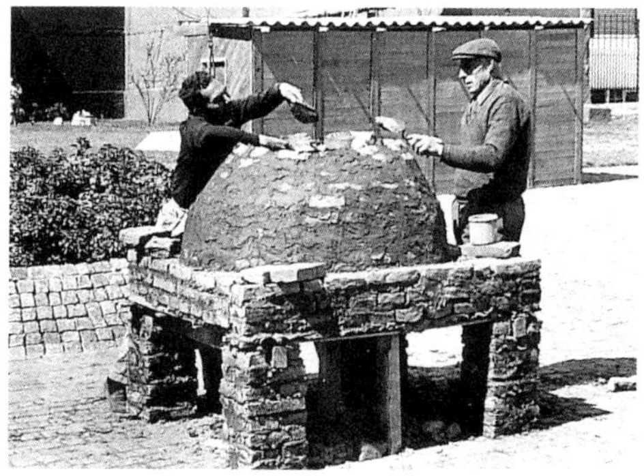
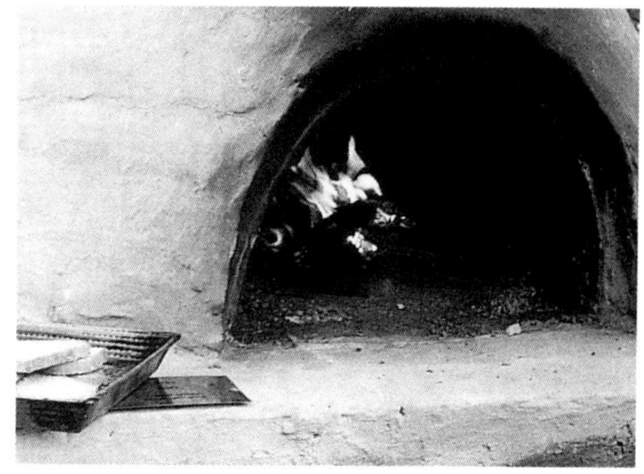
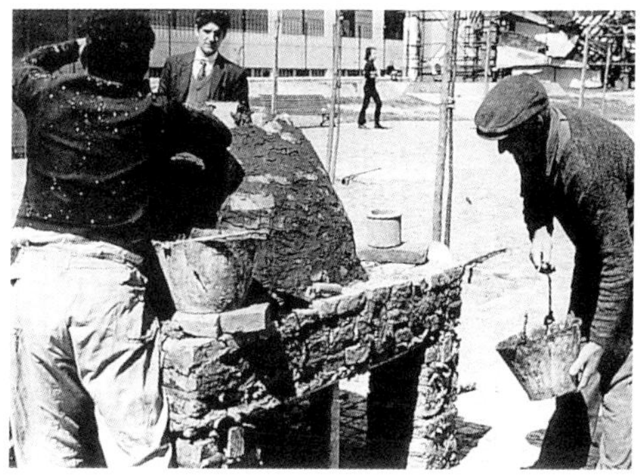

Figure 40.
Víctor Grippo, *Construcción de un horno popular para hacer pan (Construction of a Traditional Rural Oven for Making Bread)*, 1972, black-and-white documentary photographs.

Artists who subscribed to this version (Jacoby, Costa, Escari, Tucumán Arde) appropriated the existing structure of mass media—whether in the form of newsprint, billboards, television, or other technological means of communication—in order to produce a work in which the medium does indeed become the message.

The last feature of Latin American conceptualisms to be discussed here concerns their redefinition of audiences as integral components of the conceptual program. The notion of an idea-based art of broad communicational reach was intrinsic to these practices from the very beginning. What was at stake in them, however, was not the potentially unlimited material accessibility of the work (a feature that also lay at the core of many North American practices), but the conscious effort to counter-circulate messages or communicate new values to audiences. This outstanding trait further distinguishes Latin American conceptual practices from the "telepathic" model prevalent in the United States, a model characterized by its "non-availability" and resistance to producing audiences.[21] In all the cases considered here, *telepathy* is substituted by *pathos* (contamination) or *pathia* (participation). Beyond the metaphysical aspirations of the telepathic model, our artists searched for alternative, participatory systems of communication. Proceeding from a complex critical understanding and application of information, communication, and reception theories, a number of Latin American artists and groups (Barrio, Oiticica, Meireles, Manuel, Tucumán Arde, Grippo [fig. 40], and even Los Grupos) deliberately grounded their tactics in the vernacular matrices of their local contexts. For instance, in the Declaration of Avant-Garde Principles that preceded the exhibition *Nova objetividade brasileira* (1967), the signatories proclaimed: "Our movement, in addition to endowing creative work with a cultural sense, will adopt all means of communication with the public, from newspapers to public forums, from streets to parks, from salons to factories, from leaflets to cinema, from transistor radio to television."[22] Undoubtedly, the work of these artists/groups again anticipated metropolitan insights, such as the analysis of audiences later introduced by North American conceptualists.

ON ADVERSITY WE THRIVE!

In Brazil today (in this way it would also resemble DADA), in order to have an active cultural position that counts, one must be against, viscerally against, everything that could be, in sum, cultural, political, ethical, and social conformity. ... ON ADVERSITY WE THRIVE!
—Hélio Oiticica, "General Scheme of the New Objectivity," 1967

As with any major paradigm shift, the emergence of conceptualism in Latin American countries responded to a complex series of socio-artistic circumstances. Nonetheless, for the purposes of this study, I wish to briefly highlight the following three factors: (1) the failure of the expectations created by the hegemonic project of *desarrollismo* (developmentalism); (2) the simultaneous emergence of authoritarian military regimes; and (3) a major shift in the understanding of the role of the avant-garde in the Latin American context. Parallel to the general climate of unrest that marked the decade of the 1960s—emblematically captured by the anti–Vietnam War movement, the fight for civil rights in the U.S., the success of the Cuban Revolution, and the

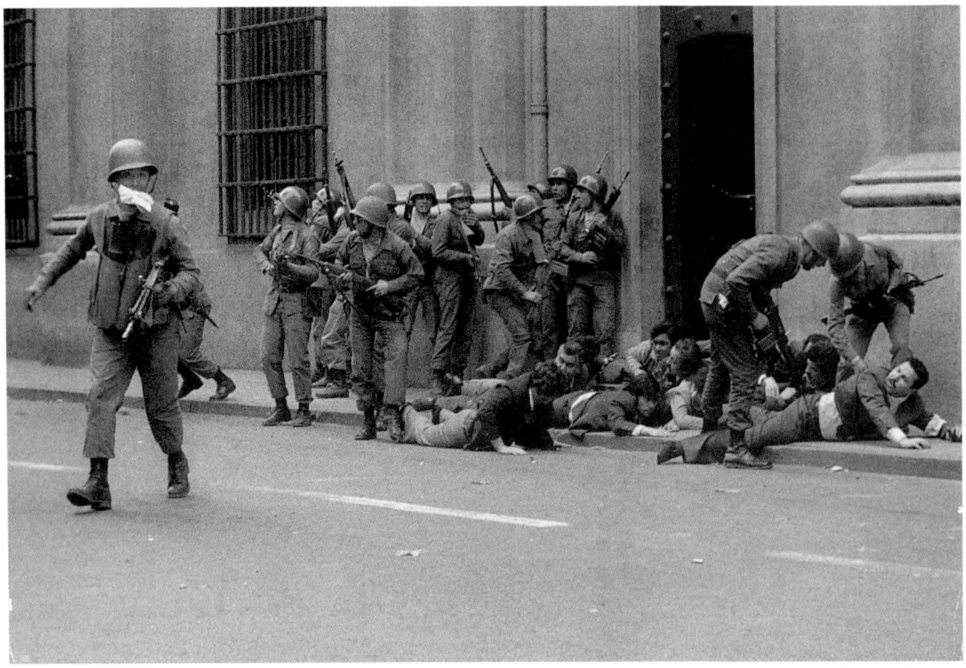

Coup in Chile, September 1973, in which Pinochet assumes power after the execution of Salvador Allende. Courtesy of Sygma. © S. Julienne/Sygma.

events of May and October 1968 in France and Mexico—each of these processes contributed to the consolidation of a new artistic paradigm exemplified by conceptualism.

The majority of artists who engaged conceptual practices came of age in the midst of postwar *desarrollismo* (1950–70). In addition to advanced industrialization and a more sustained level of economic development, this period was characterized by accelerated urban growth, the introduction of mass-media communication technologies (particularly television), a significant expansion of higher education, and a more visible role for art and culture.[23] These factors not only nurtured the hope of liberation from the political and economic stranglehold of the United States, but also the illusion of an emancipated role for Latin America in the First World order. The promise of *desarrollismo* was particularly relevant for Argentina and Brazil, two countries largely constituted by a broad racial mixture of European, African, and indigenous groups. Unlike many other Latin American countries (with the exception of Mexico), Argentina and Brazil had participated in the international avant-garde of the 1920s, contributing highly original paradigms to the movement. Besides, that legacy translated into the emergence of "export-quality" vanguard movements in the 1940s and '50s. Argentina's Grupo Madí as well as the concrete poetry and visual constructivist movements in Brazil were rational experiences linked to the postwar developmentalist boom and long-sought dreams of modernization, an illusion that, at least in Brazil, led to the design and construction of a prospective capital in Brasilia.

Accompanying this actualizing impulse was the creation of a cultural infrastructure to support and promote contemporary art. In 1951, for instance, the São Paulo Bienal was established and Buenos Aires saw the opening of the most important avant-garde center of the period, the Instituto Torcuato di Tella, in 1958. Furthermore, these institutions, wielding the banner of internationalism, entered into an active circuit of cultural and artistic exchange with the United States, particularly New York. Linked to higher standards of socioeconomic development, the presence of cultural modernization projects helped to bridge what Néstor García Canclini has characterized as the significant gap between Latin American modernisms and modernization, thereby prompting the reemergence of active avant-garde movements in specific countries. This partly explains why conceptualism, as the most defiant form of art, thrived relatively early in Argentina and Brazil. At least initially, other countries of the region, lacking similar sociocultural projects, remained somewhat indifferent to the conceptual shift.

Mexico, in particular, presents a peculiar profile. There, artistic modernization occurred in

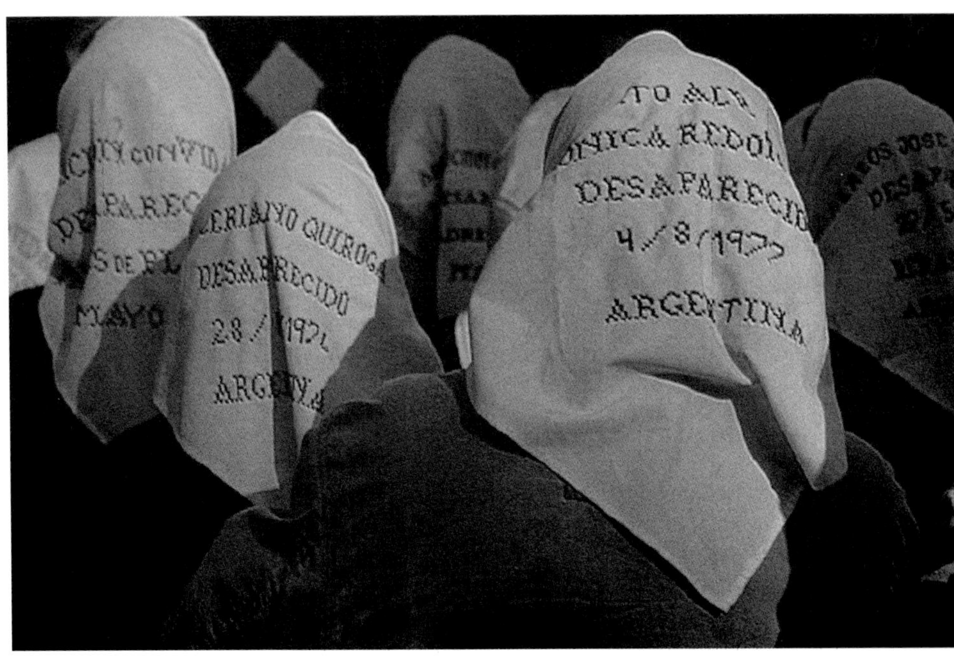

Argentinean mothers protest the disappearances of civilians under the military regime, Buenos Aires, c. 1990. Photograph by Dave G. Houser, courtesy of Corbis.

the context of a centralized and omniscient state apparatus whose forty-year reliance on single-party rule posed serious questions about the nature of democracy, a situation reflected in the arts. Since the 1920s, the identification and subsequent institutionalization of the legacy of Mexican muralism with the state significantly stifled the emergence of experimental artistic production until well into the 1970s. The lag separating Mexican artists from the international avant-garde was reflected both in their subordination to the system and in the following justification by a noted critic: "In Mexico, tradition was so strong ... that painting and the processes that derive from it could be considered to be in dialogue with muralism in order to exalt, correct, or contest it." According to the same critic, this legacy imprinted a particular retardataire logic on artistic developments, which in the 1960s and after were characterized by the triumph of figurative modes and the late appearance of abstraction. This process not only exalted traditional practices and supports, but significantly delayed the emergence of alternate forms of artistic production.[24] The government-led military onslaught against the student movement in 1968—which resulted in the massive killing of protesters—shocked Mexican artists and intellectuals, severely demoralizing them.

It was not until the mid-'70s, with the abrupt appearance of Los Grupos on the urban metropolitan scene, that the full impact of this catastrophic event on artists was revealed. Los Grupos consisted of more than fifteen groups of diverse social backgrounds, objectives, and artistic interests that included, among others, performance, photography, neomuralism, books, urban poetry, and urban theater. The majority of the groups' members came from the ranks of the university-based leftist student movement and had participated directly or indirectly in the events of 1968. Despite their far-ranging eclecticism, however, they all shared an anti-institutional agenda that called for the breaking down of traditional media categories in favor of interdisciplinary work, the abolition of individualism in art, the collectivization of artistic practice, the democratization of systems of art production and distribution, and the development of new audiences. While several of the groups incorporated conceptual strategies (No-Grupo, Peyote y la Compañía, Proceso Pentágono), their understanding of conceptualism was rather limited, and their impact was circumscribed to the critique of institutions as it applied to the specific context of Mexico, rather than to the production of radical forms of idea-based art. Notwithstanding the genuine impulse that generated this movement, by 1980 the majority of Los Grupos seemed to have either succumbed to internal disagreements or were coopted by the official state apparatus, which created a special Salón Anual de Experimentación to present their work on a regular basis.[25]

Even before the first half of the decade was over, political adversity cut short the optimism of the *desarrollista* generation. Between 1964 and 1976, six major countries in South America fell under military rule, including Brazil, Argentina, Uruguay, Peru, and Chile. Authoritarian regimes not only abolished the

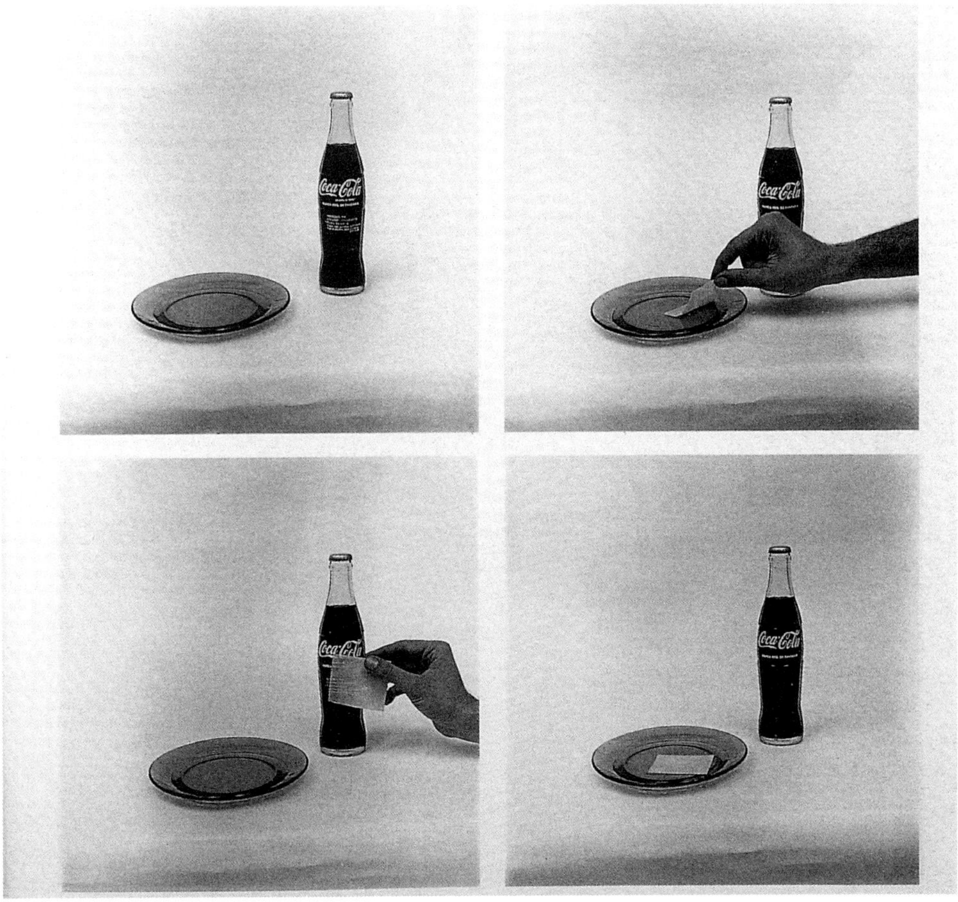

Figure 41.
Cildo Meireles, *Inserções em circuitos ideológicos: Proyecto Coca-Cola (Insertions into Ideological Circuits: Coca-Cola Project)*, 1970, silkscreen on Coca-Cola bottles. Collection of the artist.

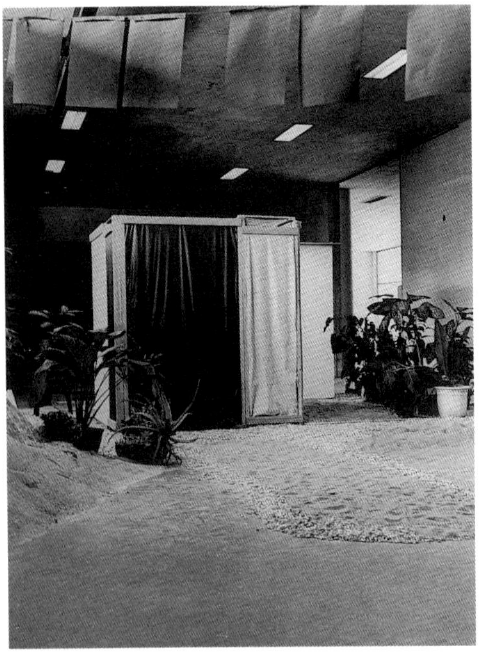

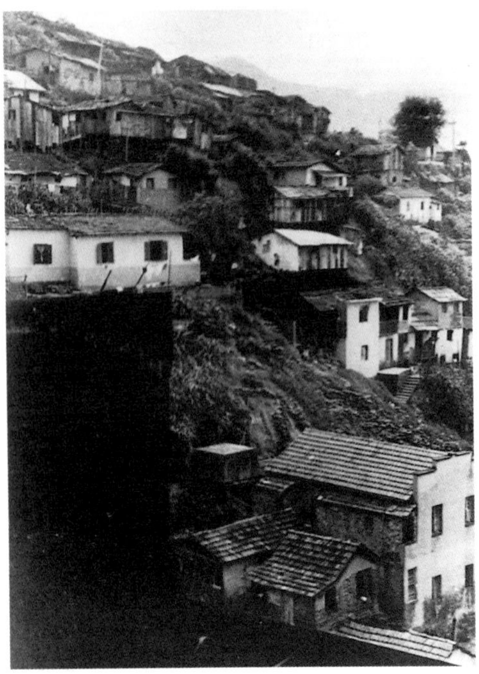

Figure 42. (TOP)
Hélio Oiticica, *Tropicália, Penetrables PN2 and PN3*, 1967, installation at Museu de Arte Moderna, Rio de Janeiro, 1967.

Figure 43. (BOTTOM)
Morro de Mangueira, Rio de Janeiro, 1965, depicting the organic architecture of Rio's favelas.

rights and privileges of bourgeois democracy but also institutionalized torture, repression, and, censorship. All of the artists discussed here experienced authoritarianism in its psychological and material forms, either as internal or external exiles. In Argentina, artists' offensives against the regime of General Onganía, paradigmatically embodied in the collective event Tucumán Arde, called for "a complete rearticulation of artistic practices [in tandem with] new institutional frameworks, new audiences, new means, and new messages."[26] For Juan Pablo Renzi, one of the theoreticians of this Rosario avant-garde group, this new posture called, in turn, for "a conscious incorporation of political action into artistic practice."[27] In Brazil, Cildo Meireles defined this practice early on as one of *inserção* (insertion) into political or cultural circuits, or even as a *transgressão* (transgression) of "the real," understood either as an ideological representation or as actual space.[28] In this context, conceptualism's ideatic thrust proved to be a valuable asset in the development of politically subversive insertions or countercultural artistic transgressions. As demonstrated by both the Brazilian and Argentinean cases, the frequently abrupt substitution of the art object with conceptual forms was the result of a reflexive (not self-reflexive) process that accompanied the displacement of artistic practices from the strictly institutional to the sociopolitical arena.[29]

The interplay between the successes and failures of *desarrollismo* is fundamental for the origins of our conceptualism. In turn, the advent of authoritarianism can also be credited with having stimulated an additional feature in Latin America: its self-conscious status as radical political and artistic avant-garde. In contrast to other parallel avant-garde tendencies centered on formal innovation (local versions of op, pop, etc.), the outstanding feature of the conceptual avant-garde was the merging of art and politics into a socio-artistic project of emancipation, that is, a project in which the creation of new forms of art would go hand in hand with the hypothetical transformation of everyday life and the construction of an alternative society. The main purpose of the new objectivity, in Oiticica's words, was thus "to foster a general creative state, which would be called Brazilian avant-garde, in a cultural consolidation (even if specifically anticultural methods are used for this)."[30] In Buenos Aires, Roberto Jacoby called for an avant-garde that would "permanently negate art" while "permanently affirming history."[31] This formula, by its very nature, challenged both authoritarianism and its accomplice, transnational capitalism.

For many of these artists, only an art that participated in such a "complete sociopolitical reformulation" could resolve the dilemma confronting cultural producers at that particular moment in time. In Oiticica's view: "how to, in an underdeveloped country, explain and justify the appearance of an avant-garde, not as a system of alienation, but as a decisive factor in its collective progress?" The conscious attempt by these artists and groups to contest the institutional world of art and bridge the gap that separated them from society as a whole situates them within the framework outlined by Peter Bürger for the European historical avant-gardes. This trait, in turn, further distinguishes Latin American practices from both the mainstream model of conceptual art and parallel manifestations of the so-called neo-avant-gardes of the 1960s. As demonstrated by Tucumán Arde, these movements were in many ways closer to the heroic impulses that animated the historical avant-garde than to the market-driven phenomenon of the neo-avant-garde.[32]

The origins of this anti-art avant-garde consciousness can be traced back to the mid- to late 1950s when a number of groups and individuals in different countries of the region began to question the function of the art object and its systems of circulation and distribution in noncentral societies. Unlike the United States, where minimalism provided the grounds for the emergence of conceptual art, in Latin America the passage from object- to idea-based art originated in a wide array of sources grounded in informalism, pop, and modes of geometric abstraction. In Brazil, as early as the mid-'50s, the manifestos of Ferreira Gullar as well as the visual/corporeal experiments of the neoconcrete group established powerful precedents for the iconoclastic Brazilian conceptualists. To these must be added Waldemar Cordeiro's *Popcrete* works (1961–66), which synthesized formal and functional concerns into assembled objects where the idea was already more important than the object itself.

Other countries also registered early anti-art manifestations by artists previously associated with informalist tendencies. In Venezuela, for instance, the political, literary, and visual arts collective El Techo de la Ballena (1961–68) provided the stimulus for radical artists like Claudio Perna (fig. 215), who would quickly evolve into a leading exponent of conceptualism. In Mexico City, Los Hartos (the "Fed-Ups"), a group of artists led by Mathias Goeritz, proclaimed their disgust with both the institution of art and its forms in a sacrilegious manifesto-exhibition in 1961. Even earlier, the work of the Chilean emigré filmmaker and theater artist Alejandro Jodorowsky—centered on the notion of "ephemeral panic" and its potential to unleash unexpected reactions in viewers—opened up an important line of performative experimentation. The same type of anti-institutional revulsion that animated the Mexicans served as the impulse for Alberto Greco's iconoclastic *Vivo dito* series (1962–65; figs. 44, 147). The latter consisted of extemporaneous performances in the streets of Madrid, Buenos Aires, Florence, and elsewhere where Greco, in a manner that paralled Piero Manzoni's "art certificates," either signed his name on people and objects or marked chalk circles around them, thereby turning them into "living works of art."[33] Greco's "living art" found a later echo in Oscar Bony's *La familia obrera* (*Proletarian Family*, 1968; fig. 148), in which a working-class family posed as a work of art during exhibition hours, in the process earning twice the salary of their regular jobs.

The avant-garde status of these practices, in turn, poses a series of paradoxes involving continuities and ruptures with established traditions in specific countries of Latin America. Perhaps the most important achievement of conceptualism was establishing the "continuity of rupture" with an avant-garde legacy (Duchamp, dada, the Brazilian *antropofagia* movement, etc.) that, despite its isolated precedents in Latin America in the 1920s and '30s, had been lost for several generations.[34] As the notion of avant-garde itself, this kind of radical precedent did not exist in the U.S. and England, an inconceivable gap in the two countries generally credited with the birth of conceptual art. This fact, in turn, justifies the autonomy with which conceptualism erupted in Latin America—the key argument of this essay. However, the continuity which the 1960s avant-garde established with previous models was not predicated on a notion of style or even tradition, but on the persistence of the type of radical conceptual and artistic operations whereby art became a means toward sociopolitical emancipation. This was the case in Rosario, where the '60s avant-garde recovered the political tradition of Antonio Berni and the Mutualidad artists of the 1930s.[35] In Brazil, it resulted in the assimilation of Oswald de Andrade's notion of *antropofagia* (a cannibalistic impulse of self-determination through appropriation), which the new objectivists declared their "defense" against cultural colonialism.[36]

Nevertheless, the deep sense of rupture that animated these artists and groups was nowhere more explicit than in their proclamation of anti-art as the starting point for their practice. Therefore, it is not the idea of an avant-garde in itself that must be stressed here, but the radical nature of the shift which the conceptualist version brought about in the redefinition of art and artistic practice in many Latin American countries. As noted by Juan Acha, "the most important aspect of the postmodern *no-objetualismos* consisted in destroying in us the humanist Renaissance tradition."[37] In this respect, we must consider that in some Latin American countries conceptualism not only contested existing forms of bourgeois art, but was simultaneously redefining an earlier model of the Latin American avant-garde. This model—exemplified by the art and theories of David Alfaro Siqueiros and Joaquín Torres-García—postulated avant-garde

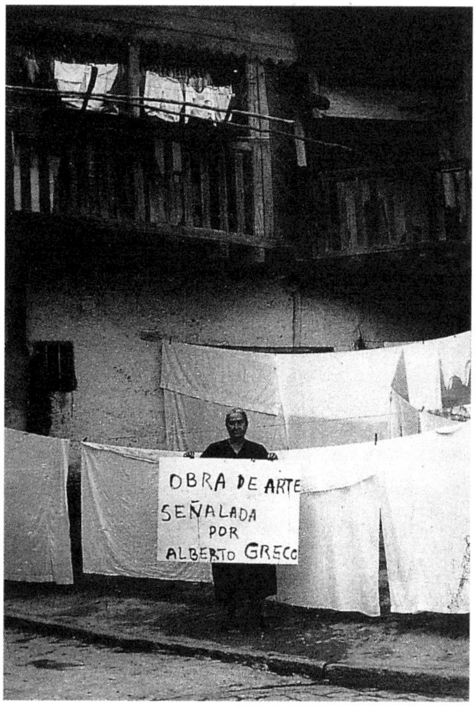

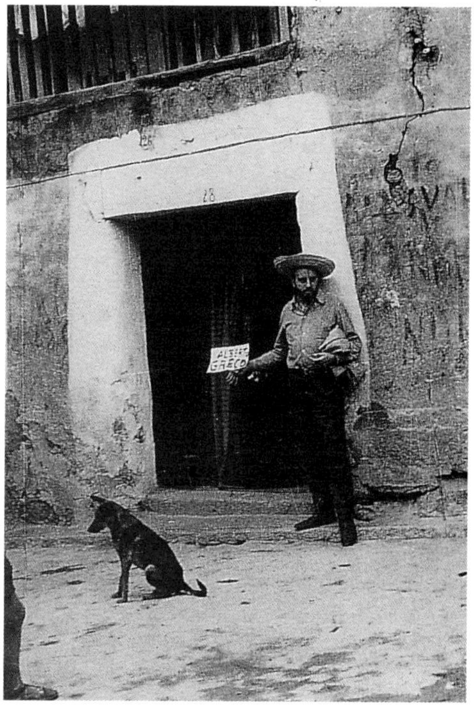

Figure 44.
Alberto Greco, from the series *Vivo dito,* 1962, documentary photographs.

tendencies in opposition to the original concept of rupture with the past that motivated the European historical avant-garde. It favored, instead, a paradoxical form of avant-garde art based on an unusual notion of tradition, understood as the "actualization" of the legacy of Western art from the untainted perspective of New World societies.[38] With the exception of Brazil and Argentina, the prevalence of this model in Latin America largely explains why dada and its legacy had scant influence in the region until this decade.

Resignifying Adversity

Art will be neither beauty nor novelty, art will be effectiveness and disturbance. The successful work of art will be that which, in the context in which the artist moves, has an impact similar to that of a guerrilla attack in a country on its way to liberation.
—León Ferrari, *El arte de los significados,* 1968

If, as I have argued so far, the determining feature of conceptualism in Latin America is the analysis of its relationship to the sociopolitical context, i.e., the ideological dimension, the latter does not imply an abandonment of artists' formal investigations. After all, art is a form of ideology and its mechanisms can also constitute the "material identity" of idea-based practices. Despite the profound questioning of art carried out by British and North American conceptualists, their attempts in this regard failed precisely because they ultimately clung to the "idea of art." Both Kosuth's "art as idea as idea" and Weiner's dictum "the definition of my art is my art" circumscribed the contribution of this mainstream model to what Benjamin Buchloh termed "the aesthetics of the administered world." By contrast, the more ample structural and contextual focus of the investigations carried out by Latin American artists can be considered to have significantly expanded the context for the redefinition of art outside the strict parameters of the artistic sphere. In terms of both the historically rough circumstances that generated it, as well as its profound search for redefinition, this trend could be understood as an attitude of resignifying adversity. In what follows, I will discuss some of the most paradigmatic proposals this attitude generated in the Buenos Aires, Rosario, and Rio de Janeiro contexts.

Sensorial Interaction

The conceptual bent of Lygia Clark and Hélio Oiticica's oeuvre lies, on the one hand, in their incorporation of the body and the senses as materials for conceptual propositions, and on the other hand, in their redefinition of *pathia* as applied to a new type of spectator or audience. These two aspects find their source in the theories concerning object/body/language relations of the neoconcrete poet and theoretician Ferreira Gullar. For both Clark and Oiticica, this process is the result of the systematic disintegration of the primary structures of the traditional work of art (space, time, etc.). However, the body is not a performative entity unto itself but the vehicle for a complex dialectic between artist/participant, whose ultimate purpose is to bring about a transformation of consciousness. Clark's interactive, wearable structures, based on a sensorial "reconstitution of the body," are vehicles for the type of synthetic *vivencia* conducive to the "experimental exercise of liberty" (figs. 46, 149, 198). Similarly, Oiticica's *Parangolés* recycle primal pictorial structures into a form of playful, collective participation that envisions a "return to myth" (fig. 150).

Participation, then, assumes a critical dimension associated with the need to actively transform the socio-ethical-political field. These investigations are grounded in the avant-garde notion of art as an integral element of a "social totality." In themselves, both aspects carry important implications for conceptualism. On the one hand, by considering the body and the senses as material for the conceptual proposition, they opened the possibilities for bridging the mind/body dichotomy that had plagued Western art since the Renaissance. This option was unthinkable in a North American context still fighting the orthodox legacy of puritanism. On the other hand, the notion of semantic participation paved the way for researching sensorial interaction as the basis for conceptual practices.

A further line of investigation, developed mostly by artists in Brazil (Meireles, Caldas [fig. 45] and Argentina (Lamelas [fig. 207], Porter [fig. 47], was that provided by the reinterpretation of Duchamp's legacy in terms of a

Figure 45.
Waltércio Caldas, *Condutores de percepção (Conductors of Perception),* 1969, mixed media. Private collection.

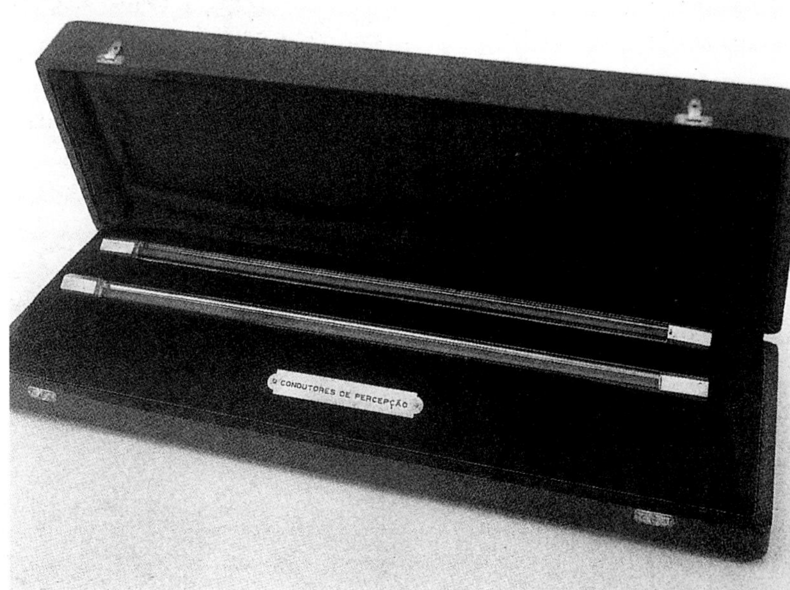

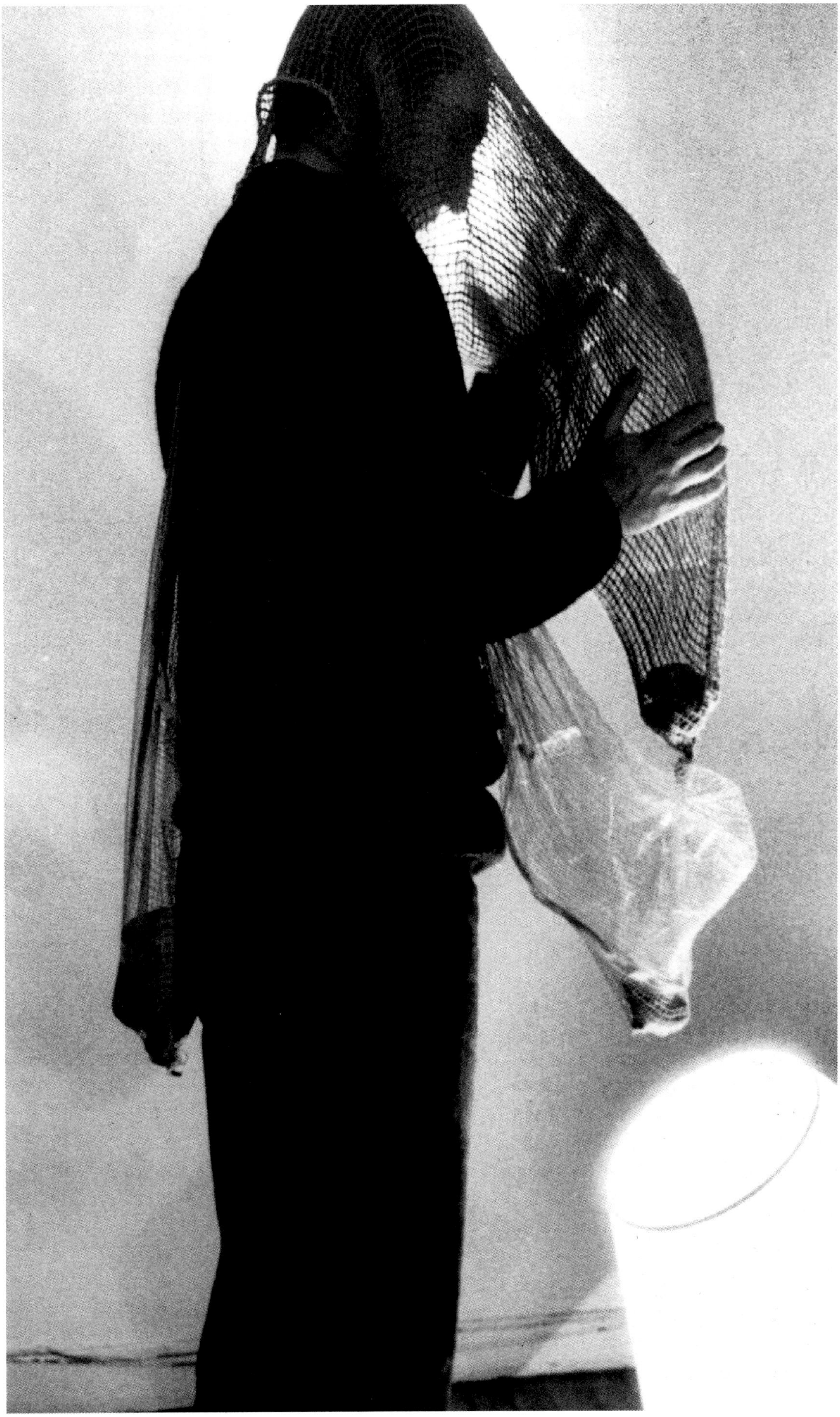

Figure 46.
Lygia Clark, *Máscara-Abismo* (*Mask-Abyss*), 1968, mesh mask with weights. Courtesy of the Estate of Lygia Clark.

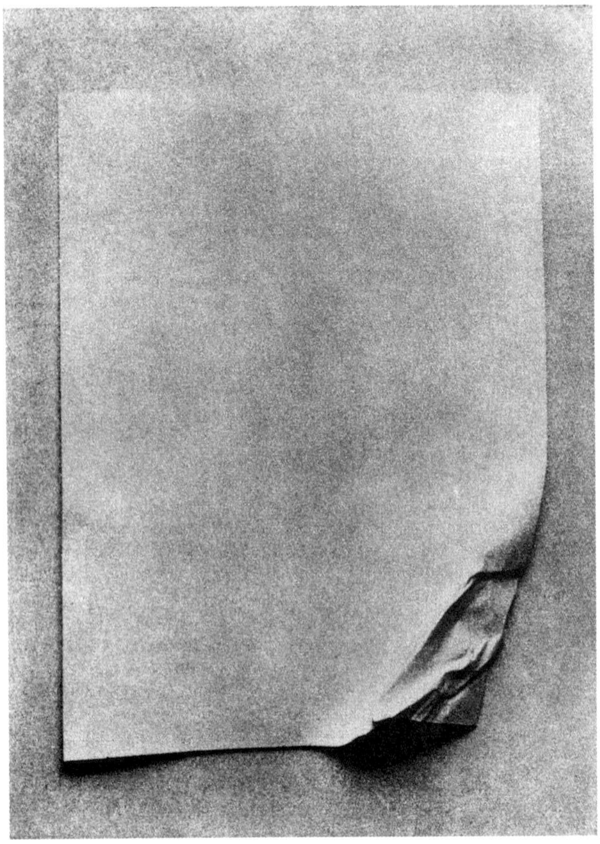
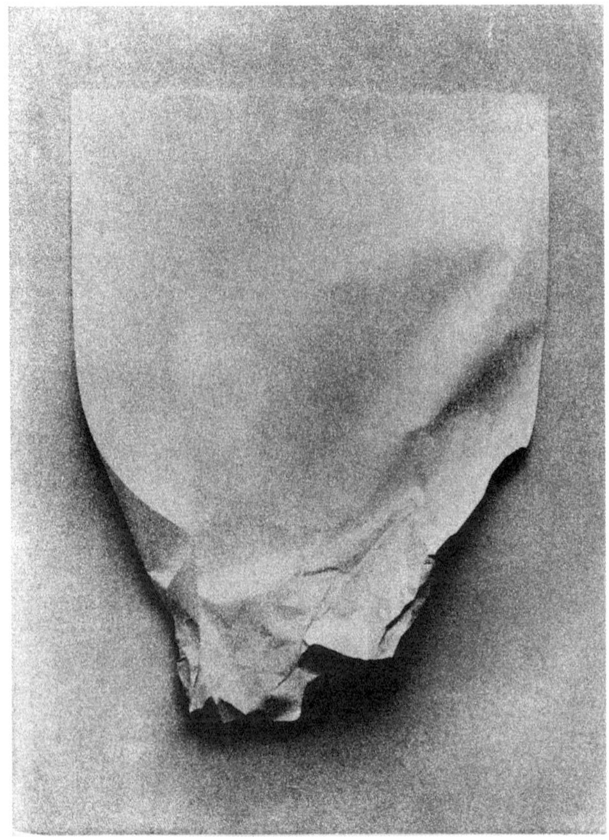
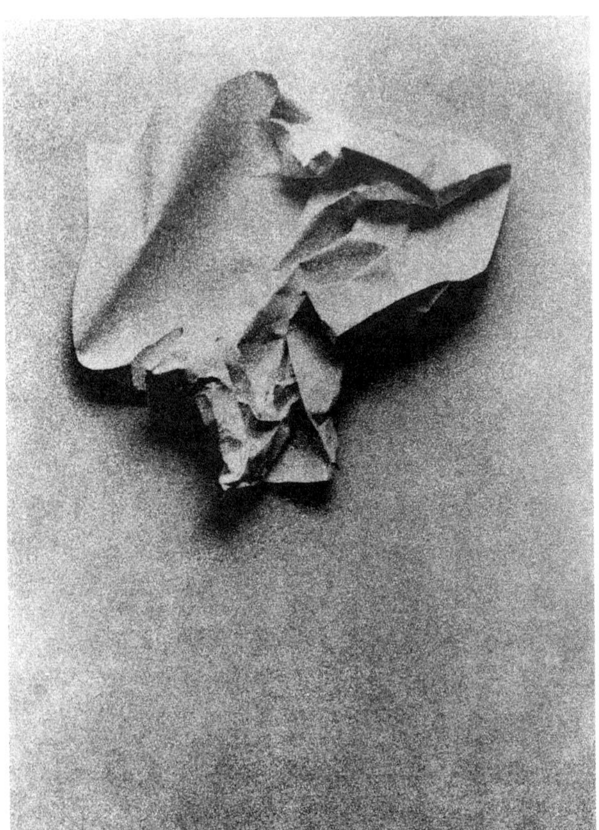
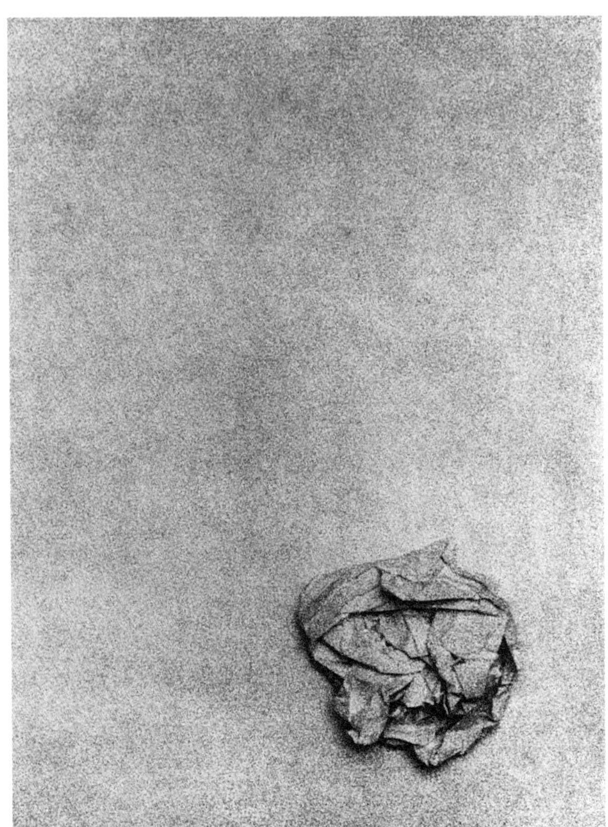

Figure 47. (LEFT)
Liliana Porter, *Wrinkle,* 1968, ten photoengraved etchings with an interview by Emmett Williams, New York Graphic Workshop. Collection of the artist.

sensorial/tactile-based practice parallel to language. Particularly in Brazil, a number of artists subscribed to the idea that "vision, sound, touch, smell, and taste were forms of language, thought, and communication." The work of these artists extended Duchamp's search for a nonretinal form of art into a material and perceptual "laboratory of language." For instance, the Experimental Unit of the Museu de Arte Moderna, Rio de Janeiro, was created in 1969 by Frederico Morais, Cildo Meireles, Guilherme Vaz, and Luis Alphonsus with the intention of "searching for a total language; [and] centralizing experiences concerning the decodification and codification of languages ..." For more than a year, the EU organized debates with artists and intellectuals, and conducted surveys of the museum's audiences.[39]

Language Displacements

While most of the artists considered here agreed that language was the key factor in the understanding of reality, only a few limited themselves exclusively to the empirical properties of language. The majority chose instead to use text as a mere support for transmitting new axiologies. According to such values, the artist as an "administrator who classifies"[40] the results of the preestablished textual program is substituted by the artist as "encoder" or "organizer" of meaning.[41] In the adverse context of Latin America, for many this was the only possible option for art, one that provided the means to extend its limits beyond the "dead-end" of mainstream tendencies, including conceptual art itself.[42] Thus, Wittgensteinian positivism as well as Barthes's idea of the "death of the author" were not only absent from the production of Latin American language-based conceptualism, but their premises were reevaluated through the (re)insertion of the active social subject into the communicational circuit. These tactics included: exploitation of the contextual and referential dimension of language, the substitution of tautology in favor of metaphor and analogy, the incorporation of the human (subjective) referent, the exaltation of the image and perceptual value of words, and the production of irony.[43] León Ferrari's suspension of the distinction between the acts of "seeing" and "reading" a work, as exemplified by his *Cuadro escrito (Written Painting)* series (1964; figs. 36, 151), not only preceded the xerographic tautologies of Joseph Kosuth,[44] but already differentiated both versions of language-based art. Through his referentially charged, idiosyncratic handwriting—which synthetically merged the visual, auditory, and connotative properties of words into a single proposition—Ferrari reinserted subjectivity into the conceptual proposal.

This ironical handling of the presumed "objectivity" of writing must be seen within the instrumentalization of language elicited by both mass media and authoritarianism. The Colombian Antonio Caro (figs. 48, 152) also utilized baroque calligraphy as a statement of subjectivity in *Homenaje a Manuel Quintín Lame (Homage to Manuel Quintín Lame,* 1972–). In this case, by retrieving and duplicating the indigenous leader's signature from oblivion, Caro is underscoring the inequities of recent Colombian history. In Luis Camnitzer's language-based work, tautology was only a formal vehicle to "package" the idea. By combining objects, images, and text into a single format, exemplified by his series of text/object works of 1967–69, Camnitzer reversed the analytic principle of Kosuth's Duchampian propositions into synthetic statements that exploited the referential—mostly ironic—qualities of word/object/image relationships. The introduction of perceptual elements into the structure of words (*Horizon,* 1968), as well as the spatialization of language exemplified by the "word installations," further transformed the self-referential form into a vehicle for socio-political issues. By contrast, Antonio Dias's "word" paintings and objects (1968–73; figs. 144, 200) explode the structural linkage

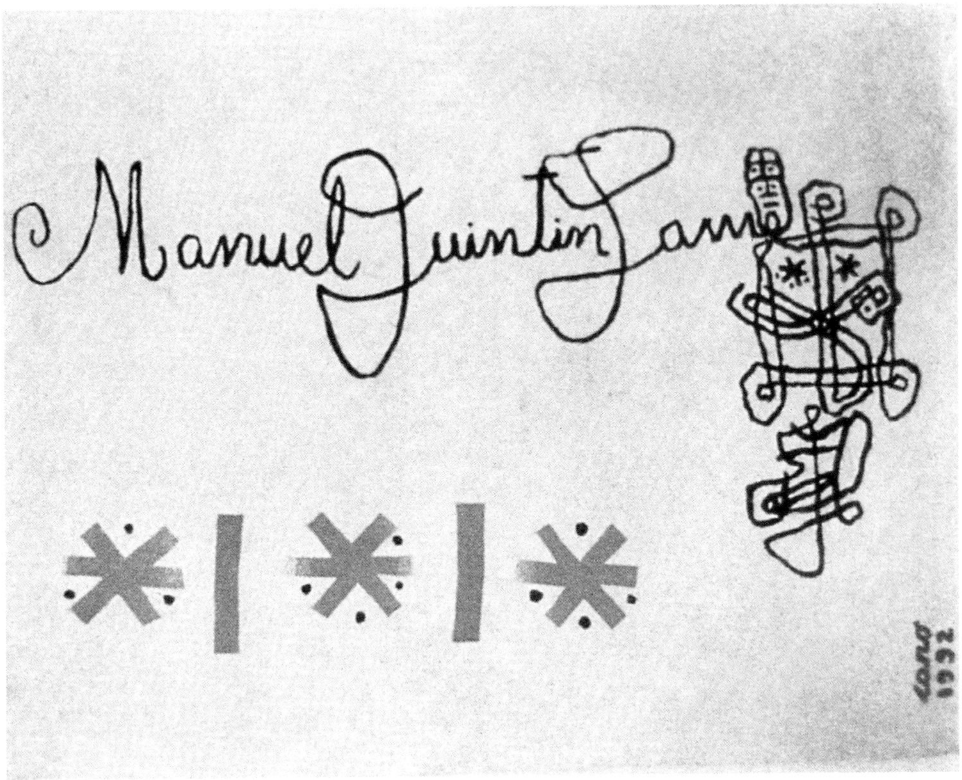

Figure 48.
Antonio Caro, *Homenaje a Manuel Quintín Lame (Homage to Manuel Quintín Lame),* 1972–, ink on cardboard. Collection of the artist.

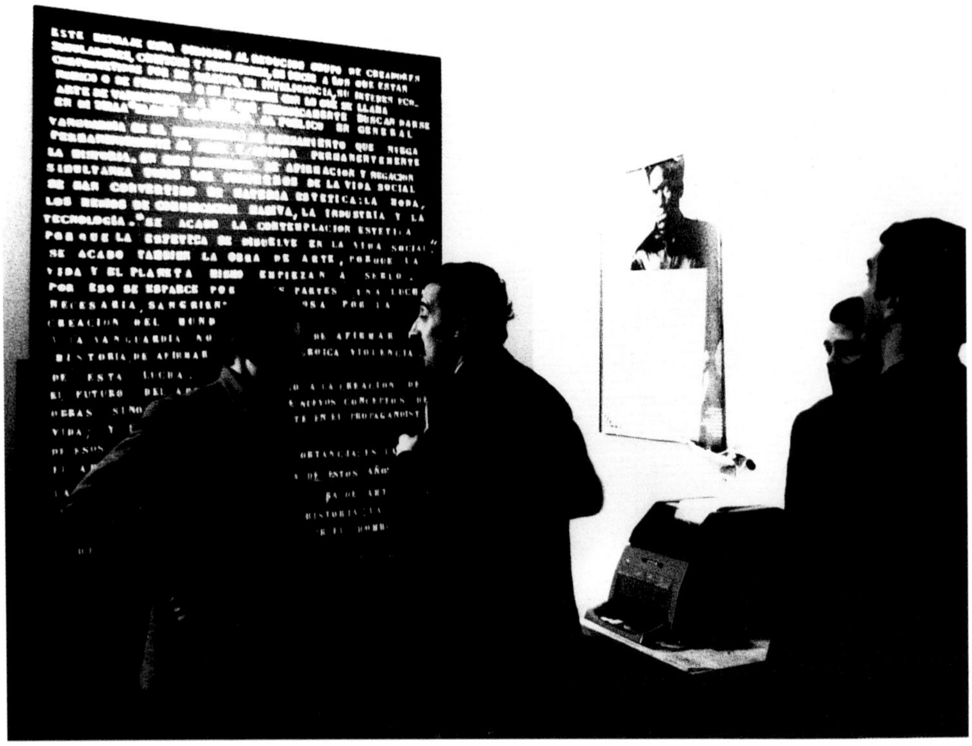

Figure 49.
Roberto Jacoby, *Mensaje en el di Tella (Message at the Tella),* 1968, installation with poster, blackboard, text, and teletype machine. Collection of the artist.

between words/images/society, thereby problematizing the function of the painting-as-painting and opening an ambiguous space for the communication of meaning.

Arte de los medios

Language was also a central trait of the Argentinean *arte de los medios* (mass-mediatic art), a new strategy that coalesced in Buenos Aires in 1966 with the avowed intention of "constituting the work inside mass media itself."[45] By privileging the "act of transmission" over the factual "constitution" of the work, this mass-mediatic art carried to its logical extreme the ultimate feature of conceptual art, that is, the dematerialization of objects and their substitution by language. In the words of Oscar Masotta, one of the principal theoreticians who accompanied its development, "after pop we [in Argentina] dematerialized art." From this angle, *arte de los medios* is perhaps the only enactment of the abolition of the object in the Latin American context. More importantly, mass-mediatic works were structurally prepared to receive and convey political messages, thereby carrying the potential to fuse both "revolutionary" and "aesthetic" praxis into a radical form that resisted institutionalization. The fact that these works only existed in the consciousness and memory of the receptors,[46] also made them extremely appealing for the increasingly critical aims of the Argentinean avant-garde after the military coup of 1966.

Arte de los medios, like Brazilian *nova objetividade,* encompassed a broad range of tendencies. Those pertinent here consisted of experiences in which artists appropriated the productive means of mass communication in order "to project them as critical alternatives" to the social effects of mass media and the subtle manipulation of messages that they embodied.[47] As stated by Jacoby himself, in order to be distinguishable from the normal effect of media-produced messages, the "context" of the processes had to be altered in a perceptible way.[48] In the first mass-mediatic work, known as *Happening para un jabalí difunto (Happening for a Dead Boar,* 1966), Eduardo Costa, Jacoby, and Raúl Escari sent out to news media a detailed photographic and written report of a nonexistent event, enticing the media to transmit it, then denouncing its falseness. What was distinctive about this type of investigation was neither the information itself nor the manner in which it was circulated, but the extent to which it succeeded in ridiculing the media as media.[49]

Roberto Jacoby's *Mensaje en el di Tella (Message at the Tella,* 1968; fig. 49) took this strategy a step further. Through the juxtaposition of three political messages—that of a young North American black man, that of the broadcasting agencies transmitting news of May 1968, and his own—it established ideology as a valid material for the conceptual proposal.[50] Closely paralleling the format of Dan Graham's *Homes for America* (1966–67), Eduardo Costa's *Fashion Fictions* (1966, Buenos Aires; 1967, New York; fig. 153) centered on the notion of "wearable art." However, whereas Graham's intention was to expose the contextual nature of media representation, Costa's proposal played upon a "fiction" that is communicated as "fact" by the media, thereby exposing the fallacious and manipulative character of mass communication. By contrast, León Ferrari's *Palabras ajenas (Others' Words,* 1967) systematically retrieved information and used it to create a political work based on notions of appropriation and resignification.

In its appropriation, exaltation, and critical use of mass media, *arte de los medios* was emblematic of the aims and failures of the postwar Argentinean modernization project. In this sense, it can be seen as an art that turns upon itself the very tools of the utopian dream that constituted it. This inversion is nowhere more evident than in the avant-garde collective action known as Tucumán Arde (figs. 37, 38). This mass-mediatic event, which integrated artists and workers from Rosario, Buenos Aires, and Santa Fé, took place at the Argentinean CGT (Workers' Central Union) in November 1968 in Rosario and Buenos Aires. Tucumán Arde, however, was the culmination of a series of radical developments that had been slowly coalescing in the Buenos Aires/Rosario artistic axis since 1965 as a result of a general climate of dissatisfaction with artistic institutions and in response to political repression. By November 1968, the group consisted of more than thirty artists, including Juan Pablo Renzi, Graciela Carnevale, Eduardo Favario, Noemí Escandell, Roberto Jacoby, Margarita Paksa, León Ferrari, Pablo Suárez, and Ricardo Carreira. The group joined the CGT unions to denounce labor conditions in Tucumán, an impoverished province where riots had been censored by the national press. Their protest took the form of an exhibition, preceded by a period of careful documentation in which the artists broke into teams to research the social and political factors affecting workers' conditions in Tucumán. One team traveled to Tucumán with the purpose of establishing contacts and gathering visual and oral testimonies. For the final event in Rosario, the group took over the CGT space with mural-scale photographs, films, newspapers, banners, posters, letters, leaflets, slogans, and mimeographed pamphlets that presented the full spectrum of the exploitive conditions confronting the people of Tucumán. In addition to the use of mass media itself, the group deployed to full advantage strategies derived from publicity to entice viewers to the event.[51]

Beyond the explicitly political dimension of the group's work, the significance of Tucumán Arde in the broader context of global conceptualism lies in its having effected a transference of artistic action from the aesthetic to the political public sphere through the unprecedented use of mass media. It must be stressed, however, that for these artists, the end product was not the exhibition itself but the huge counter-informational circuit it generated based on visual and written investigative reports that denounced the false information circulated by the national media. This notion of art as information, independent of traditional supports or art world infrastructure (which two years later would constitute the theme of *Information* at the Museum of Modern Art, New York) can be seen as an optimal product of the conceptual strategy. Yet unlike many other instances of this trend, which either passively registered information flows or formally appropriated mass-media structures for artistic purposes, Tucumán Arde reclaimed informational circuits away from centralized powers, placing them in the service of a collective endeavor that sought to actively transform reality. In this process, it reasserted the value of human agency in the midst of the instrumentalization of language and communication set in motion by the media spectacle. The notion of art as a "total experience" was intrinsic to the avant-garde impulse of this group of artists. In this context, the work becomes "the nucleus that integrates and unifies all the elements that constitute human reality: economic, social, political."[52]

Tucumán Arde embodied what Juan Pablo Renzi called a *situación límite* (limited situation), i.e., a fragile space outside both political and artistic institutions that allowed, if only momentarily, for the visualization of a revolutionary practice at both levels.[53] However short-lived, this space marked a unique moment in Latin America. Pioneer conceptual art advocate and chronicler Lucy Lippard, who visited Rosario in 1968, considered the group's work "a revelation" which led to her subsequent politicization.[54] The "dissolution of art into the social" (Jacoby), however, tested the limits of art and politics, underscoring the contradictions at the core of the avant-garde project of Tucumán Arde. As Ana Longoni has observed, the issue was not how political art could become, but to what extent politics tolerated "aestheticization." The role of artist and political activist thus canceled each other out, leading many members of Tucumán Arde to abandon art altogether for other forms of cultural practice.[55]

Insertions into Circuits

In Rio de Janeiro, what may be considered a strategy akin to mass-mediatic art assumed a different form related to the Duchampian line of investigation that characterized a large sector of the Brazilian avant-garde. The key concept, *inserção* (insertion)—first elaborated by Cildo Meireles in a 1970 text, and exemplified by his *Insertions into Ideological Circuits: Coca-Cola Project* (1970; fig. 41) and *Insertions into Ideological Circuits: Banknote Project (Who Killed Herzog?)* (1973; fig. 186)—was that of direct intervention in a circuit in order to counter-circulate information. Unlike *arte de los medios,* the transgression here consisted of removing readymade objects (soda bottles, banknotes, subway tokens) from preestablished circuits, inscribing subversive messages on them, and returning them to the circuit. Although both strategies shared a similar objective (to communicate messages under extremely repressive conditions), the format of the insertion strategy or "information exchange," as well as the daily-life vehicles it utilized, opposed the technological emphasis of *arte de los medios.* Because the entire operation was designed to defy centralized systems of control, mass media itself was rejected due to its dependence on and/or complicity with the state apparatus. This condition, while also present in Argentina, was paramount to the Brazilian experience of authoritarianism.

Additionally, the tactics that informed this strategy reference popular communication systems, for instance, religious chain letters and shipwreck bottles.[56] In this sense, Meireles's *Insertions* invert McLuhan's informational utopia: they bet on the possibility of removing the control of communication processes from the manipulative network industry. In his own words, tactics of insertion are nothing less than a "mechanism of expression of the subject against society."[57] Furthermore, in Meireles's *Insertions,* the readymade is displaced from its anti-art status to its semiotic role as carrier of referential meanings within a larger structure or circuit. The artist's role, then, is to activate this process through a type of cultural practice that constantly exposes the innuendos of ideology. The series of interventions carried out by Antonio Manuel in newspapers (1966–76; fig. 39), as well as his *Urnas quentes (Hot Ballot Boxes,* 1968; fig. 154) and *O corpo é a obra (The Body Is the Work,* 1970; fig. 208), can be seen as early formulations of the insertion strategy at the level of state-controlled public information circuits. *O corpo é a obra* ultimately asserted the value of authenticity as the irreducible core of the individual and his/her most valuable weapon against any system of social control, including art.

Art or Cultural Practice?

If Marcel Duchamp intervened at the level of Art (logic of phenomena), what is done today, on the contrary, tends to be closer to Culture than to Art, and that is necessarily a political intervention ...

—Cildo Meireles, Rio de Janeiro, April 1970

Within this panoramic framework, conceptualism's appeal for artists in Latin America rested mainly on two factors. First, the understanding of art as a form of knowledge enabled artists not only to explore problems and issues related to concrete sociopolitical conditions, but to develop a series of tactics to subvert their impact on the public; and second, the conceptualist critique of traditional art institutions and the substitution of object- with idea-based art paved the way for the elaboration of a practice suited to both the political immediacy and economic precariousness of Latin America. Rather than serving exclusively as a vehicle for dissecting the commodification of art under late capitalism, conceptualism became a strategy for exposing the limits of art and life. All of these shooting tactics developed under conditions of marginalization and, in the majority of cases, official repression.

Despite its unique achievements, however, conceptualism in Latin America could not escape the intrinsic contradictions of its utopian project. Its success as a mode of thought also announced its failure. On the one hand, its positive aspects opened up novel territories for artists whose legacy is very much alive today. On the other hand, the notion that art could completely exchange its "pure use value" for "communication value"[58] situates these practices in a different register no longer tied to aesthetics or to the autonomous sphere of art. In these circumstances, art ceases to be art in order to become a type of "limit experience" more akin to anthropology or cultural practice. To the extent that this transformation is linked to an ethico-socio-political project, it substantially differs from the idea of the artist as ethnographer popularized by contemporary multiculturalism. In its place, it opens up a space for art to critically engage the social and artistic framework in which it is inscribed.

Perhaps no other single artist in Latin America understood this fact better than Hélio Oiticica who, from an anti-art perspective, was able to identify or refunctionalize alternate forms of art production in the social matrix that surrounded him (figs. 42, 212). Today, Oiticica's production remains a forceful reminder of the artist's power to transform elements of individual and collective daily experience into the basis for a dialectical model of artistic production. This primal paradigm was also at work in the achievements of Tucumán Arde and those of all the artists represented in this exhibition. As illustrated by Tucumán Arde, however, the price of crossing this "threshold" implied a point of no return. Indeed, many artists involved with radical conceptual experiences abandoned art in favor of other experiences, including a return to traditional modes of art. Others continued to produce on the margins of a revitalized art establishment that ignored them. The rest struggled with the ethical considerations of the "artistic bubble" in which they were trapped. While this situation was not unique to conceptual practices in Latin America, its impact was stronger in this region, given the emphasis artists here placed on bridging the gap separating them from society. These contradictions continue to plague conceptual-based practices today.

With a few exceptions, Latin American conceptual practices remained in the long run marginal activities largely appreciated and supported by intellectual elites within their own countries.[59] As Marta Traba foresaw, conceptualism was poorly understood by audiences and, while conceptual artists never entered the market, they were forced to depend on precarious cultural infrastructures for their survival. In this sense, Benjamin Buchloh's retrospective assessment of the "critical naiveté" with which mainstream conceptual artists subscribed to the "illusion that the transformation of the artwork into a linguistic and textual intervention would necessarily engender a greater number of readers, a greater politicization of cultural practice," may also hold true for Latin American conceptualists.[60] The difference, however, resides in the way in which Latin Americans, foreseeing this limitation from the start, proceeded early on to shape their practices on the communicational and ideological potential of their conceptual propositions. Conceptualism here meant the reshaping of these practices and was translated as: TACTICS FOR THRIVING ON ADVERSITY. This fact indeed saved Latin American conceptualism from the tautological impasse and sterile academicism that came to characterize Anglo/North American forms of conceptual art.

Finally, the relationship between conceptualism and authoritarianism awaits a full assessment. While early conceptual practices were largely spurred by repressive governments, the latter can also be credited with the eventual dissolution of these practices. This was particularly evident in Argentina. Thus, perhaps the greatest contradiction confronted by conceptualism in Latin America is embodied in a painful irony: the advent of democracy brought about its demise. This leads me to raise an admittedly unfair question. Had authoritarianism not existed, would conceptualism have achieved the same high profile in Latin America? While it could be argued that the fate of this movement was the same worldwide, in Latin America the passage from authoritarianism to democracy imprinted a particular fate on these practices, significantly curtailing the radical investigations which they had opened. But despite these shortcomings and limitations, the origins of conceptualism in Latin America stand out as one of the most brilliant chapters in the history of 20th-century art on the continent. That paradigm was nothing less than the struggle to create meaning in a self-absorbed world.

Notes

1. This text expands my perception of conceptualism in Latin America as put forward in "Blueprint Circuits: Conceptual Art and Politics in Latin America," in *Latin American Artists of the Twentieth Century,* ed. Waldo Rasmussen et al. (New York: Museum of Modern Art, 1993), 156–67. Time and additional research have reinforced my conviction about the autonomous development of conceptual practices in our continent.

2. In Latin America, the word *conceptualism* first appeared as a result of a critical retrospective operation that sought to determine the specificity of Latin American practices vis-à-vis the center-based discourse of conceptual art. Neither *conceptual* nor *conceptualism* appear in artists' writings or in the critical literature surrounding their work until the mid- to late 1970s. Indeed, some artists self-consciously resisted the term for fear of being absorbed by the mainstream or providing state censors with an easily identifiable label. (Conversation with Luis Camnitzer, April 21, 1998.) In many countries, the term's popularization occurred after the international dissemination of Joseph Kosuth's ideas in specialized journals *(Studio International)* and regular weeklies *(Newsweek)*. Something similar seems to have happened in Europe, as suggested by Claude Gintz, "El arte conceptual, una perspectiva: Notas para un proyecto de exposición," in *El arte conceptual, una perspectiva,* ed. Claude Gintz (Madrid: Fundación Caja de Pensiones, 1990), 10. *Conceptualism* is used throughout this essay to denote a larger cultural and artistic phenomenon that is distinctly independent from the canonical model exemplified by North American conceptual art.

3. With the exception of a few general essays published in recent exhibition catalogues, there exists no comprehensive overview of the development of this phenomenon in the region. For early forays into this territory, see Jacqueline Barnitz, "Conceptual Art and Latin America: A Natural Alliance," in *Encounters/Displacements: Luis Camnitzer, Alfredo Jaar, Cildo Meireles* (Austin: Archer M. Huntington Art Gallery, University of Texas, 1992), 35–47; Ramírez, "Blueprint Circuits"; and Luis Camnitzer, "Una genealogía del arte conceptual latinonamericano," *Continente Sul/Sur,* no. 6 (November 1997): 179–230.

4. Marta Traba, *Dos décadas vulnerables en las artes plásticas latinoamericanas* (Mexico City: Siglo Veintiuno Editores, 1973), 87–153.

5. My intention here is not to endorse a deterministic model of art historical development, but to stress the originality and autonomy of the Latin American model.

6. As noted by Oiticica, new objectivity was a *chegada* (approach) constituted by multiple tendencies where the "lack of unity of thought," as in dada, was the most important characteristic. These tendencies included the group of conceptual artists discussed here. See Hélio Oiticica, "General Scheme of the New Objectivity" (1967), in *Hélio Oiticica* (Rio de Janeiro: Projeto Hélio Oiticica, 1992), 110–20. For the contradictory origins of the term *nova objetividade,* see Frederico Morais, *Artes plásticas: A crise da hora atual* (Rio de Janeiro: Editora Paz e Terra, S.A., 1975), 91–93, and Frederico Morais, *Cronología das artes plásticas no Rio de Janeiro, 1816–1994* (Rio de Janeiro: Topbooks, 1995), 294.

7. Juan Acha, "Teoría y práctica no-objetualistas en América Latina," in *Ensayos y ponencias Latinoamericanistas* (Caracas: Ediciones GAN, 1984), 221–42.

8. In Brazil, specifically Rio de Janeiro, a first stage of artists' collective engagement—marked by exhibitions *(Opinião 65, Opinião 66, Nova objetividade brasileira),* demonstrations, and large public events *(Arte no aterro, Apocalipopótese)*—took place between the military coup of 1964 and the Institutional Act No. 5 that abolished the Constitution, abrogated civil rights, and instituted censorship in 1969. A second period corresponds to 1969–71 *(Salão da bússola, Do corpo à terra* [Belo Horizonte], XIX Salão de Arte Moderna, and a series of individual exhibitions organized by the Petite Galerie under the title *Agnus Dei*). After a three-year interim marked by artists' absences or migrations, a third stage begins in 1974 with the publication of *Malasartes.* See Francisco Bittencourt, "A vanguarda visual carioca dos años 70," *Vozes* 72, no. 5 (June–July 1978): 29–42.

9. In the case of Argentina, Andrea Giunta has identified the following three stages, which closely follow the political developments of the period: 1965–75: political and artistic avant-garde project; 1976–85: resistance to violent military dictatorship; 1986–present: reinstatement of democracy. See Andrea Giunta, "Arte y (re)presión: Cultura crítica y prácticas conceptuales en Argentina," in *Arte, historia e identidad en América: Visiones comparativas,* ed. Gustavo Curiel et al. (Mexico City: UNAM, Instituto de Investigaciones Estéticas, 1993), 875–89.

10. In New York, Latin American conceptualism first appeared in 1966–67 in the work of Luis Camnitzer and the New York Graphic Workshop, which included artists Liliana Porter and José Guillermo Castillo. Other Latin American conceptualists who developed their careers in New York were Leandro Katz and Eduardo Costa. A number of Brazilians (Hélio Oiticica, Cildo Meireles, Guilherme Vaz, Rubens Gerchman) also spent time in New York in the early '70s. See Barnitz, "Conceptual Art and Latin America," 37, and Carla Stellweg, "'Magnet–New York': Conceptual, Performance, Environmental, and Installation Art," in *The Latin American Spirit: Art and Artists in the United States, 1920–1970,* ed. Luis Cancel et al. (New York: Bronx Museum and Abrams, 1988), 284–311.

11. In Chile, with the exception of some works by Juan Pablo Langlois (alias Rogelio Vicuña) and the poetry-based work of Cecilia Vicuña, conceptualism does not appear until the late 1970s. In 1971 Joseph Kosuth lectured at the Universidad de Santiago, Chile, where he assumed a political stance, probably enticed by the Unidad Popular government of Allende. This lecture, however, does not seem to have produced echoes in the local artistic community. See Joseph Kosuth, "Painting versus Art versus Culture," in *Art After Philosophy and After: Collected Writings, 1966–1990,* ed. Gabriele Guercio (Cambridge, Mass.: MIT Press, 1991), 89–92.

12. In tandem with other non-object-based manifestations (video, performance), the degree to which these practices quickly spread throughout the region was the subject of a large exhibition that accompanied the *Primer coloquio Latinoamericano de arte no-objetual y arte urbano* (The First Latin American Colloquium of Non-Object-Based and Urban Art). Both events took place on June 17–21, 1981, at the Museo de Arte Moderno in Medellín, Colombia, and coincided with the IV Bienal de Arte in Medellín. See Juan Acha's summary in "El coloquio," *Revista del Arte y la Arquitectura en América Latina* 2, no. 7 (1981): 26.

13. See Mari Carmen Ramírez, "Rematerialization," in *Universalis: 23. Bienal Internacional São Paulo* (São Paulo: Fundação Bienal de São Paulo, 1996), 178–89, and "CONTEXTURAS: Lo global a partir de lo local," paper presented at the symposium *Globalization and Latin American Art,* ARCO, Madrid, February 1997, n.p.

14. Oiticica, "General Scheme," 117–18.

15. "I want to demonstrate that contents, especially those that are explicitly ideological or social, possess in the consciousness of the receptors a material identity. To the same extent that one used to work with diverse materials (paint, gesso, wood), it is possible to work with ideological contents." Roberto Jacoby, *Mensaje en el di Tella,* c. 1968, n.p., Roberto Jacoby Papers, Buenos Aires. León Ferrari also noted: "Clear meanings, social commitment, ideology, came to constitute what [Luis Felipe] Noé considered the most eternal and irremovable anti-aesthetic." León Ferrari, *El arte de los significados,* I Encuentro Nacional de Arte de Vanguardia, Rosario, 1968, typescript, León Ferrari Papers, Buenos Aires, 5.

16. Simón Marchán Fiz, *Del arte objetual al arte de concepto, 1960–1974* (Madrid: Ediciones Akal, 1988), 269–71.

17. María Teresa Gramuglio and Nicolás Rosa, *Tucumán Arde,* manifesto, Rosario, November 1968, n.p., Graciela Carnevale Archives, Rosario. See also Ana Longoni, "Arte y violencia en los últimos años sesenta: Entre la representación y la acción," in *Arte, sociedad, cultura e identidad: I Jornadas de Sociología y Antropología del Arte* (Buenos Aires: Facultad de Ciencias Sociales, n.d.).

18. Luis Camnitzer, "Arte colonial contemporáneo," *Marcha,* July 3, 1970, n.p.

19. Ibid.

20. See Marchán Fiz, *Del arte objetual,* 270.

21. Stephen Melville discusses the "non-availability of much conceptual work—either its appearance only through the detour of documentation or its absolute non-appearance—as resistance to or refusal of current conditions of visibility." In his view, this trait engendered the "political fantasy dreams of a telepathic community, i.e. a community not riven by the act of beholding or by its ability to engender an audience." Stephen Melville, "Aspects," in *Reconsidering the Object of Art, 1965–1975,* ed. Ann Goldstein and Anne Rorimer (Los Angeles: Museum of Contemporary Art, 1995), 232.

22. Morais, *Cronología,* 295 (my translation).

23. See Néstor García Canclini, "La modernidad después de la posmodernidad," in *Culturas híbridas: Estrategias para entrar y salir de la modernidad* (Mexico City: Consejo Nacional para la Cultura y las Artes, 1989), 223.

24. Rita Eder, "El arte no-objetual en México," *Revista del Arte y la Arquitectura en América Latina* 2, no. 7 (1981): 14–20. As is well known, José Luis Cuevas exemplifies the triumph of figurativism in the Mexican scene from the 1960s until very recently.

25. For a critical history of Los Grupos, see Dominique Liquois, *De los grupos los individuos: Artistas plásticos de los Grupos Metropolitanos* (Mexico City: Instituto Nacional de Bellas Artes, 1985); Felipe Ehrenberg, "En busca de un modelo para la vida," in Liquois, *De los grupos los individuos.* See also Eder, "El arte no-objetual," 16–20; *Artes Visuales,* no. 23 (January 1980); and Shifra Goldman, "Elite Artists and Popular Audiences: The Mexican Front of Cultural Workers," in *Dimensions of the Americas: Art and Social Change in Latin America and the United States* (Chicago: University of Chicago Press, 1994), 123–39.

26. *The New Argentine Cultural Vanguard,* statement drafted by the Organizing Committee for the Revolutionary Imagination, distributed at the Tucumán Arde event, Buenos Aires, November 1968, Graciela Carnevale Archives, Rosario (my translation).

27. Juan Pablo Renzi, *La obra de arte como producto de la relación conciencia ética—conciencia estética,* I Encuentro Nacional de Arte de Vanguardia, Rosario, 1968, cited in Ana Longoni, "Tucumán Arde: Encuentros y desencuentros entre vanguardia artística y política," in *Cultura y política en los años '60,* ed. Enrique Oteiza et al. (Buenos Aires: Oficina de Publicaciones del CBC, 1997), 318.

28. Ronaldo Brito and Eudoro Augusto Macieira de Sousa, *Cildo Meireles* (Rio de Janeiro: Edição FUNARTE, 1981), 24.

29. Guillermo Fantoni has analyzed the implications of this process for the specific case of the Rosario avant-garde in "Rosario 1966: Episodios de vanguardia y fragmentos de conversaciones," in *Serie 10: Arte y estética* (Rosario: Universidad Nacional de Rosario, Facultad Humanidades y Artes, 1993), 4–5.

30. Oiticica, "General Scheme," 110.

31. Jacoby, *Mensaje en el di Tella,* n.p.

32. Peter Bürger, *Theory of the Avant-Garde* (Minneapolis: University of Minnesota Press, 1984). See also Guillermo Fantoni, "Horizontes problemáticos de una vanguardia de los años sesenta: Un movimiento artístico entre el heroísmo y las crisis," in *Anuario, Segunda Epoca* (Rosario), no. 13 (1988): 137–48.

33. See Angel Rama, *Antología de El Techo de la Ballena* (Caracas: FUNDARTE, 1987); *Los ecos de Mathias Goeritz: Catálogo de la exposición* (Mexico City: Antiguo Colegio de San Ildefonso, 1997), 242; Francisco Reyes Palma, "Oratorio monocromático: Los Hartos," in *Los ecos de Mathias Goeritz: Ensayos y testimonios* (Mexico City: Instituto de Investigaciones Estéticas, 1997), 121–29; Alejandro Jodorowsky, *Hacia el efímero pánico o iSacar al teatro del teatro!,"* unpub. ms., 1963, n.p.; and *Alberto Greco* (Valencia: Instituto Valenciano de Arte Moderno, Centre Julio González, 1991).

34. I owe this insight to my conversations with Héctor Olea concerning the role and function of the avant-garde in Latin America, Austin, February–March 1998. The oxymoron being stressed here—"continuity of rupture"—points to the "continuity of disenchantment" represented by the loss of aura.

35. See Guillermo Fantoni, "Rupturas en perspectiva: Modernismo y vanguardia en el arte de Rosario," *Cuadernos del Ciesal* 2, no. 2–3 (1994): 177–84.

36. Oiticica, "General Scheme," 110–11.

37. Acha, "Teoría y práctica no-objetualistas," 236.

38. My point is that they both theorized these innovations under the notion of "actualization" and not "rupture" with past artistic traditions, whether they referred to the art of Pre-Columbian cultures or to European art from the Renaissance onward.

39. Morais, *Cronología,* 309–10.

40. Sol LeWitt, cited in Buchloh, "De la estética de la administración a la crítica institucional," in *El arte conceptual,* ed. Gintz, 23.

41. On the notion of the artist as such, see Ferrari, *El arte de los significados:* "Meaning in itself does not make the work of art. The daily press is full of meaningful information that people read indifferently every day. Our work will thus consist of organizing those meanings ..." (p. 5).

42. See Nadja Tilinsky, "Antonio Dias in Conversation," in *Antonio Dias: Trabalhos, Arbeiten, Works, 1967–1994,* ed. Paulo Sergio Duarte et al. (Ostfildern: Cantz, 1994), 53.

43. These tactics also appeared in the language-based work produced in the early 1970s by several members of the CAYC-based Grupo de los Trece (Group of the Thirteen). See Centro de Arte y Comunicación, *Hacia un perfil del arte latinoamericano muestra del Grupo de los Trece e invitados especiales organizada por Jorge Glusberg* (Buenos Aires: El Centro, 1972).

44. It should be noted that in 1964, neither Kosuth nor Weiner had begun their linguistic investigations. Weiner opened an exhibition of painting at Seth Siegelaub's gallery that year, while Kosuth did not begin his dictionary series until 1966. A precedent for Ferrari's *Written Paintings* is Yoko Ono's *Instructions for Painting* (1961–64), first exhibited at the Sōgetsu Art Center in May 1962. See Alexandra Munroe, *Japanese Art After 1945: Scream Against the Sky* (New York: Abrams, 1994), 226–27.

45. Eduardo Costa, Roberto Jacoby, and Raúl Escari, *Un arte de los medios de comunicación,* manifesto, Buenos Aires, July 1966. Reprinted in Oscar Masotta, *Happenings* (Buenos Aires: Editorial Jorge Álvarez, 1967), 118.

46. Oscar Masotta, *Conciencia y estructura* (Buenos Aires: Editorial Jorge Álvarez, 1969), 16.

47. María José Herrera, "En medio de los medios: La experimentación con los medios masivos de comunicación en la Argentina en la década del 60," in *Arte argentino del siglo XX* (Buenos Aires: Fundación para la Investigación del Arte Argentino, 1997), 97.

48. Cited in ibid., 90.

49. Costa, Jacoby, and Escari, *Un arte de los medios,* 118.

50. Jacoby's *Message at the Tella* paralleled David Lamelas's *Office of Information About the Vietnam War,* presented at the 1968 Venice Biennale, where Lamelas's use of a teletype machine won him notoriety. A later instance of the utilization of this format was Hans Haacke's *News* at Prospect '69 in Düsseldorf.

51. See Mariano Mestman and Ana Longoni, "Tucumán Arde: Una experiencia de arte de vanguardia, comunicación y política en los años sesenta," *Causes y Azares,* no. 1 (1994): 75–85; Ana Longoni, "La intervención política como programo estético: Una lectura de Tucumán Arde," in *El arte entre lo público y lo privado: VI Jornadas de Teoría e Historia de las Artes* (Buenos Aires: Centro Argentino de Investigadores de Arte, 1995), 389–401; and Guillermo Fantoni, "El impacto de lo nuevo en los primeros sesenta: Conformación y emergencia de un grupo de vanguardia," *Anuario, Segunda Epoca,* no. 14 (1989–90): 321–39.

52. Gramuglio and Rosa, *Tucumán Arde.*

53. Juan Pablo Renzi, *La obra de arte como producto de la relación conciencia ética–conciencia estética,* cited in Longoni, "Tucumán Arde: Encuentros y desencuentros," 317.

54. Lucy Lippard, "Escape Attempts," in *Reconsidering the Object of Art,* ed. Goldstein and Rorimer, 20, and Lucy Lippard, *Six Years: The Dematerialization of the Art Object* (New York: Praeger, 1973), 263–64.

55. These contradictions have been analyzed by Longoni, "La intervención política como programa estético."

56. See Brito and Macieira de Sousa, *Cildo Meireles,* 24.

57. Interview with Cildo Meireles, in Marí Bartomeu and Nuria Enguita, *Cildo Meireles* (Valencia: IVAM, 1995), 23.

58. Benjamin Buchloh, "The Political Potential of Art," in *Politics-Poetics: documenta X—the book* (Ostfildern-Ruit: Cantz, 1997), 386.

59. See Acha, "Teoría y práctica no-objetualistas," 237.

60. Buchloh, "The Political Potential of Art," 385.

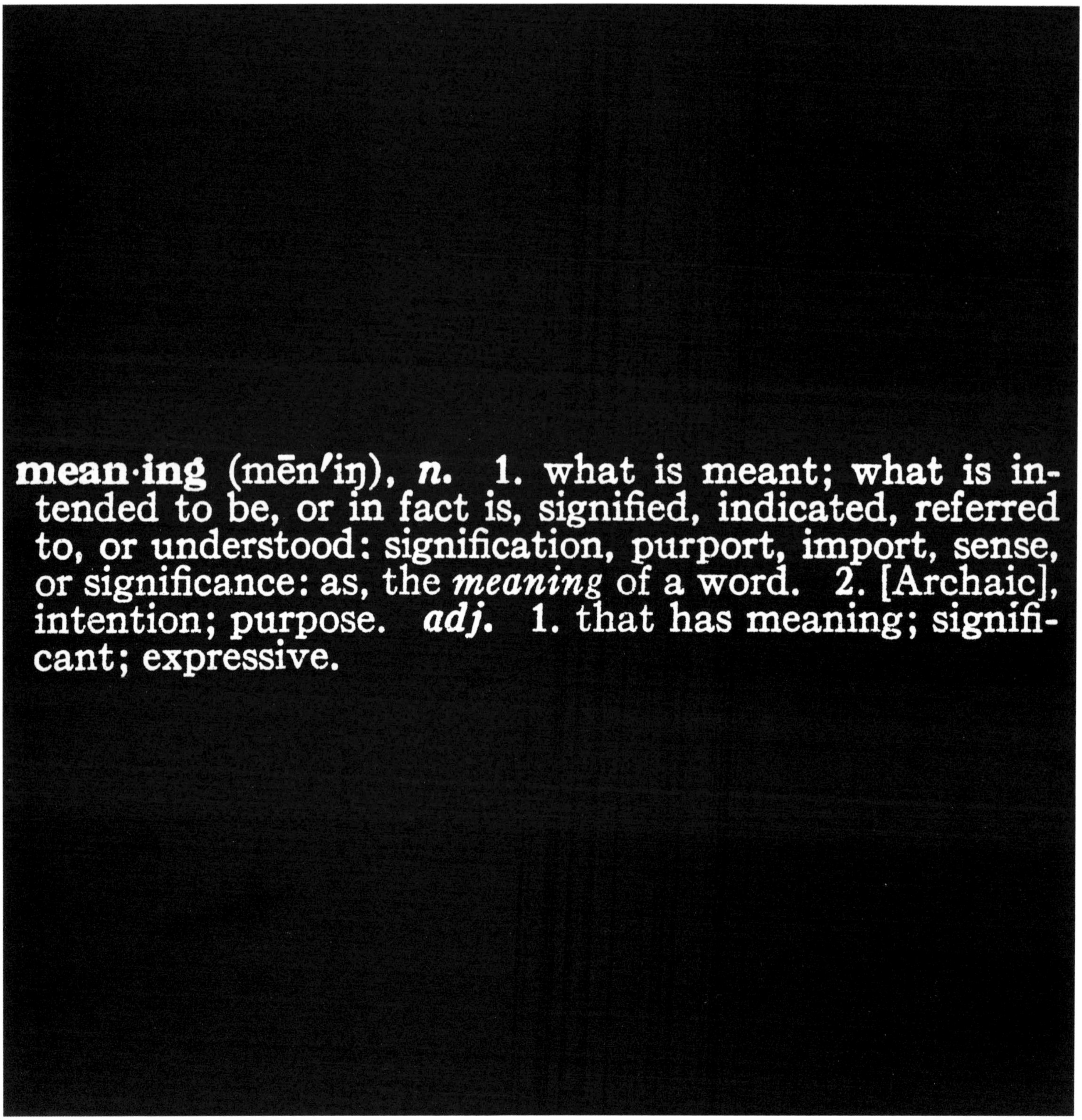
mean·ing (mēn′iŋ), n. 1. what is meant; what is in-
tended to be, or in fact is, signified, indicated, referred
to, or understood: signification, purport, import, sense,
or significance: as, the meaning of a word. 2. [Archaic],
intention; purpose. adj. 1. that has meaning; signifi-
cant; expressive.

Global Conceptualism and North American Conceptual Art

Peter Wollen

Conceptualism, as this exhibition suggests, was a global movement. However, unlike surrealism, which had important adherents and followers in the Caribbean, Mexico, Japan, and the Arab world, it did not simply spread out from a center in Europe or the United States—in other words, from the traditional art capitals of Paris or New York. Conceptualism was a genuinely broad-based trend—Japanese or Latin American conceptualism, for example, had their own quite distinct local trajectories with their own unique characteristics. But it is important to note that conceptualism's global reach is a product of both its multipolar origins and the impetus initially given to it by New York–based conceptual artists. This very small but very vocal and productive phalanx of artists, strategically situated and committed to a typically avant-garde strategy—complete with manifestos, journals, theoretical statements, and an atmosphere of powerful group solidarity riven with contention—set the theoretical parameters that consequently made it possible for conceptual art to transform the landscape of the global art world in an enduring way. North American conceptual art, then, inevitably came to play a disproportionate role in the emergence of the much broader conceptualist movement.

Conceptual art sealed the fate of modernism in the visual arts, but paradoxically it also brought back into currency the avant-garde ideas of Marcel Duchamp and the Russian constructivists, particularly Rodchenko and Tatlin. Moholy-Nagy's telephone paintings played their part too. Without these avant-garde commitments and its base in the Manhattan art world, conceptual art would not have been able to perform its historic role as a new avant-garde (imitating the model of past avant-gardes) that finished off modernism, thus revealing how different their respective missions had always been.

Traditionally, avant-gardism had been seen not as an ongoing artistic tendency with a history of its own, but as a series of isolated outbursts, each of which was eventually subsumed into the ongoing narrative of modernism itself. These avant-gardes had never been content simply with finding artistic means appropriate to modernity, to the massive changes that transformed our culture and society from the mid-19th century onward. Rather, they sought, as Peter Bürger has long since established, to expand their frontiers beyond the core of the art world itself (painting, sculpture, visual design), to make forays into the neighboring arts and into much broader cultural and political arenas. Essentially, these avant-gardes proposed a series of new methodologies and ontologies, new theoretical foundations for art, which were subsequently ransacked for useful technical tricks and formal strategies by the mainstream of modernism. Conceptualism, as this exhibition suggests, was a worldwide movement with many different tendencies in different countries and continents, which were only retroactively herded together to form an *ism* fit to take its place alongside cubism, expressionism, dadaism, surrealism, popism, minimalism, etc., all tributaries flowing into the greater

FIGURE 50.
Joseph Kosuth, *Titled (Art as Idea as Idea) [meaning]*, 1967, photographic enlargement. The Menil Collection, Houston.

stream of modern art history. But by so doing, critics and historians robbed conceptual art of its paradoxical distinction, that of being the last avant-garde of all, the one modernism found it impossible to digest, whose impact had to be smoothed out and rationalized by the invention of a new period hold-all, "post-modernism," somewhat pathetic in its prepositional dependence on its great predecessor.

The time has come, with this exhibition, to look back at the history of conceptual art and to grasp its significance in a new light, one that challenges the everyday assumptions underlying the historiography of 20th-century culture. I will say at the outset that here I am writing specifically about North American art, in New York primarily but also in San Francisco, San Diego, Los Angeles, Toronto, Vancouver, and elsewhere, each developing in significantly different ways. The history of conceptual art in other regions of the world is still more diverse, reflecting their very different circumstances, antecedents, and preoccupations, even if the New York terminology (which we owe principally to critics' efforts to understand the work of Joseph Kosuth and Sol LeWitt) eventually superceded that of arte povera, systems art, language art, information art, and so on. The example of North America would cast a long shadow over developments elsewhere, until all were conveniently huddled together under the same elastic rubric, *conceptualism.* From this totalizing point of view, conceptual art might canonically seem to have begun in New York in 1967 with the opening at the Museum of Normal Art of an exhibition organized by Joseph Kosuth entitled *Normal Art.* Kosuth assembled the work of a number of artists who later became central figures in the history of the movement—Mel Bochner, Hanne Darboven, Dan Graham, Kosuth himself, Christine Kozlov, Sol LeWitt, and Lee Lozano—together with others who would more likely be grouped as minimalists or land artists such as Carl Andre, Eva Hesse, Donald Judd, Robert Morris, Robert Ryman, Robert Smithson, and even Frank Stella.

Or perhaps, purists would argue, New York conceptual art began in 1968 with the *Xeroxbook* show organized by Seth Siegelaub and John W. Wendler, which featured work in the form of a xeroxed catalogue and no on-site gallery exhibits at all (fig. 158). The artists included were Andre, Robert Barry, Douglas Huebler, Kosuth, LeWitt, Morris, and Lawrence Weiner. This show was followed by another, opening in the first week of 1969 when Barry, Huebler, Kosuth, and Weiner showed their work in a rented office space on 52nd Street, intended only as an adjunct to the catalogue descriptions.

But the movement clearly took off in 1969, culminating in an exhibition entitled *Conceptual Art and Conceptual Aspects* in which Barry, Bochner, Kosuth, Kozlov, and Weiner were joined by a more cosmopolitan contingent—Art & Language, Iain Baxter, Daniel Buren, Jan Dibbets, Hans Haacke, On Kawara, Adrian Piper, Ian Wilson, and others. In this year, too, significant exhibitions were held in North American cities other than New York. A show in Newport Beach, California, with Michael Asher, John Baldessari, Barry Le Va, and Allen Ruppersberg, opened in April. In July, *Conception-Perception* at the Eugenia Butler Gallery in Los Angeles featured works by Baldessari, Huebler, Kosuth, Le Va, and Weiner. That same month, Siegelaub initiated a show organized "at various locations throughout the world": five in Europe, three in the United States (Baltimore, Los Angeles, and Niagara Falls), two in Mexico (U.S. artists though: Kosuth and Smithson), and one in Canada (N. E. Thing Company in Vancouver), or two if you count the other side of Niagara Falls! Then in February 1970, Tom Marioni founded the Museum of Conceptual Art in San Francisco, which housed not only a vigorous art scene with members and exhibitions, but also an art collection, always a telltale sign that a movement has arrived.

Three things struck me as I studied this chronology. First, 1967–69 was a period of unusually intense political militancy and cultural upheaval, ranging across Black Power, the student movement, solidarity with Third World struggles, the beginnings of feminism, the Summer of Love, and organized opposition to the Vietnam War. Second, the speed with which the movement crystallized was

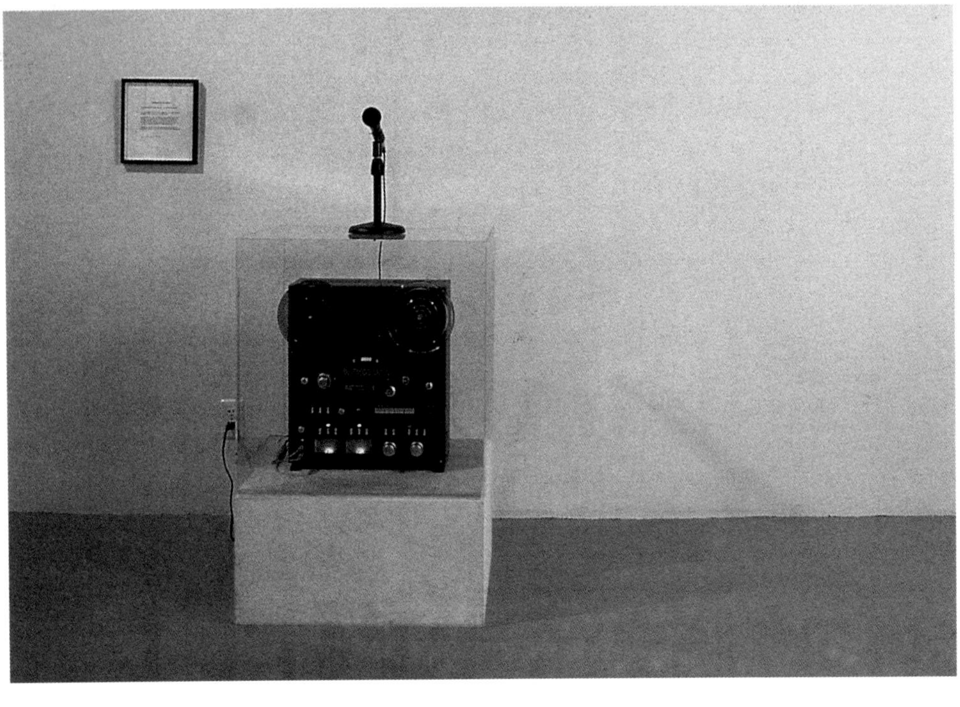

FIGURE 51.
Christine Kozlov, *Information No Theory,* 1970, tape recorder and statement. Collection of the artist.

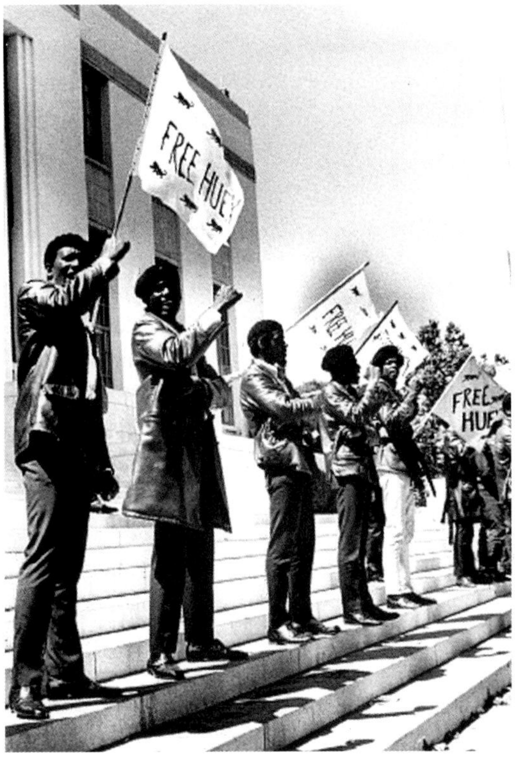

Supporters of Huey Newton demonstrate outside courtroom in Oakland, California, July 15, 1968. Courtesy of UPI/Corbis-Bettmann.

Chicago, National Guardsmen with rifles drawn against antiwar protestors outside the Democratic National Convention, August 1968. Courtesy of Magnum Photos, Inc. © 1968 Raymond Depardon.

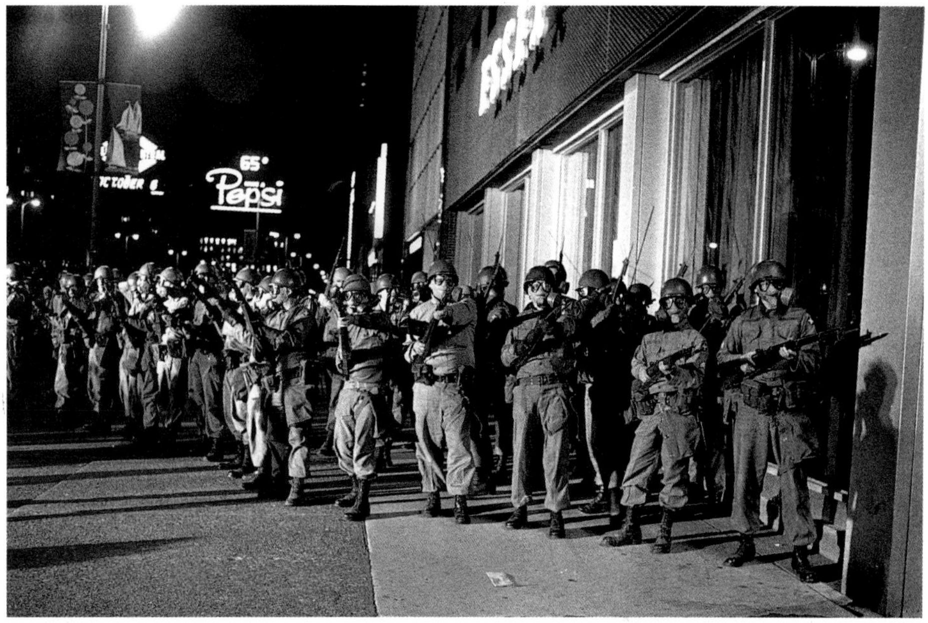

New York City, antiwar protest outside the Internal Revenue Service, 1972. Courtesy of Magnum Photos, Inc. © 1996 Charles Gatewood.

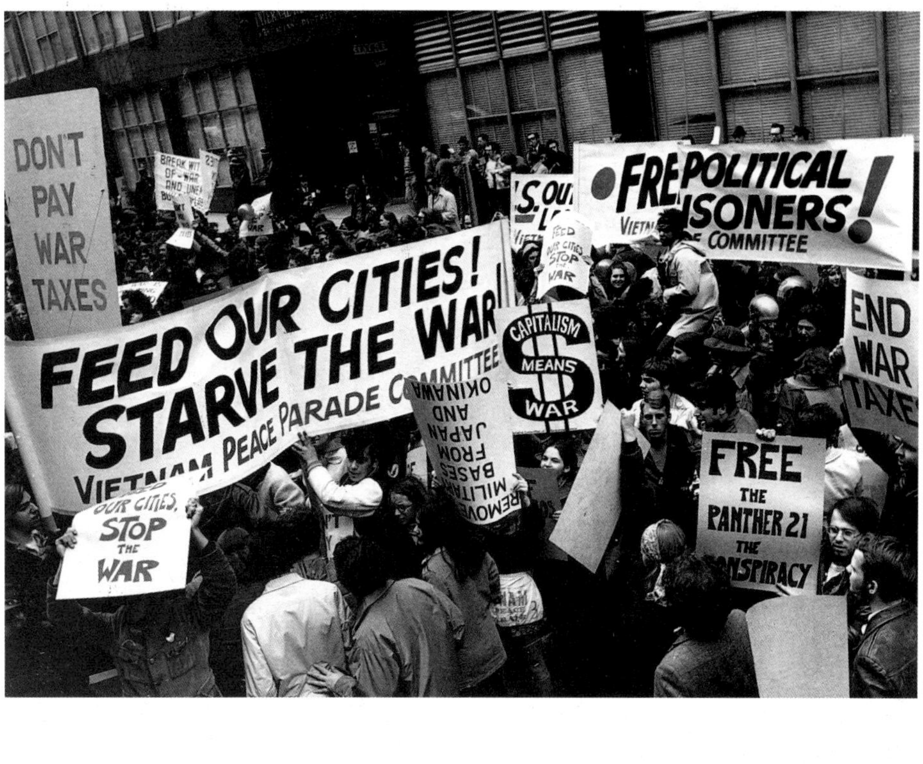

Lawrence Weiner

1. The artist may construct the piece
2. The piece may be fabricated
3. The piece need not be built

Each being equal and consistent with the intent of the artist the decision as to condition rests with the receiver upon the occasion of receivership

Figure 52.
Lawrence Weiner, statement in *Arts Magazine,* April 1970.

phenomenal, bringing together artists from many different backgrounds whose turn to conceptualism was given a special organizational impetus from the group around Siegelaub and Kosuth, functioning something like a traditional avant-garde. Third, Sol LeWitt—with the exception of the *Xeroxbook* show and representation of his work in *Information* (a big survey exhibition at the Museum of Modern Art, New York, in 1970)—seems to have pursued a somewhat solitary path, in which his published work in journals was arguably more important than actual exhibitions (although, of course, these continued). His "Paragraphs on Conceptual Art" appeared in *Artforum* in June 1967, and "Sentences on Conceptual Art" (fig. 157) was published in *0–9* (New York) in January 1969 and the first issue of *Art-Language* (Coventry) in May 1969.

In retrospect, we can see that LeWitt's crisply programmatic texts, like Kosuth's more rambling and much longer theoretical articles, were particularly important historically precisely because conceptual art differentiated itself from earlier or parallel movements by its self-reflexive character, its insistence that it required a metalanguage to be understood and that metalanguage was intrinsic to the work. The extrinsic metalanguage of LeWitt's "Sentences" and "Paragraphs" served to clarify what this intrinsic metalanguage was, and provided a rationale for it. Moreover, LeWitt's pronouncements read like philosophical theorems or, at least, lists of binding definitions. Kosuth's essays, in contrast, are much more discursive and, one might say, opinionated, but they also carry an ambitious philosophical weight, arguing for a definition of art as the necessary precondition for the making of art. Kosuth went further by actually incorporating definitions into artworks, seeming at times to make them identical, effacing the distinction between signifier and signified in a way reminiscent of Magritte's *This Is Not a Pipe* but going further, concerned not simply with the nature of visual representation but with the nature of art itself as a form of discourse. Due to the semantic loop involved, philosophical statements about art could be presented as artworks, functioning at the same time as a kind of manifesto for themselves. In fact, the manifesto, the theoretical proposal, and the artwork became three elements of an interlocking system.

This system tied together many of the threads that marked out avant-garde work from what we might think of as merely modernist work. This particular avant-garde strategy, however, was strikingly self-contained. It existed within a unique kind of semiotic circuit, knotting together art object, art theory, and art manifesto without leaving any obvious loose ends, rather like the relationship of mathematics and the theory of mathematics, complete with a proof that they are actually the same thing. To understand how this happened, we have to look at the way in which, in respect to minimalism, art already existed in a specific kind of relation both to the theory of art and to the idea of an avant-garde. With hindsight, we can now see that minimalism not only signified the demise of Clement Greenberg's theoretical system, inextricably linked to modernism as an epochal movement, but also a crucial shift toward the ideas of John Cage (Greenberg's main rival as an art theorist), which may be considered a precondition for the eventual triumph of postmodernism. Cage sought to efface the boundary between art and life, in true avant-garde style, and introduced the idea that an artwork was simply the end product of an arbitrary system of rules which could be arrived at in a number of different ways, ranging along a spectrum from pure chance to complex mathematical algorithms. It must have seemed to Greenberg that an old devil had returned in a new guise, as if dada and surrealism, with their found objects and chance procedures, had somehow mutated into a new form. Many years were to pass, however, before the truly insidious character of Cage's influence would reveal itself, as it penetrated the very heart of Greenberg's own fortress.

Minimal art was not, in any obvious sense, an organized movement or even tendency. Like most names of art movements, *minimalism* was a term applied post hoc by critics, who saw something in common among a group of artists that included Andre, Dan Flavin, Judd, LeWitt, and Morris. Insofar as these artists had something in common, it could be summed up as follows. They produced three-dimensional constructions based on simple, unornamented rectilinear forms. In general, simple units or modules were repeated to form what David Batchelor, author of the best book on the topic,[1] calls "an overall regular shape" whose underlying logic could be grasped in a moment. Usually, these works stood on the floor. If colored, they were deliberately inexpressive. As a rule they were made of industrial materials of a kind, as Batchelor notes, typically "available from builders' merchants and the like rather than a fine art or craft supplier." There was little obvious sign either of craft or the artist's hand, or of any need for self-expression through personal creativity. The works were simple, direct, and unpretentious, while giving clear evidence of thought and planning, just as building a wall would require thought and planning. By 1966, LeWitt was producing floor pieces in which the underlying generative concept of the work was no longer immediately visible, so that, in Batchelor's words, "the viewer has to complete the system in his or her mind," and "the completion of the series thus relies on the viewer's recognition of a certain logic."

Where did minimalism come from? First, there was the example of assemblage, which had already called into question the canonical distinction between painting and sculpture. Second, there was Frank Stella's painting, which we might compare and contrast, as Batchelor does, to Warhol's grid paintings. Third, there was the move toward the structuring of painting by simple stripes and strata of color, found, for instance, in work by Barnett Newman and Mark Rothko, both of whom also painted in series. Flavin's work was influenced by Morris Louis's stripes, and his move away from painting followed the example of the Russian constructivists. Among sculptors, there was the precedent of Brancusi's endless towers. LeWitt made his first modular cube piece in 1965. From early on, he wanted to make works whose structure was plain to the eye, stripping away the "surface skin" and simply showing the edges of his cubes. He wanted the work to look "hard and industrial." The result was what Batchelor calls a kind of "linearism," which led him logically to drawing, just as the use of the cube as a repeated module led him to seriality. Before constructing his three-dimensional units, LeWitt produced working drawings, just as later, as a conceptual artist, he produced sets of verbal instruction, preliminary to making drawings. Constructions were drawings in space; drawings were translations of words and numbers.

In some respects, conceptual art can be seen as the logical extension of minimalism. In other ways, however, there was a definite break or rupture, a shift onto quite new ground. Like minimalism, conceptual art challenged the canonical boundaries between painting and sculpture, adopted modularity and seriality as working methodologies, and envisioned the finished artwork as simply the

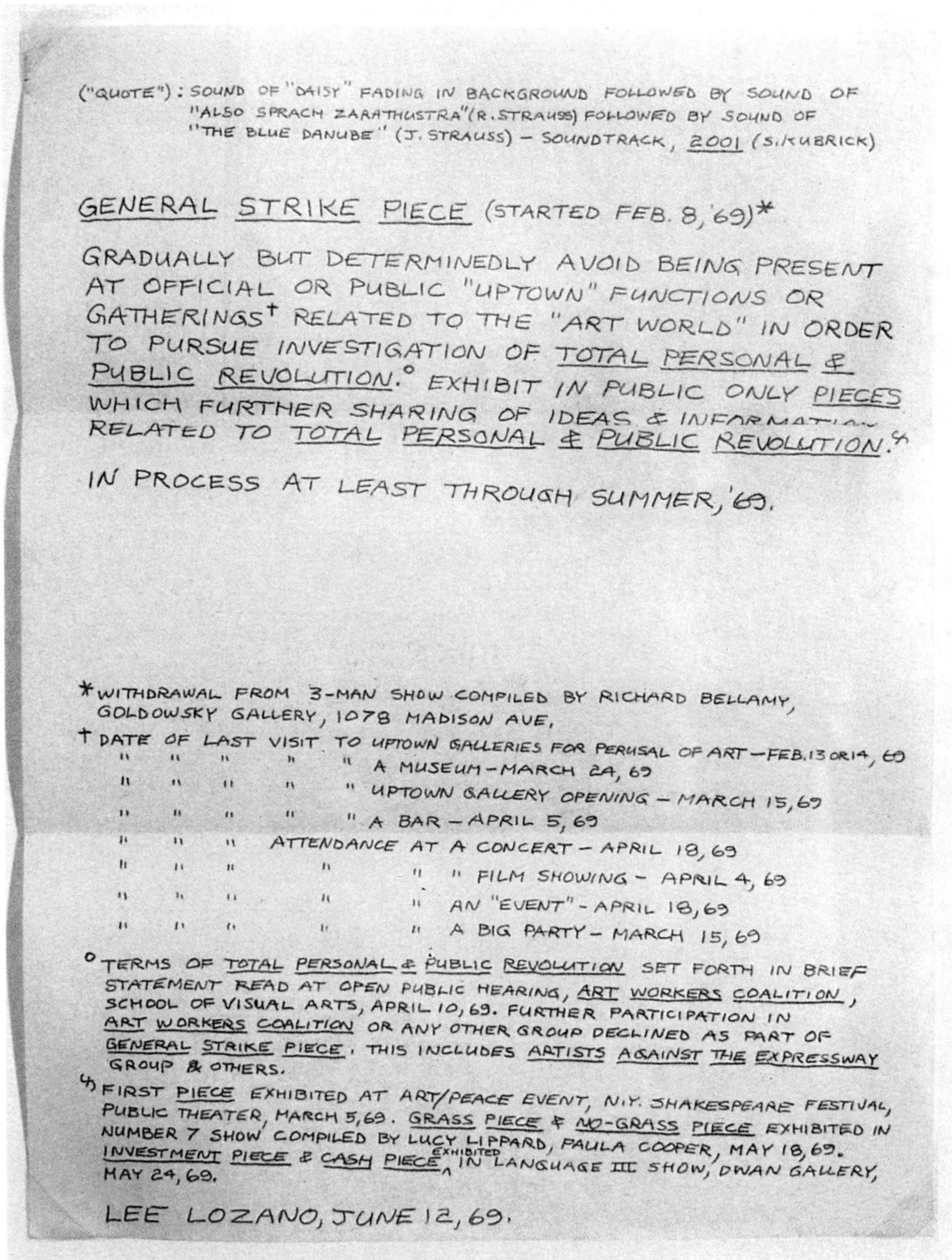

("QUOTE"): SOUND OF "DAISY" FADING IN BACKGROUND FOLLOWED BY SOUND OF "ALSO SPRACH ZARATHUSTRA" (R. STRAUSS) FOLLOWED BY SOUND OF "THE BLUE DANUBE" (J. STRAUSS) – SOUNDTRACK, 2001 (S. KUBRICK)

GENERAL STRIKE PIECE (STARTED FEB. 8, '69)*

GRADUALLY BUT DETERMINEDLY AVOID BEING PRESENT AT OFFICIAL OR PUBLIC "UPTOWN" FUNCTIONS OR GATHERINGS† RELATED TO THE "ART WORLD" IN ORDER TO PURSUE INVESTIGATION OF TOTAL PERSONAL & PUBLIC REVOLUTION.° EXHIBIT IN PUBLIC ONLY PIECES WHICH FURTHER SHARING OF IDEAS & INFORMATION RELATED TO TOTAL PERSONAL & PUBLIC REVOLUTION.§

IN PROCESS AT LEAST THROUGH SUMMER, '69.

*WITHDRAWAL FROM 3-MAN SHOW COMPILED BY RICHARD BELLAMY, GOLDOWSKY GALLERY, 1078 MADISON AVE.

† DATE OF LAST VISIT TO UPTOWN GALLERIES FOR PERUSAL OF ART – FEB. 13 OR 14, 69
" " " " " A MUSEUM – MARCH 24, 69
" " " " " UPTOWN GALLERY OPENING – MARCH 15, 69
" " " " " A BAR – APRIL 5, 69
" " " ATTENDANCE AT A CONCERT – APRIL 18, 69
" " " " " " FILM SHOWING – APRIL 4, 69
" " " " " AN "EVENT" – APRIL 18, 69
" " " " " A BIG PARTY – MARCH 15, 69

° TERMS OF TOTAL PERSONAL & PUBLIC REVOLUTION SET FORTH IN BRIEF STATEMENT READ AT OPEN PUBLIC HEARING, ART WORKERS COALITION, SCHOOL OF VISUAL ARTS, APRIL 10, 69. FURTHER PARTICIPATION IN ART WORKERS COALITION OR ANY OTHER GROUP DECLINED AS PART OF GENERAL STRIKE PIECE. THIS INCLUDES ARTISTS AGAINST THE EXPRESSWAY GROUP & OTHERS.

§ FIRST PIECE EXHIBITED AT ART/PEACE EVENT, N.Y. SHAKESPEARE FESTIVAL, PUBLIC THEATER, MARCH 5, 69. GRASS PIECE & NO-GRASS PIECE EXHIBITED IN NUMBER 7 SHOW COMPILED BY LUCY LIPPARD, PAULA COOPER, MAY 18, 69. INVESTMENT PIECE & CASH PIECE EXHIBITED IN LANGUAGE III SHOW, DWAN GALLERY, MAY 24, 69.

LEE LOZANO, JUNE 12, 69.

Figure 53.
Lee Lozano, *General Strike Piece, Feb. 8, 1969,* graphite ink and paper. Wadsworth Atheneum, Hartford, Connecticut. Alexander A. Goldfarb Contemporary Art Acquisition Fund.

realization of an initial idea that could be executed by an anonymous fabricator. But there was also a decisive shift, which occurred over a period of time and involved a number of separate issues. With this in mind, we need to tread warily around issues of precedence. I think it is safe to say that we can see the germs of conceptual art emerge from minimalism, serial art, systems art, etc., from the early 1960s onward. It began to crystallize as a separate tendency for Kosuth early in 1967 with a statement written for a show he organized at the Lannis Gallery, New York. Entitled *Non-Anthropomorphic Art by Four Young Artists,* the exhibition included Kosuth, Kozlov, Michael Rinaldi, and Ernest Rossi. This is also the year in which Sol LeWitt wrote his "Paragraphs on Conceptual Art" for *Artforum,* and the first significant statement by Art & Language, "Remarks on Air-Conditioning," was published in *Arts Magazine.*

In his "Statement" (later retitled "Notes on Conceptual Art and Models"), Kosuth made a number of important claims, among which were the following: (1) "All I make are models. The actual works of art are ideas. Rather than 'ideals' the models are a visual approximation of a particular art object I have in mind. It does not matter who actually makes the model, nor where the models end up." (2) Each "art object" is atemporal and meaningless in itself, but it does have "philosophical implications," which Kosuth does not wish to deny or reject. (3) Each art object is "concerned totally with art in as much as it is concerned with nothing else." As a consequence, it must have "an order, a logic of one kind or another," which will distinguish it from other kinds of objects. (4) Mathematics is a kind of tool that makes it "possible for a structure or object to have an order not associated with natural or useful objects." Mathematics can provide us with a type of order that is true in itself, rather than because it represents reality or because it is useful. (5) Similarly, art has a "beauty" that depends upon its "uselessness," its detachment from reality, which is "tautological for the idea of pure or total existence."

What is immediately striking about these claims is their remorseless aestheticism, well within the modernist tradition. As Victor Burgin remarked, looking back thirty years later, Kosuth's concern was with "the whole question of self-reflexivity, which is nothing other than art for art's sake." The way Burgin saw it, this was Kosuth "identified totally with Ad Reinhardt."[2]

Burgin's view, expressed in 1997 but describing what he thought at the end of the 1960s, implies that Kosuth's position at that time reflected a wish to provide an art-for-art's-sake theorization of minimalism as the construction of pure objects analogous to the conceptual objects of pure mathematics, but anonymously fabricated to give them a form in space. It was only a step from this position, of course, to include conceptual elements of the theoretical definition of art within the object itself in textual form, as Kosuth famously did in his 1967 *Titled (Art as Idea as Idea)* (fig. 50), with its dictionary definition of *meaning* photostatted, blown up, and incorporated into the art object—in a sense, *being* the art object. LeWitt's approach in his "Paragraphs on Conceptual Art" is significantly different from Kosuth's in that he is concerned not with the concept of art as such, but with the conceptual basis for the making of the work, as Cage had long been. "This kind of art," LeWitt wrote, "is not theoretical or illustrative of theories; it is intuitive, it is involved with all types of mental processes and it is purposeless." Significantly, there is agreement on the uselessness or purposelessness of art (though these concepts are slightly different) but, whereas Kosuth came increasingly to think of the work as theoretically self-reflexive, LeWitt was not at all interested in its "philosophical implications." Instead, he was interested in its practical implications as a method of work—the artist has an idea, which is then executed in a mechanical kind of way. The idea, in itself, might be intuitive or irrational. It certainly does not need to stand up to theoretical scrutiny. It simply needs to be "interesting."

LeWitt's approach, like Kosuth's, was committed to the uselessness of the art object, but not to its aesthetic beauty or tautological self-reflexivity. In this sense, LeWitt was less radical than Kosuth, more concerned with pushing back the limits of minimalism by stressing the initial conceptual plan rather than the finished work. LeWitt was never drawn into the post-Duchampian questions about the definition of art that absorbed other conceptual artists. Whereas Kosuth complicated both his theory and practice as time went on, developing them by introducing new ideas and procedures, LeWitt soon settled on a relatively simple way of working—producing formulas for potential drawings and then having them executed. In fact, LeWitt sometimes seems like a manic-obsessive version of a Fluxus artist, endlessly having whimsical ideas for drawings but stripping them of any "philosophical implications" and anything that might suggest caprice or madcap humor. In this sense, he was like Duchamp—he wanted to remain, in his own words, "emotionally dry" and to eliminate subjectivity.

The concept *conceptual art* appears to have entered the discourse of the art world in a substantial way only from 1969 onward. In that year, Germano Celant used the term for his exhibition *Arte Povera: Earthworks, Impossible Art, Actual Art, Conceptual Art,* and Gillo Dorfles reiterated it in the title of an article for *Art International* in which he tried to make a distinction between *arte concettuale* and *arte povera.* Soon afterward, an exhibition in Leverkusen (with a catalogue introduction by Sol LeWitt) was titled *Konzeption-Conception;* then Catherine Millet wrote on "L'art conceptuel" for *Opus International* in Paris and Harald Szeemann used the word *Concepts* after the colon in the title of his exhibition in Berne, *When Attitudes Become Form,* linking it with Works, Processes, Situations, and Information.[3] By 1970, critical essays on conceptual art were widespread in the U.S., Europe, and Australia. In America, there was an article in *Harper's Bazaar* and a piece on Joseph Kosuth in *Newsweek.* The first U.S. exhibition to refer (indirectly) to *conceptual art* as such appears to be Eugenia Butler's show in Los Angeles in July 1969. This was followed in November by the Leverkusen exhibition mentioned above and in the next two years by shows in New York, Turin, Jerusalem, Innsbruck, Milan, and Basel (Buenos Aires also had *El arte como idea in Inglaterra*). However, although these shows used the term *concept* or *conceptual* or *idea,* their interpretation of what this might mean was still extremely fuzzy. *Conceptual art* would gradually become a typical art world label, applied with a broad brush to a spectrum of works that seemed to break new ground and go beyond the limits of existing *isms.*

It seems to have taken about two years for historians, critics, and curators to catch up with artists. The story, however, does not end with its beginning. Kosuth, in particular, has himself taken a retrospective look at the history of conceptual art and made his own distinctions. In effect, he has defended the tendency he supports as the "real" version of conceptual art and discarded the rest as false heroes. In 1971, Kosuth gave a lecture in Salvador Allende's Chile, entitled "Painting versus Art versus Culture (or, Why You Can Paint If You Want To, But It Probably Won't Matter)."[4] In this talk, he already took pains to differentiate conceptual art from minimalism, describing the former as "a competitive paradigm or model of artistic activity" with, as its task, "the dismantling of the mythic structure of art as posited in present-day cultural institutions." In effect, Kosuth was now making a claim for conceptual art as an avant-garde tendency rather than just another art movement. He wanted to draw a clear divide between conceptual art and minimalism, even to mark a moment of rupture from modernism itself.

In the second issue of "his" journal, *The Fox* (1975), Kosuth distinguished between "Theoretical Conceptual Art" (TCA) and "Stylistic Conceptual Art" (SCA).[5] TCA, of course, followed the agenda outlined above and remained oppositional. On the other hand, the "deterioration of the movement into a popular SCA," Kosuth wrote, "pointed, at

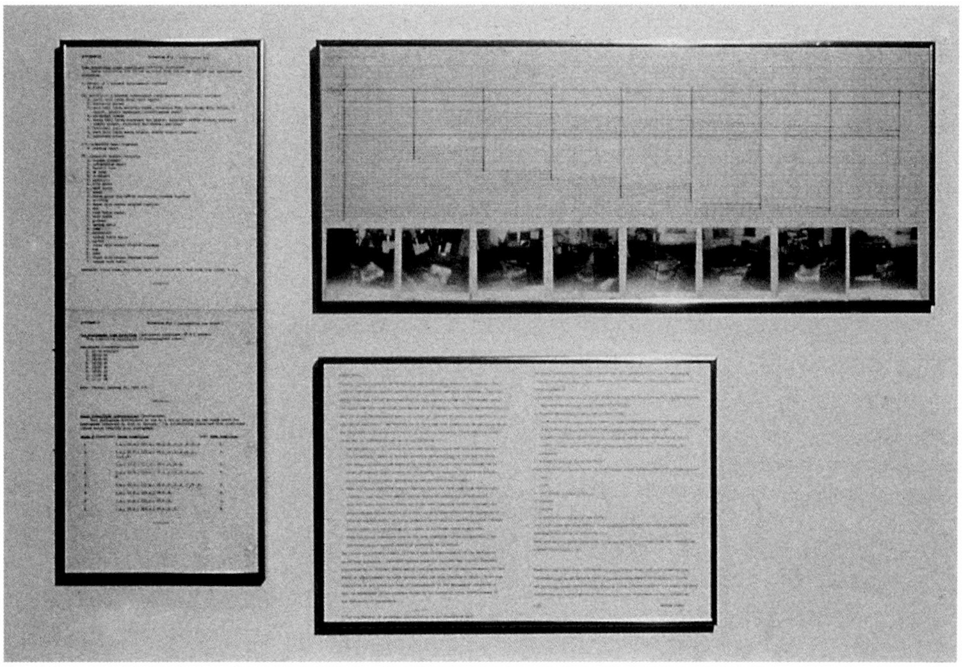

Figure 54.
Adrian Piper, *Hypothesis Situation #19,* 1969–70, photograph, text, chart collage. Collection of the artist.

least on the surface, to an ultimate victory by the establishment. The form the victory takes is one of annexation." TCA, he later explained in a paper studded with references to Habermas, Marcuse, Jameson, etc., should be a "critical practice" concerned with the "demystification" of art and the "restoration of meaning"; it should be "political" in the sense that "our very conceptions of both culture and politics, as part of a discourse which trivializes both, must be critically understood as they are re-made for human use."[6]

In a further phase, Kosuth took the final step of redescribing SCA as simply a form of post-minimalism.[7] From the start, he argued, conceptual art had been defined "in the language of minimalism" and naturally developed, in the context of the art world, into a movement that "provided the Modernist agenda with a revitalized 'avant-garde' face without letting go of the premise that the repository of central artistic concern was still in the object, if only in its absence. In this regard, post-Minimalism's primary concern is with a radicalization of alternative materials rather than alternative meanings." That is, as I understand it, language and even concepts were treated as the materials of a new kind of "negative" art object, rather than as instruments for the critical investigation (and subversion) of the underlying premises of art within North American culture. In other words, as Kosuth put it,

> What separates Conceptual art from both [postminimalism and political message art] is the understanding that artistic practice locates itself directly in the signifying process and that the use of elements in an art proposition (be they objects, quotations, fragments, photographs, contexts, texts, or whatever) functions not for aesthetic purposes (although, like anything in the world, a proposition can also be aesthetic), but rather as simply the constructive elements of a test of the cultural code.

Test is further defined here as "a questioning process." In other words, the function of art is to question the cultural codes within which it operates, is institutionalized and received, including, of course, the codes that give art its political power and meaning.

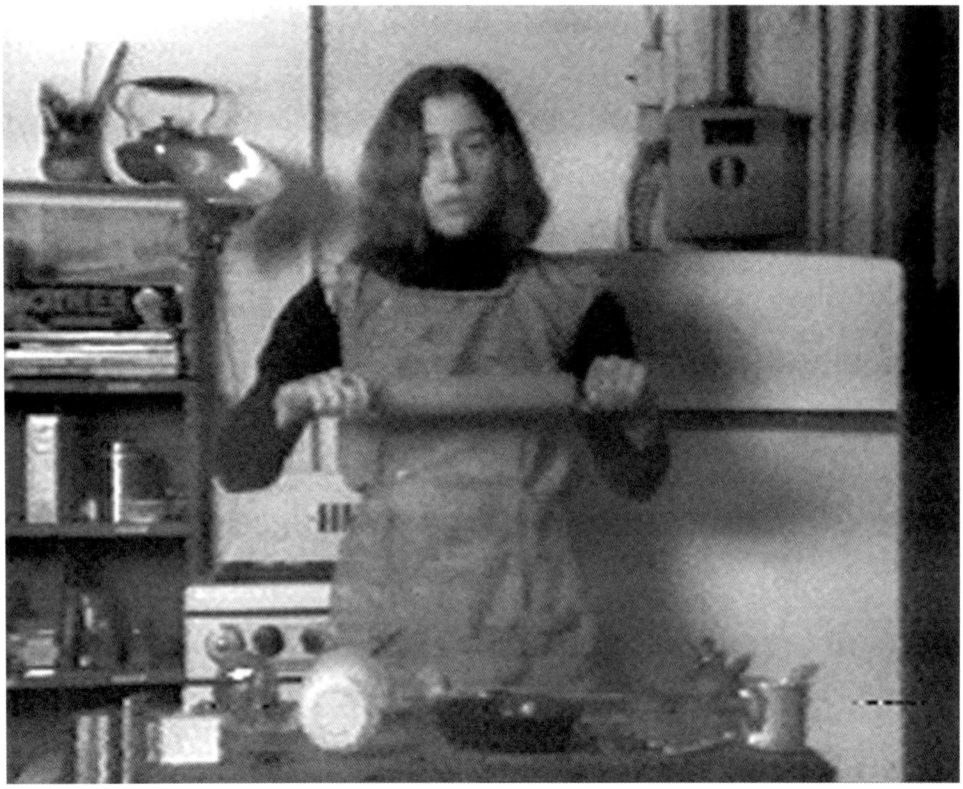

Figure 55.
Martha Rosler, *Semiotics of the Kitchen,* 1975, videotape. Courtesy of Electronic Arts Intermix, New York.

As I read Kosuth's polemics, I couldn't help but suspect that his critique of postminimalism had concealed implications for our judgment of Sol LeWitt. After all, LeWitt was canonical for both Lucy Lippard (herself almost one of the minimalist group) and Rosalind Krauss, a founding editor of *October* who writes about LeWitt as though he were a postminimalist—in *Grids* and *The Originality of the Avant-Garde*—even though she herself deploys a very different set of theoretical arguments drawn from psychoanalysis, Bataille, and poststructuralism. What should we really think of all those elegant wall drawings, with their densely packed collocation of colored pencil lines? Could this be the heartland of SCA? My own view is that Kosuth's development from postminimalism to TCA, to art as cultural critique, represents what actually happened more accurately than the SCA version embraced, according to him, by the art world.

In contrast to Kosuth, LeWitt stayed much closer to his original theory and practice, and consequently had the lesser general influence in the long run. By broadening the borders of the movement, Kosuth prepared the ground for *conceptualism,* a tendency that both emerged from the crisis of modernism and superceded it. Indeed, there is a sense in which the whole of the art world is now dominated by conceptualism—by work driven by "art ideas," by installation, by art viewed as a form of cultural criticism. In saying this, I do not want to minimize the importance of LeWitt's early role. Moreover, his theoretical positions on conceptual art are much more rigorous than the mainstream reception of his work would suggest. When asked in 1981 whether he felt he had to endorse every wall drawing that followed his instructions, he replied, "If someone did a work of mine, unknown to me? I think it's fine. It's not like painting a picture, where each is unique. Much work today can be done by anybody." LeWitt's view, it seems, is that the actual drawings are analogous to the performance of a score. The artist is like a composer, the draftsperson or fabricator like a performer. The works go out into the world for multiple performances, some better, some worse.

Rather than the legacy of Duchamp, which influenced Kosuth, we are dealing here with the legacy of Cage, deflected in the direction of Moholy-Nagy's telephone paintings or Rodchenko's call for (fabricated) industrial art. The art object itself is not completely rejected, but its uniqueness is challenged. At the same time, LeWitt's multiples are usually site-specific and frequently (in museum shows, mostly) painted over. His "sale" of works is really payment for authentication, which is not strictly necessary. In this sense, despite LeWitt's own distance from political artmaking, his work inevitably raises political questions about the institutions of the art world. On the other hand, the wall drawings in themselves are plainly postminimalist art objects, which are indeed regarded as objects of pure aesthetic contemplation rather than challenges to the ideology of art—its absolute uniqueness, its physical creation by the artist, its assumed hierarchy of artist and "anybody."

Conceptual art problematized and decentered—even at times erased—the traditional art object, the painting or the sculpture. In place of the object it substituted a discourse, often modeled on the critical apparatus of the historian or the theorist (written text plus photographic documentation) or the contextualizing practices of the curator and exhibition designer (selecting and arranging a series of items to create significant correlations). As the British-based artist Mary Kelly (fig. 155) pointed out in 1978, these procedures could be described in terms drawn from the new discipline of semiotics, as codified by Roland Barthes. Conceptual art shifted the axis of meaning in art from the "metaphoric" to the "metonymic," from the semantic to the syntactic, from the message to the code (or, in Kosuth's terms, also cited by Kelly, from the "synthetic" to the "analytic").[8] Art installations not only made use of verbal language, but

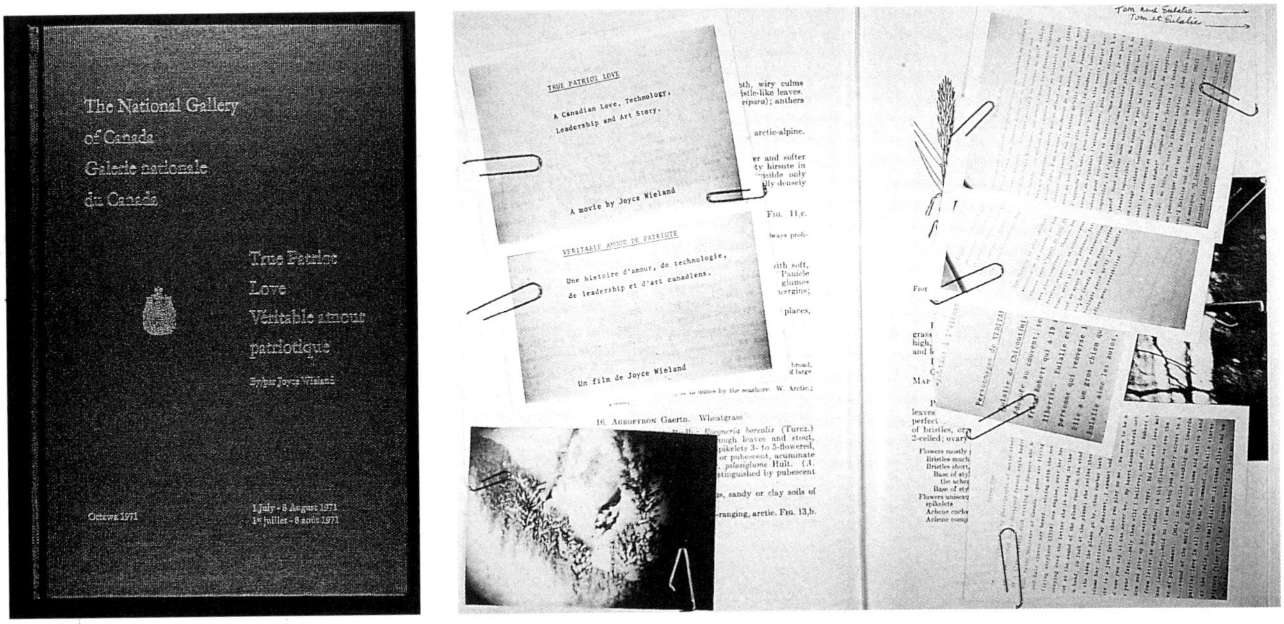

FIGURE 56.
Joyce Wieland, *True Patriot Love,* 1971, book (exhibition catalogue) published by the National Gallery of Canada, Ottawa.

themselves became languagelike in the way they strung a series of items together to make a significant sequence, as words are combined in a linear fashion to make a sentence. This was not simply a formal shift. It brought with it a new way of referring to the world, through complex forms of narrative, documentation, and metalanguage, far removed from traditional modes of visual representation. Painting and sculpture were not simply problematized but replaced by text, photography, and performance. Artmaking was seen as a cultural and political activity, rather than an aspect of personal creativity.

This long-term impact of conceptual art, it seems to me, is still underestimated. It was not simply the successor to color field painting or minimalism or serial art, for instance, although undoubtedly conceptual art would never have occurred without the influence of Johns or Reinhardt or Morris or Andre or Judd. It was not simply a new style or a new movement. It was the single greatest shift in art since the Renaissance: it successfully dethroned painting and sculpture from their "natural" position in the hierarchy of the arts. (In 1970, John Baldessari burned his paintings and put the ashes in an urn as a work of conceptual art [fig. 156]). It challenged the primacy they had enjoyed, as of right, for centuries and transformed the art world into a field of unprecedented semiotic complexity, whose effects are still with us in the form of installation art—the new genre that emerged from the combination of conceptual art with elements of assemblage, environment, performance, photo-text, and video. As has often been recognized, the vision that made this new hybrid possible was provided, in the first instance, by Marcel Duchamp, but it was conceptual art that broke apart the time-honored structures of the old art world

FIGURE 57.
Michael Snow, *Wavelength,* 1966–67, 16mm film.

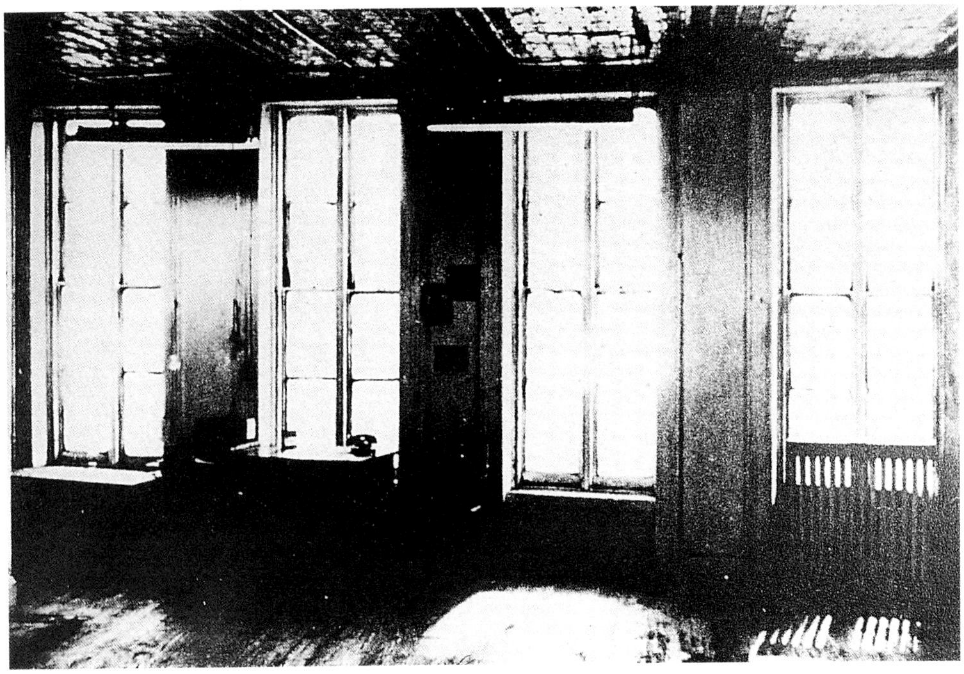

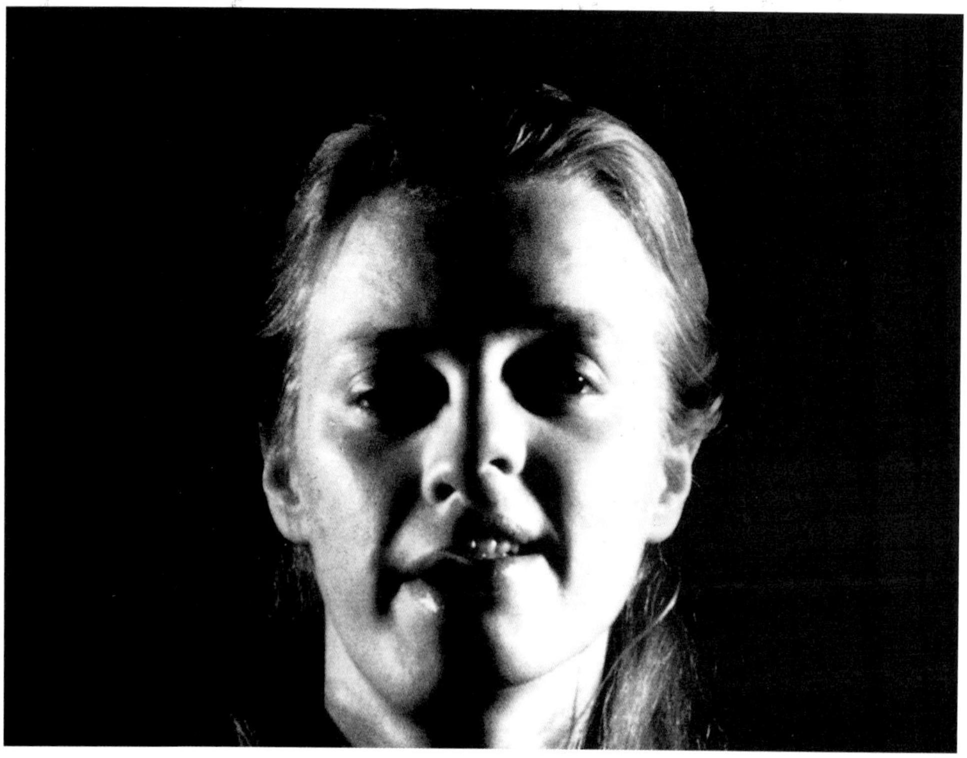

FIGURE 58.
Hollis Frampton, *Zorns Lemma,* 1970, 16mm film, 60 min., color, sound. Courtesy of Anthology Film Archives, New York.

and decisively undermined the leading role of painting and sculpture.

Looking back on it, we can see that, paradoxically, there was a logic to this break, which came from within the tradition of painting itself. Greenberg's call for art to emancipate itself from easel painting led inexorably to a further call for art to liberate itself from painting of any type. The crucial precedent for this further act of emancipation was found in the rediscovered example of Duchamp and the Russian experimentalists of the 1920s, among whom Rodchenko can now be seen as the most relevant. But the most important step was the turn to theory—first the theory of art itself, seen still in post-Kantian terms, but soon the theory of art as a social and semiotic phenomenon. In retrospect, we might think that conceptual artists often used the wrong theory. It seems strange that during the heyday of semiology, the rise of Barthes and Lacan, the rediscovery of Peirce, and the bitter wars around Chomsky that racked linguistics, artists should have turned to Wittgenstein and A. J. Ayer. Nonetheless, theory it was. It is not so much that one kind of theory is intrinsically better than another, but that some theories offered more possibilities than others, were simply much more useful. Victor Burgin, for instance, has noted how his interest in semiotics began when he came back from Yale in 1967, where Judd, Morris, and Reinhardt were all teaching at the time, and "stumbled across this little Jonathan Cape translation, Roland Barthes's *Elements of Semiology,* and it changed my life."

The explanation Burgin gives is that semiology (or "semiotics," as it was later redubbed) was not only "a non-anecdotal, non-subjective criticism," but also

> a theory which was able to turn its attention, almost indiscriminately, to advertising, to cinema, to literature. This seemed to me to offer a broad base where you could actually connect with other people and other fields and have a discussion in common. So naturally my fantasy was that art would become reintegrated into the broader field of cultural criticism.[9]

As we have seen, this was exactly the move that Kosuth was later to make, although on the basis of a different kind of theory. Doing so meant acknowledging that a clean break had to be made with the logic of modernism, certainly in its Greenbergian version, which had, so to speak, led to a narrowing of art to an increasingly reflexive preoccupation with its own ontology and an increasing absence of any substantive relationship with the world. The break with modernism meant not simply the downgrading of visuality, although this was extremely significant, but also the opening up of art to extrinsic political and cultural issues, formerly considered irrelevant or inappropriate, a state of affairs largely the legacy of McCarthyism and the Cold War.

The turn to cultural theory, however, arose in a very specific context. Conceptual art, as Lucy Lippard has often stressed, appeared at a time of unusual political turbulence and confrontation, which swept through the North American art world as it did through the universities and the ghettos. This political climate had a direct impact on the initial formation of conceptual art and it decisively shaped its development. From very early on, the attack on the traditional art object (especially painting) was seen, in political terms, as an attack on the commodification of the art world. The denigration of vision by conceptual artists also carries a clear echo of the denunciation of the Society of the Spectacle by the Situationists, what Martin Jay refers to as the latter's "iconophobia." For the Situationists, the world of the visual had been more or less entirely colonized by the media and by the culture of the market. New artistic techniques were necessary to escape incorporation into the world of the spectacle. Conceptual artists, too, wanted to create a new kind of relationship between artist, gallery, and public, a relationship that would challenge not only the commercial nature of the art world but also the idea of the viewer as passive consumer of sensations rather than thoughtful interlocutor. Text, photography, and found objects were incorporated into artwork not simply because they were interesting new media with which to work, but because they offered specific ways of engaging the attention of the art public and, as Burgin observed, opportunities to reintegrate art into a wider cultural field of discourse, from which modernism had increasingly abstracted it.

At the same time, the New York art world itself was changing. Women and artists from a diverse range of cultural and ethnic backgrounds were demanding access and recognition. Always sidelined during the history of modernism, its crisis gave them new opportunities. Conceptual art, in particular, offered a new arena, one that encouraged artists to ask fundamental questions about both art and the art world, about the politics and sociology of art. Moreover, conceptual work was relatively cheap to produce, portable, and lacking in the self-conscious heroism of previous modernist movements. Women quickly became prominent in the world of conceptual art (fig. 60). As we have seen, Christine Kozlov and Lee Lozano were there from the beginning. Kozlov's piece for an inaudible tape (fig. 51) and Lozano's work in which she instructed herself as to how to behave socially in the art world and ethically in her personal and political life (fig. 53) were early classics of conceptual art. Adrian Piper, an African-American woman with a training in philosophy, was present very early on within the conceptualist movement (fig. 54). Eleanor Antin's conceptual works were among the first to tackle the intersection of public and private, and the social construction of the self (fig. 191). Yoko Ono (figs. 109–111), like Shusaku Arakawa (fig. 159) and On Kawara (fig. 108), provided an important link between Japan and the United States. Beginning as a Fluxus artist, Ono subsequently made the transition from Fluxus to a broader conceptualism, with an increasingly political dimension. Similarly, Hans Haacke, coming to New York from Europe, quickly perceived the potential conceptual art offered as a means of social criticism and analysis (fig. 161).

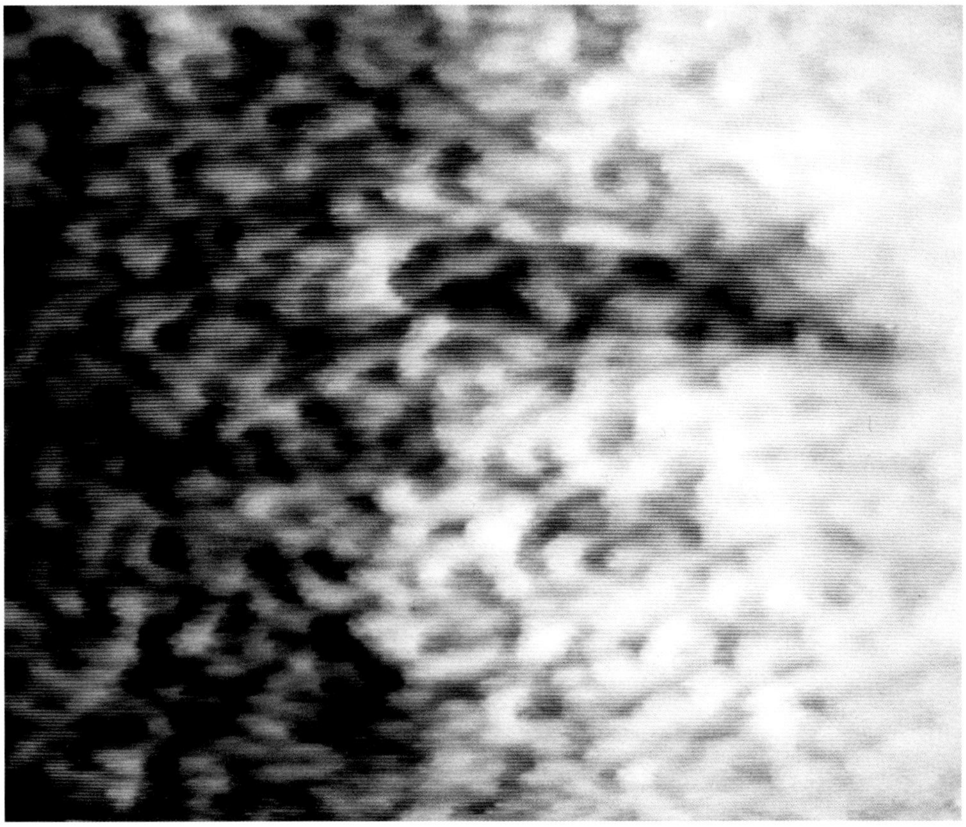

Politics and social criticism were to become increasingly important in shaping the history and geography of conceptual art. In Los Angeles, the guerrilla artists' collective Asco (Spanish for "disgust"), which included Harry Gamboa, Jr. (fig. 202), Willie Herrón, Gronk, and Patssi Valdez, protested the exclusion of Chicano artists by spraypainting the Los Angeles County Museum of Art and signing it graffiti-style as an artwork. In New York, Faith Ringgold, an African-American member of Art Workers Coalition and the Guerrilla Art Action Group, renamed a wing of the Museum of Modern Art the Martin Luther King Wing, noting the absence of black artists in its exhibition schedule and permanent collection, an action vividly recounted by her daughter Michele Wallace in her book *Invisibility Blues.* Gamboa also moved into film and video, making his conceptualist series entitled *No Movies* which, given the lack of resources to complete them as films, only existed as ideas in phototext form. That same year, 1971, Robert Morris organized the Art Strike protest against the Venice Biennale's selection of all male white artists and the extension of the war into Cambodia. Another group of artists, led by Poppy Johnson and Lucy Lippard, demonstrated against the Whitney Biennial to demand 50 percent representation of women.

These actions, designed to challenge the covert political role of museums, paralleled the critique of the fetishized modernist art object implicit within conceptual art. Questioning the art object led logically to challenging first the gallery show, then the museum exhibition. Conceptual art inherited the mantle of protest from the early activities of Henry Flynt, a fluxartist who had invented the term *concept art* back in 1963 in relation to the Fluxus movement, and also inaugurated the first wave of '60s demonstrations against the policies of New York museums.

Figure 59.
Theresa Hak Kyung Cha, still from *Mouth to Mouth,* 1975, videotape. Courtesy of Art Museum, University of California, Berkeley, Gift of the Theresa Hak Kyung Cha Memorial Foundation.

FIGURE 60.
Lucy Lippard,
C. 7,500, 1973,
exhibition catalogue:
30 printed index
cards. Collection of
Lesley Dick, Los
Angeles.

Inevitably there will be complaints about the sexual limitation of this show, to which I can only say that all curatorial limitations or whims ("German Art Since 1945", "Color Painting", "The Cat in Art", "American Artists Under 35", etc.) are equally ridiculous and, for the curator, equally necessary. One simply hopes that the audience is interested enough in art to pay attention to the art rather than to the superficial framework within which the art is presented. It should also be added that the artists in this show are of no single ideological persuasion. Some are feminists, some are not. All are artists. Their ages, backgrounds, even nationalities range too broadly to succumb to generalization.

The kind of work included here has, for better or worse, been labeled "conceptual art", that is, art in which the idea is paramount, in which permanence, formal or decorative values, are secondary if of any concern at all. The first two shows in this series also included sculpture, earthworks and a few "paintings"; the third show, like this one, included only "conceptual artists" working with written, photographic, or taped material, none of whom was in the first two shows; this fourth show includes only women artists, by way of an exasperated reply on my own part to those who say "there are no women making conceptual art". For the record, there are a great many more than could be exhibited here.

C. 7,500

AN EXHIBITION ORGANIZED BY LUCY R. LIPPARD
AT

The California Institute of the Arts, Valencia, California

The Wadsworth Atheneum, Hartford, Connecticut

Moore College of Art, Philadelphia, Pennsylvania

The Institute of Contemporary Art, Boston, Massachusetts

Walker Art Center, Minneapolis, Minnesota

Smith College Museum of Art, Northampton, Massachusetts

May 1973 - February 1974

<u>Participating Artists</u>

Renate Altenrath	Suzanne Kuffler
Laurie Anderson	Pat Lasch
Eleanor Antin	Bernadette Mayer
Jacki Apple	Christiane Möbus
Alice Aycock	Rita Myers
Jennifer Bartlett	Renee Nahum
Hanne Darboven	N.E.ThingCo. Ltd.
Agnes Denes	Ulrike Nolden
Doree Dunlap	Adrian Piper
Nancy Holt	Judith Stein
Poppy Johnson	Athena Tacha
Nancy Kitchel	Mierle Ukeles
Christine Kozlov	Martha Wilson

The demand for access by historically peripheral social groups occurred in tandem with the extension of art into peripheral media—photography (in the work of Dan Graham, Hans Haacke, and Allan Sekula), film, and video (Martha Rosler [fig. 55]). The '60s was a period of great vitality for avant-garde film and, at the end of the decade, a new paradigm was created with the emergence of structural film, which itself derived from the combined influence of minimalism, serial art, Duchamp, Warhol, and Fluxus. While conceptual art and structural film are rarely connected by critics or historians, it is clear that they were in fact closely related. They can be seen, in effect, as two sides of the same coin. The apparent division between them simply reflects the two different discourses inhabited by historians of art and film, each approaching their own field of expertise without taking the other into account. In fact, like Duchamp, Warhol, and the makers of fluxfilms, many experimental filmmakers also made gallery art. The work of Michael Snow (fig. 57) and Joyce Wieland (fig. 56), for example, can be seen as positioned within the paradigm of conceptual art as logically as within that of structural film. Hollis Frampton's *Zorns Lemma* (1970; fig. 58) brought together influences from the art world—especially Frank Stella and Carl Andre, who were both close friends of Frampton—with an interest in language, serialism, a mathematically based systematicity, and conceptual photography.

Frampton's xerograph series, *Reasonable Facsimiles* (1971), was an archetypal conceptual work, a set of authentications, cancellations, lists, and propositions on the subject of art. *Zorns Lemma* is based on an axiom of set theory which proposes that, given a set of sets, there is a further set composed of a representative item from each set. The structuring set of sets in the film consists of twenty-four repetitions of a twenty-four-letter alphabet. At first each letter is represented by a "found" photographed word with the appropriate initial letter, presented in alphabetical order. Each set of words is then systematically replaced by a set of fragments of a filmed scene or activity, according to an underlying protocol, as in a LeWitt floor or wall piece. Another conceptual artist, Robert Huot (fig. 187), a former minimalist who made invisible and therefore unsalable works as a protest against the art market, appears in the film as a painter painting a wall within a fixed time span. Structural film involved an investigation of the conditions of possibility of film itself, in the same way that conceptual art saw itself as an investigation of the conditions of possibility of visual art. Somewhat later and in another vein, Theresa Hak Kyung Cha (fig. 59) used language as a crucial component of her video work in order to investigate her own paradoxical place within American culture.

The original focus on the semiotics of visual representation, central to the development of conceptual art but also pursued with great depth and seriousness by artists such as Shusaku Arakawa and Agnes Denes, gave way, as we have seen, to a much broader redefinition of art as a social construct. Just as it decentered the traditional aesthetics and semantics of visual representation, conceptual art also decentered New York itself from its hegemonic position in the global art world. Among the early shows, Lucy Lippard's exhibitions in Seattle and Vancouver (and later Buenos Aires) deliberately set out to shift the art world's center of gravity. Canadian artists such as Carole Condé and Karl Beveridge (fig. 160), Les Levine, Vincent Trasov (Mr. Peanut [fig. 216], and those involved in collaborative groups such as N. E. Thing Company and General Idea, played an important role in the history of conceptual art. San Francisco opened its own Museum of Conceptual Art and there were centers also in Los Angeles (Michael Asher, John Baldessari) and San Diego (Martha Rosler, Allan Sekula), where conceptual art blended with the political influence of Herbert Marcuse. Conceptual art had a significant impact in challenging the geographical as well as ethnic and gender hierarchy of core and periphery in the art world. Decentralization, I believe, was the direct effect of the crisis of modernism which, due to its close links with the art market and museum culture, had traditionally played a strongly centralizing role.

Conceptual art provided a timely vehicle for artists determined to break down the elite world of modernism. As a result of this ongoing process of democratization, the historic role of conceptual art cannot be understood simply by rehearsing the early work of its avant-garde pioneers. It very rapidly burst its Lower Manhattan bounds and became the site of an extremely complex and dynamic movement, with far-reaching implications geographically, politically, and semiologically. It was as if the initial New York cohort created a crack in a dam that eventually broke and released a flood of innovative new art. We are still trying to grasp what happened, to chart its sudden eddies, its deviant surges, its confusing cross-currents. During the 1960s, the flow of information within North America and around the world increased dramatically as a result of cheaper international air travel and improved communication networks. Consequently, the picture that emerges, taken as an ensemble, is that of a complex movement with very different roots—in Europe, in Japan, in North America—which branched out with the second generation in new and exciting directions. "Pure" conceptualism soon shattered on the jagged rocks of theory and politics, driving Kosuth into a different camp from LeWitt and setting Art & Language, Burgin, and Haacke on a different track from both of them. Conceptual art cannot and should not be compressed into a movement with an unproblematic origin and a single master trajectory. In reality, it quickly broke out of what Mel Bochner already in 1968 was calling its "solipsism."

For Claude Gintz's exhibition, *L'art conceptuel, une perspective* (1989), the Los Angeles conceptual artist Michael Asher submitted a text arguing that the exhibition was

> as much a view of Conceptual Art as it is a perspective of the institutions used for the maintenance and historical reproduction of that practice. What are the forces and conditions driving the historical analysis which are beyond conceptual art practice's own definition of its historical context and production procedures? Historical objectification ought to be accelerated while there is still a collective experience and memory which can assist in the clarity of an analysis, simultaneously opening up a space to ask fundamental questions about history making.[10]

This new exhibition gives us an opportunity both to ask these fundamental questions and to introduce new perspectives. The persistent influence of conceptual art is still far from exhausted. It retains the potential to surprise us. Conceptual art, seen as a historic avant-garde, may now be dead but global conceptualism, as a broad movement embracing installation, video, film, sound tape, performance, and text, continues to flourish. It offers us the possibility of making and responding to a form of art that has proved resistant to the powerful forces of homogeneity which have come inevitably with economic and cultural globalization.

Notes

1. David Batchelor, *Minimalism* (London: Tate Gallery, 1997).

2. Victor Burgin, interviewed by John Roberts, *The Impossible Document: Photography and Conceptual Art in Britain, 1966–1976* (London: Camerawork, 1997).

3. Germano Celant, *Arte Povera: Earthworks, Impossible Art, Actual Art, Conceptual Art* (New York: Praeger, 1969); Gillo Dorfles, "Arte concettuale o arte povera?" *Art International* 13, no. 3 (March 1969): 35–38; *Konzeption-Conception: Dokumentation einer heutigen Kunstrichtung/Documentation of Today's Art Tendency* (Leverkusen: Städtisches Museum, 1969); Catherine Millet, "L'art conceptuel," *Opus International* (Paris), no. 15 (December 1969): 20–23; *When Attitudes Become Form: Works, Concepts, Processes, Situations, Information: Live in Your Head*, ed. Harald Szeemann (Berne: Kunsthalle, 1969).

4. Published in Joseph Kosuth, *Art After Philosophy and After: Collected Writings, 1966–1990*, ed. Gabriele Guercio (Cambridge, Mass.: MIT Press, 1991).

5. Joseph Kosuth, "1975," *The Fox*, no. 2 (1975): 87–96.

6. Joseph Kosuth, *Within the Context: Modernism and Critical Practice* (Ghent: Coupure, 1977).

7. Joseph Kosuth, "No Exit," *Artforum* 26 (March 1988): 112–15.

8. Mary Kelly interviewed by Terence Maloon, *Artscribe* 13 (August 1978).

9. Burgin in Roberts, *The Impossible Document*.

10. Claude Gintz et al., *L'art conceptuel, une perspective* (Paris: Musée d'Art Moderne de la Ville de Paris, 1989), 112.

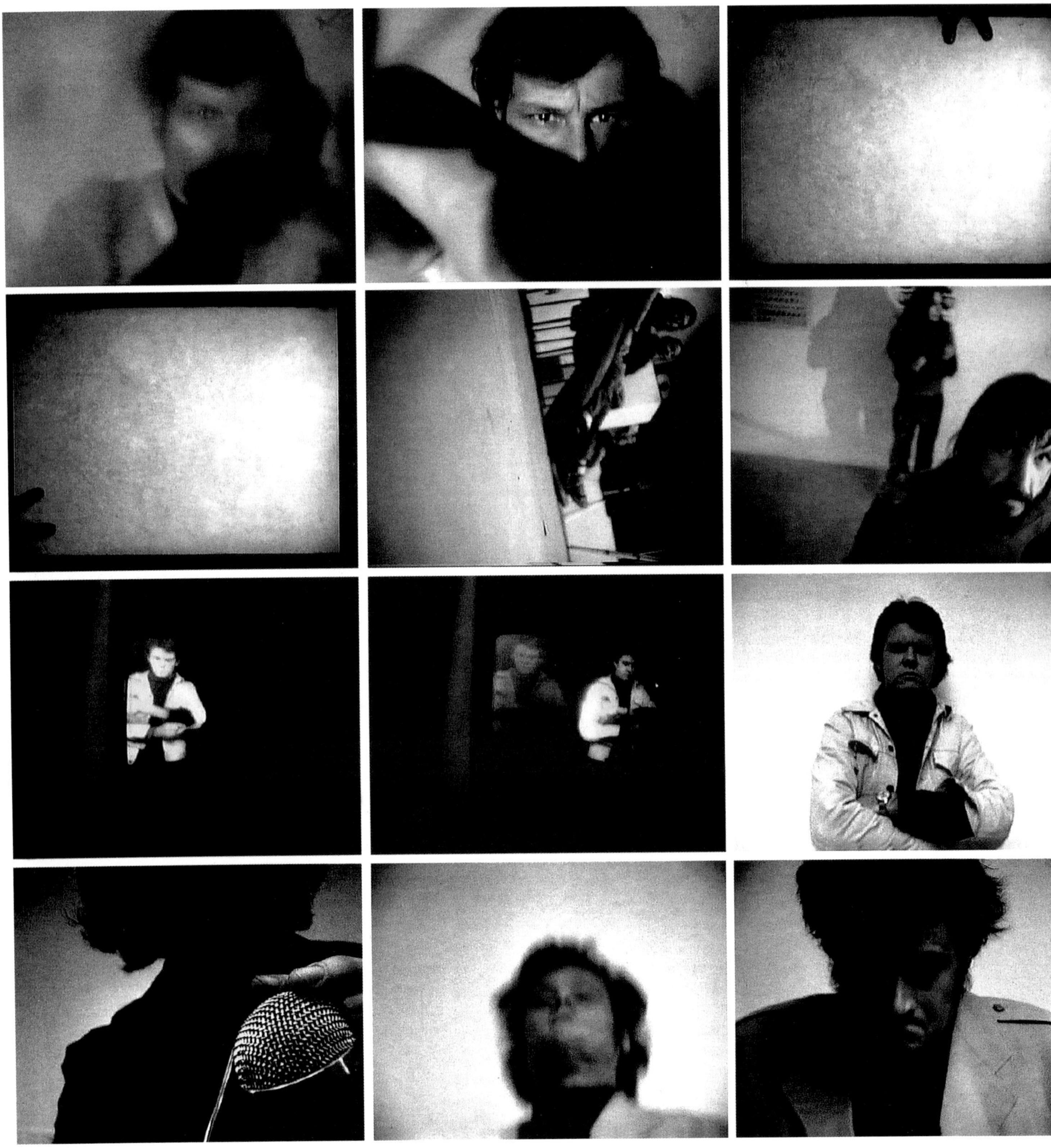

Peripheries in Motion: Conceptualism and Conceptual Art in Australia and New Zealand

Terry Smith

The presumption that there was a single metropolitan center of invention, out from which artistic innovation spread as a style to be adopted by provincial art worlds, is being tested by this entire exhibition. I believe it will show that, on the contrary, there was a roughly simultaneous emergence in a number of art centers and art communities around the world of a conceptual questioning of the nature of art. In every case, but differently, these seem to have been set against both generalizing notions of art, and modernism perceived as an orthodox, international art discourse. Artists such as Terry Atkinson, Michael Baldwin and others in Coventry, Ian Burn and Mel Ramsden in Melbourne, were responding to certain developments in avant-garde art, especially in New York and particularly the antiform aspect of minimalism. The crucial distinction here may be that they did not reproduce a local version of minimalism but used some of its less mainstream aspects to question art itself.

One of the original conditions of mid-1960s conceptualism is that it was produced in cities such as London and New York by artists such as Ian Burn from Melbourne and Billy Apple from Auckland, that is, by individuals striving to define an art practice distinctive for travelers between the peripheries and centers of cultural power. Much art of this period came out of a suitcase, or could be made on the spot by people in transit. Regions such as the southern Pacific are also important in that they exemplify another worldwide phenomenon: the impact of conceptualism—especially as it became institutionalized as Conceptual Art—on younger artists in local art worlds tied to metropolitan centers. International in form, their work was local in content. This moment still marks out advanced art in the region and, as such, has been subject to commentary by certain Aboriginal artists.

Context

Since the settlement of Terra Australis and New Zealand by British colonists in the late 18th century, the fundamentals and outer boundaries of art practice have been set by commitments to certain subjects (above all landscape), to specific media (especially painting), and to Romantic, self-expressive conceptions of what it is to be an artist. Western European visual forms and institutions dominated national cultural agendas, tying settler and immigrant artists to a framework of provincial dependence on metropolitan centers, especially London. Indigenous visual cultures were posited as exotic others and as generalized emblemata.

All of this began to unravel in the 1960s: popular and high art from the United States assumed cultural leadership, but this prerogative was soon contested at home, in the colonies, and around the world. At the height of its internationalizing reach, U.S. definitions of art—including the institutionalized modernism that was its most advanced form—underwent a crisis of legitimacy. At the same time, following their own imperatives, Aborigines in Australia and Maoris in New Zealand began to assert their cultural singularity, political independence, and historical

Figure 61.
Mike Parr and Peter Kennedy, *Idea Demonstrations,* 1972, 16mm film, 40 min., black and white and color, optical sound. Collection of the artists.

precedence. Coincidentally, travel by artists back and forth on the colonial circuits, and laterally to other cultural formations, increased markedly, as did the circulation of information about what was happening in art all over the world.[1]

The conceptual "moment" in the art of Australia and New Zealand occurred in the context of these world changes, and was much marked by them. It took, however, quite specific structural forms, three of which I detail here.

1. The idea of the avant-garde emerged, arguably for the first time in the history of Australian and New Zealand art, as the leading model for innovative artmaking. Pop tendencies—themselves relatively weak compared to those in the U.S., Britain, and parts of Europe—had produced little in the way of coolly reflexive art. The junk assemblages of the Annandale Imitation Realists celebrated instinctive gatherings of nonart material, especially in the work of Colin Lanceley and Mike Brown. The third member, Ross Crothall, did produce a few works that might count as proto-conceptual. These include his cigarette abstractions, in which actual cigarettes are arrayed in op art formats on hardboard. This group—two New Zealanders and an Australian—came together in 1961–62 for two exhibitions in Melbourne and Sydney, then disbanded after less than a year.[2]

The hard-edge painters and sculptors who gathered around Central Street Gallery in Sydney from 1966—Tony McGillick, Michael Johnson, David Aspden, and others—were an institutionalizing avant-garde in that they subscribed totally to a formalist internationalism. The early conceptualism of Burn and Apple was occurring elsewhere. Whereas the conceptual, process, and performance artists who formed Inhibodress in Sydney in 1970—for instance, Peter Kennedy, Mike Parr, Tim Johnson—were an open, dematerializing avant-garde.[3] All of these developments were driven by a very specific notion of the avant-garde: the belief that, while high-profile recognition, financial success, and cultural power were evidently concentrated in the art capitals of the world, something more important and far-reaching could be achieved by artists at the margins. The nature of art itself could be transformed as a result of the efforts of a group of artists working consciously together, and this could occur in Australia, New Zealand, anywhere. The core impulse of avant-gardism was not, many artists believed, compatible with money and power, particularly not within the nexus of the military-industrial-commercial complex and the culture of high modernism.[4] Art could be rethought in one's head, with the least resources. Look at the dadaists, at Tatlin's productivists!

The idea that art work could be—indeed, *must* be—conceptual work on the concept of art had profoundly disruptive effects on art practice in Australia and New Zealand during the later 1960s. To make art that itself raises this issue is to create *theoretical objects or events*. This was done, in the mid-'60s, by a very small number of Australian and New Zealand artists in transit.

2. There is no simple shift from object- to idea-based art, anywhere in the world. To define conceptualism in such a way is to descend into banality. On the contrary, the first "step" taken by any art that deserves the name *conceptual* was to make objects—artworks—that threw perception into doubt. In the Australian case, this was expressed at the level of style as an interrogation of minimal painting (including op and hard edge), and of painted metal sculpture (together seen as formalism). This is an originary moment for conceptual art as a whole, one of many that happened spontaneously in a number of places around the world during this time. It occurred in 1966 in London, the traditional place for the continuing education of graduating Australian and New Zealand art students of ambition. Fresh from the National Gallery School in Melbourne, Ian Burn (an Australian) continued his working relationship with the English artist Mel Ramsden, who had just returned from a visit to Australia where he had studied briefly at the same school.

The step to be taken, particularly in the Australian case, was beyond an expanded kind of minimalism, itself the dominant international and local art of the moment among experimental artists. This was not an instant

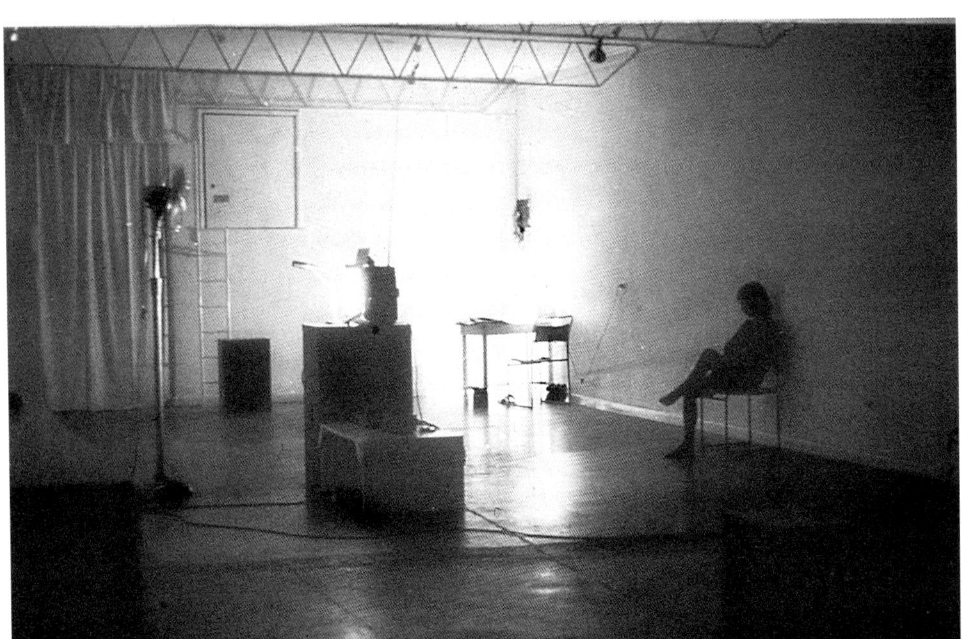

FIGURE 62.
Peter Kennedy, *But the Fierce Blackman*, 1972, sound performance, Inhibodress Gallery, Sydney.

overturning, but a *supplement,* a rendering radically provisional of the host. In New Zealand, there was a greater orientation toward installation and especially performance work in its conceptual currents, reflecting the influential examples of Billy Apple, Jim Allen, Bruce Barber, and others.

3. Conceptualism was one of the defining elements of the shift within the region from a locally focused to internationalist, specifically late modernist, orientation toward art practice. To make art that situates itself in relation to this relationship is to make *strategic objects or events.*

This, too, was done by very few artists during the mid-1960s. But it became a widespread practice throughout the region in the years around 1970. Older artists were deeply disturbed by this trend, yet younger artists flocked to its possibilities in droves. For them, strategic conceptualism was one option among others offered by the proliferation of practices around 1970. Not a choice among new styles—as things must have appeared to younger artists around 1910—but a choice of antistylistic actions. Ironically, at the very same moment, conceptualism was being defined into a style: conceptual art. The time lags of the international art circuit meant that younger artists based in Australia and New Zealand were confronted with both at once: conceptualism and conceptual art. Most chose to try out the new style, but the substantial artists among them saw that conceptualism demanded a new practice.

I will now explore each of these steps in turn.

Early Conceptualism

Barrie Bates won the National Gallery of New Zealand Traveling Scholarship in 1959 and attended the Royal College of Art in London for the next three years. This school was the site of the invention of British pop, then experiencing a burst of popular and art world attention.[5] His major focus was graphic art—indeed, advertising was how he made his living—but in 1960 he began to be interested in the idea

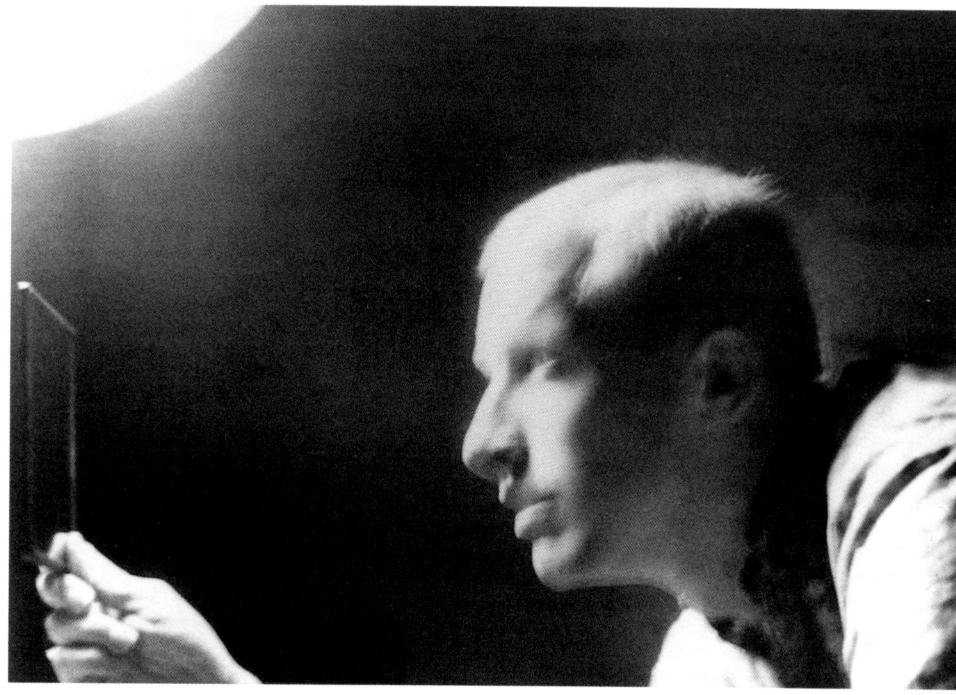

Figure 63.
Billy Apple, *Bleaching with Lady Clairol Instant Creme Whip,* 1962, photographic postcard. Collection of the artist.

that everyday activities such as shaving, bathing, even squeezing pimples might be art activities worth recording as such in photographic sequences. This threw into sharp relief the artificial nature of not only the art objects he was making, but the art system itself. A regular choice for the important survey exhibition Young Contemporaries, he turned the tables in 1962 by entering a painting entitled *Young Contemporaries 1962* (1961; fig. 162), consisting entirely of an enlarged version of the entry blank for the exhibition itself. Bates then took a step taken by few other conceptualists. In his own words:

> In London in 1961 I began an extended work which was part of my effort to break down the separation between "life activity" and "art activity." I decided to use my own identity as a vehicle with which to explore the concept of the artist as an "art object." This began by changing my name (identification) and my physical appearance. Recreating myself became the art work. I relinquished my given name Barrie George Bates and chose the name Billy Apple to replace it. Then I assumed a new appearance which was Barrie Bates' conception of Billy Apple's image [fig. 63]. At the home of

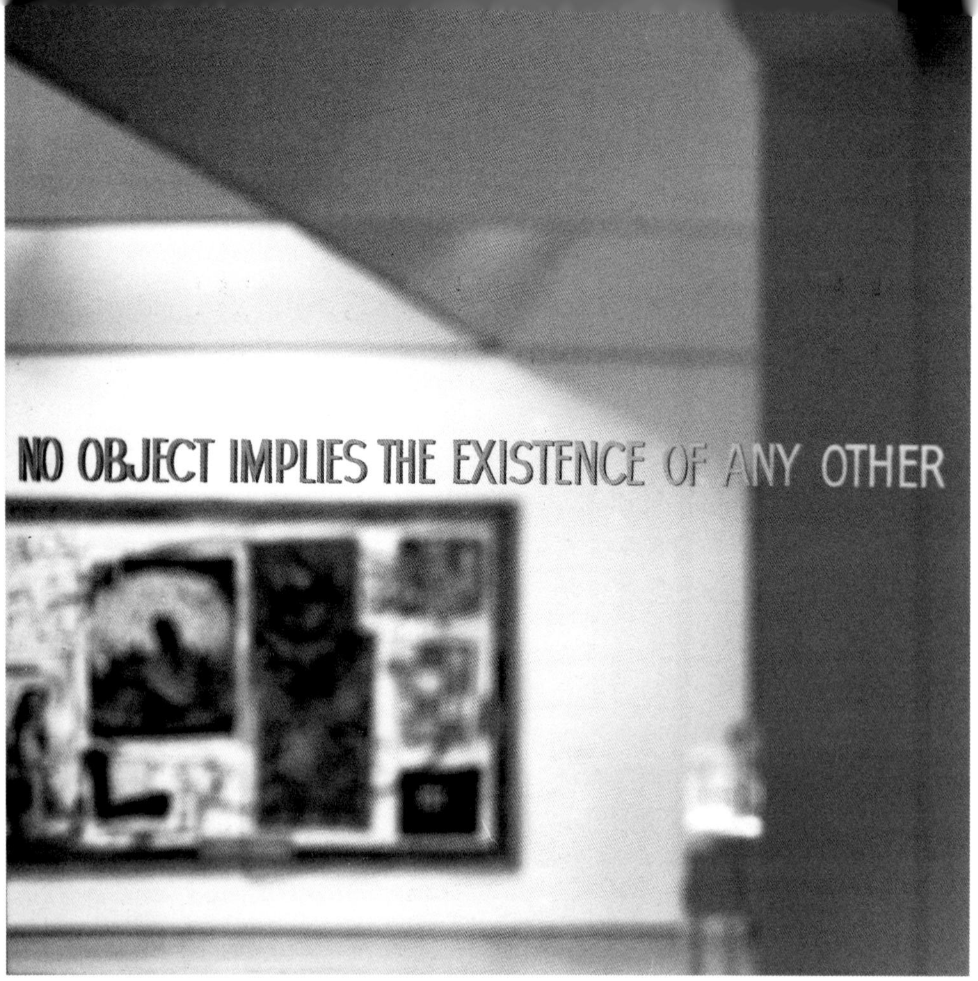

Figure 64.
Ian Burn, *No Object Implies the Existence of Any Other,* 1967, framed mirror, lettering. Collection of the Art Gallery of New South Wales, Sydney.

> Richard Smith, 13 Bath Street, London E.C. 1 in November 1962, I bleached my hair and my eyebrows yellow blonde with Lady Clairol Instant Creme Whip.[6]

In April 1963, Bates/Apple exhibited life-sized versions of his new passport photograph declaring his new identity. During the next few years he created works in various media—including bronze casts of apples and parts of his body, a pseudo-shop that sold "fruit"—punning on both his name and aspects of his identity-in-formation. Under the name Barrie Bates, he continued to show neon pieces in exhibitions in London and New York, where he moved in 1964. In October 1969, Apple opened a noncommercial space at 161 West 23rd Street, regularly showing installation and procedural pieces until it closed in June 1973. These included sweepings of roof dirt, collections of nasal and fecal matter over sustained periods, rubbish gatherings, destructions of glass tubing that were subsequently dispersed outside the city, and a number of actions that involved cleaning up specific spaces. Many other artists in New York and elsewhere were, at this time, also exploring such aspects of everyday life as art.

Ian Burn and Mel Ramsden met at the National Gallery School, Melbourne, in 1964. They both moved to London in 1965 and worked together on a daily basis, as they did after moving to New York in 1967 (their collaboration continued until 1977, when Burn moved to Sydney and Ramsden to England). In 1966 Ramsden made a number of *Untitled* paintings consisting of heavy black enamel surfaces mounted on deep stretchers of various shapes. There is reference here to Frank Stella's canvases of the late 1950s, regarded by many as the ultimate paintings, after which all that remained to painters was comment on this culmination. Ramsden's *Secret Painting* (1967–68), a black square shown alongside a statement to the effect that the work's content is known only to the artist, was part of a series labeled *Non-Visual Art.*

In 1965 Burn moved quickly from eccentric figuration in the manner of Sidney Nolan to color field works in which areas of color were generated by numbers and could be shifted in terms of positioning. He then did a series of "minimal"-style op paintings in which each work was repeated as a "proposition" about what a painting might be, for example, the "six different exactly identical paintings" idea worked out as *Yellow Premiss* (1965). Burn then made a set of large minimal paintings of single colors painted with highly reflective enamels, followed by a series of *Mirror Pieces* (1967–68) in which the sequence of viewing was refracted by variations in the grinding, and thus reflectibility, of the glass. These were soon accompanied by texts, framed and mounted alongside the painting, which discussed the materialities of the spectator's encounter and increasingly its phenomenology, for example, *No Object Implies the Existence of Any Other* (1967; fig. 64).[7]

A little-known work that fully exemplifies this moment is *Soft-Tape* (1966; fig. 164) by Burn and Ramsden. Designed to be installed in a white room entirely empty except for a tape recorder on a white stand, the points raised by the piece were made explicit in a text displayed near the exit:

> Presentation of the work uses a tape-recorder. The sound emitted by the recorder is kept throughout at a monotonous and uniform level which is (as near as possible) at the "zero-point" between understanding the spoken words and indecipherable noise. This is a means of stabilizing and holding directions at a point of "uncertainty"—which sets up the possibility of conflicting directions.
>
> Listening along a relaxed and "normal" sound level, it will appear that the recorded sound is a soft and even blur. This is intentional and any kind of variance (i.e. from the meaning of the words to the effect of the recorded sound) will be due to (i) the physical position of the spectator, or (ii) the amount of attention he is prepared to give. For this reason, other than the recorder mechanism, the display space is kept accessible and approach to the mechanism and its environs free.
>
> Instead of merely reproducing a standard symmetrical content, a framework of tension and possibility is set up between the spectator as receiver and the recorder as transmitter of the information. This is in order that the desired spatial "pattern" be achieved ...
>
> ANY determining decisions a spectator makes while confronting the mechanism are to be considered a part of the intent of the piece.

This is John Cage without the silence, La Monte Young without the sound, Fluxus without the performance, but it is supplementary to all of them, and to minimalism itself as a coalescing style. It was prepared for exhibition at Strines Gallery, Melbourne, a short-lived, avant-garde gallery specializing in presenting visual poems as artworks during the early 1960s. Concrete poetry, a small but active part of the widespread experimental poetry movement in Australia, was a pathway into conceptualism for artists such as Mike Parr.

Soft-Tape was not, in any event, shown in 1966, but the proposal circulated among artists in Australia, and Burn and Ramsden sought other opportunities for its realization, succeeding finally at the Sydney Biennale in 1990. Nevertheless, in this context, it is worth exploring the implications of its initial conceptualization, as this will take us to the heart of a certain emphasis in conceptualism's origins.

What kind of spectator did the two artists imagine? In the words spoken on the tape, they discuss a kind of art exemplified by *Soft-Tape* itself, an art that makes its "ideas" and "entire context" explicit. Since art objects are no longer capable of speaking for themselves, they must include words. Expressionist, sublime, heroic art is "simplistic"—instead, art should be "lucid." Art exists in space, indeed, space is created as the artwork is observed, read, understood. The "active participation" of the spectator, therefore, is highly valued; her behavior as an "auditor" determines the work. This should be done without changing the "tremendous fabric" of "light, space, time, materials, motion" that currently constitutes the world.

Shortly after the making of *Soft-Tape,* New York artist Lawrence Weiner called for a cessation of objectmaking. In the aims and intentions expressed by Burn, Ramsden, and Weiner, there is a formidable challenge for art: to be about everything, but to be nothing in itself. This goes way beyond minimalism as a style, which even in its most radical forms remained a seductive reduction of previous sculpture. Nonintervention applied to the spectator as well. Is this the modernist spectator—much theorized in recent times by Jonathan Crary, Martin Jay, et al.—as the Cartesian Observer, the optical perceiver who sees the world in its entirety, who acts as a pure observing machine, that is, without changing the world in the process and without being changed in the process?[8]

In the stark directness with which it enacts the effort to understand pure spectatorship-in-process, *Soft-Tape* is a striking instance of conceptualism's concern with interrogating the

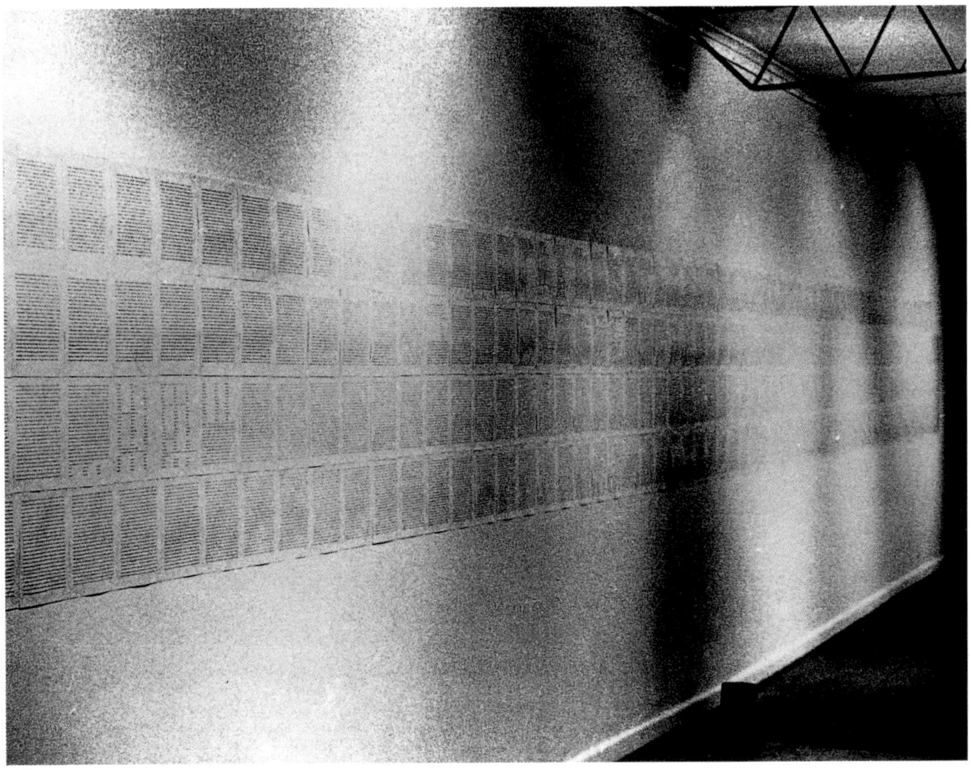

Figure 65.
Mike Parr, *Wall Definition,* 1971, 254 A4 typed pages. Collection of the artist.

relations between a perceiving subject and a perceived object. The words spoken on the tape itself, and the many notes written by Burn and Ramsden during October and November 1966 as they worked on the piece, demonstrate their acute awareness of these issues and how subtly they thought about them. It is obvious that they were fascinated with the idea of the imaginary spectator creating space by moving through time in the schematic room. In retrospect, another reading might be that *Soft-Tape* embodies the incommensurability at the base of cultural difference, that is, the great difficulties of understanding between cultures—in this case, art worlds. Hidden here is the germ of an idea that was to flower in the 1975 Art & Language exhibitions held in Melbourne and Adelaide (but not in Sydney).[9]

There are parallels here to events at the Coventry School of Art in 1965, where Michael Baldwin, working with Terry Atkinson, made a number of works consisting of mirrors mounted flush on stretchers, themselves wrapped in white canvas. Called *Untitled Paintings,* one was over life-size in height, very deep in frame, and installed hard up against a wall in the corner of a room. Another consisted of a set of four paintings installed at usual viewing height on a wall. Meanwhile, in New York, Joseph Kosuth was seeking ways of interrogating minimalism's implications in a number of well-known works. This kind of shared background reinforced the collaboration between artists in the Art & Language group from 1969 onward for a number of years.[10] Burn and Ramsden continued to make art about the conditions of observation; by 1968, their work increasingly took the form of statements about these conditions, and then statements about the conditions of making these statements. This moves into what I would characterize as second-phase conceptualism. Works such as *Six Negatives* (1968–69) are entirely language-based. In 1969 Burn and Ramsden, with English artist Roger Cutforth, established the Society for Theoretical Art and Analyses. Later that year they began to contribute to *Art-Language,* the "journal of conceptual art" produced by the British-based Art & Language group, which they joined formally in 1971. Richard Dunn, another Australian who traveled through minimal painting and installations, arrived—during his expatriate time—at similar works, for example, *The Art.Act* (1969).[11]

Around 1970: Rupture and Nexus

As conceptualism increased in intensity and diversity during the later 1960s and early '70s, and as it became an evident international style, it affected one practicing generation of Australian avant-garde painters and sculptors as a massively debilitating force while at the same time liberating another. Accomplished and subtle minimal painters such as Robert Jacks, Dale Hickey, Robert Hunter, and Paul Partos—all of whom went to New York during the moment of conceptualism's greatest impact—were traumatized. Their return to Melbourne in the mid-'70s meant an extremely tentative return to painting, one that only very slowly recovered its strength.[12]

In contrast, a younger generation of Australian and New Zealand artists responded positively to magazine-circulated information about the range of conceptual art, arte povera, performance, land art, earthworks, installation art, etc. being made around the world at the time. *Studio International* was influential in the region, as was an essay by Ian Burn, "Conceptual Art as Art," published in the standard journal *Art and Australia* in September 1970. In Sydney, critic Donald Brook actively promoted what he called "post-object art," while in New Zealand, writer Wystan Curnow argued strongly for the "new art."[13] This mix engendered an array of conceptual practices that quickly came to lead artmaking in the region in the early 1970s.

One tendency was language-based work such as Mike Parr's *Wall Definition* (1971; fig. 65), consisting of 254 quarto pages on which the Oxford English dictionary definition of the word *wall* was typed out again and again. Work on this project led Parr to recognize the implications of autism as a metaphor for the limitations of self-knowledge.[14] But despite the prominence of language in the art of the region—including the citation of ritual song

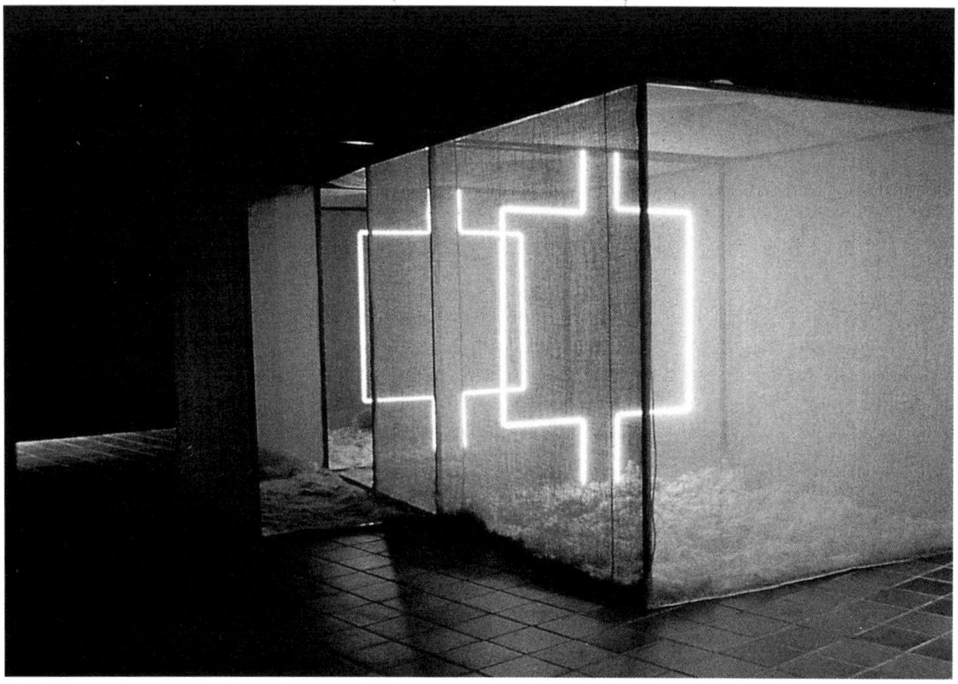

Figure 66.
Jim Allen, *New Zealand Environment No. 5,* 1969, scrim, steel tube, greasy wool, sawdust, underfelt, barbed wire, neon. Govett-Brewster Gallery, New Plymouth, N.Z.

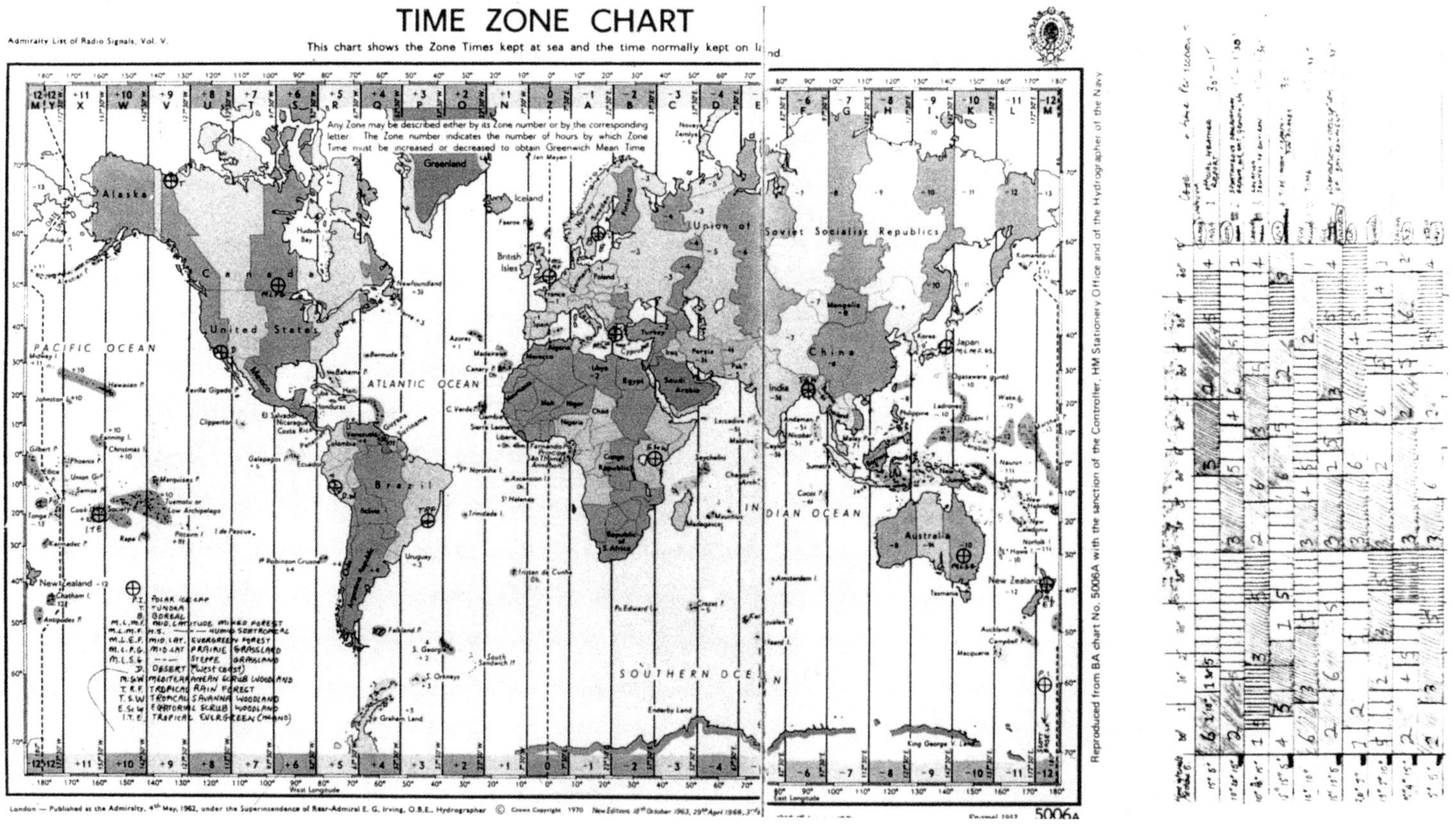

Figure 67.
Philip Dadson, *Earthworks—Timezone Map of the World, Timezone Chart,* 1971, color map mounted on stiff board. Collection of the artist.

and sign in the work of Maori artists—it was seldom used by New Zealand conceptualists as the form of the work. One rare example is Nicholas Spill's series of images of milk spilling through words such as *milk,* obviously punning on his own name.

Funky, ironic, parodic approaches to conceptual issues are another distinctive local tendency in these years. *Walk Along This Line* (1971) by Ian Milliss consisted of a strip of masking tape laid so close to a wall that anyone following the instruction would fall over. Aleks Danko's *Auto Realism* (1971), a mirror piece with its title engraved in the glass, framed the viewer's reflected face. Robert Rooney carefully photographed his folded clothes laid out on his bed each night for over three months in *Garments: 3 December 1972 to 19 March 1973,* one of a series of studies on suburban rituals.

A third major tendency was the tracing of processes as they applied to bodies, objects, and spaces. A pathbreaking example in New Zealand was Jim Allen's *New Zealand Environment No. 5* (1969; fig. 66), a sequence of rooms in which the unalloyed experience of various textures—including steel, greasy wool, sawdust, underfelt, and barbed wire—was possible for the person seeking "pure" tactility. In the virtual absence of emphasis on visuality, there is a strange parallel here to the auditory emphasis of *Soft-Tape*. The artist-run Inhibodress Gallery in Sydney was a center for experimental art that tested the limits of both communication and audience empathy in works setting propositions against bodies, objects, spaces. Founders Peter Kennedy and Mike Parr performed many actions under the heading *Trans Art,* particularly those exploring extremes of pain. These are recorded in the 1972 film by Aggy Read and Ian Stocks, *Idea Demonstrations* (figs. 61, 163). Also at Inhibodress, Tim Johnson displayed the photographic record of voyeuristic actions conducted in public, entitled *Disclosures* (1972).[15]

Sound as a delineator of space interested Peter Kennedy in pieces such as *But the Fierce Blackman* (1972; fig. 62), in which the phrase "But the fierce blackman ..." was repeated and played at varying levels through speakers set out in a staged location in the gallery. Philip Dadson worked in Cornelius Cardew's Scratch Orchestra in London in 1968, and founded the New Zealand Scratch Orchestra in 1970, an offshoot of which—From Scratch—still performs today. At 1800 hours Greenwich Mean Time on September 23 and 24, 1971, fifteen groups of people at Dadson's behest recorded the circumstances of that exact moment in fifteen locations around the world. This was his *Earthworks,* existing now as a photographic map and film record (fig. 67).

Mid-1970s

Conceptual practices all over the world turned—or, in many cases, returned—to socially embedded work in the early 1970s. This was, in part, a reaction against conceptualism becoming conceptual art. It was also a result of the dire social and political situation in most countries during the late 1960s, which could no longer be acknowledged by an equivalent or indirect artistic radicalism. Australian conceptualism was slow to respond for quite local reasons: in 1972 the Labor Party became the federal government for the first time in nearly twenty years, and along with its radical social agenda came a liberatory and internationalizing cultural policy, including the establishment of significant support for experimental art. The Labor government was dismissed from office by the Queen's representative in 1975, and the instantly intensified political climate prompted some activity among conceptual artists, for example, the Provisional Art & Language exhibitions in Melbourne, Adelaide, and Auckland in 1975–76, which addressed questions of provincialism and cultural imperialism in provocative ways. Two were closed by state governments.[16]

Another relevant development of the mid-'70s was the emergence of isolated rereadings of key currents of early avant-garde modernism. These include Imants Tillers's *Moments of Inertia* (1972–73), John Nixon's *Self-Portrait (Non-Objective Composition)* series (begun 1975), and Peter Tyndall's *detail: A Person Looks At A Work Of Art/someone looks at something* series (begun 1974). Tyndall's work returns the gaze of the Cartesian spectator by showing every viewer an impossibly generalized, humorously reduced figure of him- or herself. The specifically local take of these projects is their parodic exaggeration of the fact that provincial art cultures learn their structures of belief and their visual repertoires from reproduced images and ideas that have originated elsewhere. And then they strive to turn this adopted currency into an expressive practice.

Legacies

"Postconceptual painting" is a term that I have used to designate the main tendency in Australian art during the 1980s. Its most prominent practitioners include Juan Davila, Mike Parr, Imants Tillers, and Susan Norrie. They are all artists whose medium may be painting of one kind or another but whose content concerns the most important questions of identity and alterity, and whose aesthetic is one which makes perception itself a complex provisionality.[17]

Since the early 1970s, indigenous artists have developed and sustained an art movement matching postconceptualism as the other main current in Australian art. While Aboriginal artists living in traditional communities have shown little interest in conceptual art, certain artists of Aboriginal background whose experience has been formed in predominantly nonindigenous settings (including art schools much concerned with postmodernism) have drawn on conceptualism in striking ways. Gordon Bennett's six-panel piece *Untitled* (1989; fig. 165) uses a string of nominations typical of propositional conceptual art to underscore the impact on his people of European possession of Terra Australis.[18] Conceptual procedures also resonate in the work of Tracey Moffatt, Destiny Deacon, Fiona Foley, and others. Maori artists seem not to have drawn on the conceptual-minimal legacy to quite the same extent.

During the 1990s, a further generation of younger artists, responding in part to the above developments and to Metro Pictures–type neoconceptualism, have developed a wide-ranging and subtle array of conceptual-minimal work.[19] They are part of the conceptual-minimal nexus forged in the years around 1970, the legacy of which still shapes advanced art in Australia and New Zealand today.

Notes

1. General texts include: Bernard Smith, with Terry Smith, *Australian Painting, 1788 to 1990* (Melbourne: Oxford University Press, 1991); Christopher Allen, *Art in Australia* (London: Thames & Hudson, 1997); Gil Docking, *Two Hundred Years of New Zealand Painting,* 2d ed. (Glenfield: Bateman, 1990); Anne Kirker, *New Zealand Women Artists: A Survey of 150 Years* (Tortola: Craftsman House, 1993).

2. See Margaret Plant, *Irreverent Sculpture* (Melbourne: Monash University Art Gallery, 1985), and the entry "Annandale Imitation Realists," in *Dictionary of Art,* vol. 2, ed. Jane Turner (London: Macmillan, 1996), 120.

3. See Smith with Smith, *Australian Painting,* ch. 13, for Central Street; and Sue Cramer, *Inhibodress* (Brisbane: Museum of Modern Art, 1989).

4. This is explored in the Australian context in my interview with Jelena Stojanovic, "Conceptual Art Then and Since," *Agenda Contemporary Art Magazine,* no. 26 (November–December 1992), no. 27 (January–February 1993), supplement.

5. See the essay by Lawrence Alloway in Lucy Lippard, *Pop Art* (New York: Praeger, 1966).

6. Quoted in Arts Council of Great Britain, *From Barrie Bates to Billy Apple, 1960–1974* (London: Serpentine Gallery, 1974), 11. It is notable that David Hockney (like Andy Warhol) presented himself at this time with bleached hair, but not himself as a work of art.

7. Ian Burn, *Minimal-Conceptual Work, 1965–1970* (Perth: Art Gallery of Western Australia, 1992).

8. Jonathan Crary, *Techniques of the Observer* (Cambridge, Mass.: MIT Press, 1990); Martin Jay, *Downcast Eyes* (Berkeley: University of California Press, 1994).

9. Terry Smith, ed., *Art & Language: Australia 1975* (Banbury, Sydney, and New York: Art & Language Press, 1975).

10. See Charles Harrison, *Essays in Art and Language* (Oxford: Blackwell, 1991).

11. See *Richard Dunn: The Dialectical Image—Selected Work, 1964–1992* (Sydney: Art Gallery of New South Wales, 1992).

12. Smith with Smith, *Australian Painting,* ch. 14.

13. Donald Brook, "Flight from the Object," in *Concerning Contemporary Art,* ed. Bernard Smith (Oxford: Clarendon Press, 1975). See also Terry Smith and Paul McGillick, *The Situation Now: Object or Post-Object Art?* (Sydney: Contemporary Art Society, 1971), and Jim Allen and Wystan Curnow, *New Art: Some Recent New Zealand Sculpture and Post-Object Art* (Auckland: Heinemann, 1976).

14. See David Bromfield, *Identities: A Critical Study of the Works of Mike Parr, 1970–1990* (Nedlands: University of Western Australia Press, 1991).

15. See Cramer, *Inhibodress;* Anne Marsh, *Body and Self: Performance Art in Australia, 1969–1992* (Melbourne: Oxford University Press, 1993).

16. See Terry Smith, "The Tasks of Translation: Art & Language in Australia and New Zealand, 1975–76," in *Now See Hear! Art, Language, and Translation,* ed. Ian Wedde and Gregory Burke (Wellington: Victoria University Press, 1990).

17. Smith with Smith, *Australian Painting,* ch. 16.

18. Ian McLean, *The Art of Gordon Bennett* (Roseville East: Craftsman House, 1996).

19. See T. Smith, "Conceptual Art Then and Since," and Charles Green, *Peripheral Vision: Contemporary Australian Art, 1970–1994* (Roseville East: Craftsman House, 1995).

Circa 1973 through late 1980s

Soviet Union

Africa

South Korea

Mainland China, Taiwan, and Hong Kong

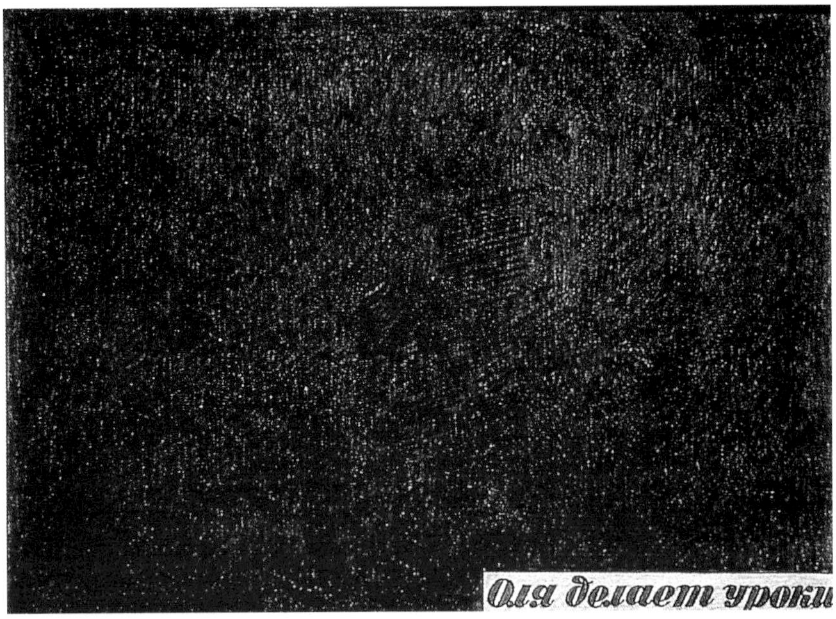
Оля делает уроки

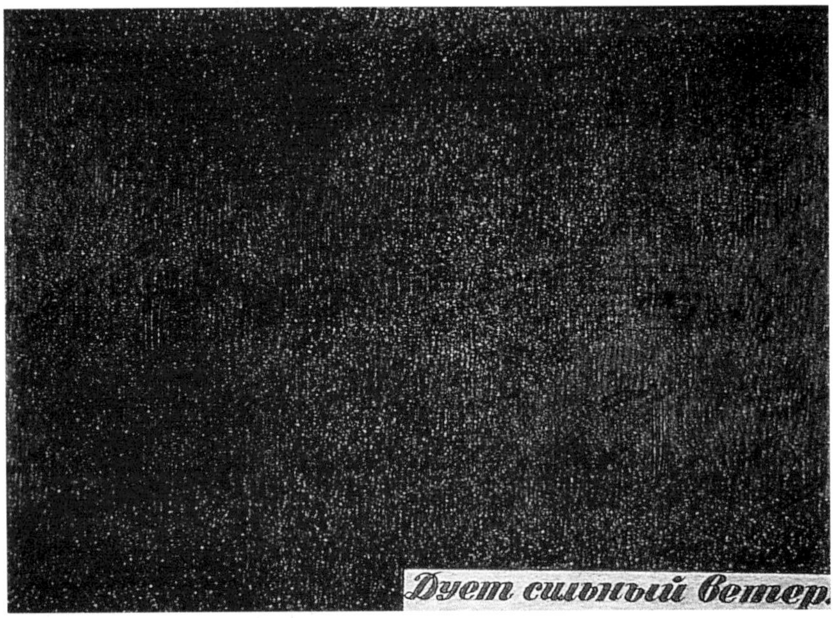
Дует сильный ветер.

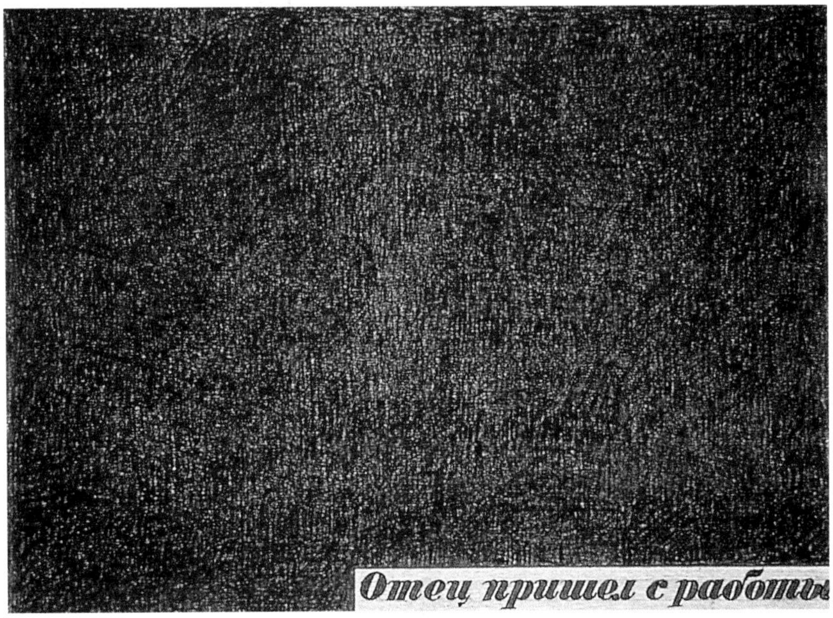
Отец пришел с работы

About Early Soviet Conceptualism

Margarita Tupitsyn

More than a decade after the appearance of Soviet dissident modernism in the late 1950s, Moscow artists Ilya Kabakov, Vitaly Komar, and Aleksandr Melamid formulated the local version of conceptual art.[1] Dissident modernists, who were the first generation of the "unofficial" art movement, originated the practical and theoretical opposition to socialist realism, the official style which held a cultural monopoly from the mid-1930s to *perestroika*. The presence of this powerful adversary unified the modernists, although their creative aspirations shared little common ground. In contrast to the one-dimensional nature of the modernists' opposition, the conceptualists Kabakov, Komar, and Melamid—who also belonged to the milieu of alternative culture—performed a dual role in resistance. First, they deviated from the modernist canons of Soviet alternative art by denying painting's privileged status and introducing elements of Soviet kitsch into their works. Second, they—particularly Komar and Melamid, who worked together as the team K/M—put themselves at odds with the Soviet cultural establishment by deconstructing its visual canons and ideological content. When considering the development of Soviet conceptualism, it is important to keep in mind this dual project of contesting the conventions of both dissident modernism and socialist realism.[2]

Unlike the first generation of alternative artists, which consisted of nonmembers of the Union of Artists, Kabakov belonged to the union's graphics division. He began his career by crystallizing his own modernist model of representation as a challenge to the familiar socialist realist canon. But, again unlike many of his Moscow colleagues, he did not adhere to any specific modernist style. Throughout the 1960s, he rapidly progressed from works that relied on purely visual sensation to those with "literal facts." Kabakov showed his distrust of pure visuality as early as 1967, when he included verbal commentaries about the image in his drawing *The Horse (Loshad')*. Then, in his drawing *Answers of the Experimental Group (Otvety eksperemental'noi gruppy*, 1969), Kabakov took a definite step toward the condition Benjamin Buchloh defined as the "withdrawal of visuality." *Answers* is a simplified rendition of a house with fragments of a landscape on either side, situated between two columns of text that in turn are divided into numbered blocks. Each block is given the name of either a female or male character who answers questions about the drawing. For example, question number 10 is attached to the presentation of a door and is connected to Vladimir Evgen'evich Markov, a "fictional beholder" of Kabakov's work, who confirms that what he sees is indeed a door.[3] In contrast to Western conceptual art, in which the operative strategy—as defined by Charles Harrison—is the "suppression of the beholder," in Soviet alternative art, the prolonged absence of the beholder caused Kabakov to invent and introduce him/her into the artwork itself.

In *Answers,* Kabakov undermined the practice of socialist realist painters who, in their concentration on constructing strict ideological

Figure 68.
Ilya Kabakov, *Primakov Sitting in a Closet (Vskafusidiaschii Primakov)*, 1972, details of album. Collection of Ilya and Emilia Kabakov.

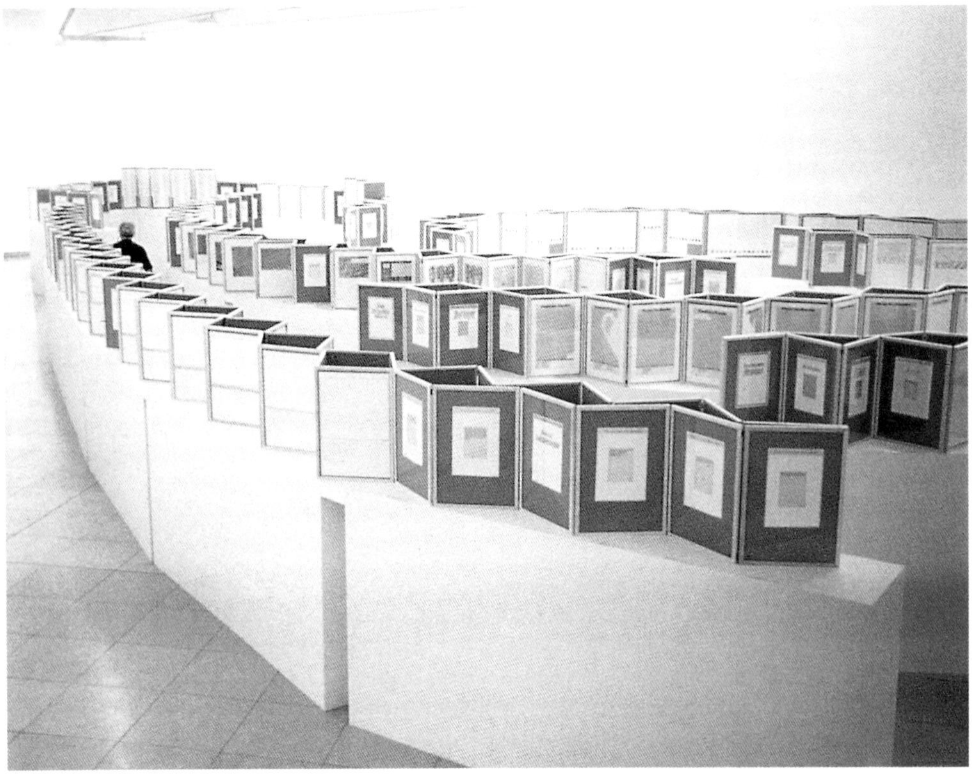

Figure 69.
Ilya Kabakov, *Primakov Sitting in a Closet (Vskafusidiaschii Primakov),* 1972, album. Collection of Ilya and Emilia Kabakov.

narratives, produced a nonretinal art but continued to operate through a visual apparatus. His next version of *Answers* (1970–71), made of enamel and masonite, eliminates pictorial images altogether. Covered with sentences imitating the language and themes of ordinary Soviet people, the work can be defined as the "aesthetic of communal babble." In another painting from the same year with the same title (fig. 166), Kabakov reintroduced pictorial images with a group of readymades—a hanger, a nail puncturing the painting's lower surface, and a toy train—all situated on the right side of the work. On the left side Kabakov employed a group of characters to discuss, comment on, and criticize his pictorial arsenal rather than simply affirming it with verbal statements. Challenging painting's exceptional status, Kabakov finally broke with the canons of Soviet alternative art. In addition to saturating his paintings with the "speech" of communal kitchens, he appropriated the shabby textures of communal interiors and the awkward, dysfunctional, and deaestheticized objects of Soviet communal households. The insertion of linguistic interpretive devices into the visual field provided the critical dialogue lacking in the Soviet alternative art movement from its inception.[4] As Kabakov points out, "The game consisted in showing on the surface the picture itself and the thoughts of the [fictional] viewers about it."[5] If the foundation of Western conceptualism was built in reaction to the overpresence of the beholder and the critic, then Soviet conceptualism was a reaction to the absence of both.

Kabakov's *Answers* series was complemented in 1972 with his work in what he called an "album" format, reminiscent of Soviet propaganda albums or portfolios designed throughout the 1930s by El Lissitzky, Varvara Stepanova, and Aleksandr Rodchenko. Each of Kabakov's ten albums, produced between 1972 and 1975, consists of a minimum of thirty-five cardboard pages of drawings and handwritten texts stacked in boxes. Each album is linked to a story about a specific Soviet character, and is intended for both viewing and reading by turning the pages. In this way, Kabakov undermined the familiar experience of optically perceiving the artwork. The first album, *Primakov Sitting in a Closet (Vskafusidiaschii Primakov,* 1972; figs. 68–70), is particularly significant in the context of conceptual art's withdrawal of visuality. It consists of forty-seven pages on which is related the story of a fictional character named Primakov, consigned to a closet in order to suppress his ability to see. Depriving him of sight and thus enhancing his ability to hear, Kabakov makes Primakov "see words instead of objects."[6] Rosalind Krauss's clarification of visual modernism as "the im/pulse to see"[7] is sacrificed for Kabakov's "im/pulse to hear." To convey the condition of "visual impairment," Kabakov begins *Primakov* with the familiar modernist model of pure visuality, the flat monochrome surface, in this case a black rectangle. By combining black rectangles with fragments of "literal facts"—"Olya Is Doing Homework," "A Strong Wind Is Blowing," "Father Came Home from Work"—Kabakov underscores Primakov's inability to optically perceive the events. Instead, he offers Primakov as an unusual beholder who, blind to the images, is concerned only with the words.

The year Kabakov began *Primakov Sitting in a Closet,* Komar and Melamid stated, "we are not artists, we are conversationalists." They later wrote that "the constant method of our work is based on conversations with each other, during which the imaginary phenomenon of art is born."[8] With these claims, K/M revealed a commitment to the operative strategy defined by Kabakov as "seeing words instead of objects." Unlike Kabakov, however, who illustrates the supremacy of the verbal with texts drawn from the reservoir of communal interactions, K/M violated the status quo of Soviet narrative (found in mass media or in bureaucratic papers) by ousting the text and altering the familiar format of its presentation. Their performance *Hamburgers "Pravda" (Kotlety "Pravda,"* 1975; fig. 4) explicitly demonstrated this process. During the performance, K/M ground up pages of the newspaper *Pravda* ("Truth"), collected its pulverized

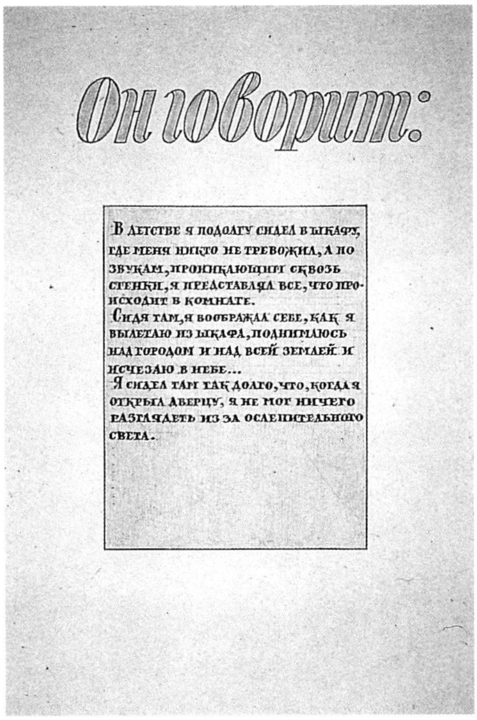

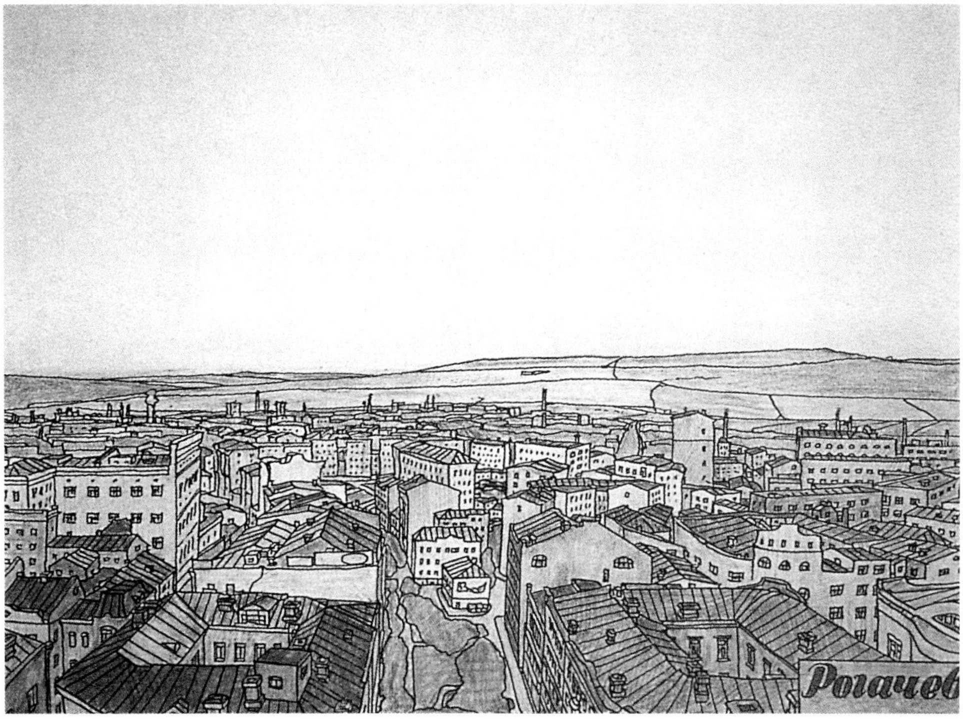

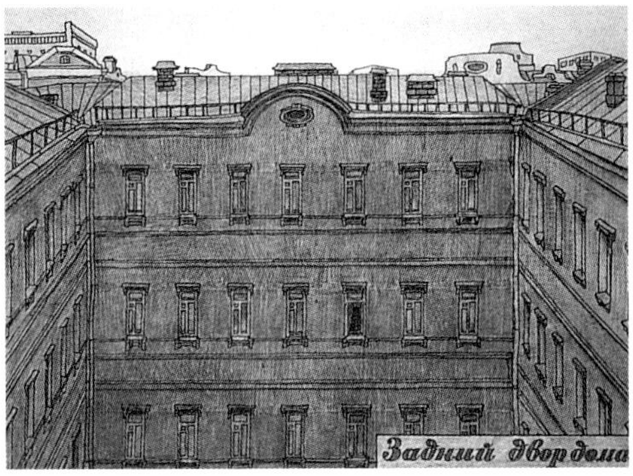

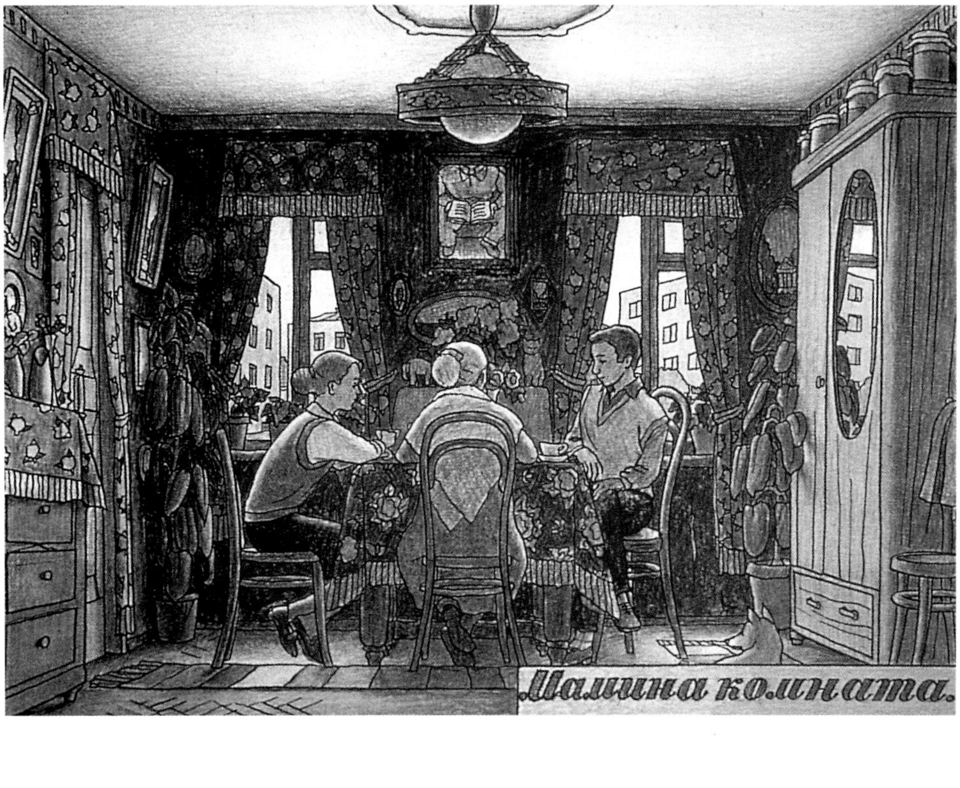

Figure 70.
Ilya Kabakov, *Primakov Sitting in a Closet (Vskafusidiaschii Primakov)*, 1972, details of album. Collection of Ilya and Emilia Kabakov.

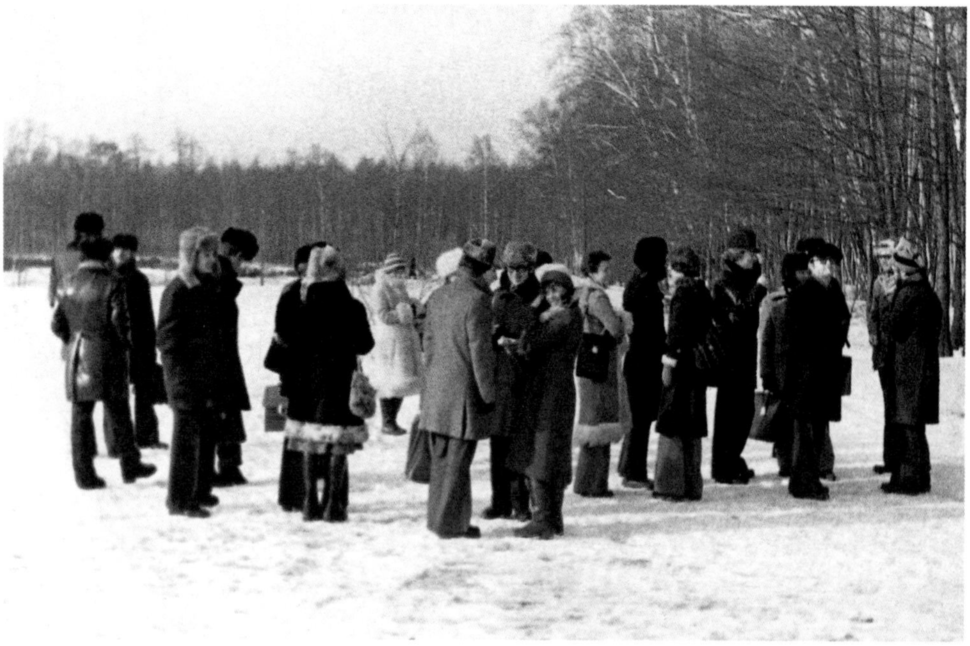

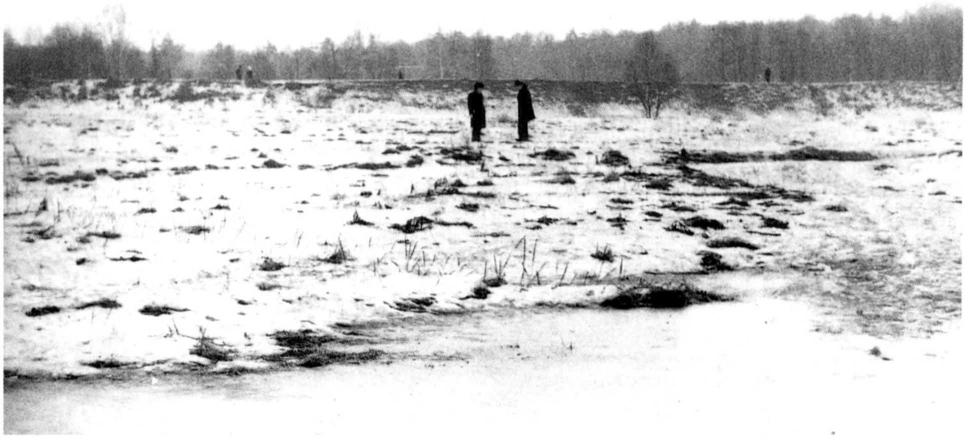

Figure 71. (top and bottom)
Andrei Monastyrskii and Collective Actions Group, *Appearance* (*Poiavlenie*), March 13, 1976.

bits and pieces, and produced a round, grayish object. The oppressive body of textual abundance had been replaced by a compact, nonthreatening geometric shape.

This neutralization of ideological objects is carried into the realm of Soviet bureaucracy with *Documents: Ideal Document* (*Dokumenty: Ideal'ny dokument,* 1975; fig. 167), in which K/M appropriated twelve types of official papers, ranging from a domestic passport and a trade-union book to marriage and birth certificates. The passport, a particularly oppressive tool, enabled the government to control the vast population by registering each citizen at a specific address, called a *propiska.* This registration, not only by city but also by specific apartment or room, made it virtually impossible for citizens to move and made them easily traceable. The trade-union card also functioned as a method of surveillance, recording every job ever held by its owner.

In *Documents: Ideal Document,* K/M negated the verbal by eliminating the text of each item. They also destroyed the documents' distinctive visual characteristics. Each document was measured, its surface area counted, and the sizes used to make twelve rectangular Plexiglas panels. A thirteenth panel completed the work, an "ideal square" (ideal document) painted red. Its size was arrived at by computing the total surface area of all the documents and dividing by twelve, which produced the arithmetic mean of the total surface area. The square root of this sum provided the measurements for the red square. This combination of specific content and abstract form served as a comment on the geometric art produced by the Soviet historical avant-garde, suggesting that postrevolutionary abstraction was constantly intruded upon by various political contents. For example, K/M's "ideal square" invokes Kazimir Malevich's *Red Square* of 1915, which appears to be a purely abstract object but in fact—as its subtitle, *Painterly Realism: Peasant Woman in Two Dimensions,* indicates—refers to a concrete image.[9] More generally, K/M allude to the fact that Malevich, Lissitzky, and Sergei Sen'kin introduced agitational slogans into their abstract canvases or posters and, later on, Stepanova, Rodchenko, and Gustav Klutsis returned to figuration in the form of photographic imagery. K/M's ironic games with political content and geometric form, recalling the two aspects of Soviet art-making since the Revolution, and their conspicuous subversion of the historical avant-garde's social ambitions and formal strategies, clashed with both Western minimalists' admiration for the Soviet nonobjective tradition and Western conceptualists' fascination with the political radicalism of Soviet culture.[10]

In *Music "Passport" (Muzyka "Pasport,"* 1976; fig. 72), from the *Codes* series, K/M further "dissected" this notorious Soviet document. The artists asked a professional musician to compose a musical piece in which each note would correspond to a letter drawn from the passport's ten regulations. By constructing a bridge between a concrete bureaucratic text and a musical composition, K/M disputed the myth (upheld by many early modernist painters) that music is the most abstract of all art forms. On the other hand, their translation of the passport's specialized rhetoric into the universal language of a musical score was, perhaps, the sharpest critique of Soviet mechanisms of control. K/M's substitution of words with notes returns us to Kabakov's "im/pulse to hear," as a substitute for the "im/pulse to see."

After the production of Kabakov and K/M's conceptual works, the homogeneity of Moscow's alternative art community radically disintegrated. Kabakov and K/M had questioned this community's prolonged devotion to easel painting as the ultimate mode of expression, and its obsession with the purely visual aspects of artmaking. Furthermore, they had crossed the carefully guarded line separating the upholder of the avant-garde spirit (Soviet dissident modernism) and the epitome of kitsch, socialist realism. Nevertheless, Kabakov and K/M continued to produce commodifiable objects in a country with no market for their consumption and no spaces for their exhibition.

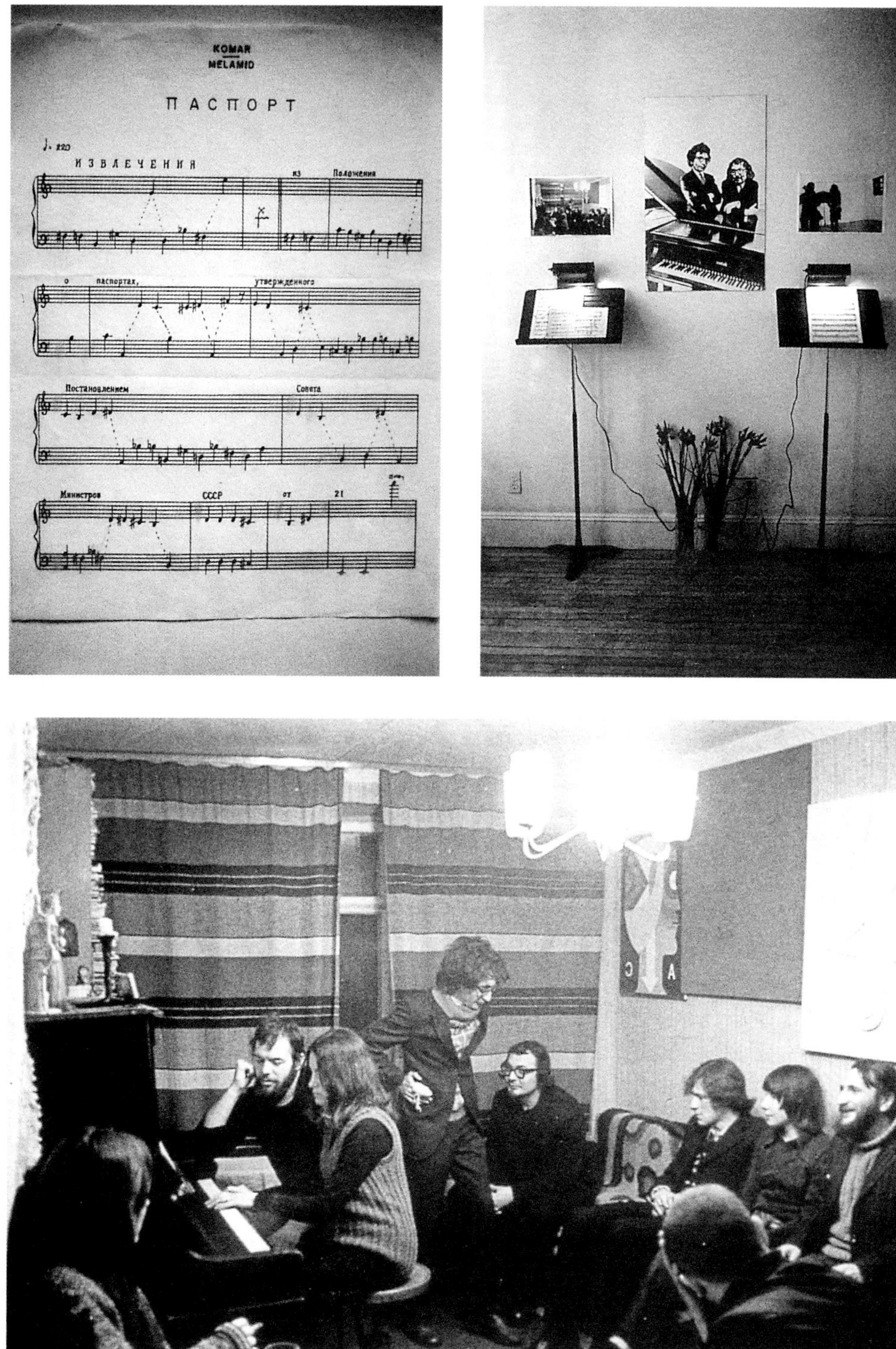

FIGURE 72.
Vitaly Komar and Aleksandr Melamid, *Music "Passport"* (*Muzyka "Pasport"*), from the *Codes* (*Kody*) series, 1976, score (left), installation with photographs, texts, audiotapes, musicstands, electric lights. Komar and Melamid Studio, New York.

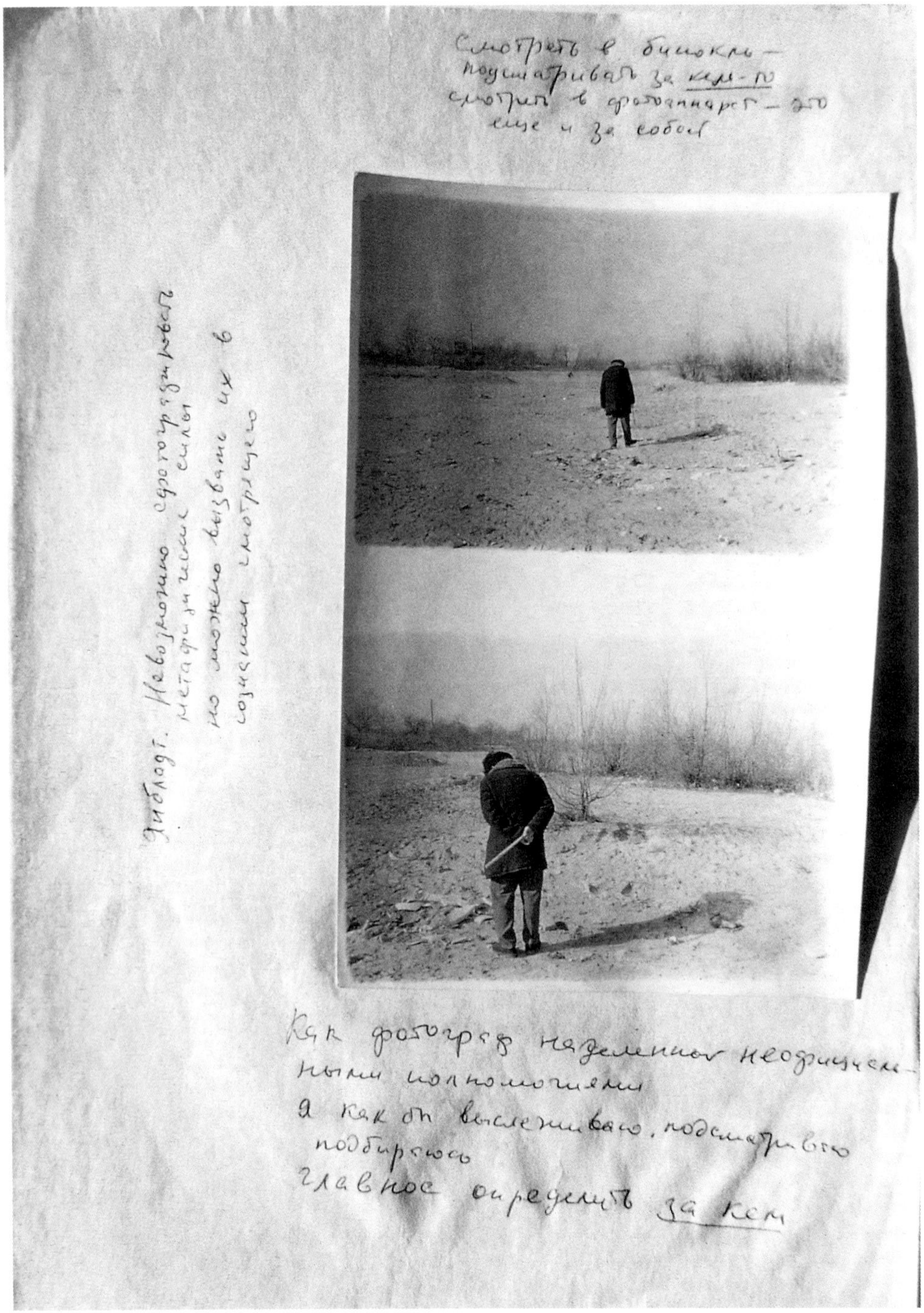

Figure 73.
Boris Mikhailov, *Unfinished Dissertation (Nezakonchennaia dissertatsiia),* 1984, one of 180 photographs. Collection of the artist.

In contrast, Andrei Monastyrskii, theoretician of the Collective Actions Group (Kollektivnye Deistviia), was committed to finding alternative spaces for alternative culture, and promoted the idea that action is a sufficient creative gesture. The group argued that it was absurd to play the role of urban artist in a country where the space for urban art was occupied by socialist realism. With the intention of moving the nucleus of alternative art from small city apartments and humble studios to the vast spaces of the countryside, the group initiated a process that inserted culture into nature, and began converting the rural no-man's land into a limitless exhibition space. Another member of the Collective Actions Group, Nikita Alekseev, explains: "If the wild life in the West is a small island among the achievements and mistakes of the culture, in Russia it is the other way around."[11]

A brief discussion of the Collective Actions Group cannot begin to convey the complexity of its theoretical background or the depth of its influence on other Moscow conceptualists. The group was formed in 1976 and originally included Monastyrskii, Alekseev, Georgii Kizeval'ter, and Nikolai Panitkov. They were later joined by Igor Makarevich, Elena Elagina, and Sergei Romashko. In the introduction to their first self-published volume, entitled *Trips to the Countryside (Poezdki za gorod,* 1980), the group's members stated:

> Most of [our] actions evolve from a scenario in which a group of people is called by us to participate in some activity unknown to them. Everything that happens in this kind of setting can be divided into two parts. The first consists of things that occur in the empirical zone (which is arranged according to the preliminary plan of the group). The second part deals with effects occurring in the realm of the psyche, that is, with the emotions arising in response to what is happening in the participants' visual field during the performance, and the emotions in regards to what precedes and accompanies the action.[12]

Furthermore, the group noted in 1983, "All our activities can be briefly characterized as a kind of 'trip in the direction of nothingness' armed with equipment of an aesthetic/psychological nature. The means for this we receive from the existence of a very closed (but permanent) circle of engaged people."[13] This circle included Moscow alternative artists and poets of several generations who were periodically asked to travel by train to the country, then walk to an enormous empty field to blow up balloons, appear and disappear in a forest, or lie down in a ditch. On the way to the performance site, they often encountered physical difficulties (deep snow or heavy rain), an ordeal intended to help them shed their urban orientation as preparation for the action.

The group's early performances illustrate the blunt simplicity and aching brevity of their plots. In *Appearance (Poiavlenie,* March 13, 1976; fig. 71), thirty invitees traveled to the field to witness two members of the group emerge from the forest, cross the field toward the spectators, and give them a "documentary certificate" confirming their presence at the event. *Liblikh* (April 2, 1976) involved twenty-five spectators who came to the same field to hear the sound of a bell, hidden underground before their arrival. The bell continued to sound after they left.[14] Each performance featured three categories of participant: author, co-author, and performer. The third category subsumed the first two: the author determined the concept of each happening, which the co-authors were required to accept. Weather conditions might also change the course of a performance and thus constituted a form of co-author. Staging these communal gatherings to fulfill the "empty actions" of their performances, the group identified emptiness as the main characteristic of Soviet existence throughout the Brezhnev era.[15]

By the late 1980s, at the end of the *perestroika* period, Collective Actions' performances, which depended on the participation of other members of the alternative cultural milieu and on the group's subsequent verbal and written analysis, became unrealistic. The climate of market-oriented values and exhibition opportunities at home and abroad eroded the communal sensibility of Soviet alternative artists. They became preoccupied with individual goals that were, as a rule, directed toward making careers in the West. At the same time, the infamous "field" site of most of the group's performances was subdivided and sold to nouveau riche clients, thus ending the "trips in the direction of nothingness."

Two years before *perestroika,* in 1984, Irina Nakhova—at the time, the only woman artist in the Moscow conceptual circle—responded to the ideas developed by her male colleagues.[16] Unlike the members of the Collective Actions Group, she considered her studio an adequate exhibition space. (Kabakov also built his first installation, *16 Strings* [1984], in his studio.) And contrary to Kabakov and K/M's "submission" to the power of speech practices, she insisted—through the construction of an installation series entitled *Rooms (Komnaty,* 1984–87; figs. 74, 168, 211)—that visual rather than verbal information should dominate the viewer's experience of art. In each of the four elaborately constructed "rooms," Nakhova covered the walls, ceiling, and floor with cutouts (ranging from handmade abstract shapes to reproductions from popular magazines) and manipulated the lighting to create unexpected visual effects. Nakhova's aim was to transgress the limits of painting's two-dimensionality and place the viewer within the pictorial space itself in order to expose her or him (so little accustomed to nonverbal experiences)[17] to an avalanche of visual information. This effect was comparable to the overwhelming nature of Soviet official texts and speeches.

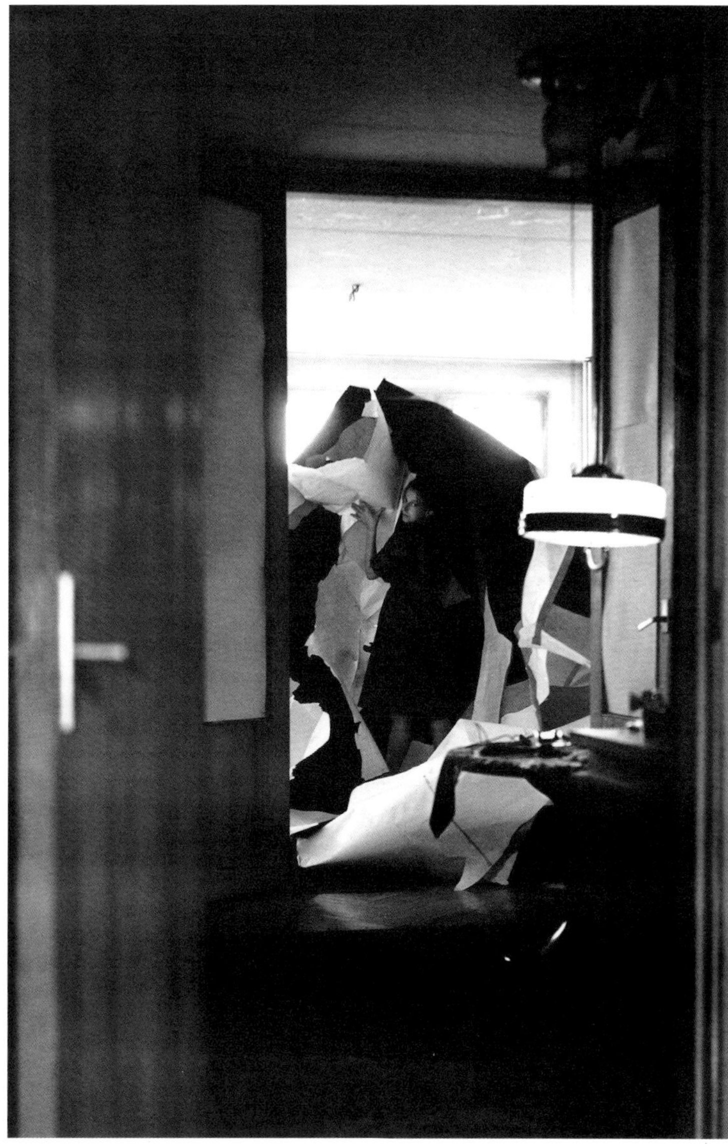

FIGURE 74.
Irina Nakhova,
Room (Komnata) No. 2,
Moscow, 1984, documentary photograph.
Collection of the artist.

However, Nakhova's project acquired a different meaning and format when her husband, critic Joseph Bakshtein, interviewed a number of visitors and used the resulting dialogues along with photographs of the installations as documentation of her experiments. The dialogues focused on *Room No. 2* (1984; fig. 74), and were almost exclusively limited to conversations with Moscow male conceptual artists, including Kabakov, Eduard Gorokhovskii, Makarevich, and Ivan Chuikov. By becoming an integral part of the project and constructing an additional meaning, the male voices shifted Nakhova's work from its concern with the hegemony of the visual to their own speech-based discourse. According to Makarevich, for instance, Nakhova's installation was "such a strong concentration of representation" that it was "pressing." Gorokhovskii was similarly disturbed. "Stay a little bit in this room," he complained, "and you can go out of your mind."[18] Such visual elements as turning the lights on and off were perceived as "psychological" and "metaphysical" experiences. Significantly, Nakhova was (voluntarily) absent during these conversations. Other women's voices were represented by the artists' wives, whose comments were limited to empty epithets such as "beautiful" and later presented parenthetically in the self-published volume. Therefore, the visual (here female) was effectively suppressed first by speech (here male) and then by its documentation, a text destined to become the final record of Nakhova's installations.

Most of these examples of early Soviet conceptualism used photography to document ephemeral projects or performances. This use of the photographic image transgressed the medium's sole function, since the late 1930s, of fulfilling the tasks of official journalism. (The only other realm in which photography was actively practiced was family life.) However, even in its capacity as a document for conceptual work, photography remained subordinate. It still held the position from which it had tried to escape in the early 20th century, namely that of handmaiden to the fine arts.

Boris Mikhailov, a photographer from Kharkov, reempowered the camera by once again directing its lens at scenes of Soviet reality, now caught without the "mythographic decor." Defining his then-unique position, Mikhailov noted in 1984: "As a photographer endowed with unofficial authority, I in some way track down, spy, sneak. Most importantly is to define after whom."[19] Like the founders of Soviet factography (Aleksandr Rodchenko, Boris Ignatovich, Elizar Langman, etc.), Mikhailov viewed the function of a photo image not as a single pictorial record of reality but as one of a series of fragmentary photo stills valid only when seen all together and supported by linguistic additions.

Unfinished Dissertation (Nezakonchennaia dissertatsiia; figs. 73, 169) is Mikhailov's earliest and longest series. It consists of several hundred photographs all taken during one dreary winter month in 1984. According to Mikhailov, this was the moment he broke from an interest in Western cultural production and began searching for local subject matter. In its final version, *Unfinished Dissertation* consists of approximately 180 sheets of cheap drawing paper, with one or two photographs casually glued to the surface. The texts that follow the images were either composed by Mikhailov or drawn from a variety of published sources, including Soviet scientific literature and books on philosophy and art. Whole paragraphs and short sentences are scribbled chaotically in the margins.

In addition to adhering to the series format, Mikhailov appropriated such primary compositional tools of the early Soviet factographers as extreme fragmentation, cropping, and capturing subjects from behind. For *Unfinished Dissertation's* subject matter, Mikhailov "revisited" monuments, landscapes, and cityscapes conceived in the 1920s and '30s, and tracked down the people who constructed them. *Unfinished Dissertation's* pictures are of a reality that might be called the "double after": it is postutopian with respect to 1920s factography, and postmythographic with respect to the photo-staging of subsequent decades.[20] Similarly, Mikhailov's individualized and philosophizing comments bypass both the dry, utilitarian language of the factographic photo images and the bureaucratic narrations attached to photo images of the later period.

Here, we are once again faced with the urge common to all Soviet conceptualists to construct and read the visual with substantial support from the verbal. In Mikhailov's case, the randomness and abundance of the verbal attests to the displaced status of his photos—or, as he calls them, *kartochki.* They are not for mass-media consumption, not for exhibition, not for appropriation by other artists. Mikhailov's inquiry "after whom" he is "spying" while taking his snapshots is investigated through the literary dimension of the photo visuals.

❖

Komar and Melamid left the Soviet Union in 1976 and, since then, have been able to realize their projects, whereas artists like Kabakov, Nakhova, and Mikhailov waited another decade, until *perestroika* opened the "window to Europe."[21] Thus the political breakdown of the Soviet Union had a direct impact on the history of Soviet conceptualism. Kabakov, Nakhova, and Mikhailov, as well as younger representatives of Moscow conceptualism—Igor and Svetlana Kopystianskii, Elagina, Makarevich, the Medical Hermeneutics Group (Meditsinskaia Germeneftika), and the Peppers (Pertsy)—were finally able to realize their conceptual installations in Western galleries and museums. However, in the West the textual parameters of their works were lost to a large degree, which resulted in Soviet culture's reception by Western viewers on an essentially visual level. Thus Kabakov's postulate "seeing words instead of objects" was ironically fulfilled in a refractive form when the Western viewer was subjected to "seeing" rather than "reading" the language-saturated works of Soviet conceptualism.

Notes

1. For a detailed and broader history of Soviet conceptualism, see my "On Some Sources of Soviet Conceptualism," in *Nonconformist Art: The Soviet Experience,* ed. Norton Dodge and Anna Rosenfeld (London: Thames & Hudson, 1995), 303–33, in which I connect the Soviet conceptualists' use of text to similar practices of the Soviet historical avant-garde. Here I would like to add that this linguistic element, intrinsic to both eras of Soviet culture, is not based on the conceptualists' knowledge of the constructivist/productivist tradition. Rather, it illustrates the prolonged dependence of Russian and Soviet culture on textual rather than visual mechanisms of artmaking. For the most part, as in the case with dissident modernists who in the late 1950s possessed no substantial knowledge of the local historical avant-garde and discovered abstraction through Western exhibitions, the Soviet conceptualists' knowledge of their domestic cultural legacy was sparse and relied primarily on visual perception or on distorted theoretical premises.

2. The conceptual movement began to actively manifest itself at the time when dissident modernism was institutionalized by the Soviet government. For a further discussion of the nature of Soviet dissident modernism, see my "Avant-garde and Kitsch," in *Margins of Soviet Art: Socialist Realism to the Present* (Milan: Giancarlo Politi Editore, 1989), 23–37, and Victor Tupitsyn, "'Nonidentity Within Identity': Moscow Communal Modernism, 1950s–1980s," in *Nonconformist Art,* ed. Dodge and Rosenfeld, 64–100.

3. On the visual level, Kabakov's colleagues often compared him with René Magritte. It seems, however, that in his early works he pursued a rather different goal. Instead of confounding pictorial reality with contradictory verbal messages, Kabakov affirmed or narrated what was already represented by pictorial means.

4. Beginning in the late 1950s, Soviet alternative artists functioned as both creators and beholders of their art. The function of the interpreter (critic) did not exist.

5. Ilya Kabakov and Yuri Kuper, *52 entretiens dans la cuisine communautaire* (Marseilles: Art Transit, Ateliers Municipaux d'Artistes, 1992), 16.

6. From a videotaped interview with Sergei Borisov, Moscow, 1986.

7. Rosalind Krauss, "The Im/Pulse to See," in *Vision and Visuality,* ed. Hal Foster (Seattle: Bay Press, 1988), 52.

8. K/M, "In Search of the Ideal," unpub. ms., 1974.

9. K/M's making of the red square by means of a precise calculation corresponds to John Milner's interpretation of Malevich's paintings as objects of carefully planned proportions. See John Milner, *Kazimir Malevich and the Art of Geometry* (New Haven: Yale University Press, 1996). Carter Ratcliff makes a parallel between K/M's red square in *Documents* and Malevich's canvas, then distinguishes them thus: "Unlike a Malevich canvas, Komar and Melamid's patterns of line, color, can be decoded if one has a key." Ratcliff fails to recognize that Malevich added a narrative subtitle to *Red Square* and thus decoded its content as well. See Carter Ratcliff, *Komar and Melamid* (New York: Abbeville Press, 1988), 99.

10. According to Benjamin Buchloh, some Western conceptualists were inspired by Camilla Grey's book *The Great Experiment: Russian Art, 1863–1922,* published in 1962, and were particularly influenced by this art's political aspirations and productivist theory. In contrast, K/M—as demonstrated in *Documents: Ideal Document* and in such other early works as *Circle, Square, Triangle* (1974)—responded to the formal and ideological strategies of constructivism/suprematism with an explicit irony and cynicism. See Benjamin H. D. Buchloh, "Conceptual Art, 1962–1969," *October* (Winter 1990): 140–41.

11. Nikita Alekseev, from a letter to Victor and Margarita Tupitsyn, 1983, Tupitsyn Archive, New York.

12. Collective Actions Group (Nikita Alekseev, Georgii Kizeval'ter, Andrei Monastyrskii, and Nikolai Panitkov), *Poezdki za gorod* (Moscow: Self-published, 1980), Tupitsyn Archive, New York.

13. Collective Actions Group (Andrei Monastyrskii, Georgii Kizeval'ter, Nikolai Panitkov, Igor Makarevich, Nikita Alekseev, Sergei Romashko, and Elena Elagina), *Poezdki i vosproizvedeniia* (Moscow: Self-published, 1983), Tupitsyn Archive, New York.

14. According to Monastyrskii, the group was initially influenced by the musical experiments of John Cage, especially his concept of "sounding silence" as expressed in *4'33"*. In 1978 Monastyrskii wrote to Cage and later received a response in which Cage was interested in a collaborative project. The letter was torn up by Monastyrskii's mother, who was frightened by the foreign address, but he managed to salvage it from the garbage.

15. In 1981, after a trip to Czechoslovakia, Kabakov wrote an essay entitled "O pustote" (On Emptiness), in which he thoroughly developed his ideas on a particular Soviet model of emptiness, distinguishing it from the European concept. See Ilya Kabakov, "On Emptiness," in *Between Spring and Summer: Soviet Conceptual Art in the Era of Late Communism,* ed. David Ross (Cambridge, Mass.: MIT Press, 1990), 53–59.

16. Nakhova was particularly influenced by Victor Pivovarov, a close colleague of Ilya Kabakov. Like Kabakov, in the early 1970s Pivovarov adopted the album format and attempted the process of verbalizing the visual.

17. For decades the Soviet public was exposed primarily to socialist realist works in museums and official galleries. Although these works did not employ texts and offered a variety of imitated realist styles (including late 19th-century realism and French impressionism), viewers were in fact "reading" paintings and receiving ideological instruction from them.

18. For the comments by Makarevich, Gorokhovskii, and others, see *MANI: Komnaty* (Moscow: Self-published, 1987), 143, 145, Tupitsyn Archive, New York.

19. Boris Mikhailov, *Unfinished Dissertation.*

20. For a history of the development of factography and mythography, see my *The Soviet Photograph, 1924–1937* (New Haven: Yale University Press, 1996). I derive the term "double after" from a popular '20s and '30s photo theme of "before and after," where "before" referred to the prerevolutionary reality and "after" the postrevolutionary one.

21. Among the important exhibitions of Soviet conceptual art in the U.S. are *Russian New Wave* (New York: Contemporary Russian Art Center, 1981); *Between Spring and Summer: Soviet Conceptual Art in the Era of Late Communism* (Boston: ICA, 1990); *The Green Show* (New York: Exit Art, 1990); and *Perspectives of Conceptualism* (New York: Clock Tower, 1991).

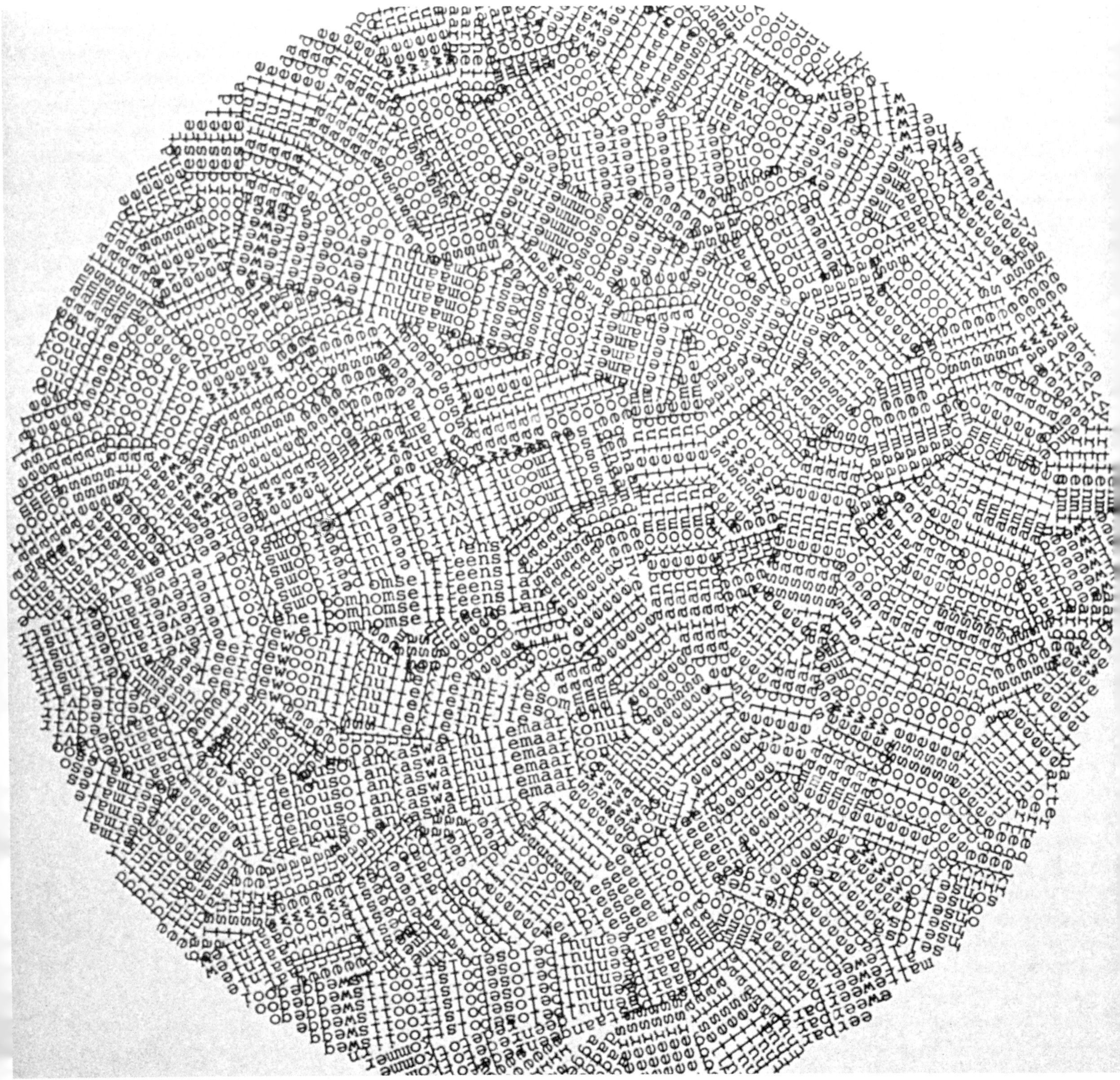

Where, What, Who, When: A Few Notes on "African" Conceptualism

Okwui Enwezor

Figure 75.
Willem Boshoff, page from *Kykafrikaans,* 1980, 95-page, soft-cover book. Ruth and Marvin Sackner Archive of Concrete and Visual Poetry, Miami.

Is There Such a Thing as African Conceptualism?

The term *conceptual art* has been so institutionalized that it has come to occupy a narrow strip of territory encompassing only discourses flowing out of very specific practices. Most of these practices are connected to or subsumed within the artistic discourses of postwar Western Europe and the United States. Moreover, the established meanings of these activities have often proceeded from the idea that what makes such art *conceptual* begins with the notion of the dematerialization of the object, as well as the privileging of language-based art, institutional critique, the nonvisual, and on the litany goes. My intention here is neither to rehearse this litany nor simply to displace its firmly rooted meanings, but to add to it and, where possible, to enlarge its constricted art historical certitude. Hence, what would it mean, this late in the day, to nominate as "conceptualist" something that acts like, looks like, and resembles those practices, but whose chief concerns may lie elsewhere? Such is the question one must pose for anything called African conceptualism.

Given the complex perceptual issues that are its fundamental organizing principles, conceptual art, as elaborated in the U.S. and Western Europe, would seem to exclude Africa. Such an exclusion would, of course, be in line with the already prevailing disqualification of African aesthetic thought from the broader argument of modernism. Despite the different experiences of modernity globally, this art historical conceit remains firmly entrenched in different institutional and epistemological operations. Thus the notion of pleading a particular area's case for inclusion remains a fraught one. There has still not been a way to remedy that neglect, and here will not be the venue to do so.

It is crucial to state this from the outset, because our assignment as curators for this exhibition is to locate the particular point at which the attitude called *conceptualism* made its first appearance in different areas of the world. If the claim for conceptual art has always been made in reference to its relationship to the dominant language of modernism, and if its institutional valorization has situated it as the most significant artistic breakthrough of the 20th century after cubism, then it must be allowed that this shift is deeply engrained in the earlier opportunity which African sculptural objects offered the early modernists to escape the convoluted mise-en-scènes of impressionism and classical European art. This is an old story, but worth reiterating. Indeed, how does Africa participate in this exercise in constructive revisionism at the core of which resides the idea of the avant-garde, with so clear a history located in the metropolitan identity of the Western city?

To ask this invites a series of other questions. To wit: What *is* conceptual art as applied to the conditions that exist in Africa? So identified, would these artistic practices, which might

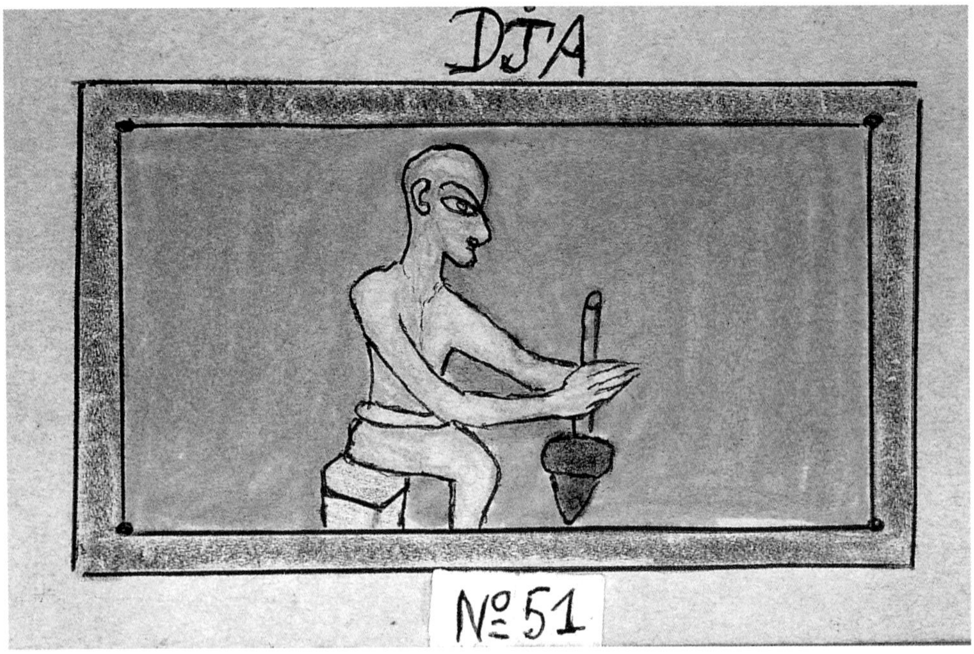

Figure 76.
Frédéric Bruly Bouabré, *Relevés des signes observés sur noix de cola (Readings from Signs Observed on Kola Nuts)*, 1981–94, colored pencil and ballpoint on cardboard. Contemporary African Art Collection (C.A.A.C.), in collaboration with André Magnin, courtesy of Frédéric Bruly Bouabré.

also be "corroded" and "contaminated" by other cultural and political/ideological principles, alter the definition, indeed the material and intellectual manifestation of what is or is not conceptual art? Would conceptualism in Africa, like its Euro–North American counterpart, constitute a significant shift within the dominant institutional framework as to posit a new language or paradigm? If so, what specific labels were applied to this shift, how were they received and discussed? Do these labels constitute a movement in which many artists participated? Quite simply, is there such a thing as conceptual art in Africa, or is it just a term imported as part of a neocolonial enterprise of modernist art history? Most importantly, in deciding what is conceptual in Africa, whose model of thought and what methods of distinction should be applied in dismissing or admitting works, attitudes, actions, and propositions?

These are vexing questions, yet pursuing them is key to broadening the place of African modernity within the larger discussions of 20th-century art. One way to address these questions is to ignore all preset rules. But a more promising strategy is to set up a critical correspondence between the disjunctive temporalities of the African imaginary and the highly differentiated space of Western institutional and epistemological reflections on modern art.

Conceptual art, as commonly understood, attempted a fundamental restructuring of the viewer's relationship to the art object. First, its critique of systems of representation and presentation pitched artmaking toward the dematerialization of the object, thereby placing less value on the perceptual codes through which art is traditionally received. This strategy sought to challenge the autonomous value placed on objects, which value is, in turn, connected to cultural ways of looking. Second, conceptual art privileged linguistic, informational, and philosophical systems over materialist modes of production, making communication, performance, documentation, process, actions, and the world outside the studio part of the intensive phenomenology of process. It should be added, however, that this understanding of conceptual art—in view of alternative information that has since become available—is only a partial account. Still, there is a reality—hegemonic or not—that is not so easily evaded.

My task, then, is to examine how this understanding of conceptualism relates or corresponds to the fundamental philosophical questions of African systems of signification. And we find that in classical African art, conceptualism would seem oxymoronic. While many African cultures produced exquisite objects, many of which clearly permitted early Western modernists to explore different forms of representation through spatial disembodiment, it bears remarking that African objects were never ends in themselves, nor did they acquire any form of autonomy as sculpture through their objecthood. While in Western art, the cycle of art is completed in the aesthetic realm of display, in African traditions this finale is achieved through a desublimination strategy that perpetually displaces the object and places greater significance on nonvisual codes and performative actions, particularly through linguistic puns and aphoristic utterances. By repeatedly making contingent the status of the object as an autonomous signifier, the artwork functions within a fluid system of exchanges and relationships among object, artist, and audience.

In African art, two things are constantly in operation: the work and the idea of the work. These are not autonomous systems. One needs the other and vice versa. A paraphrase of an Igbo idea will clarify this relationship: where there is something standing which can be seen, there is something else standing next to it which cannot be seen but which accompanies the object. In its material basis, African art is object-bound, but in its meaning and intention it is paradoxically anti-object and antiperceptual, bound by the many ways of conveying ideas whereby speech or oral communication are highly valued. The work of an artist such as Frédéric Bruly Bouabré is an extension of this idea. And if Bouabré sought to put his words and ideas on paper, there is a clear ideological motivation for doing so. Yet evidence of the dematerialized object does not in itself mean that the object is not valued or that the culture of visual memory is deadened by the weight of sight. I certainly cannot identify a self-reflexivity in which artists deliberately sought to remove their work from functioning on the visual level. More to the point, in African art there is an interpellation of the object and language.

While the argument laid out so far would seem to ground conceptualism in the classical art of Africa, contemporary practice is actually a much trickier and even contradictory enterprise. The conceptual work of the Senegalese group Laboratoire Agit-Art and the South African artists included in this exhibition was never directed at maintaining a relationship with older African philosophical systems, as in Bouabré's case. In many ways, they deploy the same conceptualist strategies prevalent in the West. The reason for this perhaps is their shared relationship with concepts of modernity. But this is where the comparison ends, since the motivations supporting each strategy were different and the results sought were widely divergent. Malcolm Payne, for example, resorted to conceptualist tactics—dematerialization, language works, and a process he calls "confusion acts"—as a response to political conditions under apartheid. In African conceptualism, it is crucial to acknowledge the role of politics and responses to political institutions by artists operating under dictatorships.

As far as I can tell, there has never existed anything that can be definitively declared a conceptual "movement" in Africa, at least one in which everybody agrees as to its parameters. A sustained investigation has yielded only a few artists, and in the case of Laboratoire Agit-Art, a single group. Hence, conceptualism in Africa is a practice associated with scattered, isolated, and solitary examples and never blossomed into a full-fledged artistic discourse. Along with the received definitions of conceptualism as propagated by the Euro–North American axis, the mid-1960s has often been "universally" accepted as its point of periodization and entrance into "art world" currency. For the artists considered here, the conceptualist moment begins in the early 1970s.

Figure 77.
Malcolm Payne, *Past, Present, Future,* 1973, still from videotape. Collection of the artist.

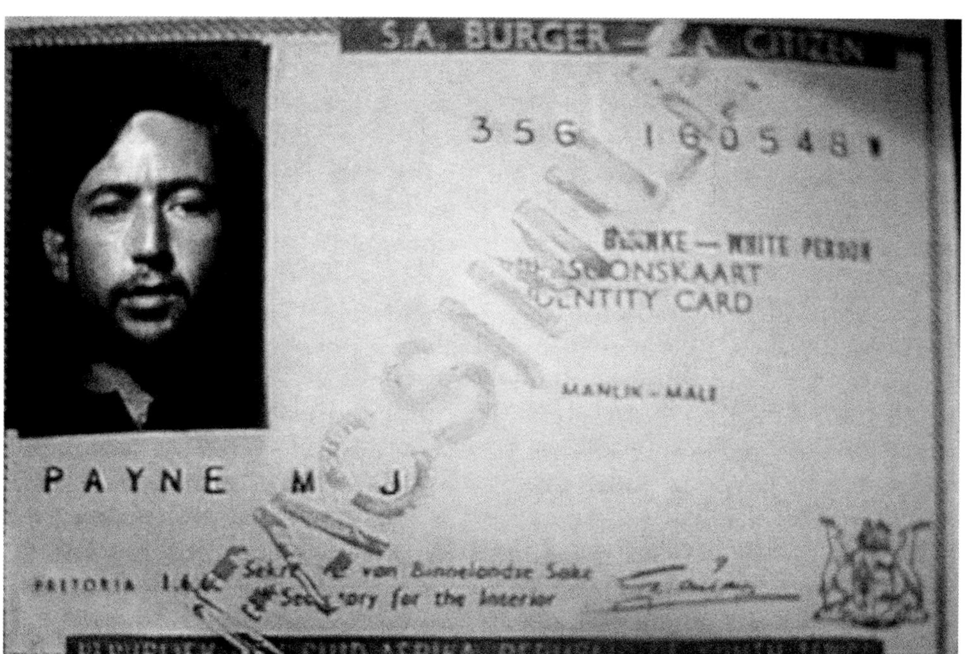

Laboratoire Agit-Art: Excavating the Social and the Political in the Postcolony

The 1960s was the moment of Africa's emergence, a decade of incredible political, social, and cultural ferment. As many countries agitated for and gained independence from years of debilitating colonial domination by Europe, it is fair to say that they shared a political context connected to the processes of decolonization and the struggle against Western hegemonic influence. Throughout Africa, the urgent political and ideological questions of the postindependent nation-state, accelerated and pressurized by rapid urbanization, gave rise to new concepts of identity and the individual. Linked to this sociopolitical complexity was the tense relationship between ideas of modernity and a nationalistic sense of tradition and culture. At one end of the continent, a Pan-Africanist notion of modernity, led by Ghana's first prime minister Kwame Nkrumah armed with scientific socialism, became a readymade context from which the significant reformulation of Africanism was proposed. In North Africa, the Suez Canal crisis launched Gamal Abdel Nasser's Pan-Arab movement. Nasser's aim, like Nkrumah's in Ghana, was to rally unity against Western imperialism.

But by the mid-1970s, the political transformation that swept the colonial powers out of Africa was in crisis. The prospects of, and euphoria over, the social and political reconstruction of the independent countries had dimmed considerably as a series of dictatorships and repressive regimes entered the scene. It is within this troubled era of the postcolony that the most significant expression of avant-gardism, and a practice that can be labeled conceptual, would emerge.

The Dakar-based Laboratoire Agit-Art was founded in 1973–74 by an interdisciplinary group of artists, writers, filmmakers, performance artists, and musicians. Laboratoire's aim was to transform the nature of artistic practice from a formalist, object-bound sensibility to practices based on experimentation and agitation, process rather than product,

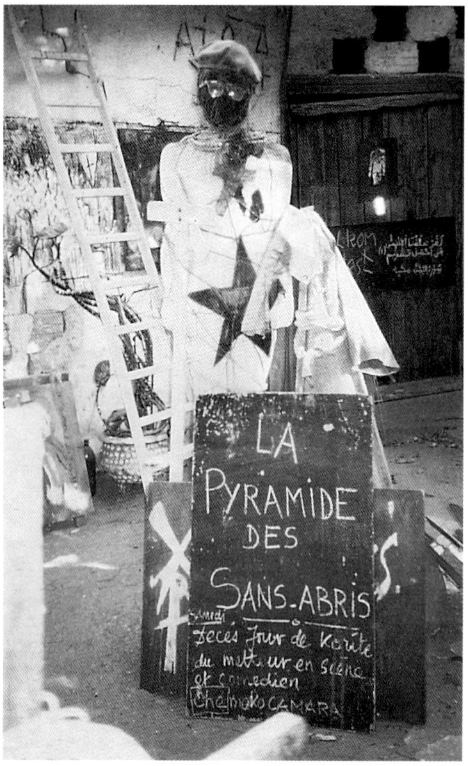

Figure 78.
Issa Samb of Laboratoire Agit-Art, 1994.

ephemerality rather than permanence, political and social ideas rather than aesthetic. Audience participation was of paramount importance to the group's work, which privileged communicative acts over the embodied object. Neither utopian nor self-referential, Laboratoire grounded its actions in the immediate sociopolitical situation (fig. 78). Whether or not the group was aware of similar practices in the West, Laboratoire's position on art after the object is supremely consistent with Lucy Lippard's assertion that conceptual art was "emerging from two directions: art as idea and art as action." In this sense, according to Ima Ebong, Laboratoire Agit-Art

> has attempted nothing less than a reshaping of both the language of Senegalese art and the terms on which artistic production occurs in that country ... the group engages aspects of Western modernism, but it concerns itself with the conceptual ideologies of the avant-garde rather than with Modernist formalism. Its tactics of provocation and agitation in keeping with its name, suggest a connection with the Western anti-art performance aesthetic. These artists work outside the government-sponsored system of galleries and museums, distancing their collaborative creations from the painting on canvas, an art form subject to a deeply rooted system of commodity control.[1]

An important precursor to Laboratoire Agit-Art can be found in the work of Nigerian musician, performer, political activist, and social iconoclast Fela Anikulapo Kuti. From the mid-1960s, Fela's relentless critique of the postcolonial state and his challenge to the corrupt political order were exemplary links to the strategies later adopted by the group. Throughout his career, which included founding a political party and running for president in 1979 (before being disqualified by the military regime), Fela never made a distinction between his music, life style, and political resistance. Revered by the public and constantly censored by the government, in the early '70s Fela declared his complex of buildings in Lagos—living quarters, a nightclub, and a recording studio—an independent territory, which he named Kalakuta Republic. All actions, he stated (especially as related to drugs and sex), were legal in his republic, and all applicable Nigerian laws declared null and void.

In 1977, two members of Laboratoire Agit-Art, El Hadji Sy and Issa Samb (a.k.a. Joe Ouakam), visited Kalakuta Republic. According to Issa, they were drawn by Fela's courage and his avant-gardism, which went well beyond mere aesthetic reaction.[2] Laboratoire's focus on the impermanent, contingent character of actions informed by a critique of institutional power "corresponds in great part to this notion of the socialization of an aesthetic, in the form of an activist avant-garde that inserts itself within the wider cultural discourse of Senegal but refuses to follow its institutional and formal criteria."[3] This aggressively contextual relationship to regimes of legitimation and power distinguishes Laboratoire Agit-Art from many other African groups of the same period which were operating within a proto-modernist framework directed at recovering lost origins, rather than problematizing the meaning of "origin" in the broader analysis of contemporary culture in the postcolony.

Signs and Systems: Frédéric Bruly Bouabré

While the practices of Laboratoire Agit-Art were concerned with communication through the "socialization of an aesthetic" and activism against the postcolonial state, Frédéric Bruly Bouabré's work is embedded in the traditional conceptual issues of classical African art. His interest in signs and systems, language and symbology, subjectification over representation, vision over sight, classification, documentation, lists, codification, etymology, archival practices, and experimentation with written text as opposed to the production of images—all are related to his attentive transcription of the oral culture of his people, the Bété.

Bouabré was born in 1923 in Zéprégühé, Ivory Coast. Originally a translator and colonial informant for Western anthropologists and ethnographers, in 1948 he was convinced by a vision to abandon this work and dedicate himself to recording, transcribing, and translating the rapidly disappearing oral culture of the Bété. According to the dictates of his vision, Bouabré christened himself Sheik Nadro (One Who Does Not Forget), and his activities shifted completely and permanently to that of taxonomist and artist. Language, for Bouabré, is the supreme tool for preserving memory and reconstructing history, and also serves as a model of representation through which ideas and the everyday life of a dynamic society can be explored and explained. This commitment to instrumentalizing language ultimately led to his invention of a Bété alphabet. His quest, it seems, is to make transparent the meanings buried in obscure phenomena, to make them available as source material for the writing of history. Bouabré is a decipherer of dreams, of images that hover at the edge of consciousness. He is equally a cosmologist of signs and numbers, a taxonomist of ethnographic knowledge, a recorder of his people's history.

In Bouabré's work, there is a cabalistic attention to the structure of numbers and words, their multiple associative meanings and permutations used to delve into the murky depths of the unconscious. He proposes theories and explanations, constructs maps, compiles indexes, writes compendia. He has created a pictographic alphabet of more than 450 characters, dedicated to excavating and preserving the disappearing oral history of his people. Bouabré's unique narrative form, composed on tarotlike cards, often combines text and image in a detailed elaboration of complex systems of communication (fig. 172).

However, Bouabré does not only make images in the quasi-naive form that has led many to view him as some kind of mystic of the primeval African world, or as an untutored curiosity. For almost fifty years, he has produced an astonishing array of books on classical African systems of representation, for instance, *Le langage des symboles africains dans les musées* (The Language of African Symbols in the Museum, 1975), *Le calendrier du "monde noir" d'origine (Bété)* (The Calendar of the "Black World" of [Bété] Origin, 1982), *Le musée du visage africain* (The Museum of the African Face, 1975), etc. But the singular character of his work lies in his sensitivity to the most mundane elements. For example, he sees in discarded leaves of kola nuts (fig. 76) and orange rinds signs and meanings that could be transposed to readable visual propositions. As an archivist and deconstructionist, he has studied the staggering meanings of scarifications on African faces, revealing them to be as much a linguistic form as a communal rite of passage.

The Language Project of Rachid Koraïchi

Born in Algeria but now living in exile in Tunisia, Rachid Koraïchi has relentlessly produced works in which he utilizes the Arabic script to delineate urgent political questions. Like the classical forms of Islamic art, Koraïchi's art is devotional but resistant to ideological fundamentalism. Spare and austere, his works are rendered on expansive sheets of paper, fields of black text on white laid out in alternating vertical and horizontal bands that surge, deviate, retreat, invert, detour, and veer all over the page like a musical score (fig. 79). The structure of Koraïchi's work is both graphic and calligraphic, expository and nonsensical, what Abdelkebir Khatibi characterized as the "metamorphosis of the visible ... these transmutations, these translations from one sign system to another, one image to another ... a spatial paradigm oriented towards all languages, from pictographs to a form of writing resembling ideographs, by way of Arabic graphic (here exquisite), whether it be legible or illegible, whether it be inverted or even rove in all directions ... as if seeking escape from the confines of the unframed images."

Yet Koraïchi's art is not to be reduced to writing alone. His investment in signs and symbols means also that he has worked assiduously to decompose the script, to turn its cursive elegance into personal codes and concrete poetry. It would appear that with this decomposition, Koraïchi writes on the margins of his own psychic exposition, sublimating his public political concern into the limits of the individual voice. His program is often both romantic and grand, as in his banners of gold-decorated texts that may seem like propaganda productions. Or it can be caustic and pensive, tough and combative, melancholic and mournful, as in his responses to political injustice and exile.

Throughout a career that has spanned at least three decades, Koraïchi has set out a rigorous intellectual program from which he simultaneously works inside and outside the parameters of institutional authority. His drawings and writings, at once lyrical and iconoclastic, borrow from classical Islamic texts and the work of contemporary writers and poets. His attentiveness to language as the repository of individual and collective action is manifested in his adoption of both traditional lyrics and subversive political rhetoric to critique the repressive regimes of his region. Yet Koraïchi is not a heretic, nor is he interested in that ugly, stereotypical image of Islam as fundamentalist, obdurate to new forms of discourse. He comes from a tradition of "enlightened Islam," which in recent years has begun to gather steam in many Islamic countries where the subject of Islam's ethical humanism is vigorously debated.

Still, in encountering Koraïchi's work in the realm of contemporary art, how do we resist the temptation to read it as decorative motif and not language? Because non-Roman-derived script may be confused with the decorative (what I will call the recourse to the sign as calligraphy), it is often difficult to assess the proper place of art that works inside its formal basis. In the context of this exhibition, then, Koraïchi's work is somewhat of a paradox. It raises the question of what to do with works which, if we strictly adhere to the judgment of classical conceptual matrices in Europe and the United States, both understand and deracinate that judgment. This

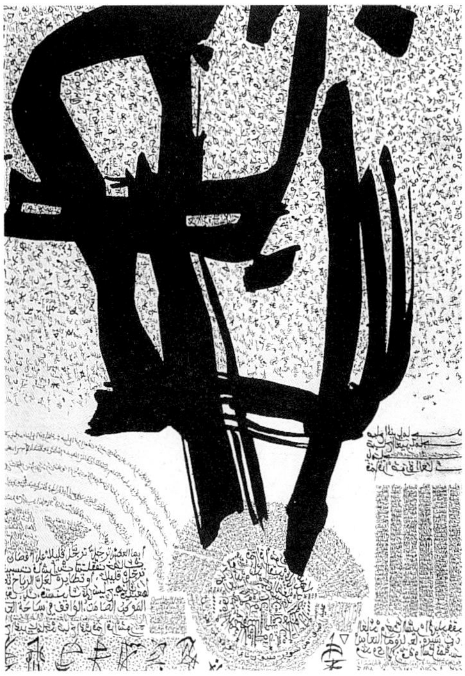

FIGURE 79.
Rachid Koraïchi, *Print and Calligraphy* from *A Nation in Exile* (Amman: Darat al Funun, Abdul Hameed Shoman Foundation, 1997).

stems from the fact that what may be appreciated as conceptual in Islamic art—especially in its relationship to text (calligraphy) and language (discourse) as the fundamental basis of both representation and signification—is more in tune with the tradition of, as opposed to rebellion against, the materialized image. But if the meaning of the sign is contained in the text, in the sublimity of language rather than in the image—particularly with regard to the Islamic anaconic mandate, which sublimates the representation of the human form into rapturous devotional songs and words of the Prophet—how can we then characterize the work of an artist such as Koraïchi, an artist who seemingly has obeyed this rule as conceptual, when the very problematic conceptualism sets for itself is an insistent philosophical and anarchic program intent on destroying such authority? First it would be important to understand that the reading of works by artists like Koraïchi presents a problem not only within this context, but also for the larger context of that rigid body known as the Western canon.

The rendering of "pure conceptualism" in the reductive vocabulary of institutional critique and language systems as the procedural condition of understanding art after the image, must then also contend with works like Koraïchi's. His attitude from the beginning has been both political and personal, often veering far from hard resistance to celebratory, incantatory poetry. Over the years he has worked in collaboration with some of the most brilliant contemporary Arab writers of his generation, including the great Palestinian poet Mahmoud Darwish. His work with literature favors delicate and complex meditations over reactive protest. Yet it is clear that Koraïchi's work is set along the edges of a corpus of art and writing that not only compares with the Western canon, but also without which what we call the history of the West would not be possible.

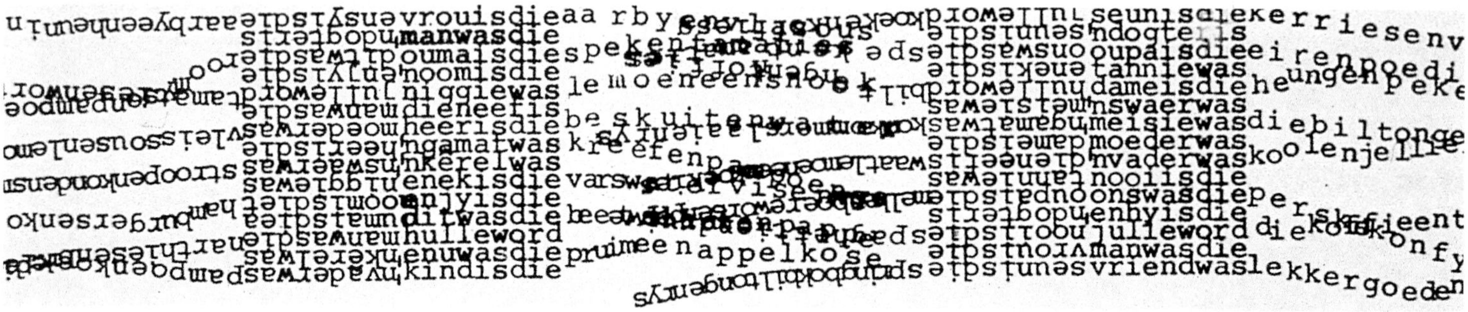

Figure 80.
Willem Boshoff, pages from *Kykafrikaans*, 1980, 95-page, soft-cover book. Ruth and Marvin Sackner Archive of Concrete and Visual Poetry, Miami.

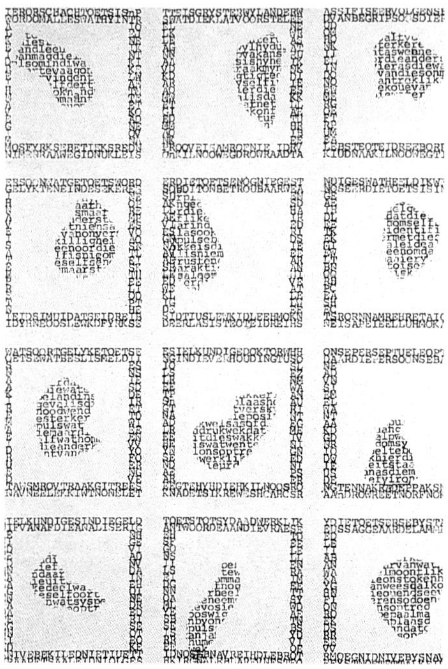

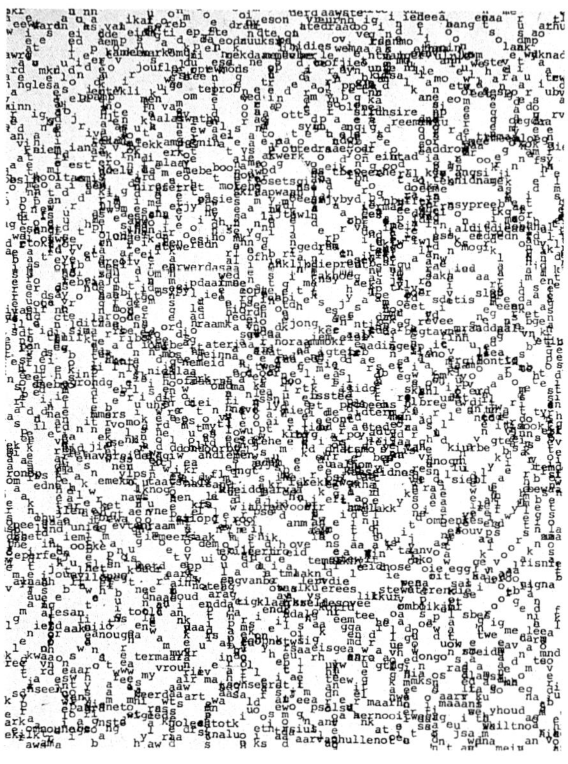

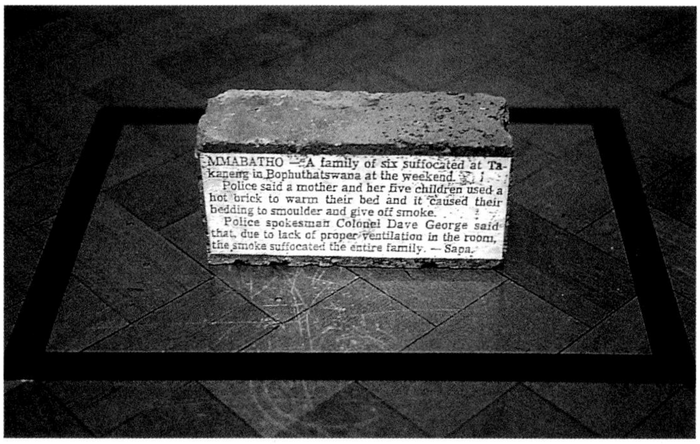

FIGURE 81.
Kendell Geers, *Brick,* 1988, mixed media installation. Private collection.

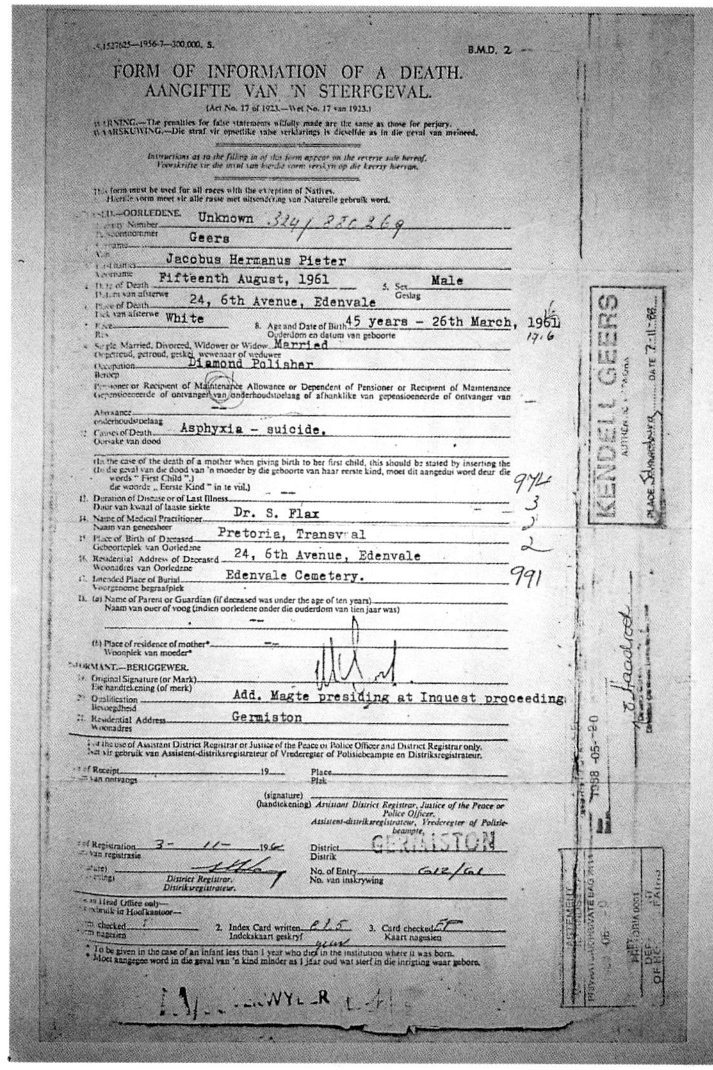

FIGURE 82.
Kendell Geers, *Death Certificate,* 1961–88, found object. Private collection.

South Africa

Until the official end of apartheid in 1994, South Africa suffered under an often violently enforced system of racial segregation, and was for years culturally isolated from the rest of the world. The work of the South African artists in this exhibition—Willem Boshoff, Malcolm Payne, and Kendell Geers—must therefore be considered in the light of this unique history. The reason for such an examination is not to fetishize what is obvious about South Africa's historical memory and its exile from the rest of Africa, but because of the ways in which the work of these artists critically implicates and interrogates that history.

Willem Boshoff's conceptual practice is an elaborate effort dedicated to the study of ignorance, that is, pushing to the point of dissolution the idea that the world is knowable. Imprisoned by South African authorities for his refusal to serve in the military (the micrographic work, *Kleinpen I* [fig. 171], was produced in prison as a way to maintain mental equilibruim), Boshoff considers rational knowledge a useless mechanism for mapping its revelation. Described as an orthodox conceptualist, in the sense that he keeps, in Gerardo Mosquera's apt phrase, a clean concentration on language, Boshoff finds in obscure and obsolete words a way to construct a map that denies sight but empowers knowledge.

Boshoff compiles extensive dictionaries and encyclopedia of names, words, plants. The laborious exactitude of his compositions (fig. 194), collocations, and accumulations does not operate on the thrill of esotericism, but on the recognition of the vastness of the world and the ideological systems that circumscribe it. Paradoxically, Boshoff insists he is not interested in teaching: "I write dictionaries of words that I hope nobody will understand."[4] The very invention of these dictionaries, far from reanimating interest in what they seek to represent or reveal, is first intended as a detour, a way of denying the rationalist's persistent will to knowledge. Mosquera has characterized this process as a kind of imaginary travel: the artist in his room, ruminating, chewing over, constructing and deconstructing, calculating, as "he stages the relations between words, meanings, and visual and tactile images, and discusses language and its material base and representation. ... possessed by insomnia ... he navigates dictionaries, and tries to open routes through the oceans of language."[5] Here language becomes buried in language, referring only to itself.

But Boshoff is not content to leave things as they are. He seeks other strategies for making available what words represent, how their semantic meaning might be reconstituted. His study of linguistics and Wittgensteinian

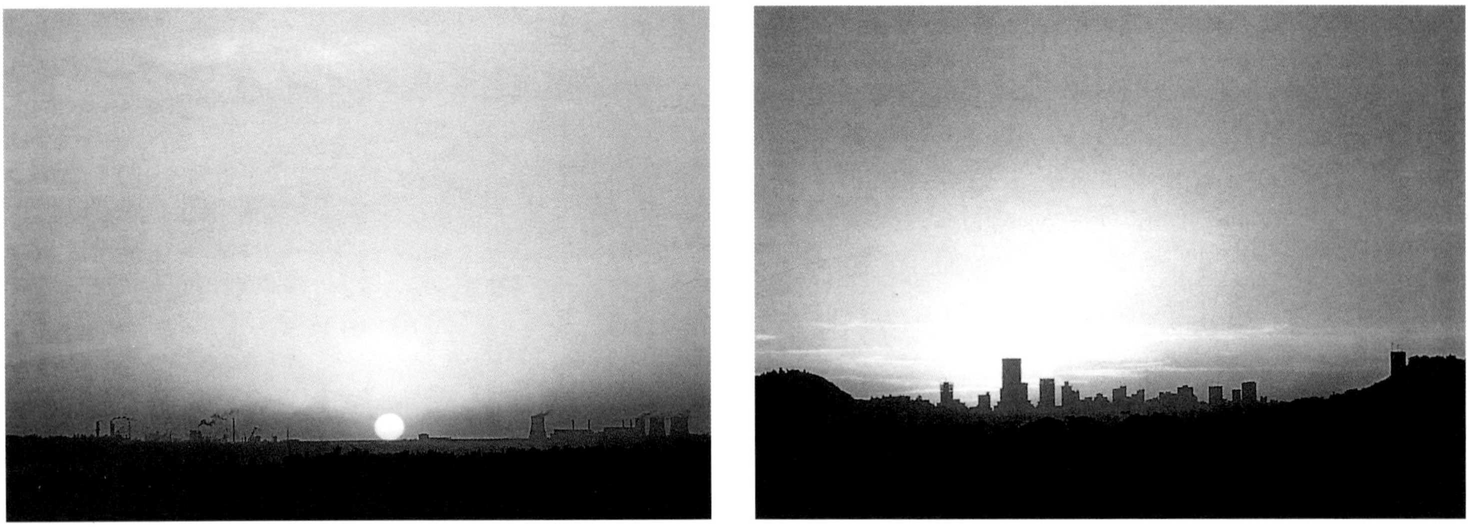

FIGURE 83.
Malcolm Payne, *Good Mourning; Good Night,* 1973, slide projections.

philosophy led him to explore other ways of rendering words into pulsating signs, resulting in *Kykafrikaans* (1980; figs. 75, 80), a serial work of concrete poetry and his most sustained inquiry into the nature of words and obsolescence.

If Boshoff, like Bouabré, keeps a clean concentration on language, Malcolm Payne's very complex and critical work keeps a clean concentration on the political and subversive. Here the political functions not on a literal level, but as an act of contamination. Rather than responding to an oppressive regime via the cliched fist-and-guns of the revolutionary artist, Payne engages in acts of subterfuge by penetrating ideological spaces, "carefully contrived confusion ... [as] the only weapon to keep my creative impetus vaguely alive."[6] This struggle to maintain creative independence has typically been perceived as anarchic. For the 1973 Aquarius Art Festival in Durban, for instance, he proposed to explode underwater a huge quantity of red dye as part of the festivities marking the Afrikaner celebration of Blood River Day, during which they commemorate their defeat of the Zulus. According to Payne, "The idea was further nuanced to include the ultimate irony, to sell the idea to the organizers, explaining to them that they could achieve for themselves and followers an enhanced spiritual and religious experience if the river ran red."[7] The organizers rejected the proposal.

Of all the African work included in this exhibition, Payne's early projects seem conclusively *conceptual,* in their orientation and rejection of the material base of what he called "an overdose of Greenbergian and late Caro modernism." This he endured as a student at St. Martin's School of Art in London in 1973. Partly because of his early exposure to the critical discourse of Western conceptualism, and his contact with the work of artists like Beuys, the practices of Art & Language, and others who were seeking broader spaces for their ideational propositions, Payne sought ways to transpose some of their theories to the situation in his own country.

Upon his return to a South African art scene still enthrall to Clement Greenberg, Payne turned increasingly to performance, using endurance as a metaphor for the individual's quest to transcend the political and intellectual fragmentation imposed by apartheid (fig. 83). Payne was among the first young artists to explore systems of representation of the self, and the state's overwhelming control over defining that self. Identity as an intense site of subjectification thus became a basis for resistance. Appropriating the tools of surveillance, Payne began to meld video, slide projections, photographs, and facsimiles of his body and face into a conceptually sophisticated practice, the goal of which was to deny the state's final right of adjudication in the construction of identity (figs. 77, 170). Payne's intense meditation on the political possibility of subversion laid the groundwork for many artists who would delve into similar questions twenty years later.

One such artist is Kendell Geers. Following Payne's stellar example, Geers has channeled his provocative and vigilant sensibility into an art that acts as an incendiary device within systems of representation (fig. 81, 82). If art is activity, then Geers has made his own existence the signal vector of its convergence, completely blurring the distinction between his life and art, and by extension, self-regulation and institutional administration. Hence, Geers's art is an activity located not inside the solitude of the studio but in the rough-and-tumble world of actions, of political, social, and cultural engagement. In 1995 Geers was invited to exhibit his work at the Johannesburg Art Gallery, *the* institutional showcase of South African art, its classical architectural design by Edwin Lutyens a reminder of the country's ugly and continuing colonial domination. Rather than making anything that might be construed as an object or merit consideration as an artwork, Geers offered *Title Withheld (Boycott),* in which he emptied an entire room within the museum of its contents. With this attack on the institution (and by extension, some of his fellow artists), Geers asserted that art could refuse and resist the ideology of museological practice. Thus, the seemingly empty room questioned the pervasive modernist hunger for market-oriented postcolonial objects. As an amplification of this debate, *Title Withheld (Boycott)* returns us to the vault of the museum, to its ethnographic storage rooms and holding docks, where art and cultural objects await dispersal into the myriad networks of institutional recontextualization. It is precisely what has been cleared and evacuated from the gallery's walls that is the subject of this intensely aware intervention.

Moving away from Geers's longstanding relationship with the traditions of the modernist avant-garde (an example is his alteration of his birthday to May 1968 as a gesture of solidarity with the students who initiated the summer of civil disobedience in Europe), we return to his position via postmodernism as it neatly converges on the question of identity. In *Untitled (ANC, AVF, AWB, CP, DP, IFP, NP, PAC, SACP)* (1993–94), a work whose genesis is directly linked to the political chaos and violence that ravaged South Africa in the months leading to the country's first democratic elections, Geers staged an elaborate set of political actions in the wake of the murder of a member of the Inkatha Freedom Party. On July 19, 1993, the day of the killing, in defense of the political rights of the individual within an intolerant political culture, Geers decided to join all the official parties of South Africa. He would comment that, in this way, it would be impossible to lose. Of course, this response to the institutionalization of politics through party affiliation is an ironic one, for it is the very basis of belonging that produces the kind of rigid fetishization of identity that continues to plague his country with violence. By joining all these parties—culminating on February 7, 1994, when the ultra right-wing Afrikaner Weerstandsbeweging (AWB) issued him an identity card—Geers sought not only to claim all these false identities, but to mark them suspect beyond measure.

As we begin to sift through the material that accompanies this exhibition, we will find new networks and connections will emerge, some familiar, some obscure. In this way, *Global Conceptualism: Points of Origin* will have accomplished its goal of illuminating the forces that propelled artists to find a detour and, in effect, change the ground rules regulating art production and the very language of art itself. At their most critically aware, the African artists considered here have met those challenges, and the richness and acuity of their interventions have left their own indelible mark. Perhaps now we can begin to embrace other accounts of conceptualism that do not always adhere to the strict regimes of orthodox conceptual art, but document the multivalent strategies and diverse motivations behind its appearance globally. This section on African conceptualism should thus be seen as a source for future investigation, which no doubt will uncover other practices that I have overlooked.

Notes

1. Ima Ebong, "Negritude: Between Mask and Flag, Senegalese Cultural Ideology and the 'Ecole de Dakar,'" in *Africa Explores: 20th Century African Art,* ed. Susan Vogel (New York: Center for African Art, 1991), 198.

2. Interview with Issa Samb by the author, Dakar, April 1998.

3. Clémentine Deliss, "7+7=1: Seven Stories, Seven Stages, One Exhibition," in *Seven Stories About Modern Art in Africa* (Paris and New York: Flammarion, 1995), 19.

4. Quoted in Ashraf Jamal, "Willem Boshoff: Blind Alphabet," in *Object Lessons* (São Paulo: 23rd São Paulo Bienal, 1996), 4.

5. Gerardo Mosquera, "Important and Exportant," in *Trade Routes: History and Geography* (Johannesburg and The Hague: 2nd Johannesburg Biennale, Africus Institute of Contemporary Art and Prince Claus Fund for Culture, 1997), 270.

6. Malcolm Payne, "Fault Lines—Breakwater Conference," speaker's notes for a visual presentation at the Breakwater Conference, Cape Town (unpublished).

7. Ibid.

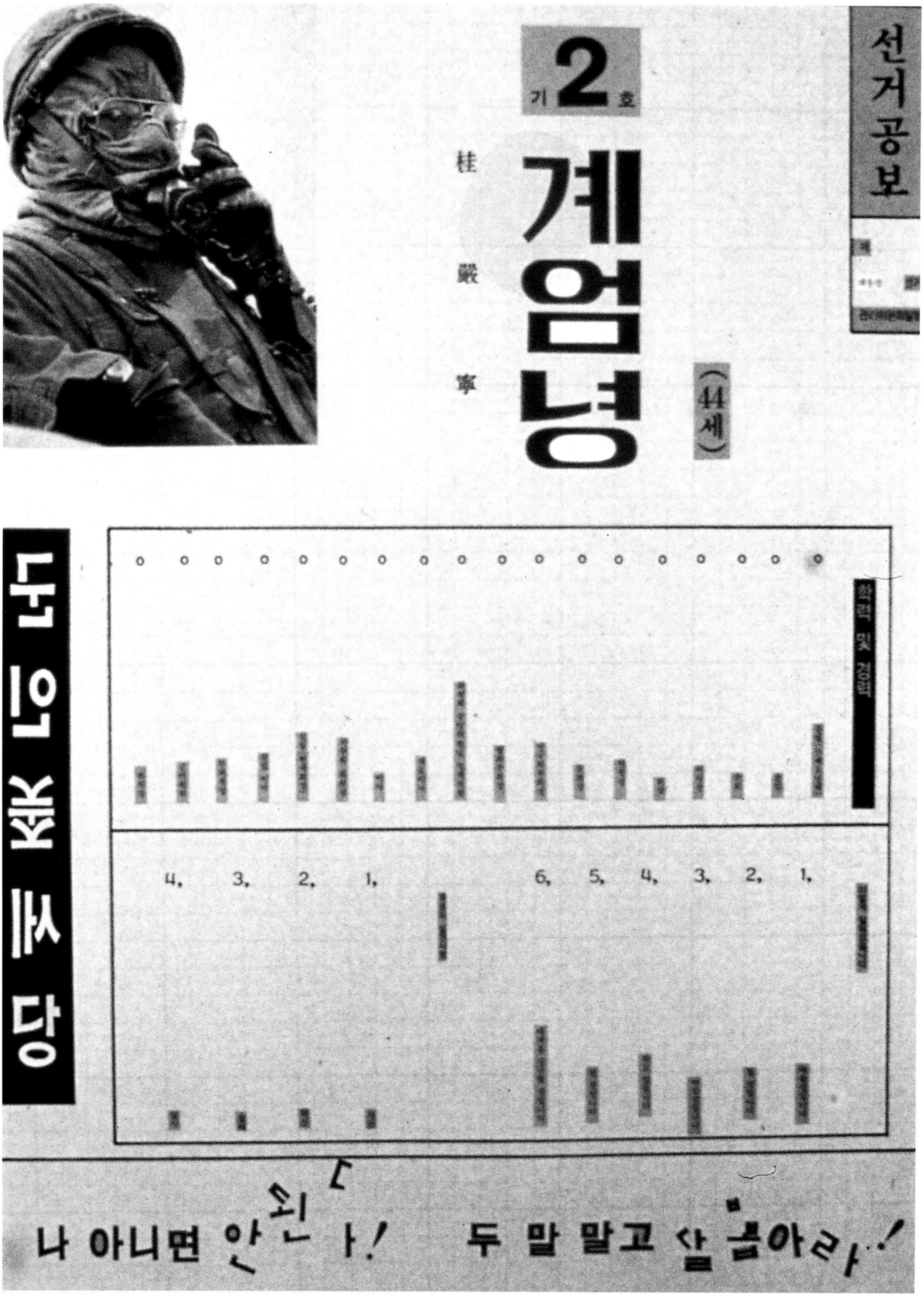
선거공보
기 2 호
계엄령
桂 嚴 寧
(44세)
학력 및 경력
나 아니면 안된다!

From the Local Context: Conceptual Art in South Korea

Sung Wan-kyung

I mention here my debt to Park Chan-kyung for his advice, and Kwon Eun-kyung, Kim Soo-yeon, Ahn Mi-hee, and Park Shin-eui for their assistance in research and translation of reference materials.

Figure 84.
Park Bul-dong, *Nightmare No. 2 (Electoral Campaign Poster)*, 1985, collage of photograph and text on paper. Collection of the artist.

Conceptualism developed in South Korea neither as a clearly definable aesthetic practice nor as a distinct art movement. In fact, conceptual art is probably the most ambiguous artistic phenomenon in both the modernist and Min Joong (People's Art) movements of South Korea. Nevertheless, it is possible to identify conceptualist tendencies or strategies in the work of diverse artists since the end of the 1960s.

Western conceptual art, notably that of the United States, came to the attention of South Korean artists primarily during the 1970s via Japan. Although scant information afforded but a limited introduction, conceptualism in Japan proved influential to a number of South Korean artists, who generally lacked access to global developments in contemporary art. In addition, an "antiform" sensibility flourished among younger artists from the late '60s onward, a consequence of what might be called the "Duchamp effect," which reached East Asia through various intermediaries. Antiform was a rebellious manifestation against conventional mainstream art, and expressed a critical attitude toward academicism, the institutional apparatus, and aesthetic idealism.

Two points should be made about this early period. First, in Korean artists' initial contacts with Western conceptualism, the latter was vaguely understood as another variation of antiform, together with happenings, earthworks, and process art. The antiform revolt of the younger generation was more passionate than the formalist one of older artists, who had rebelled against premodern academicism through informel painting a decade before. But although younger artists were extremely active during the late '60s and early '70s, their overall production lacked consistency and remained ephemeral, failing to generate a meaningful vocabulary within the Korean context.

Second, although more consistency can be found in work produced during the second half of the 1970s, this cohesion came at a price. During this time, "conceptual" strategies were in vogue among artists who dubbed themselves "white monochromists." Born under the influence of Lee U Fan, a Korean-born artist and theoretician based in Japan, white monochromism was then considered a major aesthetic achievement of the era. But one of the criticisms leveled against Lee U Fan by the later Min Joong artists is that he was insensitive to the anti-institutional nature of Euro–North American conceptual art. Lee crafted his own brand of conceptualism out of Eastern philosophy and a kind of nationalistic minimalism. Thus, the white-gray colors of white monochromism ostensibly induced reflection on a Korean "essence." Regardless of Lee's original assertions, the pseudo-minimalist/conceptualist works of the white monochromists demonstrated a profound misunderstanding of conceptualism. Ultimately, these works were nothing more than hybridized local aesthetic commodities that contradicted the

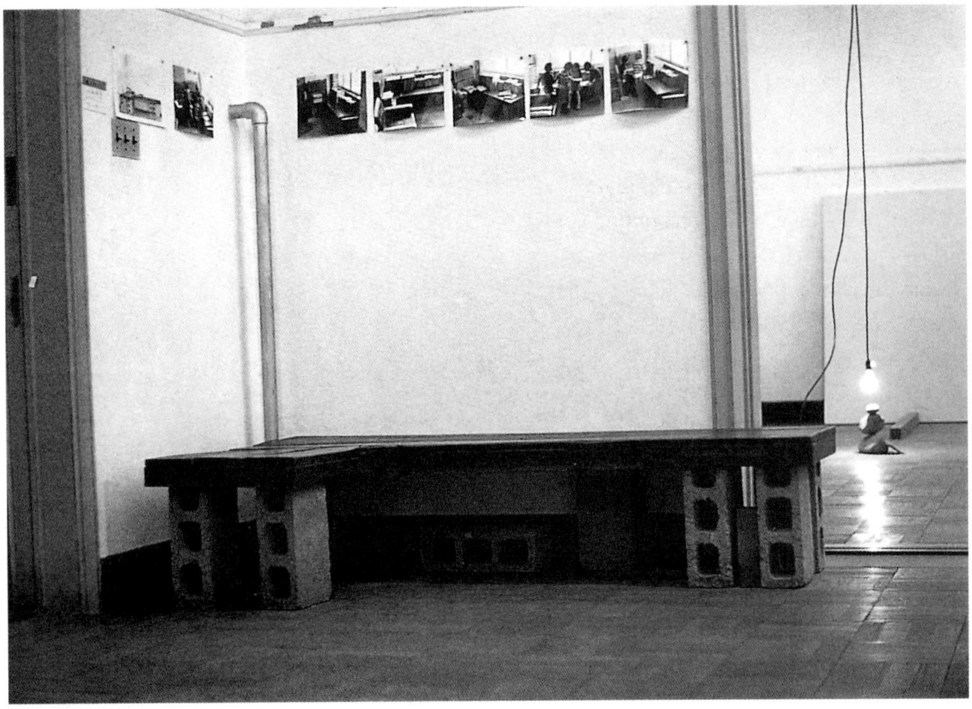

FIGURE 85.
Kim Yong-min, *Floor,* 1975, installation. Collection of the artist.

principles of conceptualism itself. However, once the formalist aesthetic of white monochromism gained hegemony in the local contemporary art scene, other tendencies—Fluxus-like happenings, land art, etc.—rapidly declined and are now barely remembered.

Although most antiform artists basically mimicked European or Japanese modernists, a noteworthy few stand out, in particular, those belonging to the S.T. (Space and Time) group, founded in the mid-1970s. Kim Yong-min, an occasional participant in S.T. exhibitions, consistently deployed antiform and conceptualist strategies. For instance, in one performance he simply mopped a floor. In another, he installed a bench in a gallery, took instant snapshots of seated spectators, and pinned the photos on the walls (fig. 85). This type of work reflects the artist's commitment to dematerialization and his critical stance toward the tautological nature of experiencing art within the gallery or museum. Another S.T. member, Sung Neung-kyung, scrupulously removed every printed line of a newspaper, discarded them in the trash, then attached the mutilated remains of each page to four panels on the gallery wall. The performance was repeated daily, with each day's edition of the newspaper, for the duration of the exhibition. Entitled *After the 1st of June 1974* (1974; fig. 173), the work mocked the violent political censorship of the military government by punning on the popular phrase, "the truth can be read between the lines."

Kim Yong-min and Sung Neung-kyung, as well as Kim Yong-ik, belong to the generation of artists who initiated a localized version of conceptual art (defined in the Western sense). The emergence of this tendency parallels a similar movement in Korean modern literature, in particular, the antipoetry of Kim Soo-young, who as early as 1966 submitted a provocative thesis on the "dialectical tension between the negation of bourgeois language and the apprehension of social reality." The conflict between formalism and social engagement enacted in the literature of the '70s also became a critical issue in the art world. Although this debate reiterated an old literary argument, still it signified the beginning of a more generalized left cultural praxis and laid the groundwork for the modernism-versus-realism polemic prevalent in the Min Joong movement of the 1980s.

Before pursuing further the traces of conceptualism in South Korean art, it is necessary to provide a brief historical survey of the phenomenon called Min Joong. As a cultural movement, Min Joong first gained public attention in 1980 with the founding exhibition of the artist collective Hyunsilgwa-Baron (Reality & Utterance). The exhibition, held at a government-supervised gallery, was immediately shut down by authorities, the second such closing since the "liberation" of 1945. In the first case, in 1969, a show entitled *Reality* organized by a group of college students—one of whom would later form Reality & Utterance—was closed at the urging of school authorities. The rationale for such censorship was that the artworks were not "pure" enough for the then-dominant art-for-art's-sake ideology because they included satirical themes and social criticism. Quite simply, they were viewed as subversive. This nebulous criteria has been maintained and reinforced: in 1985, the exhibit *Hihm-Jeon* (Power of the Younger Generation) resulted in the confiscation of artworks and the detention of some participants, and the 1987 National Security Law has been used to convict artists who address anti-U.S. struggles and national reunification in their work.

It should be noted that in addition to government officials, mainstream art groups were quick to condemn this "subversiveness." Eminent artists, critics, professors, and journalists complained that political motifs "contaminated" art, might even harm the national interest. Moreover, they claimed, the lack of aesthetic sophistication degraded the dignity uniquely required for a work of art. In a country whose government policies are based on virulent anticommunism, the word *subversive* easily translates into *red* (i.e., communist or pro–North Korea). It is hardly surprising, then, that art professionals informed on the "subversives" to government officials, and critics who lent rhetorical support to the negative campaign encouraged a policing of the art world.

All of this was happening in the context of a general government crackdown. On May 17, 1980, the South Korean government declared nationwide martial law and banned all political activities and assemblies. Colleges and universities were closed, and newspapers, radios, and other media rigorously censored. Students protesting these restrictions were soon joined by tens of thousands of ordinary citizens in massive demonstrations in the city of Kwangju. Hundreds died when this uprising was brutally suppressed by the military, and the event became a rallying point for artists as well as the general populace.

Originally a pejorative term coined by pro-government journalists and critics, Min Joong, or People's Art, refers to the broad network of cultural workers and collectives—for instance, Reality & Utterance, Durung (Levee), Imsulnyun, Seoul Art Community, People's Art School—committed to democratic ideals and overt struggle against the military regime. After the 1985 *Power* exhibition, the press began to cover the movement, generally in disparaging terms. But the quantitative expansion and vitality of Min Joong activities helped to offset the negative press. In 1985, Minmihyup (Association of Min Joong Artists) was hastily formed in Seoul to devise a theoretical framework as well as methods for effectively responding to both government suppression and conservative modernist attacks. The Council organized frequent symposia, published journals, opened a gallery, and sponsored exhibitions such as *Tong-il* (Unification) and *Antitorture* (both 1987). These shows attracted large audiences, although the quality of much of the work was often criticized.

To return to our discussion of conceptualism: Largely due to the general cynicism of Korean modern art, during the 1980s the term *conceptual art* was understood by the majority of artists and critics as another strand of formalism. Thus, its possible relationship to Min Joong was not investigated until now. Hence, any attempt to emphasize conceptualism as a prescriptive term for Korean art of the '80s can lead to inconsistencies and contradictions. Presuming Min Joong to be a localized form of "idea-based" art would generate further conflicts and ironies in the recounting of this important cultural movement. For example, within the wide-ranging spectrum of Min Joong production, there were many artists who, con-

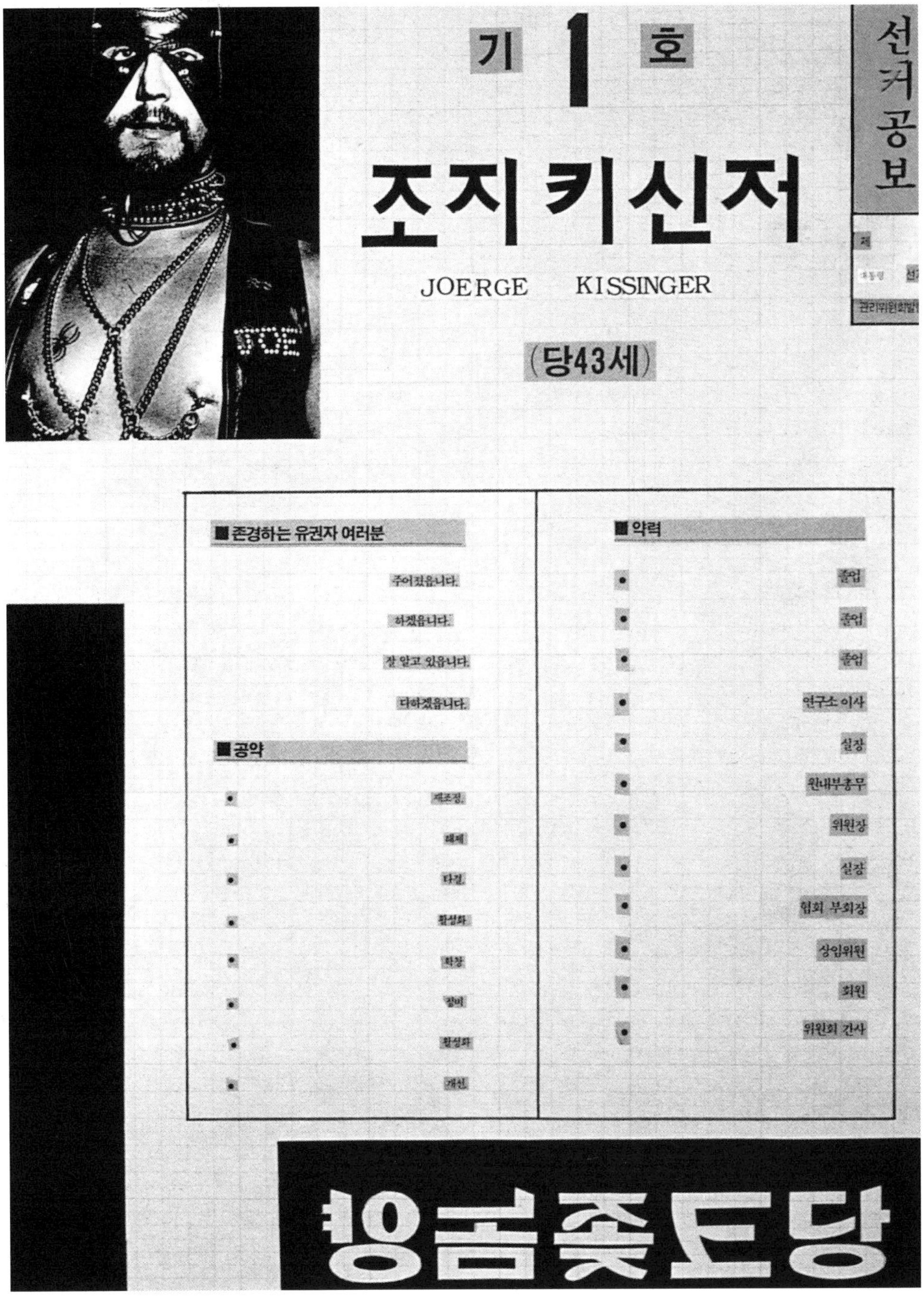

Figure 86.
Park Bul-dong, *Nightmare No. 1 (Electoral Campaign Poster)*, 1985, collage of photograph and text on paper. Collection of the artist.

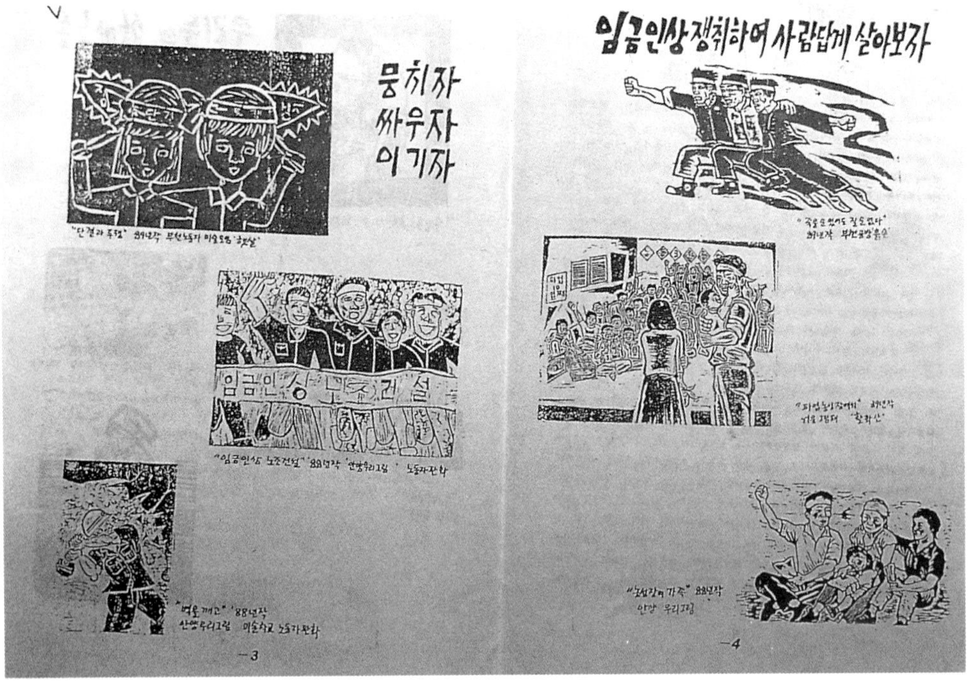

FIGURE 87.
Kim Bong-joon, catalogue for traveling exhibition of the Labor Unions. Collection of the artist.

sciously or not, employed tenets of socialist realism and critical realism. There were also art collectives and individuals within the movement who considered their work a crucial component of a comprehensive agit-prop program, although their practices were more dependent on appropriating and subverting the visual strategies of mass media than on conceptualist attitudes. In fact, conceptualism was often seen as incompatible with the political endeavors of these artists.

The conceptualist aspects of Min Joong are clearly discernible only when we consider its tendency to dissolve the boundaries between art and life, criticize the institutional apparatus of art, and engage in social situations. In other words, only by inverting our perspective, from a local to global context (as proposed by the curatorial project of the Queens Museum of Art) will we discover the conceptualist vein running through the Min Joong cultural movement. Indeed, the general thesis "art of life" expands the methodological possibilities of artistic praxis. So, for instance, the work of Kim Yong-tae and Park Bul-dong, exemplars of Min Joong and members of Reality & Utterance, acquires new meaning if viewed from an international perspective.

Both Park and Kim are acutely conscious of the way "high art" produces and structures meaning within a given context, and proposed new strategies of contextual subversion based on this awareness. For one installation, Kim collected portraits of American soldiers from commercial photo salons near the local U.S. military bases and presented them as art objects in a gallery space (fig. 175). Here the images were used to provoke a reinterpretation of the American presence in South Korea, a military occupation sold to the Korean people as a peacekeeping mission. This practice of disrupting the gallery space with intrusive realities is a typical example of the socialization and politicization of found objects within the local context. It also coincides with the Kwangju Massacre, during which students and intellectuals grew more aware of the United States' role as an unofficial sponsor of South Korea's oppressive regime.

Of all the members of Reality & Utterance, Park Bul-dong is the most sensitive to the semantic order of image and word, and the potential for creating new meanings by subverting the preexisting relationship between the two. His works are generally overflown with satirical commentary and ironic intelligence. In *Nightmare,* photo-collages of fictional candidates with texts, Park investigates the metadesign of icons and the discourse of politicians during the 1985 electoral campaign (figs. 84, 86, 174). Here distortion, destruction, the ludicrous, the impossible, the absurd, the grotesque all operate together to reveal the perversity of modern Korean culture and politics.

The work of Park and Kim clearly demonstrates methodological affinities with conceptual art, broadly defined. As for Min Joong production as a whole, interpreted within the global context of conceptualism, two distinct periods can be discerned. During the early '80s, Min Joong artists focused on "vanguard actions" staged within the framework of the gallery or cultural institution as a way to recover art's communicative function and as an attack on the vanity and incompetence of mainstream art. After 1985, Min Joong artists began to systematically engage in social movements and to work with the "audience" *outside* the gallery, the audience that was discovered while addressing political issues—class struggle, unification, censorship, the relationship between Korea's military regime and the U.S.—through their art. Perhaps this was why the Min Joong movement gained wide support among intellectuals, laborers, peasants, and the general public. At the same time, previously banned Marxist literature along with translated texts dealing with reunification became widely available, and Pax America was regarded with skepticism and resentment by increasing segments of the population.

Confronted with this new audience outside the institutions of art, theoreticians, critics, and artists could no longer simply produce or interpret works of art without first addressing certain fundamental questions. A mode of artistic production that could function critically within the larger socioeconomic system, rather than the intrinsic textuality of art, emerged as the primary determinant in a search for alternative aesthetic forms. On the one hand, many artists in suburban and rural areas borrowed the images and themes of folk traditions, reinventing them as an activist form of Min Joong. In particular, these artists were attracted to the symbiotic relationship between aesthetics and production found in Korean folk music, theater, literature, and painting, and worked closely with local community activists and per-

Figure 88.
Choi Byung-soo, *Design of Funeral Procession for the Six Suicides,* May 1991, ballpoint drawing on paper and photographic documents. Collection of the artist.

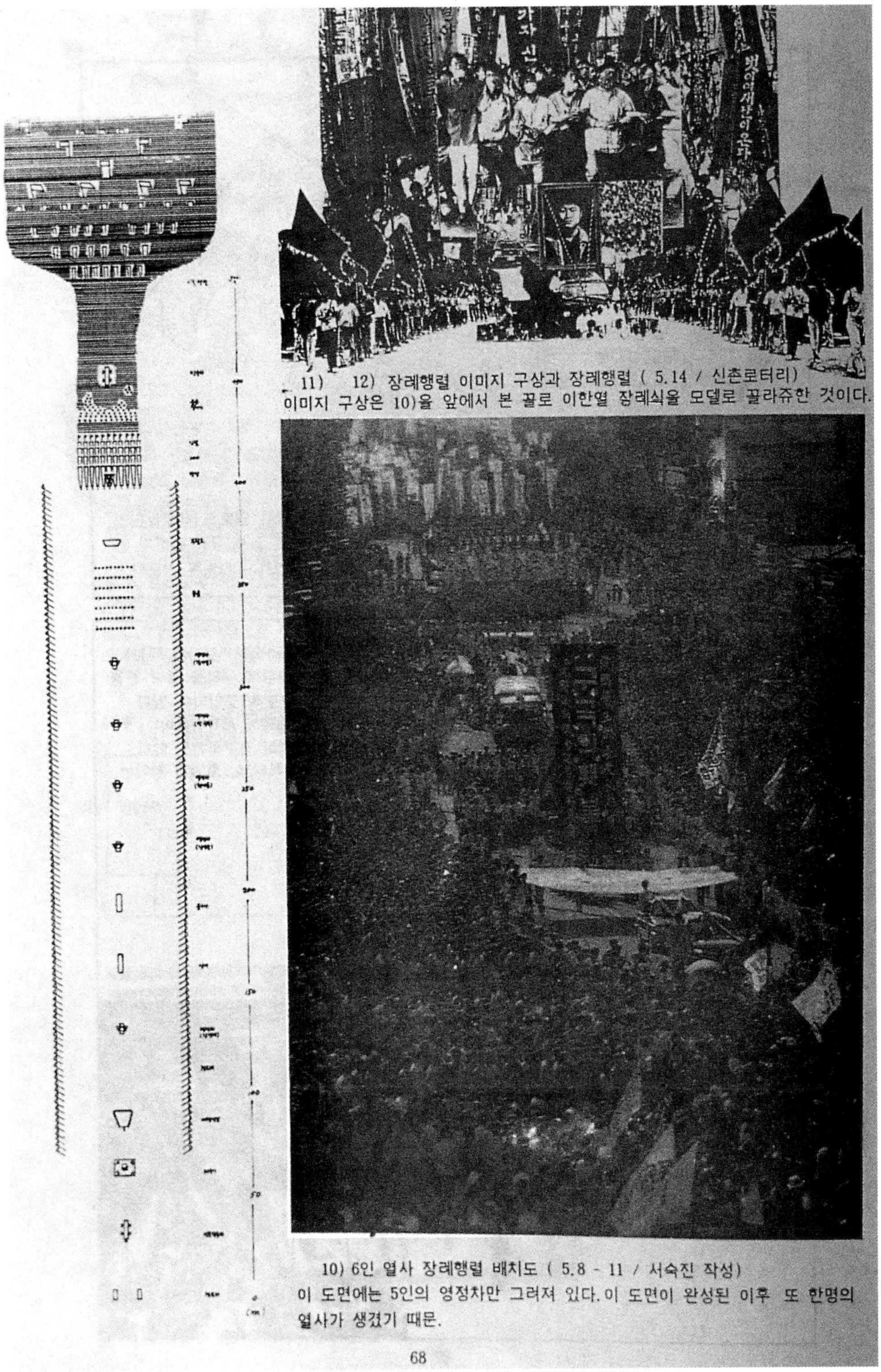

formers of traditional art. On the other hand, many artists attempted a "functional transformation" (to use Walter Benjamin's term) of mainstream media by appropriating its tools: printing, photography, video, and film.

A few significant trends during this period should be highlighted here. First, artists' collaboration with artisans and performers on mask-makings, woodcut printings, and performances improved upon the traditional theatrical style called *madang gutt.* Many Min Joong artists, including Kim Bong-joon, used this style. As a founding member of Durung, Kim expanded the aesthetic qualities of *madang gutt,* focusing on its unique relationship between artist and audience, as well as art and communal festival. Audience participation is an integral part of traditional *madang gutt.* The desire to remove the barrier between performer and audience, artist and spectator, extended to Durung's other activities and became a key tenet of the group's work in art education, in the Gongdongche (community) cultural movement, and with labor unions (fig. 87).

"Documentary as art" had become a powerful vehicle of Min Joong expression by the early 1980s. The life and work of Chun Tae-il, a self-taught unionist who galvanized the workers' movement in the 1970s by igniting himself with gasoline in a public act of suicide, provided a model for the new practice of reportage. Realistic exposés of conditions in factories, urban slums, and universities were produced by laypeople and artists who identified themselves as critical documentarists. Film/video-makers continued this practice through the late 1980s. Some of the most forceful works were created by Kim Dong-won and the Labor Newsreel group, the latter developing an efficient system of distribution that forged new links between artists and laborers. Kim's video documentary *Sanggyedong Olympics* (1986) brilliantly captures the militarylike precision with which illegal housing was dismantled in the impoverished urban district of Sanggyedong, a "city beautification project" initiated in preparation for the 1986 Asian Olympic games in Seoul. As the camera shifts between author and subjects, the work's piercing immediacy conveys the violence, hardship, and grief experienced by residents. Although Kim's documentary never achieved the status conferred on "video art," it is fair to say that his work "conceptually" challenged established notions of "beauty" more aptly than any other more stylized video in Korea.

Finally, Min Joong artists contributed directly to resistance movements in the form of blueprints for massive rallies, marches, festivals, and public funerals. The work of Choi Byung-soo is exemplary in this respect. While Choi quickly gained a reputation with his *gulgae grim,* or enormous banner paintings, he also planned, designed, and directed the visual and performative details of major political events, including the June Resistance and July–August Labor Struggle of 1987, and the funeral procession for Lee Han-ryul, who was killed by police in 1987 (figs. 88, 176). For the funeral of Kang Kyong-dai, another student killed by antiriot police, Choi mapped a march through the city, acutely sensitive to the visual dialectics of time and space. In the process, he produced blueprints for many different possible marches, which were exhibited at the Gallery Grimmadang Min in 1989.

❖

Min Joong incorporated a conceptualist dimension in various ways, for instance, disturbing the boundary between art and daily life, attacking the institutions of art, and repudiating the alliance between artmaking and the system of commodity production. To avoid misunderstanding, it is noteworthy that Min Joong encompassed a wide spectrum of activities and expressive forms: traditional arts (mask dance, theater, woodcuts), expressionist and socialist realism, pop, narrative figuration, banner and mural painting, media works (photo, printed ephemera, video, film, cartoons), cultural education programs, blueprints for mass street and campus demonstrations, and so on. Once we recognize the variety of styles, conceptual frames, and mediums employed by the movement, Min Joong's image as simplistic agit-prop—an image propagated by hostile critics, artists, and journalists—is revealed for what it is: an aspersion typically cast upon socially engaged art that undermines the institutionalized concept of art for art's sake.

Nonetheless, it is also true that the majority of Min Joong artists, who were generally suspicious of Korean modern art, paid little attention to the diverse forms of anti-art produced by the Western vanguard. Min Joong artists tended to have a narrow understanding of how art interacts with and penetrates daily life, in ways different from strategies deployed to mobilize mass struggle. This limited perspective became a major obstacle in the movement's adjustment to the ambiguous cultural geography of the 1990s.

This new situation is a consequence of profound political and economic change in the international and local arenas. The collapse of the socialist bloc and the triumph of U.S.-style neoliberalism have reverberated in every part of the world in disquieting ways. On the local level, pro-democracy forces have been disappointed by the superficial democratization accomplished under Kim Young-sam, ex-leader of the opposition party who won the 1992 election by compromising with then-president, General Roh Tae-woo. Both Roh and General Chun Doo-hwan, another former president, have since been indicted and convicted for their roles in the 1980 Kwangju Massacre and subsequent military junta. But the premature "internationalization" and frenzied economic boom begun in the previous decade have accelerated under Kim. The result: unchecked urban expansion, consumer madness, and a strange mixing of modern, postmodern, and premodern in everyday life. These international and local phenomena have been accompanied by the weakening of progressive intellectuals in Korea's political life, where for decades and throughout the '80s they had articulated the moral argument against military despotism.

South Korea

In Korea, where (as in other Asian countries) the tradition of authoritarian culture remains strong, there is a widely generalized exploitation of art in "nonartistic" contexts. We see this in the instrumentalization of art by political or other authoritarian institutions, for example, in extravagant cultural projects like the Seoul Olympic Sculptural Symposium. This instrumentalization, which reflects the value system of a feudal and colonialist past, depoliticizes art by abolishing its conceptual/intellectual dimension, reducing it to decorative fetish.

In the decade since the 1988 Seoul Olympiad, power and money have hierarchized the Korean art world as never before, a development that coincides with the proliferation of cultural exchanges with the West and the establishment of the Kwangju Biennale. In this context, the antagonism between a critical politics and flagrant careerism that existed in the 1980s has been subsumed by the competition for fame. Artists of the so-called New Generation (Shinseidae) are representative of this trend. Blending kitsch objects of premodern and modern mass culture, icons and cultural codes of nostalgia, and conceptualist devices, New Generation artists created a Korean version of pop. Hailed at first as a new cultural language, it was rapidly forgotten.

The decline of Min Joong, and thus conceptualist art, in the early 1990s must be viewed in this global context of commercialism, self-promotion, and the pursuit of (ephemeral) prosperity. A stylized conceptualism thrives, along with installation, techno art, etc., but at the expense of a critical social vision. Although there are signs of a reemergence of politically engaged cultural practices, based in the concrete reality of everyday life, this is another story to be told at another time.

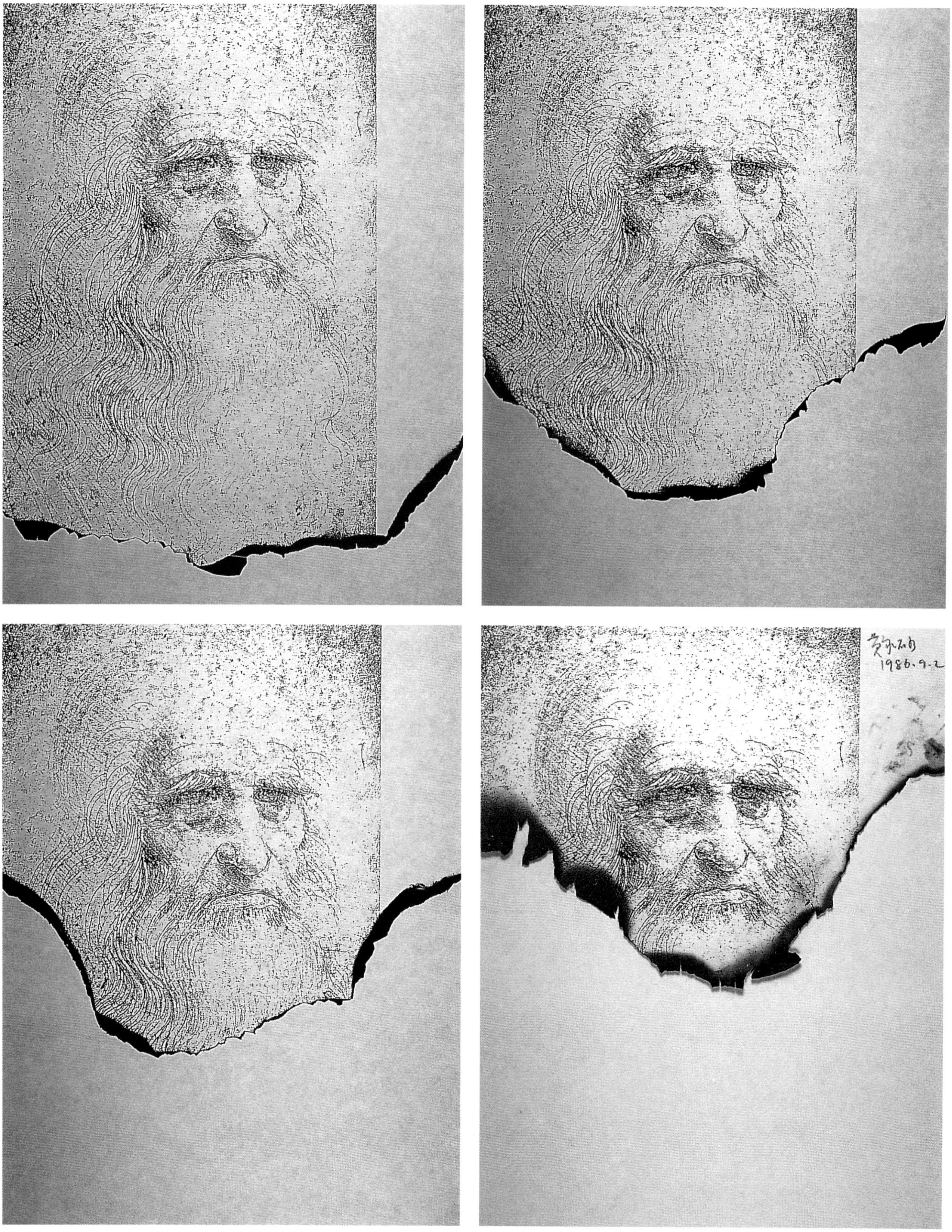
黄永砯
1986.9.2

Conceptual Art with Anticonceptual Attitude: Mainland China, Taiwan, and Hong Kong

Gao Minglu

FIGURE 89.
Huang Yong Ping, *The Beard Was Easiest to Burn (Huzi zhiyi ranshao)*, 1986, four photocopies. Collection of the artist.

As the name of a certain Western art movement of the 1960s and '70s, "conceptual art" was given two translations in Mainland China: *guannian yishu* ("idea art") and *gainian yishu* ("concept art"). *Guannian* has much broader connotations than *gainian*. The former refers to the general meaning of things in a particular context, the latter more narrowly to a specific notion or definition. Chinese conceptual art is more accurately described as *guannian yishu*.

In Taiwan during the 1960s and Mainland China in the '80s, conceptualism played a role similar to dada, that is, as a vehicle for upsetting conventions—aesthetic, social, and political. Almost all Chinese conceptual artists proclaimed an allegiance to dada. On the Mainland, they also embraced traditional Chan Buddhism, which encourages an ironic sensibility and rejects the privileging of any one doctrine in the search for enlightenment. Combined, dada and Chan Buddhism became a potent weapon in the Chinese avant-garde's assault on business-as-usual.

The conceptualist strategy of the 1980s was clarified by Mainland artist Huang Yong Ping in an essay entitled "Xiamen Dada: A Sort of Postmodernism?" (1986).[1] Here, he grounds his dadalike practice in Chan Buddhism, and declares the latter a major theoretical source of postmodernism. For Huang, Art as such has never existed, and art itself is insignificant, at least inasmuch as it has functioned as an expression of individual subjectivity. But he goes even further, advocating destruction—of doctrine, institutional authority, master texts, ideology, authorship, subjectivity—as the goal of artmaking. Huang's philosophy of art as "nothing" that creates nothing, inspired by Chan Buddhism, laid the foundation for contemporary Chinese conceptualism.

But it is important to note that, unlike its Western counterpart, this anti-art project did not develop from a logical historical progression of aesthetic avant-gardism. There has never existed in China a sphere of aesthetic autonomy as theorized by Peter Bürger for the West.[2] Euro–North American conceptual art of the late 1960s and early '70s was, in this respect, a new movement that continued a project begun in the mid-19th century: from questioning representation and the relationship between subject and object, to challenging the institutional apparatus of art, to dematerialization itself. In Mainland China and Taiwan (Hong Kong presents a different trajectory), the relationship between modern art and society has been virtually seamless and, moreover, modern Chinese art has always been informed by social concerns. So, for instance, while Mainland conceptual artists of the 1980s vehemently criticized the rationalist faith of academic painters, their aesthetic strategies became the adversarial foundation for destroying the old rationalism that framed the entire political and social order.

Finally, Chinese conceptual art represents a paradoxical negotiation between a perceptual aesthetic and its complete destruction. Again unlike most of their Western counterparts, Chinese conceptual artists did not relinquish visual power. On the contrary, they deployed that power to enhance the conceptual meaning of their work. This balancing of the visual and conceptual is a feature of all the artworks included in this section of the exhibition and, in fact, ultimately derives from traditional Chinese aesthetic theory, which discouraged extremes of any type in art practice.

Outward and Downward: Conceptualism in Taiwan

Modernist art in Taiwan flourished in the 1950s as the country opened cultural communication with the West and experienced an "economic miracle." Established in 1957, the influential Fifth Moon and Eastern Painting groups advocated a synthesis of traditional Chinese and modern Western art forms, especially abstract expressionism. In some ways, these groups continued the modernist art project begun by Chinese artists of the 1930s and '40s in Shanghai and other metropolitan areas on the Mainland, and their paintings were deemed "high" art because their art-for-art's-sake orientation could be traced back to traditional literati painting.

The advent of conceptualism in the mid-1960s represented a rebellion among young artists against these forms of elite art—literati and abstract painting—which conceptualists considered to be empty, even exhausted, and certainly distanced from ordinary life. It was also a reaction to a repressive political culture. The Taiwanese had endured martial law since 1949, when the Nationalists (Kuomintang or KMT) fled Mainland China and established a government-in-exile on the island. (Martial law was not lifted until 1987.) Thus, the iconoclasm of the Taiwanese conceptualists was partly a result of the alienation created by years of official (not to mention self-) censorship. And in their eyes, much elite art of the period, with its emphasis on "universal" principles, was a natural byproduct of a conservative culture that suppressed individualism.

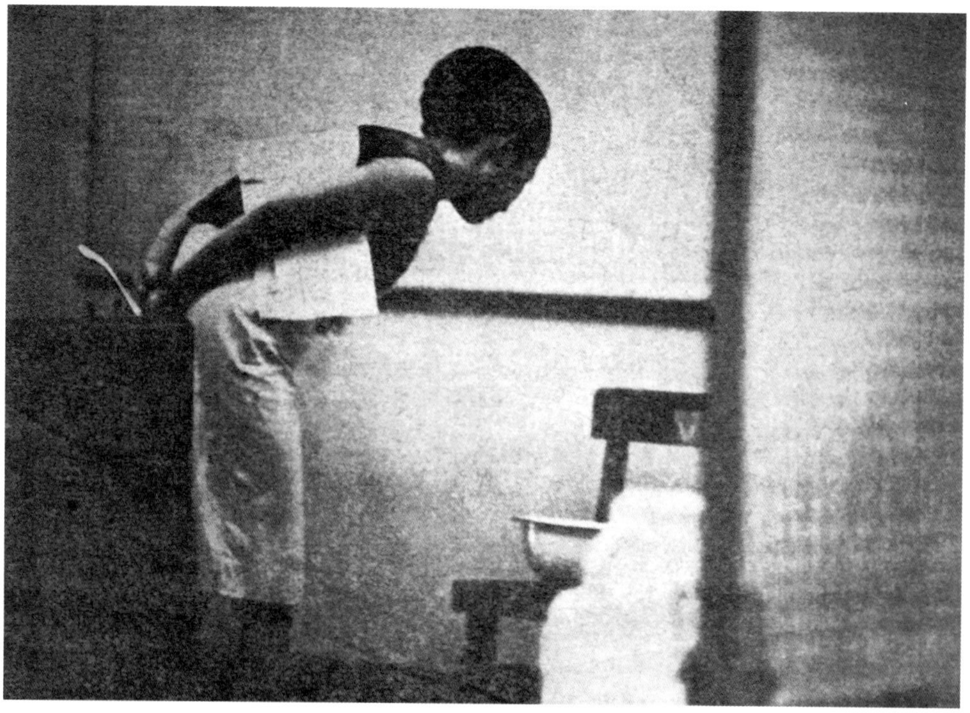

Figure 90.
Huang Huacheng, *Washing Hands* (*Xishou*), 1966, wooden chair and steel washbasin. Collection of the artist's family.

This is not to say that conceptualists, in their attempt to bridge the gap between art and everyday life, were no less elite than abstract painters, or that "life" as used here referred to a specific social condition beyond a generalized sense of alienation. Taiwanese conceptualism modified the practice of art by making new demands on visual materials and aesthetic forms rather than social function. But in the process, its outward and downward orientation laid a foundation for the "native roots," or *xiangtu,* movement of the 1970s, which in turn initiated the search for a Taiwanese political and cultural identity that reverberates to this day.

Taiwanese scholars refer to conceptualism by various terms: neodada, antipainting, multimedia art, and so on, a reflection of its multiple sources of inspiration and expansive approach to materials.[3] Philosophically, it was influenced by existentialism, and aesthetically, various Western art movements, especially dada and pop. Conceptualists organized collectives and exhibitions with a distinct anti-art edge, and adopted every available media—readymades, photography, collage, text, film, even theatrical performance—as alternatives to straight painting and as a means to radicalize the object. They challenged conventional notions of the relationship between art and life, linguistic and aesthetic forms, signifier and signified. In 1967, Huang Huacheng founded the Language Beyond Painting Society (Huawai Huahui) with several graduates of the art department at Taipei Normal University. Two years later, member Guo Chengfeng outlined the group's objectives in an article entitled "Language Beyond Painting Society: A Language Group, Not a Painting Group," implying that the linguistic/conceptual apparatus of art took precedence over the object itself.[4] In other words, "what constitutes painting is something outside of painting,"[5] a notion closely allied with the concept of "frame" proposed by Craig Owens to define the practice of Euro–North American artists like Marcel Broodthaers, Daniel Buren, Michael Asher, and Hans Haacke, all of whom investigated the institutional structure of art.[6] The difference, however, is that Taiwanese artists were primarily concerned with the broader social meaning beyond the visual image itself rather than the institution (museum, gallery) that structured the artwork. In part, this was because, until the early 1980s, Taiwan barely had an art infrastructure to criticize.

Among the most influential Taiwanese conceptualists of the '60s were Huang Huacheng, Huang Yung-sung, and Chang Chaotang. Like many of his contemporaries, Huang Huacheng created experimental artworks with various media. In 1965, he contributed to the journal *Theater,* introducing modern Western drama theory and plays to the Taiwanese public. He produced two avant-garde films in which a voiceover narrative is accompanied by a repetitive image of hands conveying a sense of sorrow or struggle. In *Eye Exam Chart (Shilibiao,* 1968), Huang transformed a familiar, mundane object into an image with new "aesthetic value," and in the photo-collage *Memory of Mother (Jinianmuqin,* 1968), he juxtaposed pictures of his mother and father to create a visual narrative of his family's history. *Washing Hands* (*Xishou*, 1966; fig. 90), an installation consisting of a washbasin, a wooden chair, and a poem by Qiu Gangjian, expressed Huang's conviction that poetry exists in the seemingly mundane activities of everyday life. As a founding member of the Language Beyond Painting Society, Huang coorganized a series of group exhibitions that conveyed a decidedly anti-art tone. For instance, *My Original Self (Zijia benlai mianmu,* 1967) was comprised principally of paintings, but many participants contributed readymades in response to the criticism of conservative museum directors and artists.[7] The Language Beyond Painting Society was formed not only to break from abstract modes of artmaking favored since the '50s, but to engage art in the practice of social criticism.

Chang Chaotang also produced multimedia works, including experimental films, photo collages, and readymades. In 1962, Chang produced the first of his "headless" portraits, photographing fellow artist Huang Yung-sung at a site on Wuzhi Mountain in central Taiwan. Huang is portrayed from the back and his head is blocked out, hence the title *Headless Back (Wutou beiying)*. Functioning as both a commentary on the insensibility of the art world (it literally has no brain), and as an existential rumination on the relationship between intellectual activity and nature, the headless motif was carried into a group of self-portraits, which were mounted as an exhibition in 1965 (fig. 91). The same theme takes on overtones of lost or obscure identity in the first entry of Chang's film series *Diary (Riji,* 1967), a surrealist nightmare featuring a headless man as well as a friend of the artist, face painted white, who cannot locate his own image in a group portrait of classmates.

Like Huang Huacheng and Chang Chaotang, Huang Yung-sung pushed the boundaries of artmaking, but unlike most of his colleagues, Huang attempted a complete break from elite formalist modes by using readymade material typically found among the lower classes.
His 1967 installation *Pawn* (*Dang,* fig. 92) consisted of several plaster statues made by the artist himself—a human head, a fragmented female body, two legs, a small figure poised on a wire coil—as well as the artist's rubber gloves, set alongside a brick carved with the Chinese character *dang* ("pawn"). One of the earliest readymade installations in Taiwan, the piece conveys an attitude of self-mockery, a commentary on the trivialization of art in Taiwanese society: artmaking here is equated with the practice among poor people of pawning their goods for survival. During the late '60s, Huang organized a series of exhibitions collectively titled UP. The title was chosen in the same spirit that prompted the word DADA: it does not convey a specific meaning but is, rather, a gesture of rebellion. More important-

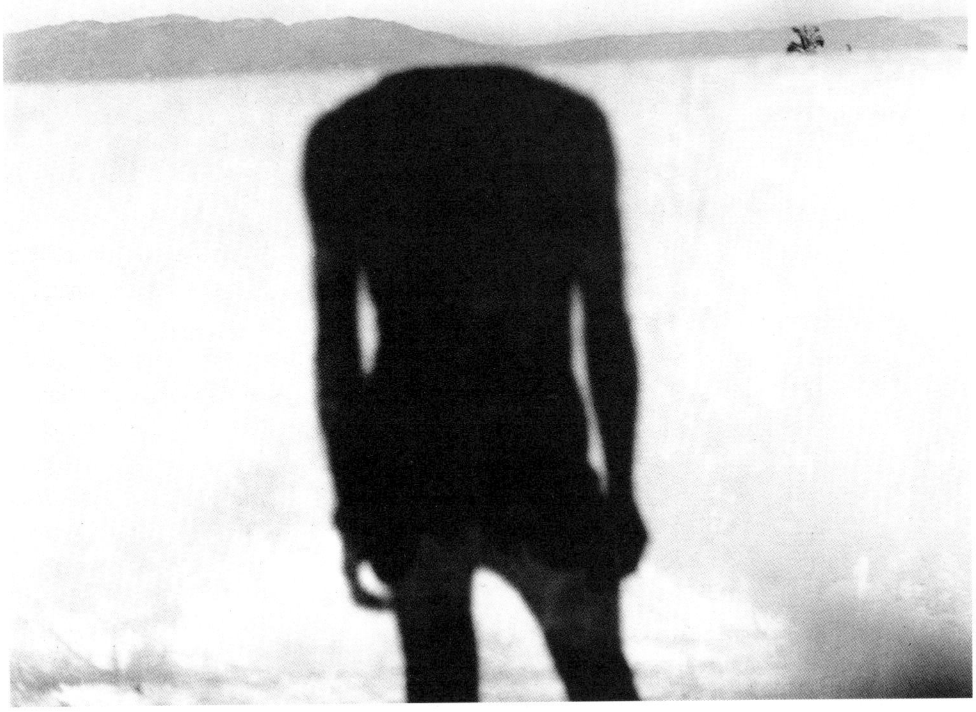

FIGURE 91.
Chang Chaotang, *Headless Self-Portrait (Wutou zihuaxiang)*, 1962, photograph. Collection of the artist.

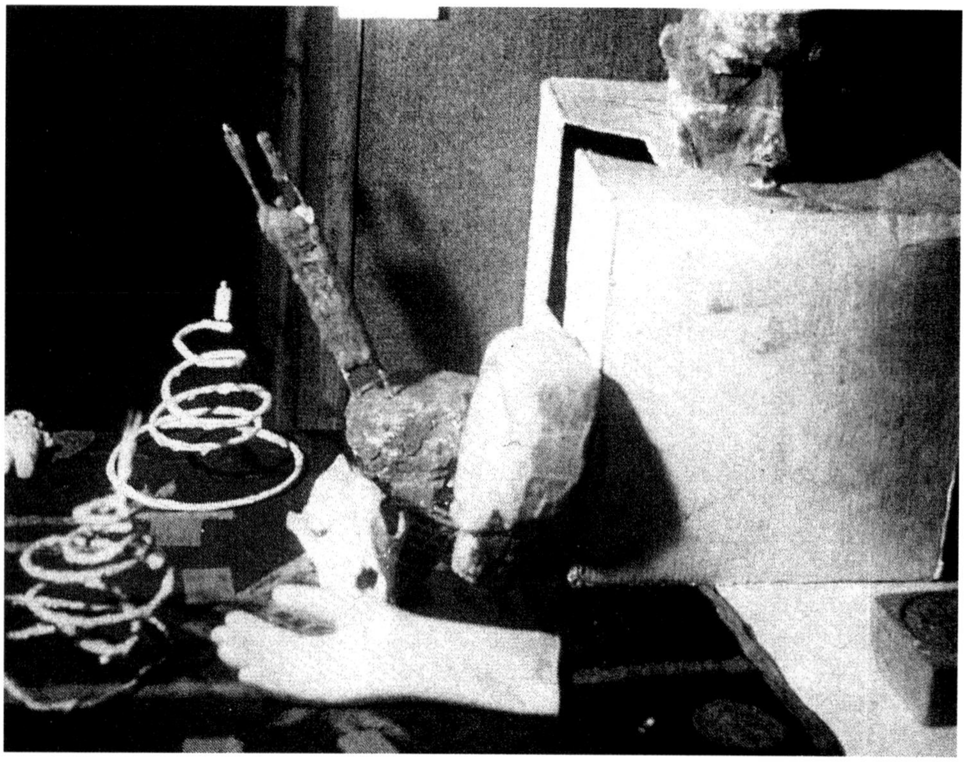

FIGURE 92.
Huang Yung-sung, *Pawn* (*Dang*), 1967, clay seal and personal objects. Collection of the artist.

ly, according to Huang, the work produced under the rubric of UP was honest.

Hsieh Tehching, a pioneer of performance art in Taiwan, was not involved in any of the groups and exhibitions described here. He began as a painter in the late 1960s, then made a dramatic debut as a performance artist in 1972 when he jumped from the third floor of a building in Taipei. The event, naturally, was considered shocking, and seems to have been the artist's most influential work in Taiwan before he emigrated to the U.S. Hsieh continued to engage in risky body "performances," including living in a state of self-imposed homelessness on the streets of New York for a year. Then, in 1986, he initiated a new project in which he has refused to engage in any art world activities (including this exhibition), claiming that everyday life itself is an aesthetic process. This project will continue through the end of 1999.

Taiwan's first (brief) wave of conceptualism ended in the late '60s (another emerged in the 1980s and continues today). Its "art for material's sake" approach, rooted in local social and cultural contexts as well as traditional concepts of the relationship between nature and spirituality, paved the way for the grassroots *(xiangtu)* cultural movements of the 1970s, in which Taiwanese artists and writers explored the indigenous (i.e., pre-Nationalist) traditions of folk art, music, and theater. Many of Taiwan's early conceptualists shifted focus as well: Huang Huacheng turned to graphic design, Huang Yung-sung made documentary films on rustic life. Both anti-Western and anti-modernist, *xiangtu* artists were often accused of provincialism. They rejected modernist idioms first introduced by Japan during its colonial occupation of the island (1895–1945) and then by the United States Information Service in Taipei, and looked to nature and everyday life among rural peoples for inspiration. On the other hand, at a time when Taiwan's booming economy reproduced many of the ugly effects of rapid industrialization, *xiangtu* artists contributed to a burgeoning environmental movement and a critique of Western concepts of modernization and progress. All of this activity would coalesce during the 1980s in a more complex joining of local and Western forms—conceptualist among them—dedicated to a renewed search for cultural identity that rejected any simple notion of "origins."

Staging Reality in Hong Kong

Frequently disparaged as a "cultural desert," Hong Kong is still struggling to overcome a legacy of colonialism and an image of Hong Kong people as shameless materialists enthrall to consumer culture. "East Meets West" has occasionally been used to define Hong Kong, mainly to promote tourism. But, simply put, a tradition of avant-gardism never developed in the territory. Nor did the social upheavals of the '60s, experienced here as elsewhere in the world, produce a parallel rebellion in the arts. Although the student movements, labor activism, and riots of 1967–68 generated a greater sense of local identity and led to modest reforms in colonial policy, not until the 1990s would a critical mass of Hong Kong artists take up the cudgel against both the conservative art establishment and a vacuous urban culture.

Meanwhile, along the way there were some exceptions to this otherwise bleak picture. Founded in 1982 by Danny Ning Tsun Yung, the collective Zuni Icosahedron adapted conceptualist and performance idioms to participatory theater. Yung himself, who studied architecture and urban design in Berkeley and New York during the late '60s, came to theater work via an interest in film and video. In 1982, he produced a single-frame film, *To Serve the People* (*Wei renmin fuwu*; fig. 93), based on the five Chinese characters—*wei, ren, min, fu, wu*—which comprise Mao's famous slogan. As the characters shimmered across the screen, various performers behind the screen enacted scenarios based on Mao's political principle.

The word *zuni* includes two Chinese characters that mean "to pursue progress." Most of Zuni's works were staged in unconventional theater spaces, actually public sites open to anyone who wanted to participate as a dancer or actor. Ideally, the group hoped the audience would become performers and the performers would appropriate the job of directing. Zuni's performers came from all walks of life—telephone operators, messengers, engineers—and brought with them experiences from their professions and neighborhoods. In a way, Zuni was attempting to bridge the gap between the "cultural desert" and the avant-garde ivory tower. This ambition, however, also produced a characteristic ambiguity between language and image, signifier and signified, actor and audience, stage and reality. For Zuni, meaning is context-specific, unfolding and expanding through the process of theater work itself. Moreover, central to Zuni's practice is a fascination with street life. Zuni attempted to extract the essence of this fascination in what might be called installations for the stage. As Danny Yung explained it, "someday Hong Kong will be a theater and a theater will be Hong Kong."[8] Zuni rejected the vocabulary of traditional theater—plot, dominant story lines, "stars"—because for them "terminology means we cannot move from the rigidness. Without terms, we have more open space, with no absolute standards."[9]

Unfortunately, the ambiguity and openness that Zuni prized struck many "ordinary" people as elitist. For this reason, Zuni's work played a role almost exclusively at the level of high culture, even receiving financial support from the colonial government and Hong Kong's elite art circles. Thus, until the 1990s, when a full-blown avant-garde movement emerged as a response to Hong Kong's handover to China, Zuni was a unique phenomenon within a society often characterized as a Big Chinatown.

From Deideologization to Dematerialization in Mainland China

Conceptual art emerged in the Mainland as part of an unprecedented groundswell of avant-garde activities known as the '85 Movement.[10] This movement, which flourished from 1985 to 1989, was very much a reflection of its historical moment, a rebellion against the authority of both state ideology and the institutional apparatus of art as represented by academics, traditionalists, and party bureaucrats. Between 1985 and 1987, more than eighty unofficial art groups declared their defiance in published manifestos, and organized some 150 avant-garde exhibitions and meetings. Over 2,000 young artists participated in such activities.[11]

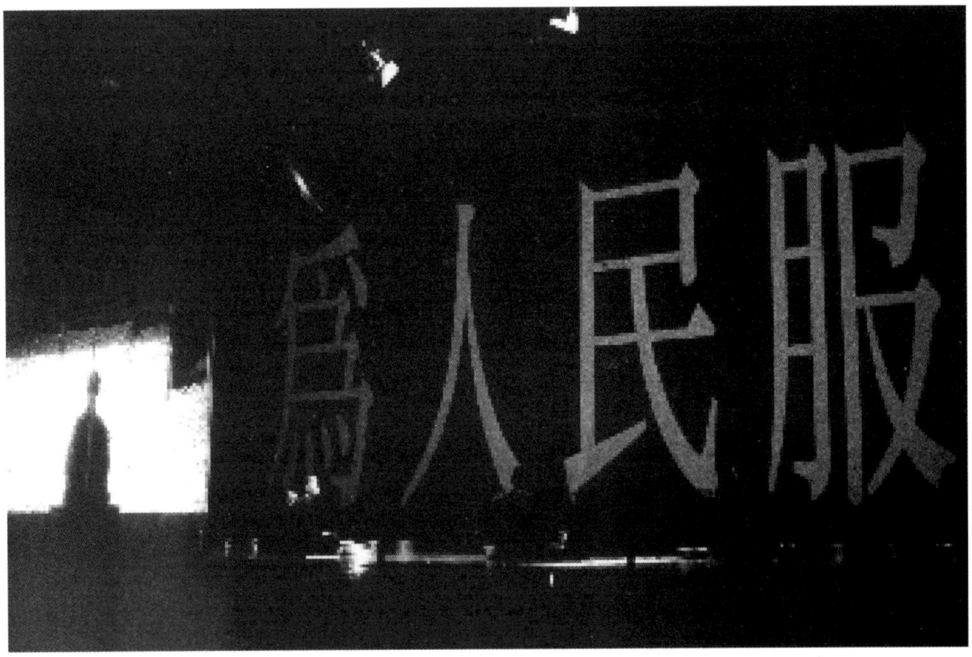

Figure 93.
Danny Ning Tsun Yung, *To Serve the People* (*Wei renmin fuwu*), 1982, videotape. Collection of the artist.

The '85 Movement arose from a specific political and cultural context, namely the end of the Cultural Revolution and the death of Mao in 1976, after which Mainland China opened its doors to the West. In addition to exposing young artists to Western art movements, the post-Mao period ushered in a wave of political and philosophical discussion on modernity, culture, humanism, and social alienation. The sources for this intense intellectual reappraisal—which touched on human value, dignity, rights, and freedom—were diverse, ranging from Karl Marx's *1844 Manuscript on Economics and Philosophy,* which was used to indirectly criticize the undervaluation of the individual in contemporary Chinese society,[12] to translated works of Western philosophy, history, aesthetics, and psychology. At the same time, ancient Chinese philosophy, history, culture, and religion were reevaluated, criticized, or sanctioned according to newly defined standards of modernity.

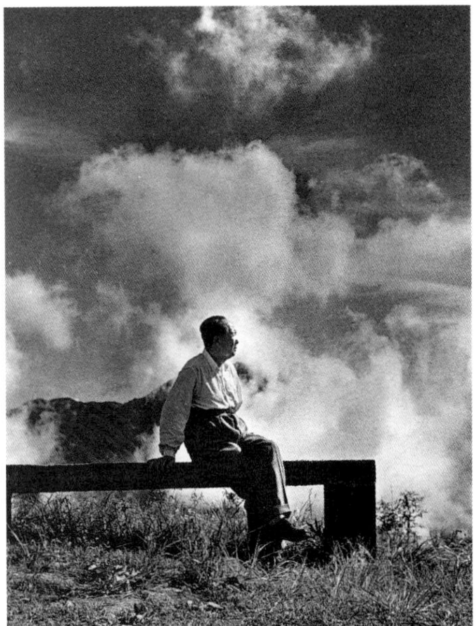

Mao Zedong at Mt. Lushan, Jiangxi, China, 1961. Courtesy of Magnum Photos, Inc.

All of this fed into the burgeoning avant-gardism that finally erupted in the '85 Movement. Two distinct tendencies can be observed among the various avant-garde groups of the movement: humanist and conceptualist. While the former emphasized utopian notions of art as a blueprint for creating a new society, the latter subscribed to a kind of anti-utopian critique of art as a social construction.

Humanists saw their art as an instrument for improving a backward society and reversing its cultural degeneration. Their theoretical foundations lay partly in traditional Confucianism and partly in modern Western philosophy, such as Nietzsche's *Übermensch,* existentialism, and Bergson's vitalism. Their aesthetic models were Western symbolism, surrealism, and expressionism. Two broad styles developed within the humanist camp, rationalist painting *(lixinghuihua)* and Current of Life painting (Shengmingzhuiliu), both of which vehemently criticized alienation from social and political reality, albeit from different perspectives. Whereas the objective of the rationalist painters was to create a new cultural and social order to replace the old, the Current of Life group sought to release suppressed emotions and instincts in order to rescue human nature from alienation. Both groups, however, shared a belief that their art could function on equal terms with science and philosophy. The humanists, thus, were simultaneously futurists, utopians, and of course modernists in the particular context of Chinese contemporary society. But the anti-Mao utopianism of the humanist avant-garde was, in fact, still the pseudo-iconoclastic myth of the artist as creator, prophet, redeemer, martyr, and social engineer.

Like the humanists, conceptual artists were "revolutionaries." However, they sought not only to go beyond the long-dominant socialist realism, but also to break with the new art schools that had emerged after the Cultural Revolution, including the humanists, their colleagues in the '85 Movement. Although conceptual artists took a strongly antagonistic stance toward state ideology, they considered their task to be, not to create a new ideology like their avant-garde counterparts, but rather to completely undermine the methodological foundation of ideological production itself. Conceptualists recognized that the first step in this program of deideologization was to demolish the illusion of subjectivity generated by Mao's revolutionary program, with its statist conception of "the people." However, the individualism longed for by avant-garde artists was not that of the "ordinary citizen" or the "little people," but a new kind of revolutionary consciousness, one critical of authority in all its guises. To that end, conceptualists adopted deconstructivist strategies such as irony, simulation, and appropriation, and created projects that were both anti-utopian and anti-authorship.

Conceptualist art of the 1980s can be divided into three major categories: language projects, anti-art projects, and performance. The first is represented by Wenda Gu, Wu Shan Zhuan, and Xu Bing, all of whom created series using Chinese characters from different critical orientations. Wenda Gu's language project aimed at destroying the underlying structure of the Chinese system of characters while maintaining its calligraphic style, thus creating a conflict between concept and aesthetic pleasure. Between 1984 and 1986, Gu produced his *pseudo characters (cobiezi;* figs. 6, 177): upside-down, reversed, restructured, or wrong-sense characters splashed in ink on huge sheets of rice paper, imitating the style of classic calligraphy masters. Gu's skepticism that any language or conceptual process can encompass the essence of nature or things has special resonance in Chinese culture, in which the written language itself—ideographic rather than alphabetic—is imbued with far greater metaphysical meaning than in other cultures. With this series, Gu sought to destroy the system of syntax and grammar that carried so many aesthetic and cultural connotations in traditional Chinese society.[13]

Unlike Wenda Gu, who questioned the general rational content of characters or texts, Wu Shan Zhuan used language to investigate the meaning of authorship. For Wu, Chinese characters, with their combination of image and concept, are themselves a form of visual art. More importantly, their meaning is given. Wu overrode his own subjectivity by juxtaposing randomly selected phrases and characters, in the process creating an oddly compelling alternative reality. In the installation *Red Humor (Hongse youmo,* 1987; figs. 94, 178, 217), he combined political, cultural, and economic information in a typical Cultural Revolution format: big-character posters designed in the red, black, and white colors of traditional China. The Maoist-period slogan, "Exercise for strength in the class struggle," stood alongside price notices, advertisements, newspaper headlines, classical poems, Buddhist texts, traffic signs, weather forecasts, and announcements such as "Mr. Wang, I am back." On the floor were printed four Chinese characters: *wu ren shuo dao,* meaning "no one can interpret them." Here were represented various contradictory discourses—serious and ironic, grand and trivial, religious and secular, revolutionary and capitalist—sans the artist's voice. Wu's insistence that an artist should not function as the dominant factor in art production, in fact, that s/he is merely material like paint or ink, greatly undermined the subjective and idealist project initiated by humanist artists.

Before shifting to installation work in the mid-1980s, Xu Bing had already established a reputation as a printmaker. In *Five Series of Repetition* (*Wuge fushu xilie*, 1987; fig. 95), Xu took up conceptualist problems through the printmaker's idiom, carving and then printing a sequence of images of village life from the same block of wood. In the final piece a set of images progresses from solid black through successive carvings to solid white, as more and more of the wood is whittled away. Thus, Xu literally dematerializes the object, deconstructing representation as he simultaneously creates and destroys the artwork. In his first major installation, *Book from the Sky* (*Tianshu*, 1987), Xu accomplished a similar disappearing act, this time with linguistic signifiers. *Book from the Sky* featured several

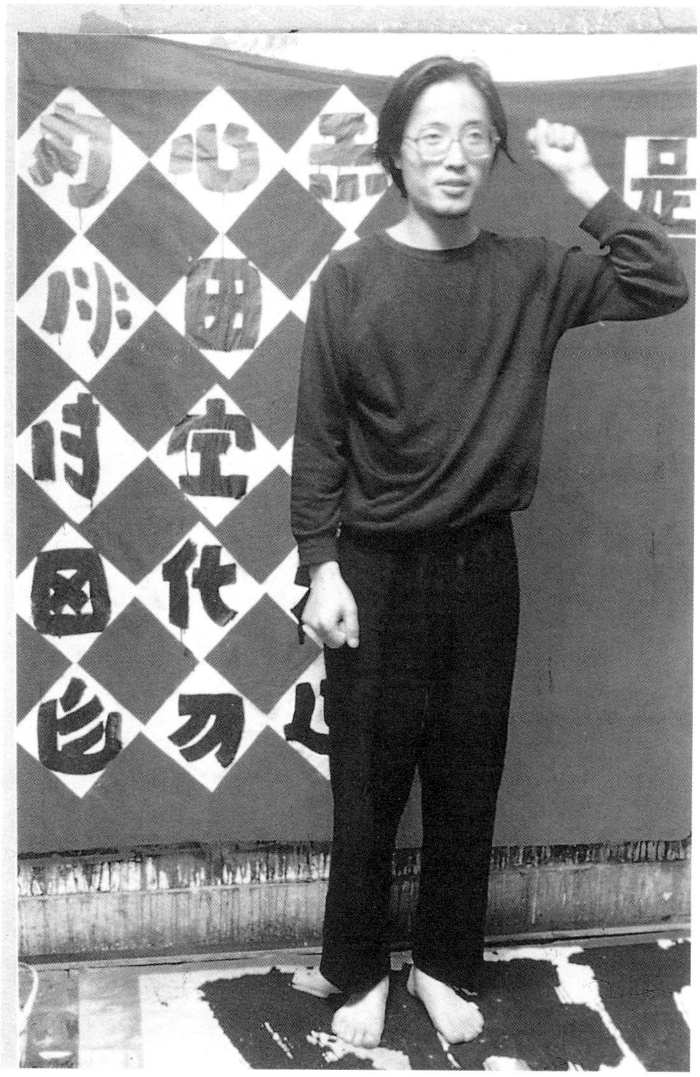

FIGURE 94.
Wu Shan Zhuan, *Red Humor Series (Hongse youmo): Big Characters (Dazibao), Swearing,* 1987, photographic documentation of installation. Collection of the artist.

FIGURE 95.
Xu Bing, *Five Series of Repetition (Wuge fushu xilie)* 1987, (details), woodcuts. Collection of the artist.

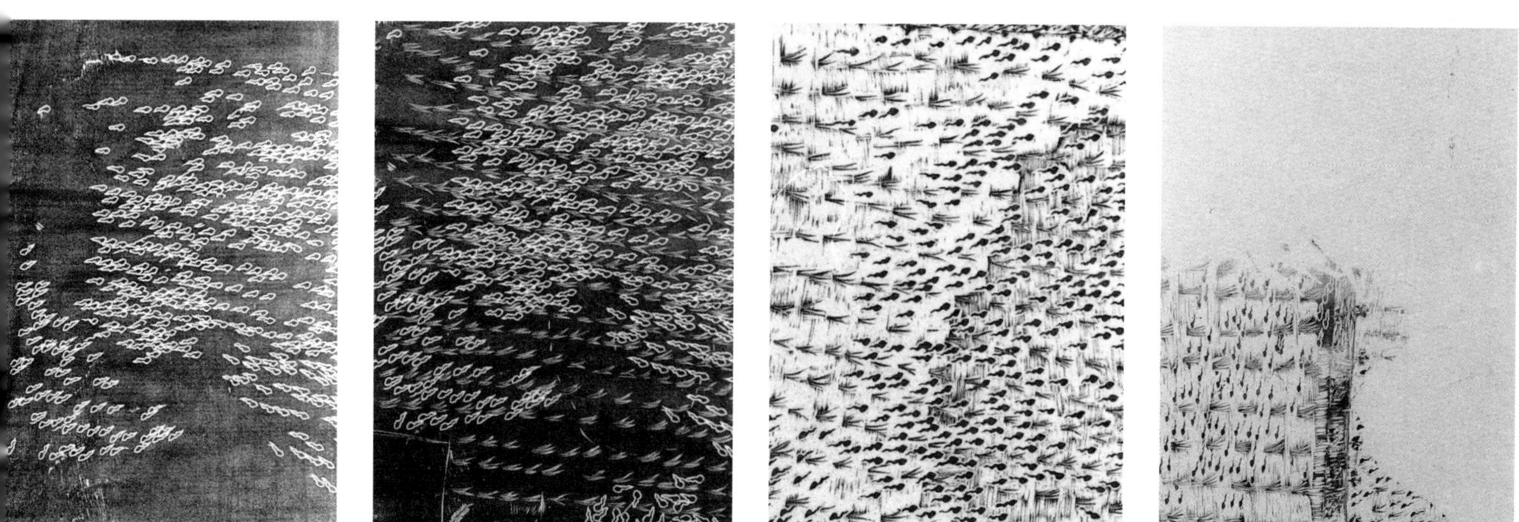

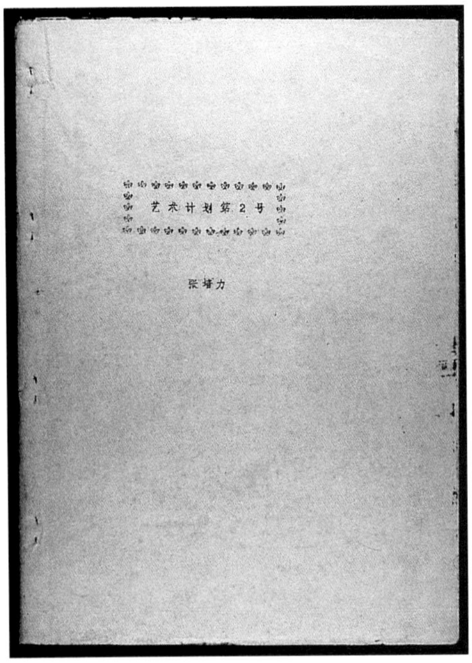

Figure 96.
Zhang Peili, *Art Plan #2 (Yishujihua erhao)*, 1987, 20-page book, print on paper. Collection of Gao Minglu, Boston.

Figure 97.
Geng Jianyi, *Investigative Forms (Diao chabiao)*, 1988, 28 sheets, ink and photographs on paper. Collection of Andreas Schmid, Berlin.

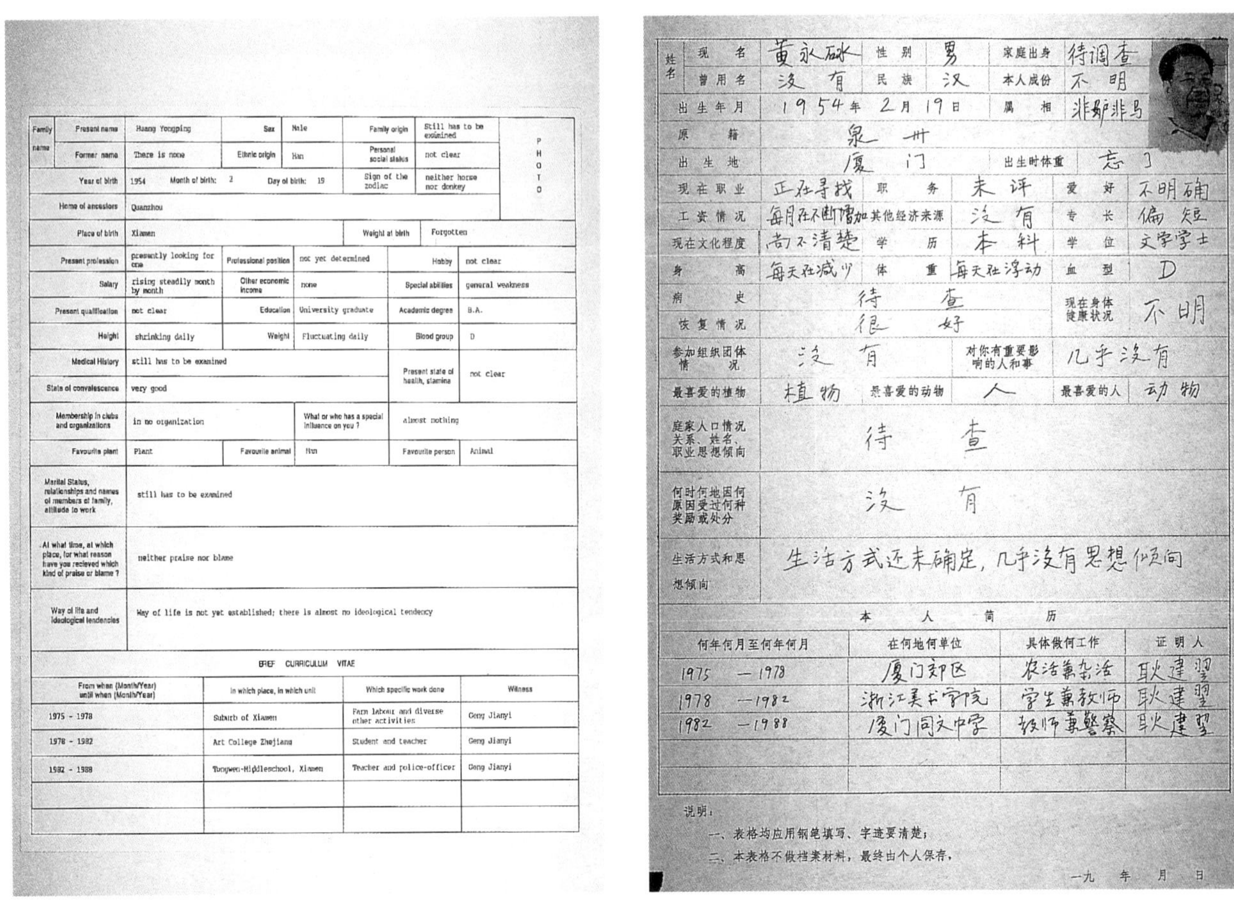

500-foot handscrolls printed with thousands of characters in monumental ink-painting style. Set in front of the scrolls were boxes of books bound in blue paper to resemble traditional Chinese books. The characters were all created by Xu himself, but seemed genuine enough to persuade the audience to attempt to read or decipher them. *Book from the Sky* evokes a crucial concept in Chan Buddhism, that of "emptiness." In Chan thought, one's realization of "emptiness" coincides with a receptiveness to a richer realm of truth, namely, enlightenment. Xu's illegible work offered the viewer a meaningless text that would function as a space of emptiness. Moreover, his complete removal of semantic meaning undercut the authority of the monumental framework, indeed, the monument itself as an ideological form and carrier of myth.

As founding members of the Pool Society (Chishe), a major avant-garde group of the '85 Movement, Zhang Peili and Geng Jianyi also took up language projects, if from radically different perspectives. Zhang spelled out his approach in the following statement: "The extension of artistic language and expansion of media seem to offer numerous possibilities: but in actuality what we really can select and make use of for our own purposes is limited. In the end, economy and sparseness of language [are] a virtue."[14] All of Zhang's projects dramatize this communicational reality. In 1987–88, he began to construct harsh and extremely rigid rules governing the exhibition and viewing of artworks. During a hepatitis epidemic, Zhang created a conceptual work called *Brown Book #1 (Hepishu yihao,* 1988), which consisted of mailing anonymous parcels containing surgical rubber gloves or parts of gloves to important figures in the Chinese art world. The last consignment included a letter informing recipients that the parcel was not a comment on their moral behavior, but that they should not attempt to contact the sender or other recipients. In *Art Plan #2 (Yishujihua erhao,* 1987; fig. 96), a twenty-eight-page list of instructions, Zhang specified in minute and tedious detail the conditions under which people should be admitted to an art exhibition. For instance, visitors must be taller than 4'3" or shorter than 5'8", refrain from speaking, and follow a route marked with mathematical precision.

Geng Jianyi also created gamelike works, in this case to structure an alternative relationship between art and public. In 1988, as the *China/Avant-garde* exhibition was being organized for the National Gallery, Geng coopted curatorial authority from museum directors by sending invitations to some one hundred artists, requesting biographical information and deliberately misrepresenting himself as an organizer of the show. Most artists filled out the forms and returned them. Geng then exhibited them as an installation—*Investigative Forms (Diao chabiao;* fig. 97)—at a well-attended art conference (which included many of the artists duped by Geng's "game"), allowing the public, rather than a panel of judges, to determine the merits of each entry.

Some conceptual artists of the '85 Movement undertook an extreme anti-art project grounded in traditional Chinese philosophy. One such artist was Huang Yong Ping, leader of the Xiamen Dada group in southern China. In his first phase of anti-art, Huang eschewed traditional media (oil paint and brush) for industrial materials (spray gun and lacquer) in a series entitled *Paint (Spray) Gun (Penqiang,* 1983), claiming that industrial mass productions were far more truthful and powerful than subjective aesthetic forms. Next he attacked the illusion of intentionality with the *Roulette Wheel Series (Zhuanpan xilie,* 1985), in which he randomly assigned number values to colors, then applied them to canvas based on the spin of a wooden wheel. Huang differentiated his method from gambling by noting that the gambler desires a particular result (winning), while the artist is indifferent to the outcome. In 1986, for Xiamen Dada's first exhibition, the group attacked the practice of collecting art by burning all the works at the end of the show. Finally, Huang turned to art history, which he denounced for creating cultural warfare, and symbolically mutilated masterworks and classical texts. *The Beard Was Easiest to Burn (Huzi zhiyi ranshao,* 1986; fig. 89), features

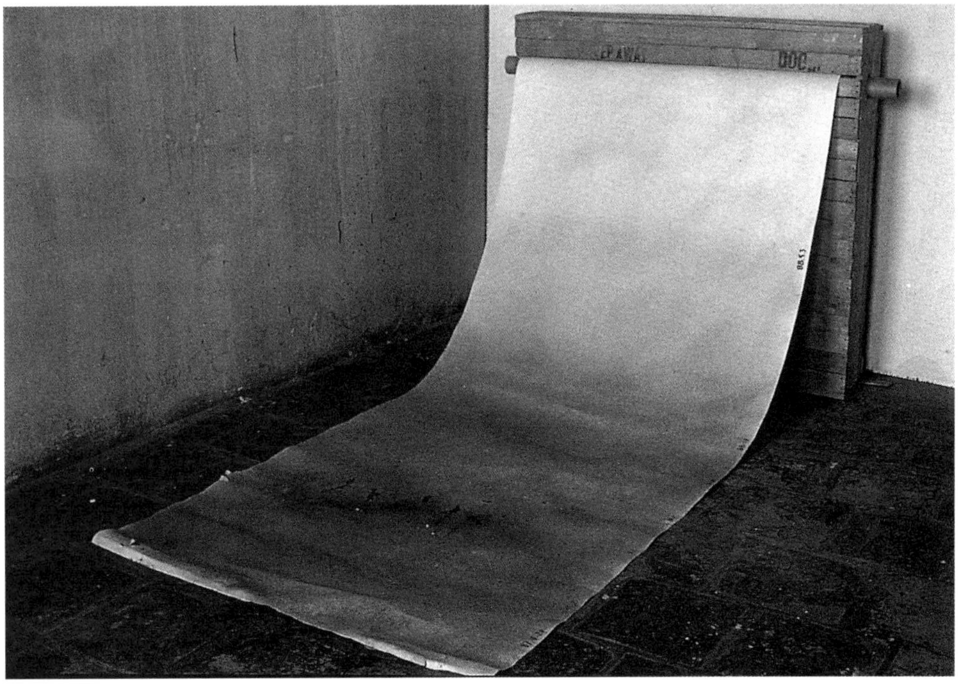

Figure 98.
Huang Yong Ping, *Dust (Zhentu)*, 1987, paper and wooden box. Collection of the artist.

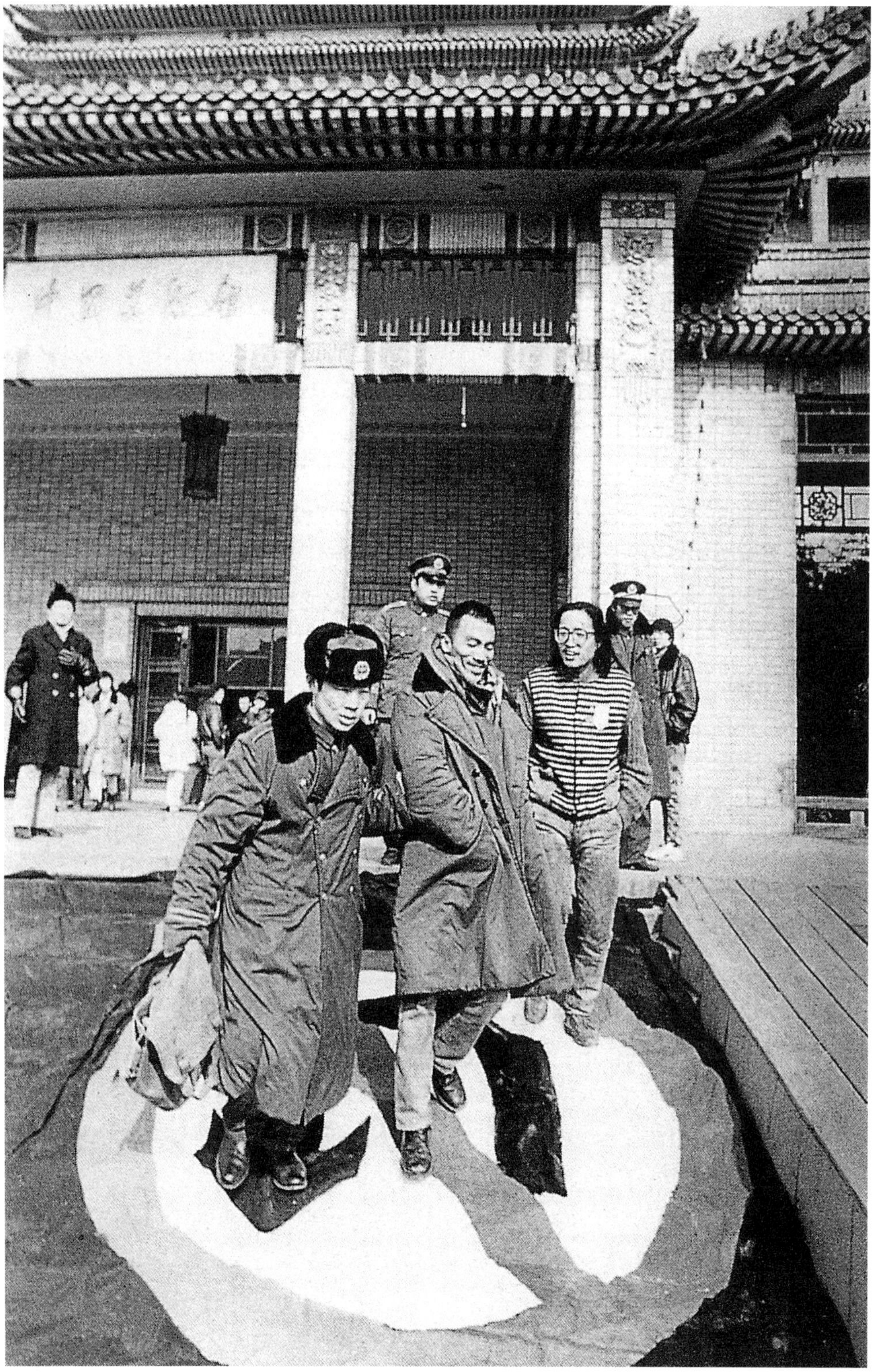

FIGURE 99.
Tang Song being arrested after shooting incident during *China/Avant-garde* exhibition, Beijing, 1989.

photocopies of a self-portrait by Leonardo with the beard singed out, and *Dust (Zhentu,* 1987; fig. 98) consists of a long scroll of paper which makes a painting by gathering dust. In 1988, Huang submitted *Drawing the National Gallery Away (Tozou zhongguo meishuguan;* fig. 179) to the organizing committee of the *China/Avant-garde* exhibition in Beijing; the committee rejected the piece.

Xiamen Dada attacked the institutional framework of art production. Some anti-artists, however, rejected this framework altogether. For instance, in *The Country Project (Xiangcun yishu huodong,* 1987; fig. 180), a group of avant-garde artists in Shanxi Province led by Song Yongping moved to remote villages to live with illiterate peasants. Resisting the elitism of professional bourgeois artists tied to academic institutions, Song and his comrades acted as the "reeducated students" advocated by Mao during the Cultural Revolution: learning to work *for* the people as they were educated *by* the people. Their motto "Serve the People," endorsed by Mao, demonstrated the paradox of populism in contemporary Chinese society. Since an art that served the people had never been a reality even in Mao's China, *The Country Project* represented a purified process of art production with neither propagandist nor commercial aims. From another perspective, these kinds of social actions popularized in the '85 Movement reflected antagonism to a booming urban commercial culture, thus the artists involved referred to their work as *xiangcun wenhua huodong,* or "village culture project."

Extreme forms of performance art flourished for a brief period during the second half of the '80s, attracting a great deal of attention and controversy. Performances often featured sadomasochistic scenarios in which artists are victimized in some way. In *Stretcher Series (Huakuang xilie,* 1986), for instance, produced by a group in Shandong Province called Black Union (Heise Lianmeng), an artist was forced into a *cangue,* an instrument used in ancient China to restrain criminals, similar to the Puritan stocks of colonial America. In this case, the *cangue* was made of canvas cut with holes and stretched on a wooden frame. M Group (M Qunti), an all-male collective founded by Song Haidong in Shanghai (the "M" of the title stands for "male"), expanded on the theme of artist as both criminal and victim in several performances, including *Ceremony (Yishi)* and *Violence (Baoligan)* (both 1986; figs. 100, 101), in which performers—representing artists—were bound, swaddled, gagged, hanged, and beaten by mobs of naked men. This sort of wild behavior was an attempt to convey the helplessness of artists and the wounded spirit of art.

Unique to Chinese performance art was the fact that it was frequently a spontaneous event staged in public space—a deliberate goad to authorities, since performance was strictly censored. These types of performances are more accurately defined as "political happenings," and the *China/Avant-garde* exhibition was viewed by some as a golden opportunity to stage such an event. No doubt artists were encouraged by the exhibition site itself: the National Gallery in Beijing is historically the most important venue for showings of official art, and the sense of danger involved in violating its near-sacred status was irresistible. So, for example, Wei Guangqing launched his *Suicide Series (Zisha xilie;* figs. 181, 189), in which he "hanged" himself in front of a series of photos, while Wu Shan Zhuan sold shrimp from a booth. Other artists threw condoms into galleries. The most provocative action occurred just two hours after the exhibition opened, when Xiao Lu and Tang Song converted their installation, *Dialogue (Duihua),* into a performance by firing two bullets into it. Public Security Bureau personnel were on the spot immediately and arrested Tang (fig. 99). Xiao escaped but later turned herself in, and the exhibition was closed for three days.

Indeed, the ambiguous status of art in the legal structure at this time made it possible to claim that within the bounds of the gallery, an otherwise serious criminal offense might not be illegal. In any case, events developed in ways the artists probably foresaw. Although the *People's Daily* initially reported the closing of the gallery as straight news, with no criticism of the artists, the authorities acted as though this were a political affair.[15] And it is probably with some justification that in subsequent government attacks on the avant-garde movement, these shots were described as the first to be fired in the events of 1989 that culminated in the Tiananmen Square Incident.

The students' defeat at Tiananmen put an end to the political and cultural modernization movement of the 1980s. Since then, increasing emphasis has been placed on the immediate economic benefit of any activity, including art. Official and popular culture have become entangled, and the new art world is dominated by a concern for commercial success to such a degree that most other criteria have been discarded. In the early 1990s, artists of the political pop *(zhengzhi popu)* and cynical realism *(wanshi xianshizhuyi)* persuasion acquired an international audience, functioning as a Chinese avant-garde on the global circuit. But these artists had virtually no influence domestically. Meanwhile, avant-garde artists for whom critical recognition rather than financial profit had been the principle goal found themselves with no public outlet for their work.

This untenable situation has given rise to new forms of conceptualism in which artists have either "privatized" their practice or gone completely public, taking their work to the streets. Whatever the venue, these artists share a distaste for China's consumption-mad society of the 1990s and the materialist aspirations of the art world, especially its glamorized international branch.

Some artists have opted for a kind of self-exile, producing small-scale installations with inexpensive materials and exhibiting them in private spaces—primarily the artists' own homes—for likeminded peers. A repudiation of the art market, apartment art *(gongyu yishu)* also represents a rejection of the grand social ambitions of the '85 Movement. Much apartment art has meditative or religious overtones. In fact, a few avant-garde artists have converted to Buddhism in recent years, especially in Shanghai, the most commercial of Chinese cities. Song Haidong, for instance, founder of the M Group who also produced readymades with overt political content during the '80s, is now a Buddhist and refuses to participate in exhibitions. Song Dong, who earns a living as a school teacher, has adapted his artwork to the cramped conditions of a ten-square-meter

A student pleads with PLA soldiers in a truck to refrain from cracking down on the demonstrators at Tiananmen Square, Beijing, 1989. Courtesy of Peter Turnley/Corbis.

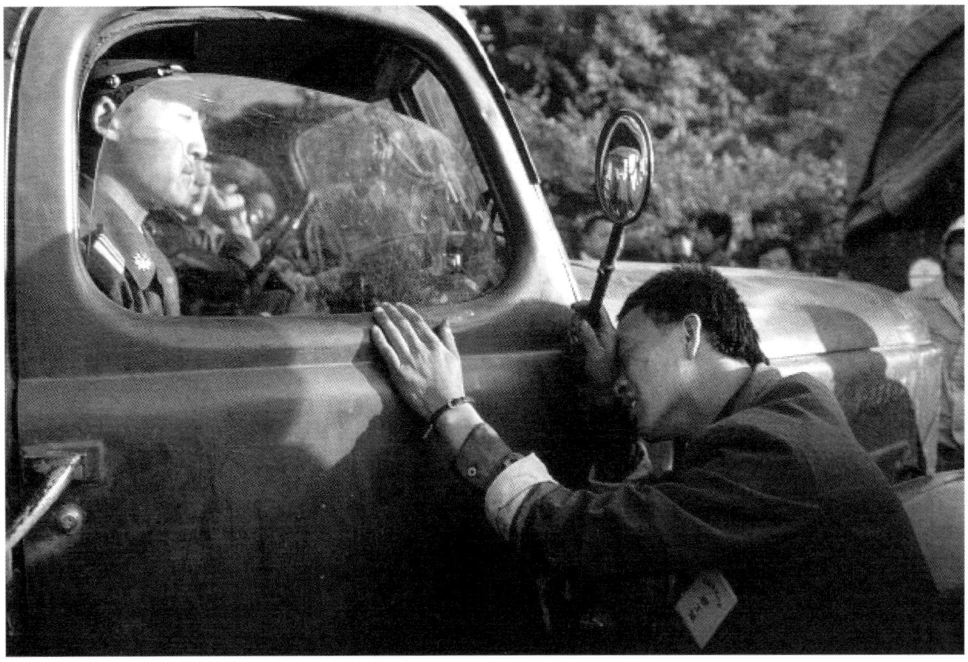

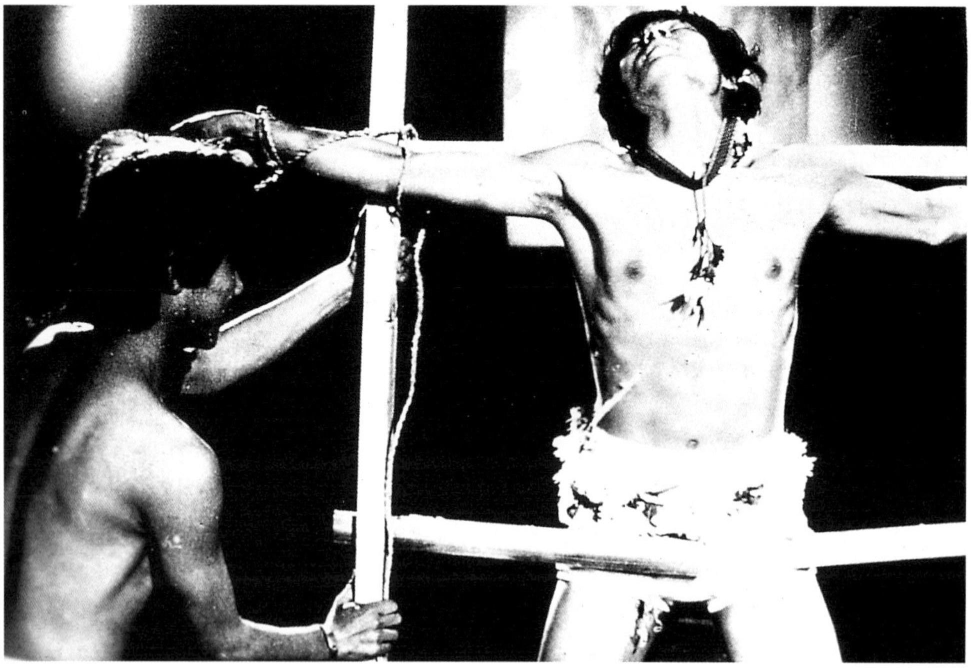

Figure 101.
M Group, *Ceremony (Yishi)*, 1986, photographic documention of a series of performances. Collection of Song Haidong.

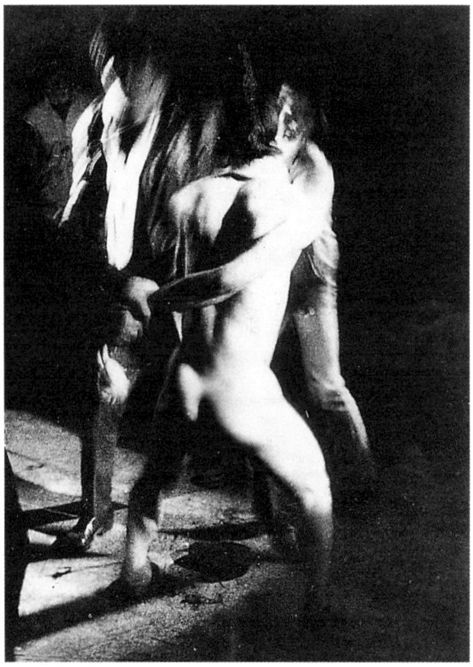

Figure 100.
M Group, *Violence (Baoligan)*, 1986, photographic documention of a series of performances. Collection of Song Haidong.

apartment (which he shares with his wife and colleague, artist Yen Xiuzhen). Song creates small installations, most sketched on paper—"proposal art," or *fangan yishu*—but has also pushed his work to the extreme limits of dematerialization. In one project, he writes Chinese calligraphy on an ordinary stone or the surface of a table, using a traditional brush with clean water rather than ink. The characters soon vanish, but their mental and spiritual impression persists. Song performs this ritual every day, much like a monk taking a morning lesson in a temple.

Street art *(jieto yishu)* takes dematerialization in another direction, attacking the commodity system itself in public venues such as plazas, stores, and restaurants. A characteristic example is Wang Jin's *Ice: Central China, 1996 (Jiuliu zhong yuang)*. Wang was commissioned by the owners of the first large shopping mall in Zhengzhou to create a monument for the opening ceremony in 1996. The artist hauled in 600 blocks of ice to construct a wall 30 meters long, 2.5 meters high, and one meter thick in the plaza fronting the mall. Embedded in the ice were hundreds of luxury consumer goods: jewelry, cosmetics, telephones, pharmaceuticals. Customers stormed the wall in a frenzy, dismantling it with every tool available to get at the goods.

❖

The conceptualist art of Taiwan in the 1960s and the Mainland during the '80s profoundly influenced the course of contemporary art in these regions. Taiwanese conceptualism broke new ground with its rejection of the previous (and still ongoing) abstract painting in favor of inexpensive, ordinary readymade materials and found objects. What some may view as bohemian cynicism in the Taiwan context was actually an anti–avant-gardism (that is, anti-elitism) aimed at rescuing art from its ivory tower prison. Similarly, two decades later on the Mainland, the conceptualism of the '85 Movement undermined both the political idealism and cultural elitism that had been dominant forces not only in Mao's revolutionary art but also in the work of the post-Mao avant-garde. On the other hand, Hong Kong's conceptualist art of the '80s did not play the same clarifying or liberating role. Rather, it functioned as a self-defined avant-garde lacking an historic context, operating in a decentralized, pluralistic art scene in which various artistic circles had little reference or relationship to one another.

Notes

1. Huang Yong Ping, "Xiamen dada: Yizhong houxiandai?" *Zhongguo Meishu Bao* (China Art Press), no. 46 (1986).

2. Peter Bürger, *Theory of the Avant-garde,* trans. Michael Shaw (Minneapolis: University of Minnesota Press, 1984).

3. Lu Qingfu, "Xiadaizhuyi de shiyanqi" (The Experimental Period of Modernism), in *Taiwan meishu xinfengmao, 1945–1993* (Taiwan's New Art, 1945–1993), ed. Ling Ping (Taipei: Taipei Fine Arts Museum, 1993), 24–31.

4. Guo Chengfeng, "Language Beyond Painting Society: A Language Group, Not a Painting Group," *Dazue Zazhi* (Universities Bulletin), no. 23 (1969): 3–4.

5. Mao Kaizhao, quoted in Lai Ying-ying, *Liushiniandai Taiwan fuheyishu yianjiu* (Taiwan's Multimedia Art of the Sixties) (Taipei: Guotai Cultural Publisher, 1996), 55.

6. Craig Owens, "From Work to Frame, or, Is There Life After 'The Death of the Author'?" in *Beyond Recognition* (Berkeley: University of California Press, 1992), 122–39.

7. Lai, *Liushiniandai Taiwan fuheyishu yanjiu,* 161–69.

8. Desiree Au, "Breaking All the Rules in the Name of Art," *Hong Kong Standard,* February 6, 1996.

9. Ibid.

10. I coined the term in "'85 Art Movement," *Meishujia Tongxun* (Journal of Artists), no. 3 (1986): 8. The authorities immediately objected to the political connotations of the term *yundong,* or movement. Consequently, "'85 Art Trend" was frequently adopted as a less objectionable alternative in publications.

11. More details on these modernist groups from 1977 to 1987 were published in Gao Minglu et al., *Zhongguo dangdai meishushi, 1985–1986* (Shanghai: Shanghai People's Press, 1991), 606–26.

12. This theme is also noted by Bill Brugger and David Kelly, "The Importance of Humanism," in *Chinese Marxism in the Post-Mao Era* (Stanford: Stanford University Press, 1990), ch. 6.

13. See Gao et al., *Zhongguo dangdai meishushi,* 207–28, and Chou Yan, "Gu Wenda's Oedipus," in *Fragmented Memory: The Chinese Avant-garde in Exile* (Columbus: Wexner Center for the Arts, Ohio State University, 1993), 20–23.

14. Quoted in *China's New Art, Post-1989/Hou pa chiu Chung-kuo hsin i shu,* ed. Valerie C. Doran (Hong Kong: Hanart T Z Gallery, 1993), 145.

15. *Renmin Ribao* (People's Daily), February 6, 1989.

1990s

South and Southeast Asia

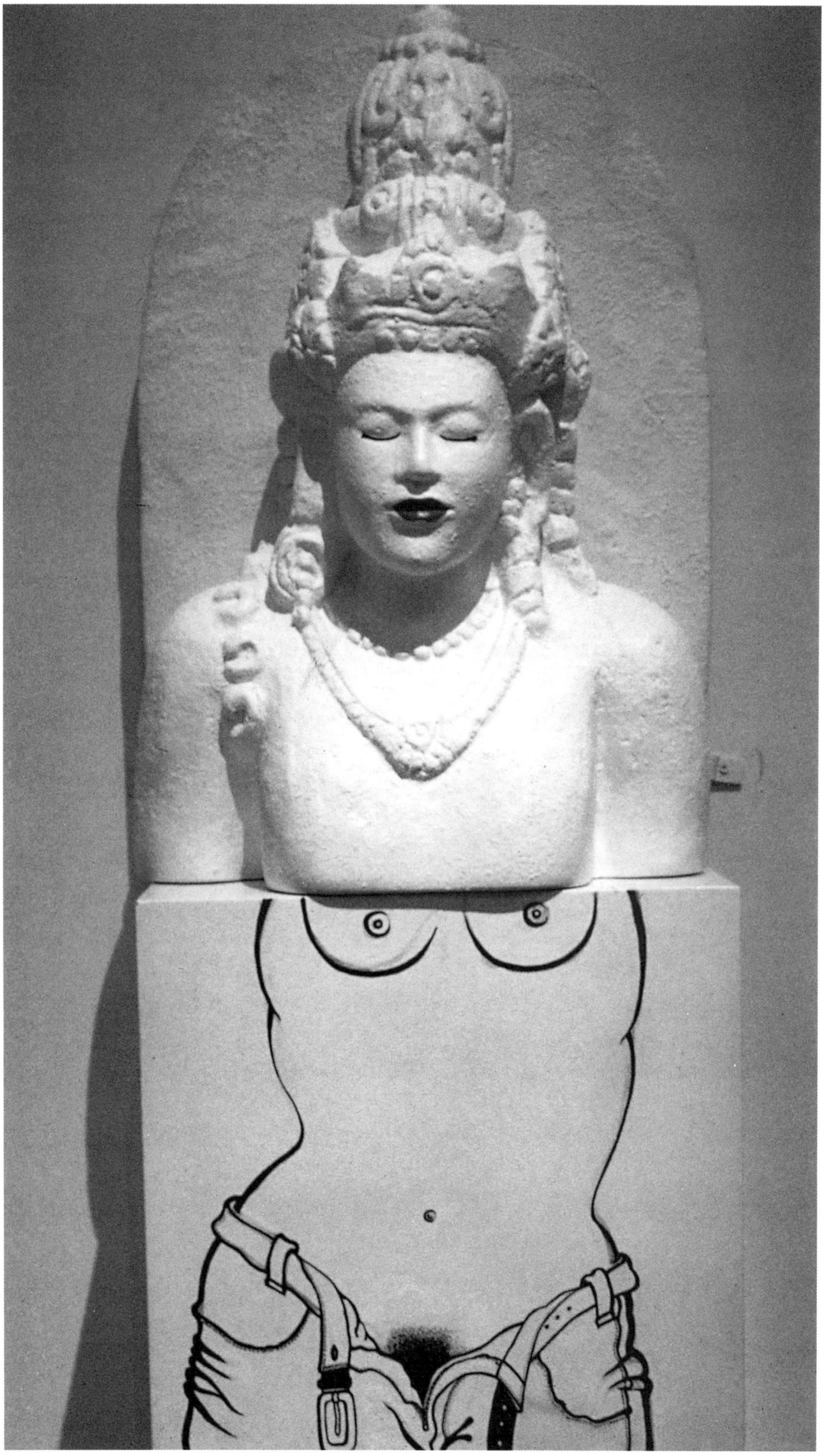

"Con Art" Seen from the Edge: The Meaning of Conceptual Art in South and Southeast Asia

Apinan Poshyananda

As a major international phenomenon, conceptual art has been recognized as a Euro–North American invention fitting neatly into linear art historical models of the West. The term *conceptualism* embraces various forms of art in which the idea of the work is considered more significant than the object itself. However, this definition of conceptualism has expanded considerably since its emergence. This article will focus on Asian artists whose work may be allied to Western "ideas" of conceptual art, but who created different "concepts" for a specific locality.

Since Western contact with modern Asian art has been limited principally to Japan, China, and South Korea, it is often assumed that conceptualist production is confined to those countries. Recently, multiculturalism has permitted some artists to find a niche along with other neglected Others. Consequently, the Western art infrastructure has become more inclusive, less hierarchical. Asian artists living abroad (e.g., Anish Kapoor, Rasheed Araeen, Wenda Gu, Xu Bing, Huang Yong Ping, Cai Guo-qiang, Rirkrit Triravanija, Vong Phaophanit, David Medalla) have been situated in relation to "mainstream" conceptual artists, while those in Asia (e.g., Miyajima Tatsuo, Yanagi Yukinori, Vivan Sundaram, N. N. Rimzon, Montien Boonma, Lee Bul, Navin Rawanchaikul, Ellen Pau, Surasri Kusolwong, Kamol Phaosavasdi, Gu Dexin, Wong Hoy-cheong, Tang Da Wu, and FX Harsono) have received attention for their attempt to redefine conceptualism in terms of local/global contextualizations. In the process, they have demonstrated that conceptualism is a nonlinear phenomenon constantly in flux.

During the 1960s and '70s, the impact of the Cold War was clearly felt in regions of South and Southeast Asia. For many countries, fear of communism and a desire for capitalism resulted in government promotion of Western curricula in arts education. For instance, many art schools in ASEAN countries offered courses on modern art adapted from English textbooks such as H. H. Arnason's *History of Modern Art.* Here, modern art is traced in chronological order stressing Euro–North American artists, with virtually no consideration of modern art in Asia. As for conceptualism, we were taught that "concept art" was peculiar to the West, along with happenings, performance, lettrism, documentation, earthworks, and body art. This practice of defining conceptual art through textbooks and lumping it with all kinds of other "isms" has often led to confusion and misinterpretation, and conceptual art was translated by Asian teachers and passed on to students in variable ways. At times, the concept behind works such as Joseph Kosuth's *One and Three Chairs* (1965) was deemed irrelevant for art practices in Asia emphasizing technical virtuosity, indigenous elements, and draftsmanship. Then again, many art schools and academies actively discouraged the exploration of conceptualism for fear that it would incite students to challenge institutional authority. In South Asia—for instance, Calcutta, Mumbai (Bombay), Madras, and

Figure 102.
Jim Supangkat, *Ken Dedes* (detail), 1975, mixed media. Collection of the National Museum, Singapore.

Lahore—a deeply entrenched colonialist pedagogy, which privileged painting and sculpture, inhibited experimentation in the arts.[1] Moreover, anti-American sentiment contributed to resistance to "pops" and "cons" from the U.S. In the 1960s, talented artists such as M. F. Husain, Tyeb Metha, and Gulam Mohammed Sheikh were more interested in European figurative painting than North American conceptualist works. Although in India and Pakistan, plenty of inspiration for "art and life" could be found in rituals and ceremonies involving the body and performance, relatively few artists ventured into the realm of conceptual art.

In Southeast Asia, conceptualism for a long time was considered less important than critical realism, surrealism, and abstraction. But as artists became discontent with mainstream art forms that emphasized national identity, decoration, and elite aesthetic values, they searched for new styles and media both at home and abroad. Many artists turned to pop, neodada, and Fluxus, experimenting with mixed media, assemblage, and found objects. These forms of expression allowed artists to escape the confines of painting, sculpture, and their conventional themes and techniques. As a result, individuals such as Andy Warhol, Robert Rauschenberg, Joseph Beuys, and Nam June Paik found a receptive audience in Southeast Asia. In particular, Beuys's notion of "social sculpture" had a powerful impact on young Indonesian and Thai artists, who saw in it a vehicle adaptable to their own cultural circumstances capable of exposing social "wounds" and initiating a "healing" process. However, it was not only inspiration from abroad or the need to catch up to the West that drove local artists to challenge the stagnation of institutionalized art.

During the 1970s, the Panchasila philosophy of Indonesia's New Order did not encourage art forms critical of society. Officially sanctioned art was characterized by art for art's sake, internationalism, and decorative realism or abstraction. In 1973, mass student unrest and criticism of the government resulted in repressive measures and the imprisonment of many students. At the same time, young artists demanded radical changes in the institutional structure of art. The Black December Incident, in which artists protested the jury selections for the 1974 Jakarta Biennial, represented the beginning of new directions and values in art production. Artists from Academi Seni Rupa Indonesia (ASRI) in Yogyagarta, Bandung Institute of Technology (ITB), and Jakarta formed a group which became known as the Indonesian New Art Movement (Gerakan Seni Rupa Baru). This movement advocated the dismantling of aesthetic hierarchies through assemblage, happenings, readymades, and found objects, and seriously questioned the relevance of the art education system in Indonesia. The manifesto accompanying its first exhibition in 1975 called for an art that reflected the entire spectrum of society as artists rejected the limitations of the abstract modernist schools. The exhibitions of the New Art Movement were open to all sorts of expression, including conceptualist.[2] For example, Jim Supangkat's entries included a framed black canvas with a single word, *dicari* ("wanted"), painted on it. His mixed-media sculpture *Ken Dedes* (1975; fig. 102) featured the head and shoulders of the legendary queen of Majapahit, the 14th-century Javanese kingdom, together with a comic drawing of a woman wearing unzipped jeans exposing pubic hair. This merging of two seemingly unrelated and contradictory sets of cultural and aesthetic values into a grotesque image shocked the public. Supangkat was accused of degrading the traditional icon, since her posture implied that she was a prostitute.

The New Art Movement's next show in Jakarta, the *Concept Exhibition* (1976), was framed by the question "How serious is our art?" It included action drawing, newspaper clippings, texts, everyday objects, and lengthy debate on art. Meanwhile, equally provocative events were shaping up in Yogyakarta, where three exhibitions—*What Identity? (Kepribadian Apa?), Experiments in Living Sculpture,* and *Spontaneous Exhibition*—were organized in 1977. Young artists such as Semsar Siahaan introduced body performance, while political satire and cynical commentary aimed at the government were conspicuous. Authorities began to suspect many artists of involvement in leftist groups. In 1978, student leaders were jailed and prominent newspapers banned after protests against President Suharto and the revival of "Sukarnoism." Artists of the New Art Movement responded with overt condemnation of Suharto and his policies in their third and largest exhibition. For instance, Hardi's photomontage *Presidential Candidate 2001* (1978) was comprised of self-portraits superimposed over the head of the late president Sukarno. Munni Ardi's *Free Speaker Platform* (1978), a performance staged in a red boxing ring, featured the text of a speech by Sukarno read aloud by visitors.

The New Art Movement was galvanized by social and political pressures within the local art scene, and not so much the desire to keep up with Western *isms.* FX Harsono later recalled that members were vaguely aware of Duchampian ideas along with the work of Warhol and Beuys through artists like Hardi, who had attended Beuys's 1977 seminar in Düsseldorf.[3] However, terms such as *conceptual art* and *installation* were widely used only later in the 1980s. The New Art Movement disbanded after 1979, but its ideas continued to motivate later artists. Its spirit was revived in 1987 in the exhibition *Supermarket Fantasy World,* a mélange of consumer objects, posters, and advertisements. Rather than direct political attacks on state authority, however, many artists shifted their focus to social issues such as consumerism, environmental degradation, and public health.

In Thailand, the student revolutions of 1973 and 1976, which toppled the military dictatorship, provided greater freedom of expression and cleared the way for experimentation by Thai artists. Although many turned to critical realism, surrealism, and neotraditional Buddhist art, some explored conceptualism by going abroad. Prawat Laucharoen, Kamol Tassananchalee, and Tana Laohakaikul, who live in the U.S., played an important role as

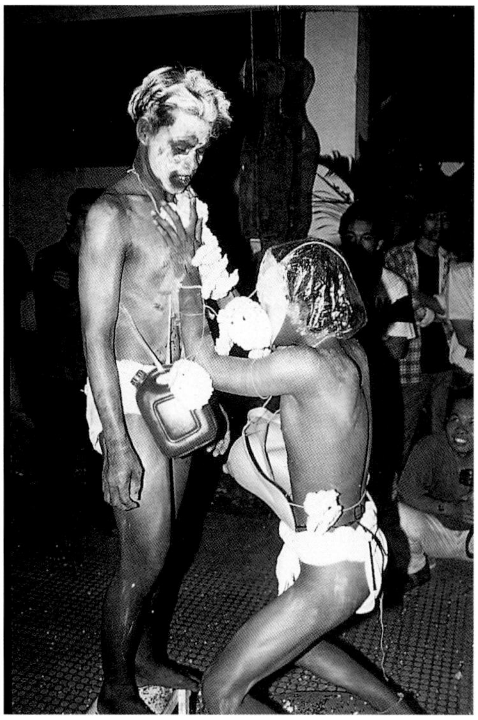

Figure 103.
Heri Dono, performance at Biennale Seni Rupa 5, Yogyakarta, Indonesia, 1997.

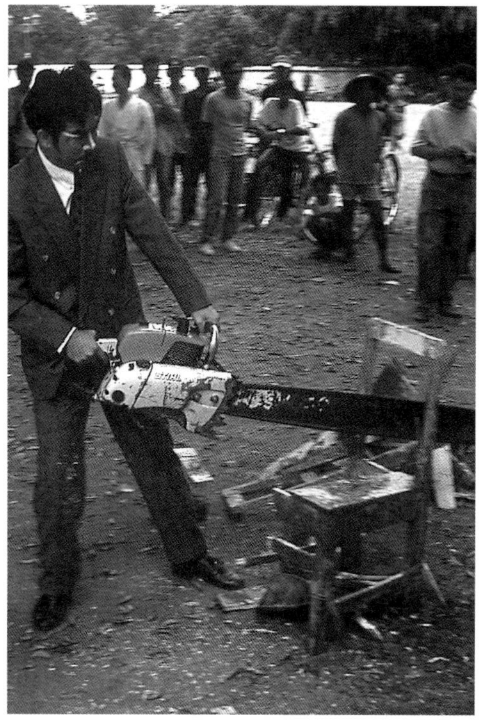

Figure 104.
FX Harsono, *Kurban/Destruksi 1:* performance in Yogyakarta, Indonesia, 1997.

Figure 105.
Santiago Bose, *Imagined Enclaves and Ephemeral Borders,* performance at Baguio Arts Festival, Philippines, 1993.

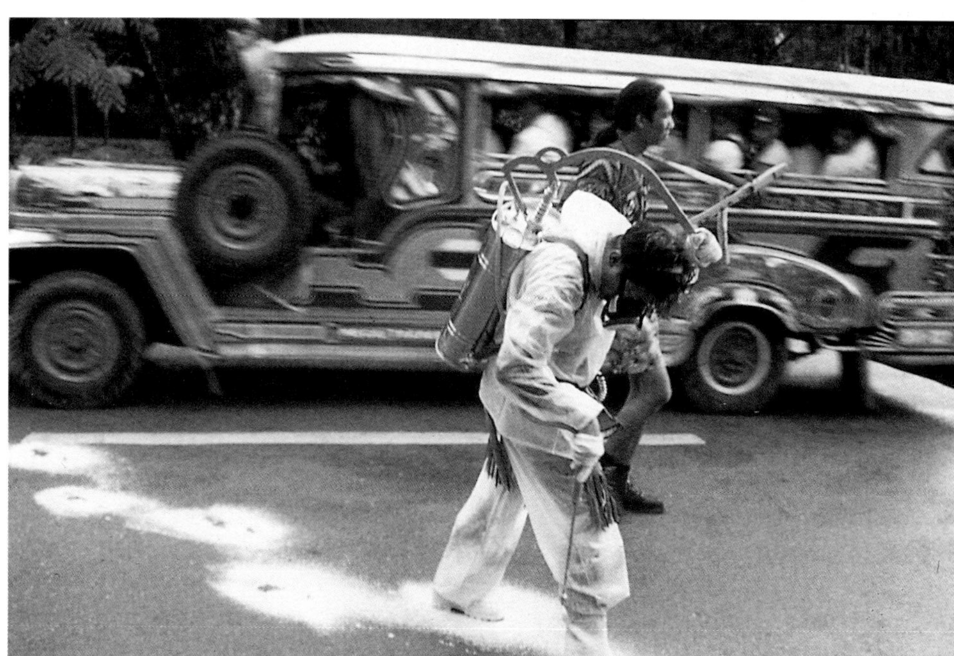

mediators, introducing conceptual art to the Thai art scene. Laucharoen collaborated with Dennis Oppenheim on the installation *Launching Station* (1981), in which chemical "missiles" were launched onto large printing plates. Laucharoen's use of chance and improvisation here and in other works derived from an interest in John Cage and Merce Cunningham. Tassananchalee created conceptual works which included pouring colored pigments in the Mojave Desert. Laohakaikul created room-size installations and outdoor site-specific works dealing with water pollution and environmental destruction. These artists visited their homeland and brought back with them innovative concepts that encouraged the production of idea-based art.

Conceptualism flourished in Thailand during the mid-'80s, as several artists, including Kamol Phaosavasdi and Chumpon Apisuk, returned from abroad to settle in Bangkok. In Thai translation, the term *conceptual art (sinlapa ruapyod)* refers variously to installation, performance, and the use of readymades (initially, it embraced any "foreign" style that inspired artists to reject conventional practice). Lively events sponsored by the Bhirasri Institute of Art in Bangkok stimulated broader interest in installation, junk, happenings, performance, and body art. Anti-art strategies were deployed by artists to attack the capitalist art market and its precious commodities. For the opening of the 1985 Thai Sculpture Exhibition, Phaosavasdi bound himself in a sack as a form of protest. Apisuk drank animal blood and shouted newspaper headlines about social conflict, sex, and money in his *Happening—Pure Communication* series. Vasan Sitthiket, a poet-painter-happening artist, drafted a neodada manifesto to accompany installations of newspapers and poems about anarchy as a creative force and death as rebirth.[4]

In the Philippines, the Baguio Arts Guild (BAG) became the nucleus for artists in search of "ethnicized" forms to counter the abstraction fostered by art schools in Manila. Filipino artists looked especially to the collaborative aspects of traditional artmaking, so different from Western standards of individualism and competition for commercial success. Indigenization, it was felt, could transform conceptualism, performance, and installation. Some Filipino artists even hailed installation as the quintessential art of the region. Roberto Villanueva, a leading member of BAG inspired by Cordillera highland culture and shamanism, created a series of site-specific works using bamboo and reeds to emphasize indigenousness as resistance to Western cultural domination. Similarly, in Singapore the Artists Village sought alternatives to the dogma of academic training. Led by Tang Da Wu, who spent some time in England, the Village produced numerous artists whose potential in idea-based art breathed new life into the sterile Singapore art scene.[5]

Conceptualist practices are now widely accepted in the art arenas of Southeast Asia and some parts of South Asia.[6] To varying degrees, artists in Indonesia, Thailand, Malaysia, the Philippines, Singapore, and India have adapted conceptual strategies as vehicles for critique and reflection on their rapidly changing societies, and several international exhibitions in Asia and Australia have legitimized these forms of conceptualism based on local idioms. In the process, conceptual artists have gained confidence that their works are not merely stylistic quotations of Western "originals." In fact, many artists dismiss Western versions of conceptualism as self-reflexive, tedious communiqués between members of intellectual cliques.

Conceptualist works convey as well as conceal political, social, and religious messages. The 1992 military crackdown in Bangkok, which caused the deaths of civilians and students, spurred Thai artists such as Vasan Sitthiket and Surapol Panyawatchira to make body art about rape and the military's abuse of power. In *The Four Elements* (1993), a series of print installations, Prawat Laucharoen confronted issues of national identity, Thai-ness, power, and democracy using images of the royal family, Buddhist symbolism, and scenes of riot and mayhem. In 1995, Philippine citizens expressed outrage over Singapore's execution of Filipina domestic worker Flore Contemplacion in heated protests and burnings of the Singapore national flag. Feminist

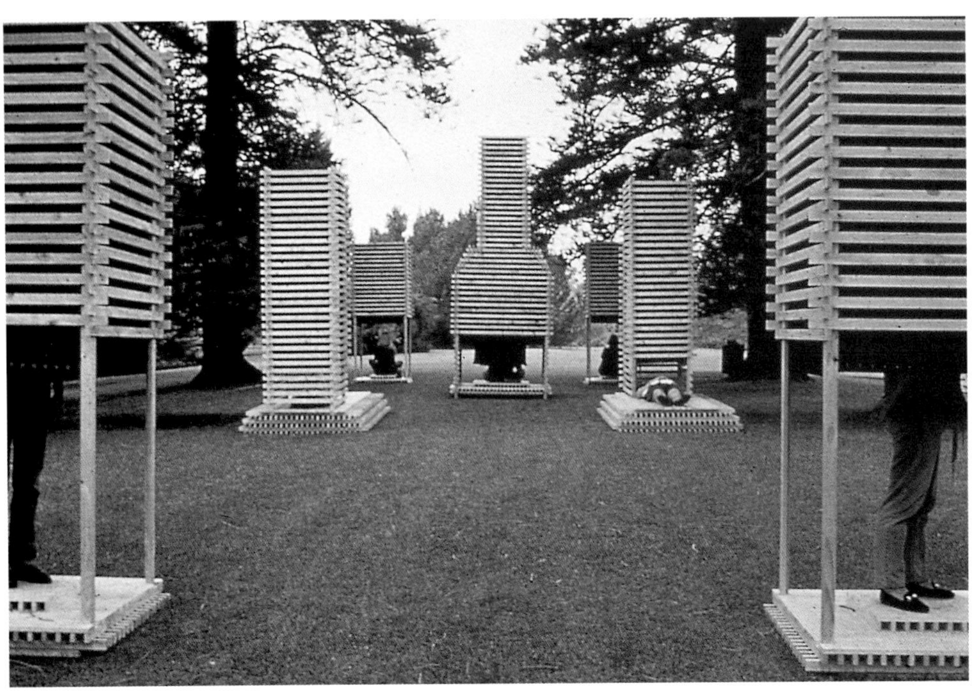

Figure 106.
Montien Boonma, *Room,* 1994, wood and cloth, as presented at the Adelaide Festival, Australia.

Figure 107.
Kamol Phaosavasdi, *Give Me a Glass of Water*, performance at Silom Art Space, Bangkok, Thailand, 1994.

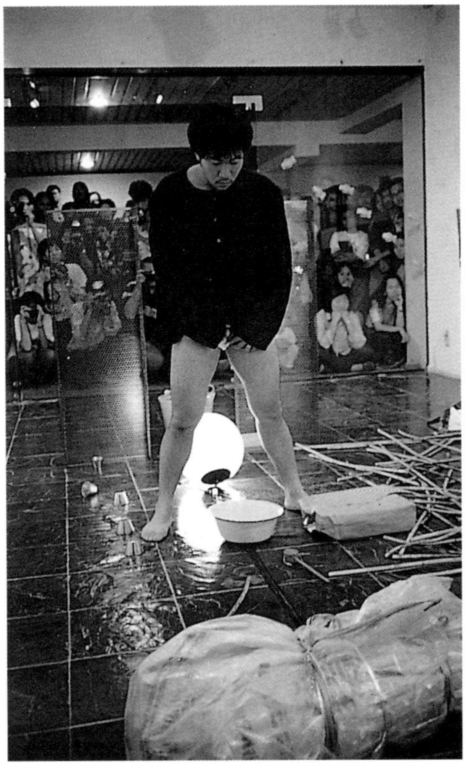

artist Imelda Cajipe-Endaya responded with a series of conceptualist works on overseas domestic workers, using quotidian objects like a chair, broom, and luggage, together with a text on the "Filipina."[7]

Religion has inspired many artists to explore ideas of faith and devotion through a conceptual framework. The site-specific installations of Thai artist Montien Boonma, which convey a sense of contemplation, void, and emptiness, often demand the viewer's participation (fig. 106). In *Breathing House* (1996–97), *House of Hope* (1996–97), and *Melting Void* (1998), enclosures and corridors filled with herbs and covered with aluminum and wax arouse the sense of smell and taste, and provoke an acute awareness of the viewer's relation to interior and exterior space.[8] India's religious turmoil of 1992–93 between Hindus and Muslims, which resulted in burning and bloodshed, became the subject of conceptualist works by Vivan Sundaram, Pushpamala N., and Sheela Gowda. Sundaram's *Memorial* (1992), an allegorical reflection on the frenzy of religious violence, is an installation with fragments of riot scenes, an image of a dead victim, and a monumental gateway. Pushpamala collected burnt books and boxes as symbols of victims of the communal riots in Mumbai. Gowda's decision to use cow dung as a medium was made during the riots of 1992–93. In India, cow dung is shit but also signifies sacredness and nonviolence, and is used as a fuel and in domestic chores. Gowda's flat cakes of manure mixed with sacred powder *(kum kum)* and gold leaf challenge the audience to define the boundaries of art and life, holiness and profanity, alternative media and aestheticized execration.

For many artists, performance offers opportunities for a fresh interaction with audiences, and they capitalize on the medium's sense of spontaneity to provide novel perspectives on social and cultural issues. In Singapore, Tang Da Wu's installations and performances reexamine Chinese traditions and myths surrounding the eating of animal parts as an aphrodisiac. Vincent Leow pushed the boundaries of censorship by drinking his own urine while Joseph Ng shaved his pubic hair. In Yogyakarta, Heri Dono collaborated with villagers to perform social rituals and satires through shadow puppet theater and trance dance as well as plays using homeless children as actors (fig. 103). FX Harsono staged a happening as a critique of deforestation and illegal logging, "slaughtering" rows of wooden chairs with a chainsaw before burning them (fig. 104). Filipino artist Santiago Bose made a labyrinthine journey through the town of Baguio, spraypainting his footsteps as he crossed many cultural borders (fig. 105). In Chiang Mai, Thailand, a group of young artists formed the Chiang Mai Social Installation, placing site-specific works in temples, cremation grounds, markets, public parks, and along riverbanks. For his solo exhibition *Give Me a Glass of Water* (1994) in Bangkok, Kamol Phaosavasdi urinated in front of the works to add layers of meaning to the problem of water pollution in the metropolis (fig. 107). Vasan Sitthiket and friends produced a short video of performers wearing penis-shaped caps raping a map of Thailand. Kosit Juntaratip focused his performance work on love and infatuation, marrying a sex doll and painting with his own blood. Navin Rawanchaikul displayed a series of found objects intended to interact with viewers in *The Zero Space That Is Not Empty* (1995). He also promoted mobile art galleries for taxis and motorized rickshaws *(tuk tuk)*. In a performance at the *Live Art* exhibition in 1997, Surapol Panyawatchira drew analogies between corrupt politicians and toilets as he urinated in a box to the accompaniment of the national anthem.

Asian artists recognize that conceptual art in the West has its distinct genealogy, but their own interpretations of such art have often derived from different trajectories. Despite the economic meltdown in Asia, artists have developed conceptualist practices to the extent that various networks have been formed within the region. A dynamic conceptualist art scene thrives in Bangkok, where events such as the *Huey Khwang Mega City, ArtPerformance Conference Bangkok,* and *Plastic & Other Waste* (which included artists from all over Asia as well as Fluxus members from Cologne) attract sizeable crowds. However, even today the response among audiences to conceptual art is mixed. Many viewers see "con art" as a stunt designed to garner attention and glorify the artist. Others argue that it broadens forms of aesthetic expression and ways of looking at art. Both readings are valid. After all, it is a matter of choosing between communication and confusion.

Notes

1. Siva Kuma, "Contemporary Indian Art: The Last Fifty Years," in *Tryst with Destiny: Art from Modern India, 1947–1997* (Singapore: Singapore Art Museum, 1997), 45–56.

2. Brita L. Miklouho-Maklai, *Exposing Society's Wounds: Some Aspects of Contemporary Indonesian Art Since 1966* (Adelaide: Flinders University, 1991), 23–77.

3. Interview with FX Harsono, Jakarta, July 16, 1998.

4. Apinan Poshyananda, *Modern Art in Thailand: Nineteenth and Twentieth Centuries* (Singapore: Oxford University Press, 1992), 207–17.

5. On Roberto Villanueva and Tang Da Wu, see *New Art from Southeast Asia* (Tokyo: Japan Foundation, 1992).

6. Julie Ewington, "Five Elements: An Abbreviated Account of Installation Art in South-East Asia," *Art and Asia Pacific* 2, no. 1 (1995): 109–15.

7. Apinan Poshyananda, "Roaring Tigers, Desperate Dragons in Transition," in *Traditions/Tensions: Contemporary Art in Asia* (New York: Asia Society, 1996), 23–53.

8. Montien Boonma, *Melting Void* (Bangkok: Marsi Gallery, 1998).

Plates

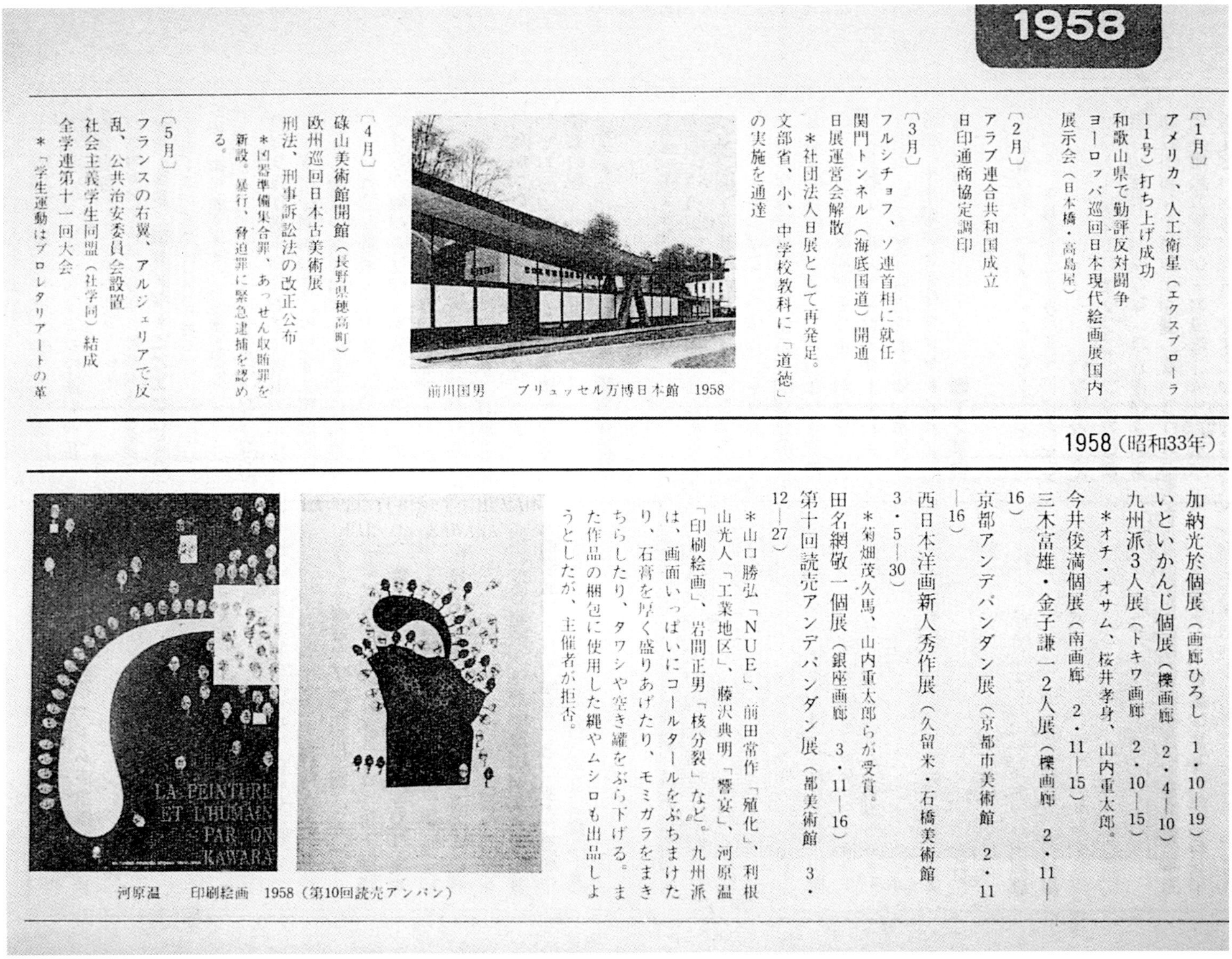

1958

〔1月〕
アメリカ、人工衛星（エクスプローラー1号）打ち上げ成功
和歌山県で勤評反対闘争
ヨーロッパ巡回日本現代絵画展国内展示会（日本橋・高島屋）

〔2月〕
アラブ連合共和国成立
日印通商協定調印

〔3月〕
フルシチョフ、ソ連首相に就任
関門トンネル（海底国道）開通
日展運営会解散
＊社団法人日展として再発足。
文部省、小、中学校教科に「道徳」の実施を通達

前川国男　ブリュッセル万博日本館　1958

〔4月〕
碌山美術館開館（長野県穂高町）
欧州巡回日本古美術展
刑法、刑事訴訟法の改正公布
＊凶器準備集合罪、あっせん収賄罪を新設。暴行、脅迫罪に緊急逮捕を認める。

〔5月〕
フランスの右翼、アルジェリアで反乱、公共治安委員会設置
社会主義学生同盟（社学同）結成
全学連第十一回大会
＊「学生運動はプロレタリアートの革

1958（昭和33年）

加納光於個展（画廊ひろし　1・10—19）
いとかんじ個展（櫟画廊　2・4—10）
九州派3人展（トキワ画廊　2・10—15）
＊オチ・オサム、桜井孝身、山内重太郎。
今井俊満個展（南画廊　2・11—15）
三木富雄・金子謙一2人展（櫟画廊　2・11—16）
京都アンデパンダン展（京都市美術館　2・11—16）
西日本洋画新人秀作展（久留米・石橋美術館　3・5—30）
＊菊畑茂久馬、山内重太郎らが受賞。
田名網敬一個展（銀座画廊　3・11—16）
第十回読売アンデパンダン展（都美術館　3・12—27）
＊山口勝弘「NUE」、前田常作「殖化」、利根山光人「工業地区」、藤沢典明「響宴」、河原温「印刷絵画」、岩間正男「核分裂」など。九州派は、画面いっぱいにコールタールをぶちまけたり、石膏を厚く盛りあげたり、モミガラをまきちらしたり、タワシや空き罐をぶら下げる。また作品の梱包に使用した縄やムシロも出品しようとしたが、主催者が拒否。

河原温　印刷絵画　1958（第10回読売アンパン）

Figure 108.
Yasunao Tone, Hikosaka Naoyoshi, and Akatsuka Yukio, *Chronology: Five Decades of Contemporary Art, 1916–1968 (Nenpyō: Gendai bijutsu no 50-nen)*, 1972, published in *Bijutsu Techō* (April, May 1972), pt. 2; p. 48, illustrating On Kawara's *Printed Paintings*. Bijutsu Shuppan-sha Publisher Collection, Tokyo.

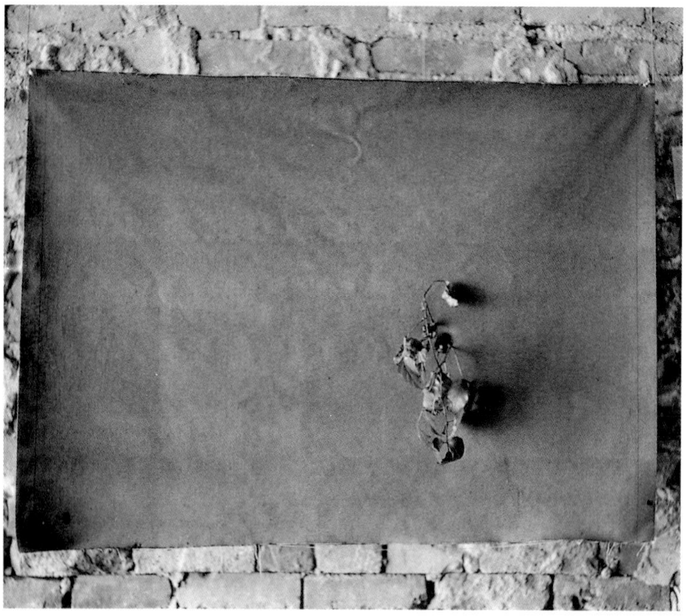

Figure 109.
Yoko Ono, *Painting in Three Stanzas, as exhibited at AG Gallery, New York* (from *Instructions for Painting series*), 1961, black-and-white photograph by George Maciunas. The Gilbert and Lila Silverman Fluxus Collection, Detroit.

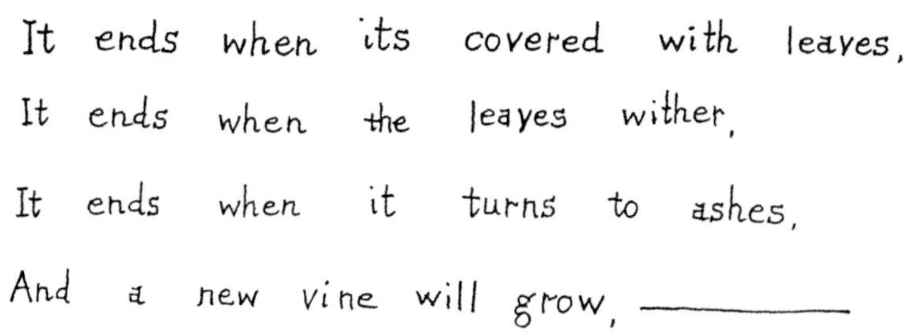

It ends when its covered with leaves,
It ends when the leaves wither,
It ends when it turns to ashes,
And a new vine will grow, ———

Figure 110.
Yoko Ono, score for *Painting in Three Stanzas* (in the form of an exhibition label written on the back of AG Gallery announcement card) (from *Instructions for Paintings* series), 1961, ink on card. Collection of the artist.

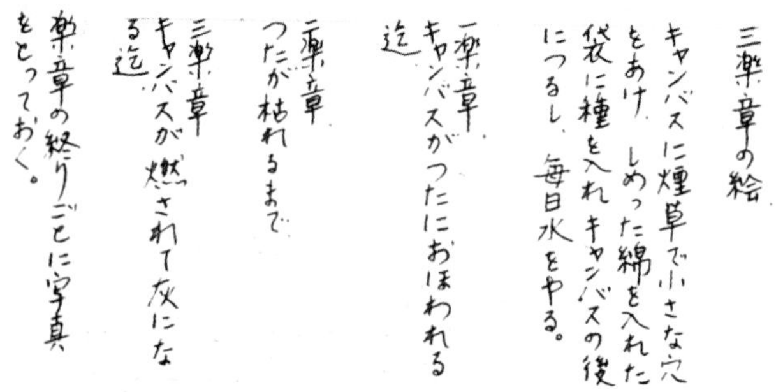

三楽章の絵
キャンバスに煙草で小さな穴
をあけ、しめった綿を入れた
袋に種を入れキャンバスの後
につるし、毎日水をやる。
一楽章
キャンバスがつたにおほわれる
迄
二楽章
つたが枯れるまで
三楽章
キャンバスが燃されて灰にな
る迄
楽章の終りごとに写真
をとっておく。

Painting in Three Stanzas

Make a small hole in the canvas with a cigarette, hang a sack that contains wet cotton and seeds behind the canvas, and water every day.

The first stanza—till the canvas is covered by the vine.
The second stanza—till the vine withers.
The third stanza—till the canvas is burned to ashes.

Photograph the canvas at the end of each stanza.

(*translated by Reiko Tomii*)

Figure 111.
Yoko Ono, *Painting in Three Stanzas, as exhibited at Sōgetsu Art Center, Tokyo, May 24, 1962* (from *Instructions for Painting* series), ink instructions on paper. The Gilbert and Lila Silverman Collection, Detroit.

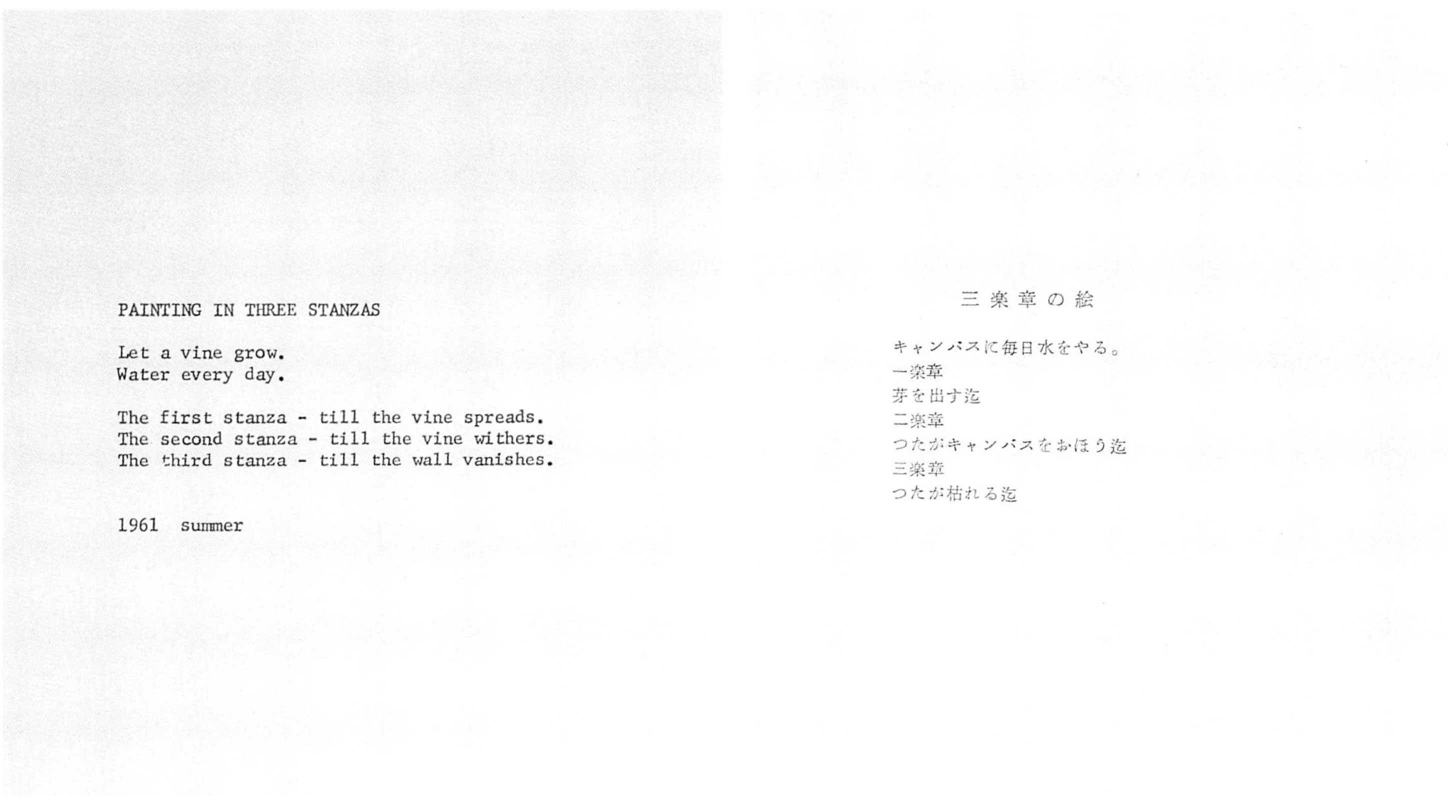

PAINTING IN THREE STANZAS

Let a vine grow.
Water every day.

The first stanza - till the vine spreads.
The second stanza - till the vine withers.
The third stanza - till the wall vanishes.

1961 summer

三 楽 章 の 絵

キャンバスに毎日水をやる。
一楽章
芽を出す迄
二楽章
つたがキャンバスをおほう迄
三楽章
つたが枯れる迄

Figure 112.
Yoko Ono, *Grapefruit,* 1964, book, pages for *Painting in Three Stanzas*. Collection of Jeff Rothstein and Reiko Tomii, New York.

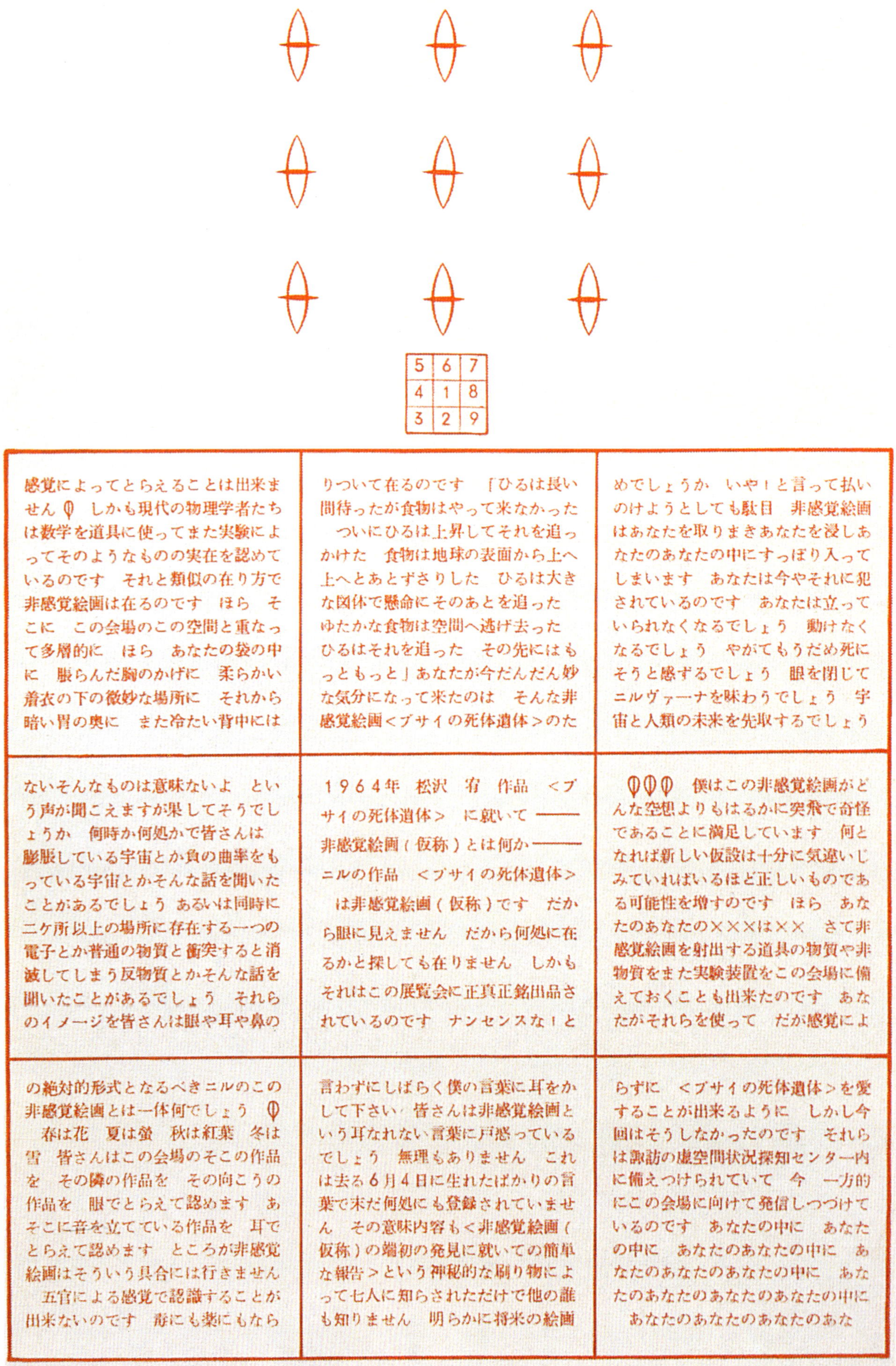

5	6	7
4	1	8
3	2	9

１９６４年　松沢　宥　作品　<プサイの死体遺体>　に就いて ——
非感覚絵画（仮称）とは何か——
ニルの作品　<プサイの死体遺体>　は非感覚絵画（仮称）です　だから眼に見えません　だから何処に在るかと探しても在りません　しかもそれはこの展覧会に正真正銘出品されているのです　ナンセンスな！と言わずにしばらく僕の言葉に耳をかして下さい　皆さんは非感覚絵画という耳なれない言葉に戸惑っているでしょう　無理もありません　これは去る６月４日に生れたばかりの言葉で未だ何処にも登録されていません　その意味内容も<非感覚絵画（仮称）の端初の発見に就いての簡単な報告>という神秘的な刷り物によって七人に知らされただけで他の誰も知りません　明らかに将来の絵画の絶対的形式となるべきニルのこの非感覚絵画とは一体何でしょう　Ψ

春は花　夏は螢　秋は紅葉　冬は雪　皆さんはこの会場のそこの作品を　その隣の作品を　その向こうの作品を　眼でとらえて認めます　あそこに音を立てている作品を　耳でとらえて認めます　ところが非感覚絵画はそういう具合には行きません

五官による感覚で認識することが出来ないのです　毒にも薬にもならないそんなものは意味ないよ　という声が聞こえますが果してそうでしょうか　何時か何処かで皆さんは膨脹している宇宙とか負の曲率をもっている宇宙とかそんな話を聞いたことがあるでしょう　あるいは同時に二ケ所以上の場所に存在する一つの電子とか普通の物質と衝突すると消滅してしまう反物質とかそんな話を聞いたことがあるでしょう　それらのイメージを皆さんは眼や耳や鼻の感覚によってとらえることは出来ません　Ψ　しかも現代の物理学者たちは数学を道具に使ってまた実験によってそのようなものの実在を認めているのです　それと類似の在り方で非感覚絵画は在るのです　ほら　そこに　この会場のこの空間と重なって多層的に　ほら　あなたの袋の中に　脹らんだ胸のかげに　柔らかい着衣の下の微妙な場所に　それから暗い胃の奥に　また冷たい背中にはりついて在るのです　「ひるは長い間待ったが食物はやって来なかった

ついにひるは上昇してそれを追っかけた　食物は地球の表面から上へ上へとあとずさりした　ひるは大きな図体で懸命にそのあとを追った　ゆたかな食物は空間へ逃げ去った　ひるはそれを追った　その先にはもっともっと」あなたが今だんだん妙な気分になって来たのは　そんな非感覚絵画<プサイの死体遺体>のためでしょうか　いや！と言って払いのけようとしても駄目　非感覚絵画はあなたを取りまきあなたを浸しあなたのあなたの中にすっぽり入ってしまいます　あなたは今やそれに犯されているのです　あなたは立っていられなくなるでしょう　動けなくなるでしょう　やがてもうだめ死にそうと感ずるでしょう　眼を閉じてニルヴァーナを味わうでしょう　宇宙と人類の未来を先取するでしょう

ΨΨΨ　僕はこの非感覚絵画がどんな空想よりもはるかに突飛で奇怪であることに満足しています　何となれば新しい仮設は十分に気違いじみていればいるほど正しいものである可能性を増すのです　ほら　あなたのあなたの×××は××　さて非感覚絵画を射出する道具の物質や非物質をまた実験装置をこの会場に備えておくことも出来たのです　あなたがそれらを使って　だが感覚によらずに　<プサイの死体遺体>を愛することが出来るように　しかし今回はそうしなかったのです　それらは諏訪の虚空間状況探知センター内に備えつけられていて　今　一方的にこの会場に向けて発信しつづけているのです　あなたの中に　あなたの中に　あなたのあなたの中に　あなたのあなたのあなたの中に　あなたのあなたのあなたのあなたの中に
あなたのあなたのあなたのあな

Figure 113.
Matsuzawa Yutaka, *Ψ Corpse (Pusai no shitai itai)*, 1964, flier. Collection of the Queens Museum of Art, 1999.6.

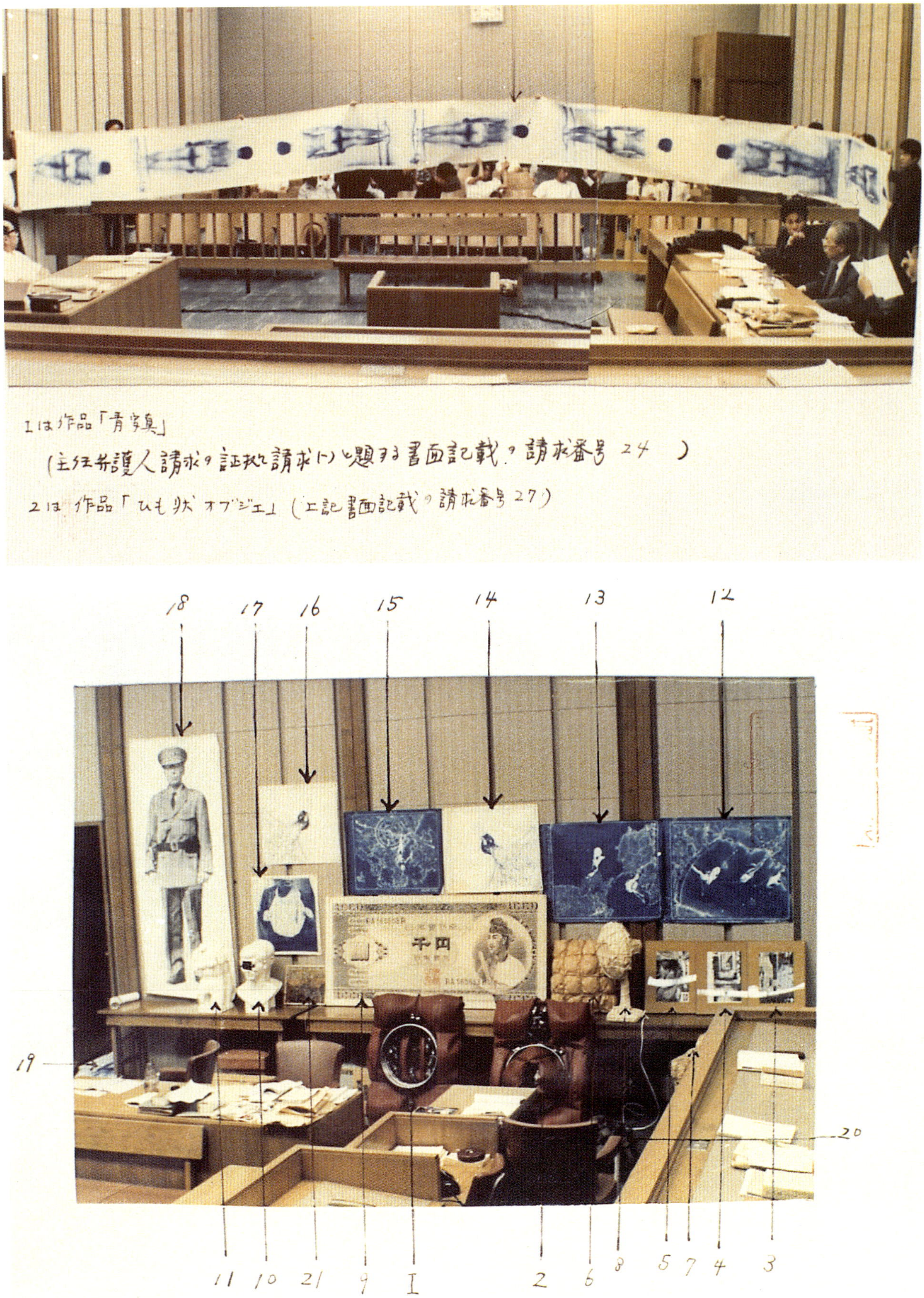

FIGURE 114. Akasegawa Genpei and Company, *Model 1,000-Yen Note Incident (Mokei sen-en-satsu jiken): Trial (defense evidence)*, 1966/1999. Collection of the Queens Museum of Art, 1999.2.

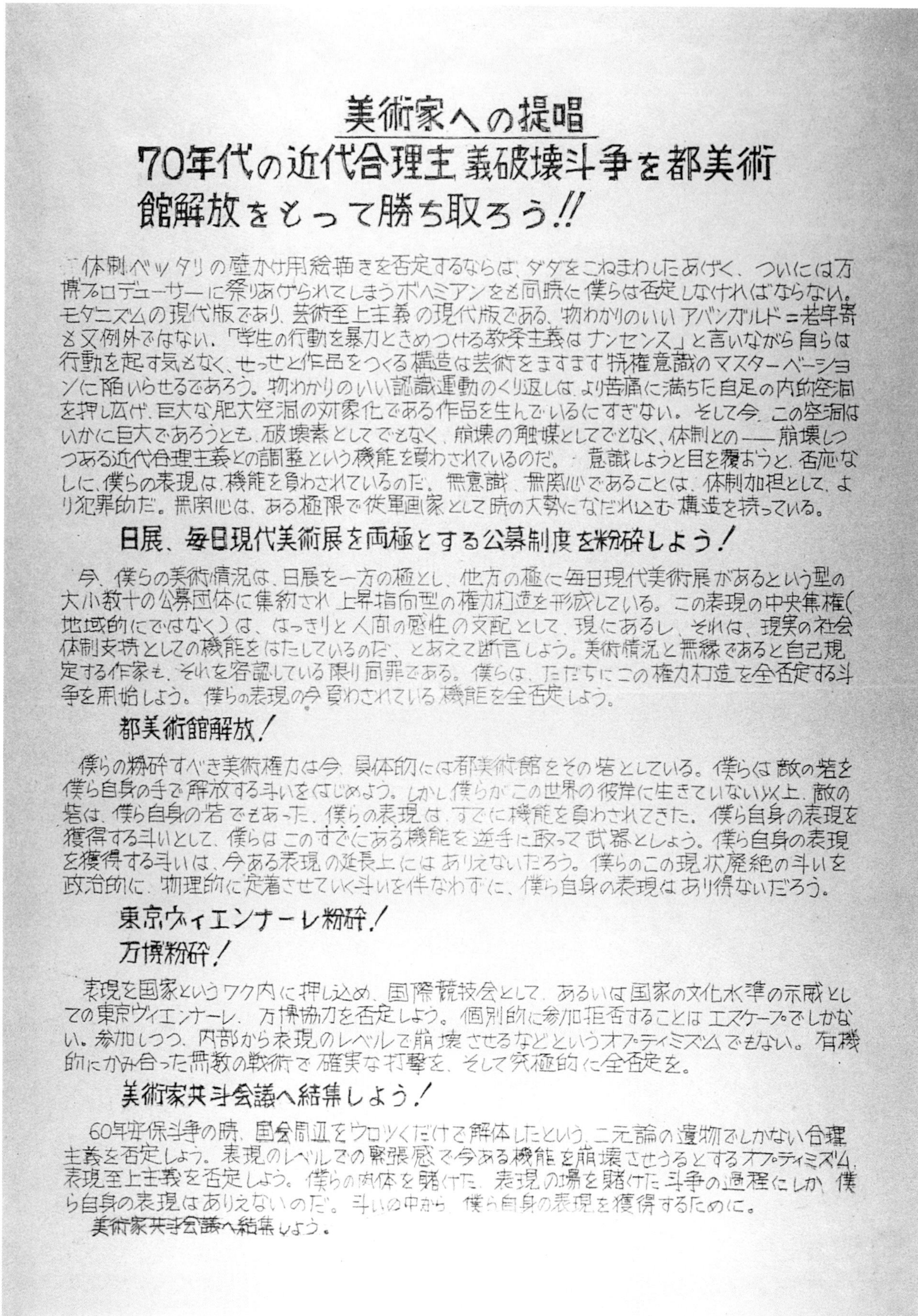

美術家への提唱
70年代の近代合理主義破壊斗争を都美術館解放をもって勝ち取ろう!!

体制ベッタリの壁かけ用絵描きを否定するならば、ダダをこねまわしたあげく、ついには万博プロデューサーに祭りあげられてしまうボヘミアンをも同時に僕らは否定しなければならない。モダニズムの現代版であり、芸術至上主義の現代版である、物わかりのいいアバンガルド＝若年寄も又例外ではない。「学生の行動を暴力ときめつける教条主義はナンセンス」と言いながら自らは行動を起す気もなく、せっせと作品をつくる構造は芸術をますます特権意識のマスターベーションに陥いらせるであろう。物わかりのいい認識運動のくり返しは、より苦痛に満ちた自足の内的空洞を押し広げ、巨大な肥大空洞の対象化である作品を生んでいるにすぎない。そして今、この空洞はいかに巨大であろうとも、破壊素としてでもなく、崩壊の触媒としてでもなく、体制との——崩壊しつつある近代合理主義との調整という機能を負わされているのだ。意識しようと目を覆おうと、否応なしに、僕らの表現は、機能を負わされているのだ。無意識、無関心であることは、体制加担として、より犯罪的だ。無関心は、ある極限で従軍画家として時の大勢になだれ込む構造を持っている。

日展、毎日現代美術展を両極とする公募制度を粉砕しよう！

今、僕らの美術情況は、日展を一方の極とし、他方の極に毎日現代美術展があるという型の大小数十の公募団体に集約され上昇指向型の権力構造を形成している。この表現の中央集権(地域的にではなく)は、はっきりと人間の感性の支配として、現にあるし、それは、現実の社会体制支持としての機能をはたしているのだ、とあえて断言しよう。美術情況と無縁であると自己規定する作家も、それを容認している限り同罪である。僕らは、ただちにこの権力構造を全否定する斗争を開始しよう。僕らの表現の今負わされている機能を全否定しよう。

都美術館解放！

僕らの粉砕すべき美術権力は今、具体的には都美術館をその砦としている。僕らは敵の砦を僕ら自身の手で解放する斗いをはじめよう。しかし僕らがこの世界の彼岸に生きていない以上、敵の砦は、僕ら自身の砦でもあった、僕らの表現は、すでに機能を負わされてきた。僕ら自身の表現を獲得する斗いとして、僕らはこのすでにある機能を逆手に取って武器としよう。僕ら自身の表現を獲得する斗いは、今ある表現の延長上にはありえないだろう。僕らのこの現状廃絶の斗いを政治的に、物理的に定着させていく斗いを伴なわずに、僕ら自身の表現はあり得ないだろう。

東京ヴィエンナーレ粉砕！
万博粉砕！

表現を国家というワク内に押し込め、国際競技会として、あるいは国家の文化水準の示威としての東京ヴィエンナーレ、万博協力を否定しよう。個別的に参加拒否することはエスケープでしかない。参加しつつ、内部から表現のレベルで崩壊させるなどというオプティミズムでもない。有機的にかみ合った無数の戦術で確実な打撃を、そして究極的に全否定を。

美術家共斗会議へ結集しよう！

60年安保斗争の時、国会周辺をウロツくだけで解体したという、二元論の遺物でしかない合理主義を否定しよう。表現のレベルでの緊張感で今ある機能を崩壊させうるとするオプティミズム、表現至上主義を否定しよう。僕らの肉体を賭けた、表現の場を賭けた斗争の過程にしか、僕ら自身の表現はありえないのだ。斗いの中から、僕ら自身の表現を獲得するために。

美術家共斗会議へ結集しよう。

FIGURE 115. Bikyōtō (Artists Joint-Struggle Council), *An Appeal to Artists, July 5, 1969*, mimeographed flier. Collection of Hori Kosai.

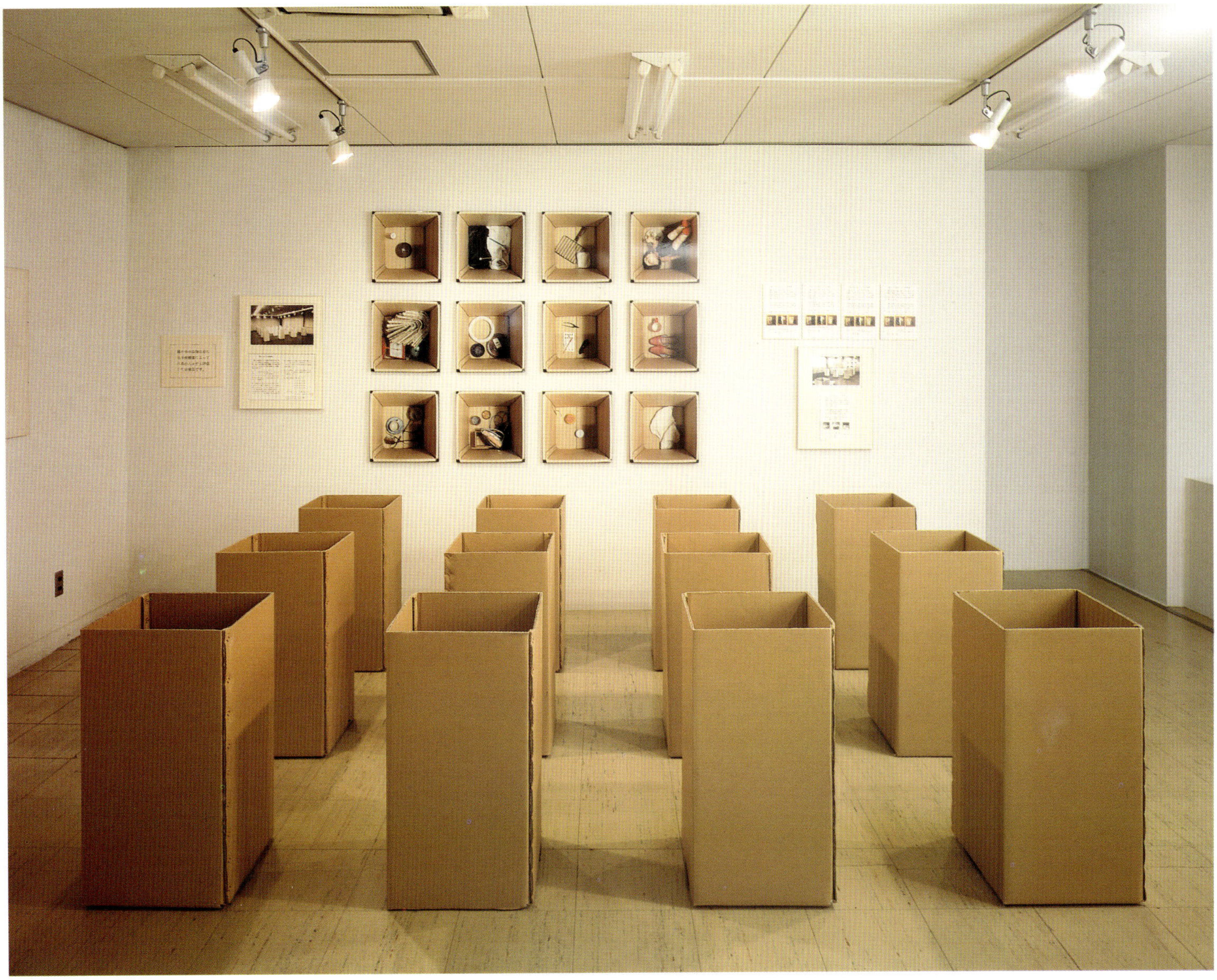

Figure 116.
Kashihara Etsutomu, *Exhibition (Rumination Version)*, 1971/1991, mixed media installation. Collection of the artist.

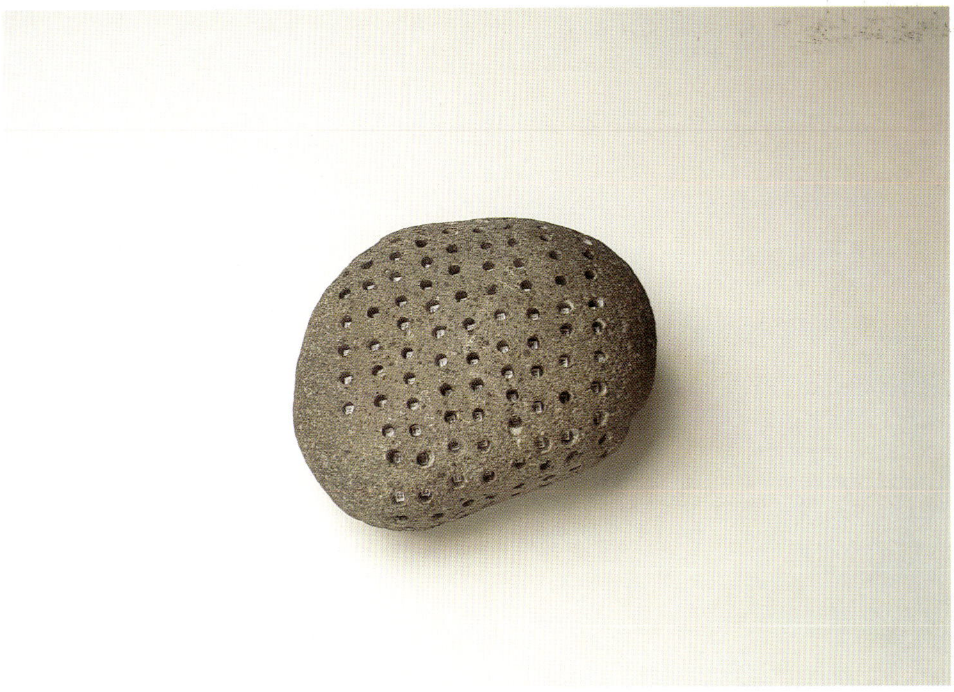

Figure 117.
Kashihara Etsutomu, *Rock*, 1970, rock, paper. Collection of the artist.

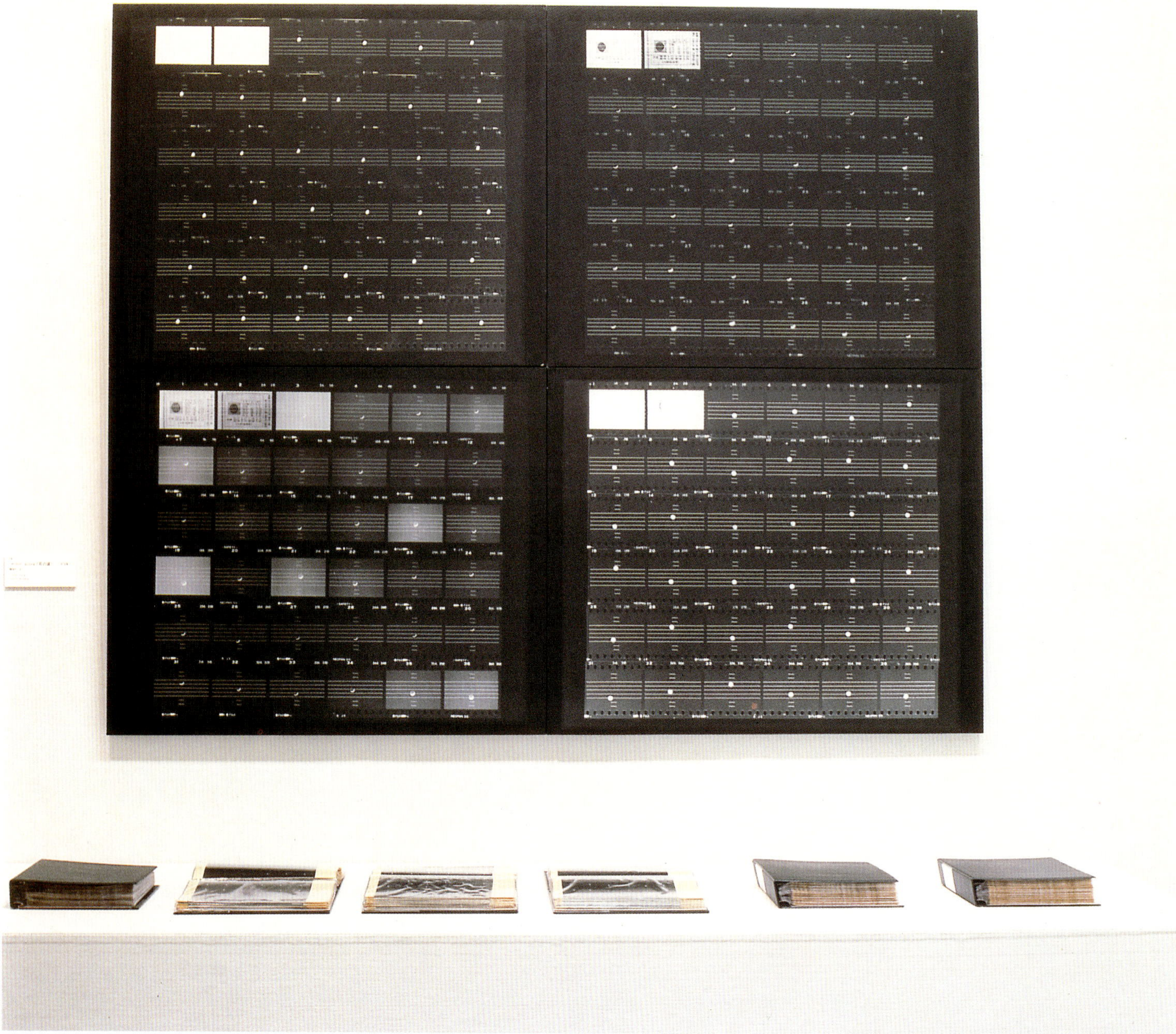

FIGURE 118.
Nomura Hitoshi, *'moon' score,* 1975–80, four photographs, six photograph files. Collection of The National Museum of Modern Art, Tokyo.

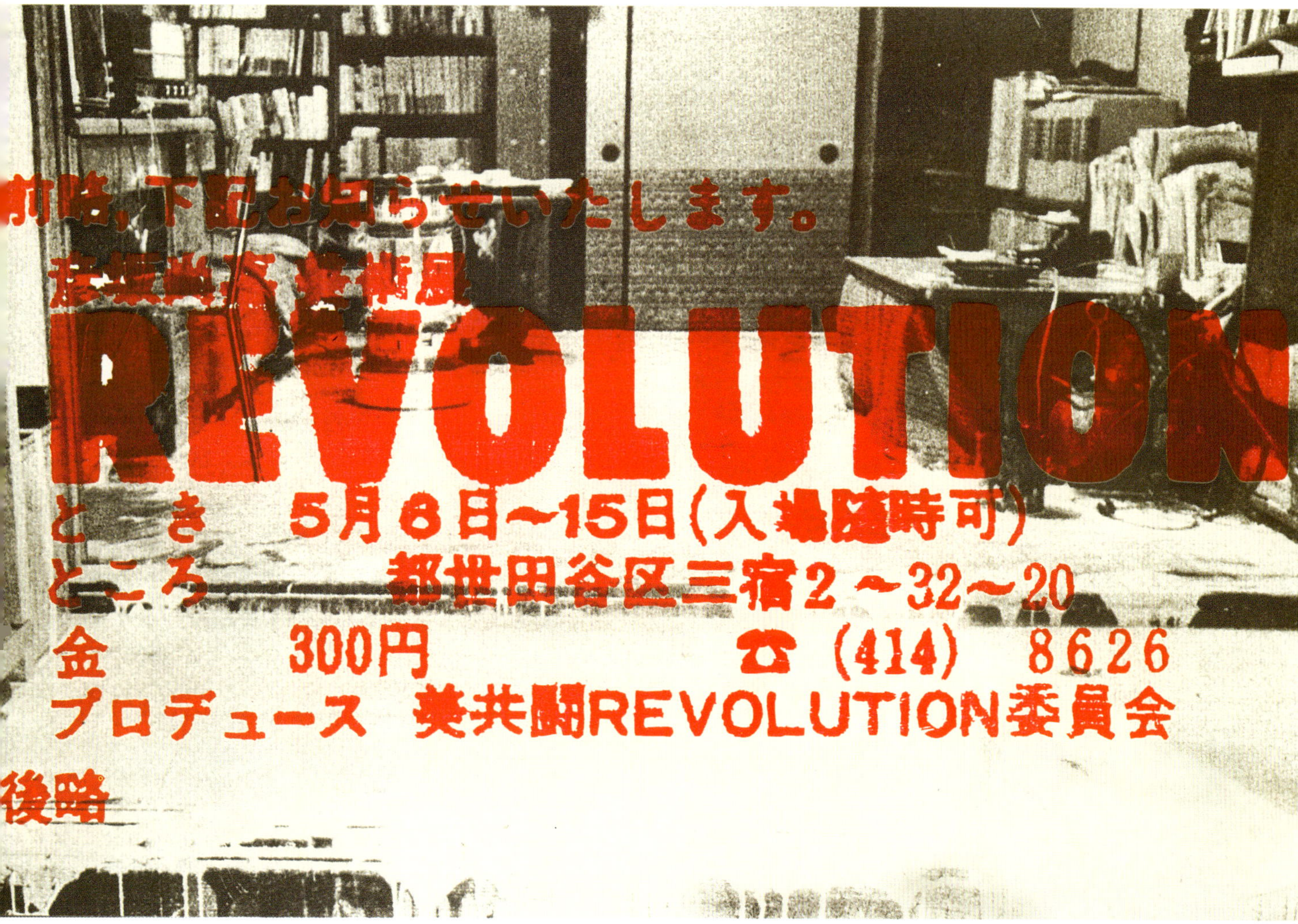

FIGURE 119.
Hikosaka Naoyoshi, invitation to *Floor Event (Furoa ivento)*, 1971, postcard. Collection of the artist.

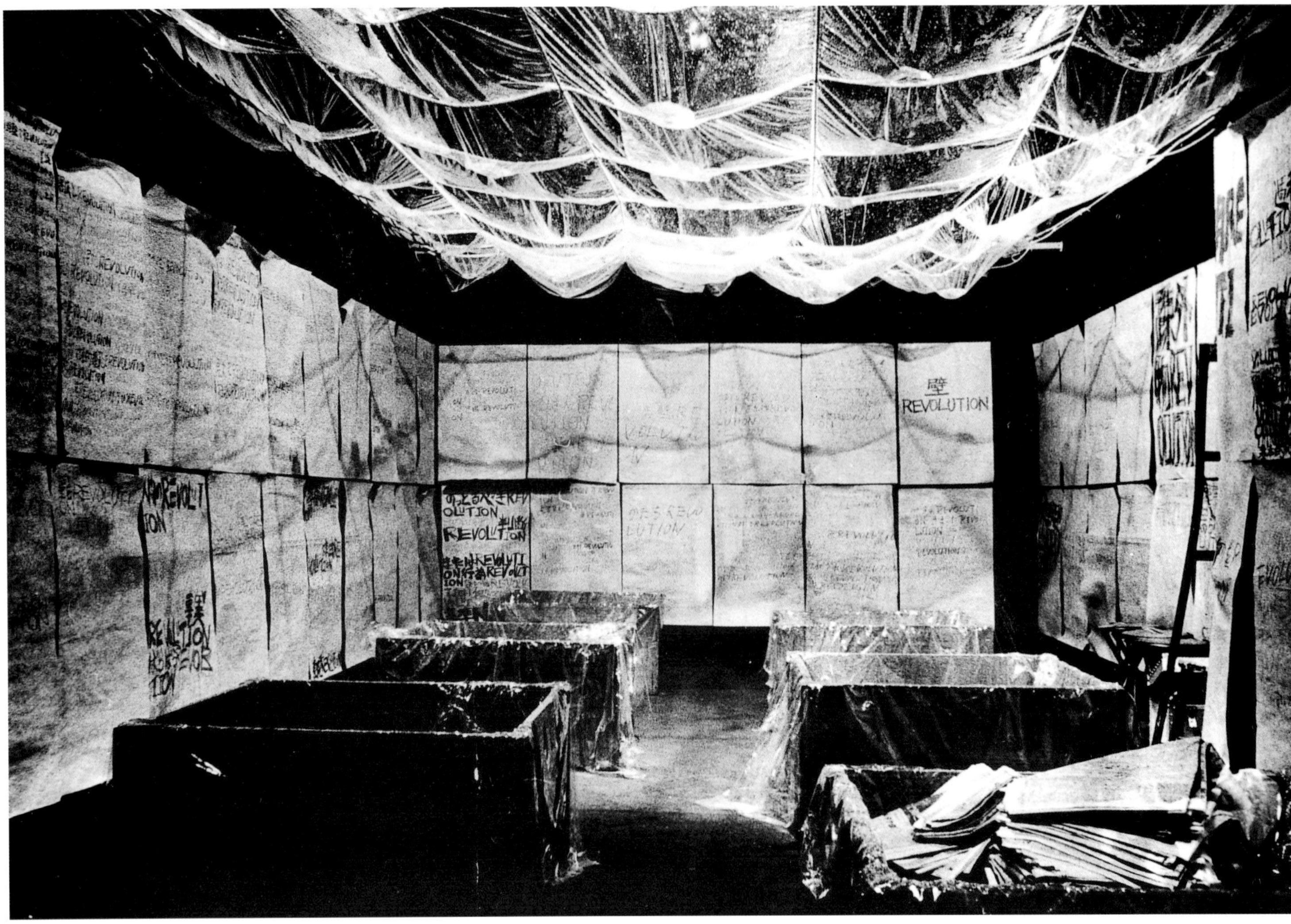

Figure 120.
Hori Kosai, *Revolution: Ceiling, Wall, Floor (Revolution: Tenjō, kabe, yuka)*, 1971, documentary photograph. Collection of the artist.

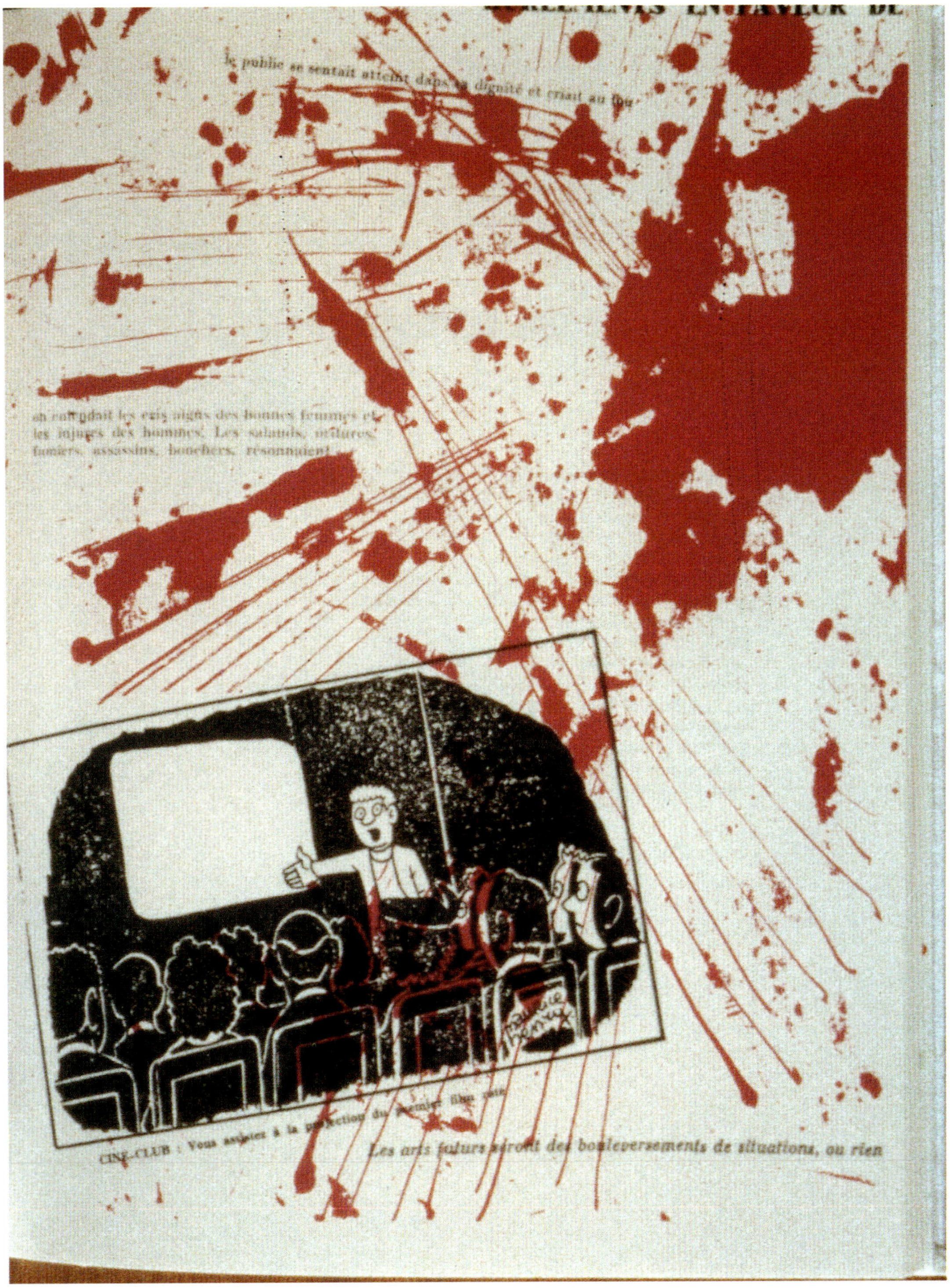

Figure 121.
Guy Debord, *Mémoires*, 1958/1993, book.
Private collection.

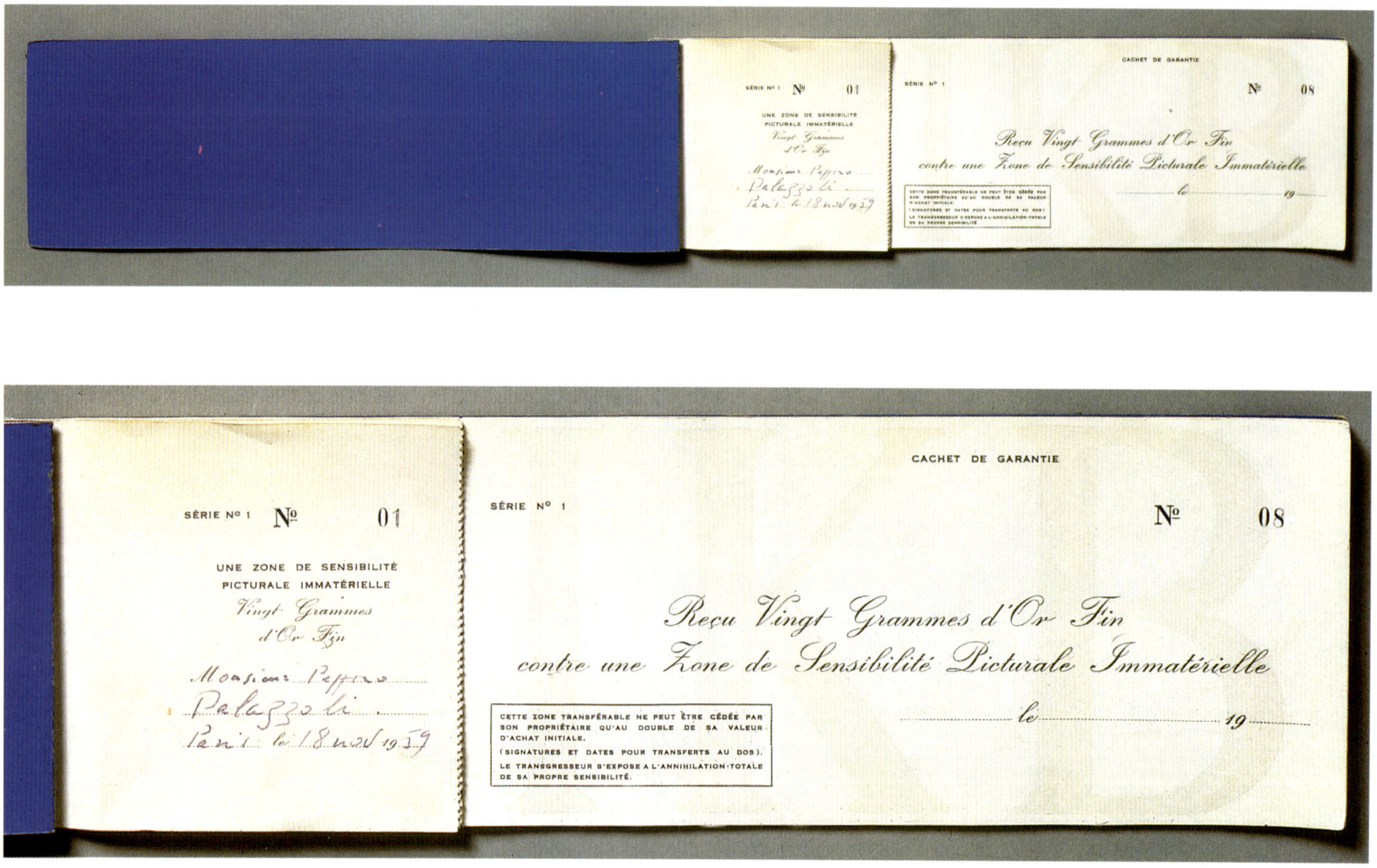

FIGURE 122.
Yves Klein, *Certificat d'un volume de sensibilité picturale immatérielle (Receipt Book for Zones of Immaterial Pictorial Sensibility)*, partially used, 1959, printed on paper (originally ten numbered receipts, each for 20 grams of gold). Collection of Ildiko Erdes, Paris.

Figure 123.
Piero Manzoni, *Linea m. 10, dicembre 1959 (Line 10 Meters Long, December 1959)*, 1959, ink on paper in cardboard cylinder. Gilbert and Lila Silverman Collection, Detroit.

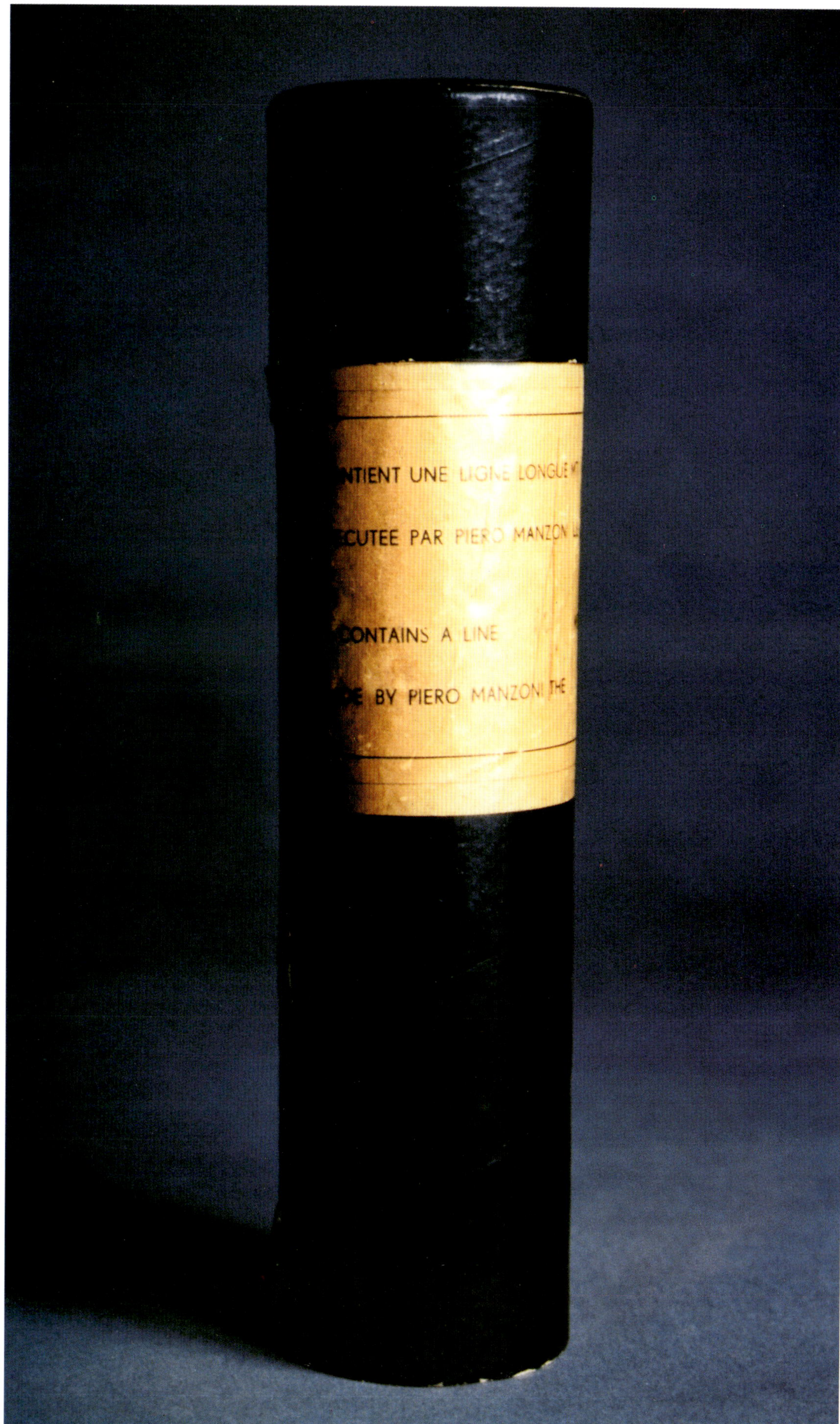

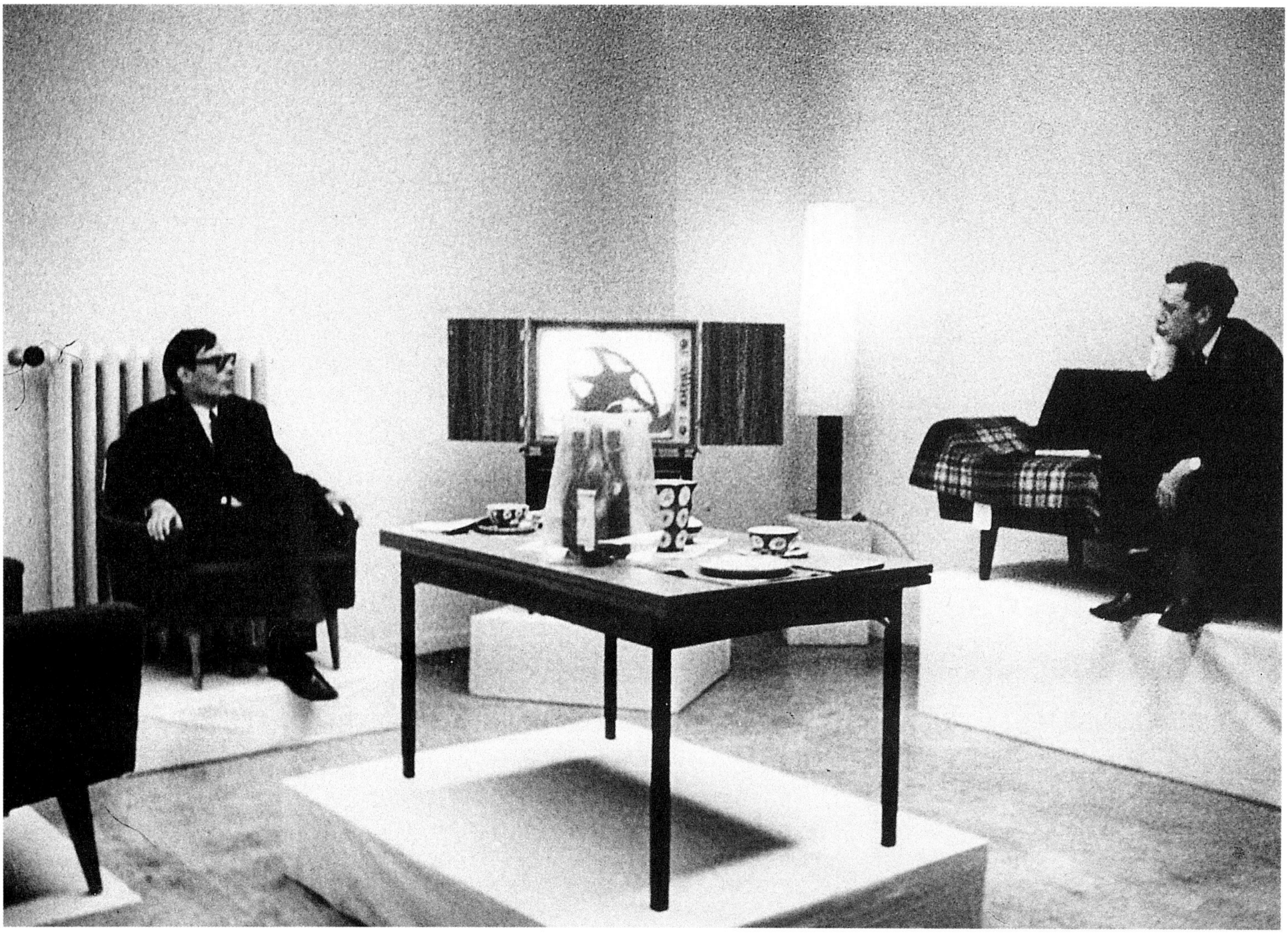

FIGURE 124. (ABOVE)
Gerhard Richter and Konrad Lueg, *Life with Pop: A Demonstration for Capitalist Realism (Leben mit Pop: Eine Demonstration für den kapitalistischen Realismus)*, October 11, 1963, photograph of performance. Collection of the artist.

FIGURE 125. (RIGHT)
Gerhard Richter and Konrad Lueg, *Program for Life with Pop: A Demonstration for Capitalist Realism (Leben mit Pop: Eine Demonstration für den kapitalistischen Realismus)*, ink on paper. Collection of the artist.

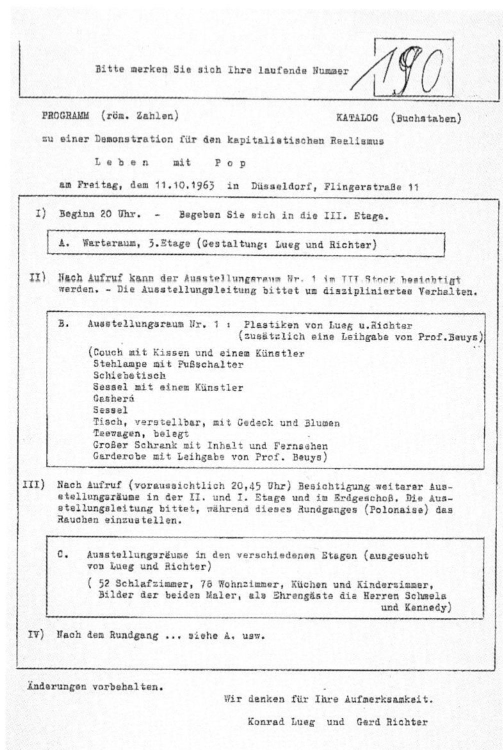

Bitte merken Sie sich Ihre laufende Nummer 190

PROGRAMM (röm. Zahlen) KATALOG (Buchstaben)

zu einer Demonstration für den kapitalistischen Realismus

L e b e n mit P o p

am Freitag, dem 11.10.1963 in Düsseldorf, Flingerstraße 11

I) Beginn 20 Uhr. - Begeben Sie sich in die III. Etage.

A. Warteraum, 3.Etage (Gestaltung: Lueg und Richter)

II) Nach Aufruf kann der Ausstellungsraum Nr. 1 im III.Stock besichtigt werden. - Die Ausstellungsleitung bittet um diszipliniertes Verhalten.

B. Ausstellungsraum Nr. 1 : Plastiken von Lueg u.Richter (zusätzlich eine Leihgabe von Prof.Beuys)

(Couch mit Kissen und einem Künstler
Stehlampe mit Fußschalter
Schiebetisch
Sessel mit einem Künstler
Gasherd
Sessel
Tisch, verstellbar, mit Gedeck und Blumen
Teewagen, belegt
Großer Schrank mit Inhalt und Fernsehen
Garderobe mit Leihgabe von Prof. Beuys)

III) Nach Aufruf (voraussichtlich 20,45 Uhr) Besichtigung weiterer Ausstellungsräume in der II. und I. Etage und im Erdgeschoß. Die Ausstellungsleitung bittet, während dieses Rundganges (Polonaise) das Rauchen einzustellen.

C. Ausstellungsräume in den verschiedenen Etagen (ausgesucht von Lueg und Richter)

(52 Schlafzimmer, 78 Wohnzimmer, Küchen und Kinderzimmer, Bilder der beiden Maler, als Ehrengäste die Herren Schmela und Kennedy)

IV) Nach dem Rundgang ... siehe A. usw.

Änderungen vorbehalten.

Wir denken für Ihre Aufmerksamkeit.

Konrad Lueg und Gerd Richter

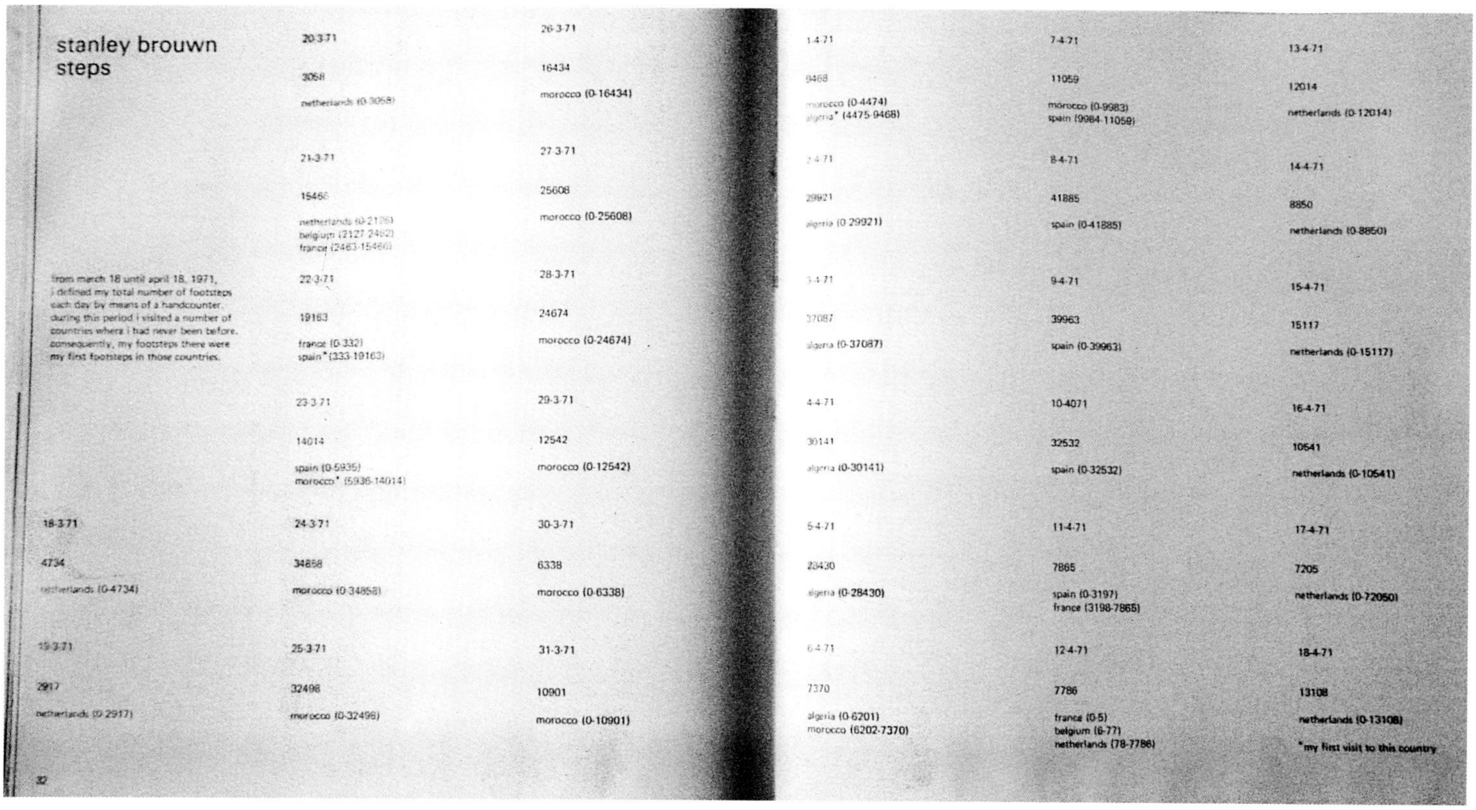

stanley brouwn
steps

from march 18 until april 18, 1971, i defined my total number of footsteps each day by means of a handcounter. during this period i visited a number of countries where i had never been before. consequently, my footsteps there were my first footsteps in those countries.

18-3-71
4734
netherlands (0-4734)

19-3-71
2917
netherlands (0-2917)

20-3-71
3058
netherlands (0-3058)

21-3-71
15466
netherlands (0-2126)
belgium (2127-2462)
france (2463-15466)

22-3-71
19163
france (0-332)
spain* (333-19163)

23-3-71
14014
spain (0-5935)
morocco* (5936-14014)

24-3-71
34858
morocco (0-34858)

25-3-71
32498
morocco (0-32498)

26-3-71
16434
morocco (0-16434)

27-3-71
25608
morocco (0-25608)

28-3-71
24674
morocco (0-24674)

29-3-71
12542
morocco (0-12542)

30-3-71
6338
morocco (0-6338)

31-3-71
10901
morocco (0-10901)

32

1-4-71
9468
morocco (0-4474)
algeria* (4475-9468)

2-4-71
29921
algeria (0-29921)

3-4-71
37087
algeria (0-37087)

4-4-71
30141
algeria (0-30141)

5-4-71
28430
algeria (0-28430)

6-4-71
7370
algeria (0-6201)
morocco (6202-7370)

7-4-71
11059
morocco (0-9983)
spain (9984-11059)

8-4-71
41885
spain (0-41885)

9-4-71
39963
spain (0-39963)

10-4-71
32532
spain (0-32532)

11-4-71
7865
spain (0-3197)
france (3198-7865)

12-4-71
7786
france (0-5)
belgium (6-77)
netherlands (78-7786)

13-4-71
12014
netherlands (0-12014)

14-4-71
8850
netherlands (0-8850)

15-4-71
15117
netherlands (0-15117)

16-4-71
10541
netherlands (0-10541)

17-4-71
7205
netherlands (0-7205)

18-4-71
13108
netherlands (0-13108)

*my first visit to this country

FIGURE 126.
Stanley Brouwn, *steps*, 1971, as printed in *Avalanche* 4 (Spring 1972): 32–33.

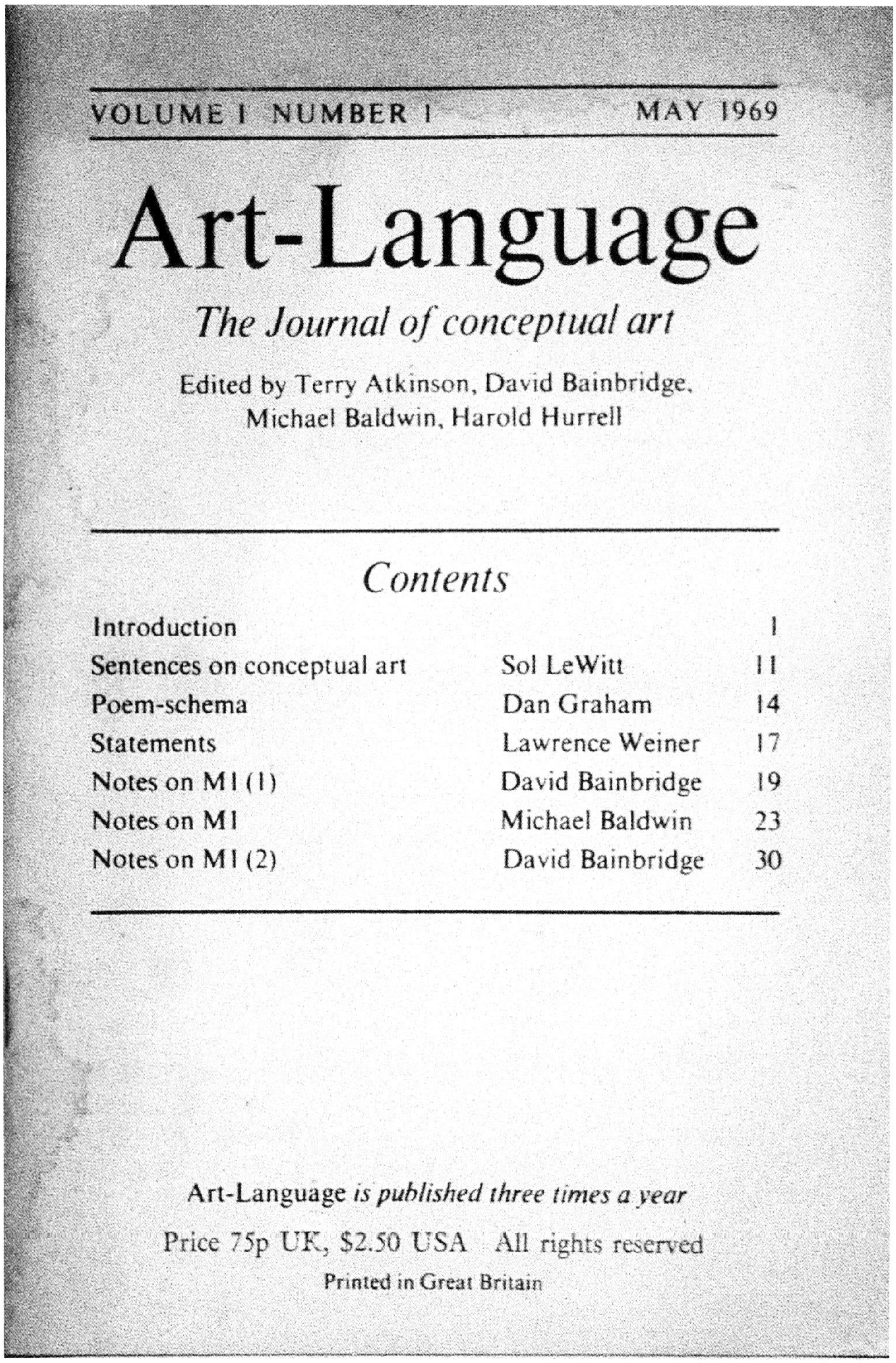

VOLUME I NUMBER I MAY 1969

Art-Language

The Journal of conceptual art

Edited by Terry Atkinson, David Bainbridge, Michael Baldwin, Harold Hurrell

Contents

Art-Language *is published three times a year*

Price 75p UK, $2.50 USA

Printed in Great Britain

Figure 127.
Art & Language, *Art-Language* 1, no. 1 (May 1969). Private collection.

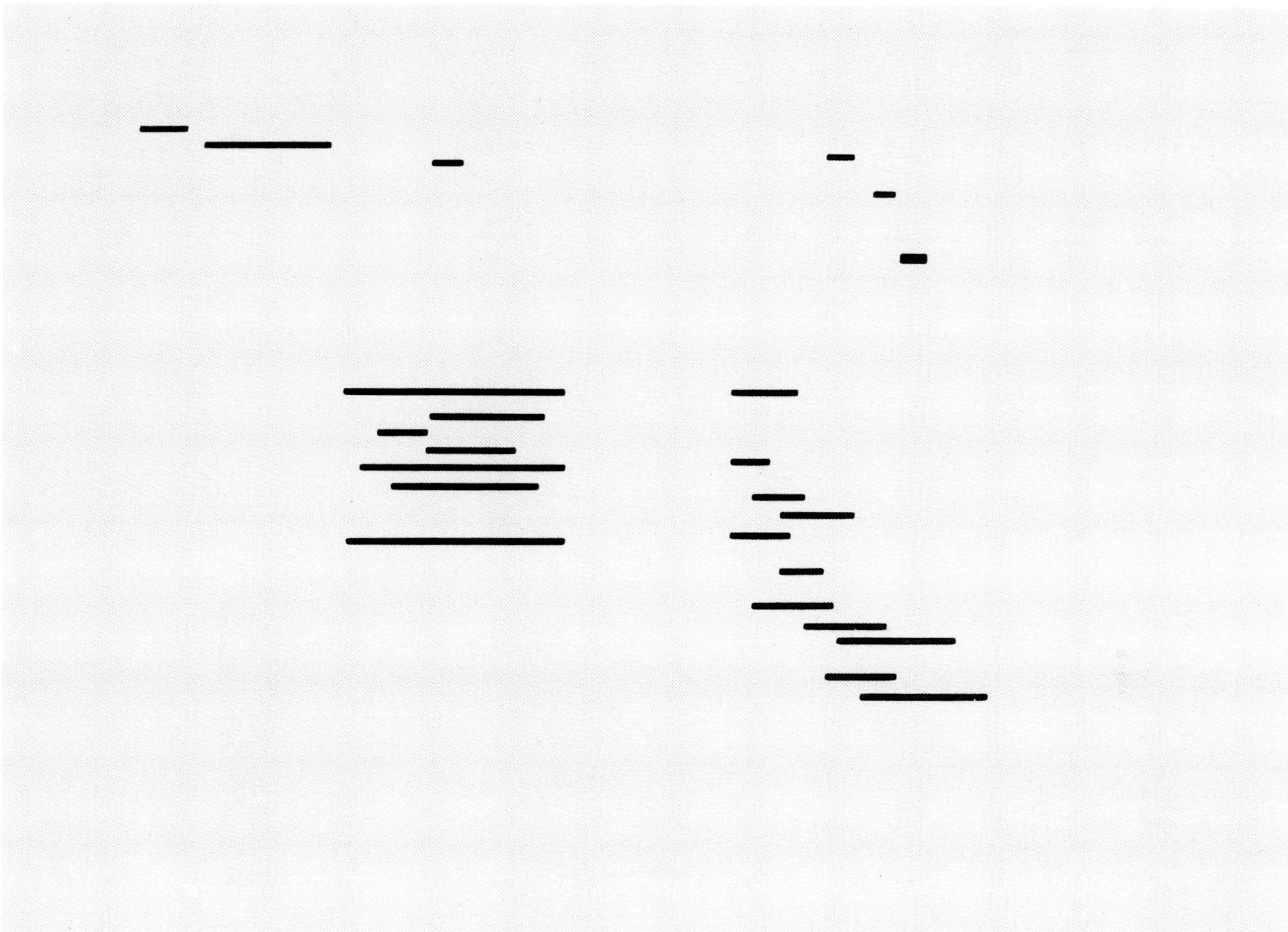

Figure 128.
Marcel Broodthaers, *Un coup de dés jamais n'abolira le hasard (Image)*, 1969, aluminum. Private collection.

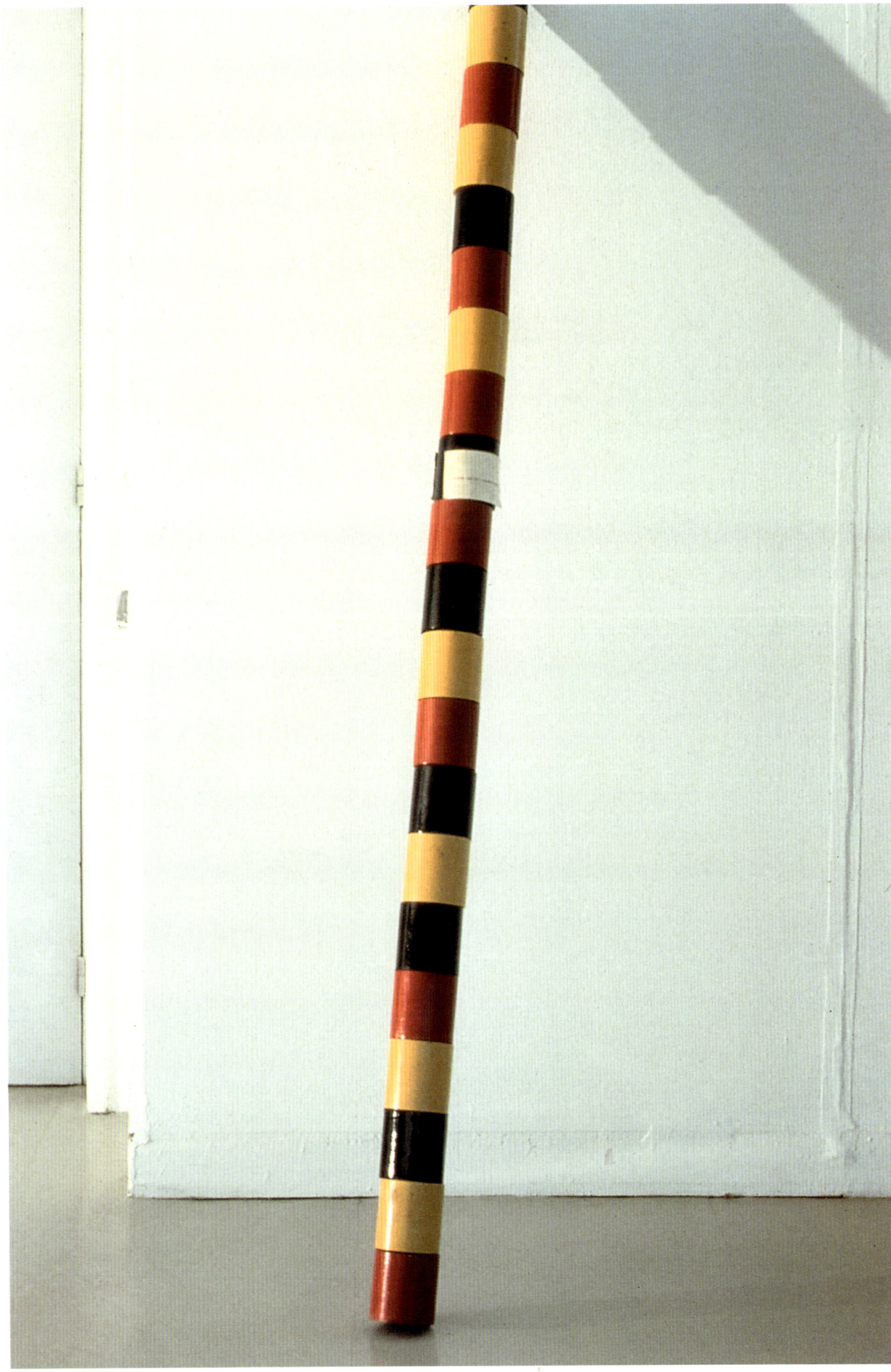

FIGURE 129.
André Cadere, *Untitled,* 1973, wooden bar painted black, white, green, and red. Collection L. & M. Durand-Dessert, Paris.

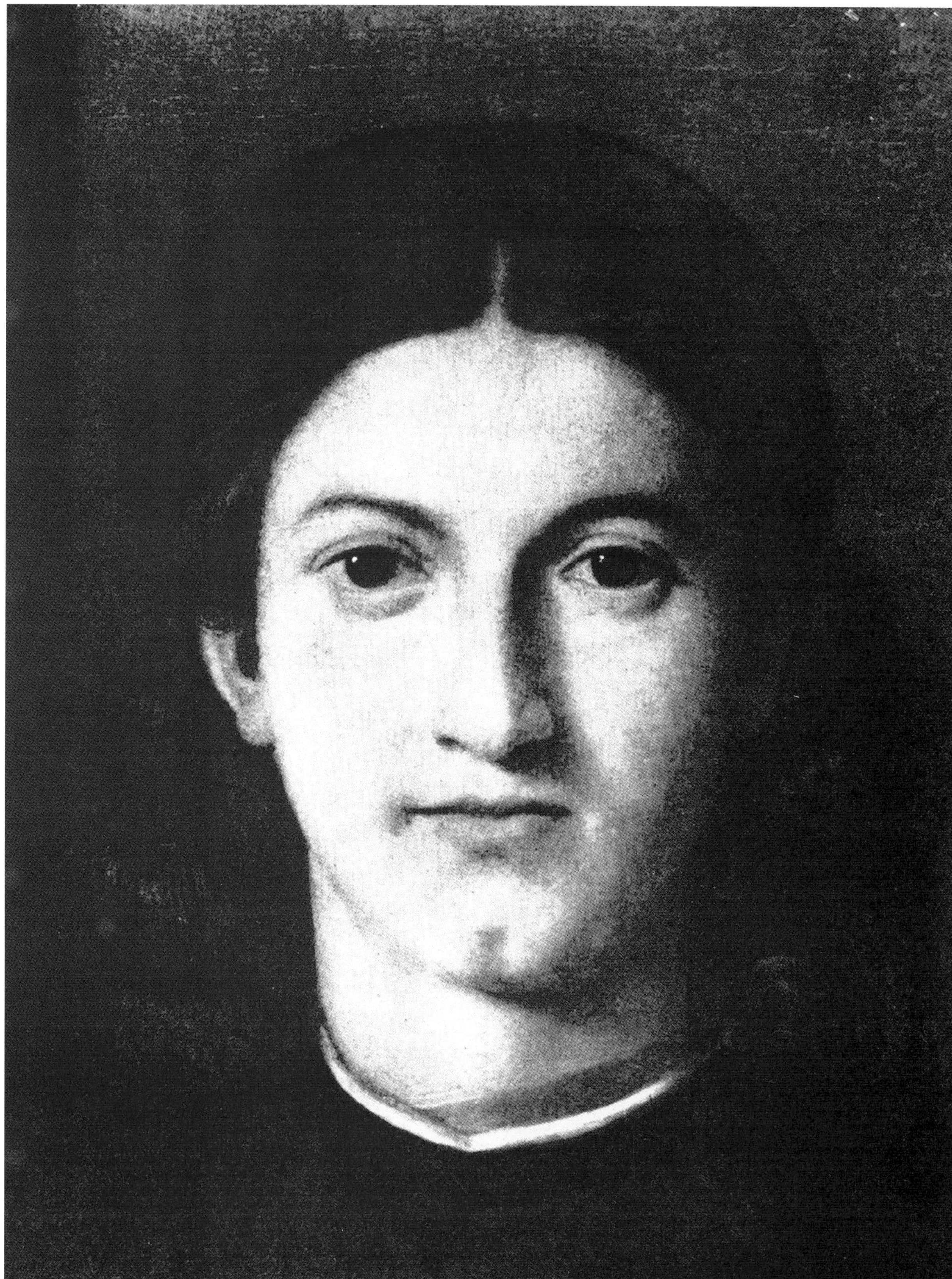

Figure 130.
Giulio Paolini, *Giovane che guarda Lorenzo Lotto* (*Young Man Watching Lorenzo Lotto*), 1967, proof on photographic paper. Collection of the artist.

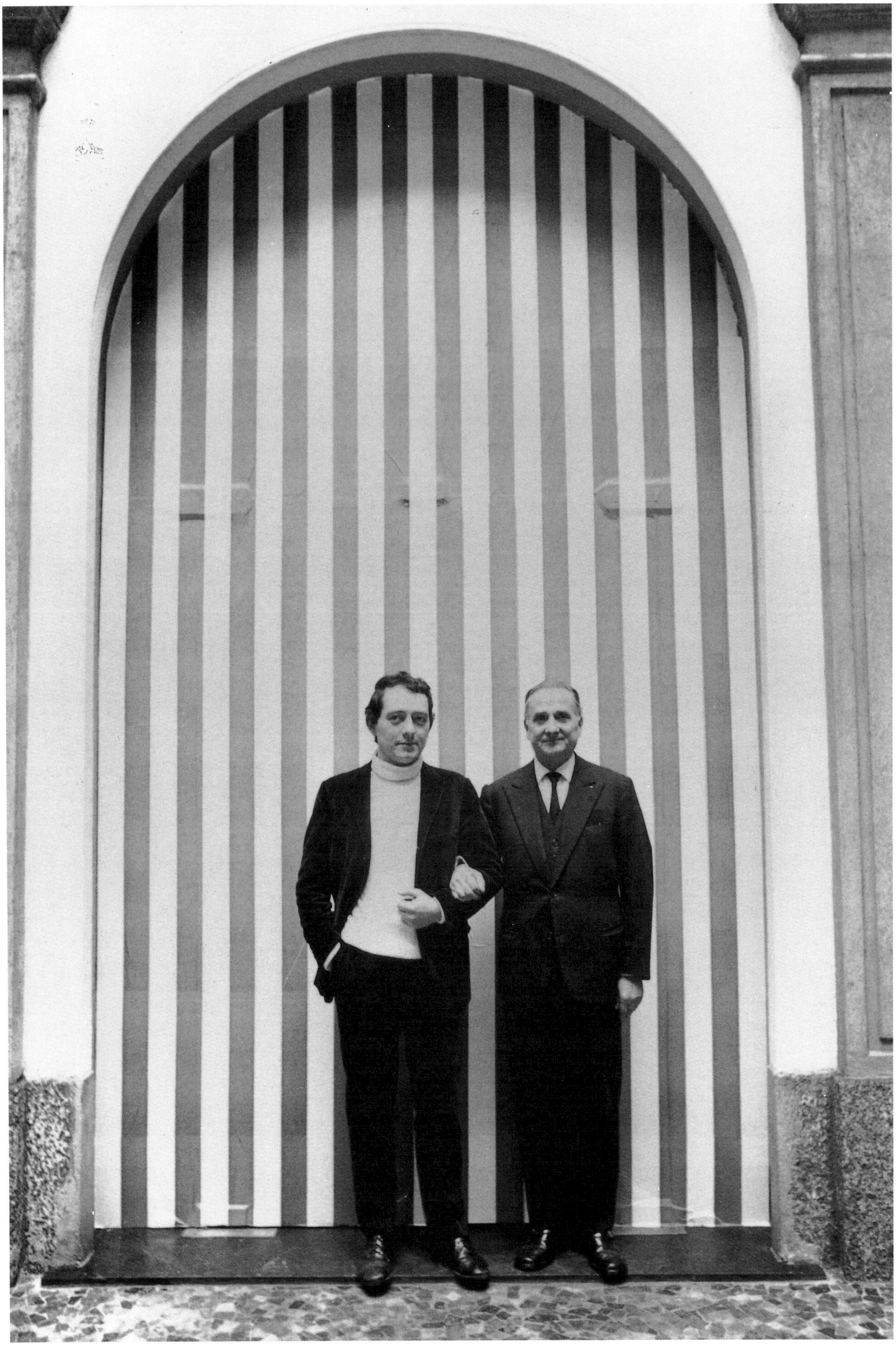

Figure 131.
Photo-souvenir: Daniel Buren and Guido Le Noci, in front of Galerie Apollinaire during the show of Daniel Buren, October 1968, Milan.

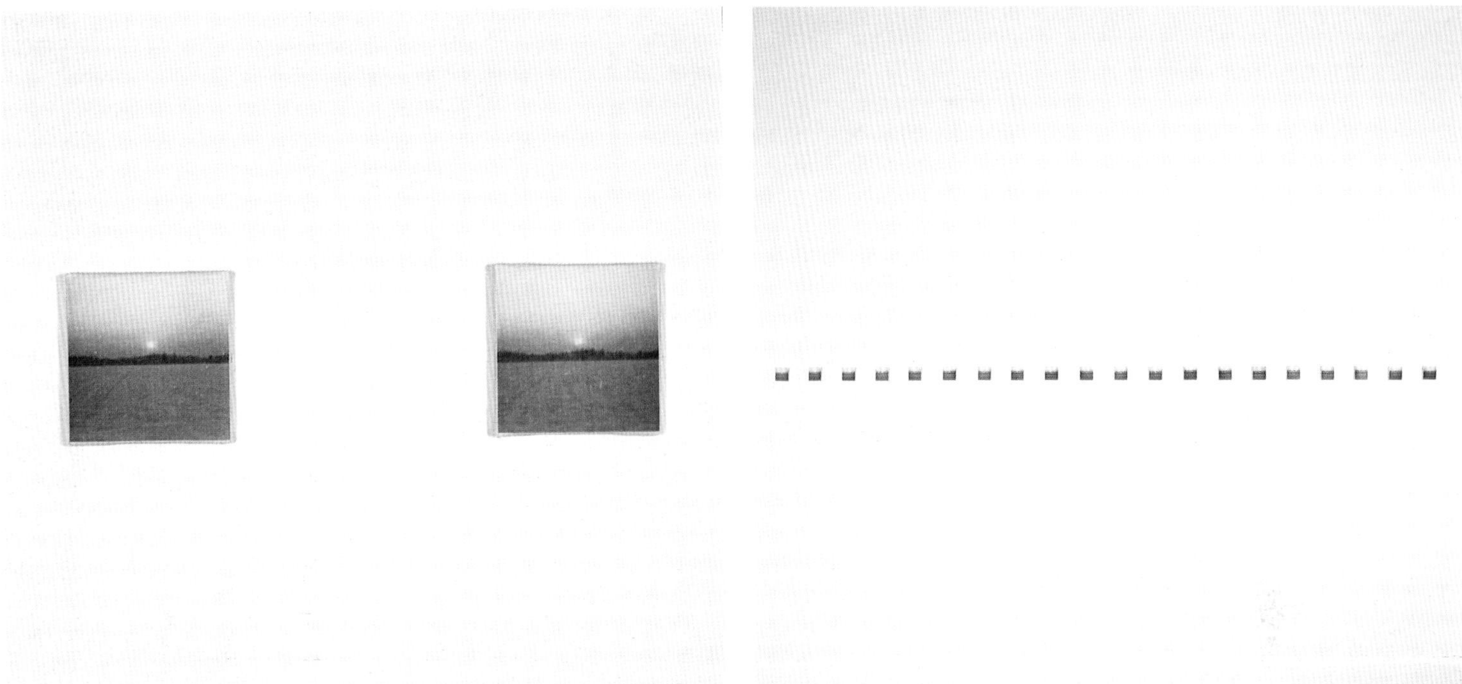

FIGURE 132.
Giovanni Anselmo, *Interferenza nella gravitazione universale (Interference with Universal Gravity)*. 1969, twenty photographs. Collection of Musée Départemental d'Art Contemporain de Rochechouart, France.

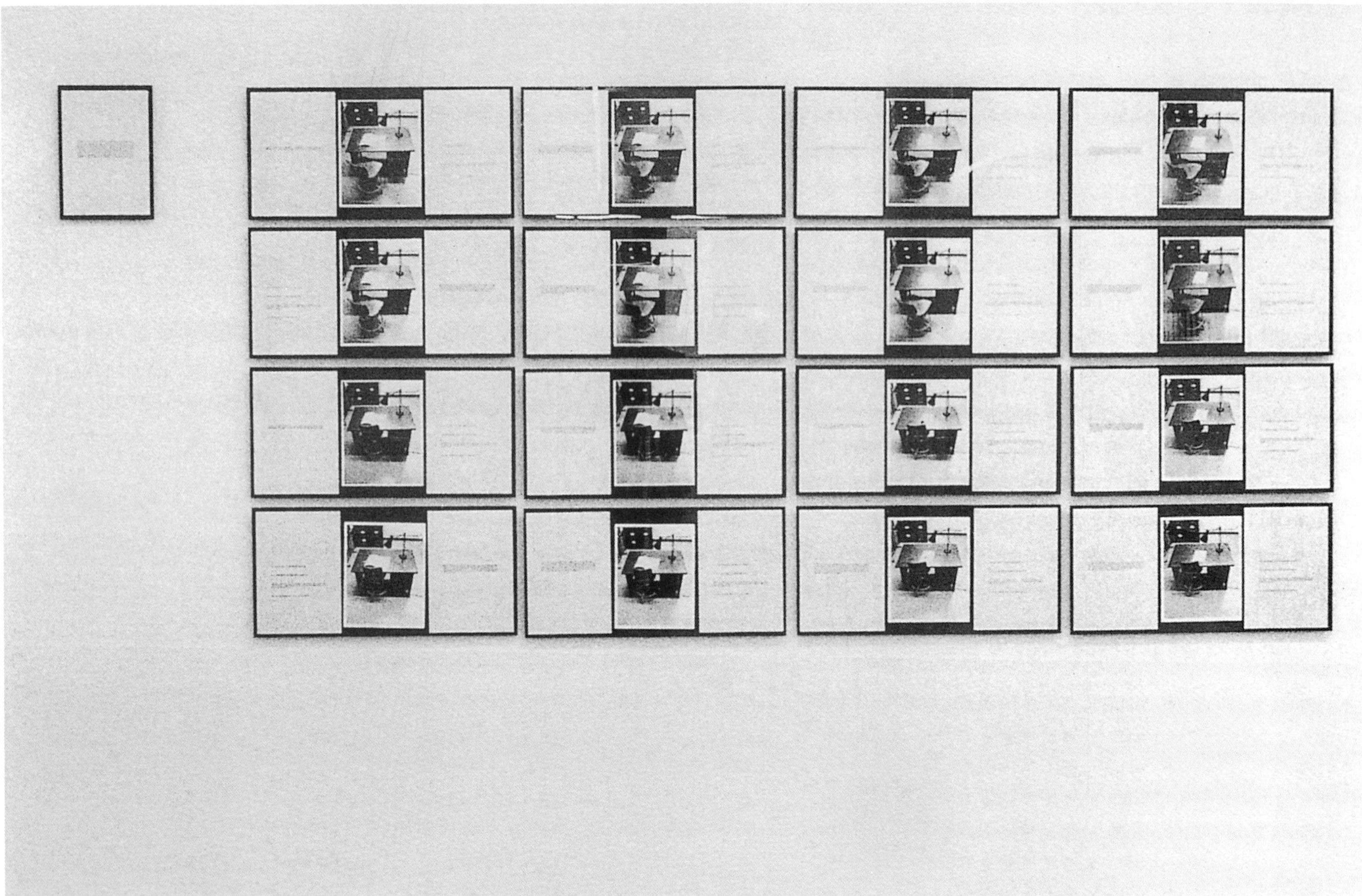

FIGURE 133.
Victor Burgin, *Performative/Narrative,* 1971, photographs and printed text on paper. Collection of Ghislain Mollet-Viéville, Paris.

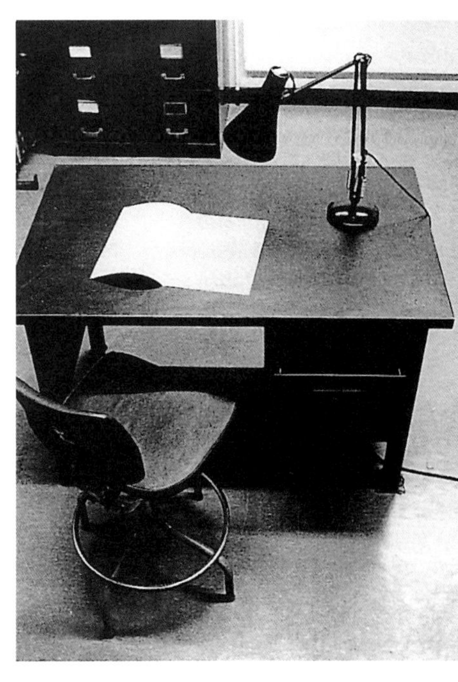

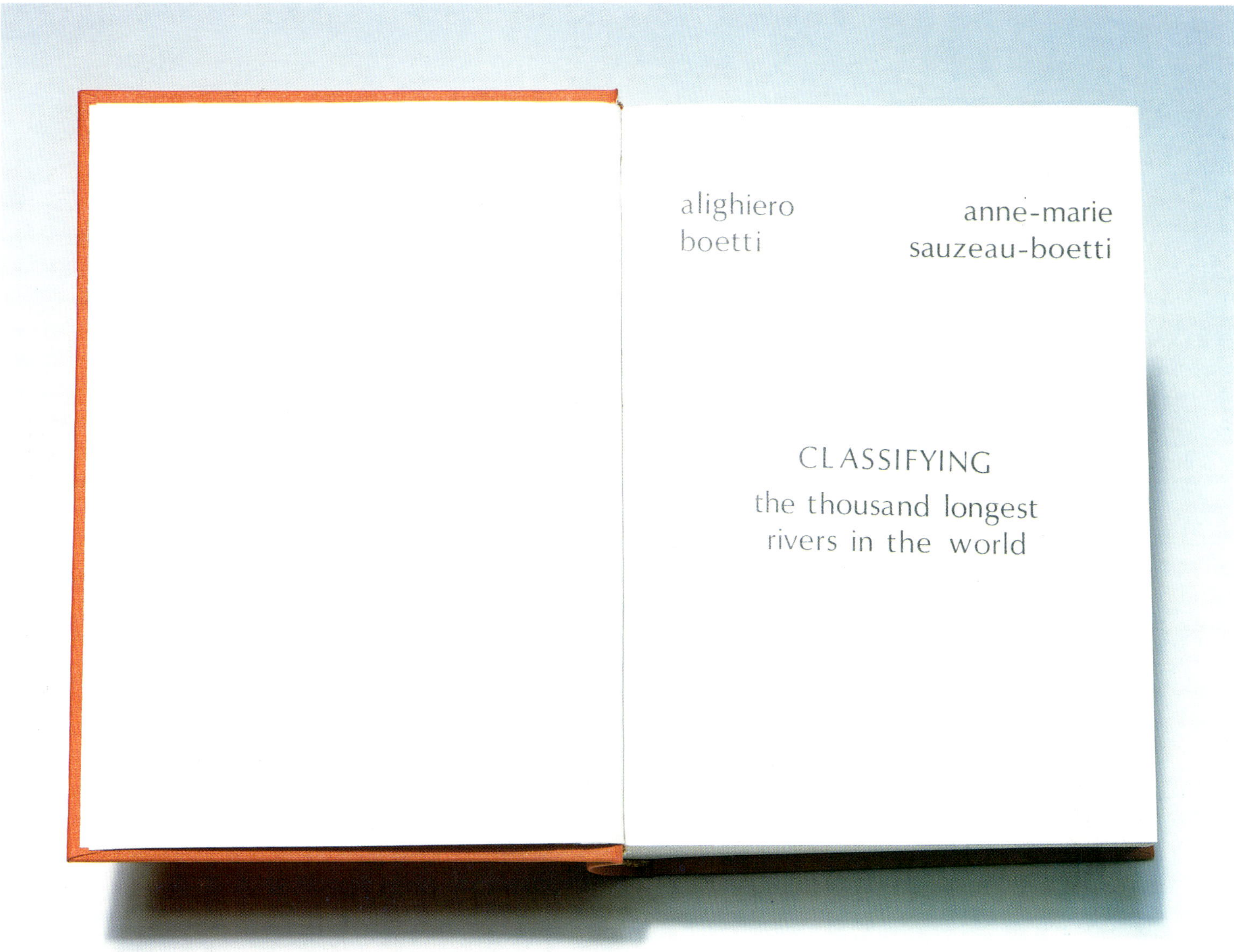

FIGURE 134.
Aligheiro e Boetti, *Classifying the Thousand Longest Rivers in the World,* 1973, 1,000-page book. Courtesy of Jennifer Bacon and Filippo Fossati, Esso Gallery, New York.

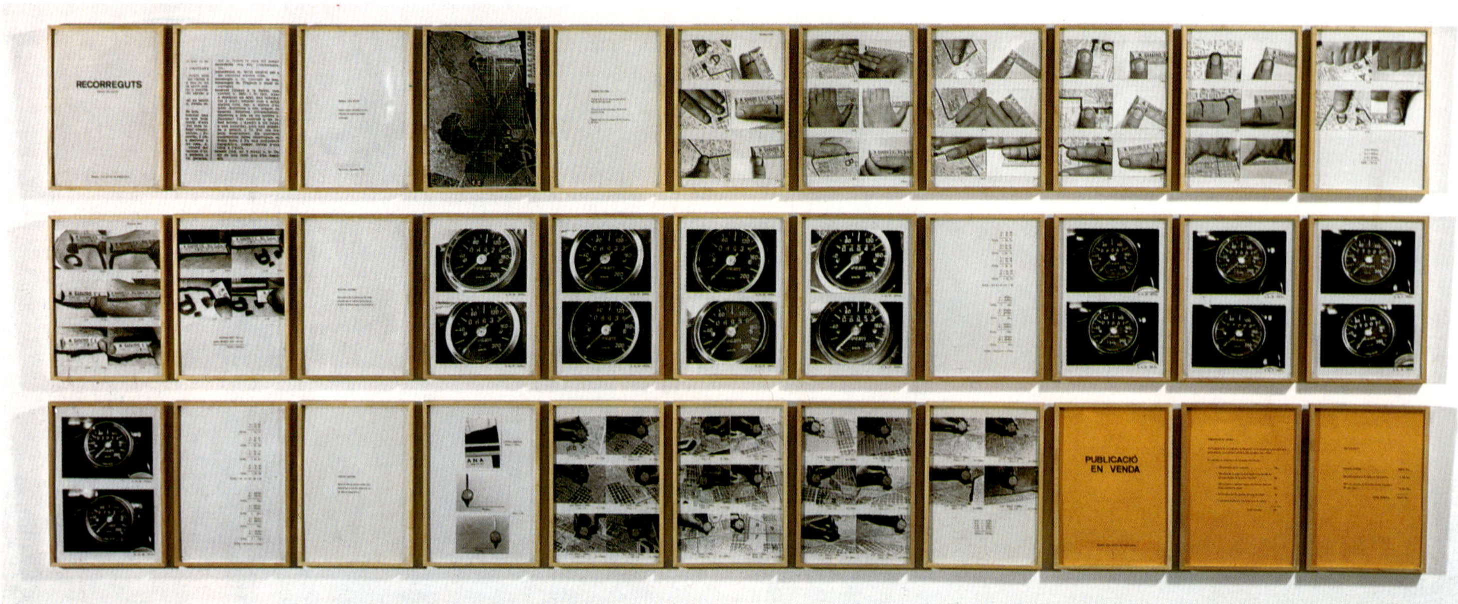

Figure 135.
Grup de Treball (Working Group), *Recorreguts (Distances Traveled),* 1973, 34 photographic collages, ink and impression on thin cardboard. Collecció Museu d'Art Contemporani de Barcelona, Procedent del Fons d'Art de la Generalitat de Catalunya, Barcelona.

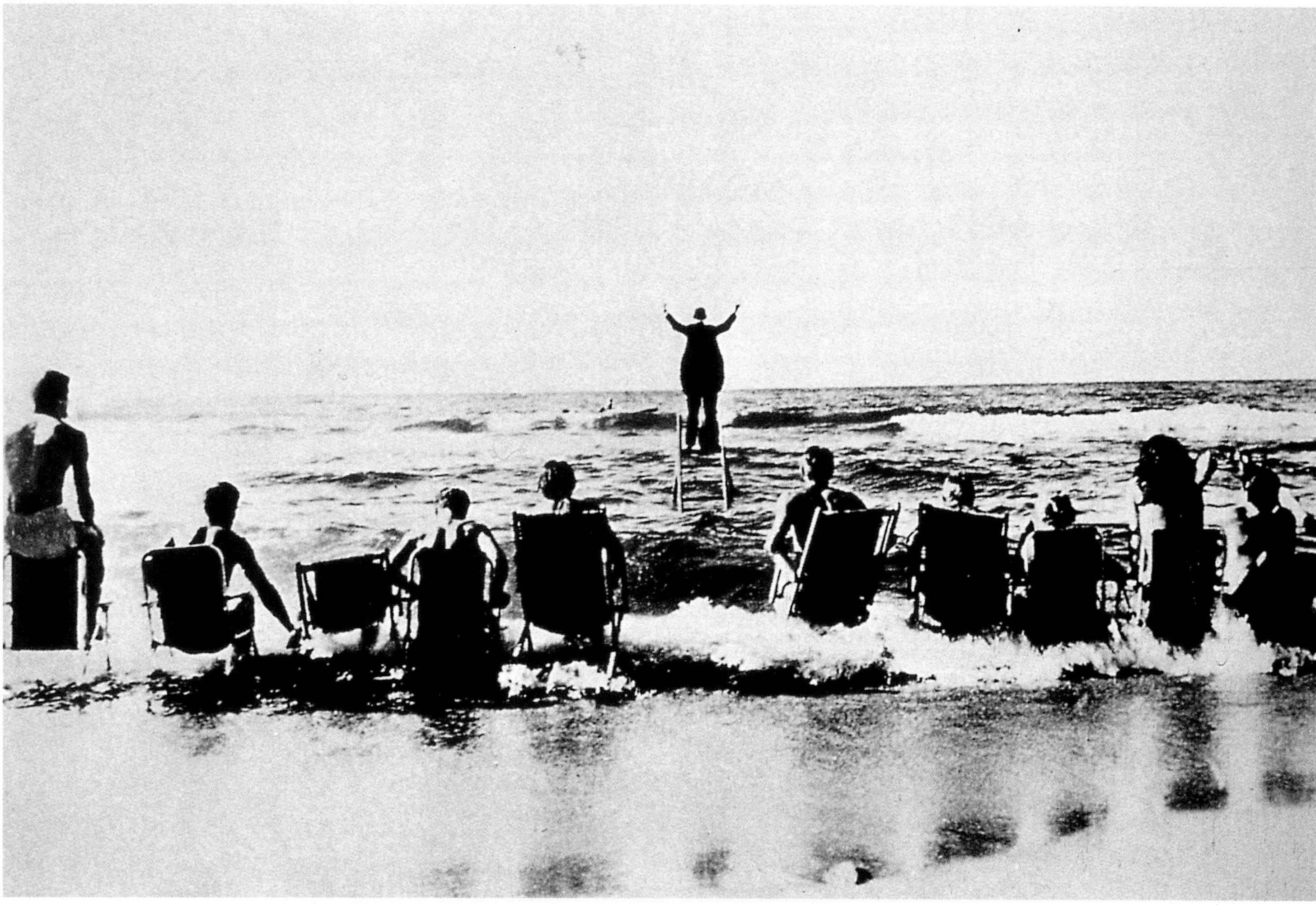

FIGURE 136.
Tadeusz Kantor, *The Sea Concerto* (*Koncert morski*), 1967, signed. documentary photograph by Eustachy Kossakowski. Cricoteka Collection, Cracow.

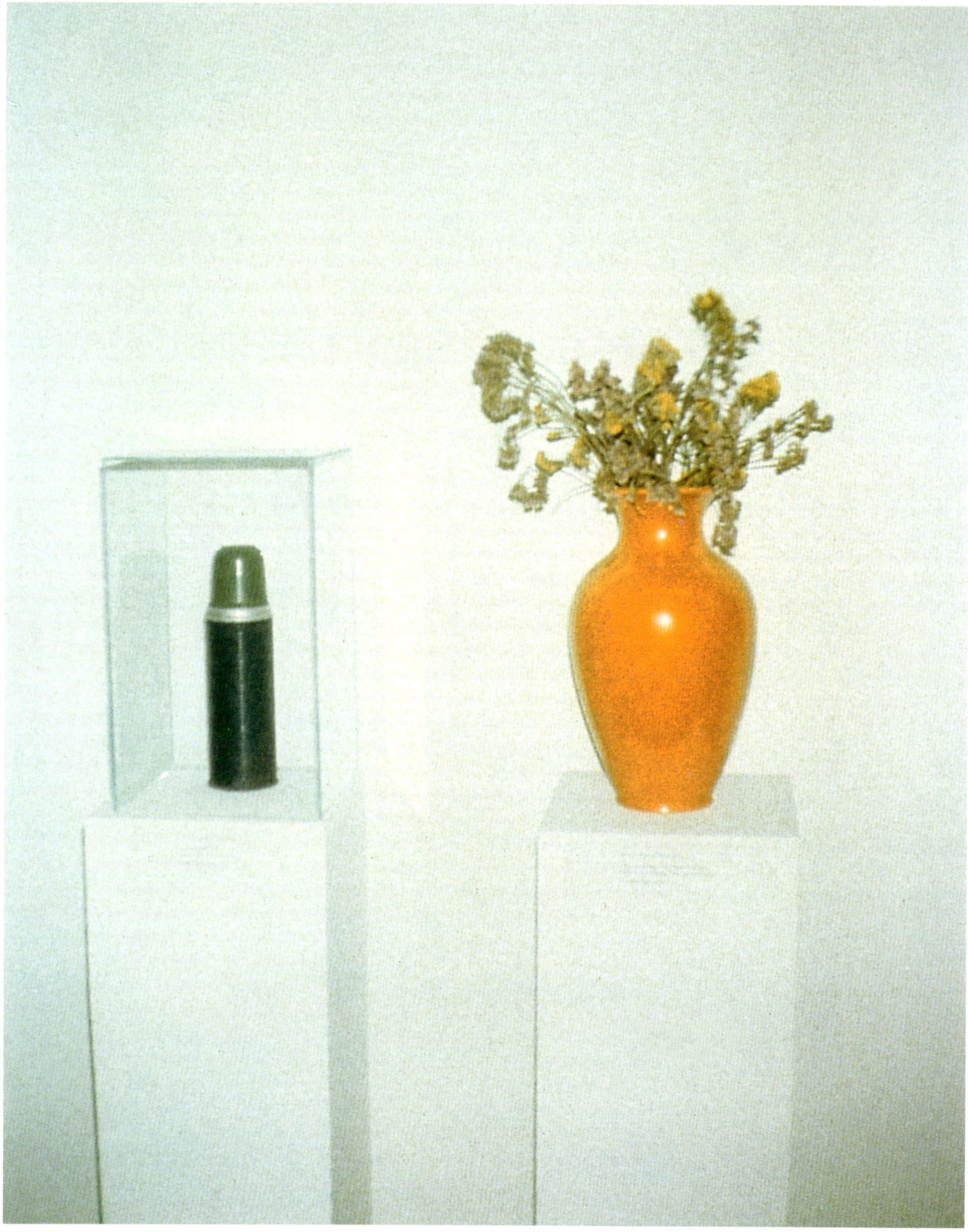

Figure 137.
Miklós Erdély, *Snow of Last Year (Tavalyi hó)*, 1970, object at left (reconstruction). Collection of Miklós Erdély Foundation, Budapest.

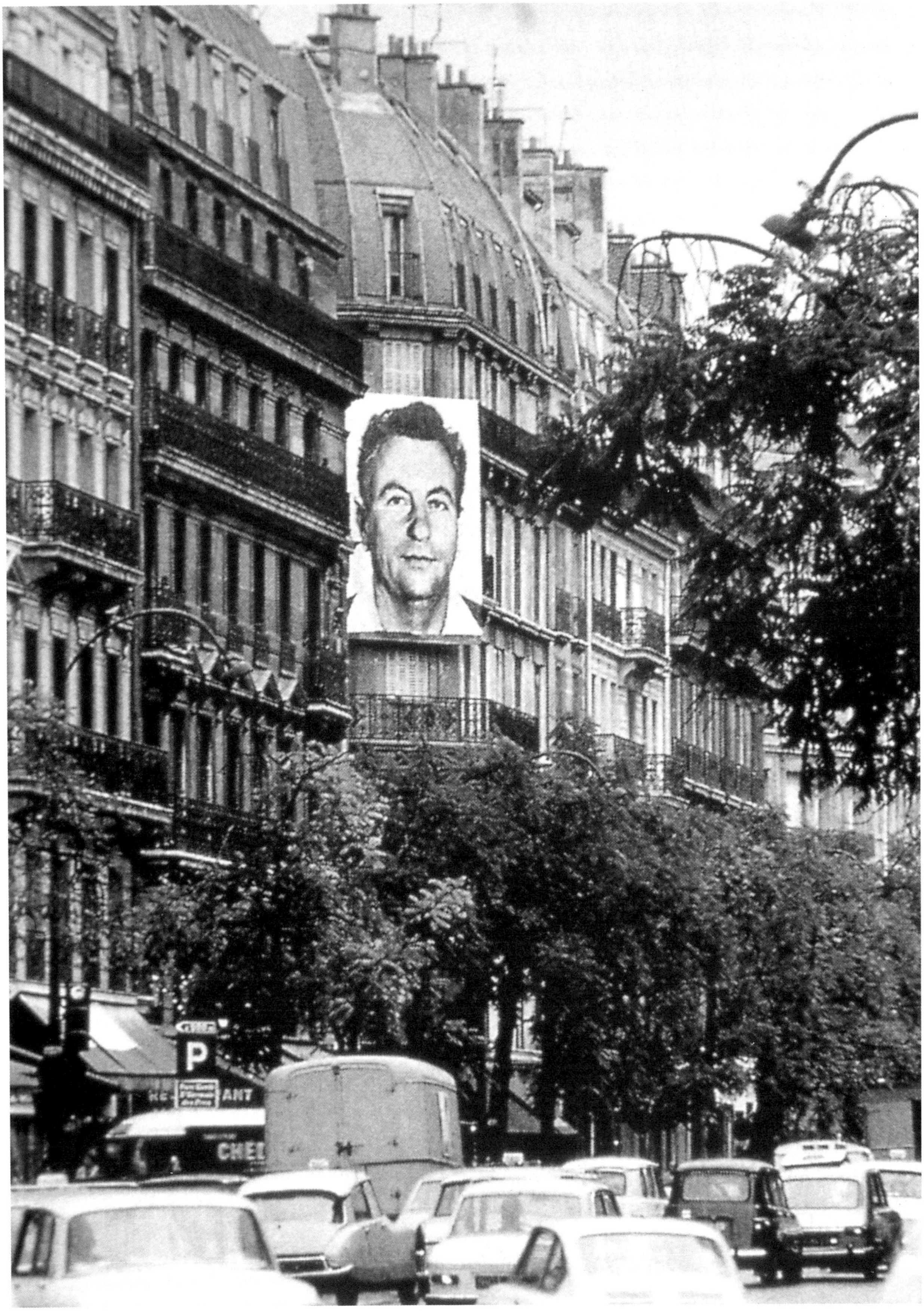

FIGURE 138.
Braco Dimitrijević, *Casual passerby I met at 11:09 pm, Paris, 1971*, 1971, documentary photograph. Collection of the artist.

Figure 139.
Goran Trbuljak, *"From time to time I stuck my finger through a hole in the door of the Modern Art Gallery without the management's knowledge" ("Skozi luknjo v vratih Galerije Moderne Umetnosti sem vsake toliko pomolil prst, ne da bi vodstvo galerije vedelo, kaj počnem")*, 1969, photograph. Collection of the artist.

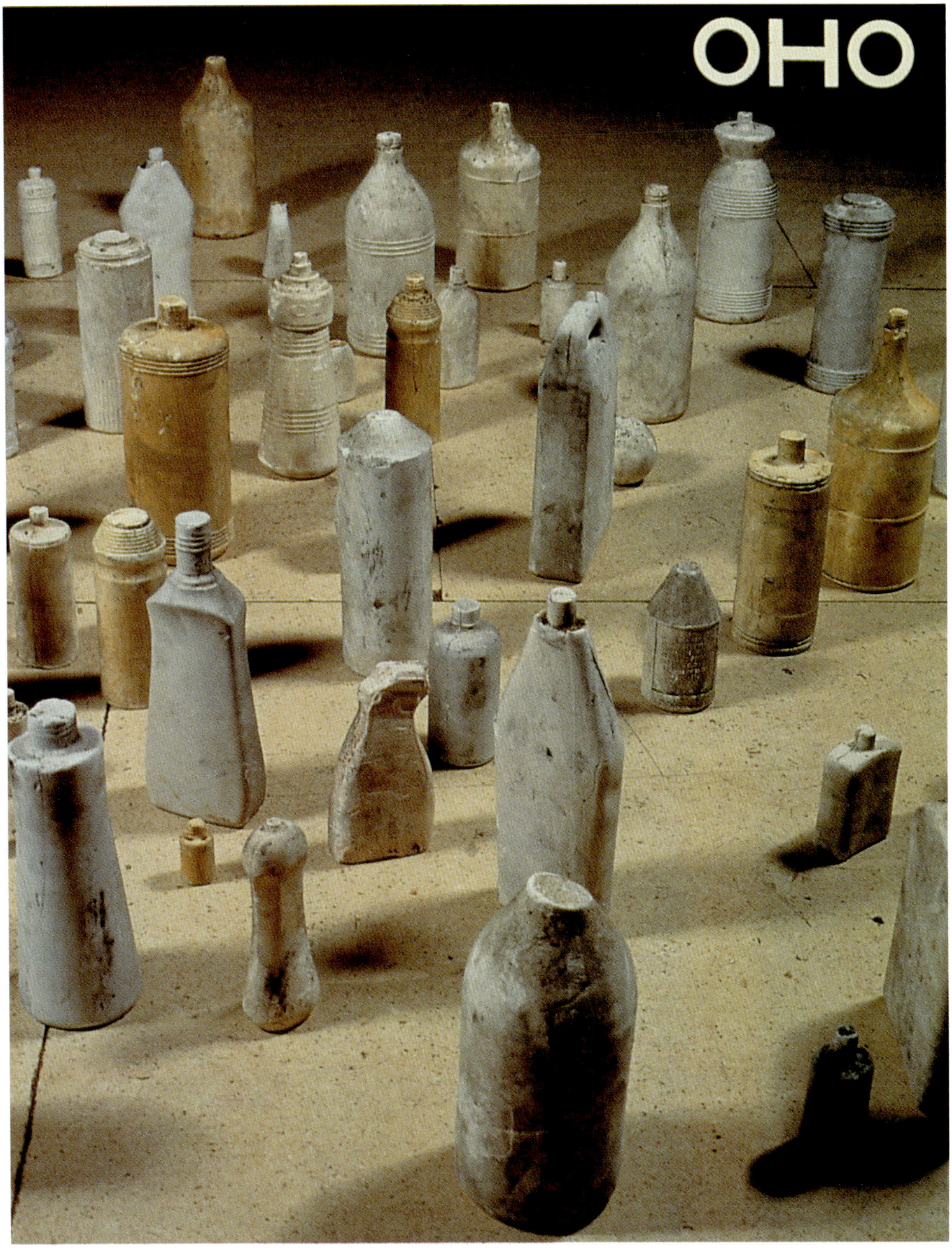

FIGURE 140.
OHO group, *Cast Bottles* (*Mavčni odlitki stetlenick in drugih predmetov*), 1965–68, approximately twenty pieces, plaster of Paris. Collection of Marko Pogačnik, courtesy of Moderna Galerija, Ljubljana.

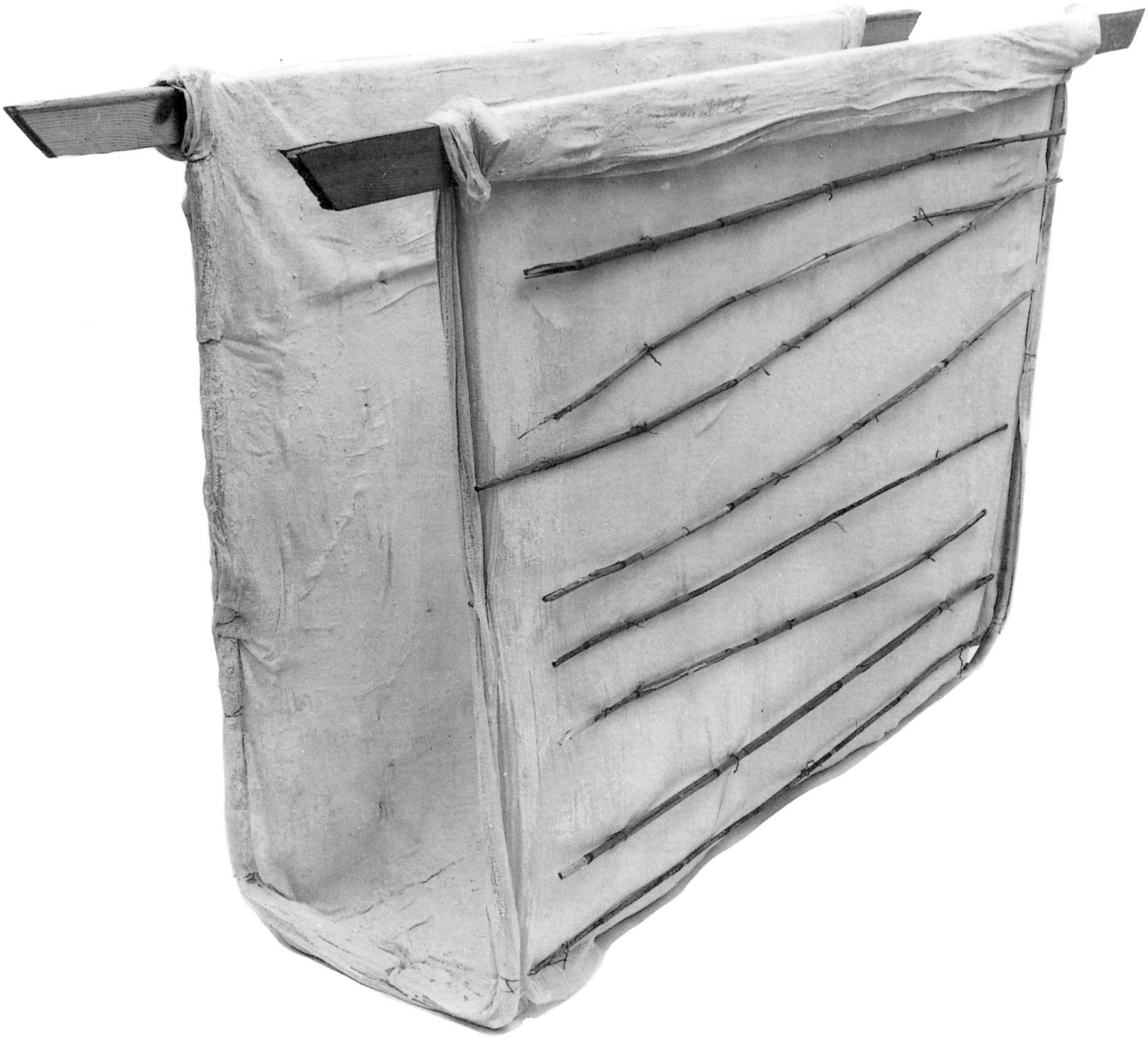

Figure 141.
Tamás Szentjóby, *Portable Trench for Three Persons* (*Háromszemélyes hordozható lövészárok*), 1969, gauze, wood, reed, sulphur, and aluminum. Magyar Nemzeti Galéria, Budapest.

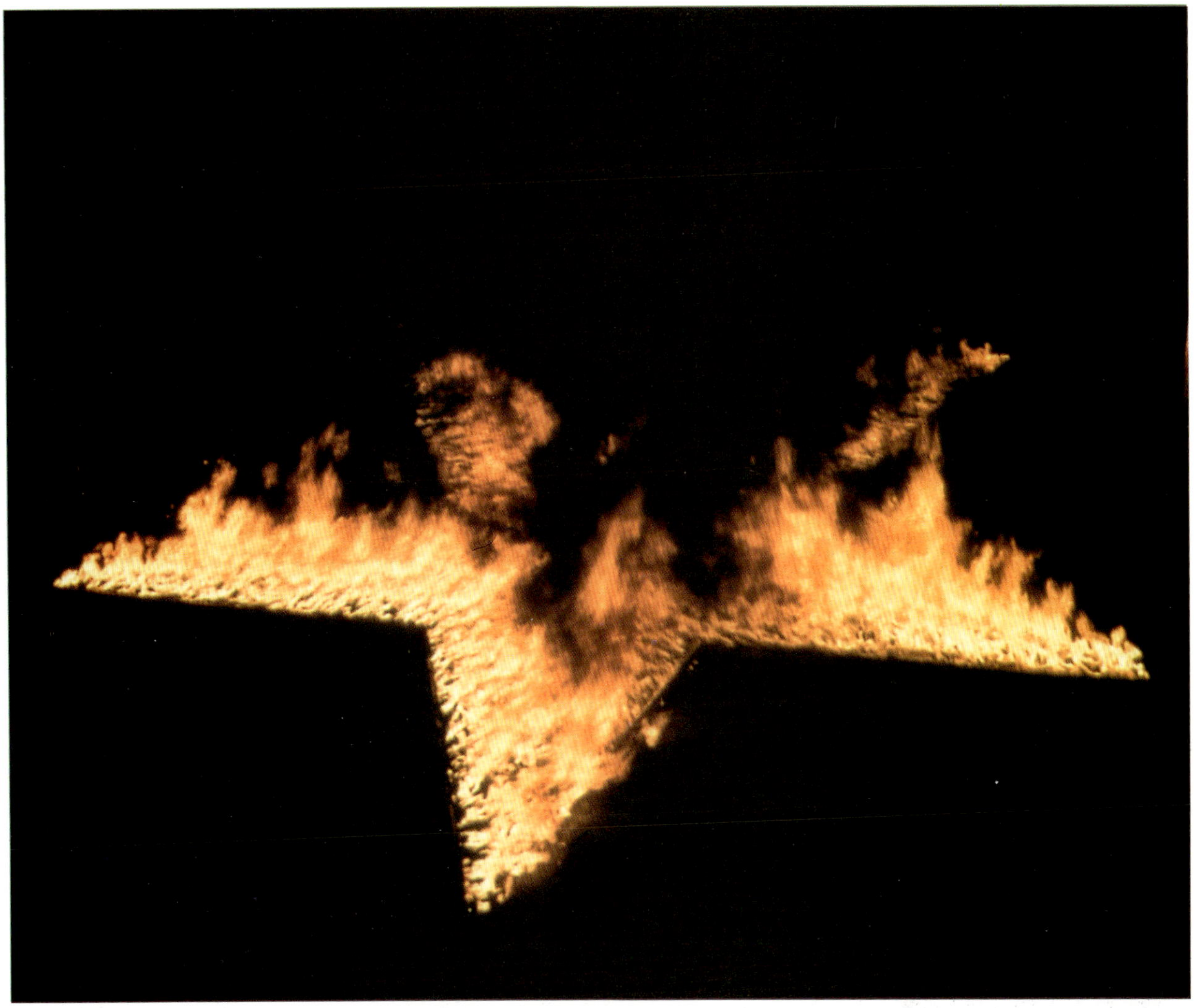

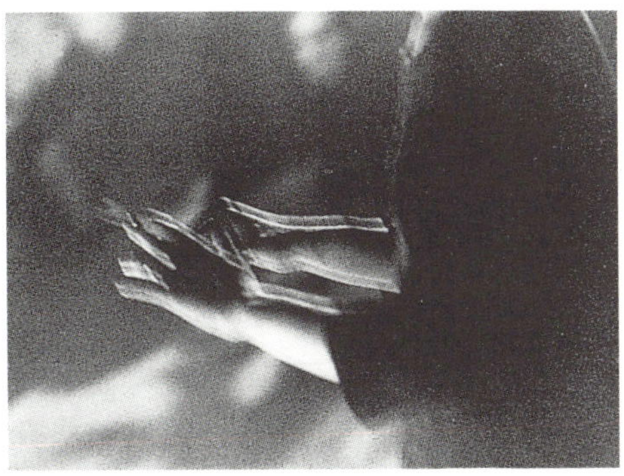

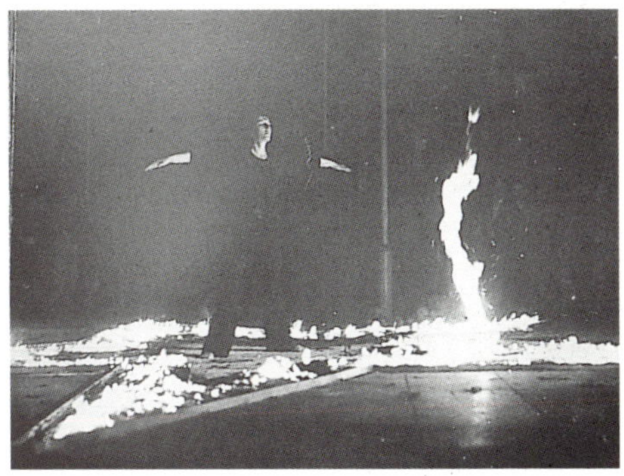

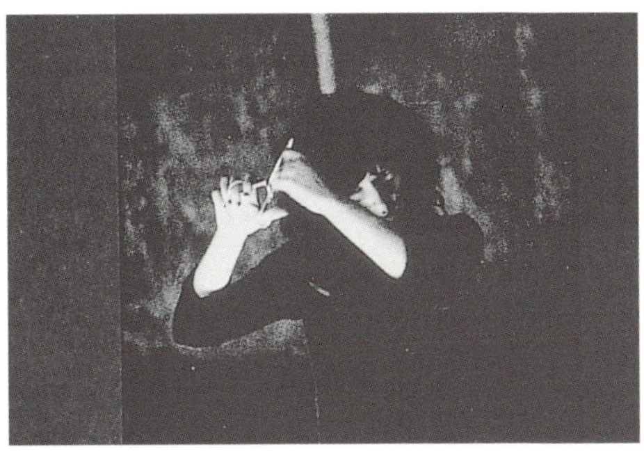

FIGURE 142.
Marina Abramović, *Drawing and Positioning/ Rhythm 5*, c. 1970, clockwise from top: *Bright Burning Star, Lighting Fire Star, Cutting Hair,* and *Cutting Fingernails*, documentary photographs. Courtesy of Sean Kelly Gallery, New York.

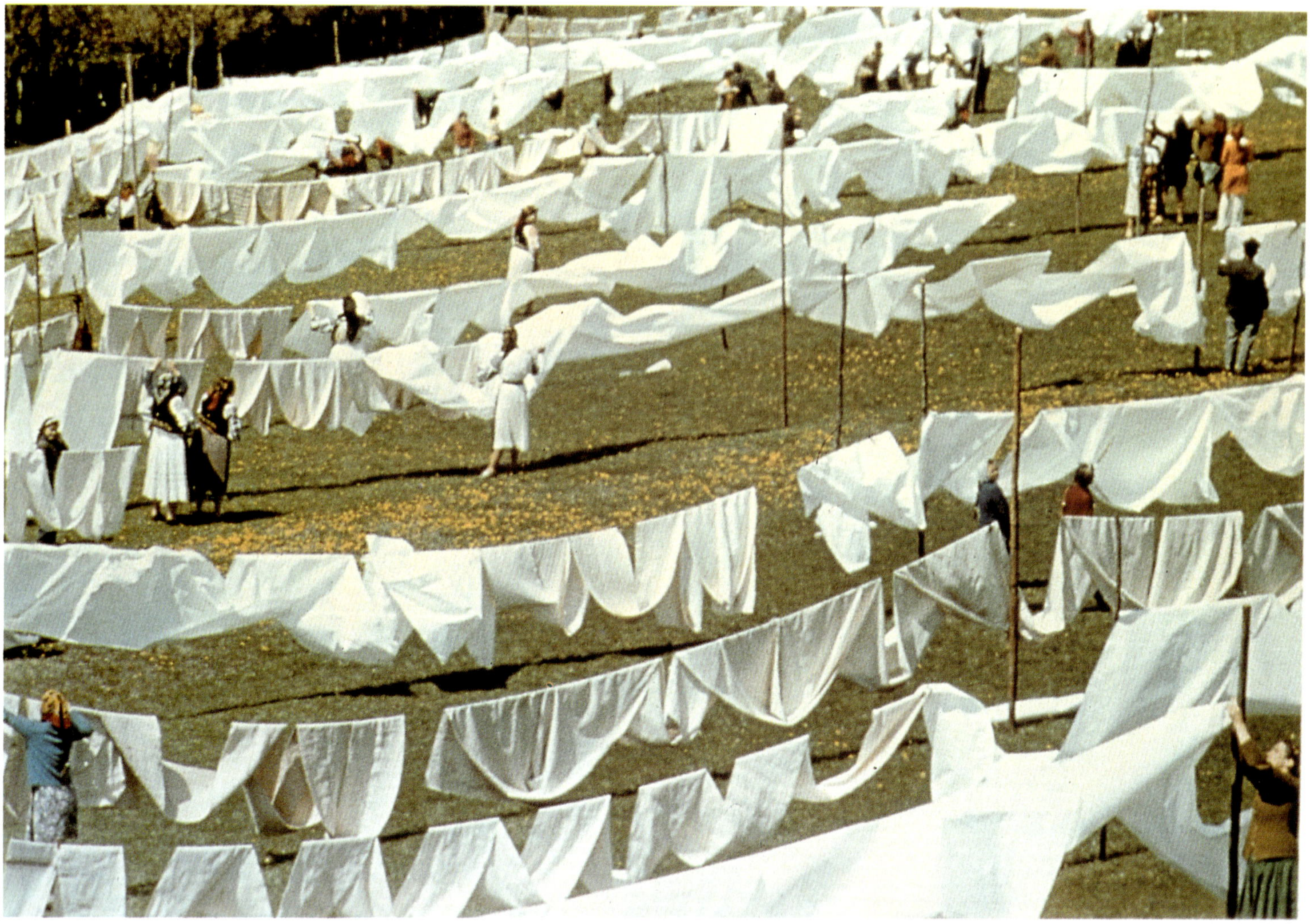

FIGURE 143.
Ana Lupaş, *Humid Installation (Instalatie umedă)*, action in the Village Margau, Transylvania, Romania, 1970, documentary photograph. Collection of the artist.

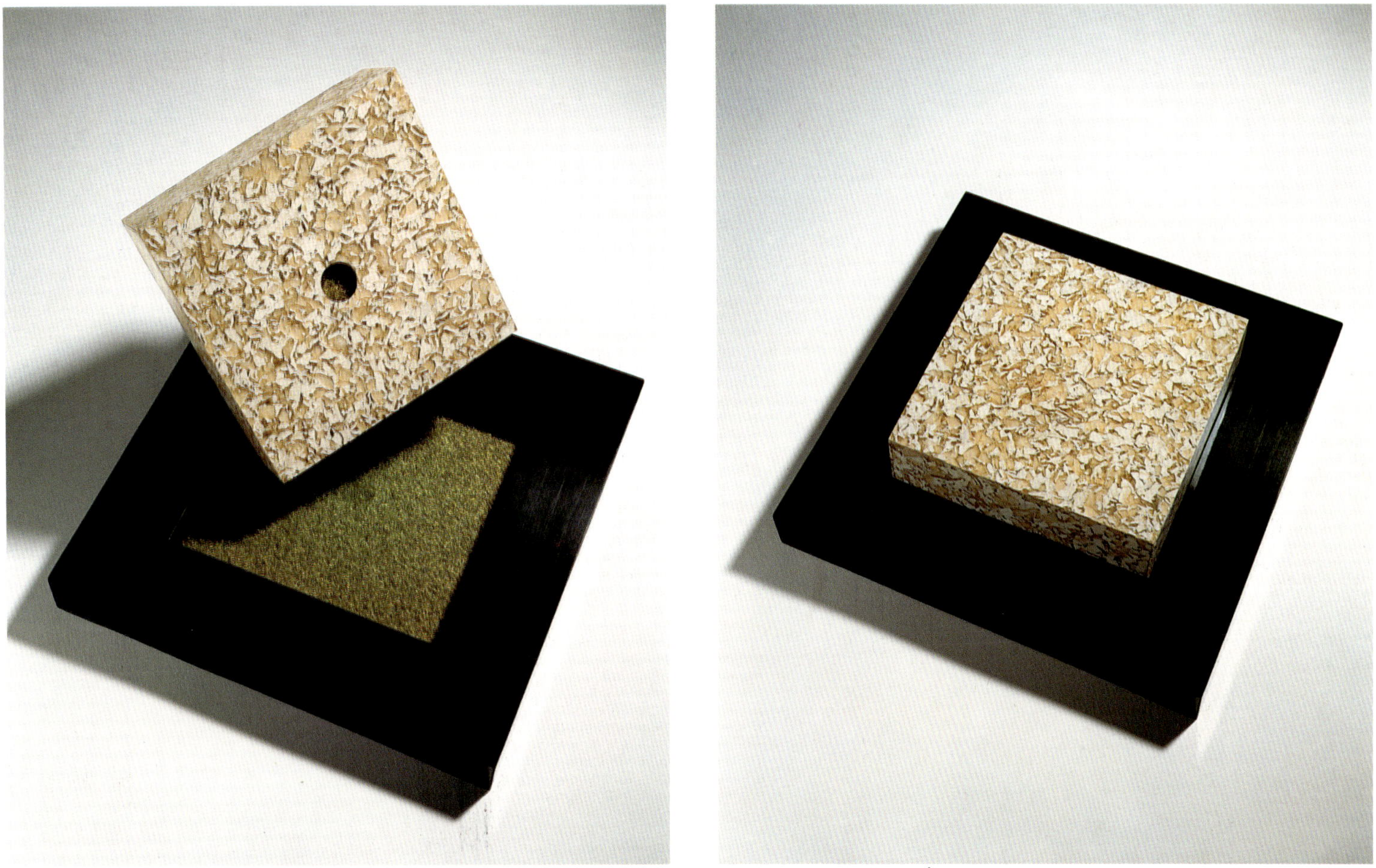

FIGURE 144.
Antonio Dias, *Oppressor/Oppressed,* 1968, wood, Formica, synthetic grass, and linoleum. Collection of the artist.

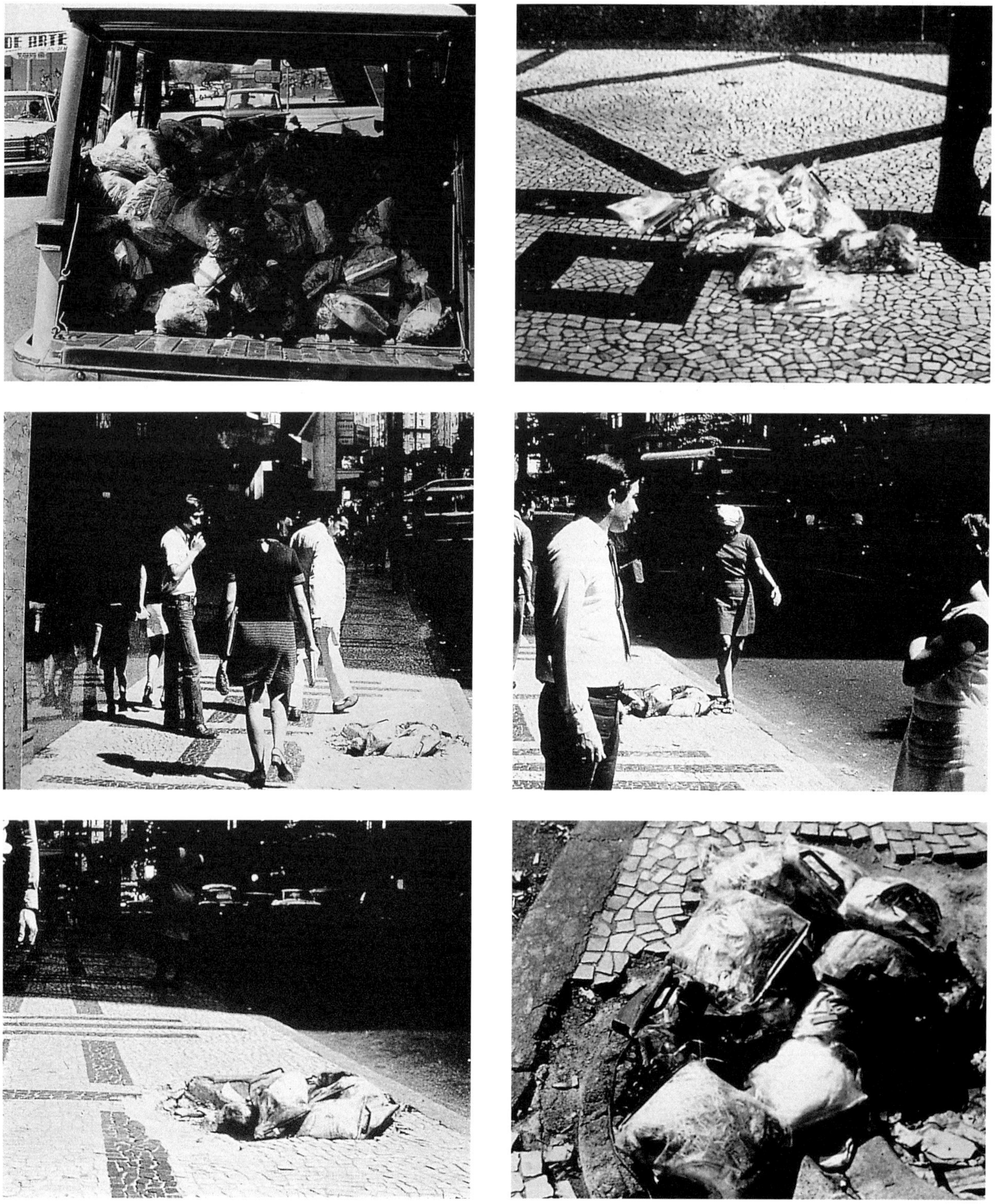

Figure 145.
Artur Barrio, *DEFL ... —situação ... +s+ ... ruas,* April 1970, documentation in slide projections. Collection of the artist.

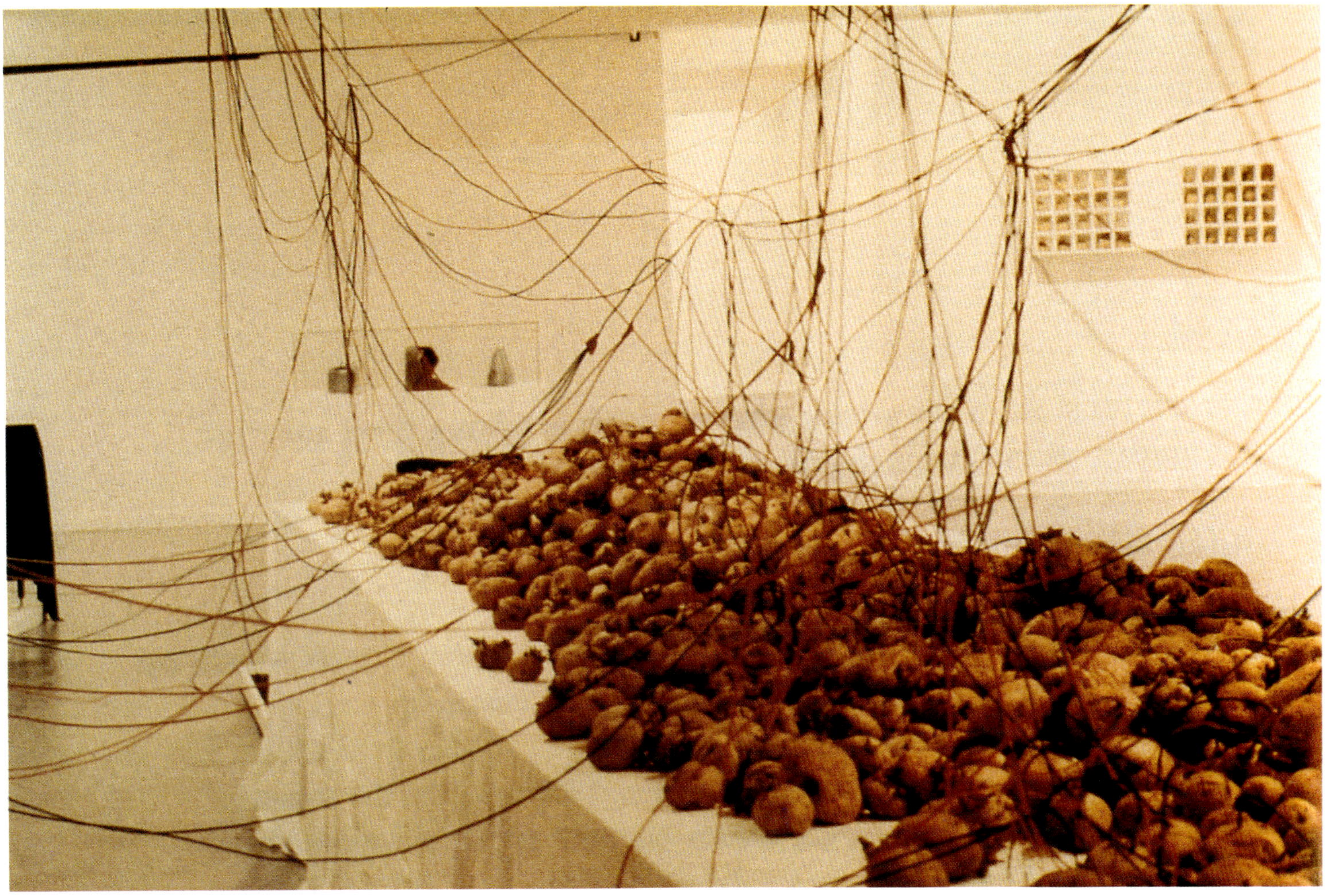

FIGURE 146.
Víctor Grippo, *Analogía I (Analogy I)*, 1970-71, (on right), potatoes, zinc and copper electrodes, electrical wires, instrument to measure a continuous low-voltage current, push-button, text, and wood. Ruth Benzacar Galería de Arte, Buenos Aires.

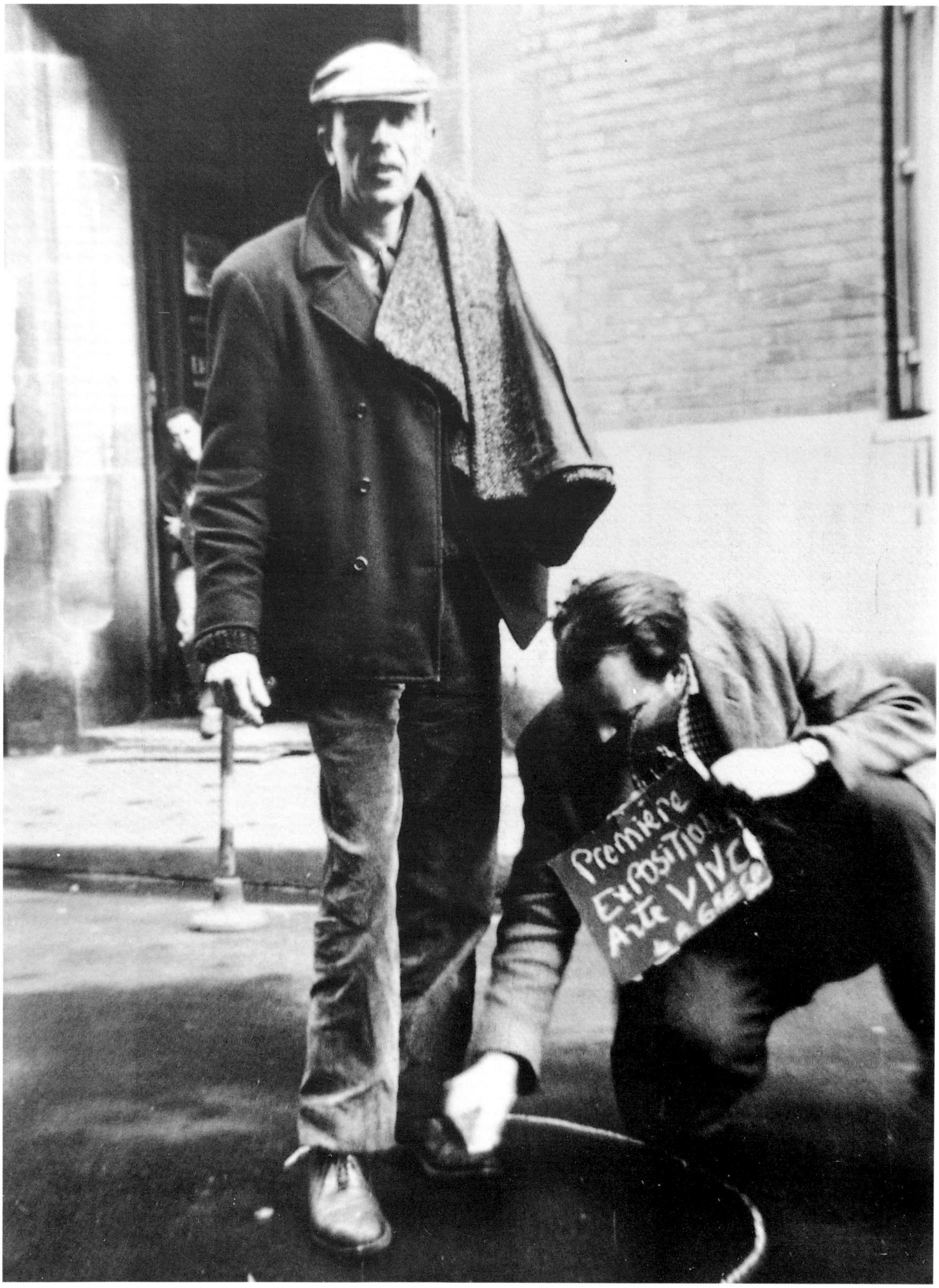

Figure 147.
Alberto Greco, from the series *Vivo dito,* 1962, documentary photograph.

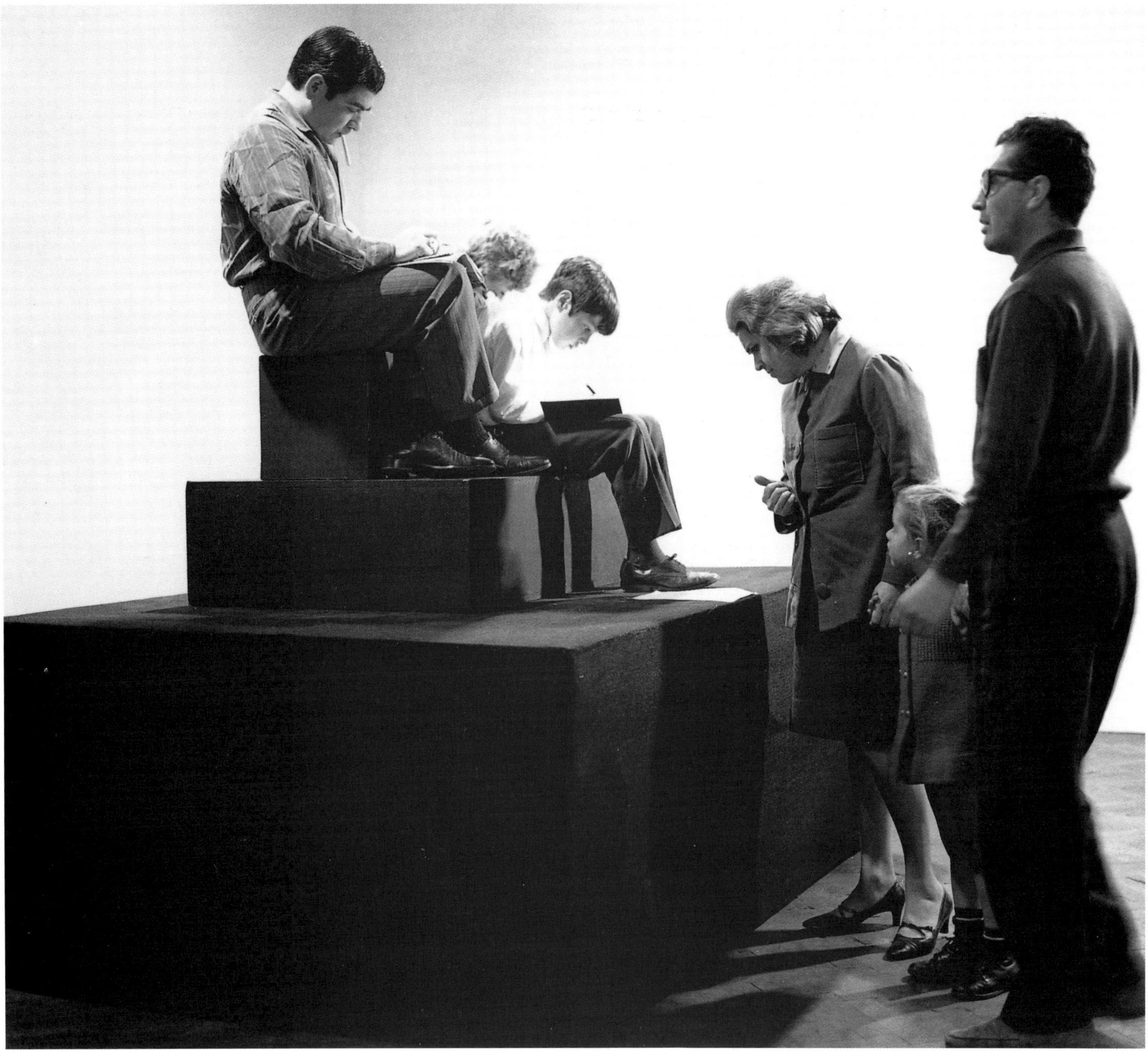

Figure 148.
Oscar Bony, *La familia obrera (Proletarian Family),* 1968, documentary photograph of performance held at Experiencias 68 Instituto Torcuato di Tella, Buenos Aires. Collection of the artist.

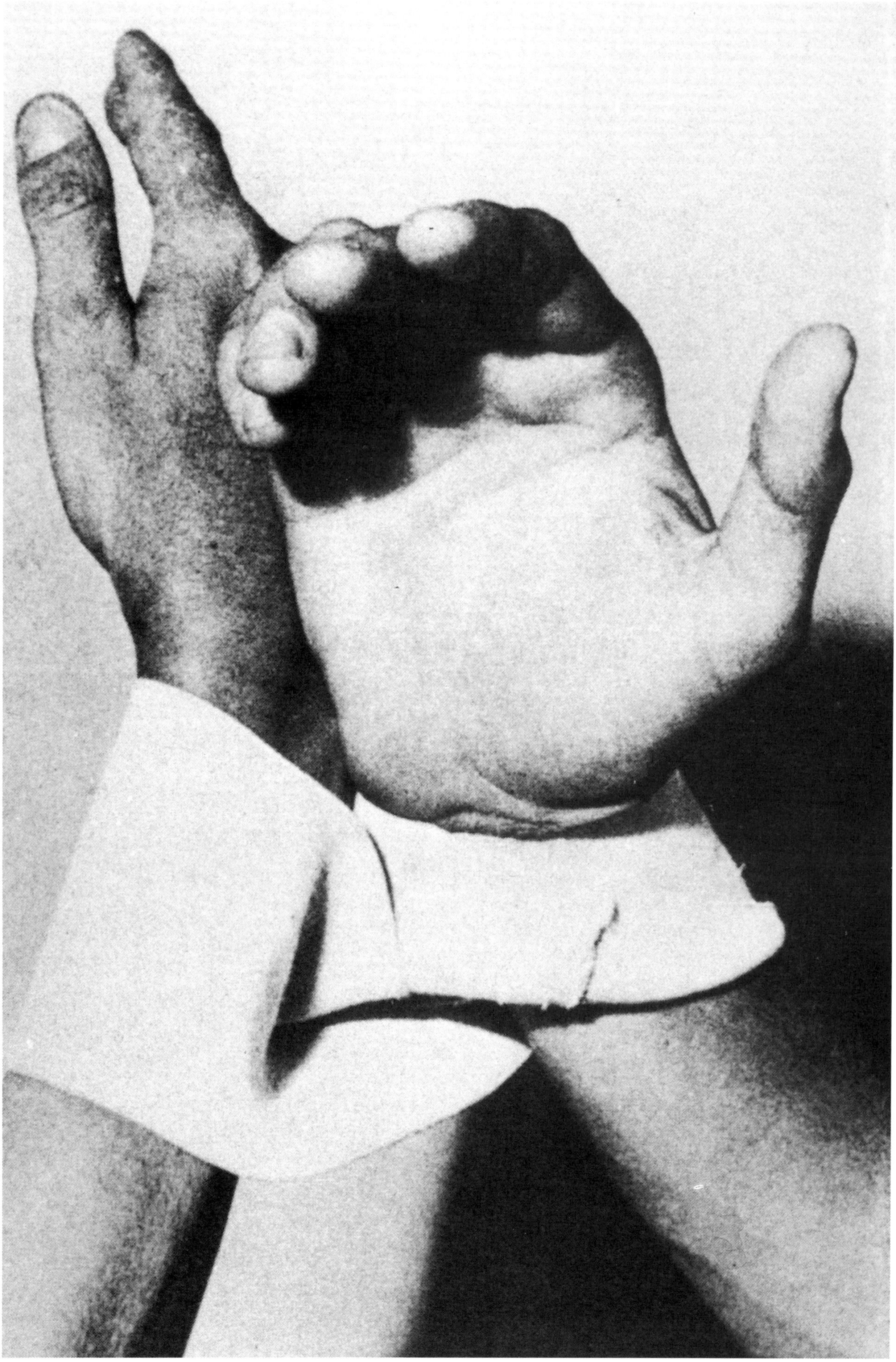

FIGURE 149.
Lygia Clark, *Dialogo (Dialogue of Hands)*, 1966, photograph of elastic mobius strip. Estate of Lygia Clark, Rio de Janeiro.

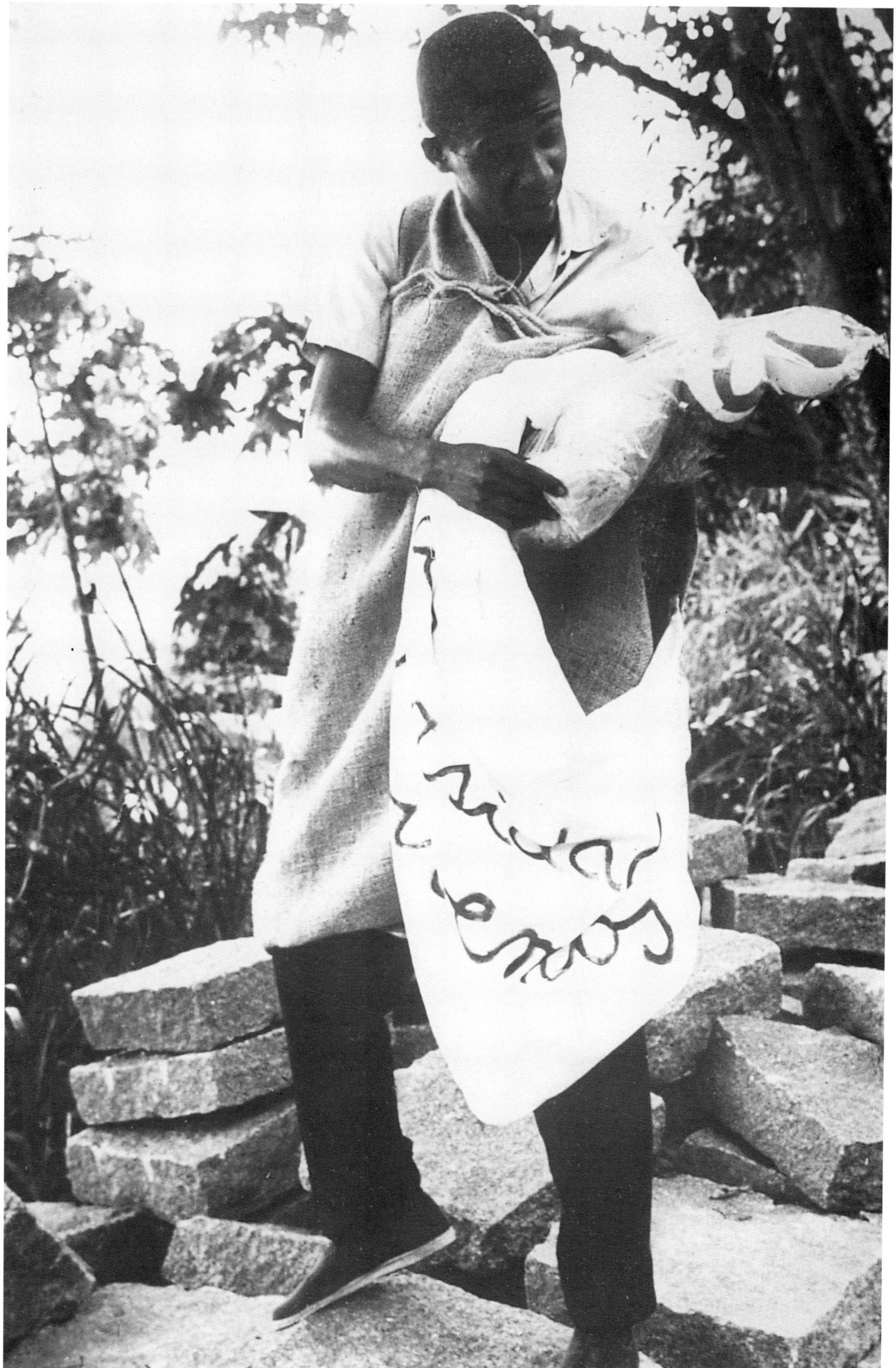

FIGURE 150.
Hélio Oiticica, *Parangolé, Nildo of Mangueira with P-16 Cape 12, "On Adversity We Thrive,"* 1967, acrylic on canvas with plastic, newspaper, burlap, and pigment. Projeto Hélio Oiticica, Rio de Janeiro.

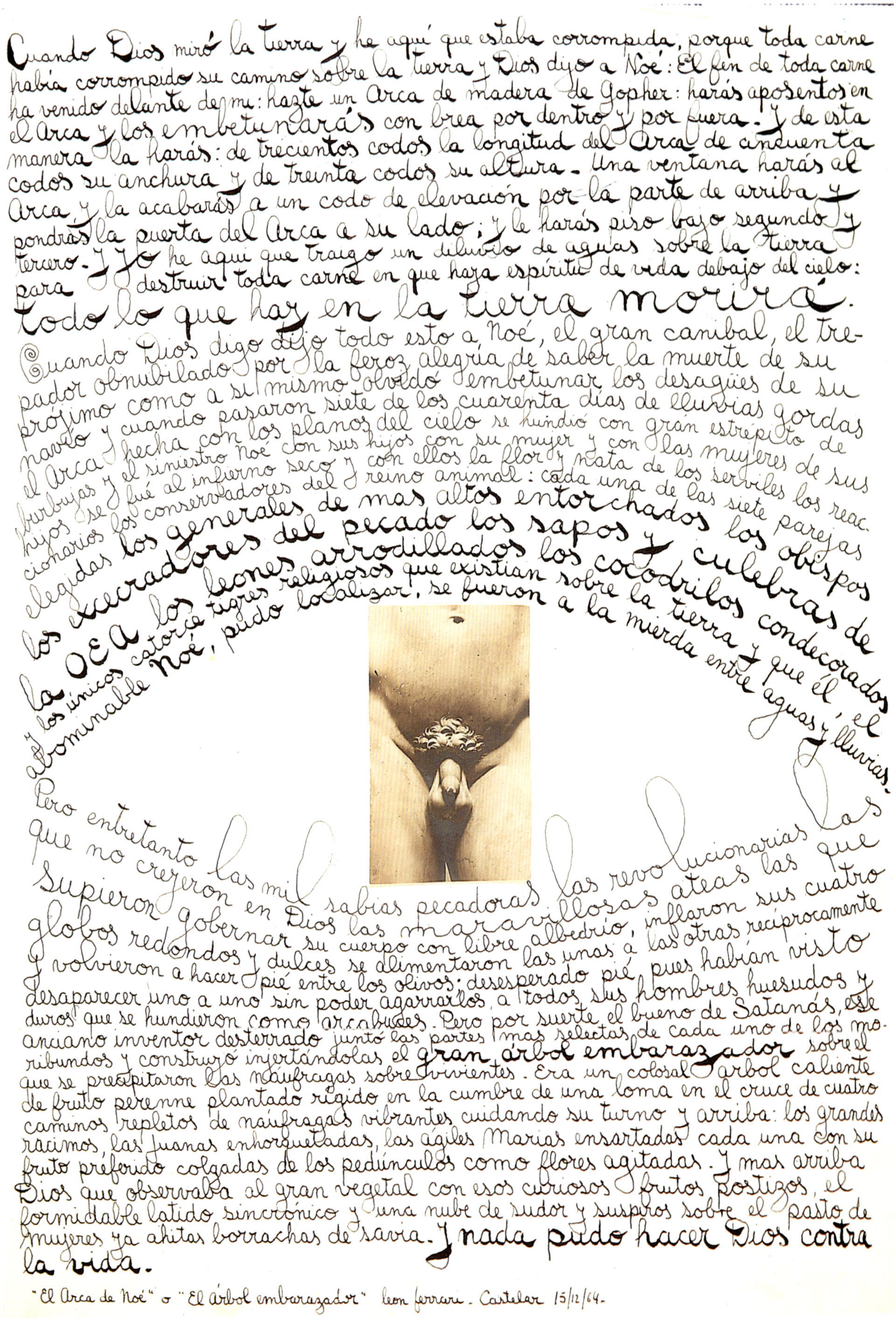

FIGURE 151. León Ferrari, *"El arca de Noé" o "El árbol embarazador" 15/2/64*, 1964, ink with collaged photograph on paper. Collection of the artist.

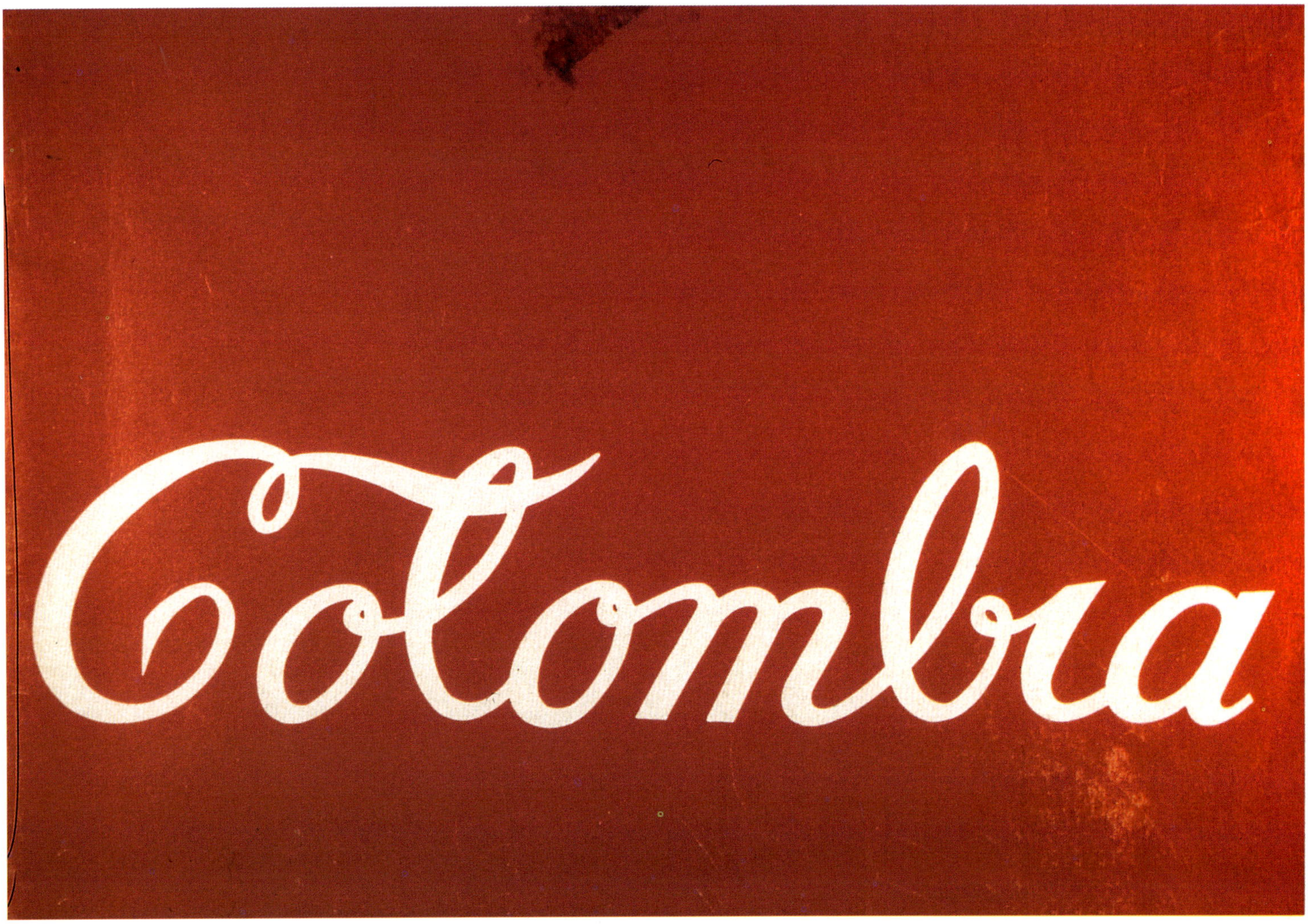

Figure 152.
Antonio Caro, *Colombia/Coca Cola,* 1976, enamel paint on tin. Collection Museo de Arte Moderno, Bogotá.

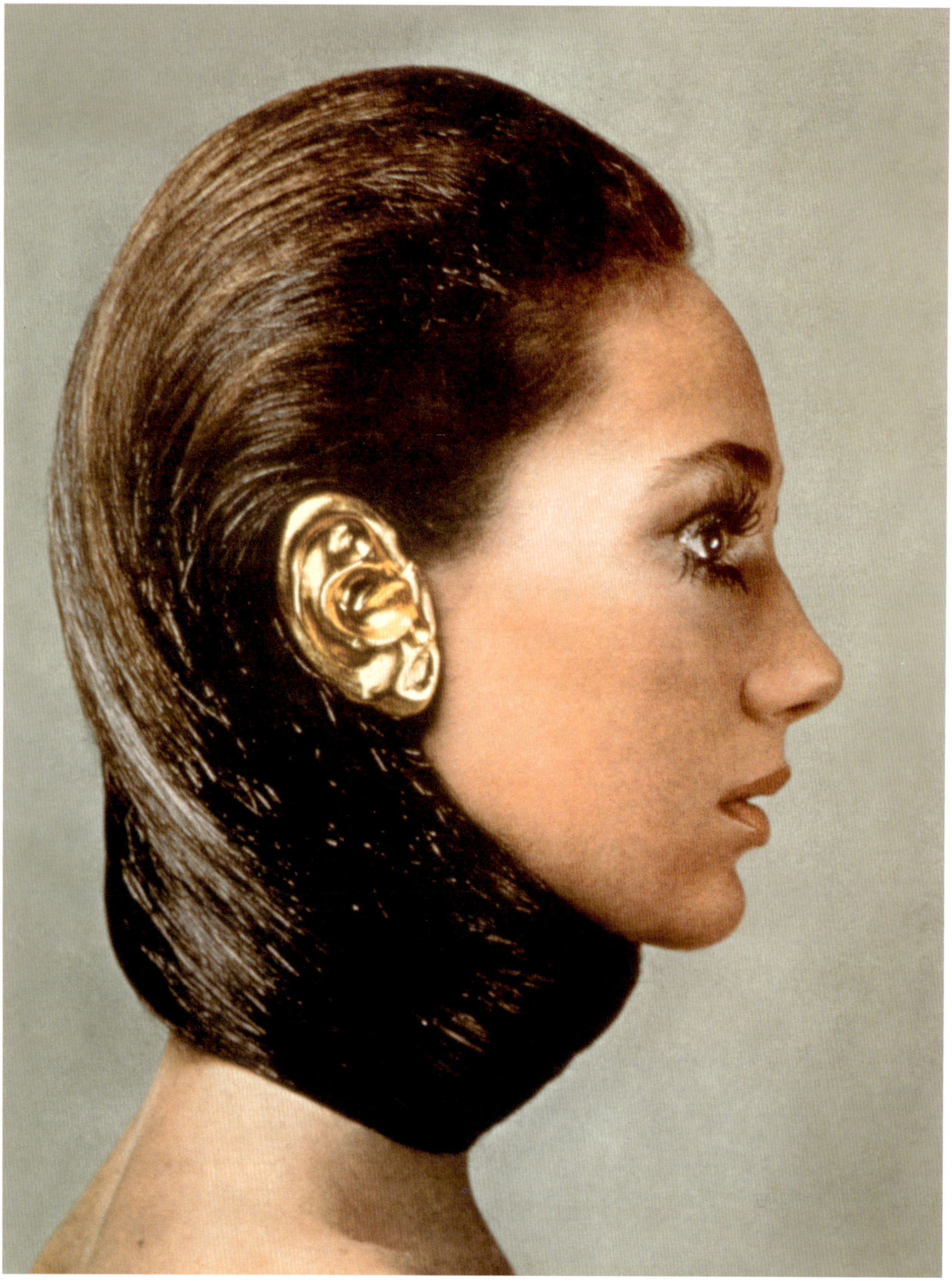

FIGURE 153. Eduardo Costa, *Fashion Fictions,* 1966–69, gold props as published in *Vogue* magazine (3.5 million copies). Collection of the artist.

Figure 154.
Antonio Manuel, *Urnas quentes (Hot Ballot Boxes),* 1968, wood, sealing wax, tape, and photographs. Collection of the artist.

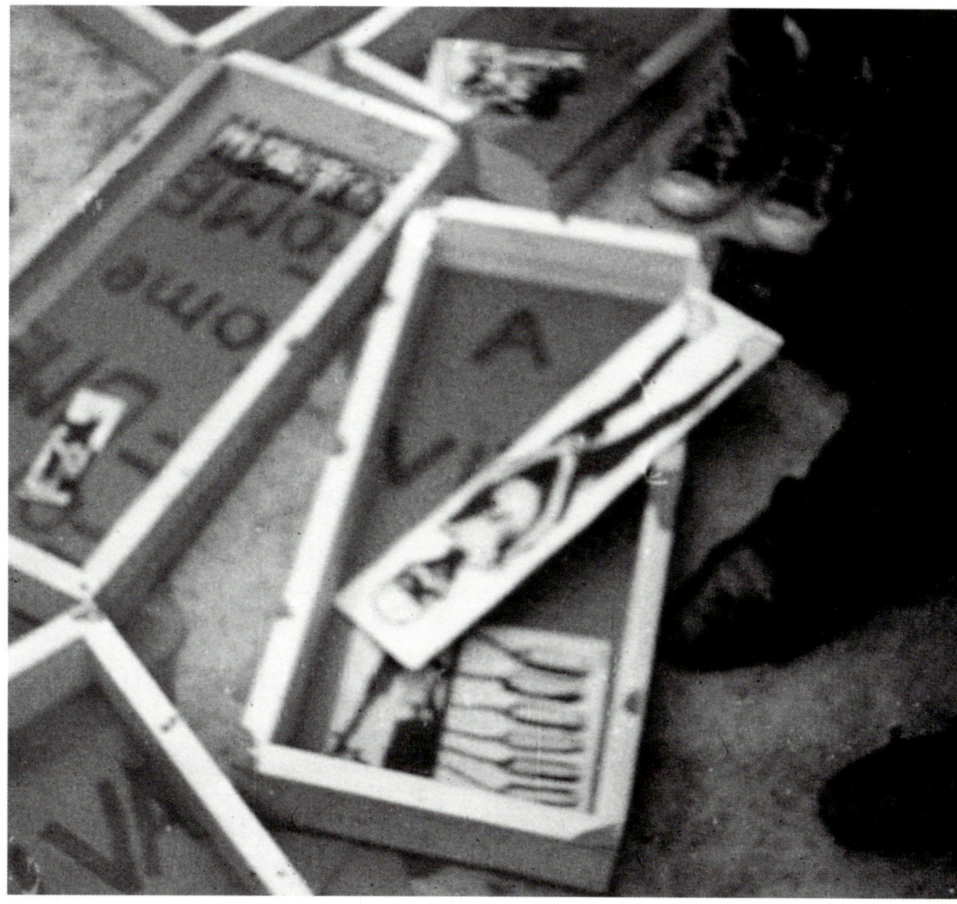

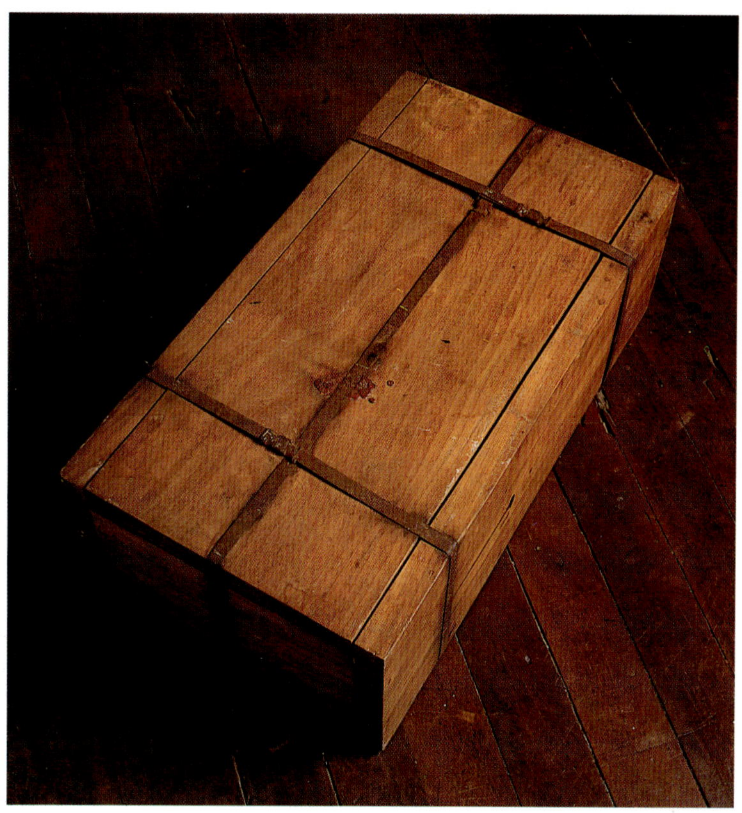

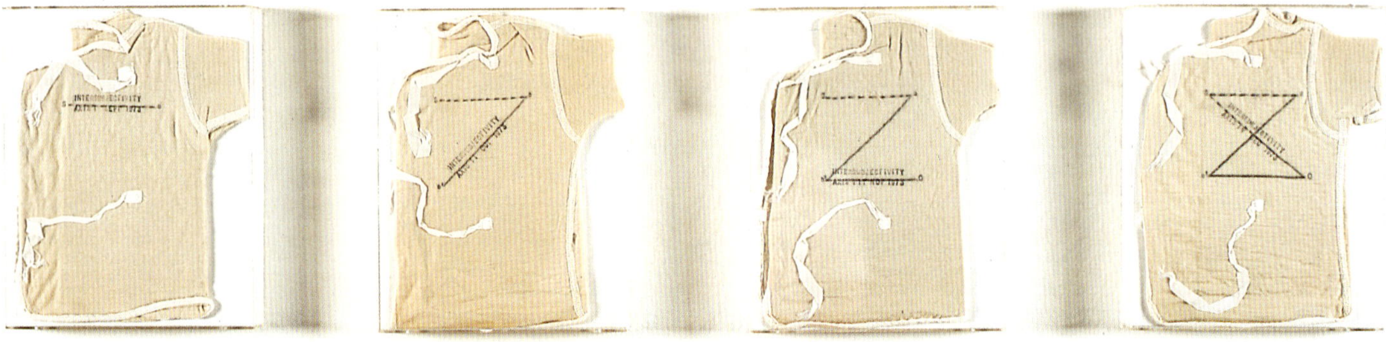

FIGURE 155.
Mary Kelly, *Post-Partum Document Introduction,* 1973, Perspex units, white card, wool vests, pencil, ink. Collection of Eileen and Peter Norton, Santa Monica.

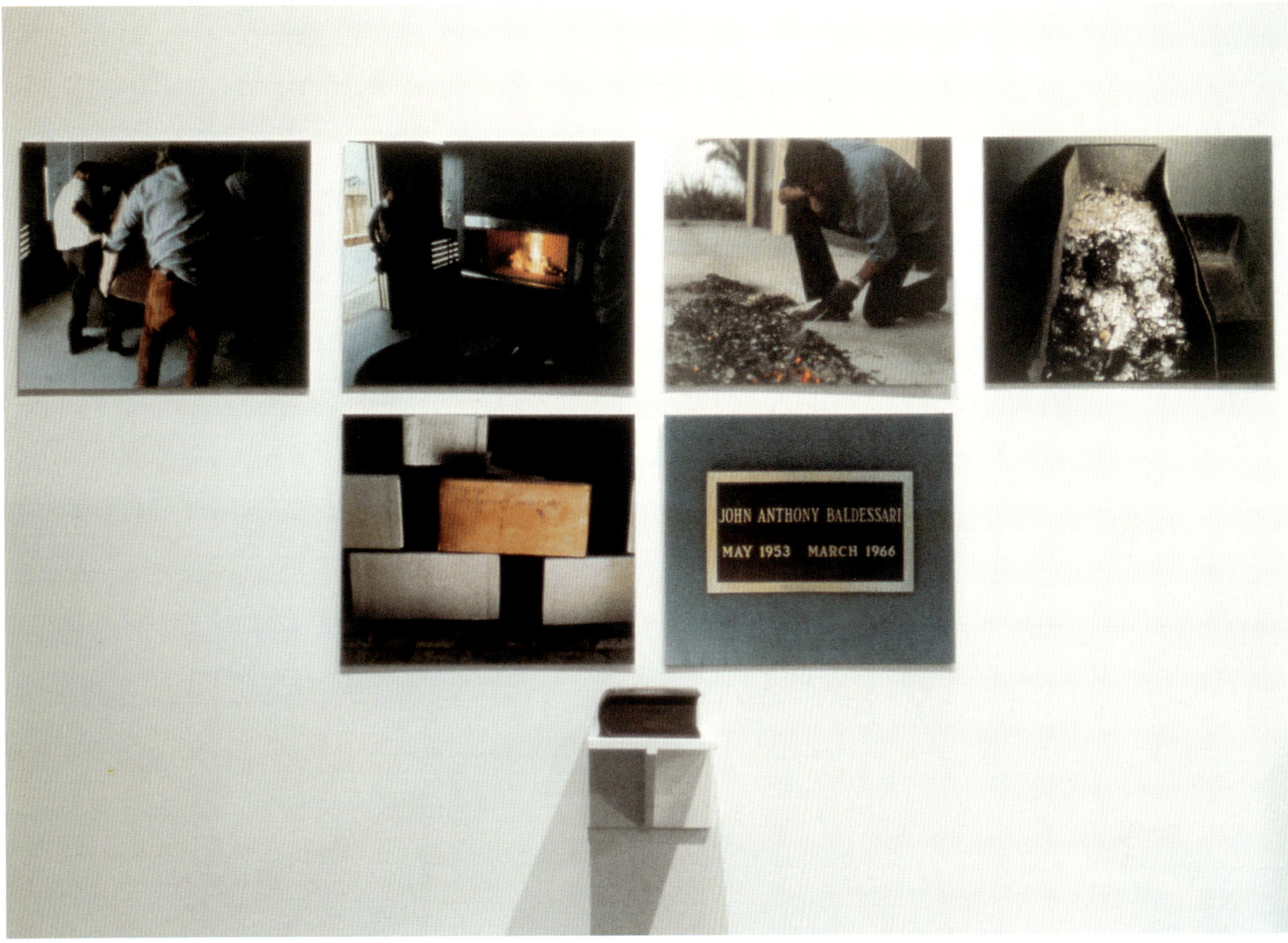

Figure 156.
John Baldessari, *Cremation Project, July 24, 1970,* 1970, bronze urn in the shape of a book, framed photographs of cremation, framed graphic, mounted affidavit giving notice of the cremation of works of art by the artist. Collection of the artist, courtesy of Sonnabend Gallery, New York.

Figure 157.
Sol LeWitt, *Sentences on Conceptual Art,* January 1969.

Sentences on Conceptual Art

1 Conceptual artists are mystics rather than rationalists. They leap to conclusions that logic cannot reach.

2 Rational judgments repeat rational judgments.

3 Irrational judgments lead to new experience.

4 Formal art is essentially rational.

5 Irrational thoughts should be followed absolutely and logically.

6 If the artist changes his mind midway through the execution of the piece he compromises the result and repeats past results.

7 The artist's will is secondary to the process he initiates from idea to completion. His willfulness may only be ego.

8 When words such as painting and sculpture are used, they connote a whole tradition and imply a consequent acceptance of this tradition, thus placing limitations on the artist who would be reluctant to make art that goes beyond the limitations.

9 The concept and idea are different. The former implies a general direction while the latter is the component. Ideas implement the concept.

10 Ideas can be works of art; they are in a chain of development that may eventually find some form. All ideas need not be made physical.

11 Ideas do not necessarily proceed in logical order. They may set one off in unexpected directions, but an idea must necessarily be completed in the mind before the next one is formed.

12 For each work of art that becomes physical there are many variations that do not.

13 A work of art may be understood as a conductor from the artist's mind to the viewer's. But it may never reach the viewer, or it may never leave the artist's mind.

14 The words of one artist to another may induce an idea chain, if they share the same concept.

15 Since no form is intrinsically superior to another, the artist may use any form, from an expression of words (written or spoken) to physical reality, equally

16 If words are used, and they proceed from ideas about art, then they are art and not literature, numbers are not mathematics.

17 All ideas are art if they are concerned with art and fall within the conventions of art.

18 One usually understands the art of the past by applying the convention of the present, thus misunderstanding the art of the past.

19 The conventions of art are altered by works of art.

20 Successful art changes our understanding of the conventions by altering our perceptions.

21 Perception of ideas leads to new ideas.

22 The artist cannot imagine his art, and cannot perceive it until it is complete.

23 The artist may misperceive (understand it differently from the artist) a work of art but still be set off in his own chain of thought by that misconstrual.

24 Perception is subjective.

25 The artist may not necessarily understand his own art. His perception is neither better nor worse than that of others.

26 An artist may perceive the art of others better than his own.

27 The concept of a work of art may involve the matter of the piece or the process in which it is made.

28 Once the idea of the piece is established in the artist's mind and the final form is decided, the process is carried out blindly. There are many side effects that the artist cannot imagine. These may be used as ideas for new works.

29 The process is mechanical and should not be tampered with. It should run its course.

30 There are many elements involved in a work of art. The most important are the most obvious.

31 If an artist uses the same form in a group of works, and changes the material, one would assume the artist's concept involved the material.

32 Banal ideas cannot be rescued by beautiful execution.

33 It is difficult to bungle a good idea.

34 When an artist learns his craft too well he makes slick art.

35 These sentences comment on art, but are not art.

First published in *0-9* (New York), 1969 and *Art-Language* (England), May 1969.

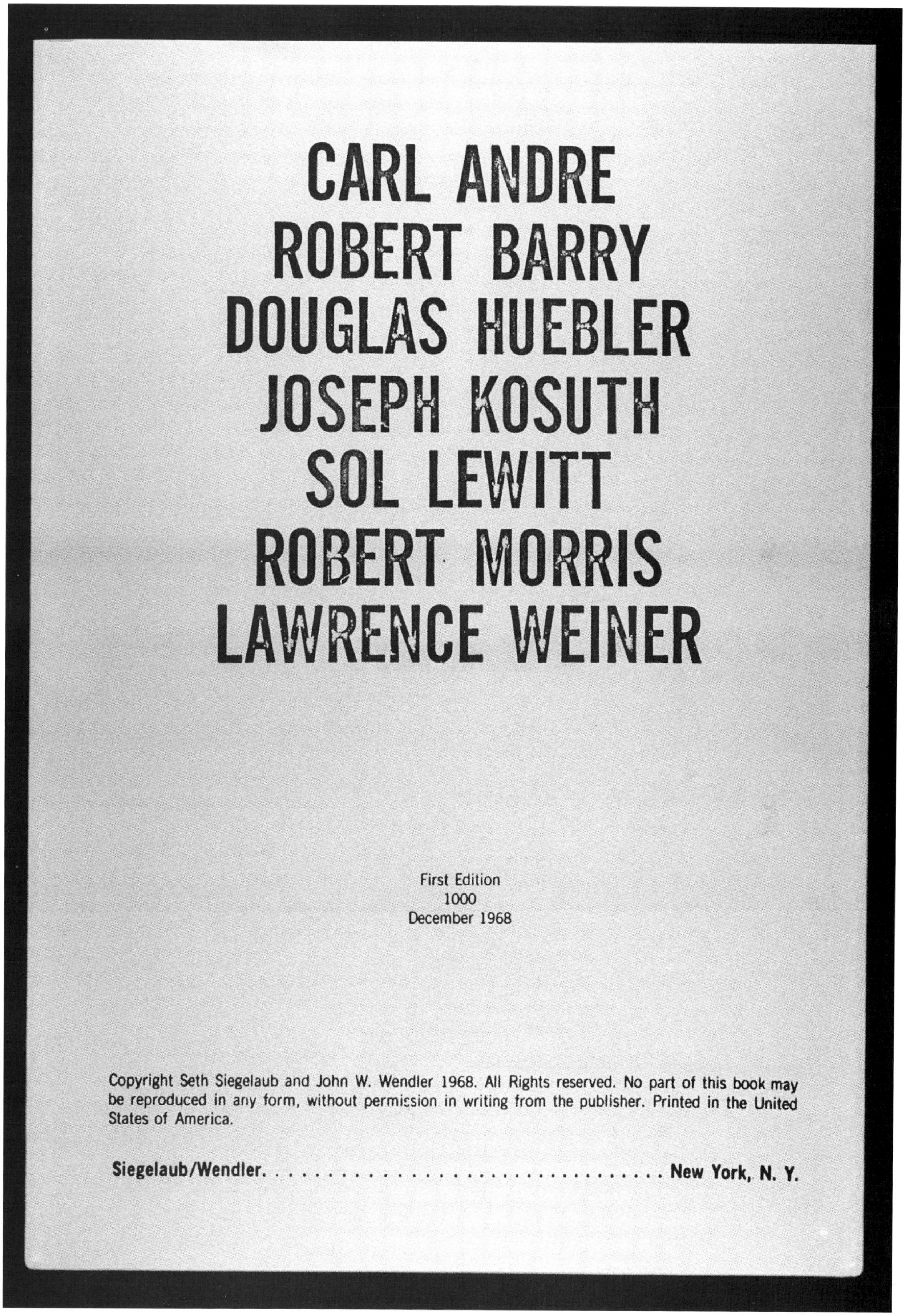

CARL ANDRE
ROBERT BARRY
DOUGLAS HUEBLER
JOSEPH KOSUTH
SOL LEWITT
ROBERT MORRIS
LAWRENCE WEINER

First Edition
1000
December 1968

Copyright Seth Siegelaub and John W. Wendler 1968. All Rights reserved. No part of this book may be reproduced in any form, without permicsion in writing from the publisher. Printed in the United States of America.

Siegelaub/Wendler. . . . . New York, N. Y.

Figure 158. Seth Siegelaub and John W. Wendler, *Carl Andre, Robert Barry, Douglas Huebler, Joseph Kosuth, Sol LeWitt, Robert Morris, Lawrence Weiner* (a.k.a. *Xeroxbook*), December 1968, book of photocopies. Collection of Walker Art Center Library, Minneapolis.

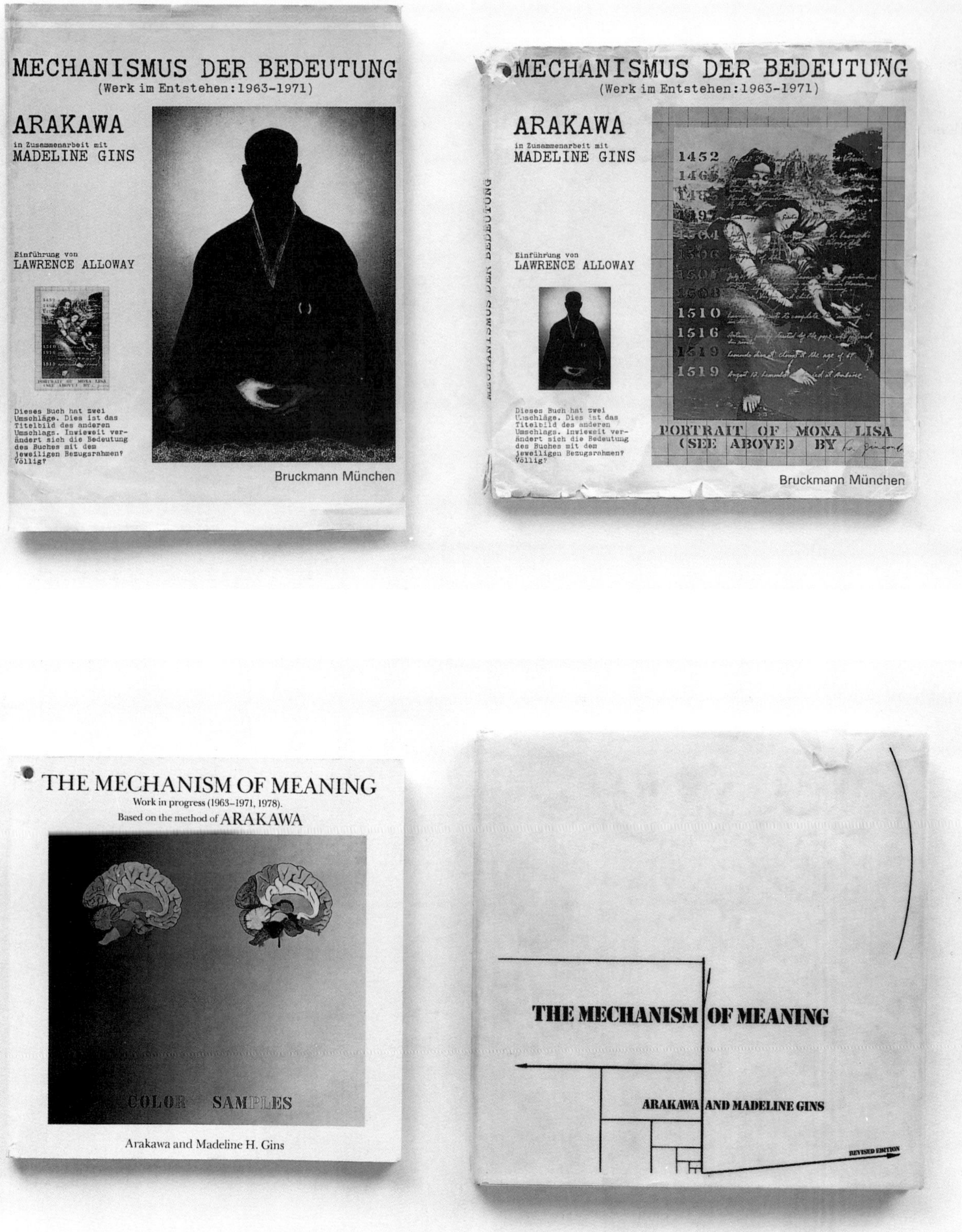

FIGURE 159.
Shusaku Arakawa and Madeline Gins, *Mechanismus der Bedeutung* (Ist ed., Munich: Bruckmann, 1971); *The Mechanism of Meaning* (2d ed., New York: Abrams, 1979, and 3d ed., New York: Abbeville Press, 1988), exhibition catalogues and books. Collection of the artists.

Figure 160.
Carol Condé and Karl Beveridge, (top and center) ... *It's Still Privileged Art,* 1976; (bottom) *Red Women's Detachment* (Chinese comic book after which it was modeled), 1966. Private collection.

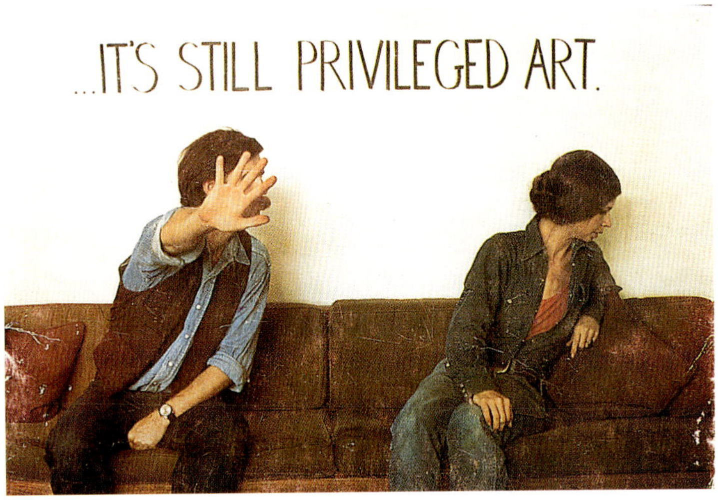

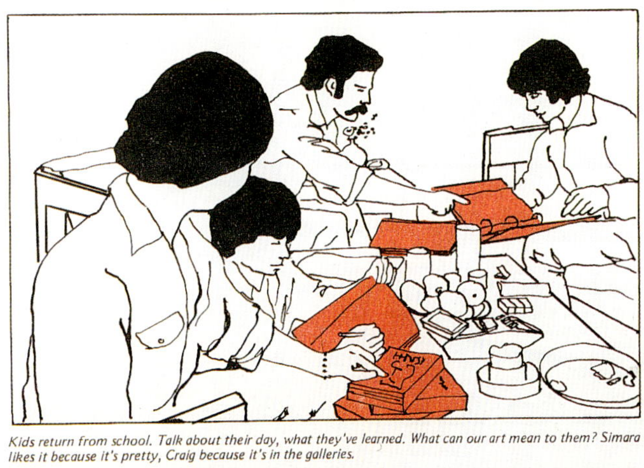

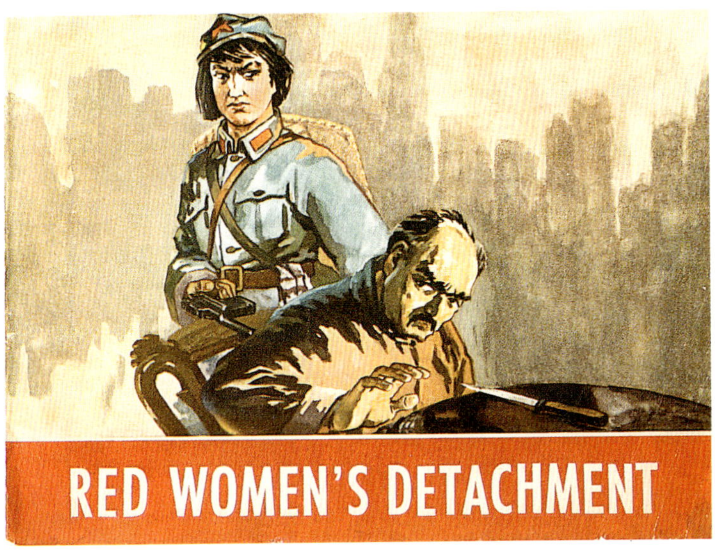

FIGURE 161.
Hans Haacke, *Milwaukee Visitors' Profile*, 1971, survey questionnaire.

These questions and your answers are part of

Hans Haacke's VISITORS' PROFILE

a work in progress during "Directions 3: Eight Artists", Milwaukee Art Center, June 19 through August 8, 1971.

Please fill out this questionnaire and drop it into the box by the door.
DO NOT SIGN.

---

1) Do you have a professional interest in art, e.g. artist, student, critic, dealer, etc.? yes no

2) How old are you? years

3) Should the use of marijuana be legalized, lightly or severely punished? legal light severe punishment

4) Do you think law enforcement agencies are generally biased against dissenters? yes no

5) What is your marital status? married single div. sep. widowed

6) Do you sympathize with Women's Lib? yes no

7) Are you male, female? male female

8) Do you have children? yes no

9) Would you mind busing your child to integrate schools? yes no

10) What is your ethnic backround, e.g. Polish, German, etc.? ____________

11) Assuming you were Indochinese, would you sympathize with the Saigon regime? yes no

12) Do you think the moral fabric of the US is strengthened or weakened by its involvement in Indochina? strengthened weakened

13) What is your religion? ____________

14) In your opinion, are the interests of profit-oriented business usually compatible with the common good? yes no

15) What is your annual income (before taxes)? $____________

16) Do you think the Nixon Administration is mainly responsible for our economic difficulties? yes no

17) Where do you live? city/suburb county state

18) Do you consider the defeat of the supersonic transport (SST) a step in the right direction? yes no

19) Are you enrolled in or have graduated from college? yes no

20) In your opinion, should the general orientation of the country be more conservative or less conservative? more less

Your answers will be tabulated later today together with the answers of all other visitors of the exhibition. Thank you.

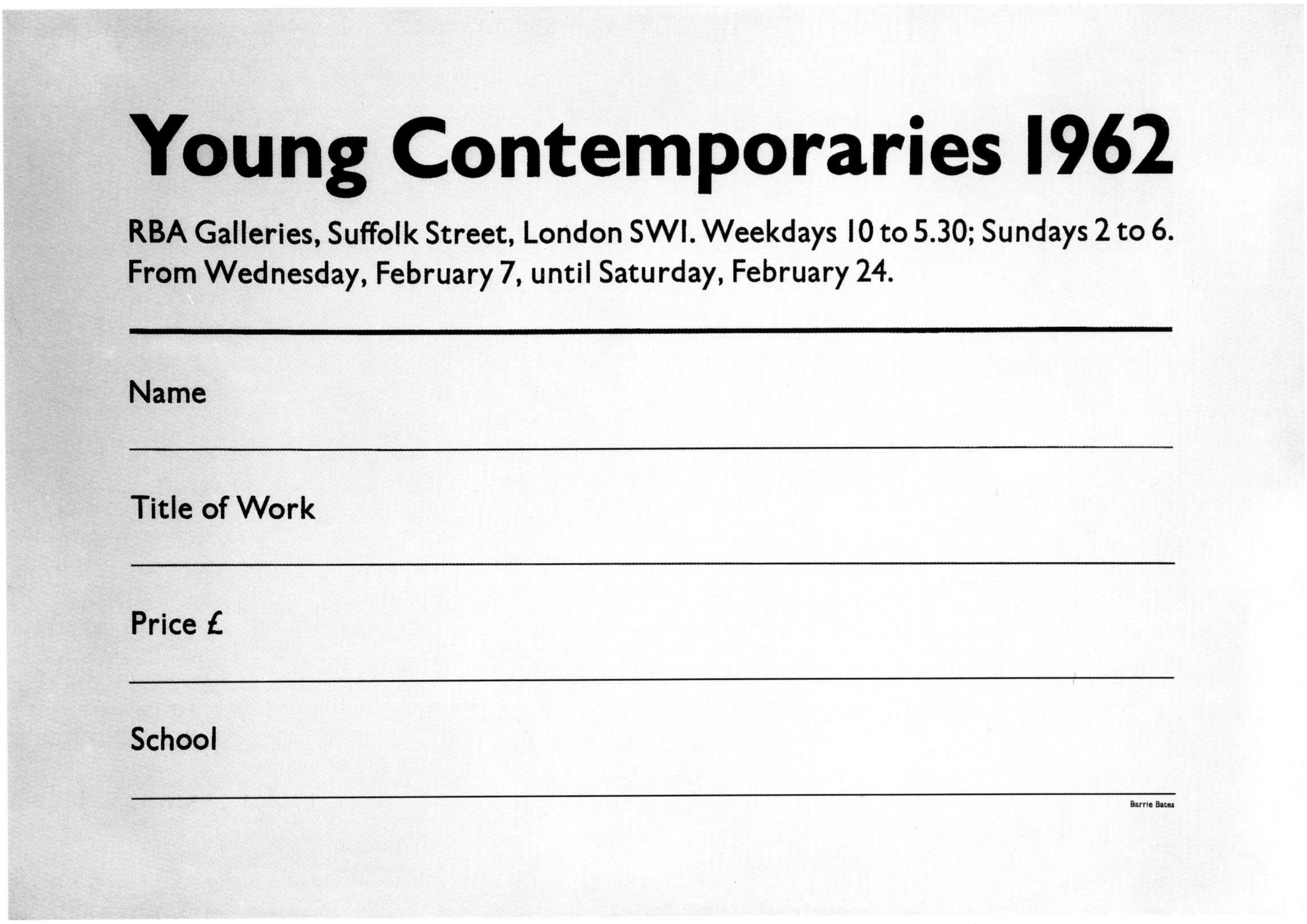

Young Contemporaries 1962

RBA Galleries, Suffolk Street, London SWI. Weekdays 10 to 5.30; Sundays 2 to 6.
From Wednesday, February 7, until Saturday, February 24.

Name

Title of Work

Price £

School

Barrie Bates

FIGURE 162.
Barrie Bates (Billy Apple), *Young Contemporaries 1962*, 1961, offset lithograph on canvas (printed by Roy Crossett, Royal College of Art). Collection of the artist.

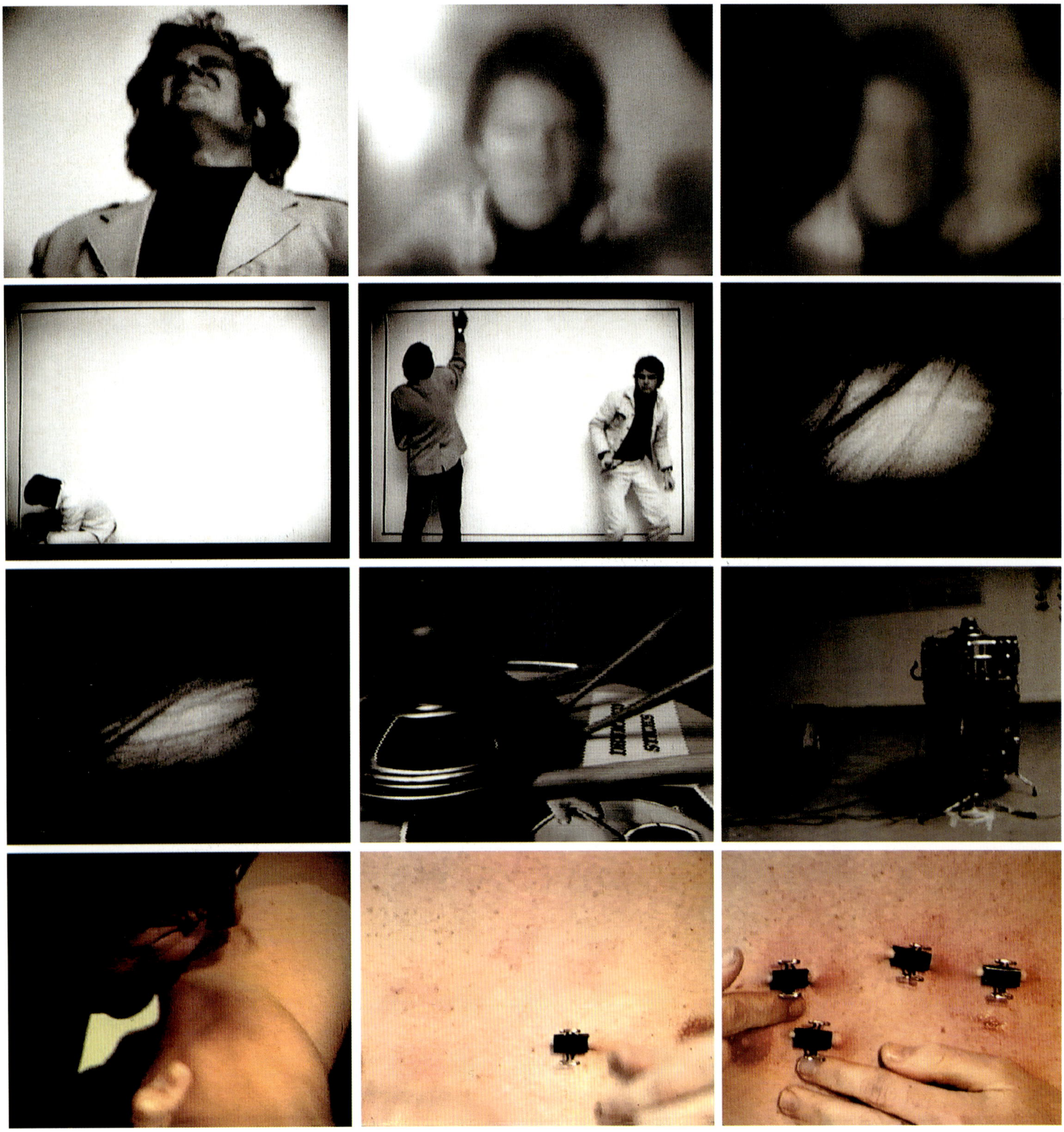

Figure 163.
Mike Parr and Peter Kennedy, *Idea Demonstrations,* 1972, 16mm film, 40 min., black-and white and color, optical sound. Collection of Mike Parr.

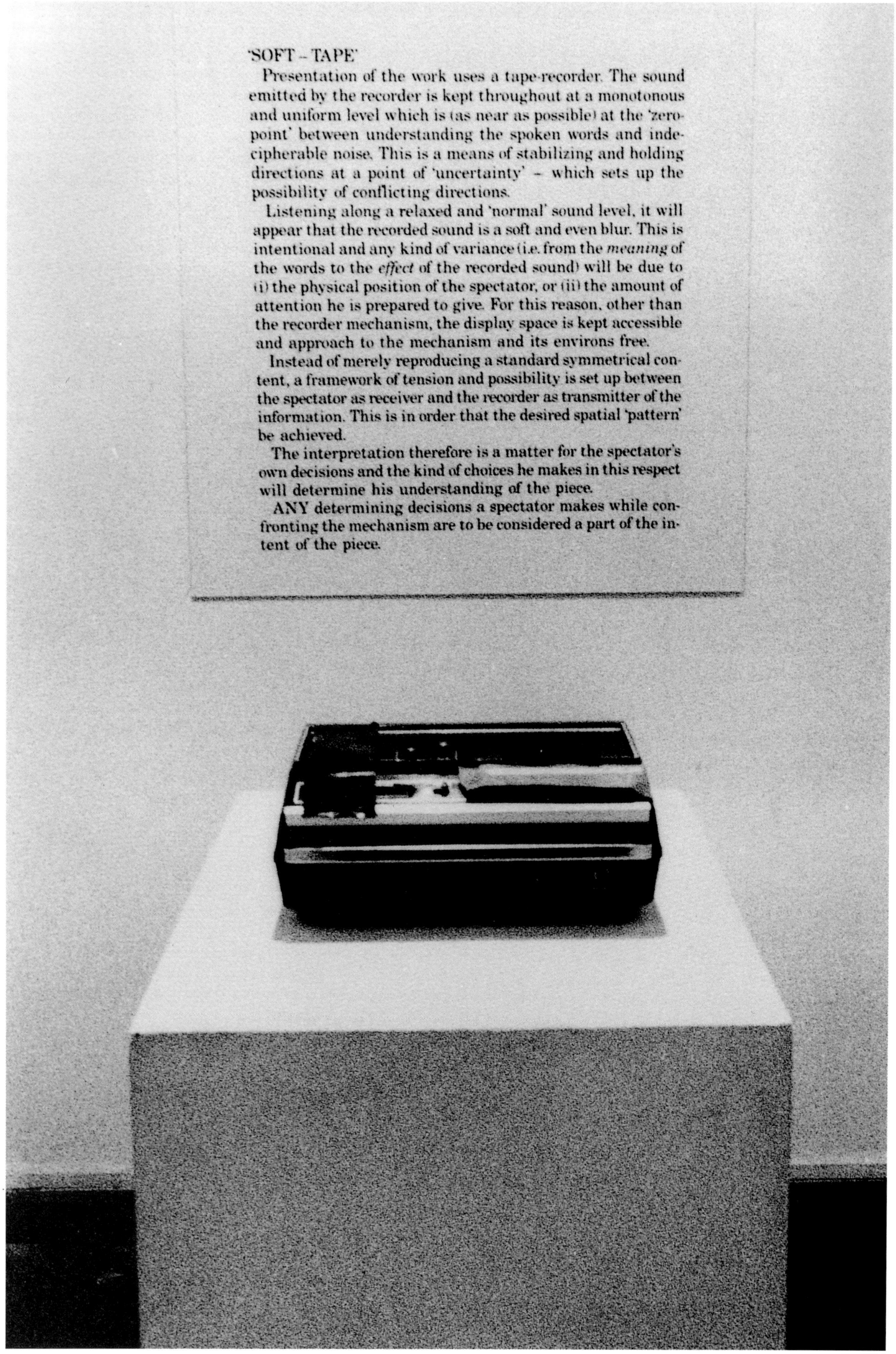

Figure 164.
Ian Burn and Mel Ramsden, *Soft-Tape*, 1966/1990, tape recorder and photostat of wall notice. Courtesy of Avril Burn and Mel Ramsden.

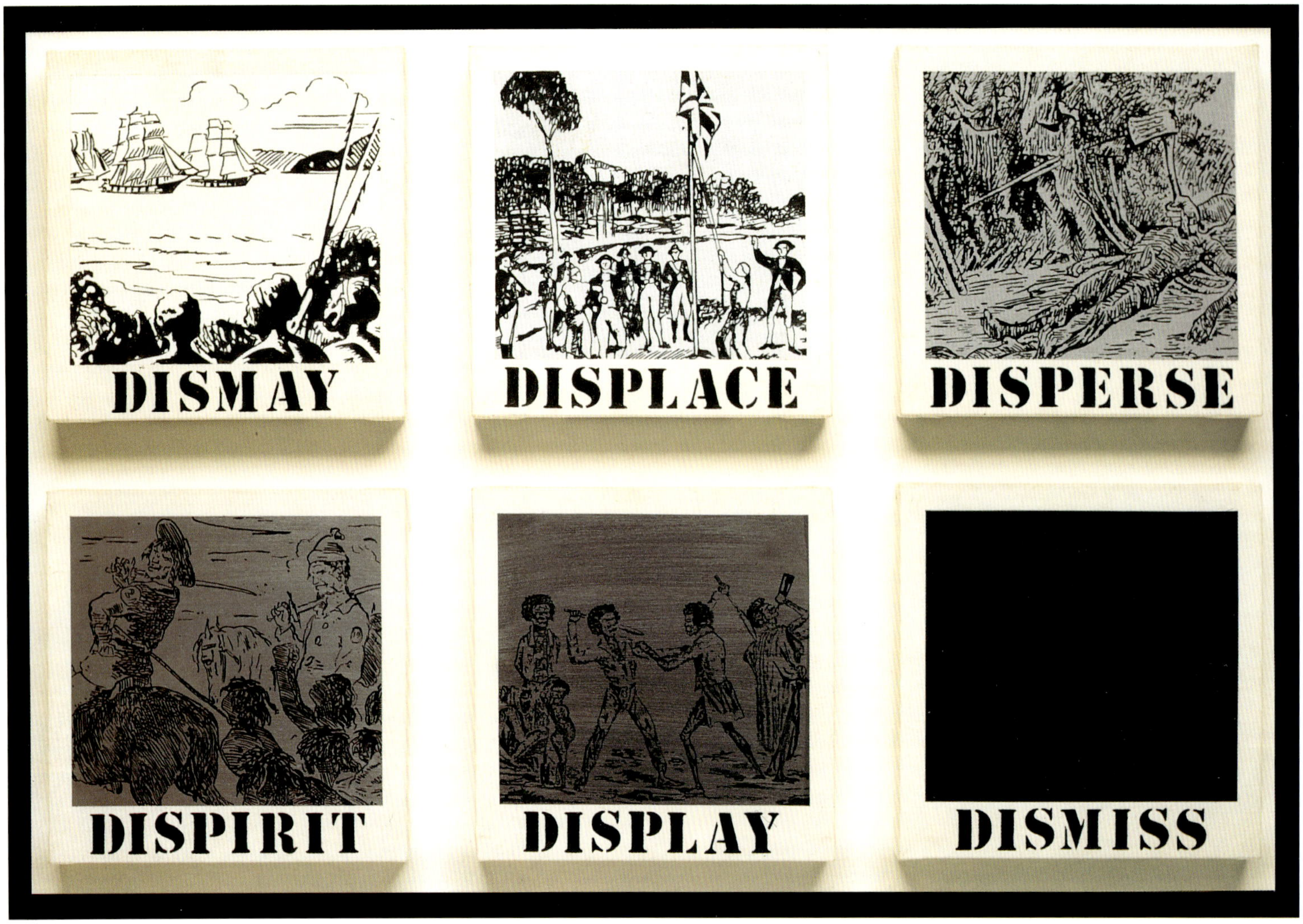

FIGURE 165.
Gordon Bennett, *Untitled (Dismay, Displace, Disperse, Dispirit, Display, Dismiss),* 1989, six panels, oil and synthetic polymer paint on 6 canvases. Museum of Contemporary Art, Sydney.

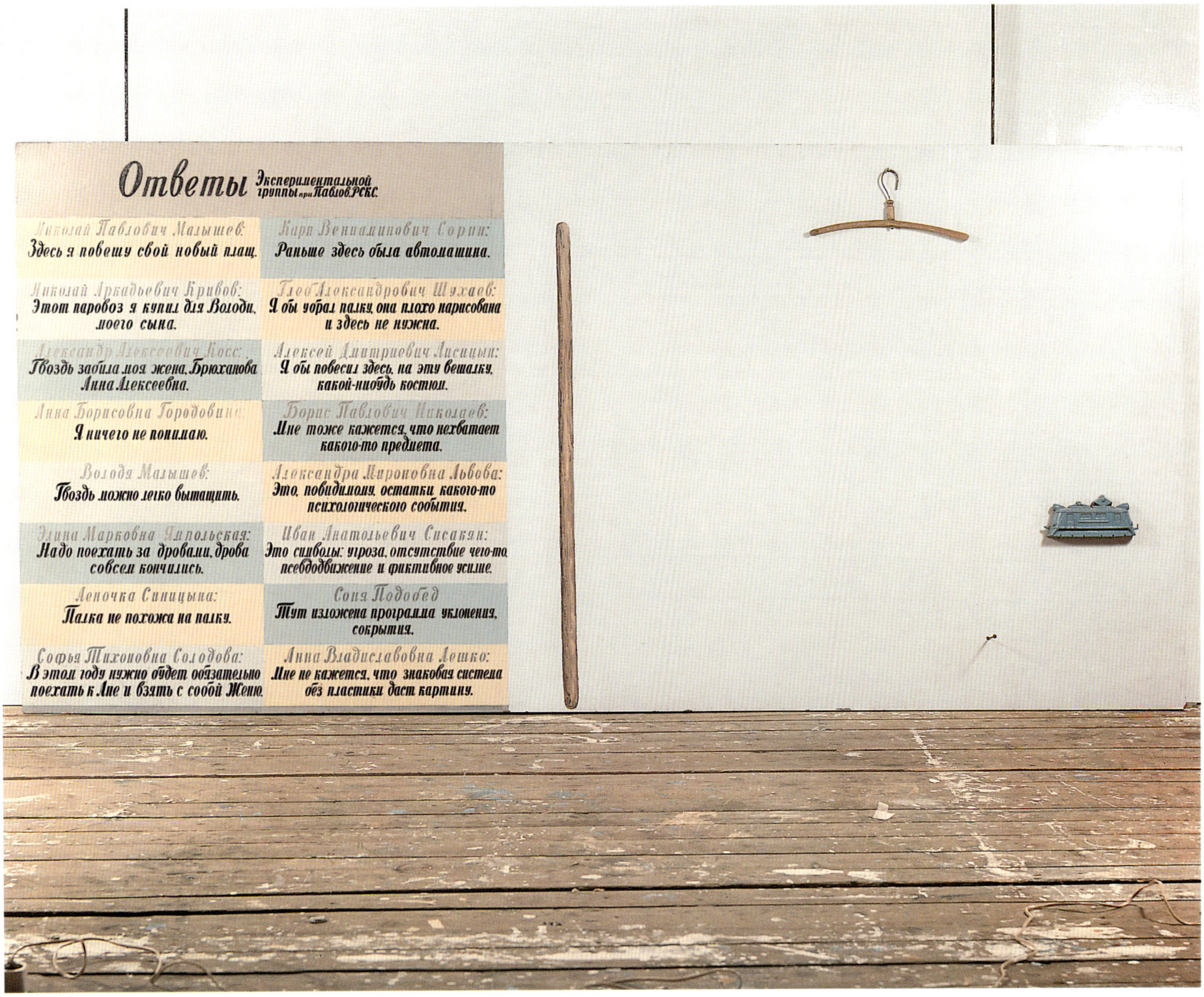

FIGURE 166.
Ilya Kabakov, *Answers of the Experimental Group (Otvety eksperemental'noi gruppy)*, 1970–71, mixed media on Masonite. The John L. Stewart Collection, New York.

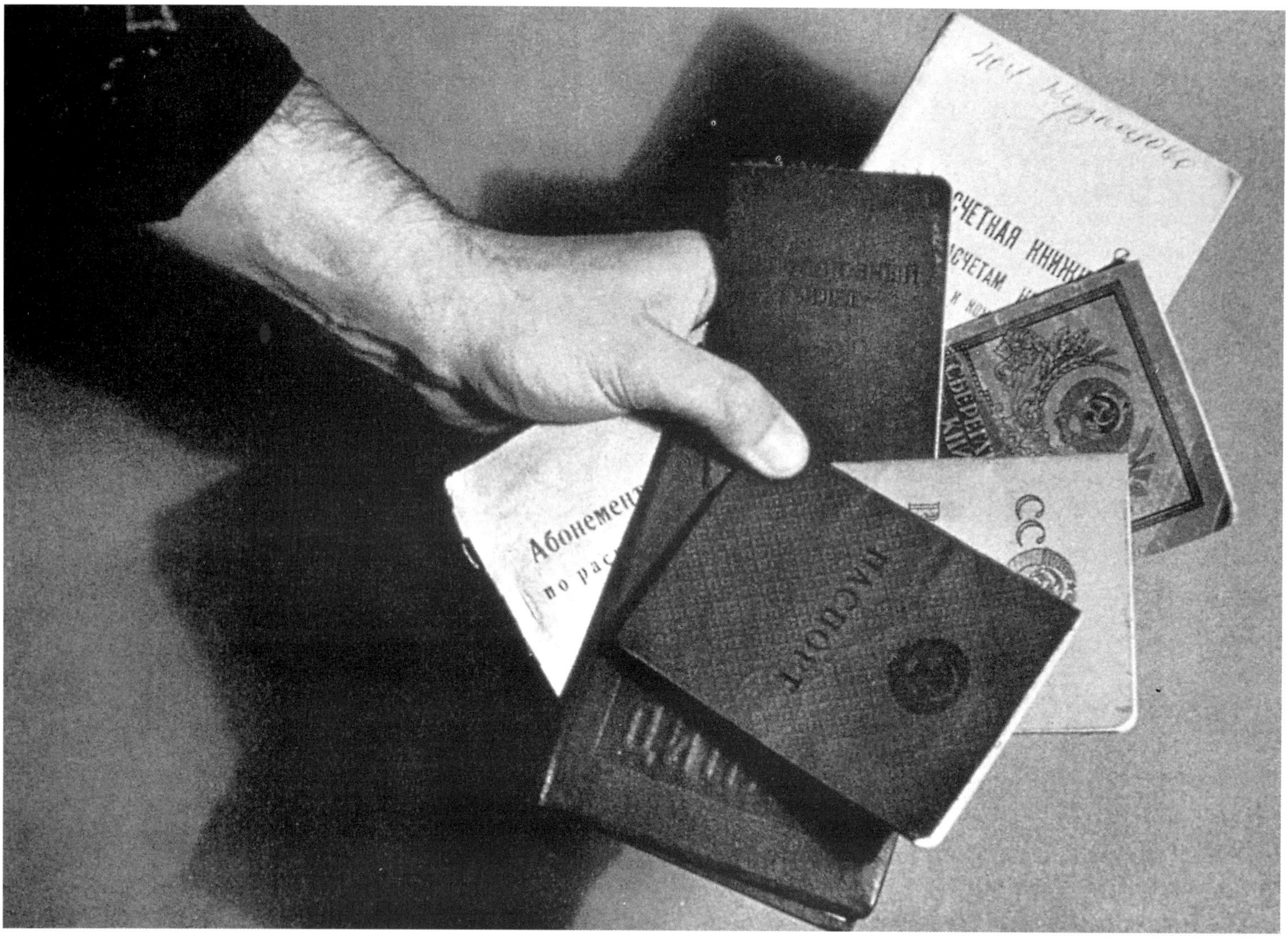

FIGURE 167.
Vitaly Komar and Aleksandr Melamid, *Documents: Ideal Document (Dokumenty: Ideal'ny dokument),* 1975, thirteen Plexiglas panels, text, and three photographs. Collection of the artists.

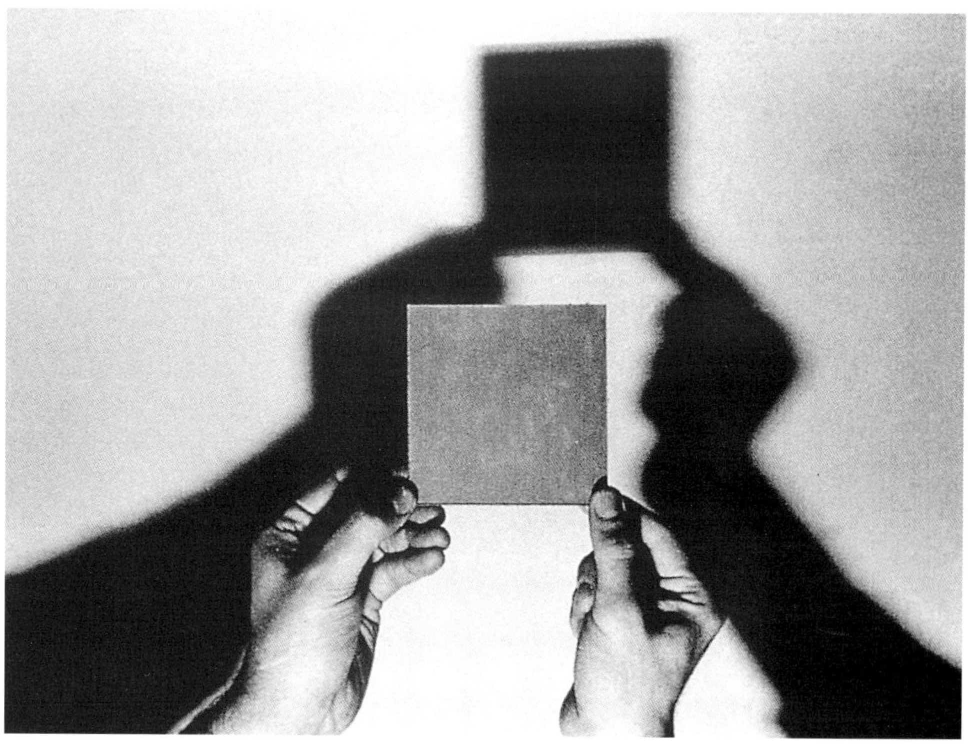

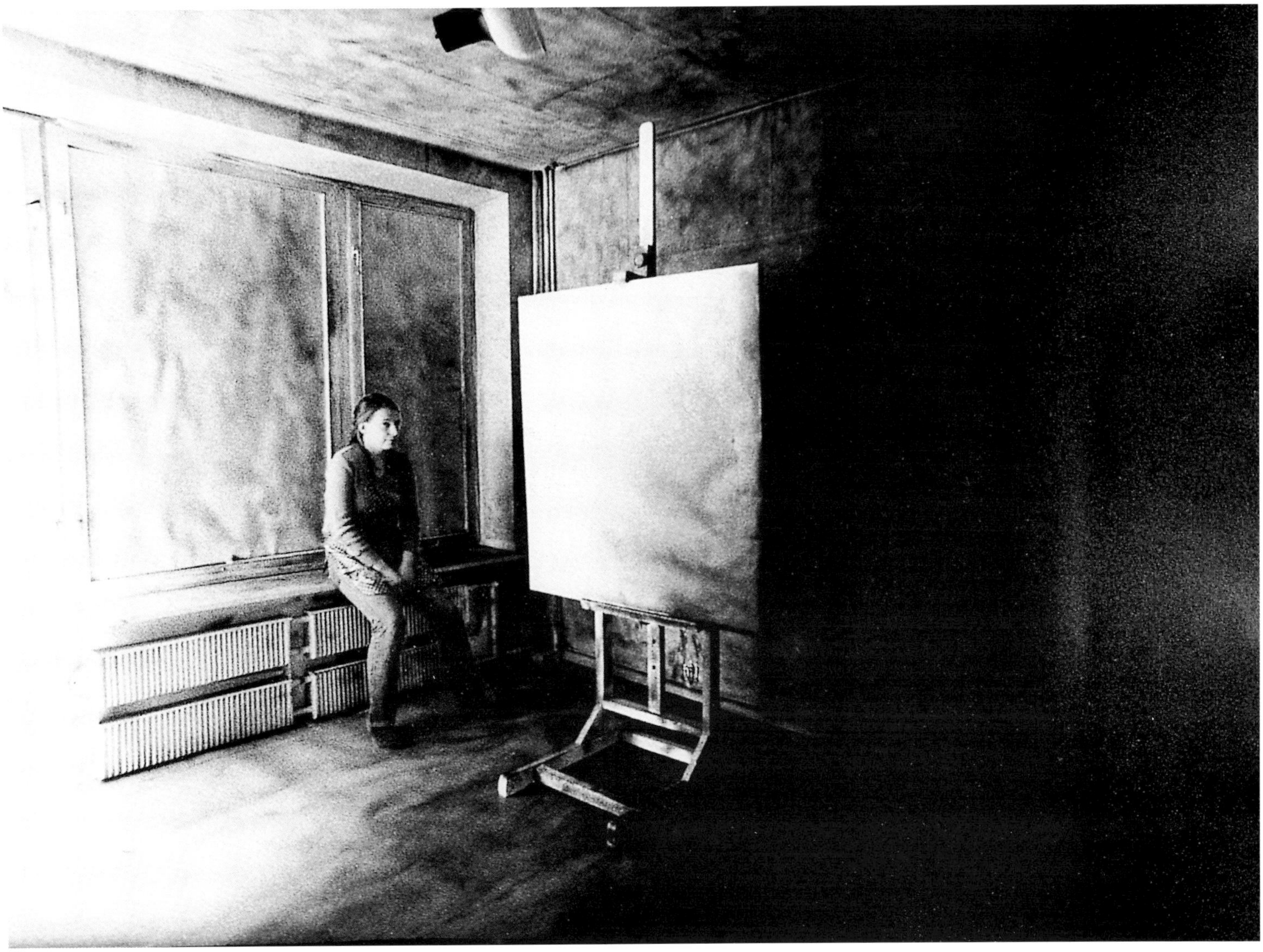

Figure 168.
Irina Nakhova, *Room (Komnata) No. 3*, Moscow, 1986, documentary photograph. Collection of the artist.

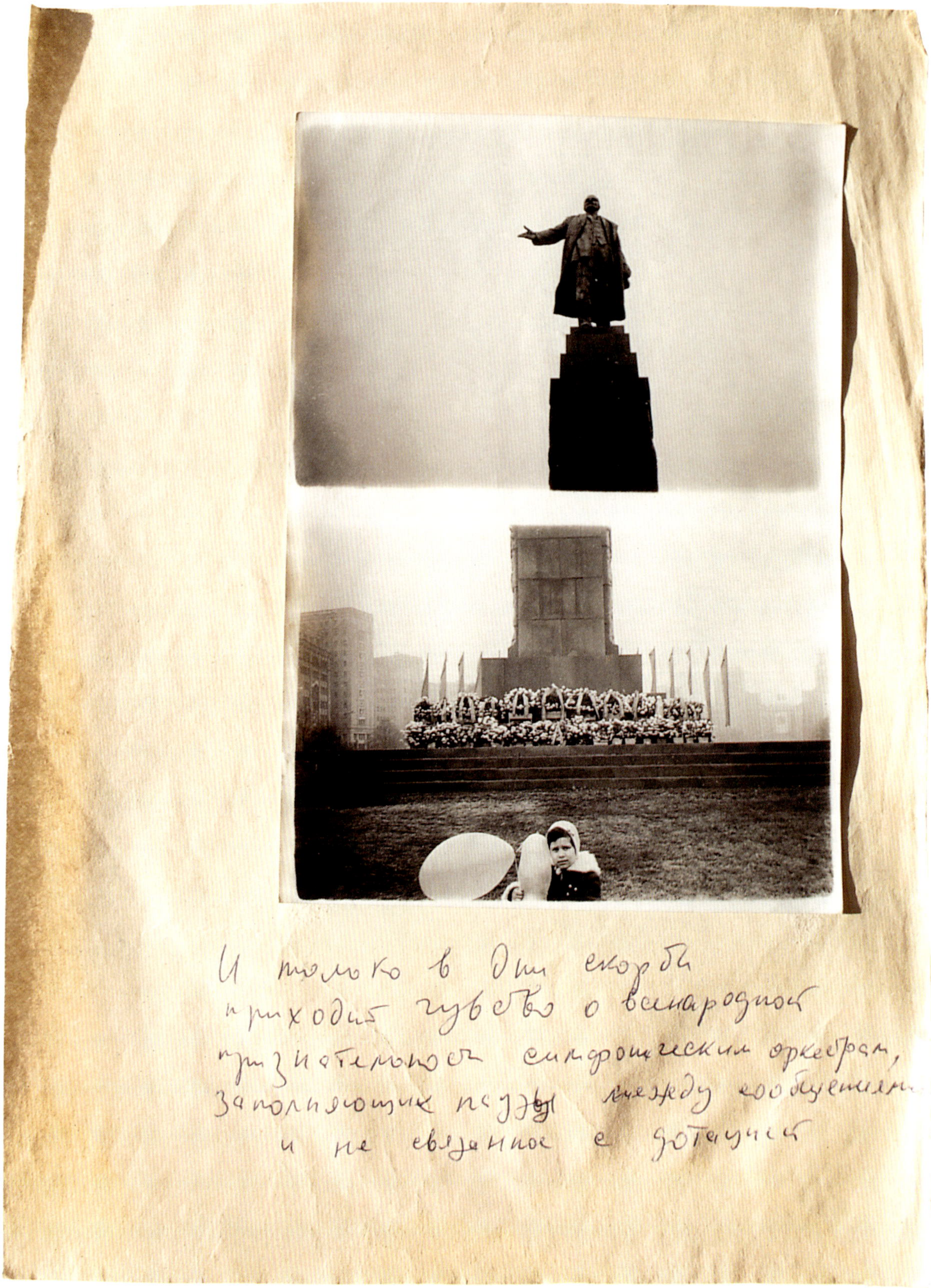

FIGURE 169.
Boris Mikhailov, *Unfinished Dissertation (Nezakonchennaia dissertatsiia)*, 1984, one of 180 photographs, on paper with text. Collection of the artist.

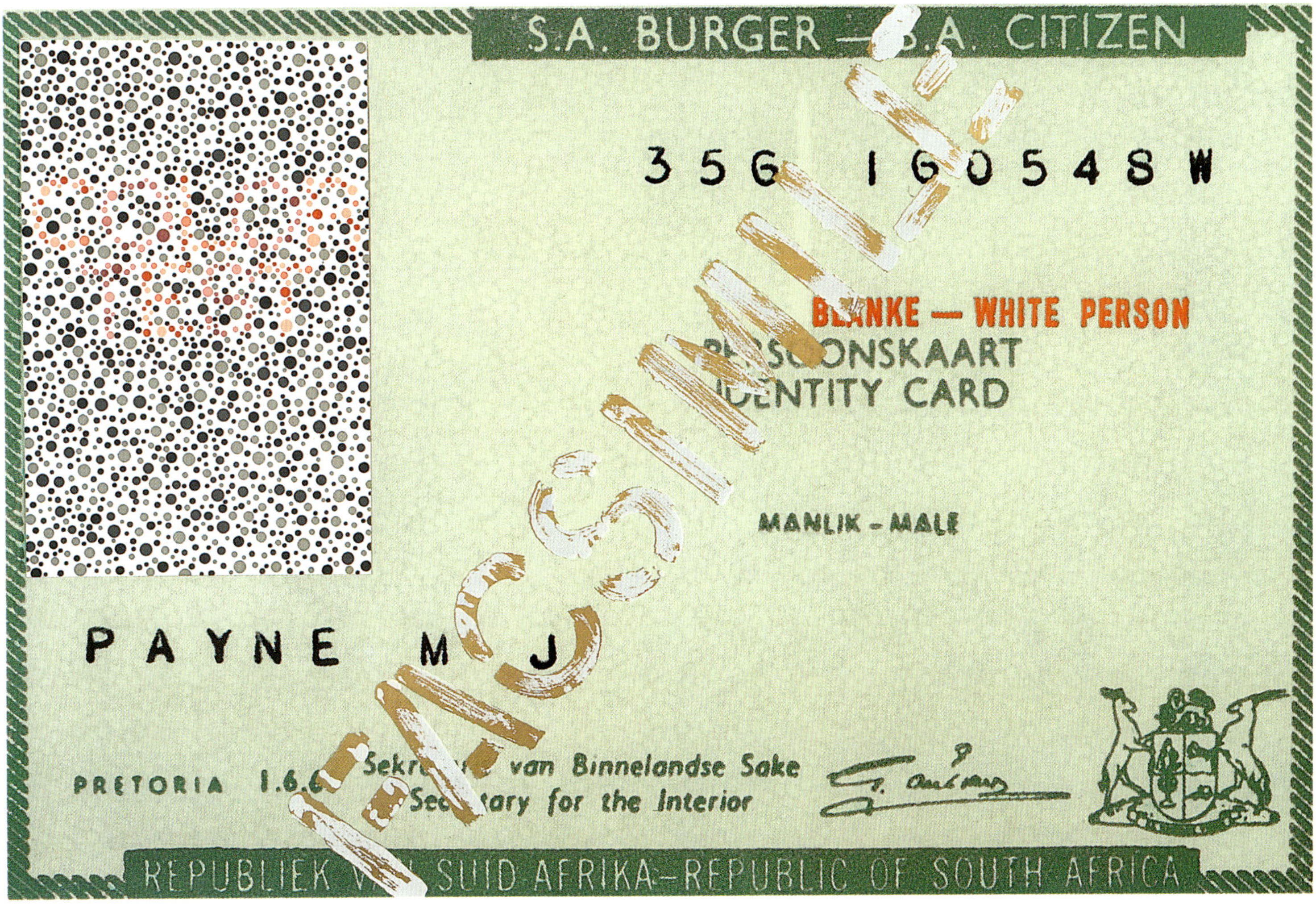

FIGURE 170.
Malcolm Payne, *Color Test*, 1973–74, screenprint.
Collection of Willem Strydom.

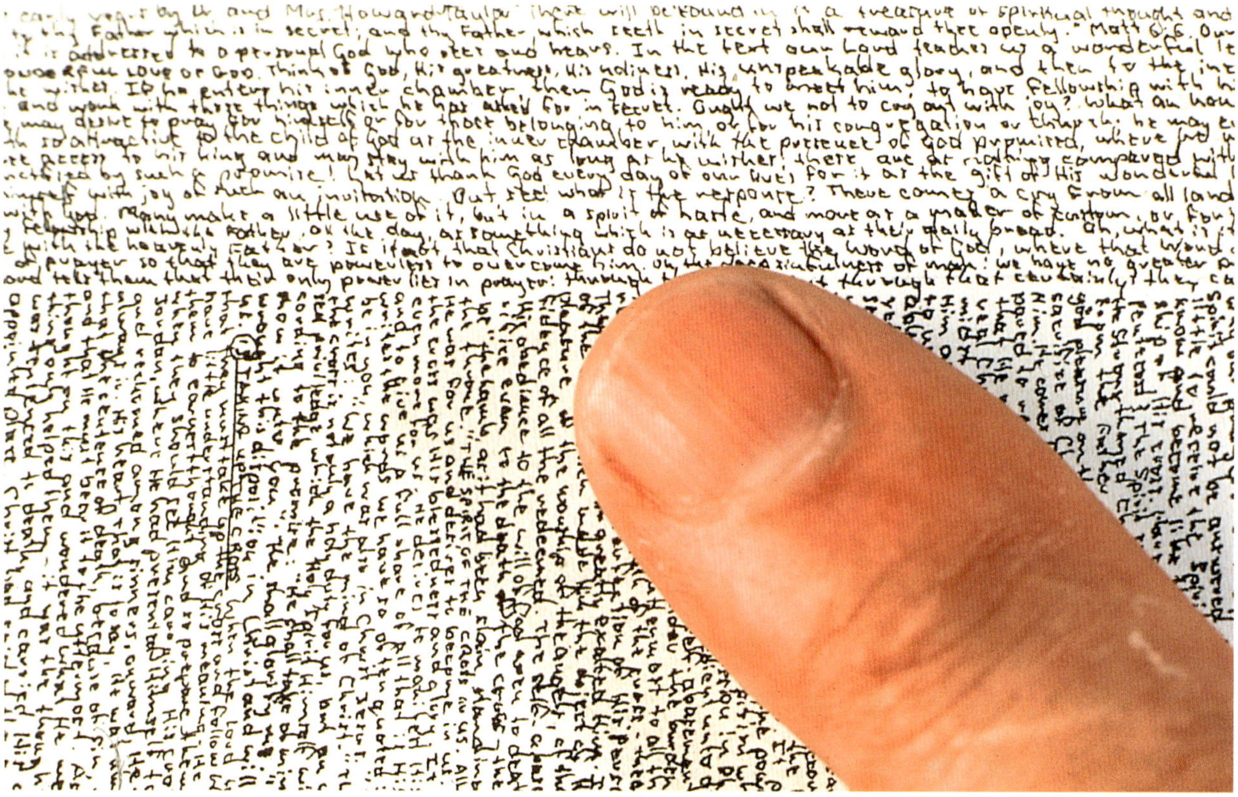

FIGURE 171.
Willem Boshoff, *Kleinpen I (The Small Pen I)*, 1979, ink, paper, microscopic writing. The Ruth and Marvin Sackner Archive of Concrete and Visual Poetry, Miami.

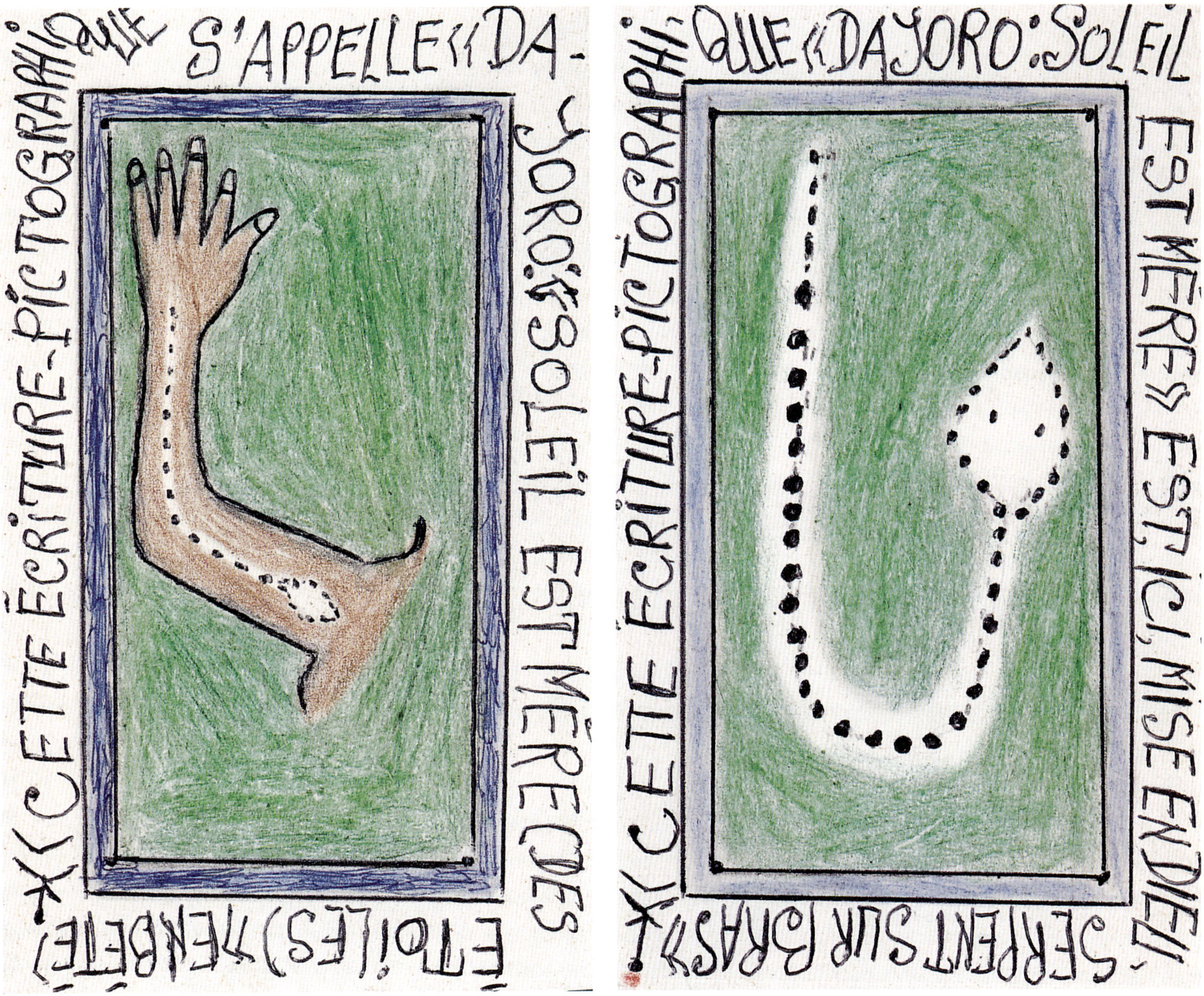

Figure 172.
Frédéric Bruly Bouabré, *West African Alphabet (The Bété)*, 1982, colored pencil and ballpoint on cardboard. Contemporary African Art Collection (C.A.A.C.), in collaboration with André Magnin, courtesy of Frédéric Bruly Bouabré.

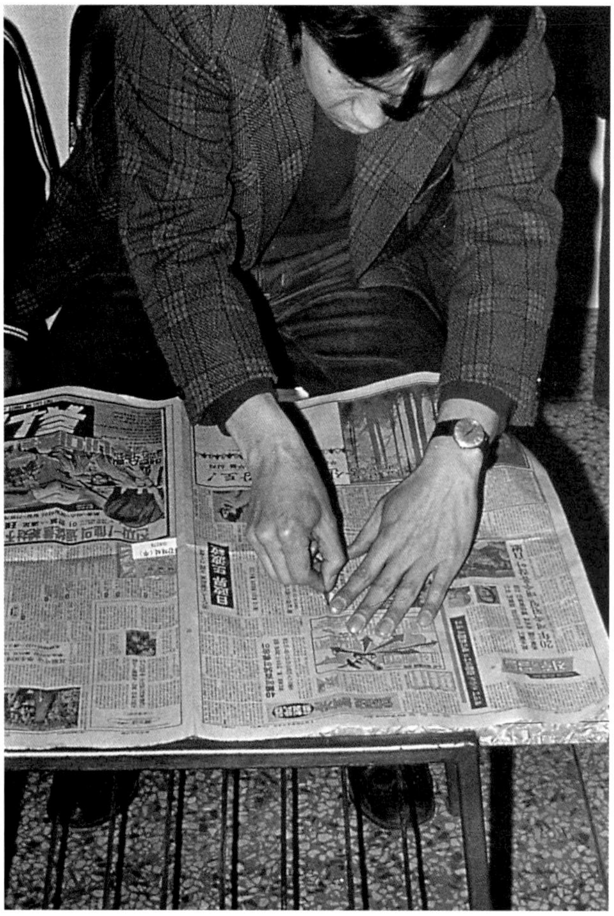

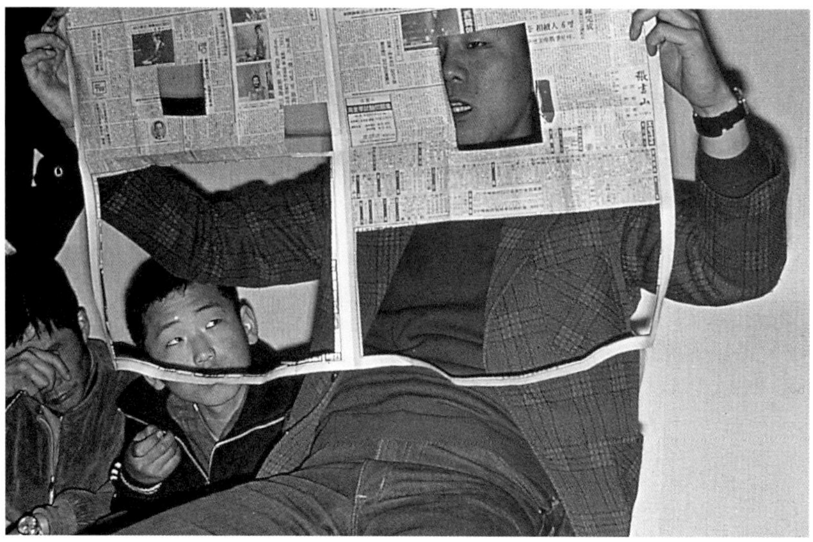

FIGURE 173.
Sung Neung-kyung, *Newspaper: After the 1st of June 1974*, 1974, documentary photographs. Collection of the artist.

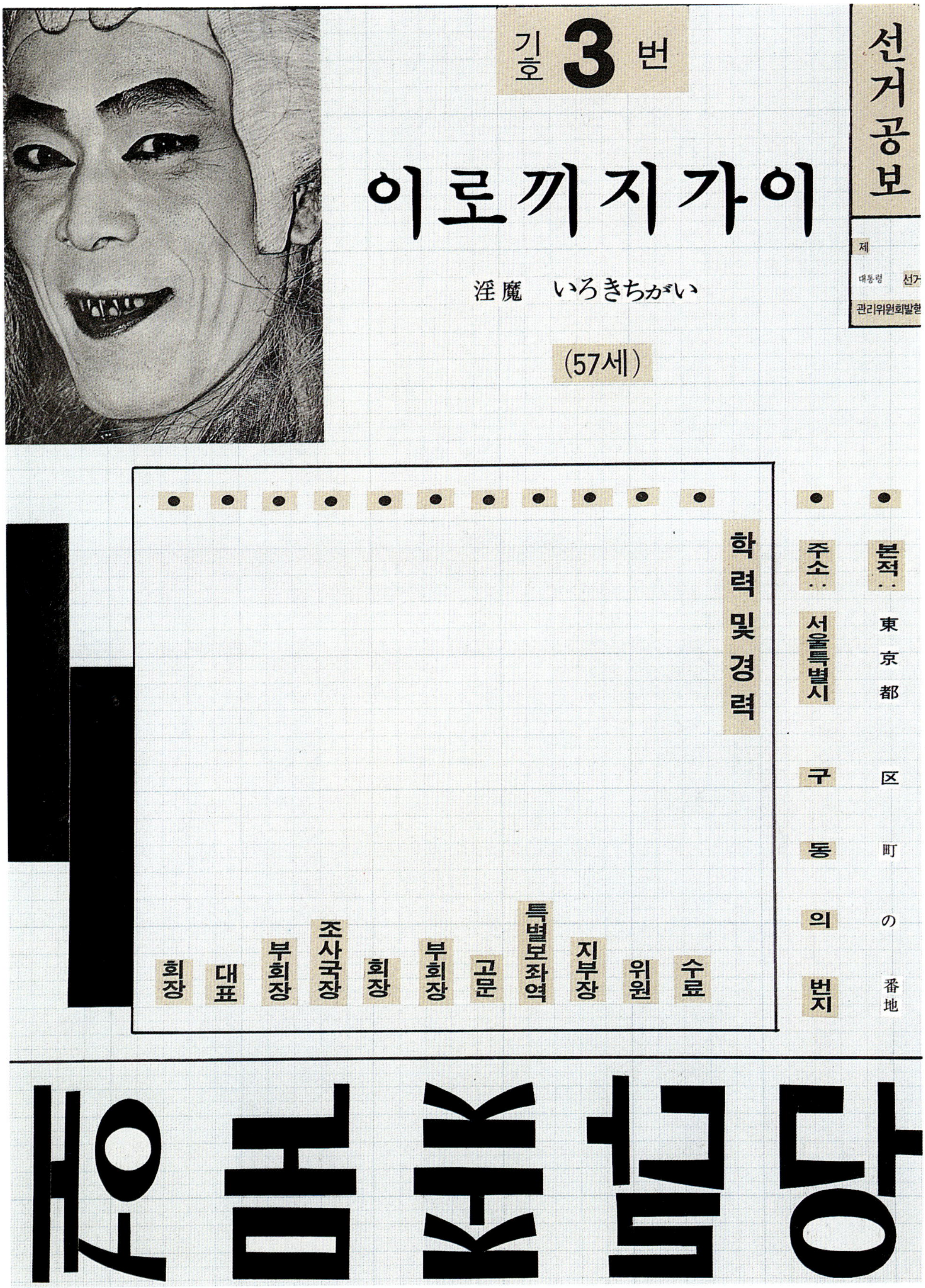

FIGURE 174.
Park Bul-dong, *Nightmare No. 3 (Electoral Campaign Poster)*, 1985, collage of photograph and text on paper. Collection of the artist.

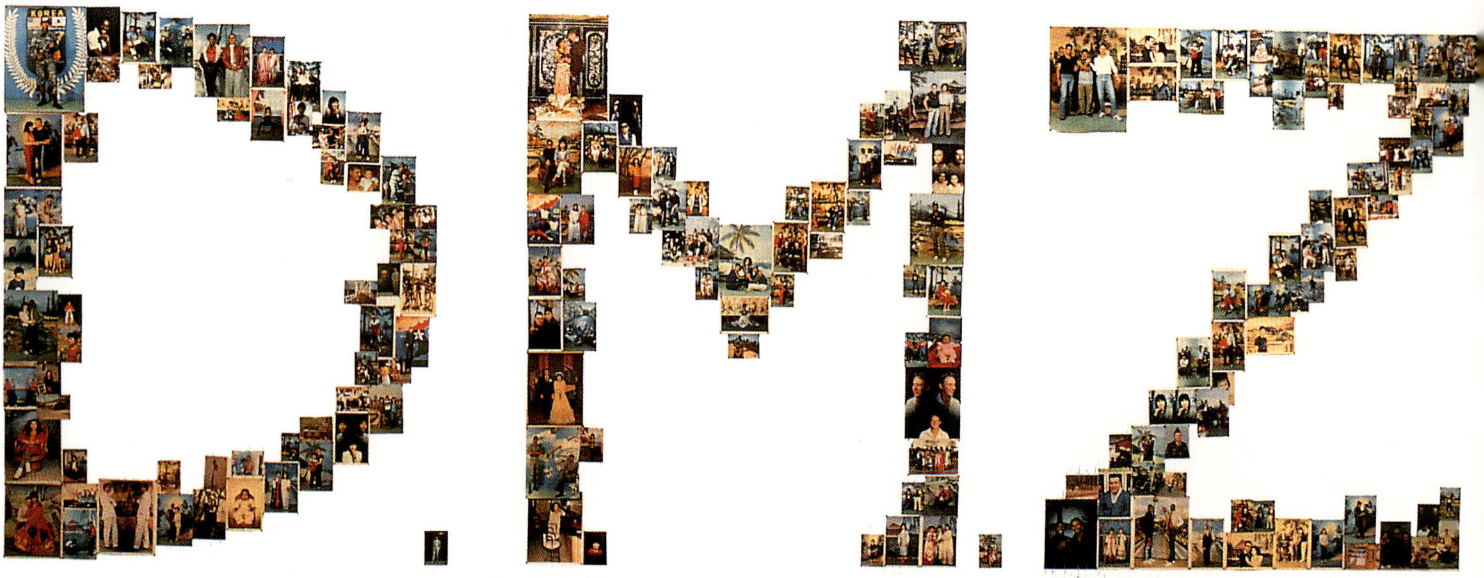

Figure 175. (above and right)
Kim Yong-tae, *Pictures from the Dongduchon Photograph Salons,* 1984, installation of found photographs from U.S. military camp district. Collection of the artist.

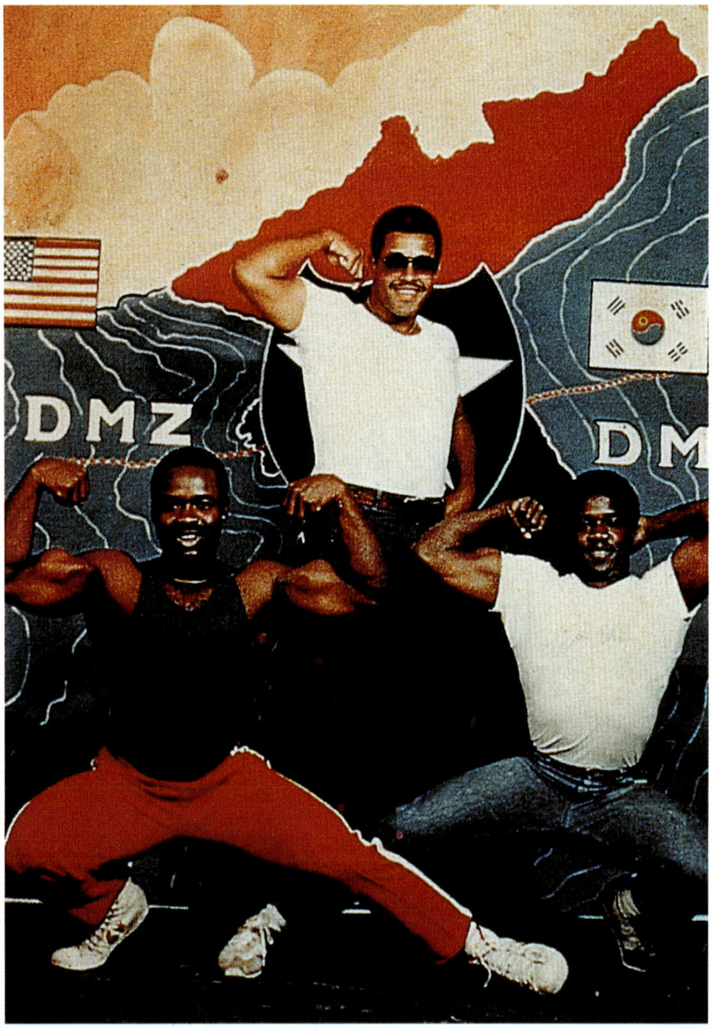
DMZ

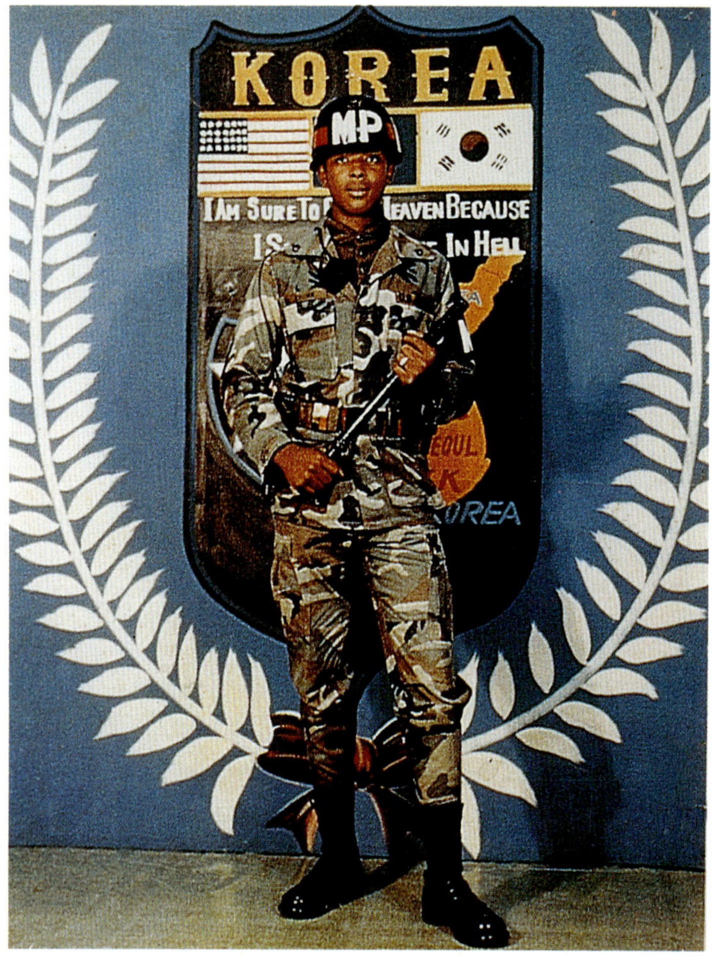
KOREA
MP

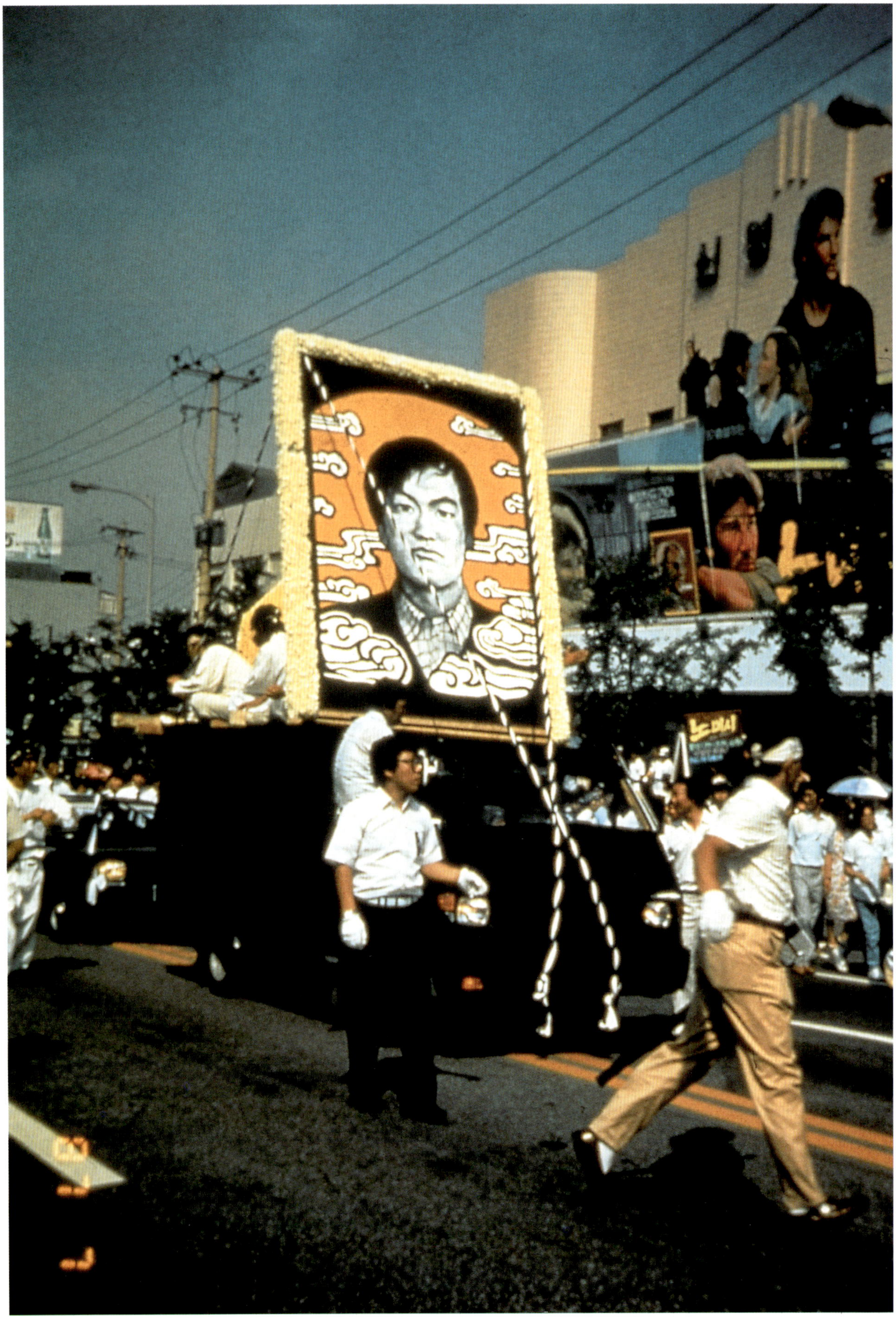

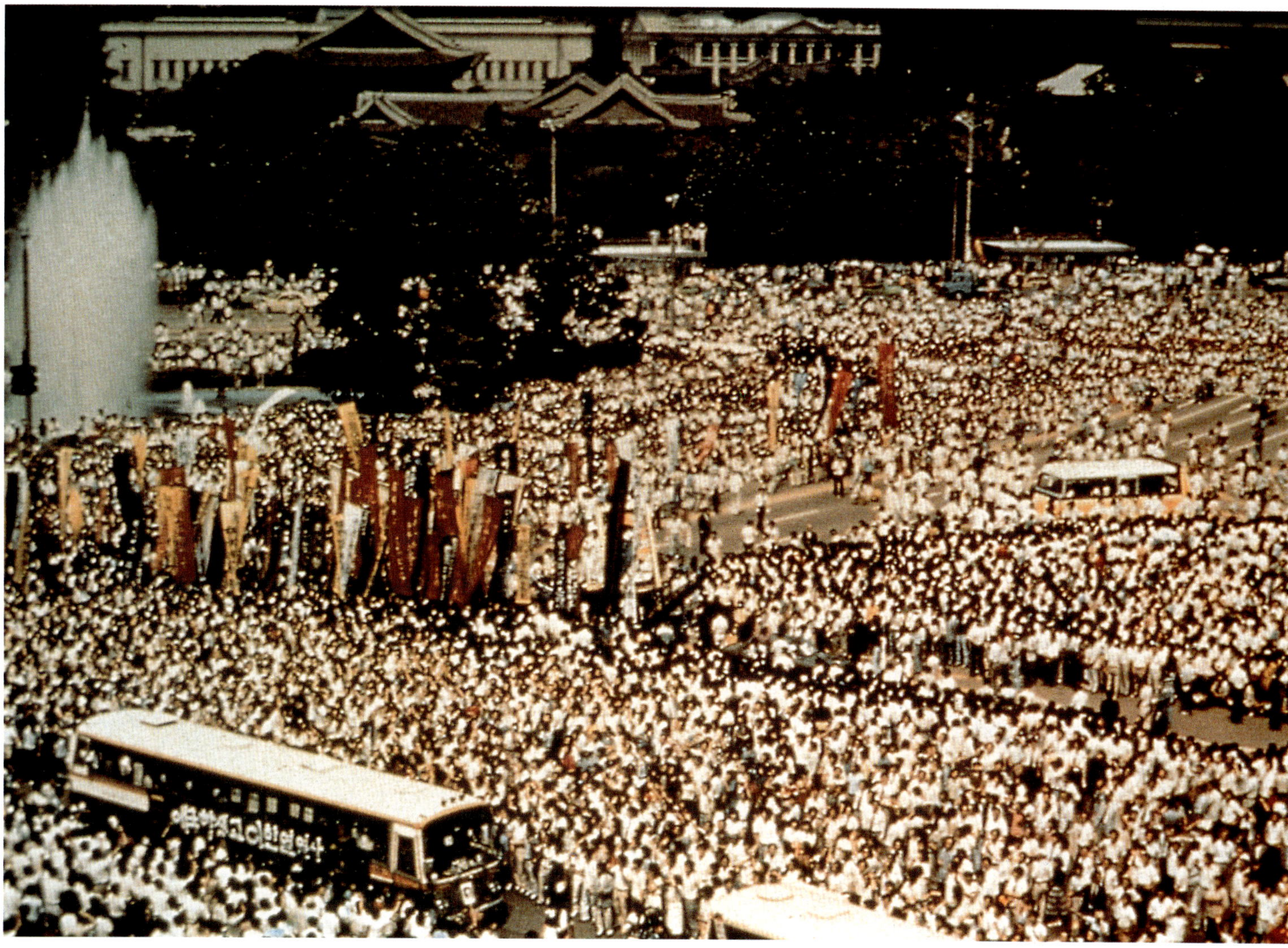

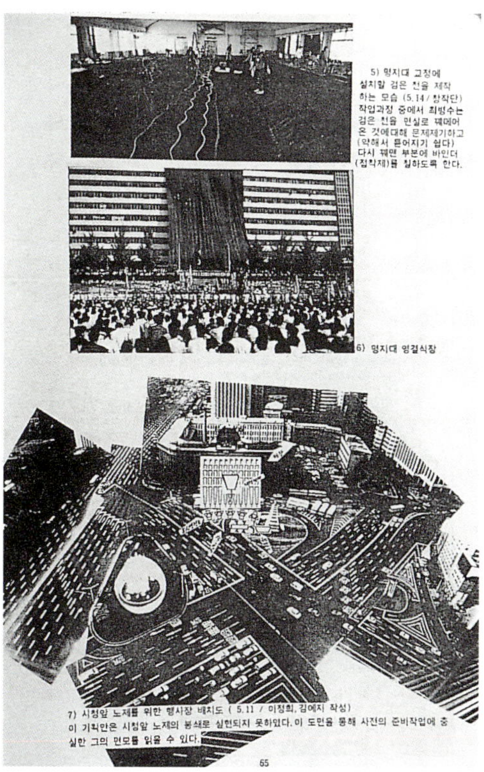

FIGURE 176. (LEFT AND ABOVE)
Choi Byung-soo, *Funeral Procession for Lee Han-ryul,* 1987, ballpoint drawing on paper and photographic documents. Collection of the artist.

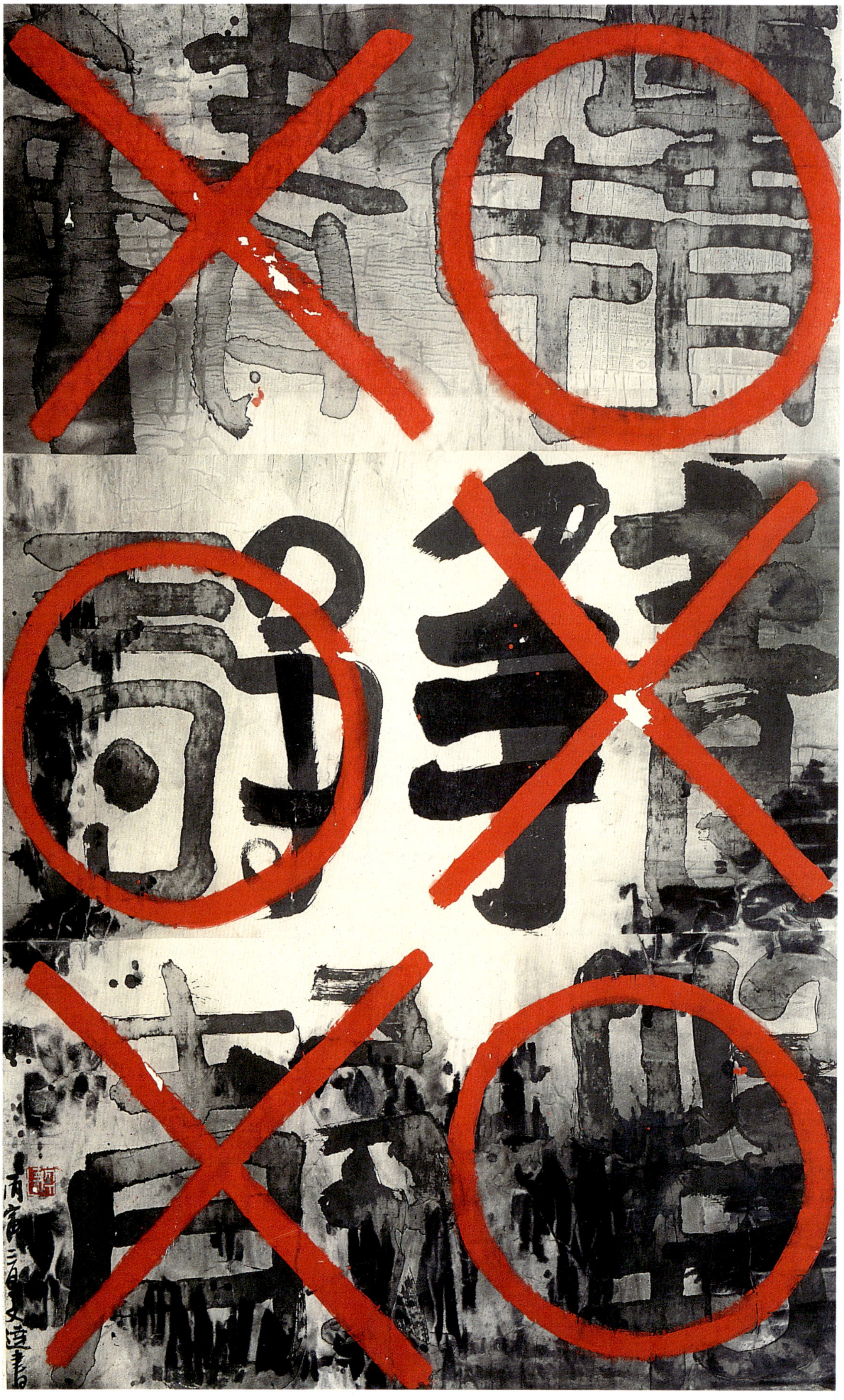

FIGURE 177. Wenda Gu, *pseudo characters of "still" written by three men and three women (san nan san nu shu xie de jing zi)*, 1986, ink and acrylic on rice paper, mounted on silk scroll. Collection of Zhen Guo, New York.

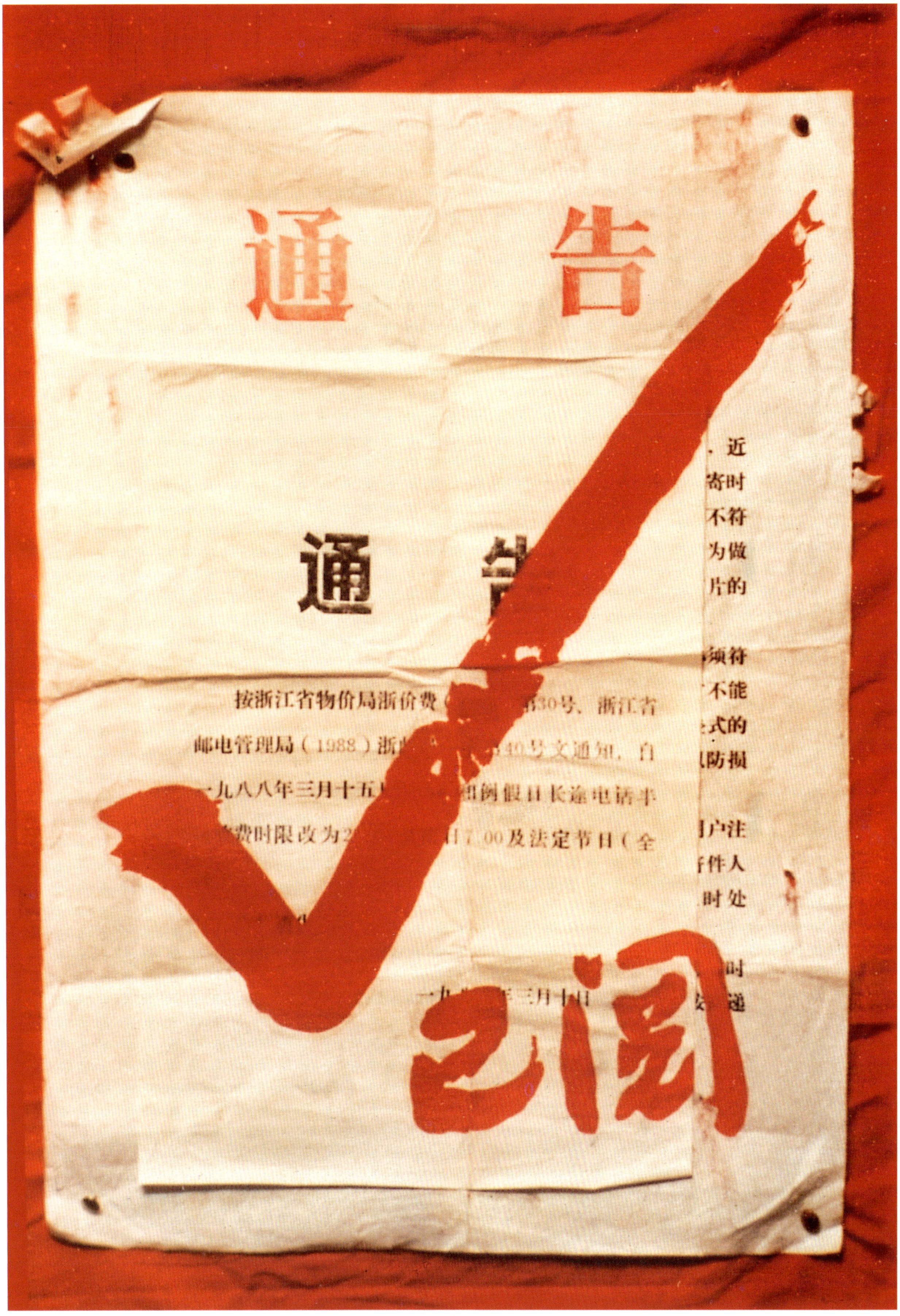

Figure 178.
Wu Shan Zhuan, from *Red Humor Series (Hongse youmo): Big Characters (Dazibao)*, 1987, installation. Collection of the artist.

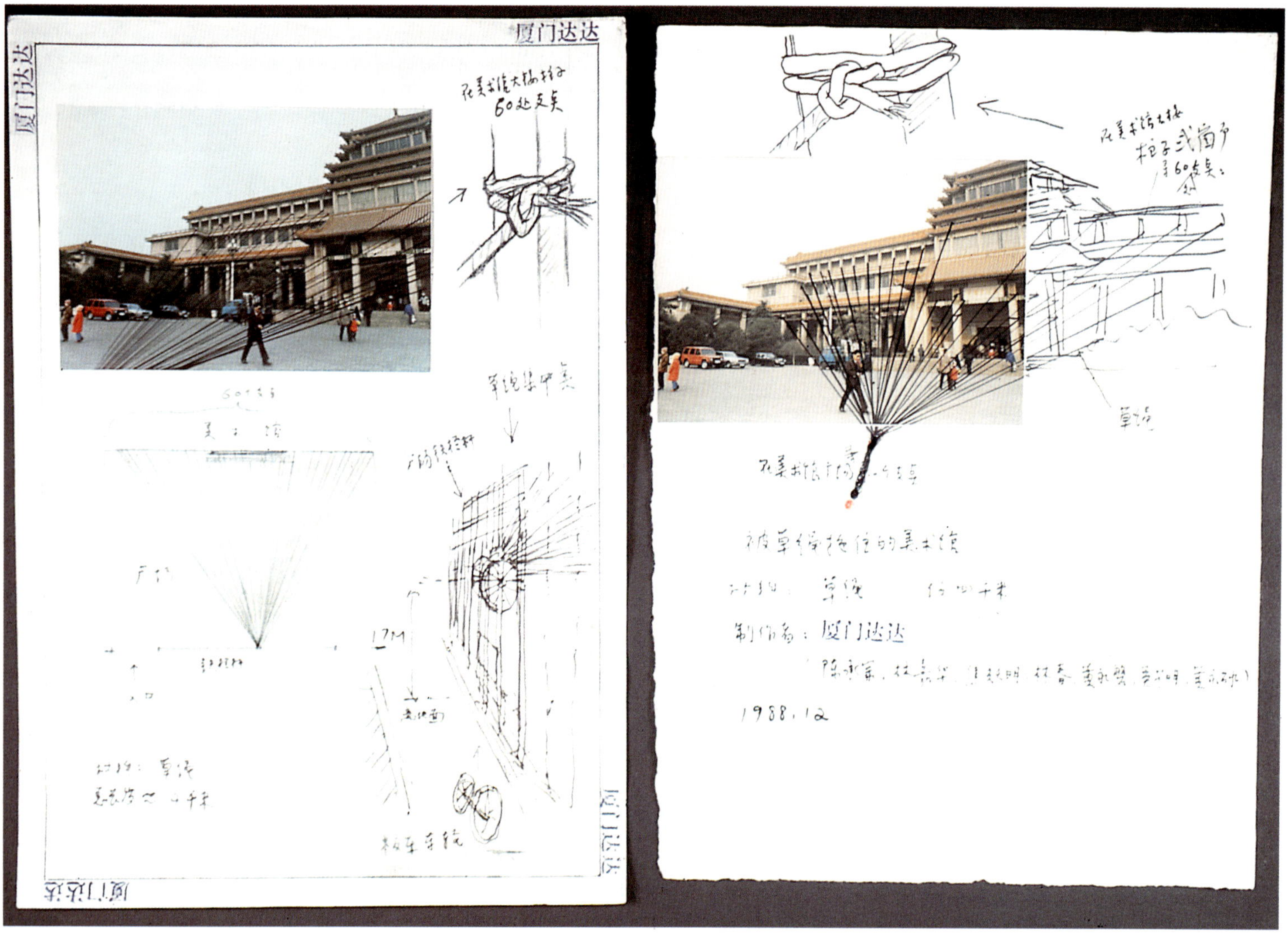

FIGURE 179.
Huang Yong Ping, *Drawing the National Art Gallery Away (Tozou zhongguo meishuguan)*, 1988, color photographs and drawing on two sheets of paper. Collection of the artist.

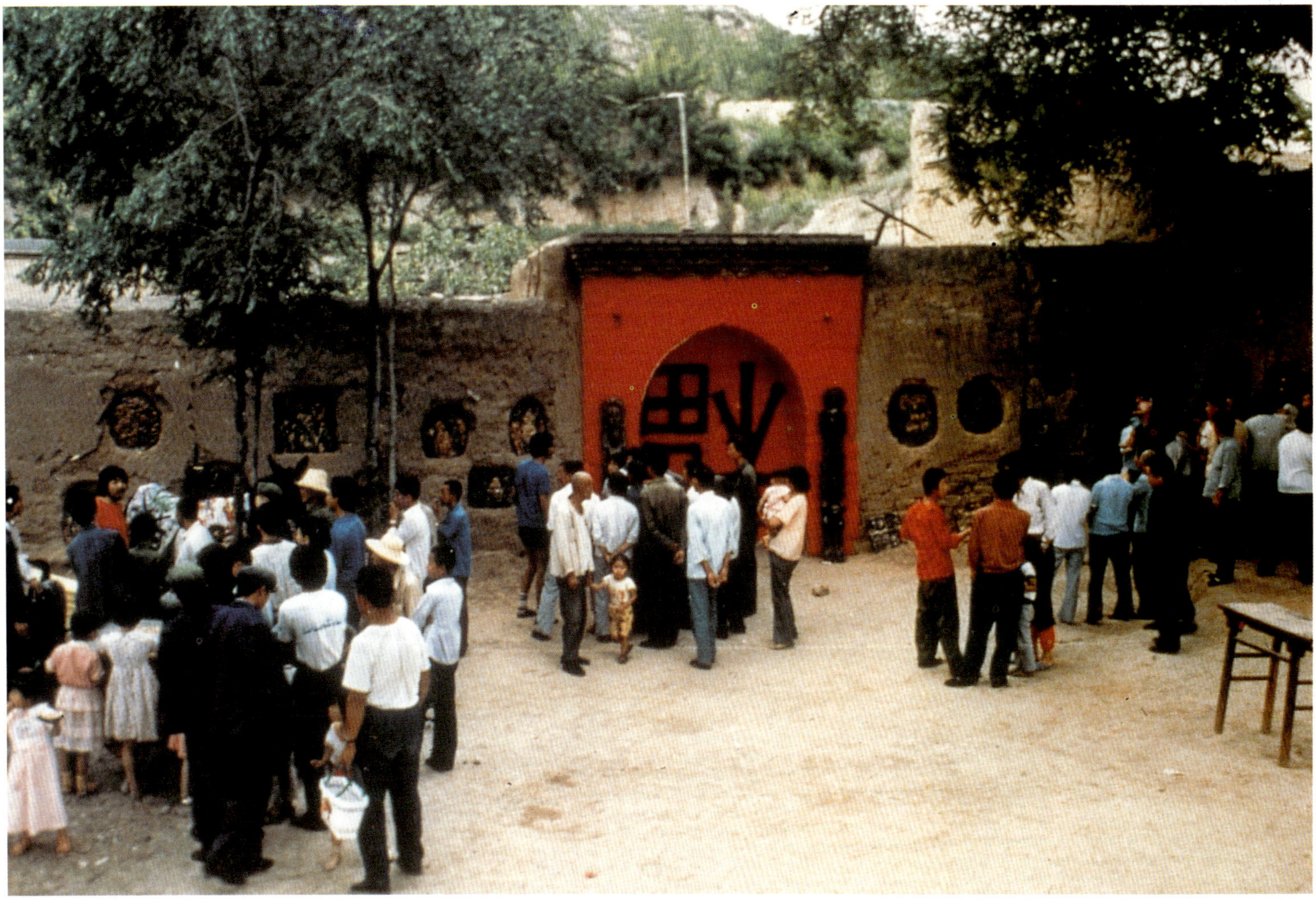

Figure 180.
Song Yongping and others, *The Country Project (Xiangcun yishu huodong),* 1987, documentary photograph. Collection of the artist.

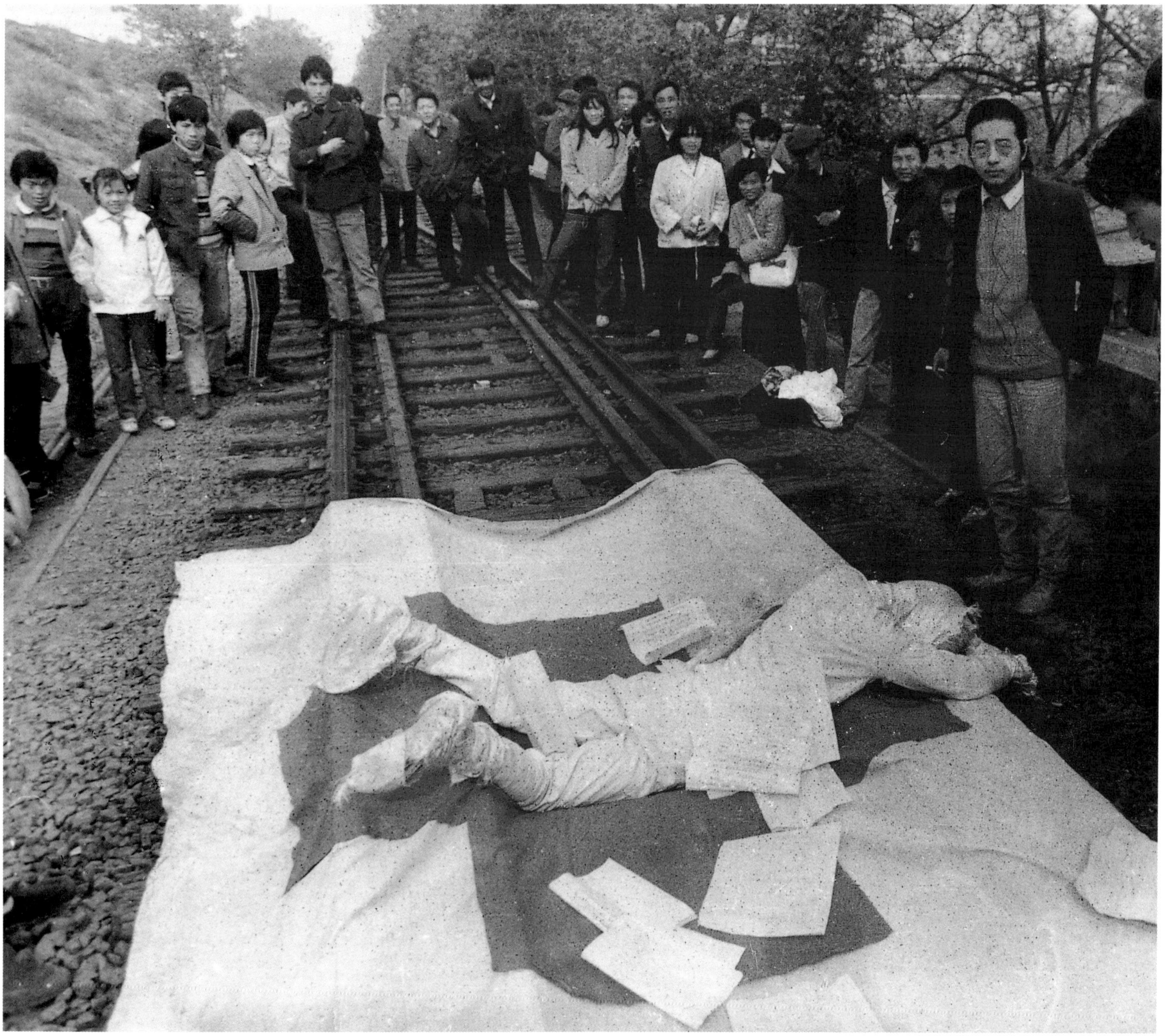

Figure 181.
Wei Guangqing, *Suicide Series (Zisha xilie)*, October 1988, one of eighteen documentary photographs. Collection of the artist.

Chronology

Japan

1954
Formation of Gutai Art Association (Gutai Bijutsu Kyōkai) in Ashiya.

1955
Founding of pro-American, conservative Liberal Democratic Party launches the 1955 System, which lasts until 1993. Japan Council Against Atomic and Hydrogen Bombs founded, the first of several anti–nuclear weapons organizations.

First open-air Gutai exhibition held in Ashiya. On Kawara, Ikeda Tatsuo, and others form Producers Discussion Group (Seisakusha Kondankai), dedicated to liberating realist art from the taint of socialist realism.

1956
Economic Planning Agency declares the end of the "postwar" era in its annual white paper. Japan joins the United Nations; reestablishes diplomatic relations with the Soviet Union.

Life magazine publishes an article on Gutai.

1957
Japan's first nuclear power plant begins operating at Tōkai Village.

First Kyoto Independent Exhibition held at Kyoto Municipal Museum of Art. Michel Tapié and others introduce art informel to the Japanese public.

1958
Nitten Foundation assumes administration of Nitten, the governmental annual salon.

1959
Prince Akihito marries Shōda Michiko.

1960
Violent protests staged against the renewal of Anpo (U.S.–Japan Security Treaty).

Neo Dada group formed by Akasegawa Genpei, Shusaku Arakawa, and others.

1962
Tokyo becomes the first city worldwide to boast a population of 10 million. Nationwide, television subscribers reach 10 million, with household penetration of 48.5 percent.

Mainichi Newspaper institutes the open-entry section in the biennial Contemporary Art Exhibition of Japan. Tokyo Metropolitan Museum of Art institutes exhibition regulations that effectively ban anti-Art works.

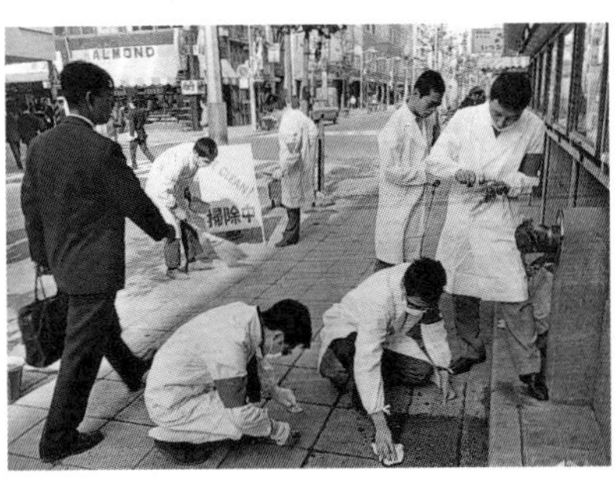

Figure 182.
Hi Red Center, *Cleaning Event (Chō-sōji ivento),* an entry to *Tone-Prize Exhibition,* 1964, documentary photograph. Collection of Akasegawa Genpei, courtesy of Nagoya City Art Museum.

1963
Restrictions on trade and foreign exchange eased.

National Museum of Modern Art, Kyoto, opens. Police investigation of Chi-37 Counterfeit 1,000-Yen Note Case intensifies. Hi Red Center founded by Takamatsu Jirō, Akasegawa Genpei, and Nakanishi Natsuyuki.

1964
Restrictions on foreign travel eased. Bullet train begins operation between Tokyo and Osaka. Olympics held in Tokyo.

Akasegawa Genpei investigated in *Model 1,000-Yen Note Incident.* Yomiuri Newspaper terminates the annual Yomiuri Independent Exhibition. *Independent '64* opens at Tokyo Metropolitan Museum of Art; *Off Museum* at Tsubaki Kindai Gallery; and *Jury Event* at Naiqua Gallery. The Venus de Milo is exhibited at the National Museum of Western Art, Tokyo.

1965
Beheiren (Citizen's League for Peace in Vietnam) founded. Leftist protests staged against ratification of Japan-Korea Treaty. Tomonaga Shin'ichirō receives Nobel Prize in physics.

1966–67
Akasegawa Genpei tried for currency fraud in the *Model 1,000-Yen Note Incident.*

1967
Japan's population reaches 100 million. Pollution Countermeasures Basic Law is enacted.

Nihon Gallery, Tokyo, mounts *War (Sensō),* organized by Haryū Ichirō. *Unfreedom of Expression* opens at Maramatsu Gallery, Tokyo.

1968
Centennial of Meiji Restoration, commonly assumed to mark the beginning of Japan's modern history. Kawabata Yasunari receives Nobel Prize in literature. Agency of Cultural Affairs established.

1968–69
Nationwide university conflicts; emergence and rapid demise of Zenkyōtō (All-Campus Joint-Struggle Councils) movement.

1969
New building of National Museum of Modern Art, Tokyo, completed. Bikyōtō founded. Hanpaku (Anti–Expo '70) teach-ins organized in Osaka and Tokyo.

1970
Expo '70 held in Osaka. U.S. returns some 150 war-record paintings to Japan on permanent loan. Japan Red Army hijacks JAL's *Yodo* plane. Leftists protest Anpo's decennial renewal.

Supreme Court upholds Akasegawa's guilty verdict. *Nirvana: For Final Art* opens. *Between Man and Matter: 10th Tokyo Biennale* features arte povera, conceptual, mono-ha, and postminimal artists. Prefectural museums of modern art open in Kōbe and Wakayama; other cities and prefectures soon follow suit.

1971
Dollar Shock; fixed dollar-yen exchange rate ends. Japan House Gallery opens in New York.

Bikyōtō Revolution Committee I and Group of Five form in Tokyo.

1972
Sapporo Winter Olympics held. Japan-China relations normalized. U.S. returns Okinawa to Japan. Japan Foundation established.

Bijutsu Shihyō (Art History-Criticism) and *Kirokutai* (Document Zone) publish first issue. Yasunao Tone and Hikosaka Naoyoshi publish *Chronology: Five Decades of Contemporary Art, 1916–1968.*

1973
Oil Shock triggers the "crazy prices." Kim Dae-jung kidnapped from Japan. Ezaki Reona receives Nobel Prize in physics.

'73/5: Affair and Practice by 12 opens at Pinar Galleries, Tokyo. Matsuzawa Yutaka launches the Suwa workshop for Tokyo's Bigakkō art school. Bikyōtō Revolution Committee II forms.

1974
Country experiences the first negative GNP growth in the postwar years. Former prime minister Satō Eisaku receives Nobel Peace Prize.

Mona Lisa exhibited at the National Museum, Tokyo.

1975
Former prime minister Tanaka Kakuei arrested in Lockheed scandal. Postwar record set for corporate bankruptcy.

New building of Tokyo Metropolitan Museum of Art completed; curatorial department added to the mecca of open-entry exhibitions.

1976
Soviet MiG-25 forced to land in Hakodate.

1977
National Museum of Art, Osaka, opens at the former Expo '70 site, Japan's third national museum specializing in modern art.

1978
Tokyo International Airport opens at Narita despite persistent leftist opposition. Japan-China Peace Treaty signed. Yamanashi Prefectural Museum of Art opens, heralding a construction boom of regional museums.

1979
Country suffers second Oil Shock. Tokyo Summit held.

1980
Japan's automobile production becomes largest worldwide.

Western Europe

1951
France Isidore Isou, leader of the Lettrists, presents his film *Traité de bave et d'éternité (Treatise on Slime and Eternity)* at the Cannes Film Festival. Guy-Ernest Debord, a young student in philosophy, meets Isou and other Lettrists at the festival. First exhibition of Cobra group held at Librairie 73, Paris. **Spain** First Hispano-American Biennial of Art, inaugurated by Franco, prompts a counter-biennial by exiled artists in Paris.

1952
England Independent Group founded in London by Reyner Banham, Alison and Peter Smithson, and others. **France** Gil J. Wolman, a Lettrist, screens *L' anticoncept* in Paris. Debord shows *Hurlements en faveur de Sade* at Musée de l'Homme, Paris, but the screening is interrupted by a hostile audience; Yves Klein attends second showing in October. Wolman, Debord, and other Lettrists insult Charlie Chaplin during a press conference at the Ritz Hotel held on the occasion of *Limelight's* European premiere, causing a rift within the group. Debord, Wolman, and others split from Isou and found the Lettrist International. **Italy** Enrico Baj and others distribute the Manifesto BUM at their exhibition in Milan. **Spain** Admitted to United Nations. **West Germany** Radio Free Europe begins transmission from Munich.

1953
France Roland Barthes publishes *Le degré zéro de l' écriture* in Paris. **Italy** Asger Jorn, a former member of Cobra, and Enrico Baj announce the formation of Imaginist Bauhaus, to be distinguished from New Bauhaus, initiated by Max Bill in West Germany.

1954
France Front de la Libération Nationale (FLN) revolts against French rule in Algeria, mobilizing widespread support among French intellectuals. France defeated in Vietnam. Edgar Varèse's *Déserts,* the first musical performance to combine recorded sounds and orchestra, presented at Théâtre des Champs-Elysées, Paris.

1956
Delegates from Algeria, Belgium, Denmark, France, Great Britain, Holland, Italy, and Czechoslovakia meet in Alba, Italy to merge the Lettrist International and Imaginist Bauhaus and create a common platform.

1957
Treaty of Rome establishes the European Economic Community. **England** Screening of Debord's *Hurlements* at ICA, London, provokes outrage. **France** Anonymously lacerated posters collected by Raymond Hains and Jacques Villeglé exhibited at Galerie Colette Allendy, Paris; the interest shown here in the assault on the image is similar to Lettrist sensibility. **Italy** Unification Conference—comprised of Ralph Rumney, London Psychogeographical Association; Debord, Lettrist International; and Asger Jorn and Giuseppe Pinot-Gallizio, Imaginist Bauhaus—held in Cosio d'Arroscia, to found Situationist International. **Spain** Workers and students demonstrate in Barcelona.

1958
Austria The Wiener Gruppe realizes its "total theater" work, *Cabaret littéraire.* **Belgium** Brussels World Exposition, the first since 1939, draws 41 million visitors. Situationist tract against art critics delivered at general assembly in Brussels, presided over by John Sweeney. **Denmark** Debord produces *Mémoires* (with Asger Jorn), a book of appropriated visual and textual fragments. **France** General de Gaulle elected president of the Fifth Republic. Yves Klein's *Void* opens at Galerie Iris Clert, Paris. **Italy** Pinot-Gallizio exhibits "mass-produced" paintings for a solo show at Galleria Notizie, Turin.

1959
France André Malraux named Minister of Culture. François Truffaut's *400 Blows* wins the grand prize at Cannes; Truffaut, Godard, Chabrol, Rivette, etc., all former members of the editorial board of *Les Cahiers du Cinéma,* will soon be collectively labeled the Nouvelle Vague. Duchamp and Breton organize *Eros* at Galerie Daniel Cordier, Paris, for the 8th Exposition Internationale du Surréalisme. **Italy** Piero Manzoni introduces his "lines" at Galleria Il Pozzetto Chiuso, Albisola. Klein sells his first *Zone of Immaterial Pictorial Sensibility* to Peppino Palazzoli. **Spain** Estampa Popular formed by artists for the purpose of mass diffusion of politically informed art.

1960
England Beatles give first concert in Liverpool. **France** Algiers is barricaded; 121 French intellectuals sign a manifesto declaring support for Algerian revolution. Left journal *Tel Quel* founded by Philippe Sollers and others. *Dimanche,* a special newspaper-like publication showing Yves Klein's *Leap into the Void,* is published in Paris. Klein, Arman, François Dufrêne (a former Lettrist), Hains, Martial Raysse, Pierre Restany, Daniel Spoerri, Jean Tinguely, and Villeglé sign the Déclaration Constitutive des Nouveaux Réalistes. **Italy** Restany coins the term *nouveau réalisme* for a group show at Galleria Apollinaire, Milan. Second cycle of *L' anti-procès* closes with first European happening, Lebel-Jouffrey's *Funérailles de la chose.*

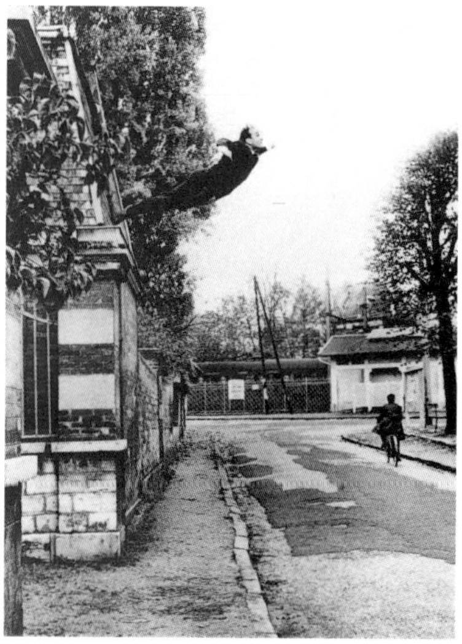

Figure 183.
Yves Klein, *Le saut dans le vide (Leap into the Void),* 1960.

1961
Denmark Manzoni presents "artist's shit" at Kopke Gallery, Copenhagen. **France** Rauschenberg exhibits *This is a portrait of Iris Clert if I say so* in Paris. **Italy** At Galleria Tartaruga, Rome, Manzoni "signs" people such as Umberto Eco and Mario Schifano as "living sculpture."

1962
Austria First public manifestation of actionism. **Belgium** Manzoni declares Marcel Broodthaers an "authentic work of art" at a gallery in Brussels. **England** Commonwealth Immigrant Act severely restricts black immigration. **France** Eight people killed in anti-OAS demonstrations. French-Algerian war ends with Algerian independence. Klein, Niki de Saint Phalle, Villeglé, and Dufrêne produce a void by removing paintings from the walls of Musée d'Art Moderne de la Ville de Paris. First public performance of Fluxus in France staged at Festum Fluxorum in Paris.

1963
Italy Manzoni dies in his Milan studio. *Piero Manzoni: Life and Works* published by Petersen Press, Glücksburg, Denmark; only the cover is printed, the inside made either of white pages, in one version, or translucent plastic material. Broodthaers pays homage to Manzoni in the *Journal des Beaux-Arts* (Brussels): "Of course, Manzoni will be in the dreadful book of the 20th century." **West Germany** *Life with Pop: A Demonstration for Capitalist Realism,* a performance by Konrad Lueg and Gerhard Richter, staged in a Düsseldorf department store.

1964
Belgium Broodthaers mounts first solo show at Galerie St.-Laurent, Brussels: "Me too, I asked myself whether I couldn't have something to sell ..." **France** Jean-Paul Sartre refuses the Nobel Prize for literature. "Flesh as material": Carolee Schneeman performs *Meat Joy* at the Festival for Free Expression, Paris, organized by Jean-Jacques Lebel.

1965
France While in Paris for his show at Galerie Ileana Sonnabend, Warhol announces his intention to "retire" from painting and focus on filmmaking instead.

1966
England John Latham and Barry Flanagan organize the chew-and-spit event with students of St. Martin's School of Art, London.

1967
France Daniel Buren, Noele Toroni, Michel Parmentier, and Olivier Mosset mount a group show at the Salon de la Jeune Peinture, Paris, in which all four use a single visual motif. André Cadere emigrates from Romania to Paris. Debord publishes *La société du spectacle.* **Greece** Military coup initiates lengthy period of repression. **Italy** Arte povera (a term borrowed from Jerzy Grotowski) is introduced to the public in an exhibition organized by Germano Celant at Galleria La Bertesca, Genoa.

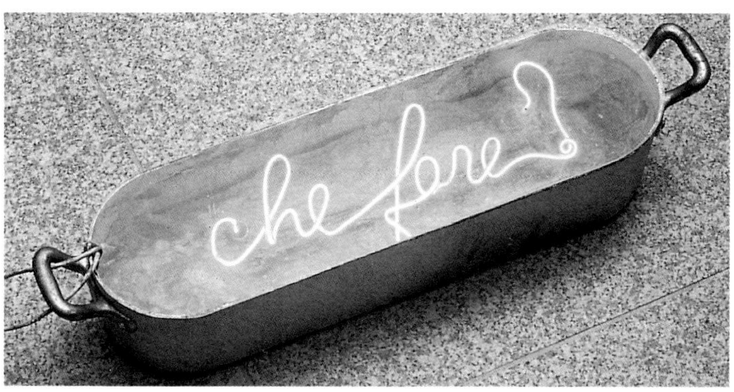

Figure 184.
Mario Merz, *Che fare? (What Is to Be Done?),* 1968, wax, neon, and metal. Collection of Musée Départemental d'Art Ancien et Contemporain, Épinal, France.

1968
Belgium Some 100 artists, including Broodthaers, occupy the Palais des Beaux-Arts, Brussels, for a day in May. Broodthaers stages the first "event" of his itinerant Musée d'Art Moderne, Département des Aigles, from his home in Brussels. **England** Art & Language formed in Coventry. **France** Events of May '68. Student uprisings begin in Nanterre, partially inspired by Situationist ideas. Revolt spreads to Paris, where students occupy the Sorbonne and École des Beaux-Arts. Millions join a general strike called by the trade unions. Duchamp dies in October.

1969
England First issue of *Art-Language: The Journal of Conceptual Art* published in Coventry by Art & Language. **France** De Gaulle resigns; Georges Pompidou becomes president. **Ireland** Violent encounters between Protestants and Catholics erupt into riots in Belfast and Londonderry; Bernadette Devlin, Catholic Deputy in Northern Ireland, arrested. **Italy** Extreme right groups suspected of orchestrating bloody attacks in Rome and Milan. **Switzerland** *When Attitudes Become Form: Works, Concepts, Processes, Situations, Information,* curated by Harald Szeemann, opens in Berne, introducing the works of North American and European conceptual artists; the exhibition provokes a national scandal and Szeemann is forced to resign. **West Germany** *Konzeption-Conception,* curated by Rolf Wedewer and Konrad Fischer, featuring American and European conceptual artists, opens in Leverkusen.

1970
England Gilbert & George perform *The Singing Sculpture* during a European tour. **France** First public demonstration of MLF (Movement for Women's Liberation) staged in Paris. **Ireland** Devlin imprisoned, sparking riots in Belfast. **Spain** Police round up anti-Franco Basque nationalists; six are condemned to death, then their sentences commuted to 30 years solitary confinement. **West Germany** Hanne Darboven presents work in progress, *Bücherei: Ein Jahrhundert,* at Galerie Konrad Fischer, Düsseldorf.

1971
France 343 women—including Simone de Beauvoir, Catherine Deneuve, Agnes Varda, Marguerite Duras, and Jeanne Moreau—sign and publish a declaration of women's rights in *Nouvel Observateur.* Daniel Buren's contribution to the Guggenheim International, New York, is removed by museum officials. Robert Wilson presents *Le regard du sourd* at the Theater Festival, Nancy. **Spain** Opposition founds the Assembly of Catalonia. Equipo Crónica organizes a series of exhibitions under the title *Policià y cultura.*

1972
France Situationist International disbands. 200,000 people attend the funeral of Pierre Overney, a militant Maoist killed by a guard at Renault-Billancourt. **West Germany** *Documenta 5,* curated by Harald Szeemann and Jean-Christophe Ammann, includes Giovanni Anselmo, Art & Language, Alighiero e Boetti, Broodthaers, Stanley Brouwn, Buren, Victor Burgin, Darboven, Jan Dibbets, Luciano Fabro. Broodthaers contributes the final section of Musée d'Art Moderne, Département des Aigles: in a space marked off with stanchions, a plaque reads "Private Property" in French, German, and English.

1973
France Michel Claura and René Denizot curate *Exposition de certains peintres qui mettraient la peinture en question (Exhibition of Some Painters Who Put Painting into Question).* Although Cadere is not invited to participate, he leaves a wooden bar in the space.

1974
England Coal miners' strike blacks out country and forces elections. **France** Pompidou dies; Valéry Giscard d'Estaing defeats left candidate François Mitterrand in presidential elections. **Greece** Democracy restored. **Portugal** Coup staged by liberal military officers; political prisoners released and censorship lifted. **Spain** Execution of anarchist Salvador Puig Antich provokes confrontations at universities. **West Germany** Chancellor Willy Brandt resigns in a scandal, and is replaced by Helmut Schmidt. Heinrich Böll and Joseph Beuys establish the Freie Internationale Universität in Düsseldorf.

1975
Portugal Armed confrontation begins between military and revolutionaries. **Spain** The Catalan Grup de Treball participate in Paris Biennal with a work documenting illegal newspapers in Spain. General Franco dies; all political prisoners liberated three days later.

1976
England Art & Language produces *Above Us the Waves: A Fascist Index,* a commentary on war images. **France** In anticipation of the opening of Centre Georges Pompidou, the Collectif Antifasciste propose that it be renamed the Centre La Commune or Centre Pierre Overney. **Spain** Socialist Workers Party sits in parliament for the first time since 1923. **West Germany** Ulrike Meinhof of the Red Army Fraction commits suicide in her prison cell. Beuys runs in parliamentary elections.

1977
France Official opening of the Centre National d'Art et de Culture Georges-Pompidou. **Spain** First free elections held with participation of the Communist Party; Catalonia becomes an autonomous region.

Eastern Europe

1945
World War II ends in Europe.

1946
Cold War begins. **Bulgaria** Stalinist candidate Georgi Dimitrov elected premier after his opponent is murdered.

1947
Romania People's Republic established.

1948
Marshall Plan implemented. **Czechoslovakia** Communists stage coup; popular foreign minister Jan Masaryk, son of the former president, murdered; Klement Gottwald elected premier. **Germany** Berlin Blockade begins. **Hungary** Local communists assume control, led by Mátyás Rákosi, a follower of Stalin. **Romania** Socialist realism, official style of the new republic, is imposed on artists; surrealism and other forms of avant-gardism are banned. **Yugoslavia** Soviets accuse local communists of "revisionism" and expel the country from the Cominform.

1949
Council of Mutual Economic Aid (Comecon) formed by the Soviet Union, Bulgaria, Czechoslovakia, Hungary, Poland, and Romania. **Bulgaria** Premier Georgi Dimitrov dies. **Czechoslovakia** Union of Artists established by minister of culture to promote socialist realism; avant-garde art forms dwindle under pressure. **Germany** Country divided into East and West; German Democratic Republic established. **Poland** First exhibition of 4F+R (Forma-Farba-Fantastyka-Faktura+Realism) held in Poznań; the group intends to reclaim cubism and surrealism. **Yugoslavia** Government appeals to, and receives aid from, the U.S.

1950
Yugoslavia Represented in the Venice Biennale.

1951
Yugoslavia EXAT 51 group forms in Zagreb, committed to abstraction and opposed to socialist realism.

1953
Stalin dies; Khrushchev assumes power. **German Democratic Republic** 10,000 Berliners protest industrial policy changes, demanding the resignation of first secretary Walter Ulbricht; martial law declared and Soviet tanks suppress revolt.

1954
Bulgaria Todor Zhivkov becomes premier.

1955
Warsaw Pact signed by Albania, Bulgaria, Czechoslovakia, East Germany, Hungary, Poland, Romania, and the Soviet Union. **Poland** Tadeusz Kantor founds Cricot 2, a group of avant-garde painters and poets, in Warsaw.

1956
Hungary Student demonstrations in Budapest set off Revolution. Soviet troops withdraw after several days of street fighting; Imre Nagy becomes president. Russian tanks return to crush revolt; János Kádár assumes control and remains first secretary of Hungarian Communist Party until 1988. **Poland** Riots erupt in Poznań; workers attack government buildings to protest social/economic conditions. Wladyslaw Gomulka becomes new party chief; initiates modest reforms.

1957
Hungary Soviets enact violent reprisals against participants in Revolution. **Poland** Official suppression of weekly *Po Prostu* galvanizes protests by students. Exhibition of Polish constructivists from between the wars held in Warsaw. Kantor founds Grupa Krakowska.

1958
Czechoslovakia New Tendencies exhibition held in Brno. **Hungary** Imre Nagy executed in Budapest.

1959
Czechoslovakia Smidroné group forms in Prague, inspired by nouveau réalisme. **Poland** Gallery of Contemporary Art, National Museum, Warsaw, presents exhibition of abstract and informel art. Krzysztofory Gallery opens in Cracow; first exhibition, organized by French revue *Phases,* features Western European avant-garde art. Jerzy Grotowski founds Théâtre-Laboratoire in Wroclaw. **Yugoslavia** Gorgona Group becomes active in Zagreb.

1960
Poland El Gallery opens in Elblag, the first gallery in the country dedicated to experimental art.

1961
German Democratic Republic Berlin Wall constructed. **Yugoslavia** Contemporary Art Gallery, Zagreb, presents *New Tendencies,* featuring work by Piero Manzoni, Group Zero, and other European avant-gardists.

1962
Czechoslovakia Milan Knížák stages his first action-protest in Prague, directly under the president's windows on Novy Svet. **Poland** Krzywe Kolo, an informal club for intellectual and artistic debate, opens in Warsaw.

1963
Poland Kantor organizes an anti-exhibition of 937 objects in Warsaw.

1964
Leonid Brezhnev becomes leader of the Communist Party in Moscow. **Czechoslovakia** Knížák and other artists draft the Aktual manifesto and organize various actions. **Poland** Od Nowa Gallery, an alternative space, opens in Poznań.

1965
Czechoslovakia City of Bratislava declared an artwork by Stano Filko, Alex Mlynárčik, and Zita Kostrová in their *Happsoc* manifestos. **Poland** Wspolczesna Gallery opens in Warsaw. Kantor stages his first happening, *Cricotage,* in Warsaw. **Romania** Nicolae Ceauşescu becomes president, notable throughout his political career for extreme corruption, cruelty, and exploitation of workers.

1966
Czechoslovakia Fluxus festival held in Prague. **Poland** Foksal Gallery opens in Warsaw. **Romania** State decree #770 bans abortion and contraceptives, and mandates a five-child quota per family. **Yugoslavia** Multimedia collective OHO founded in Lubljana.

1968
Czechoslovakia Alexander Dubček appointed first secretary of Czech Communist Party; initiates social/economic reforms, launching Prague Spring. Censorship lifted. Soviet and Warsaw Pact troops invade; censorship reimposed. Albania and Romania withdraw from Warsaw Pact in protest. **Hungary** Communists introduce liberal New Economic Policy.

1969
Czechoslovakia Dubček expelled from Party; "normalization" policies introduced by Jan Husák. **Hungary** *Movement* exhibition, held in Pécs, is closed by authorities.

1970
Poland Strikes and riots by workers at the Lenin Shipyards in Gdańsk leave 45 dead, killed by Polish police. Gomulka resigns, replaced by Edward Gierek.

1971
Hungary Tamás Szentjóby, Miklós Erdély, and others stage public action, *Liberty for Angela Davis,* in Budapest. **Yugoslavia** *At the Moment* exhibition in Zagreb brings together young Yugoslavian avant-garde artists—i.e., Braco Dimitrijević—and European conceptual artists.

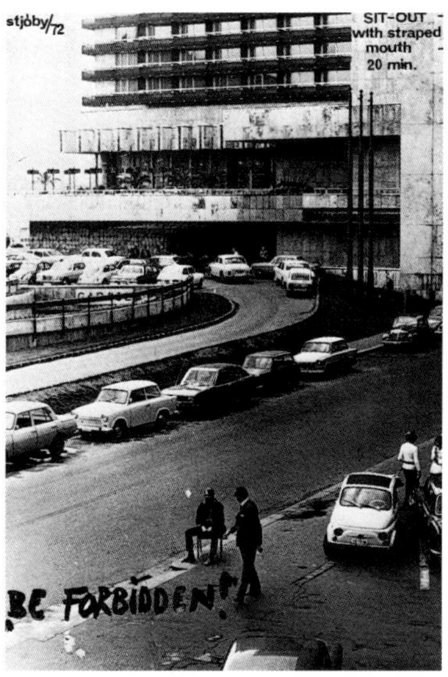

Figure 185.
Tamás Szentjóby, *Sit Out (Homage to Bobby Seale),* 1972, documentary photograph.

1973
Hungary Balatonboglár Chapel Gallery, an alternative space outside Budapest, is closed by police.

1976
Poland Workers strike in Gdańsk organized by Lech Wałęsa, who is subsequently fired from his job at Lenin Shipyards.

1977
Czechoslovakia Charter 77—drafted by Václav Havel and Jan Patočka, among others, and signed by 240 intellectuals and activists—circulates in Prague, demanding recognition of civil rights. Havel and Patočka arrested; Patočka dies as a result of police brutality. **Romania** Earthquake causes massive destruction and death. Ceauşescu grants amnesty to 19,000 political prisoners.

Director of Venice Biennale announces intention to exhibit dissident art of the Soviet Union and Eastern Europe. The Soviet ambassador to Rome protests and demands cancellation of the exhibit; director refuses, and Hungary, Poland, Czechoslovakia, and the Soviet Union boycott the 1980 Biennale.

1978
Poland Karol Cardinal Wojtyla elected Pope John Paul II.

1980
Poland Solidarnosc (Solidarity) formed after strikes led by Lech Wałęsa in Gdańsk; some 10,000 Poles join by the end of the year. **Yugoslavia** President Tito dies.

1981
Poland Lech Wałęsa arrested and Wojciech Jaruzelski declares martial law (until the end of 1982); Solidarity outlawed.

1983
Poland Lech Wałęsa receives Nobel Peace Prize. **Romania** U.S. vice-president George Bush refers to Ceauşescu as "one of Europe's good communists."

1984
Czechoslovakia Jiří Kolář's *Weekly 1968,* composed of 52 collages each devoted to a week in 1968, is exhibited at Kunsthalle Nuremberg. **Hungary** György Galántai, founder of a mail-art archive, invites artists from around the world to submit images of Hungary; director of the Budapest gallery slated to exhibit the submissions cancels the show at the last minute. **Poland** Widespread public outrage over murder of Solidarity leader Jerzy Popieluszko by security police. **Yugoslavia** IRWIN group founded in Lubljana as part of Neue Slovenische Kunst (NSK), recycling fascist, communist, folk, and kitsch imagery.

1985
Gorbachev implements *perestroika* (restructuring) and *glasnost* (openness) policies in the Soviet Union.

1986
Hungary The Inconnu art group launches *The Fighting City* in Budapest, inviting Hungarian and foreign artists to submit mementos of the 1956 Revolution. An exhibition of the items is held in the apartment of Inconnu member Tibor Philipp, with the official notice of intention to confiscate works hung prominently on the wall. **Poland** Jaruzelski releases 13,000 political prisoners but refuses to recognize Solidarity.

1987
Romania Workers storm Party headquarters to protest mass starvation caused by Ceauşescu's brutal economic policies.

1988
Czechoslovakia Twentieth anniversary of Prague Spring and aftermath remembered in thousands of events. **Hungary** Communists and opposition alike commemorate 1956 Revolution. Young Democrats Party founded by students. **Poland** Károly Grósz replaces János Kádár as first secretary of the Polish Communist Party. Solidarity legalized. **Yugoslavia** A million Serbs demonstrate in Belgrade against independence of Kosovo.

1989
Beginning of political changes in Czechoslovakia, Hungary, Poland, and other socialist countries. Fighting between Albanians and Serbs begins in Yugoslavia (March); Croatian Democratic Party formed. Imre Nagy and other martyrs of the Hungarian Revolution reburied in an official ceremony (June). Solidarity defeats the communists in the first free elections since 1949 (June). Hungary opens border with Austria (September). Berlin Wall demolished (November). Four-fifths of the Czech labor force strikes; Velvet Revolution wins in Prague (November 17–29). Sympathy demonstrations for László Tökés in Timişoara, Romania, lead to widespread pro-democracy demonstrations; hundreds of protestors are killed by police; deposed Romanian president Ceauşescu and wife executed (December). Václav Havel becomes president of Czechoslovakia (December 29).

1990
Gorbachev receives Nobel Peace Prize. **Bulgaria** Former premier Todor Zhivkov arrested. **Germany** East and West unite. **Hungary** Soviet troops withdraw. **Poland** Lech Wałęsa elected president. **Yugoslavia** Federation begins to collapse.

1991
Yugoslavia Slovenia and Croatia proclaim independence. Confrontations between Serbs and other groups escalate.

1993
Czechoslovakia Splits into Czech Republic and Slovak Republic. Czech Republic bans abortion. **Poland** Abortion banned.

1994
First McDonald's in Eastern Europe opens in Varna, Bulgaria.

Latin America

1948
Colombia Beginning of La Violencia, a period of civil war centered around the political struggle between the Liberal and Conservative parties.

1951
Brazil First Bienal de São Paulo held.

1955
Argentina Juan Perón ousted by military.

1956
Brazil Haroldo do Campos founds the concrete poetry movement.

1958
Argentina Frondizi becomes president; country experiences short-term economic expansion, modernization, and accelerated inflation. **Brazil** First nuclear reactor in Latin America begins operation. **Colombia** La Violencia ends; national accord between Liberals and Conservatives gives country a measure of consensus and stability. **Venezuela** U.S. vice-president Richard Nixon's motorcade attacked during a goodwill tour.

1959
Argentina Informalist movement founded in Buenos Aires by Alberto Greco and others. **Brazil** *Manifesto neoconcreto* and *I Exposição de arte neoconcretã* held at Museu de Arte Moderna, Rio de Janeiro. Ferreira Gullar's "Teoría do não-objeto," which launches the neoconcrete movement, published in *Jornal do Brasil,* Rio de Janeiro. **Cuba** Revolution propels Fidel Castro to power.

1960
Argentina Instituto Torcuato di Tella founded in Buenos Aires. **Brazil** Inauguration of Brasilia as new capital, designed by Lúcio Costa and Oscar Niemeyer. **Mexico** David Alfaro Siqueiros imprisoned for criticizing government policies. **Venezuela** Joins Saudi Arabia, Iran, Iraq, and Kuwait to form OPEC.

1961
U.S. and Latin American countries join in the Alliance for Progress, primarily a vehicle for suppressing communist activities. **Argentina** Experiences economic and political instability. **Mexico** Exhibition of Los Hartos (the "Fed-Ups") organized in Mexico City. **Venezuela** El Techo de la Ballena founded.

1962
Argentina Frondizi ousted by military. **Colombia** Museo de Arte Moderno founded in Bogotá. **Peru** Military coup deposes Prado Ugarte.

1963
Argentina Confrontation between "Blues" and "Reds"; proscription of Peronismo; Illia becomes president. Jorge Romero Brest named director of the Centro de Artes Visuales in Buenos Aires; remains in post until 1969. **Peru** Belaunde Terry elected president. **Uruguay** Tupamaro guerrilla group organizes.

1964
Brazil Military coup deposes João Goulart; General Castelo Branco elected president. Ferreira Gullar's *Cultural posta em questão* censored by the military. **Venezuela** At the 10th Inter-American Conference, the U.S. sponsors a resolution banning communism in the Western Hemisphere; Latin American nations call for an end to colonialism in the Americas (U.S. abstains).

1966
Argentina Military assumes power, deposes Illia; urban guerrillas organize. Controversial *Homenaje a Vietnam,* a group show in Buenos Aires, signals the beginning of artists' politicization. Roberto Jacoby organizes Week of Happenings at Instituto di Tella. **Brazil** Eduardo Costa, Roberto Jacoby, and Raúl Escari circulate manifesto, *Un arte de los medios de comunicación,* in Buenos Aires.

1967
Argentina Experiencias 67 at Instituto di Tella showcases work by some conceptual artists. **Bolivia** Che Guevara dies. **Brazil** Exhibition *Nova objetividade brasileira,* Museu de Arte Moderna, Rio de Janeiro, serves to coalesce radical artistic avant-garde; exhibition preceded by a declaration of avant-garde principles signed by more than 15 artists.

1968
Argentina Mass-mediatic collective action Tucumán Arde staged November 1–15 in Rosario and November 25 in Buenos Aires. León Ferrari publishes *El arte de los significados* for the event. Experiencias 68 at Instituto di Tella presents cutting-edge work by conceptual artists; exhibition shut down by police. **Brazil** Coup within a coup; Congress dissolved; series of Institutional Acts passed which modify (and ultimately abolish) the Constitution, thereby giving the state unlimited power. *Apocalipopótese,* a public event (happening) organized by Hélio Oiticica, presents a variety of avant-garde manifestations. **Mexico** Students massacred by military during protest at Tlatelolco Square, Mexico City. **Peru** Velasco Alvarado takes power through a military coup.

1969
Argentina Popular insurrection known as El Cordobazo. Centro de Arte y Comunicación established in Buenos Aires. **Brazil** Military government passes Institutional Act No. 5, the most severe and repressive of the reform acts. Brazilian contributions to the 6th Paris Biennal censored by authorities; Mário Pedrosa, president of the Brazilian Association (of art critics) condemns the action and calls for a boycott of the 10th Bienal de São Paulo. Frederico Morais, Cildo Meireles, and others establish Unidade Experimental at Museu de Arte Moderna, Rio de Janeiro. *Salão da bússola* held at MAM. **Uruguay** Social tension, strikes, and attacks by urban guerrillas precipitate declaration of martial law.

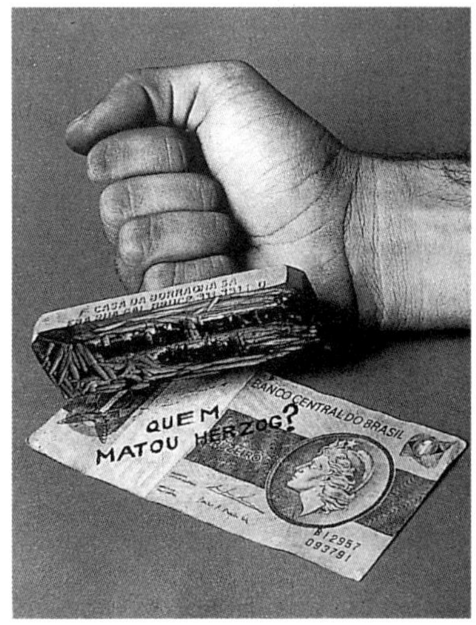

FIGURE 186.
Cildo Meireles, *Inserções em circuitos ideológicos: Proyecto cedula (Insertions into Ideological Circuits: Banknote Project [Who Killed Herzog?]),* 1973, stamped paper currency. Collection of the artist.

1970
Argentina Massacre of Trelew. Instituto Torcuato di Tella closes. **Brazil** Frederico Morais organizes *Investigation on the Nature, Meaning, and Function of Works of Art* at Galería IBEU, Rio de Janeiro, the first official exhibition of conceptual art in Brazil. *Do corpo à terra* opens in Rio. **Chile** Salvador Allende elected president, instituting radical reforms, including the nationalization of industry.

1973
Argentina Peronist restoration results in extreme repression. **Chile** Allende deposed and murdered by military, with U.S. assistance; country enters a period of bloody repression under General Augusto Pinochet, resulting in thousands of tortured, murdered, or "disappeared" civilians, and the introduction of "free-market" reforms. **Colombia** *Arte y política* opens at Museo de Arte Moderno, Bogotá. **Mexico** Peyote y la Compañía and Tepito Arte Acá, the first of Los Grupos, founded in Mexico City.

1975
Brazil Avant-garde artist-run review *Malasartes* launched in Rio de Janeiro.

1976
Argentina Military coup led by General Videla; repression intensifies, leading to thousands of tortured, murdered, or disappeared civilians.

Mexico Los Grupos come together (including Suma, Mira, Proceso Pentágono, and Taller de Arte e Ideología).

1978
Brazil Núcleo de Arte Contemporânea founded in Paraíba by Antonio Dias. **Mexico** Mexican Front of Cultural Workers (Frente de Grupos Trabajadores de la Cultura) constituted by broad coalition of Los Grupos.

1981
Colombia *Primer coloquio Latinoamericano de arte no-objetual y arte urbano* (The First Latin American Colloquium of Non-Object-Based and Urban Art), accompanied by an exhibition, held at Museo de Arte Moderno in Medellín.

1982
Mexico Fiscal collapse triggers the debt crisis in Latin America.

1983
Argentina Democracy restored under Raúl Alfonsín.

1985
Argentina Military generals responsible for reign of terror during 1976–82 sentenced to prison for violations of human rights.

1989
Chile Democracy restored.

North America

1966
Martin Luther King launches Chicago campaign to unionize ghetto dwellers against exploitive landlords. King comes out against the Vietnam War. Black Panther Party forms in Oakland, California. National Organization for Women founded. Andy Warhol makes *Chelsea Girls*.

January On Kawara produces first date painting. Yoko Ono gives a lecture at Wesleyan University in which she explains that the aim of her *Instruction Paintings* is to create "painting to construct in your head." Iain and Ingrid Baxter form N. E. Thing Company in Vancouver, B.C. **May** *Art in Process: The Visual Development of a Structure* organized by Elayne Varian at Finch College Museum of Art, New York. Joseph Kosuth and Christine Kozlov speak on the subject of "Ad Reinhardt: Evolution into Darkness" at the School of Visual Arts, New York.

1967
Martin Luther King launches Poor People's Campaign. Black uprising in Detroit. New York Radical Women founded, the first women's liberation group in the city. Summer of Love in San Francisco. Siege of the Pentagon.

February *Non-Anthropomorphic Art by Four Young Artists* held at Lannis Gallery, New York. Dan Graham publishes "Muybridge Moments" in *Arts Magazine*. **April** *One Set of Nine Pieces,* an exhibition of work by Sol LeWitt, held at Dwan Gallery, Los Angeles. **May** *Fifteen People Present Their Favorite Book* organized by Kosuth at Lannis Gallery, New York. Michael Snow completes his film *Wavelength*. **June** *Language to Be Looked At and/or Things to Be Read* held at Dwan Gallery, New York. LeWitt publishes "Paragraphs on Conceptual Art" in *Artforum*. Robert Barry travels to Baltimore throughout the summer; two years later, in 1969, he produces *Psychic Series,* which he defines as follows: "Everything in the unconscious perceived by the senses but not noted by the conscious mind during trips to Baltimore during the summer of 1967." **November** *Normal Art* organized by Kosuth at Museum of Normal Art, New York. *Art in Series* organized by Elayne Varian and Mel Bochner at Finch College Museum of Art, New York.

1968
Tet Offensive in Vietnam. Prague Spring in Czechoslovakia, suppressed by Soviet invasion. May '68 events in Paris. Worldwide student uprisings. Student revolt at Columbia University, New York. Martin Luther King and Robert Kennedy assassinated. Street fighting outside the Democratic Party Convention in Chicago. Richard Nixon defeats progressive candidate George McGovern in U.S. presidential elections; Liberal Party leader Pierre Trudeau becomes prime minister of Canada. Jean-Luc Godard's *Le gai savoir* and Stanley Kubrick's *2001: A Space Odyssey* released.

February Exhibition organized by Seth Siegelaub at Bradford Junior College (Bradford, Mass.). Kozlov begins *271 Blank Sheets of Paper,* a work in which each sheet represents a day that an art concept is rejected. Exhibition of *Portfolio of Piles* by N. E. Thing Company opens at Fine Art Gallery, Vancouver, featuring piles of dirt, chains, doughnuts, barrels, etc. Lucy Lippard and John Chandler publish "The Dematerialization of Art" in *Art International*. **May** *Language II* held at Dwan Gallery, New York. Art & Language (U.K.) contest Lippard and Chandler's concept of "matter" in a letter to *Art International*. **July** On Kawara begins series of *I Met* and *I Went* notebooks, typing out lists of every person he meets each day and making a mapped record of all his movements. **October** John Baldessari exhibits paintings executed by a sign painter at Molly Barnes Gallery, Los Angeles, bearing texts such as "A Painting That Is Its Own Documentation." **December** *Xeroxbook* exhibition organized by Siegelaub. Kosuth publishes *Titled (Art as Idea as Idea)* in five London newspapers.

1969
Woodstock and Altamont music festivals. Trial of the Chicago Eight. Radical feminist group Redstockings founded by Ellen Willis and Shulamith Firestone, as a breakaway from New York Radical Women. Michael Graves designs Benaceraf House addition, Princeton. Dennis Hopper's *Easy Rider* and Ken Jacobs's *Tom, Tom, the Piper's Son* released.

January *O Objects, O Paintings, O Sculptures* held in rented office space at 44 East 52nd Street, New York, organized by Siegelaub, with work by Barry, Douglas Huebler, Kosuth, and Lawrence Weiner. Four interviews by Arthur Rose, in which he discusses the show with the four artists involved, are published in *Arts Magazine* (February 1969). "Arthur Rose" is subsequently exposed as a fiction and the texts themselves are widely assumed to have been invented. LeWitt publishes "Sentences on Conceptual Art" in *0–9*, New York. Adrian Piper produces a series of booklets for the same press, based on maps of New York City and squares drawn on graph paper. Meetings held at the Chelsea Hotel, New York, lead to the founding of Art Workers Coalition; among those present are Carl Andre, Hans Haacke and Lucy Lippard. Image Bank founded in Vancouver, B.C., by Michael Morris and Vincent Trasov. **February** Lee Lozano creates *General Strike Piece,* in the form of an instruction to herself beginning: "Gradually but determinedly avoid being present at official or public 'uptown' functions or gatherings related to the 'art world' in order to pursue investigation of total personal and public revolution." **March** *One Month* exhibition, held at various sites around the world, organized by Siegelaub; Kozlov contributes *Information No Theory*. Exhibition of Robert Huot's work at Paula Cooper Gallery, New York, takes the form of a catalogue documenting site-specific works made in nongallery settings. "It was anti-the power structure; it was trying to take art away from places where it was bought and sold like so much official meat. When the people left the places where I did these pieces, the work stayed there and was painted out, or destroyed or whatever." **April** *Invisible Painting and Sculpture,* exhibition at Richmond Art Center (Richmond, Calif.), organized by Tom Marioni with work by several Bay Area artists. *The Appearing/Disappearing Image/Object* held at Newport Harbor Museum (Newport Harbor, Calif.). LeWitt, active in Art Workers Coalition, makes two public statements on the relationship between works of art, museums (specifically, the Museum of Modern Art, New York), collectors, and the general community. **May** Exhibition organized by Siegelaub at Simon Fraser University, Vancouver, B.C. **July** *Conception-Perception* opens at Eugenia Butler Gallery, Los Angeles. *July, August, September 1969,* held at various venues around the world, organized by Siegelaub. **September** *557,087,*

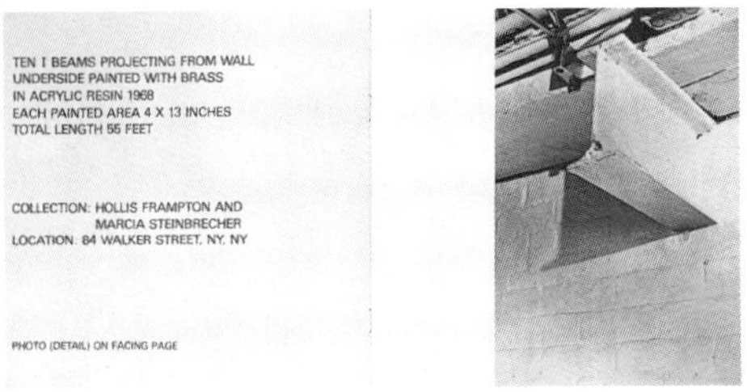

FIGURE 187.
Robert Huot, *Robert Huot at Paula Cooper* (exhibition catalogue), March–April 1969, page spread from offset catalogue, printed in black. The Museum of Modern Art Library, New York.

organized by Lippard at Seattle Art Museum, travels to Vancouver Art Museum in modified form as *955,000;* includes films by Barry, Hollis Frampton, Huot, George Landow, Paul Sharits, Snow, Joyce Wieland, and others. General Idea begins storefront exhibitions in Toronto. **October** The Museum of Modern Art, Whitney Museum, and Jewish Museum, together with many private galleries, close to mark Moratorium Day in protest against the Vietnam War. The Metropolitan Museum and Guggenheim remain open and are picketed by Art Workers Coalition. **November** *Art by Telephone* organized by the Museum of Contemporary Art, Chicago, a catalogue exhibition consisting of a 12-inch LP containing artists' telephoned statements and performances. On Kawara sends *I Got Up* postcards to Lippard every day for a month, recording the time he gets out of bed each morning. *Stolen Painting* by Shusaku Arakawa, inscribed IF POSSIBLE STEAL ANY ONE OF THESE DRAWINGS INCLUDING THIS SENTENCE, is stolen from Dwan Gallery, New York. The action is subsequently documented in *Stolen,* an artist's book prepared by the culprits, who describe the theft and return of the work, and designate their action as art in its own right. **December** Yoko Ono and John Lennon display a billboard poster in twelve cities worldwide, reading "WAR IS OVER IF YOU WANT IT. Happy Christmas from John & Yoko," in the appropriate language. Fliers are also printed with the same message. On Kawara sends his first telegram work.

1970
Kate Millett's *Sexual Politics* published. American troops invade Cambodia. Students shot dead at Kent State University. Workers strike in Gdańsk, Poland. Faith Ringgold names a section of the Museum of Modern Art the Martin Luther King Wing, dedicated to work by black artists. Robert Morris leads the Art Strike protest against the Venice Biennale's selection of all-male, all white artists (and the U.S. invasion of Cambodia). Article on conceptual art published in *Harper's Bazaar.* Peter Eisenman designs House III in Lakeville, Connecticut. Morgan Fisher releases *Production Stills.*

Yoko Ono's collected works published in the U.S. under the title *Grapefruit;* front leaf is inscribed, "Burn this book after you've read it—YOKO," and the back, "This is the greatest book I've ever burned—JOHN." Mary Kelly joins the Berwick Street Collective in London and begins work on their documentary film, *Nightcleaners,* a record of attempts to unionize women working as office cleaners. Lippard writes her novel, *I See/You Mean.* **February** Tom Marioni founds the Museum of Conceptual Art in San Francisco. **April** *Conceptual Art and Conceptual Aspects* held at New York Cultural Center. Weiner publishes statement in *Arts Magazine,* reading: "1. The artist may construct the piece. 2. The piece may be fabricated. 3. The piece need not be built. Each being equal and consistent with the intention of the artist, the decision as to condition rests with the receiver upon the occasion of receivership." **July** *Information* opens at the Museum of Modern Art, New York; Piper contributes a series of notebooks, *Context #7,* in which visitors to the exhibition are asked to make drawn or written responses to their situation as museumgoers. *Cremation Project, July 24, 1970,* a work by Baldessari, consists of the remains and notarized documentation of the cremation of all works of art produced by him between May 1953 and March 1966; affidavit to that effect published in the San Diego press, July 24, 1970. Siegelaub edits a special edition of *Studio International* with contributions by North American and European conceptual artists. **September** *Software: Information Technology: Its Meaning For Art* opens at the Jewish Museum, New York. Huebler exhibits *Variable Piece No. 4,* a participatory work involving visitors to the museum; participants' contributions are subsequently published in *Variable Piece 4: Secrets* by Printed Matter, New York, an artist-run press. Baldessari exhibits the photo-album and plaque from *Cremation Project.* **October** The Halifax Conference, organized by Siegelaub with artists from the U.S., Canada, and Western Europe, devolves into a pitched battle between the Americans and non-Americans. **November** Eleanor Antin exhibits "portraits" of *Four New York Women,* which take the form of objects, texts, or photographs with text, according to circumstances. **December** *2,972,453* held in Buenos Aires, then travels to Montevideo in May 1971; organized by Lippard as an unofficial continuation of *557,087* and *955,000,* with work by Antin and several others drawn from a wide variety of backgrounds.

1971
Attica Prison uprising. Publication of *This,* the first journal of "language writing." Ihab Hassan includes conceptualism in his essay "POSTmodernISM" *(New Literary History).*

January Lisson Gallery, London, holds *Wall Show,* with LeWitt and Weiner. **April** Antin produces *Library Science,* a nonexhibited work subsequently documented in *American Librarian* (February 1972). **May** Guggenheim Museum, New York, cancels Hans Haacke's solo exhibition as a result of objections to works such as *Shapolsky et al. Manhattan Real Estate Holdings: A Real-Time Social System, as of May 1, 1971.* Visitors' questionnaire prepared by Haacke for this exhibition subsequently used for a solo show in Milwaukee. **September** *1971 Miss General Idea Pageant* is staged at the Art Gallery of Ontario, Toronto, with a program based on the 1930s Folies Bergères.

1972
Watergate burglary. Richard Nixon elected president for a second term.

Boundary 2: Journal of Postmodern Literature and Culture launched in Binghamton, New York, a crucial event for the introduction of the concept of postmodernism into cultural discourse. Leo Steinberg discusses "postmodernist painting" in his book, *Other Criteria,* citing Robert Rauschenberg's "all-purpose picture plane" as the basis for new developments in art. *Conceptual Art* by Ursula Meyer and *Textes sur l' art conceptuel* by Catherine Millet published. *Womanhouse* exhibition held at California Institute of the Arts, Valencia. Mary Kelly elected first chair of the Artist's Union in England. Yvonne Rainer makes *Lives of Performers.* First issue of *FILE Megazine* published in Toronto. Joyce Wieland and Michael Snow, among others, participate in protest against hiring of an American as chief curator of the Art Gallery of Ontario, Toronto. Gronk and Harry Gamboa, Jr. sign the Los Angeles County Museum of Art with spraypaint, thus appropriating the museum in its entirety as a Chicano artwork, after their original proposal for representation of Chicano artists is rejected.

1973
Paris agreement to end the Vietnam War is signed. U.S. Supreme Court decision in *Roe v. Wade* grants women the right to abortion. Danièle Huillet and Jean-Marie Straub produce *History Lessons.*

Western Front founded in Vancouver, B.C., by Vincent Trasov and others as a center for performance, video, music, etc. Press of the Nova Scotia College of Art and Design established with the publication of *The Architecture of Ludwig Wittgenstein.* General Idea launches Art Metropole in Toronto with an extensive archive of Fluxus, conceptual, performance, correspondence, and other art materials. Exhibition of conceptual art by women artists, *C. 7,500*, organized by Lippard at California Institute of the Arts, Valencia. Lippard publishes *Six Years: The Dematerialization of the Art Object.* Mary Kelly begins *Post-Partum Document.* Kosuth delivers "Statement for the Congress of Conceptual Art" in Belgium. *Idea Art,* edited by Gregory Battcock, brings together texts by Bochner, Kosuth, LeWitt, Lippard, "Arthur Rose," Siegelaub, Weiner, and others.

1974
Following the Watergate hearings, Richard Nixon resigns the presidency.

Mr. Peanut (Vincent Trasov) runs for mayor of Vancouver, B.C., on the Peanut Party platform. Antin's "Autobiography of the Artist as an Autobiographer" appears in *Journal,* Los Angeles. LeWitt begins *Location* series: *The Location of a Circle, The Location of a Square,* etc.

1975
Fall of Saigon. American withdrawal from Indochina begins. Tom Wolfe's *The Painted Word* published. Chantal Akerman's film *Jeanne Dielmann 23 Quai du Commerce* and Jon Jost's *Speaking Directly* released.

First of three issues of *The Fox* published in New York, with contributions from Sarah Charlesworth, Kosuth, Piper, Carol Condé and Karl Beveridge, Martha Rosler, Ian Burn, and Kozlov. Dialogue between Carl Andre and Hollis Frampton published in *Interfunktionen* (Cologne). Three issues of *Vision* published in Oakland, California, with essays by Tom Marioni and contributions from Andre, Antin, Michael Asher, Barry, Haacke, Les Levine, LeWitt, Allen Ruppersberg, Weiner, and others. *Hans Haacke: Framing and Being Framed,* published by the Nova Scotia College of Art and Design, Halifax.

Australia and New Zealand

1965
Australia supports the U.S. by sending troops to South Vietnam. Forty percent of the Australian population is under 20.

1966
Prime Minister Menzies retires after 16 years of leadership, the longest of any single political leader in Australia. White Australia policy abandoned.

1967
Referendum gives Aborigines voting rights. Australian immigration level reaches 2 million, total population approximately 10 million.

Two Decades of American Art, organized by MoMA, New York, tours Australia. The terms *conceptual* and *funk* popularized.

1968
The Australian Council for the Arts makes its first grants. *The Field* exhibition is staged for the opening of the National Gallery of Victoria, Melbourne, introducing color field and hard-edge painting and sculpture to the Australian public. The Power Institute, University of Sydney, begins teaching, collecting, and exhibiting contemporary art.

1969
First women's liberation groups form in Sydney and Adelaide. Arbitration court approves equal pay for equal work.

Three Trends in Contemporary French Art opens at the National Gallery of Victoria. Christo's *Wrapped Coast, Little Bay, Australia* covers a quarter-mile of the Sydney harbor shoreline in polypropylene fabric/rope. Billy Apple opens Apple Gallery in New York.

1970
Antiwar demonstrations. The term "Green Bans" invented by Jack Mundey, leader of the Builders Labourers' Federation, in support of conservation of heritage sites from redevelopment by unions.

Recent British Painting tours Australian state galleries. Mike Parr and Peter Kennedy form cooperative gallery Inhibodress in Sydney. Philip Dadson founds New Zealand Scratch Orchestra in Auckland. Ian Burn publishes the influential article "Conceptual Art as Art" in *Art and Australia* (Sydney).

1971
South Africa's Springboks rugby team plays Victoria in Melbourne, setting off anti-apartheid demonstrations that escalate into riots. Australia begins withdrawal of troops from Vietnam. The push for Aboriginal land rights begins.

The Situation Now: Object or Post-Object Art? held at the Contemporary Art Society, Sydney. Harald Szeemann organizes *I want to leave a nice welldone child here (20 Australian Artists)* in Sydney and Melbourne.

1972
Labor government returns after 23 years of Liberal/Country party coalition rule in Australia. Gough Whitlam elected prime minister, beginning a period of social democracy and encouragement of the arts. Labor Party wins landslide victory in New Zealand.

1973
Cease-fire declared in Vietnam.

Sydney Opera House opens after fifteen years of troubled construction. First Sydney Biennale held. *Object and Idea* exhibition mounted at the National Gallery of Australia, Canberra. Auckland Filmmakers Co-op founded.

1974
Economic crisis in Australia and New Zealand causes inflation and unemployment. Thousands of New Zealanders emigrate to Australia.

Australia's federal budget allocates $30,000,000 for the arts, more than the state grant to the arts in Britain.

1975
Political deadlock and constitutional crisis result in sacking of the Whitlam government. National Party returns to power in New Zealand.

Provisional Art & Language exhibitions held in Melbourne, Adelaide, and Auckland (carrying over into 1976).

Soviet Union

1953
Stalin dies.

1954
Khruschev becomes general secretary of the Central Committee of the Communist Party. Ilya Erenburg publishes *The Thaw,* in which he compares talentless official artists with those who would not submit to Party rule; title of book comes to define the period of "destalinization."

1956
Central Committee issues decree, "On the Overthrow of the Cult of Personality and Its Consequences." Khruschev denounces Stalin's crimes at the 20th Party Congress. Soviet troops suppress popular uprising against communist government in Hungary.

Picasso show opens in Moscow. First examples of unofficial, nonconformist, or alternative art are recorded.

1957
Sputnik, the first satellite, launched.

International Exposition of Visual and Applied Art, held in Moscow's Gorkii

Park, features numerous Soviet and Western artists. Young Soviet artists—including Ivan Chuikov, Oskar Rabin, and Eric Bulatov—exhibit in the Sixth World Festival of Youth and Students, Moscow. Al'fred Shnitke composes his first violin concerto.

1958
Belutin Studio founded by Eli Belutin. Avant-garde composer Sonia Gubaidulina writes her first symphony.

1959
Khruschev visits the U.S.

First exhibitions of nonconformist art organized in the apartment of composer Andrei Volkonskii and collector Georgii Kostakis. Nonconformist artists begin to sell works to Westerners who visit the Soviet Union. First samizdat publications of previously forbidden poetry appear. USIA organizes an exhibition of abstract expressionism (Pollock, Rothko, de Kooning, etc.) in Sokolniki, stirring debate among intellectuals and bureaucrats.

1960
Exhibition of British art (1700–1960) held at the State Pushkin Museum, Moscow. Writer Yurii Mamleev initiates a salon in Yuzhinskii Lane which, in its bohemian activities, is reminiscent of American beat culture of the '50s. Sretenskii Bul'var group formed by Kabakov, Bulatov, Yurii Sobolev, and others.

1961
Soviet cosmonaut Yurii Gagarin is launched into space. Sino-Soviet split: Communist China publicly breaks with the Soviet Union.

Artists of the Belutin Studio exhibit at Café Molodezhnoe. Rock groups are allowed to perform.

1962
Solzhenitsyn publishes in the magazine *Novyi Mir.* Symposium on structuralist analysis held at the Academy of Science. Exhibitions of Kazimir Malevich and Vladimir Tatlin open at Mayakovsky Museum. Mikhail Chernyshov organizes *Red Truck (Krasnyi gruzovik),* featuring the first examples of Soviet pop art. Movement (Dvizhenie) group revives Soviet avant-garde traditions, including design of public interiors and outdoor performances. Unofficial art receives coverage in *Studio International. Thirty Years of the Moscow Union of Artists* opens at the Manezh; Khruschev denounces unofficial works exhibited there as anti-Soviet.

1963
Lianozovskaiia group formed by Rabin, Lev Kropivnitskii, and others.

1964
Khruschev suspended; Leonid Brezhnev becomes general secretary of the Central Committee of the Communist Party.

Literary salon forms at the apartment of Alena Basilova in Moscow. A number of scientific research institutes sponsor brief exhibits of nonconformist art. Rabin's apartment becomes a gathering place for artists and foreign visitors.

1965
Group of poets found SMOG (Union of Young Geniuses). Komar and Melamid become the team K/M and produce their first work, *Composition with Russian Medals.*

1966
Writers Andrei Siniavskii and Yurii Daniel condemned to five years house arrest for publishing work critical of the Soviet Union with a foreign press.

Studio for experimental electronic music opens in Moscow. House of Architects, Leningrad, sponsors an exhibition of kinetic art. Edison Denisov performs avant-garde music at the House of Composers, Moscow, and Leningrad Conservatory.

1967
Nonconformist artists exhibit at Klub Druzhba; the show is closed within two hours.

1968
Soviet tanks suppress reformist government of Alexander Dubček in Czechoslovakia; Soviet dissidents protest the invasion in Red Square. Brezhnev Doctrine prohibits communist regimes in Eastern and Central Europe from making significant political changes without approval from Moscow.

Francisco Infante and Nonna Gorunova stage *Forest Ritual* in the countryside near Moscow. Café Siniaia Ptitsa (Bluebird) holds one-night exhibitions of Bulatov and Kabakov. K/M exhibit at Akademgorodok (near Moscow). Mayakovsky Museum organizes shows of Olga Rozanova and Marc Chagal.

1969
State Pushkin Museum organizes Matisse show.

1970
Solzhenitsyn receives Nobel Prize for literature.

Kabakov begins *Answers of the Experimental Group.* Victor Pivovarov makes his first drawings accompanied by text, influenced by his designs for children's books. Group Argo founded by Infante.

1971
Duke Ellington performs in the Soviet Union.

1972
Kabakov begins his series of albums united under the title *Ten Characters (Desiat' personazhei).* K/M produce the first examples of sots art, which in their work often borders on conceptualism.

1973
K/M create their first installation, *Paradise (Rai),* in an apartment, and stage a performance based on the installation's narrative.

1974
Solzhenitzyn expelled from country.

Bulatov paints *Entrance–No Entrance (Vkhod–Vkhoda net),* consisting solely of words. Rimma Gerlovina makes a series of "cubes" *(kubiki),* three-dimensional structures filled with random phrases. Nikita Alekseev, a future member of Collective Actions Group, produces his first conceptual works. On September 15, unofficial artists, including K/M, organize an outdoor exhibition at which they and their works are assaulted with waterhoses and bulldozers, hence the title *Bulldozer Show.* The action generates international criticism, and on September 29 authorities allow unofficial artists to exhibit in Moscow's Izmailovskii Park. Some participants are later threatened with psychiatric hospitalization or enforced military service.

1975
K/M produce *Documents: Ideal Document.* Andrei Monastyrskii constructs a series of objects united under the title *Elementary Poetry (Elementarnaia poeziia).* Kabakov begins to present *Ten Characters* in his studio. Chernyshov and his group Red Star (Krasnaia Zvezda) give their first performance. Nest (Gnezdo) group, consisting of Mikhail Roshal', Victor Skersis, and Gennadii Donskoi, stage their first performance during an exhibition of Soviet nonconformist art at the Pavilion of the Bee Industry in VDNKh, Moscow.

1976
Major nonconformist artists are accommodated within an official organization, MOKKhG (Moscow Joint Committee of Graphic Artists). K/M produce *Music "Passport."* Leonid Sokov and Aleksandr Kosolapov make their first sots art pieces with conceptual features. Collective Actions Group present their first performance, *Appearance,* in Izmailovskii Park; poet Lev Rubenshtein participates. Kabakov begins *Kitchen Series (Kukhonnaia seriia),* in which he attaches kitchen objects to green-painted plywood.

K/M mount their first solo exhibition at Ronald Feldman Gallery, New York. Infante begins a series of performances called *Life of Triangle (Zhizn' treugol'nika)*. Exhibition of conceptual and sots art held at Leonid Sokov studio. Artist Evgenii Rukhin, who throughout the 1970s served as a link between Moscow and Leningrad nonconformist art communities, dies in a suspicious fire in his studio.

1977
Dmitrii Prigov makes graphic works based on the visual manipulation of popular Soviet texts and slogans. Rimma and Valerii Gerlovin stage a series of performances, including *Happening, Discussion (Beseda),* and *Quiz (Viktorina)*. K/M emigrate to Israel. Chuikov produces a series called *Panorama,* free-standing boxes with a painted view of a communal kitchen, and *Virtual Sculptures (Virtual'nye skul'pturi),* drawings made in the corners of his and friends' studios.

1978
Soviet Union invades Afghanistan to bolster a communist regime against an anticommunist insurgency.

Infante stages *Winter Masks (Zimnie maski)*. Igor Makarevich, future member of Collective Actions Group, makes his first conceptual works. A second generation of Soviet conceptualists emerge, including the group Toadstools (Mukhomory), Yurii Al'bert, Vadim Zakharov, and Igor and Svetlana Kopystianskii (L'vov). K/M move from Israel to New York. From the U.S., critic Victor Tupitsyn begins a regular correspondence with Andrei Monastyrskii, establishing a crucial channel of cultural networking for both Russian art communities.

1979
Natalia Abalakova and Anatolii Zhigalov begin series *Total Art (Totart)*. First issue of *A-Ya* published in Paris; becomes the mouthpiece for Soviet conceptual art. *Color Form Space,* organized by Vladimir Nemukhin, opens at MOKKhG, Moscow, with work by Kabakov, Infante, and others.

1980
Young Olympics in Moscow boycotted by 56 countries in protest against the Soviet invasion of Afghanistan.

Moscow conceptualists compile *MANI* (Moscow Archive of New Art), the first collection of materials covering their activities. Eventually three more editions are issued. First volume of *Trips to the Countryside* compiled.

1981
Boris Pasternak forbidden from going to Sweden to receive Nobel prize.

Moscou-Paris opens in Moscow, the first exhibition of the historical Russian avant-garde since before the war. *Russian New Wave,* curated by Margarita Tupitsyn, opens in New York at the Contemporary Russian Art Center, featuring work by Collective Actions, Kabakov, Pivovarov, K/M, the Gerlovins, and others. Sixty-one Leningrad nonconformist artists prepare the largest apartment exhibition in the city's history.

1982
Brezhnev dies and is replaced by former KGB chief Yurii Andropov.

Pivovarov leaves for Prague. Kabakov travels to Czechoslovakia and after his return writes an essay "About Emptiness" (O pustote). First exhibition of apt-art (i.e., apartment art) held in Alekseev's Moscow apartment. New conceptual artists such as Sergei Anufriev (Odessa), Victor Skersis, Larisa Rezun-Zvezdochetova (Odessa), Pertsy (Odessa), and Vladimir Kupriianov exhibit. Apt-Art Gallery is forced to close by the KGB. In Kharkov, Boris Mikhailov produces photographs (portraits and landscapes) juxtaposed with a variety of handwritten texts. Timur Novikov founds New Artist group in Leningrad, bringing together visual arts, music, theater, and film.

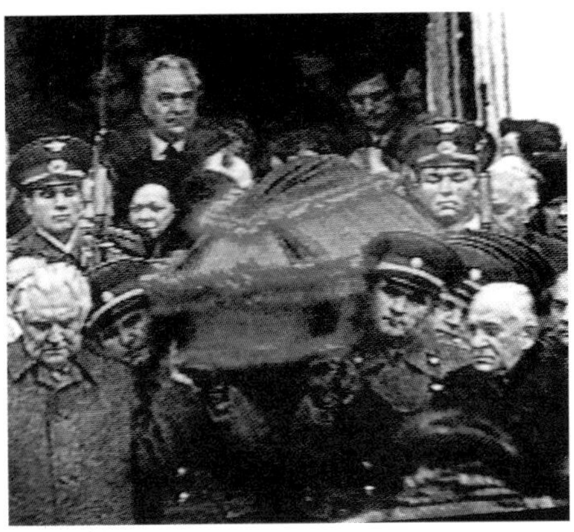

Figure 188.
Józef Robakowski, *In Memory of L. Brezhnev,* 1982, videotape, 10 min. Collection of the artist.

1983
Apt-Art en Plein Air, held in Kalistovo outside of Moscow, includes Alekseev, Al'bert, Andrei Filippov, Konstantin Zvezdochetov, and Roshal'.

1984
Andropov dies and Konstantin Chernenko becomes general secretary of the Central Committee of the Communist Party.

Members of the group Toadstools forced into military service. In Kharkov, Mikhailov produces a series of urban photographs which form the visual basis for *Unfinished Dissertation.* Irina Nakhova installs the first *Room* in her Moscow studio. Monastyrskii initiates "Wednesdays" at his apartment. Kabakov, Prigov, writer Vladimir Sorokin, and critic Joseph Bakshtein visit regularly. German collector Peter Ludwig buys Soviet official art (the so-called left wing of MOSKh) and organizes a series of exhibitions in Germany. Leningrad artist Evgenii Yufit presents his first experimental "necrorealist" films.

1985
Chernenko dies and is replaced by Gorbachev, who initiates *glasnost* (openness) and *perestroika* (restructuring) policies, drastically altering the artistic climate.

Kindergarten (Detskii Sad) group formed by younger artists from Moscow and other Soviet cities.

1986
Soviet troops withdraw from Afghanistan. Explosions at Chernobyl nuclear reactor result in 32 immediate deaths and millions exposed to radiation.

Former members of the apt-art movement form a commune in an abandoned apartment building on Furmanny Lane in Moscow. Studio 50A, Moscow, begins to exhibit Leningrad vanguard art. Novikov etablishes Club of Mayakovsky's Friends (Klub Druzei Maiakovskogo), which aims to revive the avant-garde tradition of Russian primitivism.

1987
Kabakov leaves Moscow to install an exhibition at Kunstverein Graz, and returns to Moscow once before settling in New York. Medical Hermeneutics group founded by Pavel Pepershtein, Anufriev, and Yurii Leiderman. First exhibition of Club of Avant-gardists (KLAVA) includes conceptualists.

1988
Soviet constitution rewritten, providing for elections to a newly constituted national legislature. Brezhnev Doctrine is rescinded, giving green light to political reform in communist bloc countries. Lithuania moves to declare independence; Gorbachev responds with half-hearted military efforts. Party initiates project of monuments to victims of Stalinism.

Publication in Moscow of the journal *Iskusstvo* sanctifies Soviet conceptualism. Sotheby's auctions Soviet art and spurs interest in the subject; Western collectors, curators, and museum directors begin to visit studios on Furmanny Lane. Numerous exhibitions of Soviet art held in Western museums and private galleries.

1989
First competitive elections since 1917, followed by first open parliamentary debate in 70 years.

Flash Art publishes a Russian edition. First private gallery, Pervaia, opens in Moscow. Club of Avant-gardists organize an exhibition in Sandunovskie baths where artworks are shown in a steamy neoclassical hall while the male participants swim nearby in a pool. Studios of Furmanny Lane close.

1990
Soviet republics agitate for independence. War of Laws has regional governments resisting laws passed by Moscow. Economy in chaos. Soviet constitution amended, ending monopoly of Communist Party. Gorbachev receives Nobel Peace Prize.

Club of Avant-gardists organize *Schizo-China: Hallucination of Power (Shizokitai: Galutsinatsiia u vlasti).*

1991
Hardliners in KGB, military, and Party fail in attempt to remove Gorbachev. Their arrest marks the beginning of a rapid collapse of the old communist regime and its political institutions. Boris Yeltsin, who as premier of the Russian Republic mobilizes support in opposition to the coup, subsequently declares independence for Russia, dismembering the USSR. On December 31, 1991, the USSR ceases to exist. In its place, 15 republics emerge. Boris Yeltsin is elected president. U.S. and Russia sign START accords, agreeing to reduce arsenal of nuclear weapons by 30 percent. Communist Party suspended by Yeltsin. Gorbachev resigns.

Geopolitica opens at the Museum of Ethnography, Leningrad. Tretiakov Gallery organizes *The Other Art (Drugoe iskusstvo),* a survey of Soviet nonconformist art. Artists of Furmanny Lane move to another abandoned building on Trekhprudnyi Lane, establishing studios and a noncommercial gallery.

1992
Russia begins massive privatization program following advice from American economists urging shock therapy.

Leonid Bazhanov opens the State Center of Contemporary Art, which ceases to exist within a month.

Africa

1934
L' Étudiant Noir (The Black Student), an important journal for the advancement and articulation of the ideas and philosophy of negritude, is founded in Paris by Léopold Sédar Senghor (who will become the first postindependence president of Senegal), Aimé Césaire, and Léon Damas.

1945
Nigeria Successful 37-day general strike staged by government employees throughout the country over demands for a minimum-wage increase and cost-of-living allowances.

1946
French Union created; Césaire, Damas, Senghor, Rabémananjara, Tchicaya *(père),* Sissoko, and other colonials elected to the French National Assembly. **Ghana** Constitution enacted, making Gold Coast (now Ghana) the first British African colony with an African-majority Legislative Council. **South Africa** The African National Congress forms an alliance with the South African Indian Congress to campaign against white domination.

1947
Senghor's *Chants d' ombre* published in Paris. **Nigeria** The new constitution gives a majority to Africans on the Legislative Council.

1948
Senghor's *Hosties noires* and *Anthologie de la nouvelle poésie négre et malgache* published in Paris, the latter with a preface by Jean-Paul Sartre entitled "Orphée noir." Alioune Diop founds *Présence Africaine* in Paris, a journal devoted to French African and Caribbean literature, and which will later publish the first edition of Frantz Fanon's *Black Skin/White Mask.* **Ivory Coast** Frédéric Bruly Bouabré has a vision, becomes Sheik Nadro, and begins the Bété alphabet. **South Africa** The Afrikaner National Party (later drops Afrikaner) wins parliamentary elections and introduces apartheid and white majority rule; D. F. Malan becomes prime minister.

1949
South Africa Interracial marriages banned by Prohibition of Mixed Marriages Act.

1950
South Africa Hendrik F. Verwoerd, chief architect of apartheid, appointed Minister of Native Affairs, ushering in harsh legislation against blacks. Laws include the Suppression of Communism Act; the Population Act, which classifies people on the basis of race from birth; and the Group Areas Act, which allows the forced removal of blacks from their homes and the creation of segregated suburbs and townships. The South African Communist Party is banned.

1952
UN General Assembly adopts a resolution confirming the rights of nations to nationalize industries and resources without compensation to private investors. **Kenya** Mau Mau rebellion begins; Britain declares state of emergency and sends troops. British authorities arrest Kenyan nationalist leader Jomo Kenyatta and sentence him to seven years in prison the following year. **South Africa** Beginning of defiance campaign organized by the ANC and South African Indian Congress.

1955
South Africa Freedom Charter drafted at the Congress of the People in Kliptown, attended by delegates of the ANC, South African Indian Congress, Coloured Peoples Congress, and Congress of Democrats. Document will later be used by the ANC in its push for a multiracial and equitable society in a democratic South Africa.

1957
Ghana Gold Coast becomes the first African country to gain independence—as Ghana—from Britain under Kwame Nkrumah.

1958
Congo Patrice Lumumba founds the Congolese National Movement. **Guinea** Becomes second African country to gain independence, under Sekou Touré. **Ghana** First conference of independent African states declares policy of nonalignment in Cold War struggle. **Ivory Coast** Frédéric Bruly Bouabré's Bété alphabet published by Theodore Monod. **South Africa** Hendrik Verwoerd elected prime minister.

1960
Seventeen African countries become independent from Belgium, France, and Britain. Western domination of UN ends with admission of 16 African states. **Congo** Lumumba appointed prime minister of first independent government. Katanga province secedes in a revolt led by Moishe Tshombe and aided by Belgian troops. Lumumba is removed from office. **Senegal** Senghor becomes president of newly independent country. **South Africa** Police kill 67 and wound 187 in the Sharpville Massacre during the National Anti-Pass Law Campaign; most are shot in the back. National strike to protest the massacre, called by the ANC and other political organizations, is banned. State of emergency declared and ANC leaders, including Nelson Mandela, go into exile or underground. ANC forms armed wing, Umkhonto we Sizwe (Spear of the Nation).

1961
Angola Independence struggle against Portugal begins. **Congo** Lumumba arrested and murdered by secessionist forces. **Kenya** Jomo Kenyatta released from prison. **South Africa** Becomes a republic and leaves the Commonwealth. **Tanganyika** Gains independence (later renamed Tanzania) and embarks on a sweeping socialist experiment under Julius Nyerere.

1962
Uganda Achieves independence under Milton Obote.

1963
Algeria After a brutal and bloody revolution, France grants independence to Algeria. **Ethiopia** The Organization of African Unity (OAU) founded in Addis Ababa by 30 African heads of state. **Ghana** W.E.B. Du Bois dies in Accra at age 95 and is given a state funeral by Prime Minister Nkrumah. **Kenya** Gains independence under Jomo Kenyatta. **South Africa** Nelson Mandela captured. Only country to refuse endorsement of UN resolution condemning all forms of discrimination. **Togo** President Sylvanus Olympio assassinated.

1964
South Africa Nelson Mandela sentenced to life in prison.

1965
Congo Sese Seke Mobutu stages a military coup and begins autocratic rule; country renamed Zaire.

1966
Ghana Nkrumah initiates the Volta Dam Project, then is overthrown by the military. **Nigeria** Military coup installs repressive regime. **Senegal** First World Festival of Negro Arts in Dakar presents a diverse program of the arts and cultures of Africa and its diaspora. **South Africa** Hendrik Verwoerd, apartheid prime minister, stabbed to death in Parliament in Cape Town.

1967
Nigeria Biafra declares independence and secedes. Civil war breaks out; nearly 2 million people die in a little over two years. **Tanzania** Nyerere issues the Arusha Declaration, a policy of socialist economic development based on voluntary cooperation and self-reliance *(ujamaa);* joins peasants and laborers on a 134-mile trek to Mwanza for the TANU conference.

1968
South Africa Expelled from the United Nations for its racist policy of apartheid; also banned from the Venice Biennale, beginning the cultural boycott of the country.

1970
Nigeria End of civil war; Biafra surrenders.

1971
Algeria Pan-African Festival of Arts held in Algiers to promote African cultural unity and political solidarity. **Nigeria** Fela Anikulapo Kuti, musician, performer, social and political activist, declares his estate in Lagos an independent republic, which he calls Kalakuta Republic. Beyond being a kind of political performance, this action is intended to protect his followers and visitors to his nightclub, the Shrine, from harassment by police and the military. Because the Shrine attracts many counterculture types (including Europeans and Americans) and drugs are used openly, the government perceives Fela's work and influence as subversive. **Uganda** Idi Amin, installed by a military coup, launches a reign of terror.

1973
Senegal Laboratoire Agit-Art, a group of artists, filmmakers, and dramatists led by poet/artist Issa Samb, forms around anti-art strategies against the institutionalization of art under state patronage. The group critiques the postcolonial state and its corruption through performance and unrehearsed, spontaneous actions. Most objects and props are destroyed afterwards, so as not to feed the bourgeois postcolonial economy with "African" *objets d'art.*

1975
Portugal grants independence to Angola, Mozambique, Cape Verde, and São Tomé and Príncipe.

1976
South Africa Police fire on and kill scores of unarmed school children protesting the imposition of the Afrikaans language. Hector Peterson is the first victim in what will be commemorated as the Soweto Uprising. State of emergency declared.

1977
Nigeria Second World Festival of Negro Arts (FESTAC) opens in Lagos. Issa Samb and El Hadji Sy, leading members of Laboratoire Agit-Art, arrive in Lagos, but visit Nigerian musician Fela at his Kalakuta Republic rather than attend FESTAC. **South Africa** Black Consciousness leader Steve Biko dies in police detention under mysterious circumstances.

1978
Nigeria Fela founds a political party, Movement of the People, and runs for president, attracting a large following of university students and other young people. Disqualified on the grounds of not registering his party in all required states on time, Fela challenges the decision in court and loses. Later that year, the police and military burn down Kalakuta Republic; Fela's mother dies from injuries sustained during the attack.

1979
Ghana Civilian rule restored. **Nigeria** Civilian rule restored. Fela stages a public performance in London, marrying 27 women in one day. **Uganda** Tanzanian forces depose Idi Amin.

1980
Zimbabwe White minority consents to multiparty elections. Robert Mugabe, leader of the Shona-based Zimbabwe African National Union, wins in a landslide.

1981
Senegal Police attack and destroy the Village des Artistes in Dakar, including the archives of Laboratoire Agit-Art. **South Africa** The Springboks rugby team arrives in Christchurch, New Zealand, to play against the New Zealand All Black in defiance of the cultural boycott, causing an international scandal; the rugby tour is subsequently cut short.

1983
Senegal Senghor's presidency ends after 23 years.

1985
Tanzania Nyerere resigns.

1988
Algeria Antigovernment riots prompt adoption of a new constitution allowing multiparty elections.

1989
South Africa F. W. de Klerk replaces P. W. Botha as president and begins secret negotiations with Nelson Mandela.

1990
South Africa Political prisoners released, including Nelson Mandela, who served 27 years. Cultural boycott against South Africa ends, along with ban against the ANC and other political parties.

1991
Algeria Military stages a coup to prevent an electoral victory by the Islamic fundamentalist party. Fundamentalists retaliate with a campaign of terror, aimed especially at teachers, intellectuals, and women activists. **South Africa** The ANC ends its 30-year armed struggle against apartheid. Mandela elected president of the ANC, replacing Oliver Tambo.

1992
Senegal First Dakar Biennal held.

1993
Nigeria Military government annuls election apparently won by Moshood Abiola and appoints Ernest Shonekan as president of the Nigerian Transitional Council. General Sani Abacha, a member of the Council, deposes Shonekan in a coup. **South Africa** Charismatic Communist Party leader Chris Hani assassinated; violence erupts throughout the country with scores of political killings. Kendell Geers responds with a performance that involves joining all the political parties of South Africa.

1994
Nigeria Moshood Abiola arrested and jailed for treason. **Rwanda** Ethnic strife leads to 200,000–500,000 civilian deaths, caused by extremist Hutu militias. Tutsi-led Rwandan Patriotic Front takes power in a coup, forcing an exodus of nearly 2 million Hutus into Zaire. **South Africa** First multiracial elections end 350 years of white domination. Nelson Mandela inaugurated as president. Economic boycott ends.

1995
Nigeria Abacha's government executes nine members of the minority Ogoni ethnic group, including playwright Ken Saro-Wiwa, convicted of treason in a secret tribunal. The incident causes an international scandal and many countries, including the U.S., recall their ambassadors but stop short of an economic boycott. **South Africa** First Johannesburg Biennale held.

1997
Nigeria Thousands attend the funeral of Fela Anikulapo Kuti, who dies of AIDS in Lagos.

South Korea

1950–53
Korean War.

1960
Students killed in protests against fraudulent reelection of President Lee Syng-man. Lee forced to resign and elections reheld.

Beginning of Min Joong movement, primarily a literary phenomenon at this point.

1961–65
Military coup ousts new president and installs General Park Chung-hee. KCIA established (modeled on the U.S. CIA and FBI), and effectively controls the national assembly; dissent is suppressed through censorship and torture.

1967
Joint Exhibition of Young Artists' Groups held at the National Public Information Center, Seoul.

1969
University art students organize exhibition *Reality,* and draft accompanying statement, "Theory of a National Art for Reunification." Exhibition closed by the government at the request of school authorities.

1970
First Avant-garde Group exhibition held at the National Public Information Center, Seoul.

1971
Park defeats opponent Kim Dae-jung in rigged elections.

First S.T. (Space and Time) exhibition held at the National Public Information Center, Seoul.

1972
First Independent Exhibition held at the National Museum of Modern Art, Seoul.

1973
Country embarks on a project of massive industrialization.

1974
First Seoul Biennale held at the National Museum of Modern Art, Seoul.

1975
First École de Seoul exhibition sponsored by the National Museum of Modern Art. First Festival of Seoul Modern Art, National Museum of Modern Art.

1976
Kim Yong-min, Sung Neung-kyung, and Lee Kun-yong mount group exhibition at the Press Center, Seoul.

1979
Park assassinated by the KCIA. Chun Doo Hwan, head of the security forces, assumes control of the KCIA and military.

1980
Widespread protests by students, laborers, and citizens launch pro-democracy movement. Chun declares martial law, touching off Kwangju Uprising in the provincial capital of Kwangju; brutal suppression results in massacre of hundreds. Chun becomes president and arrests Kim Dae-jung on sedition charges, removes 800 politicians from office, censors media, closes universities.

Min Joong movement, a broad network of artists, writers, and intellectuals, becomes known to the public with the premiere exhibition of the artist collective Hyunsilgwa-Baron (Reality & Utterance), held at Donganbang Gallery, Seoul; closed by authorities. Kwangju Visual Art Research Institute (KVARI) established to create visual works for use in political actions; members do not refer to their work as art or themselves as artists.

1982
U.S. Cultural Center in Pusan burns.

Avant-garde collectives Imsulnyun and Durung founded. Insulnyun mounts first exhibition at Duksoo Gallery, Seoul.

1983
People's Art School founded in Kwangju by KVARI to work with laypersons in underground movements.

1984
First exhibition of artist collective Durung held at Kyungin Gallery, Seoul. *Art of Daily Life* opens at Kwanhoon Gallery, Seoul.

1985
Association of Min Joong Artists (Minmihyup) founded. *Hihm-Jeon* (Power of the Younger Generation) opens at Arab Gallery, Seoul; works seized by authorities and many participants arrested. Seoul Film Collective organized to promote Min Joong culture and noncommercial film, spawning widespread interest among students in using film and video for activist purposes.

1987
Chun names Roh Tae-woo his successor after promising open elections in 1988. Seoul National University students Park Chong-chol dies during a police investigation. Lee Han-ryul, another student, is killed during a protest rally when he is hit by a teargas grenade. Events trigger June Resistance and July–August Labor Struggle, massive student demonstrations that soon encompass citizens of all classes across the country.

Some 100 students found the University Film Alliance in Seoul to document political events. One Film Yard, organized to distribute underground films, soon comes under government surveillance. *Unification* and *Antitorture* exhibitions held at Min Gallery, Seoul.

1988
Seoul sponsors the Summer Olympics.

Olympiad 88 International Festival of Contemporary Art organizes *The Korean Peninsula Looks at America.* Reality & Utterance mounts seventh show at Min Gallery, Seoul. Photo Collective for Social Movement formed in

Seoul to create and circulate images of political events, as well as document conditions in factories, farms, and poor neighborhoods.

1989
Thousands march in funeral procession for Kang Kyong-dai, killed by antiriot police.

1992
Dissident politician Kim Young-sam wins presidency in clean elections, and implements reforms.

1994
Korean Min Joong Arts organized by the National Museum of Contemporary Arts, Seoul.

Mainland China

1976–77
Mao Zedong dies, Cultural Revolution ends. Change in leadership does not immediately result in new cultural directions. From 1977–78, artists continue to produce work in the Cultural Revolution style, substituting new leaders for the former cast of characters.

1978–81
Deng Xiaoping introduces economic and social reforms emphasizing increased openness to capitalism and Western culture. Intellectuals and the public respond to Deng's initiatives with the Beijing Spring Democracy Movement, which flourishes from November 1978 to March 1979. Intellectuals challenge the foundations of Maoist ideology with philosophical and cultural debates on humanism and individual freedom. New art movements crop up, among them, scar painting *(shanghen huihua);* the Stars group (Xing Xing); rustic realism *(xiangtu xieshi),* a branch of new realistic painting *(xinxianshizhuyi huihua);* and new academicism, devoted to the study of European painting styles.

1982
Government launches the Anti–Spiritual Pollution Campaign to counteract Western influences, which it believes are undermining the Chinese people's commitment to communism. Campaign targets humanism in philosophy and literature, and condemns three Westernizing trends in art: individualistic values, "art for art's sake," and abstraction.

1985
Anti–Spiritual Pollution Campaign ends and the government embarks on a series of liberal reforms. Released from the constraints of the previous three years, avant-gardism flourishes across the arts—literature, dance, music, visual art, film—a phenomenon soon to be dubbed the '85 Movement.

In February, the Chinese Writers Association holds its fourth conference in Beijing, denouncing conservatism and calling for freedom of expression. A parallel development occurs in the visual arts with the widespread appearance of unofficial groups—more than 80 across the country from 1985–87—in which younger artists debate, write, and exhibit. Openly antagonistic to official culture, the groups champion individualism, freedom of expression, and a radical overhaul of aesthetic concepts and forms, rejecting both Chinese traditional art and socialist realism, deploying instead Western modern and postmodern forms such as surrealism, dada, pop, and conceptualism.

1986
Deng Xiaoping named Man of the Year by *Time* magazine in January. Deng's cover photo is reproduced as part of a collage with Rauschenberg's work *China.*

The '85 Movement continues to expand, especially the number of conceptual or anti-art *(fanyishu)* groups. Conceptualists challenge not only propagandist art and traditional academic styles, but new art schools. Their principal goal is to eradicate utopianism, subjectivity, and the artist's hand; primary media are language and readymade objects; conceptual sources are dada and Chan (Zen) Buddhism.

Last Exhibition '86, No. 1 ('86 zuihou zhanlan yi hao), opens in January at the Zhejiang Art Gallery, organized by Wenda Gu, Song Baoguo, and others; authorities close the show three hours after the opening because of the sexual content of some of the works. Wu Shan Zhuan and fellow artists in Hangzhou mount two private showings of installations entitled *70% Red, 25% Black, 5% White (Hong 70%, hei 25%, bai 5%).* The September exhibition of Xiamen Dada, a group led by Huang Yong Ping, coincides with Huang's publication "Xiamen Dada: A Kind of Postmodernism?" in *Zhongguo Meishu Bao,* in which he advocates a synthesis of dada and Chan Buddhism. Huang also produces a series of roulette wheel–like compositions based on the *Yi Jing, or Book of Changes,* which he uses to direct his painting.

Similar events—performances, happenings, installations, mixed-media exhibits—are held throughout the year by diverse groups, including *Xuzhou Modern Art Exhibition (Xuzhou xiandai yishuzhan)* in Henan Province (May); *Luoyang Modern Art Space (Luoyang yishuchang),* Henan Province (May); *To Bring into the Light (Shai taiyang)* in Nanjing (September); and *Convex/Concave (Aotuzhan)* in Shanghai (November). The Pool Society (Chishe)—formed by Zhang Peili, Geng Jianyi, and Wang Qiang—create the series *Yangshi Taichi No. 1 (Taiji xilie yihao)* on the banks of Xihu Lake and in the streets of Hangzhou. The Southern Artists Salon (Nanfang Yishujia Shalong), founded by artists in Guangzhou, organize the *First Experimental Exhibition (Diyici shiyanzhan).*

1987
Student demonstrations staged in a number of Chinese cities late in 1986 prompt a government campaign against "bourgeois liberalism," targeting all new political and cultural thought. The campaign continues through mid-1988, significantly hampering avant-garde activities.

Wu Shan Zhuan and colleagues continue the language project begun in 1986 with the *Red Humor (Hongse youmo)* exhibition. Wu himself creates a related series entitled *Big Characters (Dazibao).* Other group activities continue, even in remote areas, i.e., the *Contemporary Art Association Exhibition of Inner Mongolia (Neimenggu dangdaiyishu yanjiu hui)* in Huhehot. Important artists begin to move overseas, i.e., Wenda Gu, who mounts a solo exhibition at York University Art Gallery, Toronto, in August, then settles in New York.

1988
Campaign against bourgeois liberalism ends, and some avant-garde activities resume or new ones begin in autumn and winter. Solo exhibitions of work by Xu Bing and Lu Shengzhong open at the National Gallery, Beijing, in October. Xu's installation, *Book from the Sky (Tianshu),* consists of books and scrolls fabricated with traditional Chinese techniques, paper, and typographic styles. The thousands of hand-carved characters, however, are invented by the artist and completely unintelligible.

1989
Hu Yaobang, former general secretary of the CCP and popular among students and progressives for his support of liberal reforms, dies of a heart attack on April 15. Expressions of sympathy and grief in banner/poster form spontaneously appear across Beijing's campuses, soon blossoming into full-fledged pro-democracy demonstrations. Students and many other citizens are killed by government forces in June 4 Tiananmen Square Incident.

After delays due to political circumstances, financial problems, and conservative forces, on February 5 the first nationwide avant-garde art exhibition opens at the National Gallery, Beijing. Entitled *China/Avant-garde (Zhongguo xiandai yishuzhan),* a total of 293 paintings, sculptures, videos, and installations are exhibited by 186 artists, including Xu Bing, Wu Shan

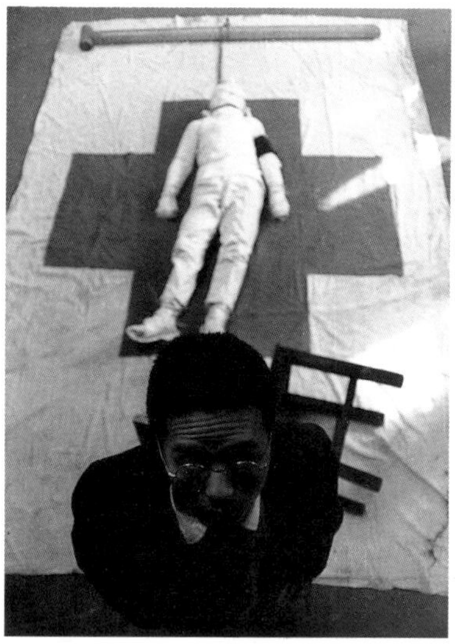

Figure 189.
Wei Guangqing, *Suicide Series (Zisha xilie),* October 1988, one of eighteen documentary photographs. Collection of the artist.

Zhuan, Huang Yong Ping, and Wenda Gu. The exhibition is closed twice by authorities during its two-week run, first when Xiao Lu and her collaborator Tang Song fire two bullets into their installation *Dialogue.* The second closing is prompted by anonymous bomb threats sent to the gallery, municipal government, and Beijing's Public Security Bureau. After the Tiananmen Square Incident and the return of conservatism, the exhibition is castigated as a typical example of bourgeois liberalism.

Huang Yong Ping participates in *Magiciens de la terre,* Centre Georges Pompidou, Paris—perhaps the first time a Chinese avant-garde artist is shown in a major international exhibition since the end of the Cultural Revolution. Huang leaves China to attend the exhibition and remains in France.

1990
As a result of the post-Tiananmen crackdown, as well as ongoing commercial pressures, idealist avant-garde activity in China declines drastically and never fully recovers.

Taiwan

1954
U.S. and Taiwan sign mutual defense treaty.

1960
Chiang Kai-shek, leader of Taiwan's only political party (the Kuomintang, or KMT) begins third term of presidency.

Modern Literature begins publication, introducing Western modernism and various "isms," including existentialism, which has a profound influence on Taiwanese literature and visual art. The Chinese Modern Art Center opens and sponsors an exhibition at the National Museum of History. The exhibition and center are forced to close when authorities claim the work of participating artist Qing Song shows anti-Kuomintang tendencies.

1961
Chang Chaotang mounts his first solo exhibition of photographs, *Xizhu Wuzhi Mountain.* Huang Huacheng publishes the short stories "Blue Stone" and "Filial Son" in *Modern Literature.*

1962
The *PUNTO International Art Movement* exhibition *(PUNTO goji yishu yundong zuopinzhan),* in which two Taiwanese artists—Xiao Qin and Li Yuanjia—participate, opens at the National Taiwan Art Museum.

1964
The Modern Poem Conference (Xiandaishi langsonghui) is held in Taipei, organized by modernist artists, including conceptualists Huang Huacheng, Huang Yongsong, and Chang Chaotang.

1965
U.S. economic aid halted. A major transnational corporation, Tongyong, invests in a Taiwanese factory, initiating a boom in foreign investment.

The avant-garde magazine *Theater,* founded by Huang Huacheng and others, gives voice to the new art movements of the late '60s. Chang Chaotang exhibits his *Headless* photographic portrait series at Meierlian Gallery, Taipei.

1966
Chiang Kai-shek begins fourth term of presidency.

Huang Huacheng publishes a manifesto on the Great Taipei School in *Theater* (January) and organizes the *Great Taipei Painting Exhibition* at Haitian Gallery. *Modern Poem* exhibition held at Taipei University. First Film Conference, organized by *Theater* magazine and held at the Wencui Cultural and Educational Academy, features two works by Huang Huacheng.

1967
Language Beyond Painting Society (Huawai Huahui), founded by Huang Huacheng and others, mounts first exhibition, *My Original Self (Zijia benlai mianmu)* at Provincial Museum of Art. Huang Yongsong organizes the first show in the exhibition series *UP* at the National Taiwan Academy of Arts, Taipei, featuring a number of readymade works. *Theater* magazine's second Film Conference, held at the National Army Art Center, includes Huang Huacheng, Huang Yung-sung, and Chang Chaotang. *Unstable Vision* exhibition, with Huang Yung-sung, Huang Huacheng, Qing Song, and Chang Chaotang, mounted at Wenxin Gallery.

1968
Taiwan enters period of "economic miracle."

Language Beyond Painting Society publishes a manifesto in *Designers* magazine, and organizes its second exhibition, *The Infinite Buddhist Power (Fofawubian),* at Wencui Cultural and Educational Academy. *Huang [Huacheng], Guo [Chengfeng], Su [Xintian]* opens at Jinggong Gallery; Huang exhibits *Memory of Mother* and *Eye Exam Chart.*

1969
Guo Chengfeng's article "Language Beyond Painting Society: A Language Group, Not a Painting Group" is published in *Universities Bulletin (Daxue Zazhi).* The group's third exhibition, *An Age Without Individuality (Meiyou gexing de shidai),* opens at Wencui Cultural and Educational Academy.

1970
Modern Qingming Festival on the River (Xiandai qingming shanghetu), the fourth exhibition of Language Beyond Painting Society, opens at the National Army Art Center. The Visual Art Association is founded by Huang Yongsong, Chang Chaotang, and others.

1971
UN ousts Taiwan and gives the China seat to the PRC. Kuomintang gradually loses support of Cold War sponsors, setting off campaign to build economic self-sufficiency which in turn leads to increasing political liberalization.

Beyond Painting '60s, the fifth and final exhibition organized by Language Beyond Painting Society, is sponsored by the China–USA Cultural and Economic Association. Major Taiwanese conceptual artists such as Zhang Zhaotang and Huang Huacheng gradually shift from a conceptual approach to graphic design and documentary film. Artists and writers turn to nature, local folk culture, and rustic subject matter in a widespread search for an authentic Taiwanese identity referred to as the *xiangtu* (grassroots) movement.

Hong Kong

1967
Months of civil disturbance—strikes, riots, bombings—force the Hong Kong government to initiate social/economic reforms, including greater attention to cultural activities.

1973
The stock market crashes; government corruption is rife. Policy changes designed to restore confidence among investors lead to rapid economic growth.

The Urban Council sponsors the first Hong Kong Arts Festival, bringing together international and local artists, musicians, and performers.

1974
Students of Hong Kong's only contemporary art program, offered by Hong Kong University Extramural Studies Department, form the Visual Art Society.

1975
The Museum of Art organizes the Contemporary Hong Kong Art Biennial, a competition open to local artists.

1977
The government expands support for art education. The Hong Kong Arts Centre opens, a not-for-profit organization that sponsors exhibitions and programs in dance, music, film, video, performance, and visual art. Hong Kong International Film Festival begins.

1981
Deng Xiaoping publicly announces intention to regain PRC control over Hong Kong. Widening gap between rich and poor spurs youth riots in the central business district.

Younger artists trained overseas begin to return to Hong Kong, representing a new generation of the avant-garde.

1982
Margaret Thatcher visits Beijing to discuss Hong Kong's future.

The performance collective Zuni Icosahedron is founded by Danny Ning Tsun Yung and others, dedicated to experimentation in the arts.

1983
First Hong Kong International Video Art Exhibition jointly organized by the Arts Centre and Goethe Institut Hong Kong. Zuni Icosahedron presents a video workshop in cooperation with the Hong Kong Arts Festival.

1984
Britain and the PRC sign the Joint Declaration, which states that Hong Kong will become a Special Administrative Region (SAR) of the People's Republic of China as of 1997.

1985
Proposal for the Daya Bay nuclear power plant stirs controversy. More than 100 community groups organize a symposium on the subject, attended by prominent politicians.

Videotage (combining "video" and "montage") is founded by artists to develop independent video production; members include Ellen Pau, May Fung, Wong Chi-fai, and Mo Man-yu. Danny Yung presents conceptual writings, "Yuen gao tze," at the arts education conference sponsored by the Arts Centre.

1986
The Art of Henry Moore, organized by the Arts Centre, British Council, and Urban Council, colonizes every public exhibition venue save one.

1987
The government rejects a public call for a referendum on direct elections.

Avant-garde artists organize the weekend exhibition *Out of Context* at the "Ghost House" on Kennedy Road, to protest the conservative exhibition policies of established art institutions.

1988
Arts Centre sponsors the *Mobile Art Show,* a public art project curated by Oscar Ho, Christine Loh, and David Clarke and featuring artists from *Out of Context. Made in Hong Kong: A History of Export Design, 1900–1960,* held at the Polytechnic's School of Design, contributes to an interest in defining a distinctive Hong Kong cultural identity. *Robert Wilson in Hong Kong,* a fictional event, is used as a cover for an art promotion campaign complete with posters and press conferences, orchestrated by Leong Manto and Fung Manyee.

1989
Arts Support, formed in solidarity with the student movement in Beijing, launches a fax-art propaganda campaign and art fair entitled *Confessions.* After the June 4 Tiananmen Square massacre, 1.5 million Hong Kong residents demonstrate across the territory; Arts Support organizes the Funeral Procession for Democracy and Democracy Strike.

Compiled by Gao Minglu with contributions and reference sources by Lai Ying-ying in Taiwan, and Danny Yung, Irene S. Leung, and Michael S. K. Siu in Hong Kong.

Artists' Biographies

Marina ABRAMOVIĆ (1946)
B. Belgrade, Yugoslavia. Graduates from Academy of Fine Arts, Belgrade (1970). Early performances (pre-1975) can be considered conceptual body works (i.e., actions with red star). Begins collaboration with Ulay (Uwe Laysiepen, b. Solingen, 1943) in 1975. Moves to Amsterdam (1976). Abramović/Ulay define their production according to period—"Warrior," "Saint," "Lovers," "Flowers." For several months during 1988, the pair walk from end to end of China's Great Wall as a performance piece.

BIBLIOGRAPHY
Abramović, Marina, with Charles Atlas. *Marina Abramović: Biography.* Stuttgart: Edition Cantz, 1994.
Abramović, Marina, and Ulay. *Relation Work and Detour.* Amsterdam: Idea Books, 1980.
Iles, Chrissie. "The Shadow and the Reflection: The Relation Works of Marina Abramović and Ulay." *In Ulay/Abramović: Performances, 1976–1990.* Exh. cat. Eindhoven: Stedelijk van Abbemuseum, 1997.
Marina Abramović. Exh. cat. Edited by Friedrich Meschede. Berlin and Stuttgart: Neue Nationalgalerie and Edition Cantz, 1993.
Marina Abramović: Objects, Performance, Video, Sound. Exh. cat. Edited by Chrissie Iles. Oxford and Stuttgart: Museum of Modern Art and Edition Hansjörg Mayer, 1995.
Marina Abramović, Ulay. Exh. cat. Paris: Éditions Centre Georges Pompidou, 1990.

AKASEGAWA Genpei (1937)

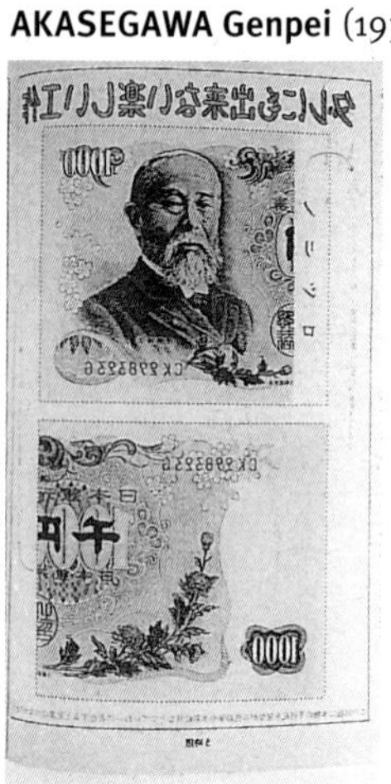

FIGURE 190.
Akasegawa Genpei, *A Course in Capitalist Realism (Shihon-shugi riarizumu kōza): Day 6, Period 5, (Conceptual Art Devoted to the State) (Kokka hi sasageru konsepucharu āto),* 1973, published in *Bijutsu Techō,* no. 371 (September 1973). Collection of the artist.

B. Yokohama, Japan. Studies painting at Musashino Art School, Tokyo (1955–58). Participates annually in Yomiuri Independent Exhibition (1958–63). Member of anti-Art groups Neo Dada (1960) and Hi Red Center (1963–64). With the latter, creates extra-gallery events, including *Cleaning Event.* For currency-based art-works, indicted, tried, and convicted for currency fraud (1965–67), in *Model 1,000-Yen Note Incident.* Works in "parodic" mode from 1967. Receives Akutagawa award for emerging novelist under pen name Otsuji Katsuhiko (1981). Teaches at Bigakkō art school, Tokyo (1970, 1972–86). Presently lives in Machida, Tokyo Prefecture, active as an artist, photographer, writer.

BIBLIOGRAPHY
Akasegawa Genpei. *Obuje o motta musansha* (An *Objet*-Carrying Proletarian). Tokyo: Gendai Shichōsha, 1970.
Akasegawa Genpei no bōken/The Adventure of Akasegawa Genpei. Exh. cat. Nagoya: Nagoya City Art Museum, 1995.
Kikan, no. 14 (1987). Special monograph issue on Akasegawa.

Giovanni ANSELMO (1934)
B. Borgo Franco d'Ivrea, Italy. Participates in first group show at Sperone, Turin (1967) along with Italian and American pop artists. Included in prescient exhibition *Arte Povera,* curated by Germano Celant (Galleria La Bertesca, Genoa, 1967) and featuring young Italian artists such as Fabro and Boetti. Exhibits widely throughout Europe during late '60s–early '70s, including Prospect 68, Düsseldorf; *Op Losse Schroeven,* Amsterdam (1969); *When Attitudes Become Form,* Berne (1969); and Documenta 5 (1972).

BIBLIOGRAPHY
Giovanni Anselmo. Exh. cat. Turin: Galleria Sperone, 1968.
Giovanni Anselmo. Exh. cat. Basel and Eindhoven: Kunsthalle and Stedelijk van Abbemuseum, 1979.
Giovanni Anselmo. Exh. cat. Lucerne: Kunstmuseum, 1973.
Giovanni Anselmo. Exh. cat. Grenoble: Musée de Grenoble, 1980.
Giovanni Anselmo. Exh. cat. Paris: Amis du Musée d'Art Moderne de la Ville de Paris, 1985.
Giovanni Anselmo. Exh. cat. Lyon: Musée d'Art Contemporain, 1989.

Eleanor ANTIN (1935)
B. New York. Creates *Blood of a Poet Box* (1965–68), a green box filled with 100 glass slides, each carrying a specimen of blood taken from one of 300 poets. Follows this homage to Duchamp and Cocteau with *California Lives* (1970), a series of biographical sculptures made from consumer goods intended to match subjects' personas. Under impact of feminism, produces a series of portraits of New York women (1971). Begins what she calls a "picaresque novel," *100 Boots,* consisting of a set of 51 postcards mailed to some 1,000 people over two-and-a-half years and describing the adventures of the rubber boots as they march from suburbia, via unemployment and military service, to a glorious finale as art stars (1971–73). Makes first video, *Representational Painting* (1972). Presents *100 Boots* at first solo exhibition, MoMA, New York (1973).

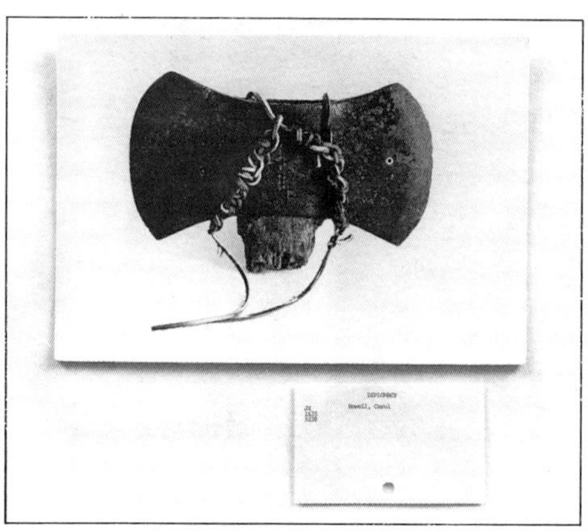

FIGURE 191.
Eleanor Antin, *Library Science,* 1972, photograph and index card. Courtesy of Ronald Feldman Fine Arts, New York.

BIBLIOGRAPHY
Antin, Eleanor. "An Autobiography of the Artist as an Autobiographer." *Journal* (Los Angeles), no. 2 (October 1974): 18–20.
___. *Being Antinova.* Los Angeles: Astro Artz, 1983.
___. "Out of the Box." *The Art Gallery* (Ivoryton, Conn.) 15, no. 9 (June 1972): 26–27, 88.
Bowen, Nancy. "On Art and Artists: Eleanor Antin." *Profile* (Chicago) 1, no. 4 (July 1981): 1–22.
Eleanor Antin: The Angel of Mercy. Exh cat. La Jolla, Calif.: La Jolla Museum of Contemporary Art, 1977.
Nemser, Cindy. "Eleanor Antin." In *Art Talk: Conversations with 12 Women Artists,* 266–94. New York: Scribner's, 1975.
Porter, Dinah. "Interview with Eleanor Antin." *Journal* (Los Angeles), no. 26 (February–March 1980): 34–37.
Raven, Arlene, and Deborah Marrow. "Eleanor Antin: What's Your Story?" *Chrysalis* (Los Angeles), no. 8 (Summer 1979): 43–51.

Billy APPLE (1935)
B. Barrie Bates, Auckland, New Zealand. Receives National Art Gallery of New Zealand Traveling Scholarship and enrolls in Royal College of Art, London (1959). Begins career as a pop artist in London, exhibiting in Young Contemporaries annual (1960–62). Changes name to Billy Apple (1962). Moves to New York (1964), where he obtains work in advertising. Runs a noncommercial gallery, Apple (1969–73). Retrospective held at Serpentine Gallery, London (1974). Returns to New Zealand (1975). Survey exhibition held at Wellington City Art Gallery (1991).

BIBLIOGRAPHY
As Good as Gold: Billy Apple—Art Transactions, 1981–91. Exh. cat. Wellington: Wellington City Art Gallery, 1991.
From Barrie Bates to Billy Apple, 1960–1974. Exh. cat. London: Arts Council of Great Britain, 1974.

Shusaku ARAKAWA (1936)
Madeline GINS (1941)
Arakawa b. Nagoya, Japan. Gins b. New York. Arakawa mounts first solo exhibition of paintings at Museum of Modern Art, Tokyo (1958). Expands production to include happenings, then ready-mades, i.e., *Box* series. Joins anti-Art group Neo Dada (1960). Moves to New York (1961) and begins *Diagram* series. Arakawa meets Gins at Brooklyn Museum School of Art (1963), and the two begin collaboration on projects such as *Mechanisms of Meaning* (1963–), *Reversible Destiny Architecture* (1973), and *The Architectural Body* (1973).

BIBLIOGRAPHY
Arakawa. Exh. cat. Berlin: DAAD-Galerie, 1990.
Arakawa, Shusaku, and Madeline H. Gins. *Mechanismus der Bedeutung.* 1st ed. Munich: Bruckmann, 1972.
___. *The Mechanism of Meaning: Work in Progress (1963–71, 1978). Based on the Method of Arakawa.* 2d ed. New York: Abrams, 1979.
___. *The Mechanism of Meaning.* 3d ed. New York: Abbeville, 1988.
Arakawa Shusaku-ten: Imi no mekanisumu (Shusaku Arakawa Exhibition: The Mechanism of Meaning). Exh. cat. Tokyo: Sezon Museum of Art, 1988.
Lyotard, Jean-François. *Que peindre? Adami,*

Arakawa, Buren. Paris: Éditions de la Différence, 1987.

Reversible Destiny: Arakawa/Gins. Exh cat. New York: Guggenheim Museum, 1997.

Taylor, Mark C. "Space as Perceiving: The Destiny of Architecture, Arakawa and Madeline Gins." *A + U* 255 (December 1991): 11–57.

Art & Language (New York)

Members included Ian Burn, Nigel Lendon, Christine Kozlov, Kathryn Bigelow, Paula Corris, Mel Ramsden, Terry Smith with the Red Crayola.

BIBLIOGRAPHY

Art & Language Foundation. *The Fox,* nos. 1–3 (1975–76).

Corris, Michael. "Inside a New York Art Gang: Selected Documents of Art & Language, New York." In *Artists Think: The Late Works of Ian Burn,* 60–71. Sydney: Power Publications, 1996.

Smith, Terry. "Art and Art & Language." *Artforum* 12, no. 6 (February 1974): 49–52.

Vries, Gerd de, comp. *Über Kunst: Künstlertexte zum veränderten Kunstverständnis nach 1965/On Art: Artists' Writings on the Changed Notion of Art after 1965.* Cologne: DuMont Schauberg, 1974.

Art & Language (United Kingdom)

After collaborating for two years on various joint projects, Terry Atkinson, David Bainbridge, Michael Baldwin, and Harold Hurrell register the name "Art & Language" in England (1968). Group begins publishing *Art-Language: The Journal of Conceptual Art* (1969), which is open to Art & Language associates and others. Invites Joseph Kosuth to act as American editor (1970). Ian Burn and Mel Ramsden join group; critic Charles Harrison becomes a proponent and collaborator (1971). *Analytical Art,* a journal edited by Philip Pilkington and David Rushton, merges with *Art-Language* (1971). Exhibits *Index 01,* an installation of eight metal file cabinets set on four gray blocks, at Documenta 5 (1972). Cabinets contain published and unpublished articles by members, while on the wall a system of indexation assesses their relative value. Continues *Index* works through 1974. Baldwin and Ramsden assume direction of Art & Language activities (1976 onward).

BIBLIOGRAPHY

The "Air-Conditioning" Show, 1966/Terry Atkinson and Michael Baldwin. Exh. cat. New York: Visual Arts Gallery, 1972.

Art & Language. Exh. cat. Eindhoven: Stedelijk van Abbemuseum, 1980.

Art & Language. Exh. cat. Los Angeles: Los Angeles Institute of Contemporary Art, 1983.

Art & Language. Exh. cat. Paris: Galerie Nationale du Jeu de Paume, 1993.

Art & Language: 1966–1975. Exh. cat. Oxford: Museum of Modern Art, 1975.

Art & Language: Proceedings I–IV. Exh. cat. Lucerne: Kunstmuseum, 1974.

Art-Language (Coventry) 1, no. 1 (May 1969)–5, no. 3 (March 1985).

Atkinson, Terry, et al. "Status and Priority." *Studio International* (London) 179, no. 918 (January 1970): 28–31.

Harrison, Charles. *Essays on Art and Language.* Oxford: Blackwell, 1991.

Harrison, Charles, and Fred Orton. *A Provisional History of Art & Language.* Paris: Éditions Eric Fabre, 1982.

Maenz, Paul, and Gerd de Vries, comps. *Art & Language: Texte zum Phänomen Kunst und Sprache.* Cologne: DuMont Schauberg, 1972.

Van Mechelen, Marga. "Language as Art, Art as Language: A Study on the Journals *Art-Language* and *The Fox.*" Ph.D. diss., Arnhem, The Netherlands, 1978.

John BALDESSARI (1931)

B. National City, Calif. Begins career as a painter (early 1960s). Gives up painting (1965) and begins to explore idea that a written description of a painting might replace the painting itself. Uses images for their informational content rather than aesthetic quality, i.e., a police photograph or children's book illustration. Makes paintings of found written texts, intended to be read rather than viewed, and executed by a commercial sign painter following artist's instructions. Produces photo-text works, some in book form (1967–68), then experiments with video and other kinetic media. Participates in *Information,* MoMA, New York (1970). "Cremates" all of his paintings July 24, 1970.

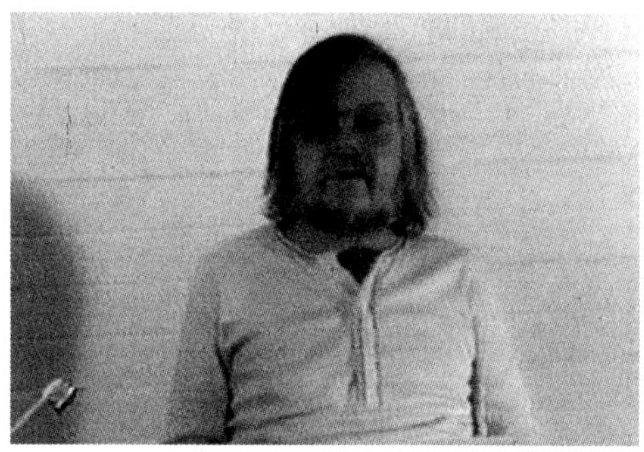

FIGURE 192.
John Baldessari, *Baldessari Sings LeWitt,* 1972, videotape, 15 min. Courtesy of Electronic Arts Intermix, New York.

BIBLIOGRAPHY

John Baldessari. Exh. cat. Eindhoven and Essen: Stedelijk van Abbemuseum and Museum Folkwang, 1981.

John Baldessari. Exh cat. Edited by Marcia Tucker. New York and Dayton, Ohio: New Museum of Contemporary Art and University Art Galleries, Wright State University, 1981.

John Baldessari. Exh. cat. Edited by Coosje van Bruggen. Los Angeles and New York: Museum of Contemporary Art and Rizzoli, 1990.

John Baldessari: National City. Exh. cat. Edited by Hugh M. Davies and Andrea Hales. San Diego: Museum of Contemporary Art, 1996.

Artur BARRIO (1945)

B. Porto, Portugal. Spends childhood in Portugal and part of adolescence in Angola (1952) before family moves to Rio de Janeiro (1955). Studies economics (1964), and registers briefly at Escola Nacional de Belas-Artes (1967). First exhibits at Galería Gemini, Rio (1967). Issues a series of manifestos calling for liberation of art from the gallery and object (1969–71). Creates books, performances, and installations incorporating garbage and human/animal waste (1969–73); continues this strategy in photography, film, and sound recording. Participates in *Information,* MoMA, New York (1970). Lives in France, Holland, and Switzerland (1974–78). Currently resides in Rio de Janeiro.

BIBLIOGRAPHY

Artur Barrio: Uma extensão no tempo. Exh. cat. Edited by Lauro Cavalcanti. Rio de Janeiro: Paço Imperial, 1995.

Barrio. Exh. cat. Text by Sheila Leirner. São Paulo: Kate Art Gallery, 1989.

Barrio, Artur. *Barrio: Texto do artista.* Rio de Janeiro: Edição FUNARTE, 1978.

Fac-símile: Projetos realizados e quase realizados. Exh. cat. Rio de Janeiro: Edição FUNARTE in association with Museu de Arte Moderna, 1981.

Pontual, Roberto. "Artur Alípio Barrio." In *Arte brasileira contemporânea: Coleção Gilberto Chateaubriand,* 317. Rio de Janeiro: Edições Jornal do Brasil, 1976.

Situações: Artur Barrio: Registro. Exh. cat. Edited by Marcio Doctors. Rio de Janeiro: Centro Cultural Banco do Brasil, 1996.

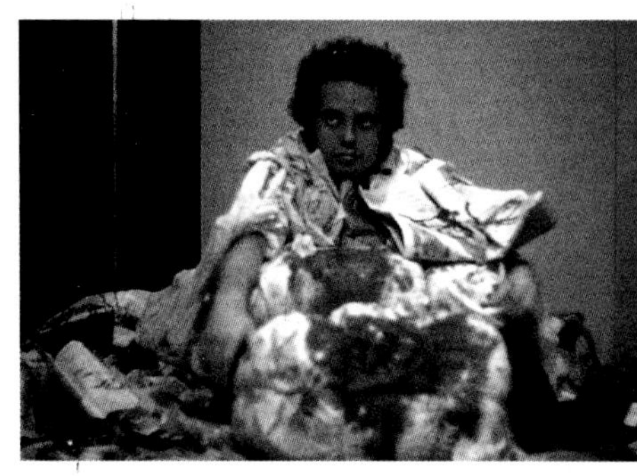

FIGURE 193.
Artur Barrio, *Situação ... ORHHHHHHHHHHHH ... 5,000 ... T.E. ... EM ... NY ... city ... 1969 ... Rio de Janeiro,* November–December 1969, documentary photograph. Collection of the artist.

Peter BARTOŠ (1938)

B. Prague, Czechoslovakia. Studies at Secondary School of Applied Arts (1956–60) and Academy of Fine Arts (1960–66) in Bratislava. Experiments with abstract expressionism for a short period, then turns to conceptual artworks in which he incorporates references to action painting processes and commentary on the object (i.e., a line painted around walls of a room, constituting painting itself). Realizes first event under title *The Gift* (1965). Mounts first exhibition (with Michal Studený) at Gallery Ciprian Majerníka, Bratislava (1967). Concentrates on art process in early 1970s, and later reduces his art to minimal gestures. Lives in Bratislava, Slovak Republic.

BIBLIOGRAPHY

Bachratý, B. "Dnes rozhovor s Petrom Bartošom" (Recent Conversation with Peter Bartoš). *Mladá Tvorba,* no. 5 (1967): 59.

Gordon BENNETT (1955)

B. Queensland, Australia. Enrolls in Queensland College of Art, Brisbane (1986). Over next ten years, achieves national and international acclaim with paintings, installations, and videos that consistently engage the most vital issues of colonialism and indigenous displacement. Mounts first solo exhibition and participates in Australian Perspecta (1989). Becomes Anniversary Creative Arts Fellow, Australian National University, Canberra (1996).

BIBLIOGRAPHY

McLean, Ian. *The Art of Gordon Bennett.* Roseville East, N.S.W.: Craftsman House, 1996.

Bikyōtō (Bijutsuka Kyōtō Kaigi = Artists Joint-Struggle Council)

Original members include Hikosaka Naoyoshi, Hori Kosai, Ishiuchi Miyako, and Miyamoto Ryūji (Tama students). Pre-Bikyōtō (1967–69) encompasses club activities, Self-Burial Ceremony, and League of Plastic Artists. Founded July 1969 by art students, artists, and critics in Tokyo and headquartered within the barricade of Tama Art University. Joins political demonstrations and organizes actions against art institutions. After Tama's lockout (October 1969), some core members leave university. Members after 1970 include Tajima Renji, Yasunao Tone, and Yamanaka Nobuo. Group reorganizes into several collectives: Bikyōtō Revolution Committee I/II (1971–74); Group of Five's Photobook *Revolution* Editorial Committee (1971–73); Bijutsu Shihyō-sha I/II, publishing the magazines *Bijutsu Shihyō I/II* (Art History-Criticism, 1971–78) and *Kirokutai* (Document Zone, 1972–77), and organizing *'73/5: Affair and Practice by 12* at Pinar Galleries, Tokyo; and Shihyō Group, contributing a slide anthology, *Art Movement That Explores Collectivity,* to Paris Biennal (1973). Hikosaka, Hori, Ishiuchi, and Miyamoto reunite in *AIR (Art In the Ruins)* exhibition series (1998–99).

BIBLIOGRAPHY

Chiba Shigeo. *Gendai bijutsu itsudatsu-shi, 1945–1985* (A History of Deviations in Contemporary Art, 1945–1985). Tokyo: Shōbun-sha, 1986.

Hikosaka Naoyoshi. *Hanpuku: Shinkō geijutsu no isō* (Recapitulation: Phases of New Art). Tokyo: Tabata Shoten, 1974.

Alighiero e BOETTI (1940–1994)

B. Turin, Italy. Self-taught. Mounts first solo exhibition at Galleria Christian Stein, Turin (1967). Included in prescient exhibition *Arte Povera,* curated by Germano Celant (Galleria La Bertesca, Genoa, 1967), and like most artists in show, distinguishes between conceptual and physical aspects of artmaking. Visits Afghanistan in 1971, and returns twice yearly through 1979. Beginning with *Mappa* (1971–72), a geographical map, has his work executed by artisans in countries with a strong craft tradition, i.e., Pakistan and Afghanistan. Participates in major exhibitions of conceptual art, including *When Attitudes Become Form,* Berne (1969) and *Conceptual Art, Arte Povera, Land Art,* Galleria Civica d'Arte Moderna, Turin (1970).

BIBLIOGRAPHY

Alighiero e Boetti. Exh. cat. Essay by Jean-Christophe Ammann. Lucerne and Turin: Kunstmuseum and Sperone, 1974.

Alighiero e Boetti. Exh. cat. London: Edward Totah Gallery, 1989.

Alighiero e Boetti. Exh. cat. Essays by Achille Bonito Oliva et al. Münster: Westfälischer Kunstverein, 1992.

Alighiero e Boetti: Opere dal 1967 al 1991. Exh cat. Rome: Galleria Giulia, 1992.

Parkett 24 (June 1990). Special issue: Alighiero e Boetti.

Worlds Envisioned: Alighiero e Boetti, Frédéric Bruly Bouabré. Exh. cat. New York: Dia Center for the Arts, 1994.

Oscar BONY (1941)

B. Posadas, Misiones, Argentina. Begins anti-art investigations in 1964. Installs *Sixty Square Meters and Their Information* at 1967 Experiencias Visuales, Instituto di Tella, Buenos Aires, in which he explores different ways of communicating with viewer through tactile, visual, and intellectual means. Receives first prize at *Salón de ver y estimar,* Museo de Arte Moderno, Buenos Aires (1967). Presents *Proletarian Family,* a living tableau in which a family earned twice their normal wage for posing as art in the gallery space, at 1968 Experiencias; exhibition closed by police. Travels in Europe and U.S. (1969–76). Wins Marcelo de Ridder Prize for Painting (1976). Invited to 1982 Venice Biennale. Lives in Milan (1978–88). Returns to Buenos Aires (1988).

BIBLIOGRAPHY

Bony, Oscar. "Oscar Bony: El gato a contrapelo" (interview). *Confirmado* (Buenos Aires), no. 408 (May 1976): 32–33.

Di Pietrantonio, Giacinto. "Oscar Bony." *Flash Art,* no. 25 (April–May 1986): 44.

"Di Tella: El vacío relleno." *Análisis* (Buenos Aires), no. 376 (May 1968): 43–44.

Herrera, María José. "'La familia obrera' como ready-made." In *Arte y poder: V Jornadas de Teoría e Historia de las Artes,* 174–82. Buenos Aires: Centro Argentino de Investigadores de Arte, 1993.

___. "Oscar Bony, una percepción mixta." *Artinf,* no. 83 (August–September 1983): 16–17.

"Premio Braque: Ausentes con aviso." *Análisis* (Buenos Aires), no. 384 (July 1968): 35–36.

Rizzo, Patricia. "David Lamelas y Oscar Bony." Unpub. ms., 1993. Patricia Rizzo Papers, Buenos Aires.

Romero Brest, Jorge. *El arte en la Argentina: Ultimas décadas.* Buenos Aires: Paídos, 1969.

Vescovo, Marisa de. "Oscar Bony." *Flash Art,* no. 102 (March–April 1981): 35.

Willem Hendrik Adriaan BOSHOFF (1951)

B. Vereeniging, Transvaal (now Guateng), South Africa. Studies at Johannesburg College of Art, where he teaches until 1997. Influenced by philosophy of Ludwig Wittgenstein. Often years in the making, his artworks are based on extensive research in linguistics, philology, and etymology and include dictionary compilations (obsolete words, manias/phobias, ethics, colors) and checklists (i.e., major botanical gardens of the world). Produces *Kleinpen I* as a form of mental therapy while imprisoned as a conscientious objector, reducing Andrew Murray's 364-page book *Prayer Life* into six pages of micrography, writing for ten minutes each day. Exhibits widely throughout Europe, U.S., and South Africa, and represents his country in the São Paulo Bienal (1996).

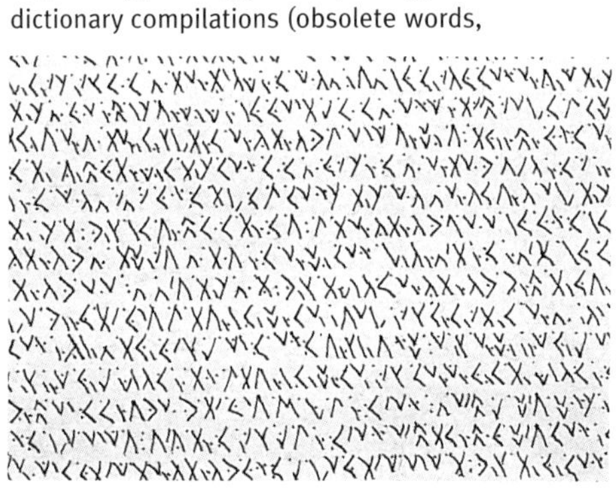

FIGURE 194.
Willem Boshoff, *Bangboek (The Book That Is Afraid),* 1977–81, ink, paper, Masonite. Billiton, Marshalltown, South Africa.

BIBLIOGRAPHY

Boshoff, Willem. *Blind Alphabet: ABC in Braille.* Johannesburg: Braille Services, 1995.

___. *Kykafrikaans.* Johannesburg: Uitgewery Pannevis, 1981.

Jamal, Ashraf. "Willem Boshoff: Blind Alphabet." In *23rd São Paulo Bienal.* Johannesburg: Africus Institute for Contemporary Art, 1996.

Kellner, Clive. "23rd São Paulo Bienal." *Nka: Journal of Contemporary African Art* (Brooklyn), no. 6–7 (Summer–Fall 1997): 14–15.

Trade Routes: History and Geography: 2nd Johannesburg Biennale. Exh. cat. Johannesburg and The Hague: Greater Johannesburg Metropolitan Council and Prince Claus Fund for Culture and Development, 1997.

Frédéric Bruly BOUABRÉ (1923)

B. Zéprégühé, Ivory Coast. Works as a translator for French ethnographers during 1940s. From 1948 onward, after a vision in which he is instructed to rename himself Sheik Nadro (One Who Does Not Forget), dedicates himself to philosophy, linguistics, and anthropology, often focusing on the impact of language on memory and history. To counteract the will to forget (hence his name), develops an alphabet of ideographic signs and symbols with which to record the oral history of his people, the Bété (first published 1958). Exhibits internationally, including Lagos (1966), Venice Biennale (1993), and New York (1994). Lives and works in Abidjan.

BIBLIOGRAPHY

L' Afrique et la lettre. Exh. cat. Lagos: Centre Culturel Français de Lagos et l'Association Fête de la Lettre, 1966.

Bouabré, Frédéric Bruly. *African School and African Language Teaching,* 1983.

___. *Bété Alphabet,* 1958–present.

___. *Le livres des lois divines revelées dans l'ordre des persecutées par le révélateur Cheik Nadro Fils de Dalo-Gbeuly officiellement appelé Frédéric Bruly Bouabré,* n.d.

___. *Le musée du visage africain,* 1975.

___. *Poids à peser l'or ou écriture–pictographique,* 1980.

___. *West African Alphabet (The Bété) Ivory Coast,* 1982.

Dalby, D. "The Indigenous Scripts of West Africa and Surinam: Their Inspiration and Design." *African Language Studies* (London), no. 9 (1968).

Magiciens de la terre. Exh. cat. Essays by Jean-Hubert Martin et al. Paris: Éditions Centre Georges Pompidou, 1989.

Magnin, André, and Jacques Soulillou, eds. *Contemporary Art of Africa.* New York: Abrams, 1996.

Monod, Theodore. "Un nouvel alphabet ouest Africain: Le Bété (Côte d'Ivoire)." *Bulletin de l' Institut Français d' Afrique Noire* (Dakar, Senegal), no. 3–4 (July–October 1958).

Worlds Envisioned: Alighiero e Boetti, Frédéric Bruly Bouabré. Exh. cat. New York: Dia Center for the Arts, 1994.

Marcel BROODTHAERS (1924–1976)

B. Brussels. Studies chemistry and writes poetry. While working as an art guide, meets Piero Manzoni (1962), who declares and signs him "an authentic work of art." Discovers pop art at Galerie Ileana Sonnabend, Paris (1963), and is particularly taken with George Segal's plaster sculpture. Presents as a sculpture 50 copies of his poetry book, *Pense-bête,* partially cast in plaster, in first solo exhibition, Galerie St.-Laurent, Brussels (1964). Responds idiosyncratically to minimal-conceptual art. Operates from his home the Musée d'Art Moderne, Département des Aigles (1968–72), staging various events, i.e., *Section XIX siècle,* a discussion on the condition of art among an installation of empty wooden crates and postcards of 19th-century masters pinned on the walls. Mounts *Section publicité* at Documenta 5 (1972). Moves to Düsseldorf, working in various media, including film, slides, books, prints, and objects. Produces a series of six exhibitions, *Décors* (Brussels 1974–Paris 1975), each intended to be viewed in its entirety as an artwork.

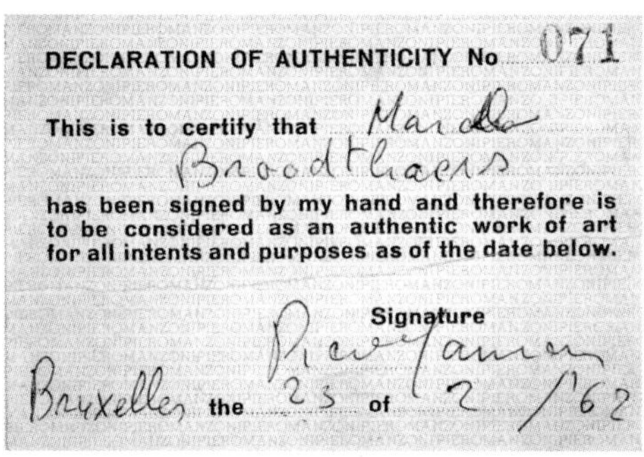

DECLARATION OF AUTHENTICITY No 071

This is to certify that Marcel Broodthaers

has been signed by my hand and therefore is to be considered as an authentic work of art for all intents and purposes as of the date below.

Signature Piero Manzoni

Bruxelles the 23 of 2 /62

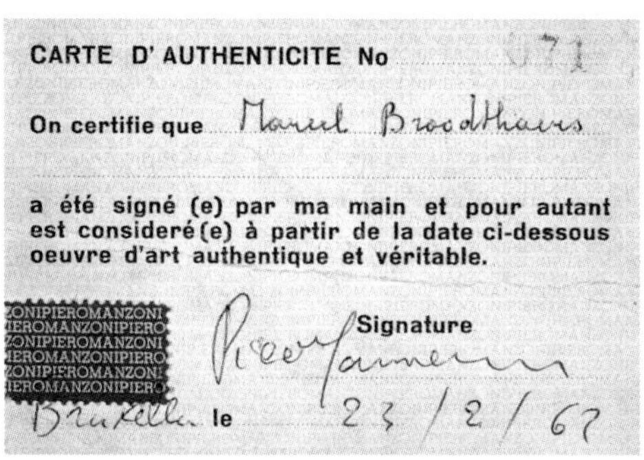

CARTE D' AUTHENTICITE No 071

On certifie que Marcel Broodthaers

a été signé (e) par ma main et pour autant est consideré(e) à partir de la date ci-dessous oeuvre d'art authentique et véritable.

Signature Piero Manzoni

Bruxelles le 23 / 2 / 62

FIGURE 195.
Piero Manzoni, *Ricevutta: Declaration of Authenticity n° 071,* 1962, ink on paper. Private collection.

BIBLIOGRAPHY

Broodthaers, Marcel. *Broodthaers: Writings, Interviews, Photographs.* Edited by Benjamin H. D. Buchloh. Cambridge, Mass.: MIT Press, 1988.
Un coup dés jamais n'abolira le hasard: Image. Exh. cat. Cologne: Galerie Michael Werner, 1969.
Marcel Broodthaers. Exh. cat. London: Tate Gallery, 1980.
Marcel Broodthaers. Exh. cat. Minneapolis and New York: Walker Art Center and Rizzoli, 1989.
Marcel Broodthaers. Exh. cat. Paris: Galerie Nationale du Jeu de Paume, 1991.
Marcel Broodthaers: Catalogue des livres/Catalogue of Books/Katalog der Bücher, 1957–1975. Exh. cat. Ghent: Imprimerie Erasmus, 1982.
Marcel Broodthaers: Der Adler vom Oligozän bis Heute. Exh. cat. 2 vols. Düsseldorf: Städtische Kunsthalle, 1972.

Stanley BROUWN (1935)

B. Paramaribo, Surinam. Educated in Paramaribo. Moves to Amsterdam and produces first *this way brouwn* (1960). Associates with Fluxus artists (from 1962). Mounts first solo exhibition at Stedelijk Museum, Schiedam (1970). Exhibits in Documenta 5 (1972).

BIBLIOGRAPHY

Art & Project Bulletin (Amsterdam) 8 (1969).
Art & Project Bulletin (Amsterdam) 11 (1969).
Brouwn, Stanley. *this way brouwn: 25–2–61: 26–2–61.* Cologne: Walter König, 1971.
100 This-Way-Brouwn-Problems for Computer I.B.M. 360 Model 95. Cologne: Walter König, 1970.
Stanley Brouwn. Venice Biennale. Amsterdam: Stanley Brouwn and the Visual Arts Office for Abroad, The Netherlands, 1982.

Daniel BUREN (1938)

B. Boulogne-Billancourt, France. Graduates from École Nationale Supérieure des Métiers d'Art, Paris (1960). Decides to strip pictorial content of his paintings to a minimum, settling on the repetition of white and colored stripes (1965). Begins trademark site-specific work (1967), in the process negating authority of the art institution, object, and artist. Creates anonymous outdoor/indoor installation for Salon de Mai 1968, Paris, with green-and-white striped posters. Mounts first solo exhibition at Galleria Apollinaire, Milan (1968), covering entrance with striped paper. Publishes various articles on the function of art, exhibitions, and museums (early '70s onward).

BIBLIOGRAPHY

Buren, Daniel. *Entrevue: Conversation avec Anne Baldassari.* Paris: Flammarion, 1987.
Daniel Buren. Exh. cat. Stuttgart: Staatsgalerie, 1990.
Daniel Buren, les couleurs, sculptures, les formes, peintures. Exh. cat. Essays by Benjamin H. D. Buchloh et al. Paris: Éditions Centre Georges Pompidou, 1981.
Daniel Buren: Les écrits, 1965–1990. Exh. cat. 4 vols. Edited by Jean-Marc Poinsot. Bordeaux: CAPC Musée d'Art Contemporain, 1991.
Daniel Buren: Metamorphoses—Works in Situ. Exh. cat. Amherst: University Gallery, Fine Arts Center, University of Massachusetts, 1987.
Daniel Buren: Photos—Souvenirs, 1965–88. Villeurbanne: Art Édition, 1988.
Daniel Buren: Senkrechte farbige und weisse Streifen, gleichzeitig zu sehen in Aachen, Dortmund, Essen. Exh. cat. Mönchengladbach: Städtisches Museum, 1971.
Francblin, Catherine. *Daniel Buren.* Paris: Art Press, 1987.
Fuchs, R. H., in collaboration with Daniel Buren. *Discordance/Cohérence.* Eindhoven: Stedelijk van Abbemuseum, 1976.
Lyotard, Jean-François. *Que peindre? Adami, Arakawa, Buren.* Paris: Éditions de la Différence, 1987.
Rorimer, Anne. "Up and Down, In and Out, Step by Step, a Sculpture, a Work by Daniel Buren." *Museum Studies* (Chicago) 11, no. 2 (Spring 1985): 140–55.
View (Oakland, Calif.) 1, no. 9 (February 1979). Special issue: Daniel Buren.

Victor BURGIN (1941)

B. Sheffield, U.K. Attends Robert Morris's seminar at Yale (1965–67). Produces *25 feet two hours* (1967–68), in which the process of its own photographic making is registered in a card file. Work remains strictly textual for two years (1969–70), as in *All Criteria;* beginning with *Performative/Narrative* (1971), image and text stand in a dialectical relationship. Publishes influential writings on art theory, visual representation, and photography, reflecting his interest in poststructuralist and psychoanalytic theory, particularly in the British journal *Screen* (1970s onward).

BIBLIOGRAPHY

Burgin, Victor. *Between.* Oxford: Blackwell, 1986.
___. *The End of Art Theory: Criticism and Postmodernity.* Atlantic Highlands, N.J.: Humanities Press, 1986.
___. "Situational Aesthetics." *Studio International* (London) 178, no. 915 (October 1969): 118–21.
___, ed. *Thinking Photography.* London: Macmillan, 1982.
___. *Work and Commentary.* London: Latimer New Dimensions, 1973.
Godfrey, Tony. "Sex, Text, Politics: An Interview with Victor Burgin." *Block* (East Barnet, Eng.), no. 7 (1982): 2–26.
Victor Burgin: Passages. Exh. cat. Villeneuve d'Ascq: Musée d'Art Moderne de la Communauté Urbaine de Lille, 1991.

Ian BURN (1939–1993)

B. Geelong, Australia. Studies at National Gallery of Victoria School, winning drawing prize (1962). Travels in Europe, Britain, and U.S. (1964); influenced by John Cage and Buckminster Fuller. Moves to New York (1967) and begins collaborative conceptual work with Mel Ramsden. Exhibits in *The Field,* Melbourne (1968), which introduces minimal/conceptual art to Australian public. Forms Society for Theoretical Art and Analyses (1969). Joins Art & Language (U.K.); with Ramsden, contributes to *Art-Language;* exhibits internationally (1970–72). Returns to Australia (1977), developing media for trade unions. Work showcased in survey *Minimal-Conceptual Work, 1965–1970* (1992), and posthumous exhibition *Artists Think: The Late Works of Ian Burn* (1993).

BIBLIOGRAPHY

Burn, Ian. "Conceptual Art as Art." *Art and Australia* (Sydney) 8, no. 2 (September 1970): 167–70.
Burn, Ian. *Dialogue: Writings in Art History.* North Sydney, N.S.W.: Allen & Unwin, 1991.
Burn, Ian. "The Sixties: Crisis and Aftermath (Or the Memoirs of an Ex-Conceptual Artist)." *Art and Text* (Melbourne), no. 1 (1981): 49–65.
Burn, Ian, et al. *The Necessity of Australian Art: An Essay about Interpretation.* Sydney: Power Publications, 1988.
Ian Burn: Minimal-Conceptual Work, 1965–1970. Exh. cat. Perth: Art Gallery of Western Australia, 1992.

André CADERE (1934–1978)

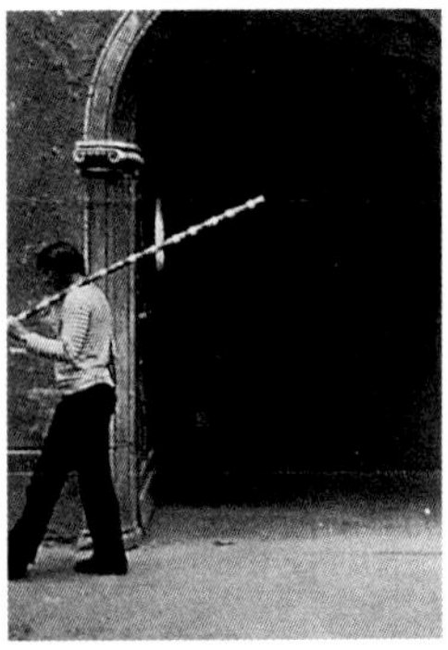

Figure 196.
André Cadere, *Histoire d'un travail,* 1982, book, printed matter. Private collection.

B. Warsaw, Poland. Family moves to Romania after World War II. Attends Academy of Bucharest. Produces semi-folkloric op art. Arrives in France (1967); previous work becomes irrelevant in new context. Behaves like a squatter in the Western art world, sojourning around Europe and U.S. with his calling card, a wooden bar. Unveils his tool for the first time at Noele Toroni's solo exhibition, Galerie Yvon Lambert, Paris, in 1970; for the last time on West Broadway, New York, in 1978, using it to enter the art world, making the story of his (its) insertion the true subject of his activity.

BIBLIOGRAPHY
André Cadere: All Walks of Life. Exh. cat. Edited by Carole Kismaric et al. New York and Paris: Institute for Contemporary Art, P.S.1 Museum, and Musée d'Art Moderne de la Ville de Paris, 1992.
Bourdon, David. "André Cadere, 1934–1978." *Arts Magazine* 53, no. 3 (November 1978): 102–03.
Cadere, André. *Histoire d' un travail.* Ghent: Herbert-Gewad, 1982.
Lotringer, Sylvère. "André Cadere: Boy with Stick." *Semiotext(e)* (New York) 3, no. 2 (1979): 140–42.
Présentation d'un travail/Utilisation d'un travail. Hamburg: Hossmann, 1975. Also published as *Presentazione di un lavoro/Utilizzione di un lavoro.* Genoa: Saman Edizione, 1975.

Waltércio CALDAS (1946)

B. Rio de Janeiro. Studies with Ivan Serpa at Escola do Museu de Arte Moderna, Rio (1964–65). Takes up printmaking (1968). Fashions readymade objects into conceptual inquiries about perception (1970–75). Mounts first solo exhibition at MAM, Rio (1973). Presents *A natureza dos jogos* at MAM, São Paulo (1975). Produces series of drawings and sculptures that denote his interest in the poetic qualities of materials and form. Cofounds and becomes editor of *Malasartes* (1975) and *A Parte do Fogo* (1980). Founds Brazilian Association of Professional Visual Artists (1977). Invited to Documenta 9 (1992) and São Paulo Bienal (1996). Teaches at Instituto Villa-Lobos, Rio de Janeiro.

BIBLIOGRAPHY
Arestizábal, Irma. *Precisão.* Rio de Janeiro: Centro Cultural Banco do Brasil, 1994.
Brito, Ronaldo. *Waltércio Caldas.* Kortrijik, Belgium: Kanaal Art Foundation, 1991.
___. *Waltércio Caldas Jr. "Aparelhos."* São Paulo: GBM Editoria de Arte, 1979.
Caldas, Waltércio. *Manual da ciência popular.* Rio de Janeiro: Edição FUNARTE, 1982.
Salzstein Goldberg, Sonia. *Waltércio Caldas.* Rio de Janeiro: Edição FUNARTE, 1988.
Waltércio Caldas. Exh. cat. Text by Paulo Sérgio Duarte. Rio de Janeiro: 110 Arte Contemporânea, 1990.
Waltércio Caldas. Exh. cat. Text by Ilse Kuijken et al. Kassel: Neue Gallery, 1992.
Waltércio Caldas. Exh. cat. Text by Lorenzo Mammi. Rio de Janeiro: Joel Edelstein Arte Contemporânea, 1995.

Antonio CARO (1950)

B. Bogotá, Colombia. Studies at Facultad de Artes, Universidad Nacional, Bogotá (1969–71). Presents controversial work *Cabeza de lleras*—a fishbowl that slowly fills with water, melting a salt-modeled bust of the ex-president—at Salón de Artistas Nacionales (1970). Distributes 5,000 drawings at the entrance to Bienal de Artes Gráficas, Cali (1971). Produces first version of *Homenaje a Manuel Quintín Lame* and other language-based works (1972–78). Creates installation series *Colombia/Marlboro* (1973–75). With Argentinean Grupo CAYC, participates in Latin American Week, ICA, London (1974). Receives prize at 26th National Salon for *Colombia* (1976). Produces second version of *Homenaje* (1978–79). Series of works with indigenous themes culminates in *Proyecto quinientos* (1987–92).

BIBLIOGRAPHY
Camnitzer, Luis. "Antonio Caro: Visual Guerrilla." *Políester* (Mexico City), no. 12 (Summer 1995): 40–45.
González, Miguel. "Todo está muy Caro." *Arte en Colombia* (Bogotá) 13 (1980): 38–41.
León, Gaspar. "Caro y su mata de maíz." *El Espectador/Magazine Dominical* (Bogotá) (1983): 26–27.
Morais, Frederico. "Colombia un país redondo." *Medellín* 1 (1978): 18–23.
Perna, Claudio. "Antonio Caro: Prefiero la pureza del viajero." *Imagen* (Caracas) 100–88 (April 1992): 34–35.
Serrano, Eduardo. "Antonio Caro." In *Un lustro visual,* 138–43. Bogotá: Ediciones Tercer Mundo, 1976.
V.R., Mili. "Antonio Caro 'Yo soy un filántropo.'" *Nueva* (Quito) (May 1984): 65–66.

Ricardo CARREIRA (1942–1993)

B. Argentina. Writer, poet, and leader of highly politicized conceptual avant-garde of Buenos Aires (1965–68), concerned with exploring visual and linguistic systems of signification and developing radical forms of anti-art. Wins prize for installation at *Salón de ver y estimar,* Museo de Arte Moderno, Buenos Aires (1966). Installs bloodstain made of red polyester resin on floor of Galería Van Riel for *Homage to Vietnam* exhibition (1966). Participates in *Premio Braque* and Experiencias Visuales (Instituto di Tella, 1967). Produces twenty-kilogram cement bags to alleviate workers' load (1967). Arrested with other artists as a result of protests surrounding *Premio Braque* (1968). Collaborates in political art actions culminating in the collective event Tucumán Arde (1968). Suffering from mental illness, disappears from art scene after 1968.

BIBLIOGRAPHY
Carreira, Ricardo. *Poemas.* Buenos Aires: Editorial Atuel, 1996.

Theresa Hak Kyung CHA (1951–1982)

B. Pusan, South Korea. Family moves to San Francisco (1962). Attends University of California, Berkeley (1968–78), where she is introduced to contemporary developments in semiotics and film theory. Begins performance, photography, and video work reflecting her own cultural and social position as a female artist from a Korean-American family, using strategies derived from sophisticated theory (1974 onward). Moves to New York (1980). Edits *Apparatus* (1980) and publishes *Dictée* (1982). Returns to Korea with brother James to film *White Dust from Mongolia* (1981; never completed). Prepares for first exhibition, a photographic series of hands as represented in art, but is murdered in 1982. Retrospective held at Whitney Museum, New York (1992).

BIBLIOGRAPHY
Cha, Theresa Hak Kyung, ed. *Apparatus—Cinematographic Apparatus: Selected Writings.* New York: Tanam Press, 1980.
___. *Dictée.* New York: Tanam Press, 1982.
___. "Personal Statement and Outline of Postdoctoral Project." University Art Museum and Pacific Film Archive, University of California, Berkeley, c. 1978.
Martin, Stephen-Paul. "Theresa Cha: Creating a Feminine Voice." In *Open Form and the Feminine Imagination: The Politics of Reading in Twentieth-Century Innovative Writing,* 187–205. Washington, D.C.: Maisonneuve Press, 1988.
Rinder, Lawrence R. "The Theme of Displacement in the Art of Theresa Hak Kyung Cha and a Catalogue of the Artist's Oeuvre." Master's thesis, Hunter College, City University of New York, 1990.

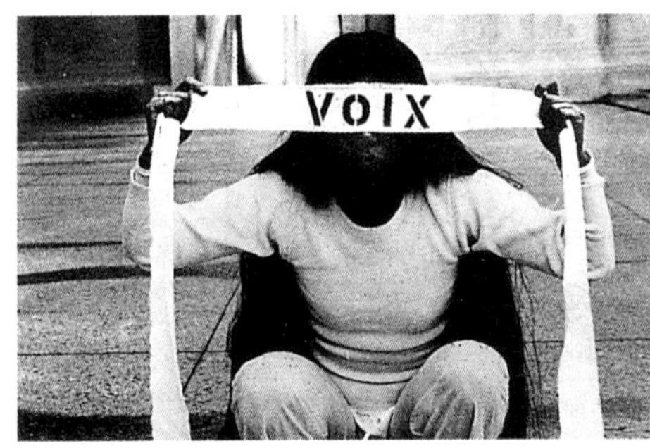

Figure 197.
Theresa Hak Kyung Cha rehearsing *Aveugle Voix* at the Greek Theater in Berkeley, California, 1975.

CHANG Chaotang (1943)

B. Taipei, Taiwan. Graduates from architecture department, Taipei University (1964). Concentrates on theater and photography (early 1960s onward). Produces and publishes a series of photographs entitled *Headless Self-Portraits (Wutou zihuaxiang);* presents series in important exhibition with photographer Zheng Sangxi (1965). Participates in several avant-garde exhibitions, including *Modern Poem* and *Theater* (both Taipei, 1966). Creates his first experimental film *Diary* (1967).

BIBLIOGRAPHY
Lai Ying-ying. *Liushiniandai Taiwan fuheyishu yianjiu* (Taiwan's Multimedia Art of the Sixties). Taipei: Guotai Cultural Publisher, 1996.
T. Photo: Beiwu Ying Xiang (T. Photo: Beiwu Image Journal), no. 1 (1996).
Umetnosti, 1982.
Konceptualna umetnost 60-ih in 70-ih let (Conceptual Art in the '60s and '70s). Ljubljana: Galerija SKUC, 1997.
The New Art Practice in Yugoslavia, 1966–1978. Exh. cat. Zagreb: Galerija Grada Zagreba, 1978.

CHOI Byung-soo (1960)

B. Seoul. Quits school at fifteen and works at various jobs, including newspaper vendor, delivery boy for a Chinese restaurant, carpenter. Makes murals, woodcuts, and banner paintings for political gatherings and demonstrations on university campuses and in the streets; arrested and early murals destroyed by authorities (1986). Participates as a planner and designer in the June Resistance (1987), July–August Labor Struggle (1987), funeral of Kang Kyong-dai (killed by antiriot police, 1989), and Labor Day commemorations. Exhibits in *JAALA,* Metropolitan Museum, Tokyo (1986); *Tong-il* (Unification) and *Antitorture,* both Min Gallery, Seoul (1987); and *Min Joong Art,* Artists Space, New York (1988). Lives in Koyang City.

BIBLIOGRAPHY

Choi Suk-tae. "Artist on Place." *Guegan Misul* (Seoul), no. 46 (Summer 1988): 128–30.

Lee Young-june. "A Critical Vision of Urban Space." *Woori Sasang* (Seoul), no. 3 (March 1992): 9–13.

Park Chan-kyung. "Gulgae Grim by Choi Byung-soo, Artist of Plaza and Street." *Saeguero Yolin Chang* (Seoul) (July 1992): 38–41.

Lygia CLARK (1920–1988)

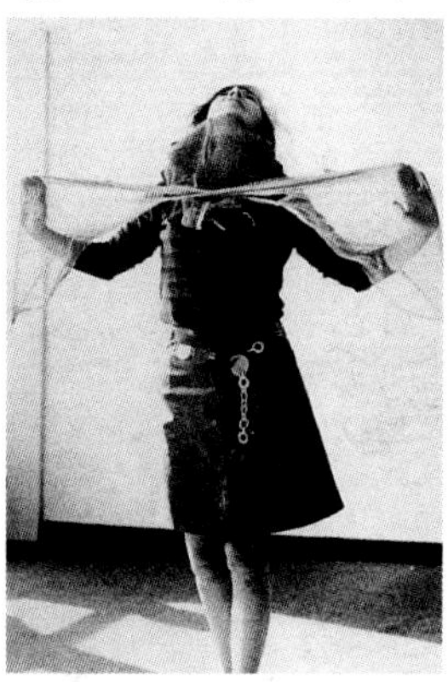

FIGURE 198.
Lygia Clark, *Camisa de força (Straightjacket)*, 1968, photographic documentation. Estate of Lygia Clark, Rio de Janeiro.

B. Belo Horizonte, Minas Gerais, Brazil. Painter, sculptor, "nonartist." Studies landscape architecture with Roberto Burle Marx in Rio de Janeiro (1947); painting with Arpad Szénes and Fernand Léger in Paris (1950–52). Joins Grupo Frente (1954–56). Produces concrete and neoconcrete paintings (1954–59). Signs Neoconcrete Manifesto with Hélio Oiticica and others (1959). First experiments with objects and performances whose meaning requires physical interaction with viewer in *Bichos* series (1960–63). Creates series of events and performances that physically engage audience with tactile and sensorial experience (1965–68). Lives in Paris (1968–77). Teaches at the Sorbonne (1970–75). Becomes interested in the therapeutic potential of art, and practices psychotherapy in Rio (1978–85).

BIBLIOGRAPHY

Bois, Yve-Alain, et al. "Lygia Clark: Nostalgia of the Body." *October* (Cambridge, Mass.), no. 69 (Summer 1994): 85–109.

Brett, Guy. "Lygia Clark: The Borderline Between Art and Life." *Third Text* (London), no. 1 (Autumn 1987): 65–94.

___. "Lygia Clark: In Search of the Body." *Art in America* 82 (July 1994): 56–63.

Cartas: 1964–1974/Lygia Clark, Hélio Oiticica. Edited by Luciano Figueiredo. Rio de Janeiro: Editoria UFRJ, 1996.

Clark, Lygia. "L'art, c'est le corps." *Preuves* (Paris) (1975): 138.

___. "Le corps est la maison—Sexualité: Envahissement du 'territoire' individuel." *Robho* (Paris), no. 8 (Fall 1971).

___. "L'homme, structure vivante d'une architecture biologique et cellulaire." *Robho* (Paris), no. 5–6 (1969): 12.

___. "Un mythe moderne: La mise en évidence de l'instant comme nostalgia du cosmos." *Robho* (Paris), no. 4 (1965): 18.

___. "The Relational Object." *Flue* (New York) 3, no. 2 (Spring 1983): 26–27.

Fabbrini, Ricardo Nascimento. *O espaço de Lygia Clark.* São Paulo: Editora Atlas, 1994.

Gullar, Ferreira, Mário Pedrosa, and Lygia Clark. *Lygia Clark.* Rio de Janeiro: Edição FUNARTE, 1980.

Lygia Clark. Exh. cat. Barcelona: Fundació Antoni Tapies, 1998.

Lygia Clark e Hélio Oiticica. Exh. cat. Rio de Janeiro and São Paulo: FUNARTE, Instituto Nacional de Artes Plásticas, 1986.

Milliet, Maria Alice. *Lygia Clark: Obra trajeto.* São Paulo: Editora da Universidade de São Paulo, 1992.

Collective Actions Group

Founded in March 1976 by members of Moscow's alternative art community, including Nikita Alekseev (b. 1953), Georgii Kizeval'ter (b. 1955), and Andrei Monastyrskii (b. 1947), later joined by Igor Makarevich (b. 1943), Elena Elagina (b. 1948), Sergei Romashko (b. 1952), and Sabina Hänsgen (b. 1955). First performance, *Appearance* (1976), staged in Izmailovskii Park, Moscow, before 30 spectators. Many subsequent performances are held outside of Moscow, with members of the alternative art community present as both participants and viewers, and actions documented by photographers Makarevich, Kizeval'ter, and Andrei Abramov. Self-publishes *Trips to the Countryside* (1980) and *Trips and Reproduction* (1983), compilations of performances with critical essays by members and viewers. Continues a steady output—i.e., *M* (1983), *Russian World* (1985), *Discussion 2* (1986)—until *perestroika,* after which the group's activities become infrequent and informal.

BIBLIOGRAPHY

Bakshtein, Joseph, Andrei Monastyrskii, and Victor Tupitsyn. *Collective Actions.* New York: Exit Art/The First World, 1999.

Kolektivnye deistviia: Poezdki za gorod. Moscow: Ad Marginem, 1998.

"Nikita Alekseev, Goga Kizeval'ter, A. Monastyrskij and Co." *Flash Art* (Milan), no. 76–77 (July–August 1977): 16–17.

Carol CONDÉ (1940)
Karl BEVERIDGE (1945)

Condé b. Hamilton, Ontario; Beveridge b. Ottawa, Ontario. Begin producing work and exhibiting as a team in early '70s. Contribute to *The Fox* (1975–76) and *Red Herring Magazine* (1977–78) as writers and editors, then return to Canada where they produce illustrated books questioning the role played by artists in political movements. Edit *Centerfold/Fuse Magazine,* Toronto (1980–82). Become active in labor politics, organizing projects with trade unions; founding members of Canadian Independent Artists' Union (1983). Mount *Oshawa: A History of Local 222, United Auto Workers of America (UAW)* at Dazibao Gallery, Montreal, a photographic reconstruction of the union's history in Canada from 1937 onward based on interviews with union members (1984).

BIBLIOGRAPHY

Condé, Carole, and Karl Beveridge. *First Contract: Women and the Fight to Unionize.* Toronto: Between the Lines, 1986.

___. *It's Still Privileged Art.* Toronto: Art Gallery of Ontario, 1975.

___. *Maybe Wendy's Right.* Toronto: [n.p.], 1979.

___. *Oshawa: A History of Local 222, United Auto Workers of America.* Special issue of *Canadian Fiction Magazine,* no. 46 (1984).

Eduardo COSTA (1940)

B. Buenos Aires. Studies at Universidad Nacional, Buenos Aires (1965). With Roberto Jacoby and Raúl Escari, writes and produces *First Manifesto and Work of "Arte de los Medios"* (1965–66) and *First Audition of Oral Language Works* (Instituto di Tella, 1966). Begins *Fashion Fictions* (1966–69). Moves to New York (1968). Participates in *Street Works I–IV* with John Perreault (1968–70). Teaches at City University of New York (1969–71). Publishes first edition of *Tape Poems* (1969) with Perreault. Participates in live and taped events at Poetry Center and WRVR Radio, New York, and Yale University (1966–69). Participates in *Fashion Show* and *Poetry Event,* Center for Inter-American Relations (1969).

BIBLIOGRAPHY

Costa, Eduardo, Raúl Escari, and Roberto Jacoby. *Un arte de los medios de comunicación* (manifesto). In *Happenings.* Edited by Oscar Masotta, 119–22. Buenos Aires: Editorial Jorge Álvarez, 1967.

Romero Brest, Jorge. *El arte en la Argentina: Ultimas décadas.* Buenos Aires: Paídos, 1969.

Philip DADSON (1946)

B. Auckland, New Zealand. Attends Elam School of Fine Arts, Auckland University (1965–67). Travels to Britain and becomes involved with Morley College Experimental Music Group, then forms an association with Cornelius Cardew and his London-based Scratch Orchestra (1968–69). Founds New Zealand Scratch Orchestra (1970) and later an offshoot, From Scratch (1974), which performs at Sydney Biennale (1979). Works in film and video, cofounding Alternative Cinema Auckland Filmmakers Co-op (1973–75). As a solo artist, performs *song stones* at Sound/Watch '92, Artspace, Sydney, and Sound Culture, Tokyo (1993).

BIBLIOGRAPHY

Dadson, Philip, and Don McGlashan. *The From Scratch Rhythm Workbook.* Auckland: Heinemann Education, 1990.

Hanne DARBOVEN (1941)

B. Munich. Attends Hochschule für Bildende Kunst, Hamburg. Meets Sol LeWitt in New York at Lannis Gallery exhibition of conceptual art organized by Joseph Kosuth and Christine Kozlov (1966). Exhibits with other minimal-conceptual artists at Museum of Normal Art, New York (1967). Mounts first solo exhibition, *Konstruktionen-Zeichnungen,* in which she develops her arbitrary system of mapping the passage of time with numbers, at Galerie Konrad

Fischer, Düsseldorf (1967). Calendar format becomes integral part of work, allowing her to create monumental works spanning months, even a century, i.e., *Bücherei: Ein Jahrhundert* (1971–75). Introduces handwritten text into her work (early '70s), then visual documentation (1978–).

BIBLIOGRAPHY

Bismarckzeit. Exh. cat. Edited by Klaus Honnef et al. Cologne: Rheinland-Verlag, 1979.

Burgbacher-Krupka, Ingrid. *Hanne Darboven: Constructed, Literary, Musical, the Sculpting of Time.* Stuttgart: Edition Cantz, 1994.

Hanne Darboven. Exh. cat. Münster: Westfälischer Kunstverein, 1971.

Hanne Darboven: Ein Monat, ein Jahr, ein Jahrhundert: Arbeiten von 1968 bis 1974. Exh. cat. Basel: Kunstmuseum, 1974.

Hanne Darboven: Primitive Zeit/Uhr Seit/Clock Time. Exh. cat. Philadelphia: Goldie Paley Gallery, Moore College of Art and Design, 1990.

Lippard, Lucy R. "Deep in Numbers." *Artforum* 12, no. 2 (October 1973): 35–39.

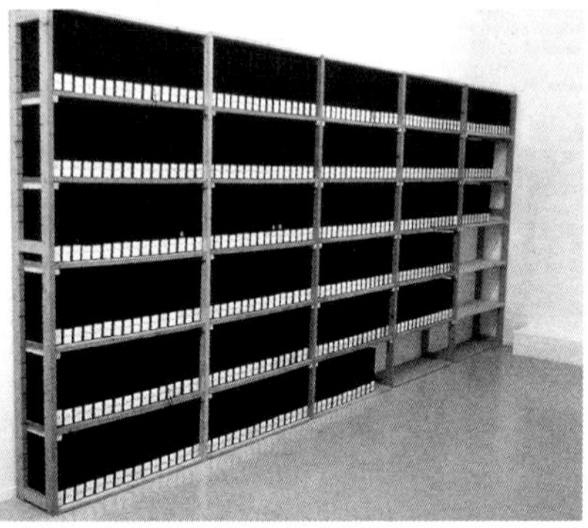

FIGURE 199.
Hanne Darboven, *Bücherei: Ein Jahrhundert (One Century in One Year)*, 1971–75, 402 filebooks on shelves and 100 index sheets on wall. Collection of Museum Moderner Kunst Stiftung Ludwig Wien.

Guy DEBORD (1931–1994)

B. Paris. Joins Lettrists (1951). Produces first film, *Hurlements en faveur de Sade;* breaks with group to form Lettrist International (LI) with Gil Wolman (1952). Launches LI journal *Potlatch* and initiates controversial anticopyright policy (1954). Asger Jorn's Imaginist Bauhaus and London Psychogeographical Association merge with LI to form Situationist International (1957). Accuses artist members of perpetuating the spectacle, and brands them right wing (1958; all expelled/resign by 1962). Publishes "antibook" *Mémoires,* bound in sandpaper (1959). Deeply influenced by Henri Lefebvre's writings on everyday life (1959–62). With Attila Kotanyi and Raoul Vaneigem, writes *Theses on the Paris Commune* (1962). Publishes *Society of the Spectacle* as a theoretical tract for SI (1967); first printing sells out by the events of May '68, in which SI plays a central role. SI disbands (1972). Debord becomes semi-reclusive (1973 onward). Commits suicide.

BIBLIOGRAPHY

Bracken, Len. *Guy Debord: Revolutionary.* Venice, Calif.: Feral House, 1997.

Debord, Guy. *Mémoires* (1959). Paris: Jean-Jacques Pauvert aux Belles Lettres, 1993.

___. *Oeuvres cinématographiques complètes, 1952–1978.* Paris: Éditions Champ Libre, 1978.

___. *La société du spectacle.* Paris: Buchet-Chastel, 1967.

Antonio DIAS (1944)

B. Paraíba, Brazil. Leaves school at 14 to work as a graphic artist in Rio de Janeiro. Studies with Oswald Goeldi at Atelier Livre de Gravura. Receives painting prize at Paris Biennal (1965)—for work addressing violence, torture, and political repression—and a travel scholarship to Paris (1967). Moves to Milan and shifts to conceptual idiom (1968). Produces word objects and paintings, films, and videos addressing representation and the art institution (1968–73). Lives in New York (1972), where he begins *The Illustration of Art* (1972–76). Travels to Nepal and learns to make organic pigments and handmade paper from Sherpa artisans (1977). Founds Núcleo de Arte Contemporânea, Paraíba (1978–81). Continues to paint in Milan, Cologne, and Rio.

BIBLIOGRAPHY

Antonio Dias. Exh. cat. Text by Mário Pedrosa. Rio de Janeiro: Galería Relevo, 1967.

Antonio Dias. Exh. cat. Text by Catherine Millet. Sydney: Fifth Biennale of Sydney, 1984.

Antonio Dias: The Invented Country. Exh. cat. Munich: Städtische Galerie im Lenbachhaus, 1984.

Antonio Dias: Trabalhos/Arbeiten/Works, 1967–1994. Essays by Paulo Sérgio Duarte et al. Stuttgart: Edition Cantz, 1994.

Duarte, Paulo Sérgio. *Antonio Dias.* Rio de Janeiro: Edição FUNARTE, 1979.

Morais, Frederico. "Antonio Dias: Obra inventiva é um colapso no entendimento." *O Globo* (Rio de Janeiro), September 10, 1985, B3.

Da Torre de Marfim/'88 Torre de Babel. Exh. cat. Text by Pierre Restany. Rio de Janeiro: Galería Relevo, 1964.

Valerio Adami, Enrico Baj, Lucio Del Pezzo, Antonio Dias, Hsiao, Gianfranco Pardi, Emilio Tadini. Exh. cat. Los Angeles: Felix Landau Gallery, 1970.

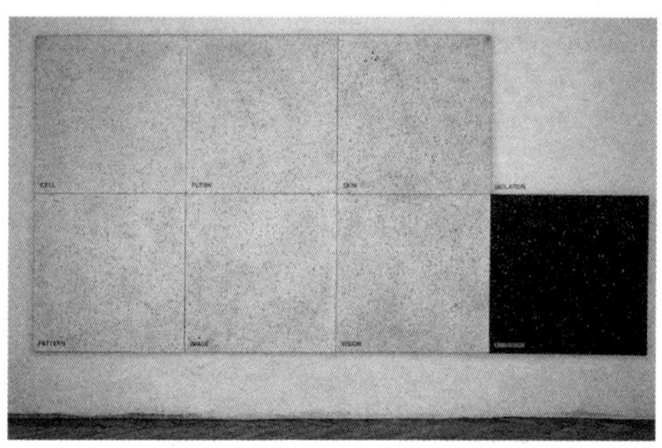

FIGURE 200.
Antonio Dias, *Biografia Alfaômega (Alfaômega Biography)*, 1968, acrylic on canvas. Collection of the artist.

Jan DIBBETS (1941)

B. Weert, Holland. Begins art career as an abstract painter. Attends St. Martin's School of Art, London (1967). Cofounds International Institute for the Reeducation of Artists, Amsterdam (1968). Participates in *Earth Art* (Cornell University, Ithaca, N.Y., 1969), although his early work does not show the empathy with nature typical of most earth artists. For *Konzeption-Conception,* organized by Rolf Wedewer and Konrad Fischer (Städtisches Museum, Leverkusen, 1969), produces *Konrad Fischer Raum,* 19 photographs recording the passage of time through changes of light and shadow, shot at regular intervals from a fixed point of view looking toward the gallery window.

BIBLIOGRAPHY

Boice, Bruce. "Jan Dibbets: The Photograph and the Photographed." *Artforum* 11, no. 8 (April 1973): 45–49.

Fuchs, R. H., and Gloria Moure. *Jan Dibbets: Interior Light, Works on Architecture, 1969–1990.* New York: Rizzoli, 1991.

Jan Dibbets. Exh. cat. Eindhoven: Stedelijk van Abbemuseum, 1980.

Jan Dibbets. Exh. cat. Essays by R. H. Fuchs and M.M.M. Vos. Minneapolis: Walker Art Center, 1987.

Reise, Barbara M. "Jan Dibbets: A Perspective Correction." *Art News* 71, no. 4 (Summer 1972): 38–41.

___. "Notes[1] on Jan Dibbets's[2] Contemporary[3] Nature[4] of Realistic[5] Classicism[6] in the Dutch[7] Tradition[8]." *Studio International* (London) 183, no. 945 (June 1972): 248–55.

Sharp, Willoughby. "Interview with Jan Dibbets." *Avalanche* (New York), no. 1 (Fall 1970): 33–39.

Braco DIMITRIJEVIĆ (1948)

B. Sarajevo, Yugoslavia. Former ski champion. Attends Academy of Fine Arts, Zagreb (1968–71) and St. Martin's School of Art, London (1971–73). Early work consists of street actions. Exhibits trademark conceptual series *Casual passersby I met ...*—oversized portraits of strangers hung on public buildings—at 1971 Paris Biennal and Documenta 5, 1972. Moves to London (1971). Participates in Documenta 6 (1971), Documenta 9 (1992) and Venice Biennale (1976). Publishes *Triptychos Post Historicos,* theoretical treaties of his work (1976). Receives award from Arts Council of Great Britain (1978).

BIBLIOGRAPHY

Braco Dimitrijević. Exh. cat. Essay by J. Harten. Düsseldorf: Kunsthalle, 1997.

Braco Dimitrijević. Exh. cat. Essay by R.H. Fuchs. Eindhoven: Stedelijk van Abbemuseum, 1979.

Braco Dimitrijević. Exh. cat. Texts by Radoslav Putar and Caroline Tisdall. Zagreb: Galerija Suvremene Umjetnosti, 1973.

Braco Dimitrijević: Against Historic Sense of Gravity. Exh. cat. Darmstadt: Hessisches Landesmuseum, 1995.

Braco Dimitrijevič: Slow as Light, Fast as Thought. Exh. cat. Vienna: Museum Moderner Kunst Stiftung Ludwig Wien, 1994.

Dimitrijević, Braco. "Casual passers-by I met." *Avalanche,* no. 5 (Fall 1972): 10-11

Miklós ERDÉLY (1928–1986)

B. Budapest, Hungary. Studies sculpture at Academy of Fine Arts (1946–47), then architecture at Technical University, Budapest (1947–51). Realizes first collaborative action, *Unguarded Money,* during Revolution of 1956. Participates in 1971 Paris Biennal. Exhibits with a group of Hungarian artists at Foksal Gallery, Warsaw (1972). Launches his series of scientific conferences (i.e., *Event Horizons,* 1974) and art training sessions (1975), both of which he considers art actions. Produces *Dream Reconstructions* (1977), first film of a trilogy, followed by *Version* (1979) and *Spring Execution* (1984). During 1980s, expands conceptual work to include painting, drawing, and installation; writes poetry and criticism; and works on architectural projects. Retrospectives held in Budapest (1986/98) and Székesfehérvár (1991).

BIBLIOGRAPHY
Erdély, Miklós. *Idő-mőbiusz* (Time-Moebius). Budapest: Magyar Műhely, 1991.
___. *Kollapszus orv.* (Coll. Med.). Paris: Magyar Műhely, 1974.
___. *Művészeti írások (Válogatott művészetelméleti tanulmányok I)* (Writings on Art [Selected Essays on Art Theory I]). Edited by Miklós Peternák. Budapest: Képzőművészeti Kiadó, 1991.
Erdély Miklós kiállítása. Exh. cat. Budapest: Óbuda Galéria, Zichy Kastóly, 1986.
Erdély Miklós (1928–1986) kiállítása. Exh. cat. Székesfehérvár: István Király Múzeum, 1991.
Miklós Erdély: Opere dagli anni '50 al 1986. Exh. cat. Rome: Spicchi dell'Est, 1992.

Luciano FABRO (1936)

B. Turin, Italy. Begins as a painter (1957–58). Attends 1958 Venice Biennale and is shocked by paintings of Fontana, Wols, and Rothko. Moves to Milan (1959) and befriends Piero Manzoni and Enrico Castellani. For first solo exhibition in Milan (1965), exhibits *Hole,* a transparent glass plate covered with a reflective surface except at its center. As he explains later, in discussing *Pavimento (Tautologia)* (1967), for the viewer, reading a work of art is to represent in his own imagination what the artist has been thinking and doing when making the work. Exhibits *Concetto spaziale (Tautologia) at Trigon 67: Ambiente Environment* (Graz).

BIBLIOGRAPHY
Luciano Fabro. Exh. cat. San Francisco: Museum of Modern Art, 1992.
Luciano Fabro. Exh. cat. Paris: Éditions Centre Georges Pompidou, 1996.
Luciano Fabro: Works, 1963–1986. Exh. cat. Edinburgh: Fruitmarket Gallery, 1987.
Sanna, Jole de. *Luciano Fabro: Biografia.* Pasian di Prato: Campanotto Editore, 1996.

León FERRARI (1920)

B. Buenos Aires. Self-taught artist and writer. Begins as metal sculptor (1955). Becomes leading member of Buenos Aires avant-garde with his calligraphic investigations (1962–64) and written descriptions of paintings and objects (1964–66). Exhibits controversial *Western and Christian Civilization*—a crucified Christ over a wooden replica of a U.S. jet bomber—at Instituto di Tella (1965); authorities close exhibition. Abandons artmaking for political action (1966–70). Composes *Palabras ajenas,* a literary collage on the Vietnam War (1967), and collaborates on Tucumán Arde (1968). Political exile in Brazil (1976–90). Produces series of Letraset city plans (1980–82); antireligious collages and installations (1983 onward); and large-scale drawings (1991–98).

BIBLIOGRAPHY
Alberti, Rafael, and León Ferrari. *Escrito en el Aire.* Milan: Vanni Scheiwiller, 1964.
Amaral, Aracy A. *Arte para quê: A preocupacão social na arte brasileira, 1930–1970.* São Paulo: Livraria Nobel, 1984.
___. "León Ferrari: A invenção e a máquina." In *Arte é meio artístico entre a feijoada é o x-burguer,* 336–38. São Paulo: Livraria Nobel, 1982.
Escrituras y esculturas de León Ferrari. Buenos Aires: Alvaro Castagnino Galería de Arte, 1991.
Ferrari, León. *El arte de los significados.* Unpub. ms., presented at Tucumán Arde, 1968.
___. "El arte político puede ser un dique ante la marea del olvido." *La Maga* (Buenos Aires), January 4, 1995, 16.
___. *Arte y poder.* Buenos Aires, 1993.
___. *La Basilica.* São Paulo: Edições Exu, 1985.
___. *Bíblia.* São Paulo: Edições Exu, 1989.
___. "Convocatoria a participar en el libro 'Veinte años' al cumplirse dos décadas del golpe de las FFAA." Unpub. ms., 1996.
___. *Cuadro escrito.* Buenos Aires: Ediciones Licopodio, 1984.
___. *Dibujos escritos y escrituras dibujadas.* Buenos Aires, 1994.
___. *Exégesis.* Buenos Aires: Ediciones Exu, 1993.
___. *Hombres.* Buenos Aires: Ediciones Licopodio, 1984.
___. *Imagens de León Ferrari.* São Paulo: Edições Exu, 1988.
___. *Nosotros no sabíamos.* Buenos Aires: León Ferrari, 1976–94.
___. *Parahereges.* São Paulo: Editora Expressão, 1986.
Giunta, Andrea. "La política del montaje: León Ferrari y 'La civilización occidental y cristiana.'" In *Cultura y política en los años '60.* Edited by Enrique Oteiza et al., 299–314. Buenos Aires: Oficina de Publicaciones del CBC, 1997.

Stano FILKO (1937)

B. Ve'lká Hradná, Czechoslovakia. Studies at Secondary School of Applied Arts (1956–59) and Academy of Fine Arts (1960–65), Bratislava. Early works are postcubist paintings, assemblages, and collages. Mounts first exhibition at Redaction of Smena, Bratislava (1964). Together with Alex Mlynárčik and Zita Kostrová, writes *Happsoc* manifestos (1965), in which they declare the city of Bratislava an artwork. During the late '60s, combines an interest in cosmology and astronomy with conceptual artworks. Emigrates to U.S. (1980). Returns c. 1990, and now lives in Bratislava, Slovak Republic.

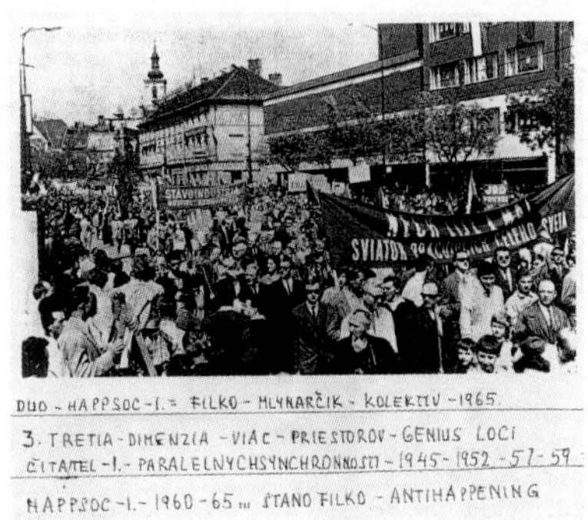

FIGURE 201.
Stano Filko, Alex Mlynárčik, Zita Kostrová, *Happsoc I, Bratislava,* 1965, photographs, typewritten text. Collection of Stano Filko, Bratislava, Slovak Republic.

BIBLIOGRAPHY
Stano Filko II, 1965–1969. Exh. cat. Introduction by Pierre Restany. Bratislava: A-Press, 1971.
Zdenek, Felix. "Z ateliéru Stano Filko." *Výtvarné Umění,* no. 7 (1967): 350–51.

Hollis FRAMPTON (1936–1984)

B. Wooster, Ohio. Attends Phillips Academy, Andover (1951–54) and Western Reserve University, Cleveland (1954–57). Moves to New York (1958), where he films *The Secret World of Frank Stella* (1958–62). Works as freelance photographer for New York galleries (1959). Hospitalized for several months, then makes *Word Pictures* (1962–63), still photographs which become the basis for *Zorns Lemma* (1970), the first feature-length experimental film to be included in the New York Film Festival. Begins making 16mm films in earnest (1966–). Produces first series of xerographs, *Reasonable Facsimiles,* and launches *Magellan* cycle (1971). Mounts retrospective of films, Anthology Film Archives, New York (1975). Designs digital hard/software for manipulating graphics, sound, and text (1977–79). Dies of lung cancer.

BIBLIOGRAPHY
Frampton, Hollis. *Circles of Confusion.* Rochester, N.Y.: Visual Studies Workshop Press, 1983.
___. "Mind Over Matter." *October* (Cambridge, Mass.), no. 6 (Fall 1978): 81–92.
Krane, Susan, and Bruce Jenkins. *Hollis Frampton: Recollections, Recreations.* Buffalo, N.Y., and Cambridge, Mass.: Albright–Knox Gallery and MIT Press, 1984.
MacDonald, Scott. "Interview with Hollis Frampton: The Early Years." *October* (Cambridge, Mass.), no. 12 (Spring 1980): 103–26.
___. "Interview with Hollis Frampton: *Zorns Lemma." Quarterly Review of Film Studies* (Pleasantville, N.Y.) 4 (Winter 1979): 23–37.

Harry GAMBOA, Jr. (1951)

B. Los Angeles. Cofounds Asco collective of Mexican-American artists (1971–87). Based on an aesthetic of "social surrealism," group stages street actions and environments designed to convey importance of Chicano life to Los Angelenos and the city, including *No Movies* series and "walking murals." Gamboa's solo efforts include work in various media—photography, installation, video, theater—and writing for numerous publications. Receives award for best experimental video, San Antonio Cinefestival (1992). Participates in *Helter Skelter* (Los Angeles, 1992), Whitney Biennial (1995), and *Contemporary Latino Photography*

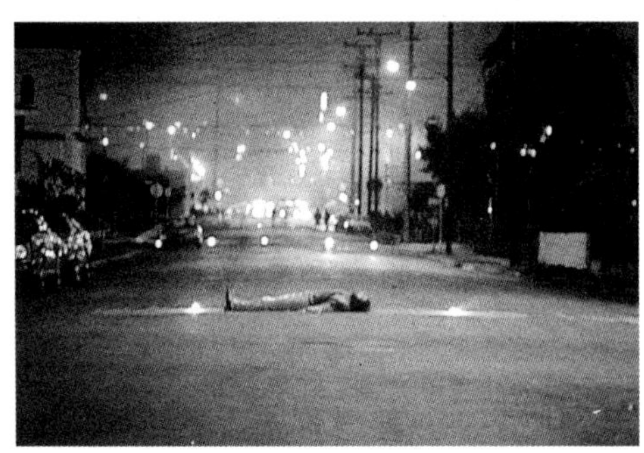

FIGURE 202.
Harry Gamboa, Jr., *Decoy Gang War Victim,* 1975, slide documentation. © 1975 Harry Gamboa, Jr.

(Smithsonian Institution, 1997).

BIBLIOGRAPHY

Chavoya, Ondine C. "Pseudographic Cinema: Asco's No-Movies." *Performance Research* 3, no. 1 (1998): 1–24.

Gamboa, Harry, Jr. *Urban Exile: Collected Writings.* Minneapolis: University of Minnesota Press, 1998.

Kosiba-Vargas, S. Zaneta. "Harry Gamboa Jr. and Asco: The Emergence and Development of a Chicano Art Group, 1971–1987." Ph.D. diss., University of Michigan, Ann Arbor, 1988.

Lippard, Lucy. *Mixed Blessings: New Art in a Multicultural America.* New York: Pantheon, 1990.

Noriega, Chon. "Talking Heads, Body Politic: The Plural Self of Chicano Experimental Video." In *Resolutions.* Edited by Michael Renov and Erika Suderburg, 207–28. Minneapolis: University of Minnesota Press, 1996.

Kendell GEERS

B. Germiston, South Africa. Graduates from University of Witswatersrand, Johannesburg (1988). Changes his birthdate to May 1968, a political performance act that essentially collapses his life and practice into one. Certain political events of 1968 become consistent references in his work: the Paris uprising, Duchamp's death, the assassination of Martin Luther King, Prague Spring, beginning of the cultural boycott of South Africa. Refuses to enlist in the army, compulsory for all white males, and briefly goes into exile in New York (1989). Returns to South Africa after the release of Nelson Mandela.

BIBLIOGRAPHY

DeBord, Matthew. "Cross/ing: Time, Space, Movement." *Flash Art* 31, no. 199 (March–April 1998).

Enwezor, Okwui. "Occupied Territories: Power, Access, and African Art." *Frieze* (London) 26 (January–February 1996): 36–41.

___, and Octavio Zaya. "Moving In." *Flash Art* 29, no. 186 (January–February 1996): 84–89.

Geers, Kendell. *Argot.* Johannesburg: Chalkham Hill Press, 1995.

___. "Art as Propaganda Inevitably Self-Destructs." In *Art from South Africa,* 23–24. Exh. cat. Oxford: Museum of Modern Art, 1990.

___. *Contemporary South African Art—The Gencor Collection.* Johannesburg: Jonathan Ball Publishers, 1997.

___. *The Horror, the Horror.* Bordeaux: CAPC, 1998.

___. "Third World Bites Back." *Art Ventilator* (Johannesburg) (September 1994): 12–15.

McEvilley, Thomas. "Report from Johannesburg: Towards a World-Class City?" *Art in America* 83, no. 9 (September 1995): 45–49.

Richards, Colin. "About Face: Aspects of Art History and Identity in South African Visual Culture." *Third Text* (London) 16–17 (Autumn–Winter 1991): 101–33.

Rosengarten, Ruth. "Inside Out." *Frieze* (London) 23 (Summer 1995): 44–49.

GENG Jianyi (1962)

B. Zhengzhou, Henan Province, PRC. Educated Zhejiang Academy of Fine Arts, Hangzhou (1981–85). Cofounds Pool Society, notable for "gray humor" paintings, and organizes its first exhibition, *New Space '85,* with colleagues Zhang Peili and Wang Qiang. Produces a series of gray humor oil paintings (1985), for instance, *The Second Situation.* Adopts conceptualist strategies to investigate institutional apparatus of art. Produces installations, i.e., *Water Factory* and *Investigative Forms* (both 1988). Participates in *China/Avant-garde,* National Gallery, Beijing (1989). Represented in numerous international exhibitions, including Venice Biennale (1993), *Configura 2,* Erfurt (1995), and *Another Long March,* Breda (1997). Currently a professor at Zhejiang Institute of Technology.

BIBLIOGRAPHY

Dijk, Hans van. "Painting in China After the Cultural Revolution: Style Developments and Theoretical Debates, Part II: 1985–1991." *China Information* (Leiden) 6, no. 4 (Spring 1992): 1–18.

Gao Minglu et al. *Zhongguo dangdai meishushi, 1985–1986* (History of Chinese Contemporary Art, 1985–1986). Shanghai: Shanghai People's Press, 1991.

"I Don't Want to Play Cards with Cézanne" and Other Works: Selections from the Chinese "New Wave" and "Avant-garde" Art of the Eighties. Exh. cat. Edited by Richard E. Strassberg. Pasadena, Calif.: Pacific Asia Museum, 1991.

Gorgona Group

Collective based in Zagreb, Yugoslavia, and active 1959–66. Comprised of artists who were almost all originally informel painters, including Dimitrije Bašičević (1921–1987), Julije Knifer (1924), Ivan Kožarić (1921), Radoslav Putar (1929–?), Duro Seder (1927), and Josip Vaništa (1924).

BIBLIOGRAPHY

Gorgona. Exh. cat. Zagreb: Galerija Suvremene Umjetnosti, 1977.

Alberto GRECO (1931–1965)

B. Buenos Aires. Studies art with C. Marcovich, Lidi Pratti, and Tomás Maldonado (1947–48). Writes poetry and fiction throughout his life. Lives in Paris (1954–56) and São Paulo (1957–58). Cofounds Argentinean informalist movement (1959). As a critique of art establishment, appropriates mass-mediatic strategies to promote himself (1960). Collaborates with K.W.Y. group in Paris (1962). Begins *Vivo dito* (1962–65), a series of street actions in which he "signs" people as art. Produces first work of "live art" (30 live rats) and *Dito Manifesto of Live Art* in Genoa (1962). Travels to New York, where he meets Duchamp (1965). Moves between Italy, Spain, France (1963–65). Commits suicide in Madrid, writing "FIN" on a barbiturate bottle as a suicide note.

BIBLIOGRAPHY

Alberto Greco. Exh. cat. Essays by Antonio Saura et al. Valencia: Instituto Valenciano de Arte Moderno, Centre Julio González, 1991.

Glusberg, Jorge. "Alberto Greco." In *Del pop-art a la nueva imagen,* 283–88. Buenos Aires: Ediciones de Arte Gaglianone, 1985.

Noé, Luis Felipe. *Greco.* Lima: Imprenta Fontana, n.d.

___. *Greco, Santantonín.* Buenos Aires: Fundación San Telmo, 1987.

Víctor GRIPPO (1936)

B. Junín, Argentina. Studies chemistry, then attends Héctor Cartier's visual arts seminars and design classes, Escuela Superior de Bellas Artes, Buenos Aires. Deploys conceptual strategies to conduct inquiries into relationship between science, art, politics, and everyday life (mid-'60s onward). Presents *Sistema,* in which he first develops integrative text/object approach to art (1966). Produces conceptual propositions/projects based on scientific hypotheses (1966–72). Joins CAYC-based Grupo de los Trece (c. 1970). Begins *Analogies* series (1970–). Constructs popular oven for baking bread in public plaza with Jorge Gamarra (artist) and A. Rossi (rural worker) (1972). Begins series of boxes with objects/text (1978). Introduces rose as symbolic element of transformation (1979). Shifts to installation art (1991).

BIBLIOGRAPHY

Brett, Guy. "Víctor Grippo." In *Transcontinental: An Investigation of Reality: Nine Latin American Artists,* 86–87. Exh. cat. London: Verso, 1990.

Di Paola, Jorge. *La comida del artista.* Buenos Aires: ICI, 1991.

Martín-Crosa, Ricardo. "Víctor Grippo." In *Arte argentino contemporâneo.* Edited by Gabriel Levinas, 161–64. Madrid: Editorial Ameris, 1979.

Pacheco, Marcelo. "Political Texts and Absent Contexts." In *Wounds Between Democracy and Redemption in Contemporary Art,* 79–83. Exh. cat. Stockholm: Moderna Museet, 1998.

___. "A Warm Conceptualist." In *Art from Argentina, 1920–1994.* Exh. cat. Edited by David Elliot, 100–05. Oxford: Museum of Modern Art, 1994.

Víctor Grippo. Exh. cat. Edited by M. Catherine de Zegher and Elizabeth A. Mcgregor. Birmingham: Ikon Gallery, 1995.

Víctor Grippo: Algunos oficios. Exh. cat. Buenos Aires: Galería Artemúltiple, 1976.

Víctor Grippo: Obras de 1965–1987. Exh. cat. Text by Jorge Glusberg. Buenos Aires: Fundación San Telmo, 1988.

Grup de Treball (Working Group)

Collective of extremely diverse artists based in Barcelona and active 1972–75. Members include Francesc Abad, Jordi Benito, Antonio Mercader, Antoni Muntadas, Francesc Torres, and Angels Ribé, motivated by growing political conflict during the last years of Franco's regime. Organizes series of exhibitions under title *Informació d'art* (1973–75). Publish first work in a catalogue of the Fifth Catalan Summer University, Prada de Conflent (1973), consisting of a list of all artists participating in Documenta 4/5 (1968/72) and amounts received from the sale of their work in 1972. Produce final collective work, *Document, Travail d' information sur la presse illégale des pays Catalans,* for Paris

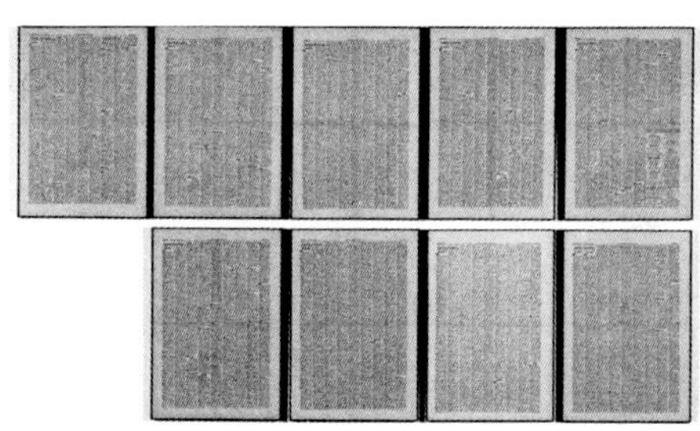

FIGURE 203.
Grup de Treball (Working Group), *Anunciamos (We Announce),* 1973, nine sheets of the newspaper *La Vanguardia* and red marking pen. Collecció MACBA, Procedent del Fons d'Art de la Generalitat de Catalunya, Barcelona.

Biennal (1975).

BIBLIOGRAPHY

Ideas & Attitudes: Catalan Conceptual Art, 1969–1981. Exh. cat. Edited by Stephen Snoddy. Manchester and Southampton: Cornerhouse and John Hansard Gallery, University of Southampton, 1994.

Wenda GU (1955)

B. Shanghai, PRC. Studies at Shanghai College of Applied Arts (1977–79) and Zhejiang Academy of Fine Arts, Hangzhou (1979–81). Lectures at Zhejiang Academy (1982–87). Plays pivotal role in "new scholar painting" movement, combining traditional Chinese ink painting and Western surrealism; begins conceptual works with nonsensical Chinese characters in ink painting format (1985). Emigrates to U.S. (1987). Begins installation work made from human materials, i.e., *United Nations* series (1993–2000), composed of hair collected from people of many different nationalities and races. Represented in *China's New Art, Post-1989,* Hong Kong/Sydney, and *Fragmented Memory,* Wexner Center, Columbus, Ohio (both 1993). Currently resides in New York.

BIBLIOGRAPHY

Chang, Danielle. *United Nations—American Division.* New York: Space Untitled, 1995.

Gebrochene Bilder: Junge Kunst aus China (Broken Pictures: Young Chinese Art). Exh. cat. Bad Honnef: Horlemann Verlag, 1991.

Levin, Kim. "Splitting Hairs: Wenda Gu's Primal Projects and Material Misunderstandings." *Artlife* (Beijing) (January–February 1997): 22–35.

Lutfy, Carol. "Asian Artists in America: Wenda Gu." *Atelier* (Tokyo) (November 1996): 49–58.

Sartor, Monique. *United Nations—Italian Division.* Milan: Enrico Garibaldi Arte Contemporanea, 1994.

Hans HAACKE (1936)

B. Cologne, Germany. While based in Europe (early 1960s), works in a number of new genres, using devices for freezing and floating. Encounters work of Group Zero (Düsseldorf) and participates in several *Zero* exhibitions. Moves to New York (1965). Assassination of Martin Luther King and Paris insurgency (1968) push him in a more political direction. Helps found Art Workers Coalition (1969). Invited to São Paulo Bienal (1969), but boycotts exhibition (along with many other artists) as a protest against the Brazilian dictatorship. Conducts polls of visitors to his exhibitions (1969–72). Guggenheim show cancelled because of controversy over installation *Shapolsky et al. Manhattan Real Estate Holdings* (1971). Continues to produce work that shows a pronounced political commitment.

BIBLIOGRAPHY

Bourdieu, Pierre, and Hans Haacke. *Free Exchange.* Cambridge: Polity Press, 1995.

Burnham, Jack. "Hans Haacke's Cancelled Show at the Guggenheim." *Artforum* 9, no. 10. (June 1971): 67–71.

Haacke, Hans. *Framing and Being Framed: 7 Works, 1970–75.* Halifax and New York: Press of the Nova Scotia College of Art and Design and New York University Press, 1975.

___. *Werkmonographie.* Edited by Edward F. Fry. Cologne: DuMont Schauberg, 1972.

Hans Haacke. Exh. cat. Oxford and Eindhoven: Museum of Modern Art and Stedelijk van Abbemuseum, 1978.

Hans Haacke: Unfinished Business. Edited by Brian Wallis. New York and Cambridge, Mass.: New Museum of Contemporary Art and MIT Press, 1986.

Siegel, Jeanne. "An Interview with Hans Haacke." *Arts Magazine* 45, no. 7 (May 1971): 18–21.

Tibor HAJAS (1946–1980)

B. Budapest, Hungary. Begins career as a poet; becomes most important representative of performance in Hungary. Stages works in Budapest, Warsaw, Arnhem, and Ghent, specializing in the use of a flash to illuminate seconds of the action. Creates conceptual works showing interest in the relationship between originals and photocopies. Retrospectives held in Paris (1985) and Székesfehérvár (1987).

BIBLIOGRAPHY

Beke, László. "A Performance és Hajas Tibor." *Mozgó Világ* (Budapest), no. 1 (1980): 98–112.

Hajas Tibor, 1946–1980. Paris: Magyar Műhely/Atelier Hongrois, 1985.

Hajas Tibor, 1946–1980: Emlékkiállítás/Memorial Exhibition. Székesfehérvár: István Király Múzeum, 1987.

Nightmare Works: Tibor Hajas. Exh. cat. Essays by László Beke et al. Richmond, Va.: Anderson Gallery, 1990.

HIKOSAKA Naoyoshi (1946)

B. Tokyo. Enters Tama Art University, Tokyo, to study painting (1967). Central member of Bikyōtō, leading post-1970 collectives (1969–78). Meets Yasunao Tone and forms Phenomenology Study Group (1969). Arrested in demonstration and released; leaves school; begins creating events, including *Floor Event* series (1970). Works with Tone to compile a history of avant-garde art in Japan (1971–72). Exhibits in Kyoto Independent (1973), Kyoto Biennale (1973/76), and Paris Biennal (1975). Lives in Kamakura, active as a painter, sculptor, performance artist, writer.

BIBLIOGRAPHY

Hikosaka Naoyoshi. *Hanpuku: Shinkō geijutsu no isō* (Recapitulation: Phases of New Art). Tokyo: Tabata Shoten, 1974.

Tomii, Reiko. *Hikosaka Naoyoshi: Gyakuritsu no jissen/Practice Against the Grain.* Tokyo, forthcoming.

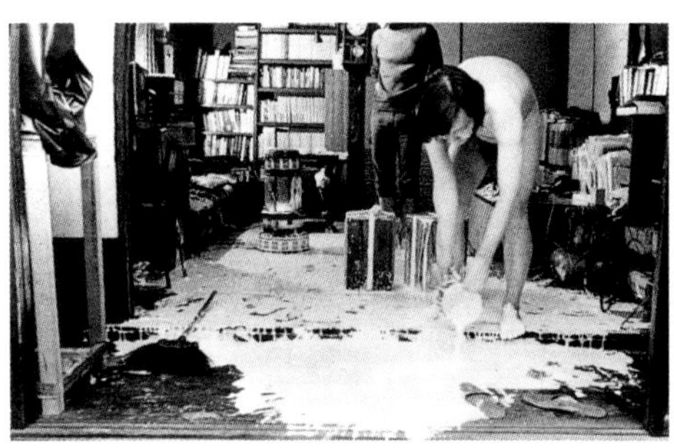

Figure 204.
Hikosaka Naoyoshi, *Floor Event* (*Furoa ivento*), 1970, documentary photograph. Collection of the artist.

HORI Kosai (1947)

B. Takaoka, Toyama Prefecture, Japan. Enters Tama Art University, Tokyo, to study painting (1967). Chairman of Bikyōtō (1969–70), participating in post-1970 collectives, except for Group of Five (1971–78). Arrested during university lockout and released (1969); expelled from school (1970). Begins creating language- and performance-based work, including *Act/Memory-Practice: Reading Affair* series (1971). Exhibits in Kyoto Independent (1973), Kyoto Biennale (1973/76), and Paris Biennal (1977). Writes plays for underground theater groups (1967–77). Presently active as painter, performance artist, writer. Lives in Tokyo.

BIBLIOGRAPHY

Hori Kosai ten: Kaze no me/The Eye of the Wind. Exh. cat. Takaoka: Takaoka Art Museum, 1996.

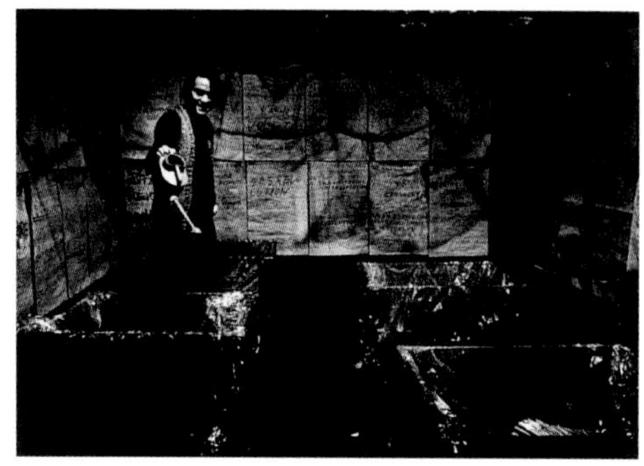

Figure 205.
Hori Kosai, *Revolution: Ceiling, Wall, Floor* (*Revolution: Tenjō, kabe, yuka*), 1971, documentary photograph. Collection of the artist.

HUANG Huacheng (1935–199?)

B. Nanjing, PRC. Moves to Taiwan (1949). Attends Taipei Normal University (1954–58). Participates in exhibition *Black and White* (1962); revolutionary ideas about design influence many Taiwan artists. Collaborates on performance and film for *Theater* exhibition (1966). Organizes the *Great Taipei Painting Exhibition* (1966)—featuring dada-type readymades with a strong direction toward anti-art—and the influential exhibition *Unstable Vision* (1967). Founds Language Beyond Painting Society (1967). Devotes himself to graphic design from the mid-'70s until his death.

BIBLIOGRAPHY

Lai Ying-ying. *Liushiniandai Taiwan fuheyishu yianjiu* (Taiwan's Multimedia Art of the Sixties). Taipei: Guotai Cultural Publisher, 1996.

HUANG Yong Ping (1954)

B. Xiamen, Fujian Province, PRC. Graduates from Zhejiang Academy of Fine Arts, Hangzhou (1982). Produces a series of anti-art projects, including *Roulette Wheel* and *The Beard Was Easiest to Burn* (1985–87). Cofounds Xiamen Dada group (1986). Creates *"A History of Chinese Art" and "A Concise History of Modern Painting" Washed in a Washing Machine for Two Minutes* (1987). Submits a proposal to *China/Avant-garde* (Beijing) entitled *Drawing the National Art Gallery Away;* rejected by organizing committee (1988). Emigrates to France (1989). Mounts first solo exhibition of installation work at École des Beaux-Arts, Rouen (1990). Represented in many international exhibitions, including

Fragmented Memory (Columbus, Ohio, 1993), *Face à l'histoire* (Paris, 1996), Kwangju and Johannesburg biennials (1997), and *Cities on the Move* (Vienna, 1997). Currently resides in Paris.

BIBLIOGRAPHY

Boussand, Juliette. "Le théâtre du monde de Huang Yong Ping ... Hors limites?" *Art Present* (Paris) 13 (Winter 1995): 30–34.

Fei Dawei. "Chine/avant-garde." *Art Press* (Paris) 141 (November 1989): 8, 28–34.

Gebrochene Bilder: Junge Kunst aus China (Broken Pictures: Young Chinese Art). Exh. cat. Bad Honnef: Horlemann Verlag, 1991.

Huang Yong Ping. "Painting with Industrial Technology: Looking for New Substitutions." *Leonardo* (Oxford) 18, no. 2 (1985): 91–92.

Huang Yong Ping. Exh. cat. Texts by Jean-Hubert Martin et al. Paris: Musée National des Arts d'Afrique et d'Océanie, 1996.

Huang Yong Ping: Trois pas neuf traces. Exh. cat. Texts by Fei Dawei et al. Marseille: Ateliers d'Artistes, 1996.

HUANG Yung-sung (1943)

B. Taiwan. Participates in important avant-garde exhibition *Modern Poem* (1966). Organizes a series of group shows under the title *UP* (1967), featuring readymade works aimed at destroying the boundary between art and life. Creates installation work *Pawn* (1967), in which personal mementos are set beside a brick carved with the Chinese character *dang* (pawn), a critical comment on the commodification of aesthetic idealism. Presents *Pawn* in *Unstable Vision* exhibition (1967). Shifts to filmmaking, in particular, documenting rustic life and folk culture (1969 onward).

BIBLIOGRAPHY

Lai Ying-ying. *Liushiniandai Taiwan fuheyishu yianjiu* (Taiwan's Multimedia Art of the Sixties). Taipei: Guotai Cultural Publisher, 1996.

Douglas HUEBLER (1924–1997)

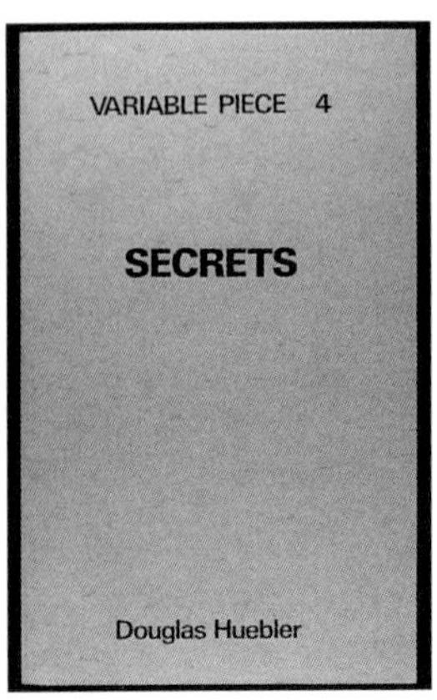

FIGURE 206.
Douglas Huebler, *Variable Piece 4: Secrets,* 1973, book (New York: Printed Matter, 1973). Private collection.

B. Ann Arbor, Mich. Begins career as a sculptor. Solo show at Seth Siegelaub's gallery in November 1968 places him at the center of developments in conceptual art. Subsequently stops producing three-dimensional work and concentrates on text and photography. Contributes 25 "drawings" to *Xeroxbook* (1968). Begins work in series—*Location, Duration, Variable* pieces—composed of typewritten or printed statements that are then photographed (1968–).

BIBLIOGRAPHY

Auping, Michael: "Talking with Douglas Huebler." *Journal* (Los Angeles), no. 15 (July–August 1977): 37–44.

Barry, Huebler, Kosuth, Weiner: [January 5–31, 1969]. New York: Seth Siegelaub, 1969.

Douglas Huebler. Exh. cat. Münster: Westfälischer Kunstverein, 1972.

Douglas Huebler. Exh. cat. Texts by Lucy R. Lippard et al. Eindhoven: Stedelijk van Abbemuseum, 1979.

Douglas Huebler: Location Pieces, Site Sculpture, Duration Works, Drawings, Variable Pieces. Exh. cat. Boston: Museum of Fine Arts and Institute of Contemporary Art, 1972.

Douglas Huebler: November 1968. Exh. cat. New York: Seth Siegelaub, 1968.

Huebler, Douglas. *Crocodile Tears (Brief Fictions Re-sounding from the Proposal in Variable Piece #70:1971 "to photographically document the existence of everyone alive")*. Exh. cat. Buffalo, N.Y.: Albright-Knox Gallery and CEPA Gallery, 1985.

Robert HUOT (1935)

B. Staten Island, N.Y. Begins art career as a minimal painter, often on transparent nylon rather than canvas (mid-'60s). Designs sets for Twyla Tharp Dance Co.; collaborates in the Chameleons performance group; produces conceptual works that approach complete dematerialization, i.e., tape pieces and empty rooms painted blue, then stops painting altogether. Organizes antiwar benefit show with Lucy Lippard and others (1968). Moves to a farm in upstate New York (1969). Exhibits anonymously, i.e., a ladder in MoMA's *Information* show (1970). Through friendship with Hollis Frampton, produces diary films notable for their emotional intensity, for instance, *Rolls: 1971*. Returns to painting (1971) with the *Diary* series, autobiographical narratives unfolding on rolls of canvas. Tours China with other New York artists and writers (1978). Produces antinuke posters for New York subway and other projects (1979–84). Lives in New Berlin, New York.

BIBLIOGRAPHY

Bob Huot. Zurich: Galerie Renée Ziegler, 1970.

Lippard, Lucy, ed. *Six Years: The Dematerialization of the Art Object from 1966 to 1972*. New York: Praeger, 1973.

Robert Huot, Allianz 8. Stuttgart: Galerie Ursula Schurr, 1980.

Robert Huot at Paula Cooper. New York: Paula Cooper Gallery, 1969.

Robert Huot Diaries. N.p.: n.p., 1979.

Roberto JACOBY (1944)

B. Buenos Aires. Studies art with Roberto Rosenfeld and Pati Blumencweig (1964), and sociology at University of Buenos Aires (1972). Works closely with theoretician Oscar Masotta and artists Eduardo Costa, Raúl Escari, León Ferrari,and Risúleo (1965–67). With Costa and Escari, writes and produces *First Manifesto and Work of "Arte de los Medios"* (1965–66). Stages Week of Happenings, Instituto di Tella (1966). Presents *Automatic Circuit*, a mass-mediatic work with answering machine (1967). Installs *Message at the Tella* in the 1968 Experiencias Visuales (Instituto di Tella). Collaborates on Tucumán Arde (1968). Contributes to underground publications, including *Sobre* (1968–69). Works as a researcher at Centro de Investigaciones Ciencias Sociales (1969–79). Produces manuscript on epistemology of revolutionary thought (1979–85). Initiates song and poetry writing; founds urban musical group Virus (1979–80). Organizes and produces experimental rock concerts (1980s).

BIBLIOGRAPHY

Costa, Eduardo, Raúl Escari, and Roberto Jacoby. *Un arte de los medios de comunicación* (manifesto). In *Happenings*. Edited by Oscar Masotta, 119–22. Buenos Aires: Editorial Jorge Álvarez, 1967.

Roberto Jacoby Papers. Buenos Aires, Argentina.

Romero Brest, Jorge. *El arte en la Argentina: Ultimas décadas*. Buenos Aires: Paídos, 1969.

Jozef JANKOVIČ (1937)

B. Bratislava, Czechoslovakia. Studies at Secondary School of Applied Arts (1952–56) and Academy of Fine Arts (1956–62), Bratislava. Earns an international reputation early on as a sculptor of monumental, simultaneously expressive and impersonal human figures. Produces a monument to Slovak partisans of World War II, *Banska Bystrica* (1967–69), a state commission subsequently demolished for being "formalist" and "inhuman." Conceptual work, begun in 1970s, consists of utopian architectural monuments containing sharp political and social criticism. Exhibits internationally, including Budapest, Vienna, Prague, Paris, and Venice. One of the first Slovak artists to incorporate computer technology into his work. Resides in Bratislava, where he teaches at the Academy of Fine Arts.

BIBLIOGRAPHY

Jozef Jankovič: Tvorba z rokov, 1958–1997. Bratislava: Slovenská Národná Galéria, 1997.

Ilya KABAKOV (1933)

B. Dnepropetrovsk, Soviet Union. Attends Moscow Art School (1945–51). Graduates with degree in book illustration from Surikov Art Institute (1957). Works for publishing houses such as Detskii Mir and Detskaia Literatura (until 1987), while producing a wealth of albums, paintings, and drawings that situate him as a pivotal figure in Moscow's conceptual art circle. Makes first trip to Western Europe in 1987 for solo exhibition at Kunstverein Graz. Subsequently lives and works in the West, participating in numerous exhibitions and projects united under the name "total installation." Presently lives in New York.

BIBLIOGRAPHY

Ilya Kabakov. Exh. cat. Berne: Kunsthalle, 1985.

Ilya Kabakov: Installations, 1983–1995. Paris: Éditions Centre Georges Pompidou, 1995.

Ilya Kabakov: Ten Characters. Exh. cat. London and New York: ICA and Ronald Feldman Fine Arts, 1989.

Morgan, Stuart. "Kabakov's Albums." *Artscribe* 75 (May–June 1989): 57–59.

Storr, Robert. "An Interview with Ilya Kabakov." *Art in America* 83, no. 1 (January 1995): 60–69, 125.

Tupitsyn, Margarita. "Ilya Kabakov." *Flash Art*, no. 126 (February–March 1986): 67–69.

Tupitsyn, Victor. "A Psychodrome of Misreading: Ilya Kabakov and Harold Bloom." *Third Text*, no. 33 (1995): 25–30.

Wallach, Amei. *The Man Who Never Threw Anything Away*. New York: Abrams, 1996.

Tadeusz KANTOR (1915–1990)

B. Wielopole, Poland. Studies at Academy of Fine Arts, Cracow (1936–39), making objects, assemblages, environments, installations, and paintings in abstract and informel modes. Serves in Polish Resistance, directing an underground theater (1940–44). Founds Cricot 2 (1955), and is founding member of artists' collective Grupa Krakowska (1957). Produces actions, happenings, and conceptual works from mid-'60s. Writes play *The Dead Class* (1975), launching career as Poland's most important theater director and theoretician of dramatic arts. Dies 1990 in Cracow, where his estate is preserved in the Cricoteka.

BIBLIOGRAPHY

Borowski, Wieslaw. *Tadeusz Kantor.* Warsaw: Wydawnictwa Artystyczene i Filmowe, 1982.

Cieszkowski, Krzysztof Z. "Illusion and Repetition: Tadeusz Kantor Interviewed." *Art Monthly* (London), no. 42 (December 1980–January 1981): 6–8.

Kantor, Tadeusz. *Halálszínház* (Theater of Death). Budapest: Magyarországi Alternatív Színházi Központ Egyesület, 1994.

___. *A Journey Through Other Spaces: Essays and Manifestos, 1944–1990.* Edited by Michal Kobialka. Berkeley: University of California Press, 1993.

___. *Tadeusz Kantor (1915–1990): Leben im Werk.* Nuremberg: Verlag für Moderne Kunst, 1996.

___. *Le théâtre de la mort.* Edited by Denis Bablet. Lausanne: Éditions l'Age d'Homme, 1977.

Klossowicz, Jan. *Tadeusz Kantor: Teatr.* Warsaw: PIW, 1991.

Plesniarowicz, Krzysztof. *Kantor: Artysta konca wieku.* Wroclaw: Wydawnictwa Dolnoslaskie, 1997.

Tadeusz Kantor: Paintings and Sculptures. Exh. cat. Cracow: Muzeum Narodowe, 1991.

KASHIHARA Etsutomu (1941)

B. Kōbe, Japan. Studies painting at Tama Art University, Tokyo (1961–65). Collaborates with Koizumi Hiroo and Maekawa Kinzō on *What Is Mr. X?* (1968–69). Produces instruction-based *Exhibition* series (1970–) and creates language works such as *This Is a Book* and *Rock* (both 1970). Edits and contributes to *Kirokutai* (1972–77); participates in *'73/5: Affair and Practice by 12* at Pinar Galleries, Tokyo. Exhibits in Tokyo (1970), São Paulo (1973), Paris (1975) biennials. Teaches at B-Semi School, Yokohama (1972–85) and Kyoto Seika University (from 1990). Publishes children's books under pen name Maki Hiroshi. Resides in Uji, Kyoto Prefecture.

BIBLIOGRAPHY

Chokkan no umi e: Kashihara Etsutomu/Toward the Sea of Intuition: Etsutomu Kashihara, 1961–1987. Tokyo: Gendai Kikakushitsu, 1987.

On KAWARA (1933)

B. Kariya, Aichi Prefecture, Japan. Produces *Bath Room* series (1953–54) and "printed painting" series before leaving Japan (1959). Begins paintings consisting of a single word such as ART (1964), and a series of "landscapes" with painted figures indicating longitude and latitude (1965). Moves to New York (1965). Initiates *Today* or "date painting" series, in which the work's date is painted in white on a colored background (January 1966–); the work is then placed in a box together with a sheet of that day's newspaper. Contributes first "I am still alive" telegram to Claura and Siegelaub's *One Month* show, Paris (1969). Begins series of found newspaper snippets (*I Read,* 1966–), xeroxed maps (*I Went,* 1968–), postcards (*I Got Up,* 1969), and so on. Continues these and other essentially interminable projects to this day.

BIBLIOGRAPHY

Mot pour mot: Les images quotidiennes du pouvoir: On Kawara au jour le jour/Word for Word: The Daily Images of Power: On Kawara from Day to Day. Exh. cat. Text by René Denizot. Paris: Galerie Yvon Lambert, 1979.

On Kawara. Exh. cat. Dijon: Le Consortium, 1985.

On Kawara: Continuity/Discontinuity, 1963–1979. Exh. cat. Edited by Björn Springfeldt. Stockholm: Moderna Museet, 1980.

On Kawara 1967. Exh. cat. Los Angeles: Otis Art Institute Gallery, 1977.

On Kawara 1973: Produktion eines Jahres/One Year's Production. Exh. cat. Berne: Kunsthalle, 1974.

Rorimer, Anne. "The Date Paintings of On Kawara." *Museum Studies* (Chicago) 17, no. 2 (1991): 120–37.

Mary KELLY (1941)

B. Fort Dodge, Iowa. Studies in Florence (1965); continues postgraduate work at St. Martin's School of Art, London, arriving just in time for the student protests of May 1968. Becomes involved in women's liberation movement, and begins to think politically and theoretically about her role as a gendered artist. Encounters Hans Haacke's *Shapolsky et al.* and *Index 2* by Art & Language, both exhibited at Hayward Gallery, London (1972), which provide models for her subsequent work. Following feminist dictum, "the personal is political," produces *Post-Partum Document* (1973–75), documenting the passage of her infant son through the early stages of child development; exhibits the work at ICA, London (1975). Moves to New York (1987).

BIBLIOGRAPHY

Kelly, Mary. "On Sexual Politics and Art." In *Art and Politics.* Edited by B. Taylor. Winchester: Winchester School of Art, 1980.

Kelly, Mary. *Post-Partum Document.* London: Routledge and Kegan, 1983.

Mary Kelly: Interim. Exh. cat. Edinburgh: Fruitmarket Gallery and Riverside Studios, 1985.

Mary Kelly. Essays by Margaret Iversen, Douglas Crimp, and Homi K. Bhabha. London: Phaidon Press, 1997.

Social Process/Collaborative Action: Mary Kelly, 1970–1975. Exh. cat. Edited by Judith Mastai. Vancouver, B.C.: Charles H. Scott Gallery, 1997.

Peter KENNEDY (1945)

B. Brisbane, Australia. Studies at National Art School, Sydney (1965–66), and moves to Sydney (1967). Exhibits neon light installations at Gallery A, Sydney/Melbourne, and establishes cooperative gallery Inhibodress in Sydney with Mike Parr (1970). Participates in Harald Szeemann exhibition, *I want to leave a nice welldone child here (20 Australian Artists),* Sydney/Melbourne; begins work as a performer/composer with AZ music (1971). Collaborates on *Idea Demonstrations* with Parr; Inhibodress closes; tours North and South America (1972). Represented in Sydney Biennale (1979/84) and Australian Perspecta (1981).

BIBLIOGRAPHY

Kennedy, Peter, with John Hughes. *Istoria: Selected Works, 1978–1986.* Hobart: Centre for the Arts Gallery, 1986.

Peter Kennedy, John Nixon: Two Contemporary Artists. Melbourne: National Gallery of Victoria, 1976.

KIM Bong-joon (1954)

B. Seoul. Studies painting at Hong-ik University, and apprentices to Buddhist master Manbong. Takes up various forms of folk art, including mask dance. Founds artists' collective Durung (1982), which aims to reestablish the relationship between artist and audience as well as between art and communal festivals. Extends group's activities into art education, the Gondongche (community) cultural movement, and the labor union movement. Various exhibitions (1984 onward) include first Durung group show, Kyungin Gallery, Seoul (1984), *Malttugi* (Itinerant) shows in Germany, and solo exhibitions in Heidelberg, Hamburg, San Francisco. Participates in *Min Joong Art,* Artists Space, New York (1988). Presently resides in Munmak.

BIBLIOGRAPHY

Sung Wan-kyung. "The Inaugural Exhibition of Durung." *Guegan Misul* (Seoul), no. 30 (Summer 1984): 186–87.

Yoon Bum-mo. *A New Horizon and a Creative Praxis of National Art: On the Works of Kim Bong-joon.* Exh. cat. Seoul: Gana Gallery, 1991.

KIM Dong-won

B. Seoul. Studies communications at Sogang University. Directs video ***Sanaggyedong Olympic*** (1986) in collaboration with the residents of Sanggyedong. Works as assistant director on the film *Tae* (Womb, 1987–88). Lives in Seoul.

KIM Yong-min (1943)

B. Chungnam Province, South Korea. Studies painting at Hong-ik University; graduates 1969. Participates in major experimental art exhibitions (1974 onward), including S.T. Group shows, festivals of modern art in Daegu and Seoul, various Seoul independents, and École de Seoul Exhibition. Produces *Floor* for 3rd Independent Exhibition, National Museum of Modern Art, Seoul (1975), one of the first Korean installation works in a conceptualist vein. Extends concept to *Fence* for 4th Independent (1976). Exhibits in 1st Seoul Biennale (1974) and São Paulo Bienal (1979). Nearly disappears from art scene (late 1980s) until a retrospective at 21st Century Gallery, Seoul (1994). Lives in Yonsan.

BIBLIOGRAPHY

Lee In-bum. "The Works of Kim Yong-min." *Gana Art Magazine* (Seoul), no. 52 (January–February 1997): 70–77.

Lee Yil. "Works and Ideas of Kim Yong-min." In *Artists in Question 1981.* Seoul: Galerie de Seoul, 1981.

KIM Yong-tae (1946)

B. Pusan, South Korea. Studies painting at Joong-ang University, then manages an art gallery and editing agency. Founds artist/critic collective Hyunsilgwa-Baron (Reality & Utterance, 1979). Participates in group's exhibitions, including its first at Donganbang Gallery, Seoul (1980), *Urban Vision 2* (1981), and *Images of Happiness 3* (1982). Works for Association of Min Joong Artists (1985–), established to fight censorship of political art, and Minyechong (Korean People's Artist Federation,

1988–). Represented in *JAALA,* Metropolitan Museum, Tokyo (1986) and *Min Joong Art,* Artists Space, New York (1988). Lives in Seoul.

BIBLIOGRAPHY

Kim Yong-tae. "The Ardent Cultural Movement for Democracy and Unification." *Hanguere Shinmun* (Hanguere Newspaper in English), May 15, 1989.

___. "Travel at Dongduchun: Souvenir Pictures." In *Hyunsilgwa Baron,* 110–17. Seoul: Yolhwadang, 1985.

Sung Wan-kyung. "On the Works of Kim Yong-tae." In *Hyunsilgwa Baron,* 118–19. Seoul: Yolhwadang, 1985.

Yves KLEIN (1928–1962)

B. Nice. Son of two painters, spends most of his youth traveling between Nice and Paris. Never attends art school, but becomes an excellent judo artist while trying to sell his parents' paintings. Moves to Tokyo (1952), where he continues practicing judo at Kōdōkan Institute and attains the Fourth Grade (1953). Returns to Paris (1954), teaching judo at the American Center (1954–59). Submits a monochromatic orange painting to Salon des Réalités Nouvelles (1955); work is rejected when he refuses to add a black dot, which jury requested in order to make it a "genuine" abstract painting. Presents his first "propositions monochromes" at Galerie Colette Allendy (1956). Stages many notable "events" over the next six years, i.e., *The Void* (1958), a show with nothing to see; first sale of a *Zone de sensibilité picturale immatérielle* (1959); and *Leap into the Void* (1960). Cofounds Nouveaux Réalistes group (1960–61).

BIBLIOGRAPHY

Restany, Pierre. *Yves Klein.* Translated by John Shepley. New York: Abrams, 1982.

Stich, Sidra. *Yves Klein.* Stuttgart: Edition Cantz, 1994.

Yves Klein, 1928–1962. Exh. cat. Paris: Éditions Centre Georges Pompidou, 1983.

Yves Klein, 1928–1962: A Retrospective. Exh. cat. Houston: Institute for the Arts, Rice University, 1982.

Yves Klein, 1928–1962: Selected Writings. Exh. cat. London: Tate Gallery Publications, 1974.

Július KOLLER (1939)

B. Piešt'any, Czechoslovakia. Attends Secondary School of Applied Arts (1955–58) and Academy of Fine Arts (1959–65), Bratislava. Incorporates words in paintings (1962–63), thereby becoming a forerunner of conceptualism in Eastern Europe. Produces actions around sports activities (tennis and ping-pong), dubbing them "antihappenings." Undertakes the public reparation of stockings as an exhibition (1968), and for similar reasons founds U.F.O. (Universal Physicultural Operation). Resides in Bratislava, Slovak Republic.

BIBLIOGRAPHY

Stephen, A., and M. Dzurik. "Czechoslovakia: The East Turns West." *Art Monthly* (London), no. 44 (1991): 14–16.

Strauss, Thomas. "Three Slovak Models for Contemporary Art Actions." In *Cross Currents Yearbook of Central European Culture.* Ann Arbor: University of Michigan, 1984.

Vitaly KOMAR (1943)
Aleksandr MELAMID (1945)

Both b. Moscow. Begin work as a team under name K/M after graduation from Stroganov Art School, Moscow (1965). Mount first solo exhibition at Café Siniaia Ptitsa (Café Bluebird, 1965). Complete first sots art series (1972). In first installation works, *Paradise* and *Biography of the Contemporary* (both 1973), develop their style of "conceptual eclecticism." Begin work in a variety of media, including photography, performance, music, and public projects (1974 onward). Participate in infamous *Bulldozer Show* in Moscow, during which their *Double Self-Portrait as Lenin and Stalin* is destroyed (1974). First solo exhibition abroad held at Ronald Feldman Gallery (1976). Move to New York (1978). Participate in Documenta 8 (1987) and Venice Biennale (1997).

BIBLIOGRAPHY

Burnham, Jack. "Komar and Melamid—Post USSR—Get Religion." *Art in America* 67 (February 1979): 13.

Fields, Marc. "Komar and Melamid and the Luxury of Style." *Artforum* 16 (April 1982): 58–63.

Indiana, Gary. "Komar & Melamid Confidential." *Art in America* 73 (June 1985): 94–101+.

Komar & Melamid. Exh. cat. Edinburgh and Oxford: Fruitmarket Gallery and Museum of Modern Art, 1985.

Komar, Vitaly, and Aleksandr Melamid. "In Search of Religion." *Artforum* 18 (May 1980): 36–46.

___. *Painting by Numbers: Komar and Melamid's Scientific Guide to Art.* Edited by JoAnn Wypijewski. New York: Farrar, Straus, Giroux, 1997.

Nathanson, Melvyn B. *Komar & Melamid: Two Soviet Dissident Artists.* Carbondale: Southern Illinois University Press, 1979.

Ratcliff, Carter. *Komar & Melamid.* New York: Abbeville Press, 1988.

Tupitsyn, Margarita. "The Red Guardians of the Tradition." *High Performance* 7, no. 4 (1984).

Tupitsyn, Victor. "Icons of Iconoclasm." *Parachute,* no. 91 (1998): 14–18.

Vitaly Komar and Aleksandr Melamid: A Retrospective. Exh. cat. Wichita, Kan.: Edwin A. Ulrich Museum of Art, Wichita State University, 1980.

Rachid KORAÏCHI (1947)

B. Ain al Baida, Algeria. Studies at the Institute of Fine Arts, Algiers, and various schools in Paris. From the early 1970s, produces elaborate works on paper, banners, and large-scale pottery adorned with combinations of Arabic script and other non-Roman-based calligraphic signs and symbols, usually in dramatically contrasting black, white, and gold colors. Drawings and writings borrow from classical Islamic texts as well as contemporary writers and poets, and also feature independently created visual imagery drawn from language symbols. Exhibits widely throughout the Arab world and abroad, including one-person exhibitions at the Galerie Sidhever, Paris (1994), and the Leighton House, London (1998), and the group exhibitions *Rencontres africaines—Exposition d'art actuel* (1994) and *Regard sur l'art contemporain tunisien* (1995), both at the Institut du Monde Arabe, Paris. Lives in Tunisia (in exile) and Paris.

BIBLIOGRAPHY

Koraïchi, Rachid, and Ethel Adnan. *Le testament de l'ennemi.* Madrid: Edition Mensa, 1989.

Koraïchi, Rachid, and Mahmoud Darwish. *L'hymne grave.* Madrid: Edition Mensa, 1990.

Koraïchi, Rachid, Pierre Restany, and Nicole de Pontcharra. *Cris-écrits.* Brussels: Éditions de Lassa, 1991.

Koraïchi, Rachid, and Michel Butor. *Salomé.* Geneva: Éditions Editart, 1992.

Koraïchi, Rachid, and Mohamed Dib. *L'enfant jazz.* Paris: Éditions Franck Bordas, 1997.

Koraïchi, Rachid, Roxane Hodes, and Nicole de Pontcharra. *Lettres d'argile.* Nîmes: Édition Corinne Maeght, 1997.

Koraïchi, Rachid, Mahmoud Darwish, Hassan Massaoudy, and Abdelkebir Khatibi. *A Nation in Exile/Un nation en exil.* Amman: Darat al Funun, Abdul Hameed Shoman Foundation, 1997–98.

Padel, Jean-Louis. *Koraïchi.* [France]: Éditions Ades Sud, 1999.

Joseph KOSUTH (1945)

B. Toledo, Ohio. Moves to New York (1965). Soon begins to use language in conjunction with found objects designated as art, printing words on sheets of clear glass and creating self-referential neon works. Embarks on *Art as Idea as Idea* series (1966), central to what he names *The First Investigation,* using photographic enlargements of words and their dictionary definitions to combine image, text, and object into a single entity, referring to an invisible concept such as "meaning" or "art." In *The Second Investigation* (1968–69), makes a series of works that appear in newspapers and on billboards and fliers, displacing the gallery or museum setting. Publishes a number of key theoretical texts and curates important exhibitions at Lannis Gallery and Museum of Normal Art, New York, gathering together a cohort of likeminded artists. Completes *Investigations* (1973) and subsequently produces billboards and installation works. Launches *The Fox* (mid-'70s), to which he makes frequent contributions.

BIBLIOGRAPHY

Barry, Huebler, Kosuth, Weiner: [January 5–31, 1969]. New York: Seth Siegelaub, 1969.

Joseph Kosuth: Investigationen über Kunst und "Problemkreise" seit 1965. Exh. cat. 5 vols. Texts by Terry Atkinson, Michael Baldwin, Mel Ramsden, and Terry Smith. Lucerne: Kunstmuseum, 1973.

Joseph Kosuth: Bedeutung von Bedeutung: Texte und Dokumentation der Investigation en über Kunst seit 1965 in Auswahl/Joseph Kosuth: The Making of Meaning: Selected Writings and Documentation of Investigations on Art Since 1965. Stuttgart: Staatsgalerie, 1981.

Joseph Kosuth: Eine grammatische Bemerkung/A Grammatical Remark. Stuttgart: Edition Cantz, 1993.

Joseph Kosuth, l'art de les idees: Una visió de trenta anys, 1965–1995. Exh. cat. Mallorca: Fundació Pilar i Joan Miró, 1995.

Kosuth, Joseph. *Art After Philosophy and After: Collected Writings, 1966–1990.* Edited by Gabriele Guercio. Cambridge, Mass.: MIT Press, 1991.

___. *Function Funzione Fonction Funktion.* Turin: Sperone Editore, 1970.

___. *Interviews, 1969–1989.* Stuttgart: Edition P. Schwarz, 1989.

Christine KOZLOV (1945)

B. New York. Begins to base work on information, using audiotapes, photographs, film, printed communications, and an array of semantic strategies, including self-referentiality, systematic ordering, diaristic chronicling, and reproduction substitution (mid-'60s). Plays central role in group of artists exhibiting at Lannis Gallery and Museum of Normal Art (New York), alongside Kosuth, where she and Hanne Darboven are often the only female artists represented. Participates in Seth Siegelaub's *One Month* show in Paris (1969), the only woman among 31 artists. Vanishes from exhibition rosters after the 1970 *Information* show (MoMa, New York). Contributes to *The Fox* (mid-'70s). Moves to London, where she lives today.

BIBLIOGRAPHY

"Christine Kozlov." In *Art conceptuel, formes conceptuelles/Conceptual Art, Conceptual Forms,* 268–70. Exh. cat. Paris: Galerie 1900▲2000 and Galerie de Poche, 1990.

Kozlov, Christine. Artist's card. In *C. 7,500.* Exh. cat. Valencia: California Institute of the Arts, 1973.

___. Artist's statement. In *Conceptual Art and Conceptual Aspects.* Exh. cat. New York: New York Cultural Center in association with Fairleigh Dickinson University, 1970.

Non-Anthropomorphic Art by Four Young Artists: Joseph Kosuth, Christine Kozlov, Michael Rinaldi, Ernest Rossi. New York: Lannis Gallery, 1966.

Laboratoire Agit-Art

Founded 1973 in Dakar, Senegal. Collective of artists, dramatists, performers, poets, and filmmakers led by poet/artist Issa Samb (a.k.a. Joe Ouakam), El Hadji Sy, and Babacar Traoré. Produces spontaneous actions, performances, and exhibitions challenging dogmatic conceptions of African identity, i.e., theories of negritude promoted by the Senegalese state under President Senghor. Rejects production of commodities for the art market, focusing instead on discussion, debate, and agitation.

BIBLIOGRAPHY

Camara, Ery. "Art et politique en Afrique: Des réalités dérangeantes." In *Face a l' histoire, 1933–1996: L'artiste moderne devant l'événement historique.* Paris: Flammarion and Éditions Centre Georges Pompidou, 1996.

Ebong, Ima. "Negritude: Between Mask and Flag—Senegalese Cultural Ideology and the 'Ecole de Dakar.'" In *Africa Explores: 20th Century African Art.* Munich and New York: Prestel Verlag and Center for African Art, 1991.

Samb, Issa. "The Social and Economic Situation of Artists of the Ecole de Dakar." In *Bildende Kunst der Gegenwart in Senegal/Anthology of Contemporary Fine Arts in Senegal.* Edited by Friedrich Axt and El Hadji Sy. Frankfurt am Main: Museum für Volkerkunde, 1989.

Seven Stories About Modern Art in Africa. Exh. cat. Edited by Clémentine Deliss, with essays by Issa Samb, El Hadji Sy, and others. Paris and New York: Flammarion, 1995.

Labor Newsreel

Founded 1989 in Seoul. Produces video reports and documentaries on current political events and social movements, including *Fired Workers* (1997), *Report on the General Strike 1 and 2* (1997), distributing 200 to 800 copies of each report to labor unions and other activist organizations.

David LAMELAS (1946)

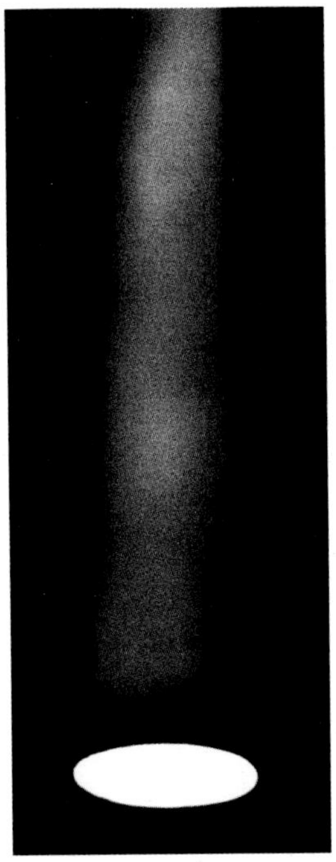

FIGURE 207.
David Lamelas, *Límite de una proyección.* 1967, Installation, Instituto Torcuato di Tella, Buenos Aires.

B. Buenos Aires. Studies at Academia Nacional de Bellas Artes, Buenos Aires (1966), and St. Martin's School of Art, London (1969). Produces minimalist site-specific sculptures (1965–67). Participates in 1967 Experiencias Visuales (Instituto di Tella) with *Situació de tiempo,* a 17-television display that signals the beginning of his investigations into media technology. Receives sculpture prize at São Paulo Bienal (1967). Installs *Office of Information About the Vietnam War* at 1968 Venice Biennale. Participates in *Information,* MoMA, New York (1970). Produces first feature film, *The Desert People* (1971). Moves to Los Angeles (1977). Returns to Europe (1988).

BIBLIOGRAPHY

David Lamelas: Fifteen Years. Exh. cat. Text by Jorge Glusberg. Buenos Aires: Centro de Arte y Comunicación, 1978.

David Lamelas: A New Refutation of Time. Exh. cat. Texts by Lynda Morris and Benjamin H. D. Buchloh. Munich and Rotterdam: Kunstverein München and Witte de With, 1997.

Lamelas, David. *Publication.* London: Nigel Greenwood, 1970.

___, and Raúl Escari. "Self Awareness." *Art and Artists* (London), no. 20 (July 1969): 18–21.

Lavandula, Labiatae, Lamiales. Exh. cat. Text by Frederick Ted Castle. Brussels: Galerie des Beaux-Arts, 1991.

Rizzo, Patricia. "David Lamelas y Oscar Bony." Unpub. ms., 1993. Patricia Rizzo Papers, Buenos Aires.

Sol LeWITT (1928)

B. Hartford, Conn. Principal figure in minimal art movement of 1960s, and generally regarded as one of the architects of conceptualism. Influenced by Muybridge and Albers, creates works using serial repetition of standardized areas of flat color (early '60s). Begins to make modular structures of cubes, employing fabricators to construct them (1965). Quickly realizes that work of this kind—based on predetermined permutations of predetermined forms with predetermined dimensions placed on a standardized grid according to a predetermined formula—can be fabricated on the basis of a set of instructions. Publishes "Paragraphs on Conceptual Art" (1967), followed by "Sentences on Conceptual Art" (1969), which propose that the exhibited work is simply a means of making the original conceptual process visible. Continues to make primarily wall drawings, realized by fabricators according to his instructions.

BIBLIOGRAPHY

Alloway, Lawrence. "Sol LeWitt: Modules, Walls, Books." *Artforum* 13, no. 8 (April 1975): 38–44.

Krauss, Rosalind E. "LeWitt in Progress." In *The Originality of the Avant-garde and Other Modernist Myths,* 244–58. Cambridge, Mass.: MIT Press, 1987.

Kuspit, Donald. "Sol LeWitt: The Look of Thought." *Art in America* 63, no. 5 (September–October 1975): 43–49.

LeWitt, Sol. "Paragraphs on Conceptual Art." *Artforum* 5, no. 10 (June 1967): 79–81.

___. "Sentences on Conceptual Art." *Art-Language* (Coventry, Eng.) 1, no. 1 (May 1969): 11–13.

Lippard, Lucy R. "Sol LeWitt: Non-Visual Structures." *Artforum* 5, no. 8 (April 1967): 42–46.

Sol LeWitt. Exh. cat. The Hague: Gemeentemuseum, 1970.

Sol LeWitt. Exh. cat. Essays by Lucy R. Lippard et al. New York: Museum of Modern Art, 1978.

Sol LeWitt: Drawings, 1958–1992. Exh. cat. The Hague: Gemeentemuseum, 1992.

Sol LeWitt: Testi critici. Rome: I Libri di AEIOU, Incontri Internazionali d'Arte, 1997.

Lucy LIPPARD (1937)

B. New York. Works as a free-lance writer on contemporary art (1964 onward), and befriends many minimal artists about whom she writes. Interest in conceptual art follows development of minimalism into conceptualism. Founding member of Art Workers Coalition, active in art world protests and women's movement. Writes "conceptual novel" *I See, You Mean* (1970), incorporating found material and tracing permutations of six characters designated A, B, C, D, E, and F. Turns organization of art exhibitions into a branch of conceptualism in its own right, for instance, *C. 7,500,* featuring predominantly conceptualist work by women (1973). Publishes *Six Years* (1973), a fascinating account of the crucial early phase of conceptual art, structured as a cross between an annotated calendar and personal journal.

BIBLIOGRAPHY

557,087: An Exhibition. Organized by Lucy R. Lippard. Seattle: Seattle Art Museum, 1969. Version titled *955,000* organized for Vancouver Art Gallery, 1970.

Lippard, Lucy, ed. *Six Years: The Dematerialization of the Art Object from 1966 to 1972.* New York: Praeger, 1973.

Lee LOZANO (1930)

B. Newark, N.J. Becomes well known in 1960s as a figurative, then abstract painter. Produces *Wave* series (1967–70), in which she develops an interest in mathematical procedures. Simultaneously produces conceptual works reflecting this interest in systems, i.e., a series of notebooks in which she records plans and principles for structuring her everyday life as an artist (1969–71). Notebooks include written instructions to herself covering such topics as what to eat and wear, who to meet, when to masturbate, and so on. Makes a conscious decision to stop painting (1970). Initiates her "boycott women" project (1971), refusing all contact with women, a project that continues to the present day. Lives in Dallas, Texas.

BIBLIOGRAPHY

Adrian, Dennis. "Lee Lozano." *Artforum* 5, no. 5 (January 1967): 60.

Benedikt, Michael. "Lee Lozano." *Art News* 65, no. 7 (November 1966): 14+.

Lee Lozano: Matrix 135. Exhibition brochure. Hartford, Conn.: Wadsworth Atheneum, 1998.

Linville, Kasha. "Lee Lozano, Whitney Museum." *Artforum* 9, no. 6 (February 1971): 81+.

Perreault, John. "Art &...." *Village Voice,* December 17, 1970, 27.

Ana LUPAŞ (1940)

B. Cluj, Romania. Attends Academy of Fine Arts, then Ion Andreescu Fine Arts Institute, Cluj (1952–62). Becomes a textile designer, writer, sculptor, performance and land artist from 1962 onward. Combines textile design with conceptual and land works with the aim of synthesizing folk and contemporary art. Refers to her work as "social therapeutics." Participates regularly in textile biennials in Lausanne, and international art biennials (1969 onward). Mounts first solo exhibition, Galeria Apollo, Bucharest (1972). Passport revoked 1985–90. Lives and teaches in Cluj, where she exerts enormous influence on Romanian art students.

BIBLIOGRAPHY

Macarevicz, Zbigniew. "Ana Lupaş/Warsaw." *Projekt* (Warsaw), no. 4 (1973).

Prut, Constantin. "Ana Lupaş." In *Dictionnar de arta moderna.* Bucharest: Editura Albatros, 1982.

M Group

All-male performance collective founded by Song Haidong and active 1985–86 in Shanghai. "M" of title stands for "male." Members include Tang Guangming, Yang Xu, and Zhou Tiehai, all of whom attended Shanghai Drama Institute (1982–85). Performances involve enactment of sadomasochistic scenarios, i.e., *Ceremony* and *Violence,* in which, for instance, several performers beat an artist as he tries to paint. Group disbands in early 1990s.

BIBLIOGRAPHY

Gao Minglu et al. *Zhongguo dangdai meishushi, 1985–1986* (History of Chinese Contemporary Art, 1985–1986). Shanghai: Shanghai People's Press, 1991.

János MAJOR (1934)

B. Budapest, Hungary. Studies graphic art at Academy of Fine Arts, Budapest, under Sándor Ék and Károly Koffán; graduates 1959. Receives awards at international exhibitions in Vienna (1966) and Vignola (1968). Participates in important avant-garde exhibitions organized under the auspices of IPARTERV (state architectural design institute) during late '60s, and produces various conceptual works combining photographs of tombstones and ironic texts on the art scene. Mounts first solo exhibition at Fényes Adolf Room, Budapest (1969). Stops making art in early '70s, and becomes official draftsman for Budapest Museum of History archaeological excavations. Returns to artmaking (1990s) in form of comic strips. Lives in Budapest.

BIBLIOGRAPHY

Krunák, Emese. "Az avantgarde grafika elõfutára, Major János mũvészetérõl" (On the Art of János Major, Forerunner of Avant-garde Graphic Art). *Mũvészet,* no. 7 (1987).

Antonio MANUEL (1947)

B. Avelãs de Caminho, Portugal. Family emigrates to Brazil (1953), settling in Rio de Janeiro. Begins to draw in 1963. Student of Ivan Serpa's workshop (until 1973), and active member of politicized *carioca* avant-garde. Participates in *Tropicália* (1967), *Apocalipopótese* (1968), *Salão da bússola* (1969), and *Do corpo à terra* (1970). Challenges censorship and mass media through newspaper interventions and distributing hermetically sealed ballot boxes to be opened only by force (1966–68). Protests rejection by National Salon jury by arriving nude at exhibition's opening (*O corpo é a obra,* 1970). Participation in Paris Biennal (1969) and solo exhibition at Museu de Arte Moderna, Rio (1973) censored by authorities. Produces site-specific installations, painting, sculpture (1980–).

BIBLIOGRAPHY

Antonio Manuel. Exh. cat. Text by Esther Emílio Carlos. Rio de Janeiro: Instituto Brasil–Estados Unidos/Galería IBEU, 1994.

Brito, Ronaldo, Frederico Morais, and Jean-Claude Bernadet. *Antonio Manuel.* Rio de Janeiro: Edição FUNARTE, 1985.

Manuel, Antonio. *A arma fálica.* Rio de Janeiro: Instituto Municipal de Arte e Cultura/Rio Arte, 1995.

O desenho moderno no Brasil. Exh. cat. Text by Reinaldo Roels, Jr. São Paulo: Galería Sesi, 1993.

Santiago, Silviano, and Antonio Manuel. *Frutos do espaço.* Rio de Janeiro: Espaço Arte Brasileira Contemporânea, 1980.

Venâncio Filho, Paulo. *Antonio Manuel: Sombras e cintilações.* São Paulo: Gabinete de Arte Raquel Arnaud, 1990.

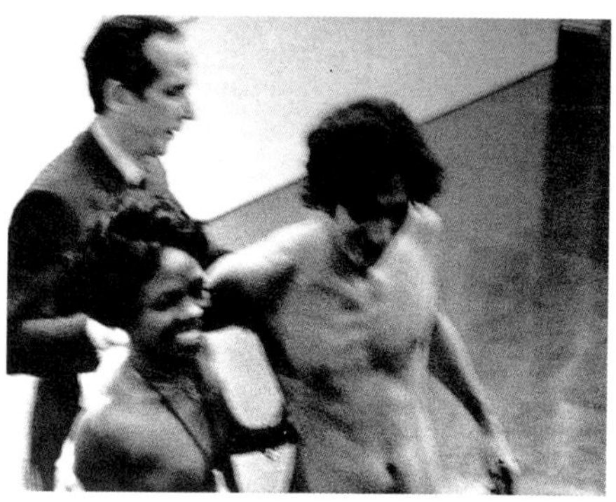

Figure 208.
Antonio Manuel, *O corpo é a obra* (*The Body Is the Work*), 1970, documentation of action staged at the Museum of Modern Art, Rio de Janeiro. Collection of the artist.

Piero MANZONI (1933–1963)

B. Soncino, Italy. Begins art career painting traditional landscapes (c. 1953). Produces achromes (1957), a series of "matierist" works made of lacerated plaster or irregular canvas, then *8 tavole di accertamento* (1958–60). Becomes acquainted with Group Zero; with Enrico Castellani, turns basement of a Milan boutique into an art gallery called Azimut (1959). Resident artist at Aage Damgard's garment factory, Copenhagen (1960). Returns to Italy and organizes an event at Azimut in which visitors are invited to consume a Manzoni artwork, i.e, hard-boiled eggs "signed" with his fingerprint (1960). In Rome, signs people as "living sculpture" and gives them a "certificate of authenticity" (1960). Mounts show entitled *Merda d'artista e opere viventi* (1961), i.e., "artist's shit," which questions in its own way the visual immediacy of the art object.

BIBLIOGRAPHY

Battino, Freddy. *Piero Manzoni, catalogue raisonné.* Milan: Vanni Scheiwiller, 1991.

Mostra de Piero Manzoni. Exh. cat. Rome: Galleria Nazionale d'Arte Moderna, 1971.

Piero Manzoni. Exh. cat. Paris: Éditions Centre Georges Pompidou, 1991.

Piero Manzoni. Exh. cat. Edited by Germano Celant. London: Serpentine Gallery, 1998.

Piero Manzoni: Paintings, Reliefs, and Objects. Exh. cat. London: Tate Gallery, 1974.

MATSUZAWA Yutaka (1922)

B. Suwa, Nagano Prefecture, Japan. Studies architecture at Waseda University, Tokyo (1943–46). Begins seriously writing poetry (1947); gives up architecture (1948); teaches mathematics at night high school (1949–84). Begins exhibiting artworks (1952). Spends two years in U.S. as Fulbright exchange professor at Wisconsin State College, Superior (1955–56) and studying religious philosophy and contemporary art at Columbia University, New York (1956–57). Participates in Yomiuri Independent Exhibition, showing collages and assemblages such as *Ψ Chamber* (1959–63). Produces *Ψ Corpse,* first text-only work (1964). Exhibits in Tokyo Biennale (1970). Organizes Bigakkō's Suwa workshop (1973–76). To date, the most consistent practitioner of conceptualism in Japan, creating antimaterialist, language-based work. Lives in Suwa.

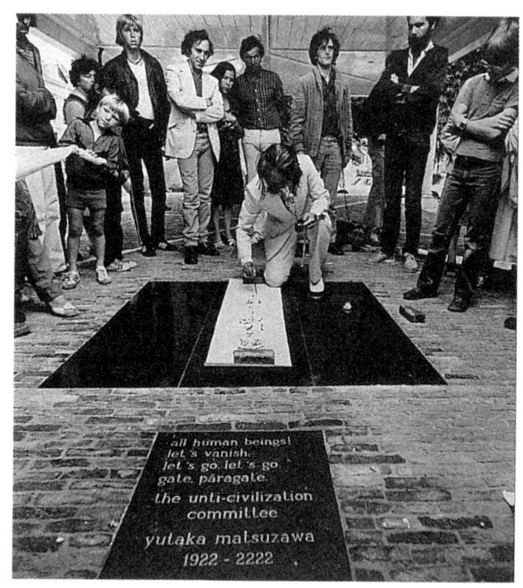

FIGURE 209.
Matsuzawa Yutaka, *Podio del Mond Per'Arte* (performance at Podio del Mond Per'Arte), June 8, 1980.

BIBLIOGRAPHY

Kikan, no. 13 (1982). Special monograph issue on Matsuzawa.

Matsuzawa Yutaka. *Ryōshi geijutsu sengen* (Quantum Art Manifesto). Tokyo: Okazaki Tamako Gallery, 1992.

Supiricharizumu e: Matsuzawa Yutaka/To Spiritualism: Yutaka Matsuzawa, 1954–1997. Exh. cat. Kawaguchi: Saitō Memorial Kawaguchi Museum of Contemporary Art, 1997.

Cildo MEIRELES (1948)

B. Rio de Janeiro. Spends childhood in Goiânia and Belém; moves to Brasilia (1958). Studies art with Félix Alejandro Berrenechea Avilez, then attends Escola Nacional de Belas-Artes (1968) and Escola do Museu de Arte Moderna, Rio (1969). Becomes active member of highly politicized Rio avant-garde. Participates in *Salão da bússola* (1969) and *Do corpo à terra* (1970). With critic Frederico Morais and other conceptual artists, founds Unidade Experimental at MAM. Produces conceptual works with readymades (1969–71). Participates in *Information*, MoMA, New York (1970) with *Insertions* series. Lives in New York (1971–73), where he produces large-scale installations such as *Eureka/Blindhotland* (1970/75). Cofounds *Malasartes* (1975) and *A Parte do Fogo* (1980). Invited to Documenta 9 (1992).

BIBLIOGRAPHY

Amaral, Aracy A. "Reflexões: O artista brasileiro II. E uma presença: Cildo Meireles." In *Arte é meio artístico entre a feijoada é o x-burguer*, 167–71. São Paulo: Livraria Nobel, 1982.

Brett, Guy, et al. *Lezarts and Through: Tunga and Cildo Meireles.* Kortrijik, Belgium: Kanaal Art Foundation, 1989.

Brito, Ronaldo, and Eudoro Macieira de Sousa. *Cildo Meireles.* Rio de Janeiro: Edição FUNARTE, 1981.

Cildo Meireles. Exh. cat. Edited by Marí Bartomeu and Muria Enguita. Valencia: Instituto Valenciano de Arte Moderno Centre del Carme, 1995.

Desvío para o vermelho. Exh. cat. Texts by Aracy A. Amaral et al. São Paulo: Museu de Arte Contemporânea, 1986.

Encounters/Displacements: Luis Camnitzer, Alfredo Jaar, Cildo Meireles. Exh. cat. Edited by Mari Carmen Ramírez and Beverly Adams. Austin: Archer M. Huntington Art Gallery, University of Texas, 1992.

Gomes, Frederico. "O território sem fronteiras da arte." *Módulo* (Rio de Janeiro) 65 (July–August 1981): 26–35.

Meireles, Cildo. "Inserções em circuitos ideológicos." *Malasartes* 1 (September–November 1975): 15.

Obscura luz: Cildo Meireles. Exh. cat. Text by João Moura. Rio de Janeiro: Galería Saramenha, 1983.

Ouro e paus. Exh. cat. Text by Paulo Venâncio Filho. Rio de Janeiro: Joel Edelstein Arte Contemporânea, 1995.

Ramírez, Mari Carmen. "Blueprint Circuits: Conceptual Art and Politics in Latin America." In *Latin American Artists of the Twentieth Century.* Edited by Waldo Rasmussen et al., 156–67. New York: Museum of Modern Art, 1993.

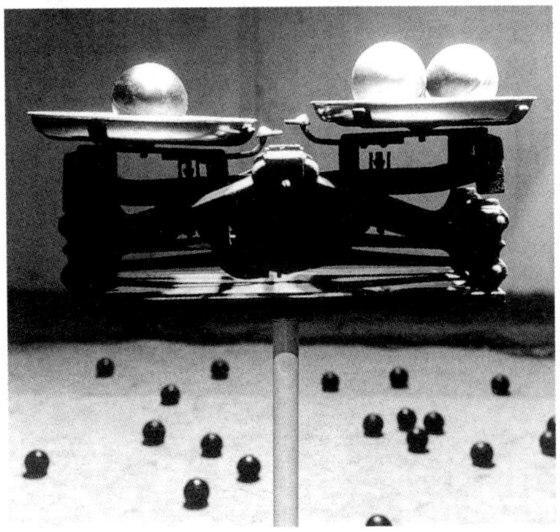

FIGURE 210.
Cildo Meireles, *Eureka/Blindhotland*, 1970–75, documentary photograph. Collection of the artist.

Juraj MELIŠ (1942)

B. Nové Zámky, Czechoslovakia. Studies sculpture at Academy of Fine Arts, Bratislava (1960–66). Becomes known for his "populist" monumental sculptures and installations, sometimes based on Slovak folk traditions and using symbols or texts in an ironic or critical fashion. Initiates and participates in a series of graphic albums with other Slovak artists, which frequently feature conceptualist work (1970s onward). Mounts first solo show at Young People's Gallery, Bratislava (1980), and exhibits several times in Hungary. Retrospective held in Bratislava (1994). Teaches at his alma mater.

BIBLIOGRAPHY

Juraj Meliš. Exh. cat. Edited by Ivan Jančár. Bratislava: Galéria Mesta Bratislavy, 1994.

Mario MERZ (1925)

B. Turin, Italy. Mounts first solo show of abstract paintings in Turin (1954). Participates in exhibition at Bologna organized by Germano Celant and other Italian critics (1968). Produces a number of works based on graffiti seen in Paris: *Che fare?* (What Is to Be Done?), from the title of a book by Lenin; *Solitario-Solidale* (Solitary-Solidary); and *Objet cache-toi* (Object Hide Yourself) (all 1968). Participates in several important shows of conceptualist work, i.e., *When Attitude Becomes Form*, Berne (1969), *Conceptual Art, Arte Povera, Land Art*, Galleria Civica d'Arte Moderna, Turin (1970), Guggenheim International (1971).

BIBLIOGRAPHY

Mario Merz. Exh. cat. Turin: Galleria Centro, 1969.

Mario Merz. Edited by Germano Celant. New York and Milan: Solomon R. Guggenheim Museum and Electa, 1989.

Mario Merz. Turin: Hopeful Monster, 1995.

Mario Merz at MOCA. Milan: Fabbri Editori, 1989.

Boris MIKHAILOV (1938)

B. Kharkov, Ukraine. Trains as an engineer, but becomes a full-time photographer by the late 1960s. Produces first series, *From an Album* and *Luriki* (1970–), the latter comprised of photos from anonymous family albums. Begins to use text with photographs, producing a series of portraits and other images, *Viscidity* (1982), which positions him within Moscow's conceptual circle. During *perestroika*, begins to travel and exhibit in Europe and U.S. Cofounds Immediate Photography group (c. 1989). Mounts solo exhibition, Central House of Cinematographers, Moscow (1990). Participates in *New Photography 9*, MoMA, New York (1993). Receives acclaim for his series *By the Ground* (1991) and *Art Dusk* (1993), which document the decline of post-Soviet society. Publishes *Unfinished Dissertation* with an Albert Renger Patzch Award (1998).

BIBLIOGRAPHY

Efimova, Alla. "Photographic Ethics in the Work of Boris Mikhailov." *Art Journal* 53, no. 2 (Summer 1994): 63–69.

Kölle, Brigitte, ed. *Boris Michajlov.* Stuttgart: Oktagon, 1995.

Mikhailov, Boris. *Unfinished Dissertation.* Zurich: Scalo, 1998.

The Missing Picture: Alternative Contemporary Photography from the Soviet Union. Exh. cat. Cambridge, Mass.: MIT List Visual Arts Center, 1990.

Mzrakova, Daniela, and Vladimir Remes. *Another Russia.* London: Thames and Hudson, 1986.

Sartorti, Rosalinde. "No More Heroic Tractors." *Aperture*, no. 116 (Fall 1989): 8–10.

Alex MLYNÁRČIK (1934)

B. Zilina, Czechoslovakia. Studies painting at private school (1947–49), then Academy of Fine Arts, Bratislava (1959–65). Travels to Paris where he meets Pierre Restany and is influenced by nouveau réalisme (1964). Organizes happenings and actions in Paris and Bratislava reflecting his "art and life" principle and incorporating traditional folkloric elements (1965–). Produces his most important conceptual work, the *Happsoc* manifesto, with Stano Filko and theorist Zita Kostrová, in which the city of Bratislava is declared an artwork (1965). Lives in Bratislava, Slovak Republic.

BIBLIOGRAPHY

Alex Mlynárčik. Exh. cat. Essay by Pierre Restany. Paris and Bratislava: Galerie Laura Vincy and Slovenská Národná Galéria, 1994.

Sest'desiate roky v slovenskom výtvarnom umení (The Sixties in Slovakian Art). Exh. cat. Bratislava: Slovenská Národná Galéria, 1995.

Straus, Tomáš. *Slovenský variant moderny* (Slovak Variation of Modernism). Bratislava: Pallas, 1992.

Irina NAKHOVA (1955)

B. Moscow. In her mid-teens, meets conceptual artist Victor Pivovarov, who introduces her to circle of Moscow conceptualists. Graduates from Moscow Polygraphic Institute (1976). Supports art activities with income earned as a children's book illustrator. Constructs installations, *Rooms*, in her Moscow studio (1984–87), which receive much attention from major artists such as Ilya Kabakov and Andrei Monastyrskii. During *perestroika*, begins to travel and exhibit extensively in Europe and the U.S., including solo exhibitions at Phyllis Kind Gallery, New York (1990/92). Becomes a permanent U.S. resident (1992). Teaches at Wayne State University, Detroit (1994–97), and works with students on large-scale site-specific installations in abandoned areas of city. Presently lives in New York.

BIBLIOGRAPHY

Hagedorn, Christine. "Cathedral of Time: Michigan Central Station." *Ground-Up*, no. 4 (May 1995).

Heartney, Eleanor. "Irina Nakhova at Phyllis Kind." *Art In America* 80, no. 10 (October 1992): 145.

Miro, Marsha. "Terminal Optimism." *Detroit Free Press,* May 12, 1995.
Powers, Mark. "Art Installation to Be Housed in Old Michigan Central." *South End* (Detroit), May 11, 1995.

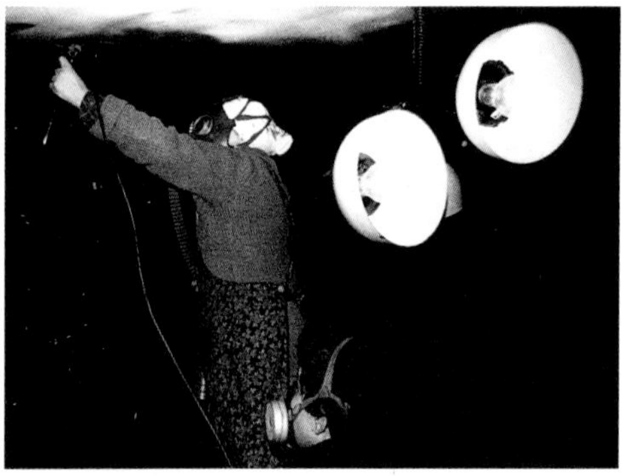

FIGURE 211.
Irina Nakhova; *Room (Komnata) No. 2*, Moscow, 1984, documentary photograph.

Paul NEAGU (1938)

B. Bucharest, Romania. Works as accountant, topographer, and electrician (1954–59), simultaneously creating photo projects, drawings, and paintings. Attends Academy of Fine Arts, Bucharest (1959–65). Expands production to include collages, sculpture, performance, and film. Moves to London; mounts solo exhibition of installations at Demarco Gallery, Edinburgh, and Amphora Gallery, Bucharest; issues *Palpable Art* manifesto (1969). Founds Generative Art Group (1972–75), "a fictional (conceptual) invention of a group of (nonexisting) artists"; works exhibited collectively, all signed by Neagu using different names and exploring diverse media/styles. Reinstates Romanian citizenship (1992). Registers Generative Art Trust in London (1995).

BIBLIOGRAPHY

Gradually Going Tornado! Paul Neagu and His Generative Art Group. Exh. cat. Sunderland, Eng.: Sunderland Arts Center, 1975.
Neagu, Paul. "Gradually Going Ahead." *Artscribe International* (London) 16 (February 1979): 48–50.
___, et al. "Palp Art." *Arta Plastica* (Bucharest) 5 (1970).
Overy, Paul. *Paul Neagu: A Generative Context, 1965–1981.* Sunderland, Eng.: Coelfrith Press, 1981.
Paul Neagu. Exh. cat. Glasgow: Third Eye Center, 1979.

NOMURA Hitoshi (1945)

B. Tatsuno, Hyōgo Prefecture, Japan. Completes graduate studies in sculpture at Kyoto City University of Arts; begins employing photography in his work, interested in time and process (1969). Regularly exhibits in Kyoto Independent, Kyoto Biennale, and Mainichi's Contemporary Art Exhibition (1969–80). Participates in *'73/5: Affair and Practice by 12* at Pinar Galleries, Tokyo. Exhibits in Tokyo Biennale (1970) and Paris Biennal (1975). Works at prop department of Asahi TV, Osaka (1969–88), which experience informs some aspects of his art. Presently lives in Toyonaka, Osaka Prefecture, and teaches at his alma mater (from 1988).

BIBLIOGRAPHY

Time-Space: Nomura Hitoshi. Kyoto: Kōrinsha, 1994.

OHO

Group of artists based in Ljubljana, Yugoslavia, and active 1966–71. Members include Marijan Ciglič (1944), Drago Dellabernardina (1948), Srečo Dragan (1944), Istok Geister (pseudonym: I. G. Plamen; 1945), Matjaž Hanžek (1949), Aleš Kermavner (1946–1966), Vojin Kovač (1949–1985), Naško Križnar (1943), Milenko Matanovič (1947), David Nez (b. U.S., 1949), Marko Pogačnik (1944), Andraž Salamun (1947), Tomaž Salamun (1941), and Franci Zagoričnik (1933). Notable for their use of diverse media, and responsible for first conceptual video works in the region.

BIBLIOGRAPHY

OHO Retrospektiva. Exh. cat. Ljubljana and Graz: Moderna Galerija and Neue Galerie am Landesmuseum–Joanneum, 1994.

Hélio OITICICA (1937–1980)

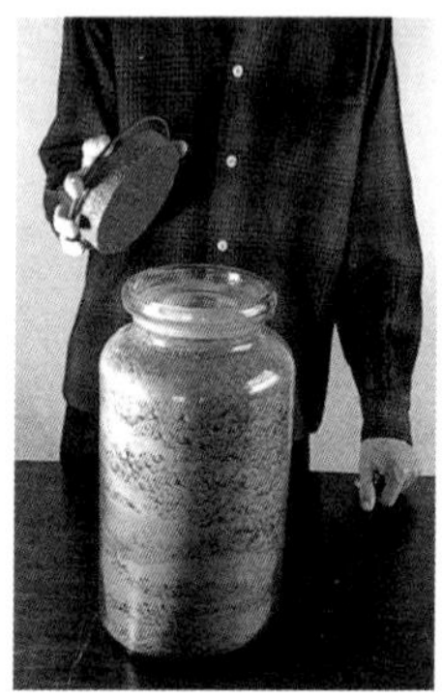

FIGURE 212.
Hélio Oiticica, *Bólide vidro 1 (Glass Bólide 1),* 1963, glass container, earth, and pigment. Collection Centro de Arte Hélio Oiticica, Rio de Janeiro.

B. Rio de Janeiro. Studies at Escola do Museu de Arte Moderna with Ivan Serpa (1954). Participates in Grupo Frente with Lygia Clark and Mário Pedrosa (1955–56). Begins *Metaesquemas* (1957). Joins neoconcrete movement and signs manifesto (1959). Produces white paintings, spatial reliefs (1959), and first *Penetrable* (1960). Begins *Bólide* series (1963). Invents *Parangolés* (1964). Joins Mangueira Samba School (1964); members of Mangueira community later participate in performances of his work. Organizes art manifestations and writes key texts of *carioca* avant-garde (1965–69). Presents *Tropicália* in *Nova objetividade brasileira,* MAM (1967). Participates in Tokyo and Paris biennials (1967), and *Information,* MoMA, New York (1970). Mounts solo exhibition at Whitechapel Gallery, London (1969). Lives in New York (1971–78), where he experiments with film. Returns to Rio (1978), and two years later suffers a fatal stroke.

BIBLIOGRAPHY

Brett, Guy. "Fait sur le corps: Le Parangolé de Hélio Oiticica." *Cahiers du Musée National d' Art Moderne* (Paris), no. 51 (Spring 1995): 32–45.
___. "Hélio Oiticica: Reverie and Revolt." *Art in America* 77 (January 1989): 110–21.
Cartas: 1964–1974/Lygia Clark, Hélio Oiticica. Edited by Luciano Figueiredo. Rio de Janeiro: Editoria UFRJ, 1996.
Favaretto, Celso. *A invenção de Hélio Oiticica.* Texto & Arte, 6. São Paulo: Editora da Universidade de São Paulo, 1992.
Hélio Oiticica. Exh. cat. Rotterdam: Witte de With, 1992.
Morais, Frederico. *Pequeno roteiro cronológico das incenções de Hélio Oiticica.* Rio de Janeiro: n.p., n.d.
Oiticica, Hélio. "General Scheme of the New Objectivity." In *Hélio Oiticica,* 110–20. Rio de Janeiro: Projeto Hélio Oiticica, 1992. Originally published in *Nova objetividade brasileira* (Rio de Janeiro: Museu de Arte Moderna, 1967).
Saccà, Lucilla. *Hélio Oiticica: La sperimentazione della libertà.* Pasian di Prato: Campanotto Editore Udine, 1995.

1,000-Yen Note Incident Discussion Group (Sen-en-satsu Jiken Kondankai)

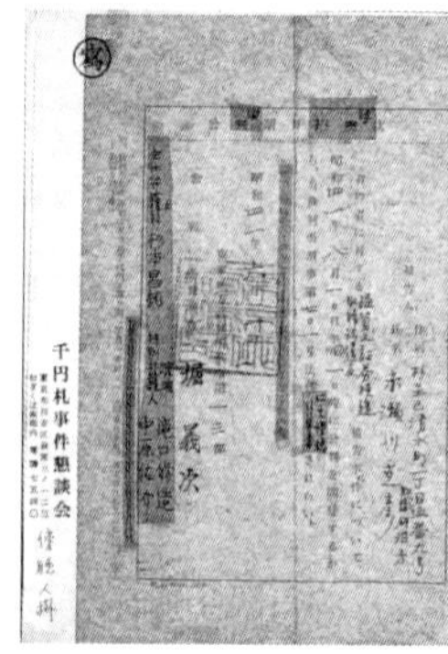

FIGURE 213.
1,000-Yen Note Incident Discussion Group, *Invitation to the Trial (Kōhan bōchō shōseijō)*, 1966, ink and rubber stamp on blueprint. Collection of Akasegawa Genpei, courtesy of Nagoya City Art Museum.

Organized in Tokyo after Akasegawa Genpei's indictment for currency fraud (1965). Members include Akasegawa, Izumi Tatsu, Nakanishi Natsuyuki, Takamatsu Jirō, and Yasunao Tone (artists associated with Hi Red Center); Imaizumi Yoshihiko and Kawani Hiroshi (editors); Sugimoto Masazumi (defense attorney); Haryū Ichirō, Ishiko Junzō, Miki Tamon, Nakahara Yūsuke, Takiguchi Shūzō, and Yoshida Yoshie (art critics). Organizes benefit events (July 1966). Mobilizes three special defenders and seventeen witnesses for eleven courtroom sessions over eleven months (1966–67). After Akasegawa's conviction, organizes *Unfreedom of Expression* at Maramatsu Gallery, Tokyo (1967).

Yoko ONO (1933)

B. Tokyo. Studies music composition and poetry at Sarah Lawrence (1953–56). Arrives in New York (early '60s), and associates with musicians and composers such as Robert Maxfield and La Monte Young. Influential in formation of Fluxus (1960–62). Co-organizes a series of concerts held in her downtown loft (attended by Duchamp, among others), in which she presents *Kitchen Piece* (1960–61). First text-only *Instructions for Painting* shown at Sōgetsu Hall, Tokyo (1962). Career changes course when she meets John Lennon (1966) and they begin collaboration on music and art projects, i.e., joint performance works supporting the peace movement. First retrospective, *This Is Not Here,* held at Everson Museum, Syracuse, N.Y. (1971). Also active as an experimental filmmaker.

BIBLIOGRAPHY

Ono, Yoko. *Grapefruit.* Tokyo: Wunternaum Press, 1964; rev. ed., New York: Simon & Shuster, 1970.
Ono, Yoko. *Instruction Paintings.* New York and Tokyo: Weatherhill, 1995.
Stiles, Kristine. "Unbosoming Lennon: The Politics of Yoko Ono's Experience." *Art Criticism* (Stony Brook, N.Y.) 7, no. 2 (1992): 21–52.
Yoko Ono: Have You Seen the Horizon Lately? Exh. cat. Oxford: Museum of Modern Art, 1997.
Yoko Ono: This Is Not Here. Exh. cat. Syracuse, N.Y.: Everson Museum of Art, 1971.

Roman OPALKA (1931)
B. Hocquincourt, France, of Polish parents. Attends Academy of Fine Arts, Łódź (1946–50) and Warsaw (1950–56). Works as a painter and graphic designer until mid-'60s, when he begins his lifelong series of number paintings, exploring passage of time as a linear phenomenon. Each painting has an aural component, a taped recording of the artist enunciating the count (in Polish). Another painting cycle, *Description of the World* (inspired by Marco Polo, 1968–), approaches the same problem from a different angle. Frequently represented in international exhibitions, including São Paulo Bienal (1969–87), Venice Biennale (1972–95), and Documenta. Lives in France.

BIBLIOGRAPHY
Kowalska, Bożena. *Roman Opalka.* Cracow: Wydawnictwa Literackie, 1976.
Opalka 1965/1–oo. Exh. cat. Warsaw: Galeria Sztuki Współczesnej Zachęta, 1994.
Opalka, Roman. *Opalka 1965/1–[infinity].* Milan: G. Politi, 1975.
Roman Opalka: Anti-Sisyphos. Stuttgart: Edition Cantz, 1994.
Savinel, Christine, et al. *Roman Opalka.* Paris: Éditions Dis Voir, 1996.

Giulio PAOLINI (1940)
B. Genoa. Produces conceptualist works concerned with the ontology of art—i.e., exhibits paintings turned to the wall or an empty canvas-frame with a can of varnish (early 1960s onward)—and with the relationship between past and present art, i.e., *The Invention of Ingres* (1968). Begins text-based works, generally more elegant than those produced by North American counterparts (mid-1960s). Participates in *Arte Povera* exhibition organized by Germano Celant for Galleria La Bertesca, Genoa (1967). Produces set designs for numerous theater productions, including *Colloquio con Malcolm X* (1968) and *Atene Anno Zero* (1970).

BIBLIOGRAPHY
Disch, Maddalena, ed. *Giulio Paolini, la voce del pittore: Scritti e interviste, 1965–1995.* Lugano: ADV Pub. House, 1995.
Giulio Paolini. Exh. cat. Text by Craig Owens. New York: Marian Goodman Gallery, 1987.
Giulio Paolini. Text by Francesco Poli. Turin: Lindau, 1990.
Giulio Paolini: Le Nouveau Musée. 2 vols. Exh. cat. Villeurbanne: Nouveau Musée, 1984.
Giulio Paolini: Survey of Works, 1960–1980. Exh. cat. Oxford: Museum of Modern Art, 1980.

PARK Bul-dong (1956)
B. Hadong, South Korea. Studies painting at Hong-ik University; graduates 1985. Participates in *Hihm-Jeon* (Power of the Younger Generation, 1985), group exhibition of young radical artists considered one of the most important art events of the '80s. Arrested with other participants, works seized by authorities. Joins Hyunsilgwa-Baron (Reality & Utterance) group (1986). Exhibits in *JAALA,* Metropolitan Museum, Tokyo (1986); *Tong-il* (Unification) and *Antitorture,* both Min Gallery, Seoul (1987); *Min Joong Art,* Artists Space, New York (1988); and various solo shows (1985/87/89). Lives in Koyangshi.

BIBLIOGRAPHY
Park Bul-dong. "Reality Needs a Sword and the Paintbrush Must Be That Sword." *Minchok Misul,* no. 3 (March 1987).
___. "The Spirit of the Comic Strip and the Praxis of Art." *Munhwa Chungshin* (December 1986).
Sung Wan-kyung. "Photo Collage of Park Bul-dong." *Gongan* (Space) (Seoul) (May 1986).

Mike PARR (1945)
B. Sydney, Australia. Mounts first solo show, *Light and Painted Constructions;* forms cooperative gallery Inhibodress in Sydney with Peter Kennedy (1970). Major protagonist of avant-garde art, especially performance. Participates in Harald Szeemann's show, *I want to leave a nice welldone child here (20 Australian Artists),* Sydney/Melbourne, and *The Situation Now,* Central Street Gallery, Sydney (1971). Collaborates with Kennedy on film *Idea Demonstrations;* Inhibodress closes (1972). Extensively represented in international and local exhibitions, including Sydney Biennale (1979/82/88/90), Australian Perspecta (1985/87), and bicentenary *Great Australian Art Exhibition* (1988–90).

BIBLIOGRAPHY
Bromfield, David. *Identities: A Critical Study of the Work of Mike Parr, 1970–1990.* Nedlands: University of Western Australia Press, 1991.
Coulter-Smith, Graham. *Mike Parr: The Self Portrait Project.* Melbourne: Schwartz City, 1994.
Kaldor, John. *An Australian Accent: Three Artists, Mike Parr, Imants Tiller, Ken Unsworth.* Sydney: John Kaldor, 1984.

Gyula PAUER (1941)
B. Budapest, Hungary. Begins as a nonfigurative sculptor (late '60s). Invents "pseudo," both a creative principle and technical method, and produces paintings, sculptures, conceptual works, films, environments, "pathosformels," and theater on that basis (1970 onward). Constructs 131 pseudo boards with slogans and inscriptions under the title *A Forest of Demonstrating Boards* for a sculpture exhibition in Nagyatád, Hungary (1978); installation destroyed by authorities. With Érmezei Zoltán and János Rauschenberger, creates landscape paintings under the female pseudonym Puci P.É.R.Y. Participates in the Olympic Games of Art, Seoul (1988). Presently teaches theater design and film at Academy of Fine Arts, Budapest.

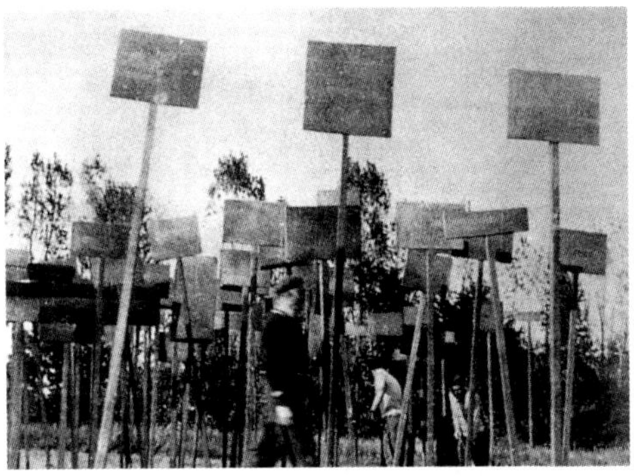

FIGURE 214.
Gyula Pauer, *A Forest of Demonstrating Boards* (*Tüntetőtáblaerdő*), 1978, documentary photograph.

BIBLIOGRAPHY
Szőke, Annamária. "Pauer: Fotó-és szövegdokumentáció" (Pauer: Photo and Text Documentation). Unpub. ms., Budapest, 1985.

Malcolm PAYNE (1946)
B. Pretoria, South Africa. Attends Pretoria Technikon; St. Martin's School of Art, London (1972–73); University of Cape Town. One of the first artists to use performance and conceptualist strategies to circumvent restrictions on individual freedom under apartheid, interrogating historical legacy of European and African identities in South Africa. Performances are often constituted as endurance pieces, operating in real time, then documented. Currently associate professor of fine art at University of Cape Town.

BIBLIOGRAPHY
Berman, Esmé. *Art and Artists of South Africa: An Illustrated Biographical Dictionary and Historical Survey of Painters, Sculptors, and Graphic Artists Since 1875.* Cape Town: A.A. Balkema, 1983.
Bunn, David, and Jane Taylor, eds. *Displacements: South African Works on Paper, 1985–1995.* Chicago: Northwestern University Press, 1997.
Hall, Martin. "From Lydenburg to Mafikeng: Appropriations of Images of the Past." In *Transgressing Boundaries: New Directions in the Study of Culture in Africa.* Edited by Brenda Cooper and Andrew Steyn. Rondebosch, S.A., and Athens, Ohio: University of Cape Town Press and Ohio University Press, 1996.
Payne, Malcolm. "Face Value: Old Heads in Modern Masks." In *Transgressing Boundaries: New Directions in the Study of Culture in Africa.* Edited by Brenda Cooper and Andrew Steyn. Rondebosch, S.A., and Athens, Ohio: University of Cape Town Press and Ohio University Press, 1996.

Claudio PERNA (1938–1997)
B. Milan, to an Italian father and Venezuelan mother. Moves to Venezuela (1955). Studies architecture but graduates in geography, which he teaches in the Universidad Central de Venezuela until retirement. First works (books with collages and assemblages of found objects) date from 1958. Works on a series of photographs (1967–68) of Caracas and of exhibits at Museo de Bellas Artes. Starts a series of interventions on a map of Venezuela (1968). In connection with extensive travel through the country, these interventions become an arena for a parallel exploration where art and geography function as metaphors for each other. Participates in events

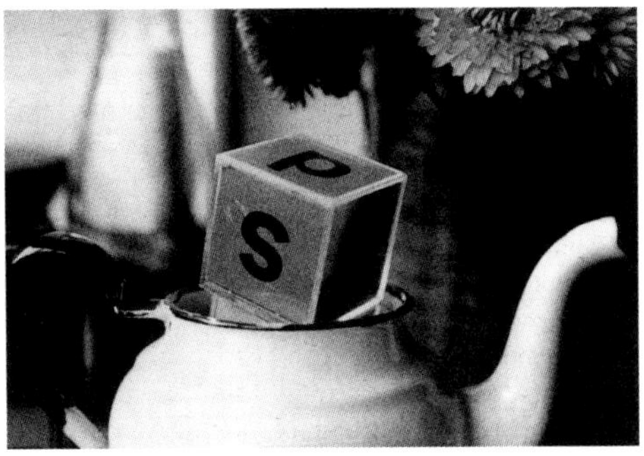

FIGURE 215.
Claudio Perna, *El objeto como concepto (Object as Concept),* 1960–70, photograph. Biblioteca Nacional de Venezuela, Caracas.

organized by Charlotte Moorman (1975) and Antoni Muntadas (1977) in Caracas. Though considered a seminal figure for Venezuelan conceptual artists, his work has been studied systematically only since his death.

BIBLIOGRAPHY

Once Tipos. Exh. cat. Caracas: Fundación Eugenio Mendoza, 1976.

Guevara, Roberto. *Claudio Perna: Re-presentaciones: Foto-grafías y acupintura.* Exh. cat. Caracas: Fundación Eugenio Mendoza, 1981.

Perna, Claudio. *El enfoque de sistemas como proposición naciente a la crisis del pensamiento tradicional (Introducción a la fotografía del futuro y del presente).* Caracas: Radar, 1994.

Adrian PIPER (1948)

B. New York. Attends School of Visual Arts, New York, and studies philosophy at Harvard (1974–77). Begins making minimalist objects. Under the influence of LeWitt and Kosuth, shifts to modular and self-referential works (1968), placing her in first wave of conceptual artists. Well read in philosophy, her work evolves in directions both innovative and theoretically astute. Produces *Hypotheses* series (1968–70), documenting her activities at specific times and places, and *Context #8* (1970), a collection of materials sent to her during one month, including announcements for antiwar protests and fliers calling for the release of Black Panther leader Bobby Seale. Begins performance work (1968). Contributes writings to many publications, including *0–9* and *The Fox* (1969 onward)

BIBLIOGRAPHY

Adrian Piper. Exh. cat. Birmingham and Manchester: Ikon Gallery and Cornerhouse, 1991.

Adrian Piper, Reflections 1967–87. Exh. cat. Essays by Jane Farver and Clive Philpott. New York: Alternative Museum, 1987.

Cottingham, Laura. "Adrian Piper." *Journal of Contemporary Art* (New York) 5, no. 1 (Spring 1992): 88–136.

Lippard, Lucy R. "Catalysis: An Interview with Adrian Piper." *Drama Review* (New York) 16, no. 1 (March 1972): 76–78.

Piper, Adrian. *Out of Order, Out of Sight,* vol. 1, *Selected Writings in Meta-Art, 1968–1992;* vol. 2, *Selected Writings in Art Criticism, 1967–1992.* Cambridge, Mass.: MIT Press, 1995.

Liliana PORTER (1946)

B. Buenos Aires. Studies printmaking at Universidad Iberoamericana, Mexico City (1958). Graduates from Escuela Nacional de Bellas Artes, Buenos Aires (1963). Moves permanently to New York (1964). Continues printmaking at Pratt Graphic Art Center. With Luis Camnitzer and José Guillermo Castillo, founds New York Graphic Workshop (1965). Investigates paradoxical nature of representation in prints, drawings, wall installations, and mail art pieces (1966–70). Begins series of mixed-media works on paper and canvas inspired by Borges, Magritte, Lewis Carroll, and Western painting traditions (mid-'70s). Turns to color photography (1995). Teaches at City University of New York, Queens College.

BIBLIOGRAPHY

Bazzano Nelson, Florencia. "Fragments of the Journey: The Art of Liliana Porter." Master's thesis, University of Texas, Austin, 1989.

Buccellato, Laura. "Porter." In *Pintores argentinos del siglo XX.* Buenos Aires: Centro Editor de América Latina, 1982.

Glusberg, Jorge. "Liliana Porter." In *Del pop-art a la nueva imagen,* 385–90. Buenos Aires: Ediciones de Arte Gaglianone, 1985.

Liliana Porter. Exh. cat. Text by Miguel González. Cali: Museo de Arte Moderno la Tertulia, 1987.

Liliana Porter: Fragments of the Journey. Exh. cat. Texts by Mari Carmen Ramírez and Charles Merewether. New York: Bronx Museum, 1992.

Liliana Porter: Obra gráfica, 1964–1990. Exh. cat. Edited by Shifra Goldman and Mari Carmen Ramírez. San Juan: Instituto de Cultura Puertorriqueña, 1991.

Mel RAMSDEN (1944)

B. Nottingham, U.K. Arrives Melbourne, Australia (1963), and commences studies at National Gallery of Victoria School, where he meets Ian Burn. Works in London (1964) and moves to New York (1967). Exhibits in *The Field,* Melbourne (1968), which introduces Australian public to minimal/conceptual work. Participates in *Language III* at Dwan Gallery, New York (1969). Writes for *Art-Language* with Ian Burn (1970). Joins Art & Language (U.K., 1971). During 1970s, exhibits internationally and lectures in Canada and New York. *Soft-Tape,* Burn and Ramsden's collaborative conceptual work (1966), reconstructed for Sydney Biennale (1990).

BIBLIOGRAPHY

Aliaga, Juan Vicente, and José Miguel García Cortés. "Michael Baldwin and Mel Ramsden on Art & Language." *Art and Text* (Melbourne), no. 35 (Summer 1990): 23–37.

Robert REHFELDT (1931–1993)

B. Stargard, Germany. Studies at Academy of Fine Arts, East Berlin–Charlottenburg (1948–53). An excellent graphic designer, becomes one of the most important East German alternative artists, developing the potential of mail art in particular. Establishes an important archive of conceptual and mail art in East Berlin (1970s), and organizes art activity within the framework of local cultural houses. Mail art actions include *Creative Workshop/ Collective Postcards, Warsaw* (1975), *Contart/Mail/ Box* (1980), and *Please Work on This Card* (1987).

BIBLIOGRAPHY

Blume, Eugene. "Robert Rehfeldt: Art Worker and Mail Artist." In *Mail Art: Eastern Europe in International Network,* 113–17. Exh. cat. Schwerin and Budapest: Staatliches Museum and Műcsarnok, 1996–98.

Mail Art Szene DDR, 1975–1990. Edited by Friedrich Winnes and Lutz Wohlrab under the direction of Birger Jesch and Joseph W. Huber. Berlin: Haude & Spener, 1994.

Robert Rehfeldt. Exh. cat. Berlin: Galerie Arkade, 1975.

Robert Rehfeldt: Kataloge, Postkarten & Künstlerkarten. Exh. cat. Text by Jürgen Schweinebraden. Berlin: Galerie Arkade, 1978.

Robert Rehfeldt: Malerei, Visuelle Poesie, Mail-Art, Grafik, Objekte, Video. Exh. cat. Text by Eugen Blume et al. Berlin: Galerie Vier, 1991.

Gerhard RICHTER (1932)

B. Dresden, Germany. Works as commercial painter (1948–51). Studies painting at Hochschule für Bildende Kunst, Dresden (1952–57). Visits Documenta 2 (1959), and admires work of Pollock and Fontana. Moves to Düsseldorf and attends Staatliche Kunstakademie (1961–64). Meets Konrad Lueg (later known as Konrad Fischer), Polke, and Palermo. Begins to make paintings with found photographs; travels to Paris with Lueg, and the pair introduce themselves to Ileana Sonnabend as German pop artists (1962). Stages *Life with Pop* in Düsseldorf department store with Lueg (1963). Begins various painting series: *Color Charts* (1966), *Grey Pictures* (1968–69), and *Atlas* (1974).

BIBLIOGRAPHY

Gerhard Richter. Exh. cat. 3 vols. Essays by Benjamin H. D. Buchloh (vol. 2), catalogue raisonné (vol. 3). Stuttgart: Edition Cantz, 1993.

Gerhard Richter: Bilder aus den Jahren, 1962–1974. Bremen: Kunsthalle, 1975.

Gerhard Richter: Bilder, 1962–1985. Edited by Jürgen Harten. Cologne: DuMont, 1986.

Küper, Suzanne. "Konrad Lueg und Gerhard Richter: 'Leben mit Pop—Eine Demonstration für den kapitalistischen Realismus.'" *Wallraf-Richartz-Jahrbuch* (Cologne) 53 (1992).

Loock, Ulrich, and Denys Zacharopoulos. *Gerhard Richter.* Munich: Schreiber, 1985.

Richter, Gerhard. *The Daily Practice of Painting: Writings and Interviews, 1962–1993.* Edited by Hans-Ulrich Obrist. London: Thames and Hudson and Anthony d'Offay Gallery, 1995.

'60 '80 attitudes/concepts/images. Amsterdam: Stedelijk Museum, 1982.

Józef ROBAKOWSKI (1939)

B. Poznań, Poland. Studies art at Mikolaj Kopernik University, Torun, and cinematography at Academy of Film and Theater Art, Lódź. Contributes to development of conceptualism in Poland with structural films, experimental videos, photo works, and important theoretical writings. Founds several artists' groups, including Gallery Mymiany (Exchange), and organizes numerous happenings, actions, and exhibitions in 1960s and '70s. Lives in Lódź, where he teaches at the Academy of Film.

BIBLIOGRAPHY

Józef Robakowski: Kinetic Energy Space. Warsaw: Centrum Sztuki Współczesnej, Zamek Ujazdowski, 1994.

Martha ROSLER

B. Brooklyn, N.Y. Attends University of California, San Diego, one of a younger generation of artists influenced by John Baldessari and Herbert Marcuse. Begins art career with politically committed phototext works, i.e., *The Bowery in Two Inadequate Descriptive Systems* (1974), then expands production into video and performance. Completes first video, *Budding Gourmet* (1974). Publishes critical writings in *The Fox* and elsewhere (1975–). Turns to installation work (1980s).

BIBLIOGRAPHY

Rosler, Martha. *If You Lived Here: The City in Art, Theory, and Social Activism/A Project.* Edited by Brian Wallis. Seattle: Bay Press, 1991.

Rosler, Martha. "Lookers, Buyers, Dealers, and Makers: Thoughts on the Audience" (1979). In *Art After Modernism: Rethinking Representation.*

Edited by Brian Wallis, 311–39. New York: New Museum of Contemporary Art and David R. Godine, 1985.
Rosler, Martha. *Service: A Trilogy on Colonization.* New York: Printed Matter, 1978.
Rosler, Martha. *Three Works.* Halifax: Press of the Nova Scotia College of Art and Design, 1981.

Michael SNOW (1929)
B. Toronto. Explores a variety of media—film, painting, sculpture—throughout '50s. Creates multimedia *Walking Woman* series (1961–67), using painting, drawing, sculpture, and decals to explore idealized image of a woman in silhouette. Produces landmark film *Wavelength (1966–67),* a 45-minute continuous zoom across his loft. Further deconstructs elements of film in *Tap* and *La region centrale,* among many others. Begins a series of music recordings, including *The Artists Jazz Band* (1974) and *Music for Whistling, Piano, Microphone, and Tape Recorder* (1977). Puts process of photographic production under the lens in *Cover to Cover* (1975), 360 photographs showing two sides of each object photographed. Lives in Toronto.

BIBLIOGRAPHY
Cornwell, Regina. *Snow Seen: The Films and Photographs of Michael Snow.* Toronto: PMA Books, 1979.
Michael Snow: A Survey. Toronto: Art Gallery of Ontario in collaboration with Isaacs Gallery, 1970.
The Michael Snow Project: Visual Art, 1951–1993. Exh. cat. Toronto: Art Gallery of Ontario and Power Plant, 1994.
The Michael Snow Project 4: Music/Sound 1948–1993. Exh. cat. Toronto: Art Gallery of Ontario and Power Plant, 1994.
Michelson, Annette. "Toward Snow." *Artforum* 9, no. 10 (June 1971): 30–37.
Presence and Absence: The Films of Michael Snow, 1956–1991. Edited by Jim Shedden. Toronto: Art Gallery of Ontario, 1995.
Snow, Michael. *Cover to Cover.* Halifax and New York: Press of the Nova Scotia College of Art and Design and New York University Press, 1975.
___. *The Michael Snow Project: The Collected Writings of Michael Snow.* Waterloo, Ont.: Wilfred Laurier University Press, 1994.

SONG Yongping (1961)
B. Shanxi Province, PRC. Educated Tianjin Academy of Fine Arts (1979–83). Chief exponent of performance work in '85 Movement. With his brother, Song Yonghong, co-authors performance piece *Experiences on a Certain Day in 1986,* staged in Taiyuan City, Shanxi Province. Organizes *Country Project* in a small village of Shanxi Province, with a group of artists (1987). Currently resides in Shanxi Province.

BIBLIOGRAPHY
Gao Minglu et al. *Zhongguo dangdai meishushi, 1985–1986* (History of Chinese Contemporary Art, 1985–1986). Shanghai: Shanghai People's Press, 1991.

Petr ŠTEMBERA (1945)
B. Plzen, Czechoslovakia. Attends University of Prague. Forerunner of body art and performance in Eastern Europe, influenced by existentialism and Chan (Zen) Buddhism. With his friend Jan Mlčoch, stages performances of an ascetic, almost autodestructive character in Budapest, Pécs, Warsaw, Lódź, East Berlin, Wroclaw, Los Angeles, and San Francisco. Produces highly reductionist, ironic conceptual works, i.e., sends Czechoslovakian weather reports to friends all over the world, or photos of classic paintings asking recipients to "reproduce this gesture" (1970s). Under the influence of Charter 77, a civil rights movement in Prague, becomes more political, then stops art activity to study yoga and Eastern martial arts. Lives in Prague.

BIBLIOGRAPHY
Miller, Roland. "The Curtain Rises II." *Variant* (England), no. 12 (Summer–Fall 1992): 18–21.
"Petr Štembera." In *Oosteuropese Conceptual Fotographie.* Exh. cat. Eindhoven: Technische Hogeschool, 1977.
Situace (Prague) 11 (1981). Special issue on Petr Štembera's performance work.
Štembera. Petr. In *Schwarz auf Weiss* (Düsseldorf), no. 3 (1976).
"Vzpominka na akcní umeni 70 let Rozhovor Ludvíka Hlaváčka s Petrem Štemberou a Janem Mlčochem." *Vytvarnč Umeni* 3 (1991): 60–68.

SUNG Neung-kyung (1944)
B. Yesan, South Korea. Studies painting at Hong-ik University; graduates 1967. Participates in major experimental art shows with performance and installation works, including S.T. Group exhibitions (1973/74), Festival of Modern Art, Daegu (1974), and École de Seoul Exhibition (1979). Invited to 1st Seoul Biennale (1974). Presents his performances *Reading the Newspaper* and *Counting Money* in *3-Man Event* (1976), which also features Kim Yong-min and Lee Kun-yong. Disappears from art scene for almost a decade, then resurfaces with a solo exhibition, *Venues* (1985), for which he produces rephotographed newspaper images. Participates in Seoul Festival of Performance and Installation (1986); *Min Joong Art,* Artists Space, New York (1988). Lives in Seoul.

BIBLIOGRAPHY
Shin Bang-hun. "Art of Sung Neung-kyung." Preface to untitled exhibition catalogue. Seoul: Samduk Gallery, 1991.

Tamás SZENTJÓBY (Saint-Auby) (1944)
B. Csomör, Hungary. Begins career as an autodidact poet. Attends École des Beaux-Arts, Geneva. Initiates first happenings in Hungary; produces conceptualist poems and objects (1966–). Makes pseudo-documentary film, *Kentaur* (1974–75). Moves to Switzerland (1976), where he founds International Parallel Union of Telecommunication (IPUT) and becomes the organization's dispatcher. Returns to Hungary after 1989. Exhibits some 3,000 "bad drawings" at Műcsarnok, Budapest, then Musée Rath, Geneva (1996). Lives in Budapest.

BIBLIOGRAPHY
Beke, László, "Kentaur: Szentjóby Tamás 'tanpályái'"; "Szentjóby Tamás: Cím nélkül"; and "Kentaur." *Magyar Műhely/Atelier Hongrois* (Paris) 44–45 (1978): 66–91.
Tamás Szentjóby. Exh. cat. Geneva: Musée Rath, 1996.

TANG Song (1962)
B. Hangzhou, Zhejiang Province, PRC. Educated Zhejiang Academy of Fine Arts (1985–89). Arrested by Chinese authorities when he and partner Xiao Lu fire bullets into their installation *Dialogue* at *China/Avant-garde,* National Gallery, Beijing (1989). Exhibition is temporarily closed, and the pair released. Represented in *Mao Goes Pop* (Sydney, 1993). Lives and works in Sydney (1989–).

BIBLIOGRAPHY
Mao Goes Pop. Exh. cat. Sydney: Museum of Contemporary Art, 1993.

Yasunao TONE (1935)
B. Tokyo. Studies Japanese literature at Chiba University and writes graduation thesis on surrealism. Joins Group Ongaku (1960). Member of Tokyo Fluxus and anti-Art circles, exploring intermedia and events. Participates in Yomiuri Independent Exhibition (1962–63) and gallery exhibitions, including *Jury Event,* Naiqua Gallery, Tokyo (1964). Principal member of 1,000-Yen Note Incident Discussion Group (1965–67). Teaches at Aoyama Design School, Tokyo; organizes Phenomenology Study Group; meets Hikosaka Naoyoshi and Hori Kosai (1969). Participates in Bikyōtō Revolution Committee I (1971). Leaves Japan for Paris (1972), and eventually settles in New York, where he continues to create and perform music.

BIBLIOGRAPHY
Tone, Yasunao. *Gendai geijutsu no isō: Geijutsu wa shisō tariuruka?* (Phases of Contemporary Art: Can Art Be Thought?). Tokyo: Tabata Shoten, 1970.

Endre TÓT (1937)
B. Sümeg, Hungary. Attends Academy of Applied Arts, Budapest (1959–65). Lives in Budapest (1965–78), West Berlin (1978–79), Cologne (1980–). Mounts first solo exhibition of paintings at Epítök Műszaki Club, Budapest (1966). Stops painting; publishes *My Unpainted Canvases* (Budapest, 1971). Produces first *Zero, Rain,* and *Gladness* works (1971 onward), in form of writings, happenings/demonstrations, books, postcards, performance, film, and video. Indefatigable maker of artist books, including *On the Next Page I Shall Say Something* (1973) and *Book of an Extremely Glad Artist* (1981). Participates in touring Fluxus West exhibition (San Diego, 1973), and represented in numerous European shows of conceptual art (1972 onward). Makes first film, *One Step* (1972), and video, *TOTalJOYS* (1974). Returns to painting (1995) in a conceptualist vein.

BIBLIOGRAPHY
Dörsel, Wilfried. "A kép távolléte." *Balkon* (May 1994).
Guest, Tim, ed. *Books by Artists.* Toronto: Art Metropole, 1981.
Semmi sem semmi (Nothing Is Nothing). Exh. cat. Budapest: Műcsarnok, 1995. Retrospective exhibition.
Straus, Tomáš. "Tót Endre legsajátosabb gondolatai." *Uj Művészet* (Art Today) (Budapest) (May 1994).
Vision (Oakland, Calif.), no. 2 (January 1976).

Vincent TRASOV/Mr. Peanut (1947)
B. Edmunton, Alberta. With Michael Morris, founds Image Bank, Vancouver (1969), a "clearinghouse" for artworks exchanged through the mail, and launching pad for Mr. Peanut (1970), Trasov's performance nom de plume. Cofounds Western Front, an alternative space for music, performance art, video programming, in Vancouver (1973). Coorganizes

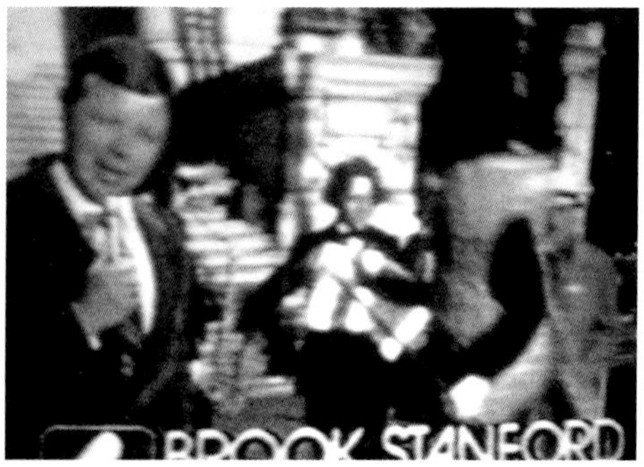

FIGURE 216.
Vincent Trasov/Mr. Peanut, still from *My Five Years in a Nutshell*, 1975, videotape. Collection of Morris/Trasov Archives, Morris and Helen Belkin Art Gallery, University of British Columbia.

Hollywood Decca Dance, the "Academy Awards of correspondence art," held in Hollywood and attended by more than 800 people (1974). Runs for mayor of Vancouver as Mr. Peanut on Peanut Party platform (P=Performance, E=Elegance, A=Ant, N=Nonsense, U=Uniqueness, T=Talent), tap dancing at rallies and meetings, accompanied by the all-female dancing/singing Ettes; receives 2,745 votes (1974). Produces video, *My Five Years in a Nut Shell* (1975).

BIBLIOGRAPHY

Art & Correspondence from the Western Front. Vancouver: Western Front Publications, 1979.

File Megazine, nos. 1–7 (1972–74).

From Sea to Shining Sea. Exh. cat. Edited by A. A. Bronson. Toronto: Power Plant, 1987.

Subtle, Susan, and Bud Lee. "Their Art Belongs to Dada." *Esquire* (August 1974).

Trasov, Vincent, and John Mitchell. *The Rise and Fall of the Peanut Party: Journal, Twenty Days in November.* Vancouver, B.C.: Air, 1976.

Goran TRBULJAK (1948)

B. Varašdin, Yugoslavia. Studies photography at School of Applied Arts, Zagreb (1963–68), then graphics at Academy of Fine Arts (1968–72). Exhibiting artist since 1970, first conceptual works focus on status of artist and role of art institutions. Declares himself a nonartist and works under pseudonyms, then "anonymous conceptual artist" or inscriptions such as "I do not wish to show anything new or original." Participates in activities of Ida Biard's Tenant Gallery, Paris (1972–). Produces first video and artist book (1973–74). Exchanges names with Swiss artist Henri Barbier. Writes for journal *Film* under various pseudonyms. Begins work as a cameraman and creates conceptual paintings in 1980s. Retrospectives held in Belgrade (1981) and Zagreb (1996). Professor of cinematography at Academy of Film and Theater, Zagreb (1988–).

BIBLIOGRAPHY

Goran Trbuljak. Exh. cat. Text by Ješa Denegri. Belgrade: Salon Muzeja Savremene Umetnosti, 1981.

G. Trbuljak. Exh. cat. Edited by Branka Stipančič. Zagreb: Muzej Suvremene Umjetnosti, 1996.

1972, artiste anonyme: Goran Trbuljak. Zagreb: Muzej Suvremene Umjetnosti, 1974.

Trbuljak, Goran. "Artiste anonyme." *Flash Art* (Milan) (June 1974).

Trbuljak, Goran. *Écrits d' un artiste.* Zagreb, 1980.

Tucumán Arde

Collective mass-mediatic political action held November 1968 in Rosario and Buenos Aires. Organized by group of artists from Buenos Aires (Ricardo Carreira, Roberto Jacoby, León Ferrari, Pablo Suárez, Margarita Paksa), Rosario (Aldo Bartolotti, Eduardo Favario, Rubén Naranjo, Emilio Ghilloni, Noemí Escandell, Graciela Carnevale, Juan Pablo Renzi, María Teresa Gramuglio, Schork, Balbé, Púzzolo, Pidustwa y Zapia), and Santa Fé (Cohen and Borthwick), in collaboration with the CGT workers' union. Work conducted in two phases: (1) research and gathering of documentation in Tucumán province by artists and affiliated sociologists; (2) publicity campaign and multimedia event involving photography, posters, film, video, fliers at CGT headquarters in Rosario (November 1–15, 1968), and in Buenos Aires (November 25, 1968). Buenos Aires event shut down by police a few hours after opening.

BIBLIOGRAPHY

"Dossier Argentine: Les fils de Marx et Mondrian." *Robho* (Paris), no. 5–6 (1969): 16–22.

Giunta, Andrea. "Tucumán Arde: Una vanguardia entre el arte y la política." In *I Bienal de Artes Visuais do Mercosul,* 520–21. Porto Alegre: Fundação Bienal de Artes Visuais do Mercosul, 1997.

Lippard, Lucy, ed. *Six Years: The Dematerialization of the Art Object.* New York: Praeger, 1973.

Longoni, Ana. "Arte y violencia en los últimos años sesenta: Entre la representación y la acción." In *Arte, sociedad, cultura e identidad: I Jornadas de Sociología y Antropología del Arte.* Buenos Aires: Facultad de Ciencias Sociales, n.d.

___. "Entre París y Tucumán: La crisis final de la vanguardia artística de los sesenta." In *Arte y poder: V Jornadas de Teoría e Historia de las Artes,* 183–93. Buenos Aires: Centro Argentino de Investigadores de Artes, 1993.

___. "La intervención política como programa estético: Una lectura de Tucumán Arde." In *El arte entre lo público y lo privado: VI Jornadas de Teoría e Historia de las Artes,* 183–93. Buenos Aires: Centro Argentino de Investigadores de Artes, 1993.

___. "Tucumán Arde: Encuentros y desencuentros entre vanguardia artística y política." In *Cultura y política en los años '60.* Edited by Enrique Oteiza et al., 315–27. Buenos Aires: Oficina de Publicaciones del CBC, 1997.

Mestman, Mariano, and Ana Longoni. "Tucumán Arde: Una experiencia de arte de vanguardia, comunicación y política en los años sesenta." *Causas y Azares* (Buenos Aires), no. 1 (1994): 75–85.

Mimeographs. Graciela Carnevale Archives, Rosario, Argentina.

Sacco, Graciela. *Acción de la vanguardia contra acción de la policía.* Rosario: Kraft Impresiones, 1987.

WEI Guangqing (1962)

B. Hubei Province, PRC. Studies at Zhejiang Academy of Fine Arts, Hangzhou (1981–85). Initiates performance work with *Suicide Series* (1988–89), which he performs in *China/Avant-garde,* National Gallery, Beijing (1989). Shifts to painting, and becomes principal exponent of political pop (early 1990s). Produces influential series of paintings entitled *Red Wall (Hongqiang xilie,* 1992). Teaches at Hubei Academy of Fine Arts, Wuhan.

BIBLIOGRAPHY

China's New Art, Post-1989/Hou pa chiu Chung-kuo hsin i shu. Exh. cat. Edited by Valerie C. Doran. Hong Kong: Hanart T Z Gallery, 1993.

Lawrence WEINER (1942)

B. Bronx, N.Y. Begins career as a sculptor, constructing works that realize verbal statements. When one such work, *A Series of Stakes Set in the Ground at Regular Intervals ...* (1968), is damaged, Weiner concludes that the work itself, as a linguistic formulation, is still intact. Subsequent works take this insight to its logical conclusion: the work need not be physically constructed nor, if it is constructed, does the artist have to be involved. Begins trademark site-specific projects, often combining a written definition of the work with its physical realization; or a definition, performance, and filmed documentation of the action performed. Statement by Weiner (*Arts Magazine,* 1970) becomes prime exhibit in Tom Wolfe's satirical hatchet job on conceptualism, *The Painted Word* (1975).

BIBLIOGRAPHY

Barry, Huebler, Kosuth, Weiner: [January 5–31, 1969]. New York: Seth Siegelaub, 1969.

Lawrence Weiner: Sculpture. Exh. cat. Paris: Musée d'Art Moderne de la Ville de Paris, 1985.

Lawrence Weiner: A Selection of Works with Commentary/Een Keuze uit sijn wek met commentaar. Exh. cat. Edited by R. H. Fuchs. Eindhoven: Stedelijk van Abbemuseum, 1976.

Lawrence Weiner: Specific and General Works. Exh. cat. Villeurbanne: Nouveau Musée/Institut d'Art Contemporain, 1993.

Lawrence Weiner: Werke & Rekonstruktionen/Works & Reconstructions. Exh. cat. Edited by Jean-Hubert Martin. Berne: Kunsthalle, 1983.

Lawrence Weiner: Works. Hamburg: Anatol AV und Filmproduktion, 1977.

Mari, Bartomeu, ed. *Show (&) Tell: The Films and Videos of Lawrence Weiner: A Catalogue Raisonné.* Ghent: Imschoot, 1992.

Schwarz, Dieter. *Lawrence Weiner: Books 1968–1989: Catalogue Raisonné.* Cologne and Villeurbanne: Walter König and Nouveau Musée, 1989.

Sharp, Willoughby. "Lawrence Weiner at Amsterdam." *Avalanche* (New York), no. 4 (Spring 1972): 64–73.

Joyce WIELAND (1931–1998)

B. Toronto. Works for Graphic Associates as an animator (1956–58), where she experiments with film. Creates stained paintings and collages (late '50s–early '60s). Lives in New York (1963–70). Attains international reputation as filmmaker, beginning with *Larry's Recent Behavior* (1963) and *Patriotism* (1964). Produces serial paintings and quilts (1965 onward), which have a filmstrip-like quality. Uses quilts as a vehicle for her political and ecological concerns, i.e., *Water Quilt,* in which a message about the politics of energy consumption is inserted under each of its 64 flaps of embroidered flowers. Mounts solo exhibition, *True Patriot Love,* National Gallery of Canada, Ottawa (1971). Completes first feature film, *The Far Shore* (1976).

BIBLIOGRAPHY

Cornwell, Regina. "True Patriot Love: The Films of

Joyce Wieland." *Artforum* (September 1971).
Joyce Wieland. Exh. cat. Toronto: Art Gallery of Ontario, 1987.
Rabinovitz, Lauren. *Points of Resistance: Women, Power & Politics in the New York Avante-garde Cinema, 1943–71.* Urbana: University of Illinois Press, 1991.
True Patriot Love. Exh. cat. Ottawa: National Gallery of Ontario, 1971.

Gil J. WOLMAN (1929–1995)
B. Paris. Member of Lettrists, group founded in 1945/46 by Isidore Isou. Screens *L'anticoncept,* projected on a helium balloon, at Musée de l'Homme; censored by government and several Lettrists arrested for attempting to show the film at Cannes (1952). Establishes more "political" Lettrist International with Guy Debord (1952). Copublishes with Debord various articles—i.e., "Mode d'emploi du détournement" (How to Use Détournement)—in *Les Lévres Nues* (Naked Lips), a Belgian surrealist journal. Purged from LI by Debord, before the latter founds the Situationist International (1957).
BIBLIOGRAPHY
Devaux, Frédérique. *Le cinéma Lettriste, 1951–1991.* Paris: Éditions Paris Expérimental, 1992.

WU Shan Zhuan (1960)
B. Zhoushan, Zhejiang Province, PRC. Studies at Zhejiang Academy of Fine Arts, Hangzhou, and Hochschule für Bildende Kunst, Hamburg. Central figure in '85 Movement. Collaborates with other artists on group exhibition entitled *70% Red, 25% Black, 5% White,* held in a private space in Hangzhou (1986). Produces a series of installations and performances entitled *Red Humor* (1987–88). Participates in *China/Avant-garde,* National Gallery, Beijing (1989) with performance *Selling Shrimp.* Emigrates to Finland (1991), and begins conceptual works dealing with global markets and transnationalism. Represented in international exhibitions at Haus der Kulturen der Welt (Berlin, 1992), Kunsthalle Rotterdam (1993), and Cable Gallery (Helsinki, 1997), among others.
BIBLIOGRAPHY
Dijk, Hans van. "Painting in China After the Cultural Revolution: Style Developments and Theoretical Debates, Part II: 1985–1991." *China Information* (Leiden) 6, no. 4 (Spring 1992): 1–18.
Gao Minglu et al. *Zhongguo dangdai meishushi, 1985–1986* (History of Chinese Contemporary Art, 1985–1986). Shanghai: Shanghai People's Press, 1991.
Wu Shan Zhuan. "About Our Art." *Meishu Sichao,* no. 1 (1987): 22–24.
___. "About the Chinese Language." *Meishu,* no. 8 (1985).

XIAO Lu (1962)
B. Hangzhou, Zhejiang Province, PRC. Attends Zhejiang Academy of Fine Arts (1984–88). Participates in *Modern Chinese Arts* (Tokyo, 1988). Arrested by Chinese authorities when she and partner Tang Song fire bullets into their installation *Dialogue* at *China/Avant-garde,* National Gallery, Beijing (1989). Exhibition is temporarily closed, and the pair released. Participates in *Mao Goes Pop* (Sydney, 1993). Lives and works in Sydney (1989–).
BIBLIOGRAPHY
Mao Goes Pop. Exh. cat. Sydney: Museum of Contemporary Art, 1993.

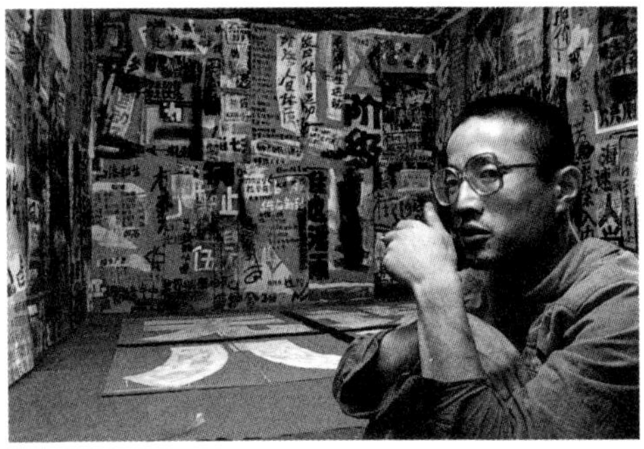

FIGURE 217.
Wu Shan Zhuan with his installation *Red Humor* (*Hongse youmo*), Hangzhou, 1986.

XU Bing (1955)
B. Chongqing, Sichuan Province, PRC. Establishes reputation as a printmaker in early 1980s. Graduates from Central Academy of Fine Arts, Beijing (1987) and teaches there until 1991, when he emigrates to the U.S. Exhibits his ambitious installation work *Book from the Sky* (1987–), composed of senseless Chinese characters, at National Gallery, Beijing (1988). Participates in *China Avant-garde,* National Gallery, Beijing (1989). Completes *Ghosts Pounding the Wall,* a series of rubbings from the Great Wall (1990). Mounts first solo exhibition at Elvehjem Museum of Art (Madison, Wis., 1991). Represented in *China's New Art, Post-1989* (Hong Kong/Sydney, 1993), and Venice Biennale (1993). Currently resides in New York.
BIBLIOGRAPHY
Lee, Benjamin. "Going Public." *Public Culture* (Philadelphia) 5 (1993): 165–78.
Taylor, Janelle S. "Non-Sense in Context: Xu Bing's Art and Its Publics." *Public Culture* (Philadelphia) 5 (1993): 317–27.
Three Installations by Xu Bing. Exh. cat. Madison: University of Wisconsin, Elvehjem Museum of Art, 1992.

Danny Ning Tsun YUNG (1943)
B. Shanghai; raised in Hong Kong. Studies architecture/urban design at University of California, Berkeley (1967) and Columbia University, New York (1969). Returns to Hong Kong (1978); produces single-frame film, *To Serve the People,* based on the five Chinese characters—*wei, ren, min, fu, wu*—which comprise Mao's famous slogan. Mounts first solo exhibition of conceptual cartoons at Hong Kong Arts Center (1979). Produces *Journey to the East,* four-part conceptual theater work (1980). Cofounds performance collective Zuni Icosahedron (1982). As director, playwright, and stage designer, mounts theatrical productions; exhibits installation and conceptual work at home and abroad; produces film and video, shown in international festivals (1982 onward).
BIBLIOGRAPHY
Yung, Daniel. "In the Presence of the Witness." *Drama Review* (Cambridge, Mass.) 38, no. 2 (Summer 1994): 53–59.

ZHANG Peili (1957)
B. Hangzhou, Zhejiang Province, PRC. Educated Zhejiang Academy of Fine Arts (1981–84). Cofounder of Pool Society and influential painter in "gray humor" mode (mid-'80s). Organizes first exhibition, *New Space '85,* with Pool Society colleagues Geng Jianyi and Wang Qiang. Shifts to conceptual work with *Art Plan #2* (1987); creates outdoor installations with Pool Society members. Participates in *China's New Art, Post-1989* (Hong Kong/Sydney, 1993), Venice Biennale (1993), *Another Long March* (Breda, 1997), and *Cities on the Move* (Vienna, 1997). Currently resides in Hangzhou.
BIBLIOGRAPHY
Dijk, Hans van. "Painting in China After the Cultural Revolution: Style Developments and Theoretical Debates, Part II: 1985–1991." *China Information* (Leiden) 6, no. 4 (Spring 1992): 1–18.
Gao Minglu et al. *Zhongguo dangdai meishushi, 1985–1986* (History of Chinese Contemporary Art, 1985–1986). Shanghai: Shanghai People's Press, 1991.
Gebrochene Bilder: Junge Kunst aus China (Broken Pictures: Young Chinese Art). Exh. cat. Bad Honnef: Horlemann Verlag, 1991.

Bibliography

Japan

Art in Japan Today. Edited by Takashina Shūji et al. Tokyo: Japan Foundation and Kinokuniya Bookstore, 1974.

Art in Japan Today II: 1970–1983. Edited by Miki Tamon et al. Tokyo: Japan Foundation, 1984.

Chiba Shigeo. *Gendai bijutsu itsudatsu-shi, 1945–1985* (A History of Deviations in Contemporary Art). Tokyo: Shōbunsha, 1986.

Dada in Japan: Japanische Avantgarde, 1920–1970, eine Fotodokumentation. Exh. cat. Edited by Shirakawa Yoshio. Düsseldorf: Kunstmuseum, 1983.

"Gainen geijutsu" (Conceptual Art). Special issue. *Geijutsu Kurabu* (Art Club), no. 8 (April 1974).

Gendai no bijutsu/Art Now 6: Shuchō suru obuje (Asserting Objets). Edited by Tōno Yoshiaki. Tokyo: Kōdansha, 1972.

Gendai no bijutsu/Art Now 11: Kōi ni kakeru (Staking Action). Edited by Haryū Ichirō. Tokyo: Kōdansha, 1972.

Haryū Ichirō. *Sengo bijutsu seisui-shi* (The Ups and Downs of Postwar Japanese Art). Tokyo: Tokyo Shoseki, 1979.

Japon des avant-gardes, 1910–1970. Exh. cat. Paris: Éditions Centre Georges Pompidou, 1986.

Japon des avant-gardes, 1910–1970: Repères chronologiques et documentaires. Paris: Éditions Centre Georges Pompidou, 1987.

Munroe, Alexandra, ed. *Japanese Art After 1945: Scream Against the Sky.* New York: Abrams, 1994.

Reconstructions: Avant-garde Art in Japan, 1945–1965. Exh. cat. Edited by David Elliot and Kazu Kaidō. Oxford: Museum of Modern Art, 1986.

Sawaragi Noi. *Nihon, gendai, bijutsu* (Japan, Contemporary, Art). Tokyo: Shinchōsha, 1998.

Tani Arata. *Kaiten-suru hyōshō: Gendai bijutsu, datsu posutomodan no shikaku* (Revolving Representation: Contemporary Art, a Post–Postmodern Viewpoint). Tokyo: Gendai Kikakushitsu, 1992.

Western Europe

L' art conceptuel, une perspective. Exh. cat. Essays by Claude Gintz et al. Paris: Musée d'Art Moderne de la Ville de Paris, 1989.

Avanguardia transavanguardia 68–77. Exh. cat. Milan: Mura Aureliane da Porta Metronia a Porta Latina in association with Gruppo Editoriale Electa, 1982.

Bonito Oliva, Achille. *Dialoghi d'artista: Incontri con l'arte contemporanea, 1970–1984.* Milan: Electa, 1984.

The British Avant-Garde. Exh. cat. New York: New York Cultural Center in association with Fairleigh Dickinson University, 1971. Also published in *Studio International* (London) 181, no. 933 (May 1971): 201–39.

Celant, Germano. *Arte Povera: Earthworks, Impossible Art, Actual Art, Conceptual Art.* New York: Praeger, 1969.

Christov-Bakargiev, Carolyn. "Arte Povera, 1967–1987." *Flash Art* (Intl. ed.) 137 (November–December 1987): 52–69.

Crow, Thomas. *The Rise of the Sixties: American and European Art in the Era of Dissent.* New York: Abrams, 1996.

Documenta 5: Belfrangung der Realität: Bildwelten heute. Exh. cat. 3 vols. Kassel: Neue Galerie und Museum Fridericianum in association with Documenta GmbH and C. Bertelsmann, 1972.

Flash Art (Int'l. ed.) 143 (November–December 1988): 87–117. Conceptual supplement.

"Fluxus: A Conceptual Country." *Visible Language* 26 (Winter–Spring 1992): 8–248.

Hobsbawm, Eric. *The Age of Extremes: A History of the World, 1914–1991.* New York: Vintage, 1994.

Identité italienne: L'art en Italie depuis 1959. Exh. cat. Edited by Germano Celant. Paris: Éditions Centre Georges Pompidou, 1981.

In the Spirit of Fluxus. Exh. cat. Edited by Janet Jenkins. Minneapolis: Walker Art Center, 1993.

On the Passage of a Few People Through a Rather Brief Moment in Time: The Situationist International, 1957–1972. Exh. cat. Edited by Elisabeth Sussman. Cambridge, Mass.: MIT Press, 1989.

Roberts, John, ed. *The Impossible Document: Photography and Conceptual Art in Britain, 1966–1976.* London: Camerawork, 1997.

Stiles, Kristine, and Peter Selz, eds. *Theories and Documents of Contemporary Art: Sourcebook of Artists' Writings.* Berkeley: University of California Press, 1996.

Szeemann, Harald, comp. *Dokumente zur aktuellen Kunst, 1967–1970.* Lucerne: Kunstkreis, 1972.

Vries, Gerd de, comp. *Über Kunst: Künstlertexte zum veränderten Kunstverständnis nach 1965/On Art: Artists' Writings on the Changed Notion of Art after 1965.* Cologne: DuMont Schauberg, 1974.

When Attitudes Become Form: Works, Concepts, Processes, Situations, Information: Live in Your Head. Exh. cat. Edited by Harald Szeemann. Berne: Kunsthalle, 1969.

Eastern Europe

Beke, László. *Művészet/elmélet, Tanulmányok, 1970–1991* (Art Theory, Essays, 1970–1991). Budapest: Blalassi Kiadó BAE Tartóshullám-Intermedia, 1994.

Beke, László, and Gábor Pataki. "The Eastern European Questionnaire for Artists, Art Historians, and Critics." In *Sub Minervae nationis praesidio: Studies on the National Culture in Honor of Lajos Németh on His 60th Birthday,* 381–84. Budapest: ELTE, 1989.

Beyond Belief: Contemporary Art from East Central Europe. Exh. cat. Chicago: Museum of Contemporary Art, 1995.

Czartoryska, Urszula. *Od pop-artu do szutki konceptualnej.* Warsaw: Wydawnictwa Artystyczne i Filmowe, 1973.

Europa, Europa: Das Jahrhundert der Avantgarde in Mittel- und Osteuropa. Exh. cat. 4 vols. Edited by Ryszard Stanislawski and Christoph Brockhaus. [Germany]: Stiftung Kunst und Kultur des Landes Nordrhein-Westfalen: Kunst- und Ausstellungshalle der Bundesrepublik Deutschland, 1994.

Fischer, Hervé. *Art et communication marginale: Tampons d'artistes.* Paris: Balland, 1974.

Groh, Klaus, comp. *Aktuelle Kunst in Osteuropa.* Cologne: DuMont Schauberg, 1972.

Kunst in sozialistischen Staaten: CSSR, DDR, VR Polen, Ungarische VR: Beitr. zu e. Standortbestimmung: Malerei, Grafik, Kleinplastik. Exh. cat. Edited by Jürgen Weichardt. Oldenburg: Isensee, 1980.

Mail Art: Osteuropa im internationalen Netzwerk/Eastern Europe in International Network. Exh. cat. Schwerin: Staatliches Museum, 1996.

Perneczky, Géza. *A háló: Alternatív művészeti áramlatok a folyóirat-kiadványaik tükrében, 1968–1988.* Budapest: Héttorung Kunyukiadó, 1991. Translated by Tibor Szendrei as *The Magazine Network: The Trends of Alternative Art in the Light of Their Periodicals, 1968–1988.* Cologne: Soft Geometry, 1993.

Poinsot, Jean-Marc. *Mail Art: Communication à distance, concept.* Paris: CEDIC, 1971.

Strauss, Thomas. *Zwischen Ostkunst und Westkunst von der Avantgarde zur Postmoderne: Essays, 1970–1995.* Munich: Scaneg, 1995.

Vision (Oakland, Calif.), no. 2 (January 1976). Special issue: Eastern Europe. Edited by Tom Marioni.

Ex-Czechoslovakia

Aktual Group. *Aktual Schmuck in Czechoslovakia.* London: Beau Geste Press, 1974.

Bénamou, Geneviève. *L'art aujourd'hui en Tchécoslavaquie.* Paris: Imprimeurs Libres, 1979.

___. *Sensibilités contemporaines: 70 artistes d'origine tchèque et slovaque hors Tchécoslavaquie, 1970–1984* (Contemporary Artistic Sensibilities: 70 Artists of Czech and Slovak Origin Living Outside Czechoslovakia, 1970–1984). Paris: Imprimeurs Libres, 1985.

Knížák, Milan. "Aktual in Czechoslovakia." *Art and Artists* (London) (October 1972).

Milan Knížák: Action as a Lifestyle—Auswahl der Aktivitäten, 1953–1985 (Selected Activities, 1953–1985). Exh. cat. Hamburg: Kunsthalle, 1986.

Riese, H. P. "Bildende Kunst in der Tschechoslowakei." *Architekt* (Vienna) 17, no. 9 (1968): 322–24.

Sest' desiate roky v slovenskom výtvarnom umení (The Sixties in Slovakian Art). Bratislava: Slovenská Národná Galéria, 1995.

Straus, Tomáš. *Slovenský variant moderny* (Slovak Variation of Modernism). Bratislava: Pallas, 1992.

Zdenek, Felix. "Die Prager Szene." *Werk* (Berne) 57, no. 5 (1970): 336–37.

Ex-German Democratic Republic

Eigenart und Eigensinn: Alternative Kulturszenen in der DDR, 1980–1990. Exh. cat. Edited by Frank Eckhart. Bremen: Edition Temmen, 1993.

Mail Art Szene DDR, 1975–1990. Edited by Friedrich Winnes and Lutz Wohlrab under the direction of Birger Jesch and Joseph W. Huber. Berlin: Haude & Spener, 1994.

Postkarten und Künstlerkarten. East Berlin: Galerie Arkade, 1978.

Hungary

Körner, Éva. "The Absurd as Concept—Phenomena of Hungarian Conceptualism." In *Joseph Kosuth: Zero at the Edge of the Known World,* 200–19. Exh. cat. Venice: 45th Venice Biennale, 1993.

Poland

Polnische Avantgarde, 1930–1990. Exh. cat. Berlin: Der Verein, 1992.

Romania

Romanian Art Today. Exh. cat. Edinburgh: Demarco Gallery, 1971.

Ex-Yugoslavia

Dokumenti o post-objektnim pojavama u jugoslavenskoj umetnosti, 1968–1973 (Documents of Post-Object Trends in Yugoslavian Art, 1968–1973). Exh. cat. Belgrade: Salon Muzeja Savremene Umetnosti, 1973.

Inovacije u hrvatskoj umjetnosti sedamdesetih godina (Innovation in Croatian Art in the 1970s). Exh. cat. Zagreb and Belgrade: Galerija Suvremene Umjetnosti and Salon Muzeja Savremene Umetnosti, 1982.

Konceptualna umetnost 60-ih in 70-ih let (Conceptual Art in the '60s and '70s). Ljubljana: Galerija SKUC, 1997.

The New Art Practice in Yugoslavia, 1966–1978. Exh. cat. Zagreb: Galerija Grada Zagreba, 1978.

Latin America

Acha, Juan. "El coloquio." *Revista del Arte y la Arquitectura en América Latina* (Medellín) 2, no. 7 (1981): 21–27.

___. "Teoría y práctica no-objetualistas en América Latina." In *Ensayos y ponencias Latinoamericanistas,* 221–42. Caracas: Ediciones GAN, 1984.

Amaral, Aracy A. *Arte é meio artístico entre a feijoada é o x-burguer.* São Paulo: Livraria Nobel, 1982.

___. *Arte para quê? A preocupação social na arte brasileira, 1930–1970.* São Paulo: Nobel, 1987.

___. "Aspectos del no-objetualismo en el Brasil." *Revista del Arte y la Arquitectura en América Latina* (Medellín) 2, no. 7 (1981): 32–35.

Artes Visuales (Mexico City), no. 23 (January 1980). Special issue: Los Grupos.

Barnitz, Jacqueline. "Conceptual Art and Latin America: A Natural Alliance." In *Encounters/Displacements: Luis Camnitzer, Alfredo Jaar, Cildo Meireles,* 35–48. Austin: Archer M. Huntington Art Gallery, University of Texas, 1992.

Bittencourt, Francisco. "A vanguarda visual carioca dos años 70." *Vozes* (Petropolis) 72, no. 5 (June–July 1978): 29–42.

Bulhões, María Amélia. "O estado militar no Brasil: Repressão e estímulo as artes plásticas." In *Arte y poder: V Jornadas de Teoría e Historia de las Artes,* 206–14. Buenos Aires: Centro Argentino de Investigadores de Artes, 1993.

Buntinx, Gustavo. "Modernidades cosmopolitas y andinas en la vanguardia peruana." In *Cultura y política en los años '60.* Edited by Enrique Oteiza et al., 267–86. Buenos Aires: Oficina de Publicaciones del CBC, 1997.

Camnitzer, Luis. "Arte colonial contemporáneo." *Marcha* (Montevideo), July 3, 1970, n.p.

___. "Contemporary Colonial Art." Paper presented at the Annual International Congress of the Latin American Studies Association, Washington, D.C., 1970.

___. *Culturas híbridas: Estrategias para entrar y salir de la modernidad.* Mexico City: Consejo Nacional para la Cultura y las Artes, 1989.

___. "Dematerialization and Resistance: The Use and Misuse of Conceptualism in Latin American Art." Unpub. ms., 1993. Luis Camnitzer Papers, Great Neck, N.Y.

___. "Una genealogía del arte conceptual latinoamericano." *Continente Sul/Sur* (Porto Alegre), no. 6 (November 1997): 179–230.

___. *New York Graphic Workshop.* Caracas: Museo de Bellas Artes, 1969.

Castrillón, Alfonso. "Reflexiones sobre el arte conceptual en el Perú y sus proyecciones." *Revista del Arte y la Arquitectura en América Latina* (Medellín) 2, no. 7 (1981): 41–44.

Curiel, Gustavo, et al., eds. *Arte, historia e identidad en América: Visiones comparativas.* Mexico City: UNAM, Instituto de Investigaciones Estéticas, 1993.

De los grupos los individuos: Artistas plásticos de los Grupos Metropolitanos. Exh. cat. Mexico City: Instituto Nacional de Bellas Artes, 1985.

Los ecos de Mathias Goeritz: Catálogo de la exposición. Mexico City: Antiguo Colegio de San Ildefonso, 1997.

Eder, Rita. "El arte no-objetual en México." *Revista del Arte y la Arquitectura en América Latina* (Medellín) 2, no. 7 (1981): 14–20.

Fantoni, Guillermo A. "Horizontes problemáticos de una vanguardia de los años sesenta: Un movimiento artístico entre el heroísmo y la crisis." *Anuario, Segunda Epoca* (Rosario), no. 13 (1988): 137–48.

___. "El impacto de lo nuevo en los primeros sesenta: Conformación y emergencia de un grupo de vanguardia." *Anuario, Segunda Epoca* (Rosario), no. 14 (1989–90): 321–39.

___. "Itinerario de una modernidad estética: Intensidades vanguardistas y estrategias de modernización en el arte de Rosario." In *Arte y poder: V Jornadas de Teoría e Historia de las Artes,* 105–13. Buenos Aires: Centro Argentino de Investigadores de Artes, 1993.

___. "Rosario 1966: Episodios de vanguardia y fragmentos de conversaciones." In *Serie 10: Arte y estética.* Rosario: Universidad Nacional de Rosario, Facultad de Humanidades y Artes, 1993.

___. "Rupturas en perspectiva: Modernismo y vanguardia en el arte de Rosario." *Cuadernos del Ciesal* (Rosario), no. 2–3 (1994): 177–84.

___. "Tensiones hacia la política: Del homenaje al Viet-Nam a la Anti-Bienal." *SiSi* (Rosario) 2, no. 2 (Summer 1990): 33–39.

___. "Vanguardia estética y vanguardia política." *Línea de Sombra* 3 (Spring 1993): 24–27.

Giunta, Andrea. "Arte y (re)presión: Cultura crítica y prácticas conceptuales en Argentina." In *Arte, historia e identidad en América: Visiones comparativas.* Edited by Gustavo Curiel et al., 875–90. Mexico City: UNAM, Instituto de Investigaciones Estéticas, 1993.

___. "Destrucción-creación en la vanguardia artística del sesenta: Entre arte destructivo y 'Ezeiza es Trelew.'" In *Arte y violencia.* Edited by Arturo Pascual Soto, 59–81. Mexico City: UNAM, Instituto de Investigaciones Estéticas, 1995.

___. "Utopía y disolución: Arte crítico en la década del sesenta." In *Artes plásticas na América Latina contemporánea.* Edited by María Amélia Bulhões and María Lúcia Bastos Kern, 97–118. Porto Alegre: Editora da Universidade Federal do Rio Grande do Sul, 1994.

Glusberg, Jorge. *Del pop-art a la nueva imagen.* Buenos Aires: Ediciones de Arte Gaglianone, 1985.

Herrera, María José. "En medio de los medios: La experimentación con los medios masivos de comunicación en la Argentina en la década del 60." In *Arte argentino del siglo XX.* Buenos Aires: Fundación para la Investigación del Arte Argentino, 1997.

Ivelic, Milan, and Gaspar Galaz. *Chile, arte actual.* Valparaíso: Ediciones Universitarias de Valparaíso, 1988.

King, John. *El di Tella.* Buenos Aires: Ediciones de Arte Gaglianone, 1985.

Jodorowsky, Alejandro. *Hacia el "efímero" pánico o ¡Sacar al teatro del teatro!* Photocopy of prologue, n.p, 1963. Blanton Museum of Art Archives, University of Texas, Austin.

López Anaya, Jorge. *El arte en un tiempo sin dioses.* Buenos Aires: Editorial Almagesto, 1995.

___. *Historia del arte argentino.* Buenos Aires: Emecé Editores, 1997.

Luis Camnitzer: Retrospective Exhibition, 1966–1990. New York: Lehman College Art Gallery, 1991.

Malasartes (Rio de Janeiro), no. 1 (September–November 1975), no. 2 (January–March 1976), no. 3 (April–June 1976).

Marchán Fiz, Simón. *Del arte objetual al arte de concepto, 1960–1974.* Madrid: Ediciones Akal, 1988.

Masotta, Oscar. *Conciencia y estructura.* Buenos Aires: Editorial Jorge Álvarez, 1969.

___, et al. *Happenings.* Buenos Aires: Editorial Jorge Álvarez, 1967.

Morais, Frederico. "Arte latino-americana da teoría a práctica." *Vozes* (Petropolis) 72, no. 5 (June–July 1972): 43–50.

___. *Artes plásticas: A crise da hora atual.* Rio de Janeiro: Editora Paz e Terra, S.A., 1975.

___. *Cronología das artes plásticas no Rio de Janeiro.* Rio de Janeiro: Topbooks, 1995.

___. *Depoimento de uma geração, 1969–1970.* Rio de Janeiro: Galería de Arte BANERJ, 1986.

___. *Do conceitual a arte contemporânea: Marcos históricos.* São Paulo: ICI, 1994.

___. *5. Opinião 65.* Rio de Janeiro: Galería de Arte BANERJ, 1985.

___. Untitled lecture given in conjunction with two exhibitions: *Objeto e participação,* Palácio das Artes, Belo Horizonte, and *Do corpo à terra,* Parque Municipal, Belo Horizonte, April 1970.

Oberto, Valentina Anselmi de, and Ignacio Enrique Oberto F., eds. *Una visión del arte contemporáneo venezolano: Colección Ignacio y Valentina Oberto.* Caracas: Fundación Noa Noa, 1995.

Peluffo, Gabriel. "Instituto General Electric de Montevideo: Medios masivos, poder transnacional y arte contemporáneo." In *Cultura y política en los años '60.* Edited by Enrique Oteiza et al., 109–30. Buenos Aires: Oficina de Publicaciones del CBC, 1997.

Pérez Oramas, Luis, and Ariel Jiménez. *La invención de la continuidad.* Caracas: Fundación Galería de Arte Nacional, 1997.

Pontual, Roberto. *Arte brasileira contemporânea: Coleção Gilberto Chateaubriand.* Rio de Janeiro: Edições Jornal do Brasil, 1976.

Rama, Angel. *Antología de El Techo de la Ballena.* Caracas: FUNDARTE, 1987.

Ramírez, Mari Carmen. "Blueprint Circuits: Conceptual Art and Politics in Latin America." In *Latin American Artists of the Twentieth Century.* Edited by Waldo Rasmussen et al., 156–67. New York: Museum of Modern Art, 1993.

___, ed. *Re-Aligning Vision: Alternative Currents in South American Drawing.* Austin: Archer M.

Huntington Art Gallery, University of Texas, 1997.
___. "Rematerialization." In *Universalis: 23. Bienal Internacional São Paulo.* São Paulo: Fundação Bienal de São Paulo, 1996.
Ramos, María Elena. *Acciones frente a la Plaza.* Caracas: Fondo Editorial Fundarte, 1995.
Reyes Palma, Francisco. "Oratorio monocromático: Los Hartos." In *Los ecos de Mathias Goeritz: Ensayos y testimonios,* 121–29. Mexico City: Instituto de Investigaciones Estéticas, 1997.
Richard, Nelly. "Margins and Institutions: Art in Chile Since 1973." *Art and Text* (Melbourne), no. 21 (May–July 1986).
Rizzo, Patricia, ed. *Instituto di Tella: Experiencias '68.* Buenos Aires: Fundación PROA, 1998.
Stellweg, Carla. "'Magnet–New York': Conceptual, Performance, Environmental, and Installation Art." In *The Latin American Spirit: Art and Artists in the United States. 1920–1970.* Edited by Luis Cancel et al., 284–311. New York: Bronx Museum and Abrams, 1988.
Traba, Marta. *Dos décadas vulnerables en las artes plásticas latinoamericanas, 1950–1970.* Mexico City: Siglo Veintiuno Editores, 1973.
Zanini, Walter, ed. *História general da arte no Brasil.* São Paulo: Instituto Walther Moreira Salles, 1983.
Zegher, M. Catherine de. *Inside the Visible: An Elliptical Traverse of 20th Century Art.* Cambridge, Mass.: MIT Press, 1996.

North America

Aliaga, Juan Vicente, and José Miguel García Cortés, eds. *Arte conceptual revisado/Conceptual Art Revisited.* Valencia: Departamento de Escultura, Facultad de Bellas Artes, Universidad Politecnica de Valencia, 1990.
Altschuler, Bruce. *The Avant-Garde in Exhibition: New Art in the Twentieth Century.* New York: Abrams, 1994.
Art & Language. Exh. cat. Eindhoven: Stedelijk van Abbemuseum, 1980.
L' art conceptuel, une perspective. Exh. cat. Essays by Claude Gintz et al. Paris: Musée d'Art Moderne de la Ville de Paris, 1989.
Art in the Mind. Exh. cat. Oberlin, Ohio: Allen Art Museum, 1970.
Avalanche (New York), nos. 1–13 (Fall 1970–Summer 1976).
Barthes, Roland. *Elements of Semiology.* Translated by Annette Lavers and Colin Smith. London: Cape, 1967.
Batchelor, David. *Minimalism.* London: Tate Gallery Publications, 1997.
Battcock, Gregory, ed. *Idea Art: A Critical Anthology.* New York: E.P. Dutton, 1973.
Buchloh, Benjamin H. D. "Conceptual Art, 1962–1969: From the Aesthetic of Administration to the Critique of Institutions." *October,* no. 55 (Winter 1990): 105–43. See also Joseph Kosuth and Seth Siegelaub, "Replies to Benjamin Buchloh on Conceptual Art," and Benjamin Buchloh, "Reply to Joseph Kosuth and Seth Siegelaub," *October,* no. 57 (Summer 1991).
Claura, Michel, and Seth Siegelaub. *18 Paris IV.70.* Paris: 66 Rue Mouffetard, 1970.
Colpitt, Francis, and Phyllis Plous. *Knowledge: Aspects of Conceptual Art.* Santa Barbara: University Art Museum, 1992.
Crow, Thomas. *The Rise of the Sixties: American and European Art in the Era of Dissent.* New York: Abrams, 1996.
557,087: An Exhibition. Organized by Lucy R. Lippard. Seattle: Seattle Art Museum, 1969. Version titled *955,000* organized for Vancouver Art Gallery, 1970.
Flash Art (Int'l. ed.) 143 (November–December 1988): 87–117. Conceptual supplement.
"Fluxus: A Conceptual Country." *Visible Language* 26 (Winter–Spring 1992): 8–248.
Flynt, Henry. "Concept Art" (1963). In *Esthetics Contemporary.* Edited by Richard Kostelanetz, 329–31. New York: Prometheus Books, 1989.
Godfrey, Tony. *Conceptual Art (Art and Ideas).* London: Phaidon, 1998.
Gregory, Katherine, Marilyn Landis, Russell F. Lewis, David Crane, and Scott R. Kahn. *Stolen.* New York: Dwan Gallery, 1970.
Information. Exh. cat. Edited by Kynaston McShine. New York: Museum of Modern Art, 1970.
In the Spirit of Fluxus. Exh. cat. Edited by Janet Jenkins. Minneapolis: Walker Art Center, 1993.
July, August, September 1969. Exh. cat. New York: Seth Siegelaub, 1969.
Leen, Frederik. "Seth Siegelaub: Conceptual Art, Exhibitions." *Forum International* 2, no. 9 (September 1991): 64–72.
Lippard, Lucy, ed. *Six Years: The Dematerialization of the Art Object from 1966 to 1972.* New York: Praeger, 1973.
Mattelart, Armand, and Seth Siegelaub, eds. *Communication and Class Struggle: An Anthology.* 2 vols. New York: International General, 1979–83.
Meyer, Ursula, ed. *Conceptual Art.* New York: E.P. Dutton, 1971.
Millet, Catherine. "L'art conceptuel." *VH 101* (Paris), no. 3 (Autumn 1970): 1–53.
Morgan, Robert C. *Conceptual Art: An American Perspective.* Jefferson, N.C.: McFarland, 1994.
Morgan, Robert C. "The Situation of Conceptual Art: The January Show and After." *Arts Magazine* 63 (February 1989): 40–50. With interviews reprinted from *Arts Magazine* 1969, and four more interviews twenty years later.
Non-Anthropomorphic Art by Four Young Artists: Joseph Kosuth, Christine Kozlov, Michael Rinaldi, Ernest Rossi. New York: Lannis Gallery, 1966.
Outside the Frame—Performance and the Object: A Survey of Performance Art in the USA Since 1950. Cleveland: Cleveland Center for Contemporary Art, 1994.
Reconsidering the Object of Art: 1965-1975. Exh. cat. Edited by Ann Goldstein and Anne Rorimer. Los Angeles and Cambridge, Mass.: Museum of Contemporary Art and MIT Press, 1995.
Roberts, John, ed. *The Impossible Document: Photography and Conceptual Art in Britain, 1966–1976.* London: Camerawork, 1997.
Siegelaub, Seth. "July–August 1970." *Studio International* (London) 180, no. 924 (July–August 1970): 1–48.
Situation Concepts. Exh. cat. Innsbruck: Galerie im Taxispalais, 1971.
Space/Time/Sound: Conceptual Art in the San Francisco Bay Area: The 1970s. Exh. cat. San Francisco: Museum of Modern Art, 1979.
Stiles, Kristine, and Peter Selz, eds. *Theories and Documents of Contemporary Art: Sourcebook of Artists' Writings.* Berkeley: University of California Press, 1996.
Vision (Oakland, Calif.), no. 1 (September 1975). Special issue: California.
Vision (Oakland, Calif.), no. 3 (November 1976). Special issue: New York.
Vries, Gerd de, comp. *Über Kunst: Künstlertexte zum veränderten Kunstverständnis nach 1965/On Art: Artists' Writings on the Changed Notion of Art after 1965.* Cologne: DuMont Schauberg, 1974.
Wallace, Michele. *Invisibility Blues: From Pop to Theory.* New York: Verso, 1990.
West Coast Conceptual Photography. Exh. cat. San Francisco: La Mamelle, 1976.
Wolfe, Tom. *The Painted Word.* New York: Farrar, Straus and Giroux, 1975.
Xeroxbook. Exh. cat. New York: Seth Siegelaub and John W. Wendler, 1968. Also known as *Carl Andre, Robert Barry, Douglas Huebler, Joseph Kosuth, Sol LeWitt, Robert Morris, Lawrence Weiner.*

Australia and New Zealand

Allen, Christopher. *Art in Australia: From Colonization to Postmodernism.* London: Thames and Hudson, 1997.
Allen, Jim, and Wystan Curnow, eds. *New Art: Some Recent New Zealand Sculpture and Post-Object Art.* Auckland: Heinemann, 1976.
Art Now: The First Biennial Review of Contemporary Art. Wellington: Museum of New Zealand Te Pap Tongarewa, 1994.
Australia: Nine Contemporary Artists: John Davis, John Dunkley-Smith, Marr Grounds, Lyndal Jones, John Nixon, Mike Parr, Redback Graphix, Stelarc. Exh. cat. Los Angeles: LAICA, 1984.
Barton, Christina. "Post-Object Art in New Zealand, 1969–1979: Experiments in Art and Life." Master's thesis, University of Auckland, 1989.
Crary, Jonathan. *Techniques of the Observer: On Vision and Modernity in the Nineteenth Century.* Cambridge, Mass.: MIT Press, 1990.
Docking, Gil. *Two Hundred Years of New Zealand Painting.* Rev. ed., with additions by Michael Dunn covering 1970–90. Glenfield, Auckland, N.Z.: D. Bateman, 1990.
Dunn, Richard. *The Dialectical Image: Selected Work, 1964–1992.* Exh. cat. Sydney: Art Gallery of New South Wales, 1992.
Green, Charles. *Peripheral Vision: Contemporary Australian Art, 1970–1994.* Roseville East, N.S.W.: Craftsman House, 1995.
Harrison, Charles. *Essays on Art & Language.* Oxford: Blackwell, 1991.
Inhibodress 1970–72. Exh. cat. Edited by Sue Cramer. Brisbane: Institute of Modern Art, 1989.
Kirker, Anne. *New Zealand Women Artists: A Survey of 150 Years.* Tortola, B.V.I.: Craftsman House, 1993.
Marsh, Anne. *Body and Self: Performance Art in Australia, 1969–92.* South Melbourne: Oxford University Press, 1993.
Plant, Margaret. *Irreverent Sculpture.* Melbourne: Monash University Art Gallery, 1985.
Smith, Bernard. *Australian Painting, 1788–1990.* With three additional chapters on Australian painting since 1970 by Terry Smith. Melbourne: Oxford University Press, 1991.
___, ed. *Concerning Contemporary Art: The Power Lectures, 1968–1973.* Oxford: Clarendon Press, 1975.

Smith, Terry, ed. *Art & Language: Australia 1975.* Banbury: Art & Language Press, 1975.

___. "Australia: Australian Art since 1900." In *The Dictionary of Art.* Edited by Jane Turner. New York: Grove, 1996.

___. and Paul McGillick. *The Situation Now: Object or Post-Object Art?* Sydney: Contemporary Art Society, 1971.

Stojanovic, Jelena. "Conceptual Art Then and Since." *Agenda Contemporary Art Magazine*, no. 26 (November–December 1992), no. 27 (January–February 1993). Supplement: Interview with Terry Smith.

Wedde, Ian, and Gregory Burke, eds. *Now See Hear! Art, Language, and Translation.* Wellington, N.Z.: Victoria University Press, for the Wellington City Art Gallery, 1990.

Soviet Union

Between Spring and Summer: Soviet Conceptual Art in the Era of Late Communism. Exh. cat. Edited by David Ross. Cambridge, Mass.: MIT Press, 1990.

Bobrinskaia, E. A. *Kontseptualizm.* Moscow: Galart, 1994.

Bown, Matthew Cullerne. *Contemporary Russian Art.* London: Phaidon Press, 1989.

Gambrell, Jamey. "Notes on the Underground." *Art in America* 76 (November 1988): 126–36.

___. "Perestroika Shock." *Art in America* 77 (February 1989): 124–34.

The Green Show. Exh. cat. New York: Exit Art/The First World, 1990.

Rosenfeld, Alla, and Norton T. Dodge, eds. *From Gulag to Glasnost: Nonconformist Art from the Soviet Union.* New York: Thames and Hudson, 1995.

Ryklin, Mikhail. "Medical Hermeneutics." *Flash Art* (Russian ed.), no. 1 (1989): 115–16.

Tamruchi, Natalia. *Moscow Conceptualism, 1970–1990.* Roseville East, N.S.W.: Craftsman House, 1995.

Tupitsyn, Margarita. *Margins of Soviet Art: Socialist Realism to the Present.* Milan: Giancarlo Politi Editore, 1989.

Tupitsyn, Victor. "Moscow Communal Conceptualism." *Parachute* 82 (1996): 25–29.

Africa

Williamson, Sue. *Resistance Art in South Africa.* Cape Town: David Philip, 1989.

Williamson, Sue, and Ashraf Jamal. *Art in South Africa: The Future Present.* Cape Town: David Philip, 1996.

South Korea

Across the Pacific: Contemporary Korean and Korean American Art. Exh. cat. New York: Queens Museum of Art, 1993.

[AG], nos. 1–3. Seoul: Korean Association of Avant-garde, 1970.

Choi Min and Sung Wan-kyung, eds. *Sigaggwa Uno 2: Hankuk Hyundae Misulgwa Bipyong* (Vision and Language 2: Korean Contemporary Art and Criticism). Seoul: Yolhwadang, 1985.

The First Seoul Biennial Organized by Korean Association of Avant-garde. Seoul: National Museum of Modern Art, 1974.

Hankukeui Chusang Misul: Isimnyoneui Guejeok (Twenty Years of Korean Abstract Art). Seoul: Guegan Misul, 1979.

JAALA (Japan/Africa/Asia/Latin America). Exh. cat. Tokyo: Metropolitan Museum of Art, 1986.

Kim Yong-ik. "Geonyomjueuiro Bon Hyundaemisul" (Contemporary Art Seen as Conceptualism). *Hongik Misul* (Seoul), no. 5 (1983): 24–33.

___. "Hankuk Hyundae Misuleui Avant-garde" (Avant-garde in Korean Contemporary Art). *Gongan* (Space) (Seoul), no. 139 (January 1979): 53–59.

Kim Yoon-soo. "Pungyowa Bingon, Mosunsogeui Kaldeung, Chilsimnyondaeui Bansung" (Abundance and Poverty, Conflict and Contradiction: Reflection on the '70s). *Wolgan Joongang* (Seoul), no. 141 (December 1979): 160–64.

Korean Min Joong Arts. Exh. cat. Seoul: National Museum of Contemporary Arts, 1994.

Lee Il. "Byunhwawa Mosack grigo Shilhum" (Change, Exploration, and Experiment). *Gongan* (Space) (Seoul), no. 113 (January 1976): 33–44.

___. *Hyundae Misuleui Guejeok* (Traces of Modern Art). Seoul: Donghwa Press Center, 1974.

Lee Kang-so. "Ilsangjeok Jonjaeui Insikronjeok Choolhyun" (Epistemological Apparition of Ordinary Existence). *Gongan* (Space) (Seoul), no. 156 (June 1980): 39–42.

Lee Kun-yong. "Hankukeui Ipchae Hangwimisul gue Charyojeok Bogoseo" (Documentary Report on Three-Dimensional Art and Performance Art in Korea). *Gongan* (Space) (Seoul), no. 156 (June 1980): 13–22.

Lee Kyung-sung. "Pungyosogae Iruerjin Joyonghan Byunhyuk: Chilsimnyondaeui Heurum" (Silent Revolution Realized in Abundance: Trend of the '70s). *Guegan Misul* (Seoul), no. 12 (Winter 1979): 59–64.

Min Joong Art: A New Cultural Movement from Korea. Exh. cat. New York: Artists Space, 1988.

Minjoongmisulul Haanghayo: Hyunsilgwa Baron Simnyoneui Baljachi (Toward Min Joong Art: Ten Years of Hyunsilgwa-Baron). Seoul: Kwahagwa Sasang, 1990.

Oh Kwang-soo. *Hankuk Hyundaemisulsa* (History of Korean Modern Art). Seoul: Yolhwadang, 1979.

___. *Hankuk Misuleui Hyunjang* (Actuality of Korean Art). Seoul: Chosun Daily, 1988.

___, with Kim Bok-young and Sung Wan-kyung. "Palsimnyondae Hubaneui Hankukmisulgwa Misuleui Saeguiryu" (Korean Art in the Late '80s and New Trend of Art). *Guegan Misul* (Seoul), no. 45 (Spring 1988): 54–64.

Park Shin-eui. "Korean Contemporary Art and the Myth of Korean Dynamism." In *Fast Forward: The Vibrant Art Scene of the Republic of Korea.* Toronto: Power Plant, 1997.

Park Yong-sook. "Silhum Yesul Yuksimnyondaewa Chilsimnyondaeui Hyundaemisul" (Contemporary Korean Art in the '60s and '70s). *Gongan* (Space) (Seoul), no. 101 (October–November 1975): 76–78.

Park Young-nam. "Hankuk Silhummisuleui Siponyoneui Baljachi" (Tracing Fifteen Years of Korean Experimental Art). *Guegan Misul* (Seoul), no. 17 (Spring 1981): 89–98.

Seo Sung-rok. *Hankukeui Hyundaemisul* (Korean Contemporary Art). Seoul: Munye Publishers, 1994.

Sung Wan-kyung. "Hankuk Hyundaemisuleui Binnagan Guejeok" (Missing Traces of Korean Contemporary Art). *Guegan Misul* (Seoul), no. 14 (Summer 1980): 133–40.

___. "Two Cultures, Two Horizons." In *Min Joong Art: A New Cultural Movement from Korea,* 9–18. New York: Artists Space, 1988.

Won Dong-suk. "Chusangwa Suyongeui Kwangue" (Relationship Between the Abstract and Its Reception). *Munye Joongang* (Seoul), no. 9 (Spring 1980): 312–17.

Yoon Jin-sub. "Chilsimnyondae Hankuk Hyundaemisuleui Jeongaewa gue Yangsang" (Development of Korean Contemporary Art in the '70s and Its Aspects). *Gueganmisul Pyongdan* (Seoul), no. 21 (Summer 1991): 16–33.

___. *Konganeui Balan: Hankugeui Ypchai Sulchi Performance, 1967–1995* (Rebellion in Space: Korean Avant-garde Art, 1967–1995). Exh. cat. Seoul: Seoul City Museum, 1995.

Mainland China, Taiwan, and Hong Kong

Andrews, Julia F., and Gao Minglu. "The Avant-garde's Challenge to Official Art." In *Urban Spaces in Contemporary China: The Potential for Autonomy and Community in Post-Mao China.* Edited by Deborah S. Davis et al., 221–78. New York: Cambridge University Press, 1995.

Art chinois. Paris: Association Française d'Action Artistique, 1990.

Art Taiwan: The Contemporary Art of Taiwan. Exh. cat. Edited by Nicholas Jose and Yang Wen-i. Sydney: G+B Arts International in association with the Museum of Contemporary Art, 1995.

China: Zeitgenössische Malerei. Exh. cat. Edited by Dieter Ronte et al. Cologne: DuMont, 1996.

China/Avant-garde (*Zhongguo xiandai yishu zhan*). Exh. cat. Beijing and Guangxi: National Gallery and People's Art Press, 1989.

China Avant-garde: Counter-currents in Art and Culture. Exh. cat. Edited by Jochen Noth et al. Berlin and Hong Kong: Haus der Kulturen der Welt and Oxford University Press, 1994.

China's New Art, Post-1989/Hou pa chiu Chung-kuo hsin i shu. Exh. cat. Edited by Valerie C. Doran. Hong Kong: Hanart T Z Gallery, 1993.

Cities on the Move. Exh. cat. Edited by Hou Hanru and Hans-Ulrich Obrist. Vienna: Secession, 1997.

Clarke, David J. *Art & Place: Essays on Art from a Hong Kong Perspective.* Hong Kong: Hong Kong University Press, 1996.

Clunas, Craig. *Art in China.* New York: Oxford University Press, 1997.

Dai Jinhua. "Redemption and Consumption: Depicting Culture in the 1990s." *Positions* (Durham, N.C.) 4, no. 1 (1996): 127–43.

Des del País del Centre: Avantguardes artístiques xineses. Exh. cat. Barcelona: Centre d'Art Santa Mònica, 1995.

Dijk, Hans van. "Painting in China After the Cultural Revolution: Style Developments and Theoretical Debates, Part II: 1985–1991." *China Information* (Leiden) 6, no. 4 (Spring 1992): 1–18.

Dis/Continuity: Religion, Shamanism, Nature. Exh. cat. Edited by Huang Hai-ming. Taipei: Taipei Fine Arts Museum, 1992.

Fragmented Memory: The Chinese Avant-garde in Exile. Exh. cat. With essays by Julia F. Andrews and Gao Minglu. Columbus: Wexner Center for the Arts, Ohio State University, 1993.

Friedman, Edward. "Democracy and 'Mao Fever.'" *Journal of Contemporary China* (Princeton) 6 (Summer 1994): 84–95.

Gao Chien-huy. *Dangdai wenhuayishu sexiang* (Fine Art: An Unrefined Visual Culture in the '90s). Taipei: Artists Press, 1996.
Gao Minglu. "Meishu, quanli, gongfan: Zhengzhi popu xianxiang" (Kitsch, Power, and Complicity: The Political Pop Phenomenon) *Xiongshi Meishu* (Lion Art Monthly) 297 (November 1995): 36–57.
___, et al. *Zhongguo dangdai meishushi, 1985–1986* (History of Chinese Contemporary Art, 1985–1986). Shanghai: Shanghai People's Press, 1991.
Gebrochene Bilder: Junge Kunst aus China (Broken Pictures: Young Chinese Art). Exh. cat. Bad Honnef: Horlemann Verlag, 1991.
Hay, Jonathan. "Ambivalent Icons: Works by Five Chinese Artists Based in the United States." *Orientations* (Hong Kong) 23, no. 7 (July 1992): 37–43.
Hinterthur, Petra. *Modern Art in Hong Kong*. Hong Kong: Myer Publishing Co., 1985.
Hou Hanru. "Towards an 'Unofficial Art': De-ideologicisation of China's Contemporary Art in the 1990s." *Third Text* (London), no. 34 (Spring 1996): 37–52.
Hsiao Ch'iung-jui. *Wuyue yu dongfang: Zhongguo meishu xiandaihua yundong ziazhanhou Taiwan zhi fazhan, 1945–1970* (The Fifth Moon and Eastern Painting Groups: Chinese Modern Art Movements in Postwar Taiwan, 1945–1970). Taipei: Dongda Press, 1991.
___. "Zhanhou Taiwan meishu dashiji" (A Chronology of Postwar Taiwanese Art). *Yanhuang Yishu* (Yanhuang Art) 10–19 (1990–91).
"I Don' t Want to Play Cards with Cézanne" and Other Works: Selections from the Chinese "New Wave" and "Avant-garde" Art of the Eighties. Exh. cat. Edited by Richard E. Strassberg. Pasadena, Calif.: Pacific Asia Museum, 1991.
Jose, Nicholas. "New Wave Art." *New Asia Review* (Westport, Conn.) (Summer 1994): 18–24.
Lai Ying-ying. *Liushiniandai Taiwan fuheyishu yianjiu* (Taiwan's Multimedia Art of the Sixties). Taipei: Guotai Cultural Publisher, 1996.
Lauk'ung Chan. "Ten Years of the Chinese Avant-garde: Waiting for the Curtain to Fall." *Flash Art* 25 (January–February 1992): 110–14.
Lin Hsing-yueh. *Art in Taiwan: Forty Years' Vicissitudes.* (*Taiwan meishu fengyun sishi nian*) Taipei: Independence Evening News Publication, 1987.
Li Xianting. "Zhengzhi popu he wanshi xianshizhuyi" (Political Pop and Cynical Realism). *Meishu Xinchao* (New Wave Art) (Taiwan), no. 1 (1993).
Lu, Sheldon Hsaio-peng. "Art, Culture, and Cultural Criticism in Post–New China." *New Literary History* (Charlottesville, Va.) 28 (1997): 111–33.
___. "Postmodernity, Popular Culture, and the Intellectual: A Report on Post-Tiananmen China." *Boundary 2* (Binghamton, N.Y.) 23, no. 2 (1996): 139–69.
Lu Peng. *Zhongguo xiandai huihua shi, 1979–1989* (A History of Chinese Modern Art, 1979–1989). Changsha: Hunan Art Press, 1992.
Lufkin, Felicity. "Images of Minorities in the Art of the People's Republic of China." Master's thesis, University of California, Berkeley, 1990.
MacRitchie, Lynn. "Precarious Paths on the Mainland." *Art in America* 82, no. 3 (March 1994): 51–57.
McIntyre, Sophie. "Made in Taiwan." *Art and Asia Pacific* 3, no. 3 (1996): 83–86.
Meishu (Art Monthly). Beijing: Chinese Artists Association, 1952–.
Meishu Sichao (Trends in Art Thought). Hubei: Hubei Artists Association, January 1985–December 1987.
New Arts, New Tribes: Taiwan Art in the Nineties. Exh. cat. Edited by Victoria Lu. Taipei: Hanart T Z Gallery, 1993.
New Phase Art of Taiwan. Exh. cat. Edited by Cheng Ming-chuan. Tainan: New Phase Art Space, 1992.
Spence, Jonathan D. *The Search for Modern China.* London: Hutchinson, 1990.
The Stars: Ten Years. Exh. cat. Hong Kong: Hanart T Z Gallery, 1989.
Taiwan meishu xinfengmao, 1945–1993 (Taiwan's New Art, 1945–1993). Exh. cat. Edited by Ling Ping. Taipei: Taipei Fine Arts Museum, 1993.
Turner, Caroline, ed. *Tradition and Change: Contemporary Art of Asia and the Pacific.* St. Lucia: University of Queensland Press, 1993.
Yorke, A. "The Role of the Artist in Contemporary China: Tradition and Modern Attitudes to Art Appreciation." *Journal of the Oriental Society of Australia* (Sydney) 20–21 (1988–89).
Zha Jianying. *China Pop: How Soap Operas, Tabloids, and Bestsellers Are Transforming a Culture.* New York: New Press, 1995.
Zhang Shaoxia and Li Xiaoshan. *Zhongguo xiandai huihua shi* (The History of Modern Chinese Painting). Nanjing: Jiangsu Art Press, 1987.
Zhongguo Meishu Bao (Chinese Art). Beijing: Central Academy of Fine Arts, July 1985–May 1991.

Checklist of Works in the Exhibition

Japan

Akasegawa Genpei
A Course in Capitalist Realism (Shihon-shugi riarizumu kōza): Day 6, Period 5 (Conceptual Art Devoted to the State) (Kokka ni sasageru konsepucharu āto), 1973
Photostat of magazine pages, *Bijutsu Techō*, no. 371 (September 1973)
3 pages, each 5 11/16 x 8 1/4 in. (14.5 x 21 cm)
Collection of the artist

Akasegawa Genpei
Greater Japan Zero-Yen Notes (Dai-Nihon zero-en-satsu), 1967
Printed matter, 2 sheets
Each 5 2/3 x 12 1/8 in. (14.4 x 30.8 cm)
Collection of the artist, courtesy of Nagoya City Art Museum

Akasegawa Genpei
Invitation to "On the Ambivalent Sea" ("Aimaina umi ni tsuite" annaijō), 1963
Printed matter, 2 sheets
Each 2 15/16 x 6 3/8 in. (7.4 x 16.2 cm)
Collection of the artist, courtesy of Nagoya City Art Museum

Akasegawa Genpei
Model 1,000-Yen Notes: Printed Work (Mokei sen-en-satsu: Insatsu sakuhin), 1963
Printed matter, court envelope
11 9/16 x 7 2/3 in. (29.3 x 19.3 cm)
Collection of the artist, courtesy of Nagoya City Art Museum

Akasegawa Genpei and Company
Model 1,000-Yen Note Trial (Mokei sen-en-satsu saiben), defense evidence, 1966/99
3 color photographs
Each 18 x 12 1/8 in. (45.7 x 55.9 cm)
Queens Museum of Art, 1999.2

Akasegawa Genpei and Company/ Tokyo District Prosecutors Office
Indictment (Kisojō), 1965
Blueprint
10 x 7 1/8 in. (25.6 x 18.1 cm)
Collection of Akasegawa Genpei, courtesy of Nagoya City Art Museum

Bikyōtō (Artists Joint-Struggle Council)
An Appeal to Artists, July 5, '69, 1969
Mimeographed flier
14 3/16 x 10 in. (36 x 25.4 cm)
Collection of Hori Kosai

Bikyōtō (Artists Joint-Struggle Council)
Bikyōtō 9/15 Meeting, 1969
Poster
29 x 20 in. (73.2 x 51.8 cm)
Collection of Hikosaka Naoyoshi

Bikyōtō (Artists Joint-Struggle Council)
We Hereby Report on the Foundation of Bikyōtō and ... July 20, 1969, 1969
Mimeographed flier
14 3/16 x 10 in. (36 x 25.4 cm)
Collection of Hori Kosai

Bikyōtō Revolution Committee II
Printing Machine, 1973
Flier
7 x 10 in. (18 x 25.5 cm)
Collection of Hori Kosai

Hikosaka Naoyoshi
Floor Event (Furoa ivento), 1970–71
2 photographs (1970), postcard (1971)
Photos: each 12 1/2 x 19 5/16 in. (32 x 49 cm); postcard: 5 11/16 x 3 15/16 in. (14.5 x 10 cm)
Collection of the artist

Hikosaka Naoyoshi
Recapitulation: Phases of New Art (Hanpuku: Shinkō geijutsu no isō), 1974
Book, dustjacket
Book: 7 11/16 x 5 1/4 in. (19.5 x 13.3 cm)
Collection of the artist

Hori Kosai
Revolution: Ceiling, Wall, Floor (Revolution: Tenjō, kabe, yuka), 1971
7 sheets of wall painting; crayon, paper, 4 documentary photographs
Wall paintings: each 53 5/8 x 23 7/16 in. (90.5 x 59.5 cm); photographs: each 6 x 9 7/16 in. (15.4 x 24 cm)
Collection of the artist

Kashihara Etsutomu
Exhibition (Rumination Version), 1971/99
Mixed media installation: documents, photographs (1971); documents, boxes, objects (1999)
Overall dimensions variable
Collection of the artist

Kashihara Etsutomu
Rock, 1970
Rock, paper
6 11/16 x 8 1/4 x 2 3/8 in. (17 x 21 x 6 cm)
Collection of the artist

Matsuzawa Yutaka
Anticivilization Exhibition (Han-bunmei ten), 1965
Flier
13 5/8 x 6 15/16 in. (34.8 x 18.6 cm)
Collection of the artist

Matsuzawa Yutaka
Humans, Let's Vanish, Gate, Gate—*Anticivilization Committee (Jinrui-yo, shōmetsu shiyō, gyatei, gyatei)—Han bunmei iinkai)*, 1966–ongoing
Banner (1966)
Approx. 590 1/2 x 35 14/16 in. (1500 x 91 cm)
Collection of the artist

Matsuzawa Yutaka
Independent '64 Exhibition in the Wilderness (Kōya ni okeru andepandan '64 ten), 1964
Advertisement in *Bijutsu Journal*, no. 51 (1964)
Image: 2 3/16 x 4 1/2 in. (5.53 x 11.43 cm); page: 8 1/4 x 5 5/8 in. (20.95 x 13.97 cm)
Collection of the artist

Matsuzawa Yutaka
Postcard Paintings (Hagaki kaiga), July 1967–June 1968
3 from set of 12 postcards
Each 5 7/8 x 3 15/16 in. (15 x 10 cm)
Collection of the artist

Matsuzawa Yutaka
Ψ Corpse (Pusai no shitai itai), 1964
Flier
15 1/8 x 10 5/16 in. (39 x 26.6 cm)
Queens Museum of Art, 1999.6

Nomura Hitoshi
'moon' score, 1975–80
4 photographs; 6 photo files
Photographs: each 31 7/8 x 39 3/8 in. (81 x 100 cm); files: each 12 1/8 x 10 x 2 1/16 in. (31 x 25.5 x 5.5 cm)
National Museum of Modern Art, Tokyo

Nomura Hitoshi
'moon' score (music), 1979
CD transfer: *Particle Creation* (20' 40") for keyboard; *Tide Force* (24' 5") for violincello
Diameter 4 3/4 in. (12 cm)
Collection of the artist

Nomura Hitoshi
Telephone Eyeshot, 1970/74
2 photographs; CD; translated transcript (1999)
Photos: each 11 x 11 in. (28 x 28 cm); CD: diameter 4 3/4 in. (12 cm); transcript: 11 x 8 1/2 in. (27.9 x 21.6 cm)
Collection of the artist

1,000-Yen Note Incident Discussion Group
Invitation to the Trial (Kōhan bōchō shōseijō), 1966
Ink, rubber stamp on blueprint
10 x 7 1/8 in. (25.6 x 18.2 cm)
Collection of Akasegawa Genpei, courtesy of Nagoya City Art Museum

1,000-Yen Note Incident Discussion Group
Toward the Trial (Chronology and Appeal) (Sen-en-satsu jiken [Jiken no keika to apīru]), 1966
Flier
11 5/8 x 16 7/16 in. (29.5 x 41.8 cm)
Collection of Akasegawa Genpei, courtesy of Nagoya City Art Museum

Yoko Ono
Cut Piece at Carnegie Recital Hall, 21 March 1965
Film by Albert and David Maysles, 9 min.
Courtesy of Maysles Films, Inc., New York

Yoko Ono
Grapefruit, 1964
Book (first edition)
5 7/16 x 5 7/16 x 1 3/16 in. (13.8 x 13.8 x 3 cm)
Collection of Jeff Rothstein and Reiko Tomii

Yoko Ono
Painting in Three Stanzas, as exhibited at AG Gallery, New York (from *Instructions for Painting* series), 1961
Black-and-white photograph by George Maciunas
Image: 10 3/8 x 10 1/2 in. (26.33 x 26.57 cm)
The Gilbert and Lila Silverman Fluxus Collection, Detroit

Yoko Ono
Score for *Painting in Three Stanzas* (in the form of an exhibition label written on the back of AG Gallery announcement) (from *Instructions for Painting* series), 1961
Ink on card
3 9/16 x 10 5/8 in. (9 x 27 cm)
Collection of the artist

Yasunao Tone
Jury Event: Tone Prize Exhibition (Shinsa ivento: Tone-shō sakka-ten), 1964
Photocopy of advertisement in *Ongaku Geijutsu* (September 1964)
3 1/3 x 2 15/16 in. (8.5 x 7.4 cm)

Yasunao Tone
Jury Event: Tone Prize Exhibition (Shinsa ivento: Tone-shō sakka-ten), an entry by Hi Red Center, Cleaning Event (Chō-sōji ivento), 1964
Documentary photograph, flier
Photo: 8 x 10 in. (20.32 x 25.4 cm); flier: 7 1/8 x 10 1/4 in. (18.1 x 26 cm)
Collection of Akasegawa Genpei, courtesy of Nagoya City Art Museum

Yasunao Tone, Hikosaka Naoyoshi, and Akatsuka Yukio
Chronology: Five Decades of Contemporary Art, 1916–1968 (Nenpyō: Gendai bijutsu no 50-nen), 1972
Published in *Bijutsu Techō*, nos. 354 and 355 (April, May 1972)
Each 5 11/16 x 8 1/4 in. (14.5 x 21 cm)
Bijutsu Shuppan-sha Publisher Collection, Tokyo

Western Europe

Alighiero e Boetti
Classifying the Thousand Longest Rivers in the World, 1973
1,000-page book
8 1/2 x 2 3/16 x 2 3/16 in. (21.5 x 5.5 x 5.5 cm)
Jennifer Bacon and Filippo Fossati, Esso Gallery, New York

Giovanni Anselmo
Dissolvenza, 1970
Iron, spotlight, slide projection
14 7/16 x 10 1/4 x 7 3/4 in. (37 x 26 x 20 cm)
Collection of L. & M. Durand-Dessert, Paris

Giovanni Anselmo
Interferenza nella gravitazione universale (Interference with Universal Gravity), 1969
20 photographs
Each 2 7/16 x 2 7/16 in. (6.5 x 6.5 cm); installation: 137 13/16 (350 cm) long
Musée Départemental d'Art Contemporain de Rochechouart, France

Art & Language
Maps, 1966–67
3 maps
25 5/8 x 20 1/2 in. (65 x 52 cm); 20 x 24 in. (51 x 61 cm); 18 1/2 x 15 in. (47 x 38 cm)
Collection of Ghislain Mollet-Viéville, Paris

Marcel Broodthaers
Un coup de dés jamais n' abolira le hasard (Image), 1969
Aluminum plates
Each 12 3/4 x 9 13/16 in. (32.5 x 25 cm)
Private collection

Marcel Broodthaers
Museum, enfants non admis (Museum, Children Not Admitted), 1968–69
2 thermopressed plastic plates
Each 32 11/16 x 47 1/4 in. (83 x 120 cm)
Private collection

Stanley Brouwn
Layout for "steps" in Avalanche 4 (Spring 1972): 32–33, 1971
Photo, type, glue, board
14 3/8 x 23 in. (36.6 x 58.5 cm)
Avalanche Archives, Gilbert and Lila Silverman Collection, Detroit

Stanley Brouwn
"steps," Avalanche 4 (Spring 1972): 32–33, 1971
Printed matter
Pages: each 9 x 9 in. (23 x 23 cm)
Private collection

Stanley Brouwn
this way brouwn, 1962
4 drawings on paper
Each approx. 8 1/4 x 11 7/16 in. (21 x 29 cm)
Fonds Régional d'Art Contemporain de Picardie, France

Daniel Buren
Les formes: peintures (The Forms: Paintings), 1977
5 white and black striped canvases, the first white stripe to the left of each painted with white acrylic paint, installed underneath five paintings from the collection of the MNAM Centres Georges Pompidou: Francis Picabia, *L' oeil cacodylate* (1921), 64 15/16 x 52 9/16 in. (15 x 133.5 cm); Maurice Utrillo, *Le jardin de Montmagny* (1908–09), 25 1/5 x 33 2/3 in. (63 x 85.5 cm); Frank Kupka, *Plans verticaux I* (1912), 61 2/5 x 38 in. (156 x 99.5 cm); Amadeo Modigliani, *Tête rouge* (c. 1915), 25 2/5 x 20 9/10 in. (64.5 x 53.1 cm); Theo van Doesburg, *Composition* (1920), 57 1/2 x 26 1/7 in. (146 x 66.4 cm). Recreated QMA: Georges-Louis Hyon, *Battle Scene* (n.d.), 37 5/8 x 43 1/2 in. (95.8 x 110.5 cm); Joseph Cornell, *Untitled Collage* (c. 1967), 15 7/16 x 13 1/2 in. (39.2 x 34.3 cm); Nassos Daphnis, *Painting #17-58* (1958), 21 3/4 x 25 9/16 (55 x 64.9 cm); and from the Walker Art Center: Florine Stettheimer, *Still Life with Flowers* (1921), 31 1/4 x 36 in. (79.38 x 91.44 cm); Yasuo Kuniyoshi, *Nude in Grey Chemise* (1929), 22 1/8 x 30 1/8 in. (56.2 x 76.52 cm); Odilon Redon, *La coupe de mystère (The Chalice of Mystery)* (1890), 28 3/8 x 19 3/4 in. (72.7 x 50.16 cm).
Courtesy of the artist

Daniel Buren
4 Photo-Souvenirs:
1) "Salon de Mai," Musée d'Art Moderne de la Ville de Paris, work in situ, April 1968, Paris
2) "Hommes Sandwiches," work in situ, April 1968, Paris
3) "Affichage Sauvage," work in situ, April 1968, Paris
4) "Affichage Sauvage," work in situ, April 1968, Paris
Documentary photographs
1–3: each 4 7/8 x 7 in. (12.3 x 17.8 cm); 4: 7 x 9 1/8 in. (17.8 x 24 cm)
Collection of the artist © D.B.

Victor Burgin
Performative/Narrative, 1971
16 photographs, printed text, paper
Each 13 x 10 in. (34 x 25 cm); Framed: approx. 13 3/8 x 26 3/8 in. (34 x 67 cm)
Collection of Ghislain Mollet-Viéville, Paris

André Cadere
Histoire d' un travail, 1982
Book
11 5/8 x 8 1/4 in. (29.5 x 21 cm)
Private collection

André Cadere
Untitled, 1973
Wooden bar painted black, white, green, red
145 1/4 x 2 3/4 in. (369 x 7 cm), in 2 parts: 94 1/2 in. (240 cm), and 50 3/4 in. (129 cm) long
Collection of L. & M. Durand-Dessert, Paris

Hanne Darboven
Sechs Filme nach sechs Bucher über 1968 (Six Films after Six Books from 1968), 1968
Film, boxed catalogues, indexes, booklet; modified variation containing catalogue and 3 duplicates of original film
Dimensions variable
Stadisches Museum Abteiberg Mönchengladbach, Mönchengladbach

Guy Debord
Mémoires, 1958/1993
64-page book
10 15/16 x 8 1/4 in. (27 x 21 cm)
Private collection

Jan Dibbets
Shadows on the Floor of the Sperone Gallery, 1971
12 black-and-white photographs
Overall dimensions: 27 1/2 x 39 3/8 in. (70 x 100 cm)
Solomon R. Guggenheim Museum, New York. Panza Collection, on long-term loan to the Solomon R. Guggenheim Foundation

Luciano Fabro
Tutto trasparente (All Transparent), 1965
Glass, iron, enamel
Glass: 70 7/8 x 39 3/8 in. (180 x 100 cm); base: 62 5/8 x 38 1/4 x 28 3/8 in. (159 x 97.2 x 72 cm)
Collection of the artist

Grup de Treball (Working Group)
Recorreguts (Distances Traveled), 1973
34 photocollages, ink and impression on thin cardboard
Each 11 3/4 x 8 1/3 in. (29.9 x 21.2 cm); framed: 12 x 9 x 1 1/16 in. (31.5 x 22.9 x 2.7 cm)
Collecció MACBA. Procedent del Fons d'Art de la Generalitat de Catalunya Barcelona

Yves Klein
Certificat d' un volume de sensibilité picturale immatérielle (Receipt Book for Zones of Immaterial Pictorial Sensibility), partially used, 1959
Print, white and monochrome blue paper (originally 10 numbered receipts for 20 grams of gold)
Closed: 3 9/16 x 11 13/16 in. (9 x 30 cm); framed: 5 1/8 x 25 4/5 x 2 in. (13 x 65 x 5 cm)
Collection of Ildiko Erdes, Paris

Yves Klein
Cession de zone de sensibilité picturale immatérielle: cession à M. Blankfort/ Série no.4, zone no. 01, Paris, 2 février, 1962 (Sale of a Zone of Immaterial Pictorial Sensibility: Sale to M. Blankfort/Series no. 4, Zone no. 1, February 2, 1962) 1962
7 Photographs, documents
Photos: each 5 x 6 15/16 in. (12.6 x 17.7 cm)
Courtesy of Pierre Descargues

Yves Klein
Dimanche, 27 novembre, 1960, Le théâtre du vide, 1960
4-page illustrated newspaper
19 1/2 x 15 1/4 in. (48 x 38 cm)
The Menil Collection, Houston

Yves Klein
Immaterial Room, 1961
Photograph
5 3/16 x 4 1/8 in. (13.5 x 10.4 cm)
Collection of Museum Haus Lange, Krefeld, Germany

Yves Klein
Le saut dans le vide (Leap into the Void), 1960
Photograph by Harry Shunk
6 3/16 x 4 1/8 in. (14.1 x 10.4 cm)
Courtesy of Shunk-Kender

Yves Klein
Le Vide (The Void), April/May 1958
4 photographs, documents
Each 5 x 5 3/8 in. (12.8 x 13.8 cm)
Courtesy of Pierre Descargues

Yves Klein
Yves Klein presenting the immaterial during the opening of "Vision in Motion" (Hessenhuis, Anvers, Belgium), March 17, 1959, 1959
Photograph
Image: 5 x 6 15/16 in. (12.8 x 17.8 cm)
Courtesy of M. Charles Wilp, Düsseldorf

Piero Manzoni
8 tavole di accertamento (8 Identification Tables), 1958–62
8 lithographs on paper *(Irlanda*, 1958; *Islanda*, 1958; *2-ABCDEFG*, 1958; *Linea*, 1959; *Impronta*, 1960; *Impronta pollice sinistro*, 1962; *Impronta pollice destro*, 1962), no. 17/60
Each 19 11/16 x 13 3/4 in. (50 x 35 cm)
Hirschl & Adler Modern, New York

Piero Manzoni
Linea m. 10, dicembre 1959 (Line 10 Meters Long, December 1959), 1959
Ink, paper in cardboard cylinder
Cylinder: height 8 7/8 in. (22.5 cm); diameter 2 1/4 in. (5.7 cm)
Gilbert and Lila Silverman Collection, Detroit

Piero Manzoni
Ricevutta: Declarations of Authenticity, n° 381-400 and n° 441-460
2 paper booklets, unused
Each 6 3/8 x 2 3/4 x 3/8 in. (7 x 17 x .4 cm)
Archivio Opera Piero Manzoni, Milan

Piero Manzoni
Stamps for Declaration of Authenticity, 1961
5 sheets of colored paper stamps in green, red, burgundy, orange, gray paper
2 3/8 x 6 15/16 in (6.2 x 17.7cm)
Archivio Opera Piero Manzoni, Milan

Mario Merz
Che fare? (What Is to Be Done?), 1968
Wax, neon, metal
5 7/8 x 19 11/16 x 7 7/8 in. (15 x 50 x 20 cm)
Musée Départemental d'Art Ancien et Contemporain, Épinal, France

OPALKA
1965/1-∞, detail: 816708–843801
Tempera on canvas
77 x 53 in. (196 x 136 cm)
Collection of the artist

OPALKA
1965/1-∞, detail: 5193063–5210330
Acrylic on canvas
77 x 53 in. (196 x 136 cm)
Collection of the artist

Giulio Paolini
The Encyclopaedia Britannica (Fourteen [th] Edition, Vol. 12), 1971
Lithograph
22 3/8 x 18 7/8in. (48 x 57 cm)
Collection of the artist

Giulio Paolini
Giovane che guarda Lorenzo Lotto (Young Man Watching Lorenzo Lotto), 1967
Proof on photographic paper
9 7/16 x 11 13/16 in. (24 x 30 cm)
Collection of the artist

Gerhard Richter and Konrad Lueg
Life with Pop: A Demonstration for Capitalist Realism (Leben mit Pop: Eine Demonstration für den kapitalistischen Realismus), October 11, 1963
Documentary photograph, program: ink, paper
Photo: 6 1/3 x 9 1/4 in. (15.5 x 23.7 cm); program: 11 5/8 x 8 1/4 in. (29.5 x 21 cm)
Collection of the artist

Gerhard Richter and Konrad Lueg
Life with Pop: A Demonstration for Capitalist Realism (Leben mit Pop: Eine Demonstration für den kapitalistischen Realismus), October 11, 1963, invitation card, 1963
Ink, paper
8 1/8 x 8 7/16 in. (20.7 x 21.5 cm)
Collection of Suzanne Küper, Berlin

Sarkis, Ida Biard, David Ebony
Short documentary films on André Cadere, 1972, 1973, 1976
Videotape, 10 min., alternately black and white and color
Courtesy of the artists

Gil Wolman
L' anticoncept, September 1951 (original form: 35mm film projected onto a weather balloon, approx. 1.5 meters in diameter)
Film, approx. 70 min., black and white
Centre National d'Art et de Culture Georges Pompidou, Paris

Eastern Europe

Marina Abramović
Drawing and Positioning/Rhythm 5, c. 1970
Documentary photographs
12 x 16 in. (30 x 40 cm); 31 x 39 in. (80 x 100 cm); 12 x 20 in. (40 x 50 cm)
Sean Kelly Gallery, New York

Peter Bartoš
Nothing, Point, Shift (Nič, Bod, Posun), 1969
Photograph
19 11/16 x 23 5/8 in. (50 x 60 cm)
Slovenská Národná Galéria, Bratislava

Braco Dimitrijević
Casual passerby I met at 11:28 pm, London, 1972, 1972
Documentary photograph (original: portrait on photographic canvas, 18 x 15 ft.)
15 3/4 x 23 5/8 in. (40 x 60 cm)
Collection of the artist

Braco Dimitrijević
Casual passerby I met at 11:09 pm, Paris, 1971, 1971
Photograph (original: portrait on photographic canvas, 18 x 15 ft.)
15 3/4 x 23 5/8 in. (40 x 60 cm)
Collection of the artist

Miklós Erdély
Snow of Last Year (Tavalyi hó), 1970
Object (reconstruction)
10 x 3 9/16 in. (25.5 x 9 cm)
Miklós Erdély Foundation, Budapest

Miklós Erdély
Unguarded Money (Őrizetlen pénz), October 26, 1956
Documentary photograph, 2 color photocopies
Each 9 7/16 x 14 3/16 in. (24 x 36 cm)
Miklós Erdély Foundation, Budapest

Stano Filko, Alex Mlynárčik, Zita Kostrová
Happsoc I, Bratislava, 1965
Photographs, typewritten text
Photos: 11 3/4 x 8 in. (29.84 x 20.32 cm), 15 1/2 x 11 3/4 in. (39.37 x 29.84 cm); folder: 19 9/16 x 12 3/4 in. (40.68 x 32.38 cm)
Collection of Stano Filko

Gorgona Group
9 Identical Photos (Gorgona, no. 1, by Josip Vaništa), 1961
Book of photographs
14 3/16 x 9 7/16 in. (36 x 24 cm)
Muzej Suvremene Umjetnosti I (Museum of Contemporary Art), Zagreb, Croatia

Tibor Hajas
Restoration 2 (Pótlások 2): Restored Money (Restaurált pénz), 1976
Bank note, photograph
18 x 13 x 1 11/16 in. (45.8 x 33 x 4.3 cm)
Tibor Hajas Estate, Budapest

Tibor Hajas
Restoration 5 (Pótlások 5): Restored Money (Restaurált Huxley), 1976
Book, photograph
18 x 12 13/16 x 1 11/16 in. (45.7 x 32.6 x 4.3 cm)
Tibor Hajas Estate, Budapest

Jozef Jankovič
Project of the Monument of Slovak Sculpture (Projekt pamätníka slovenského sochárstva), 1976
Ink, oil on paper
20 x 25 3/4 in. (50 x 65 cm)
Collection of the artist

Tadeusz Kantor
The Sea Concerto (Koncert morski), 1967, signed
Documentary photograph by Eustachy Kossakowski
18 x 24 in. (45.7 x 61 cm)
Cricoteka Collection, Cracow, Poland

Július Koller
More (Sea), 1963–64
Oil on canvas
20 x 28 in. (50 x 70 cm)
Auction Company SOGA, Bratislava, Slovak Republic

Ana Lupaş
Humid Installation (Instalatie umedă), 1970
4 offset plates, 1 color plate
Each 26 x 38 in. (66 x 96 cm)
Collection of the artist

János Major
Fact Art, c. 1970
Typewritten text, black-and-white photograph
Each 8 1/4 x 6 in. (20.95 x 15.24 cm)
Collection of the artist

Juraj Meliš
4 x P, 1970
Mixed media, welded metal sculpture, drawings
Sculpture: 8 x 5 x 5 in. (21 x 12 x 12 cm); drawings: 25 x 18 in. (63 x 45 cm)
Collection of the artist

Paul Neagu
Palpable Art, 1969
Drawings, Perspex, wood, Formica
Dimensions variable
Generative Art Trust (P.N.)

OHO group
Cast Bottles (Mavčni odlitki stetlenick in drugih predmetov), 1965–68
Plaster of Paris
Dimensions variable
Collection of Marko Pogačnik, courtesy of Moderna Galerija, Ljubljana

Gyula Pauer
Pseudo, 1970
Photo, airbrush on paper
12 x 16 x 1 in. (31 x 41 x 3 cm)
Collection of László Beke, Budapest

Robert Rehfeldt
Art Worker (Contart News 1980), 1979
Lithograph
18 x 13 3/4 in. (46 x 35 cm)
Collection of Robert Rehfeldt Estate, Berlin

Józef Robakowski
In Memory of L. Brezhnev, 1982
Videotape, 10 min.
Collection of the artist

Petr Štembera
Weather Report (Information), 1971–72
17 typewritten sheets of paper
From 2 3/4 x 5 in. (6.98 x 12.7 cm) to 8 1/4 x 12 in. (22.22 x 40.48 cm)
Collection of László Beke, Budapest

Tamás Szentjóby
Czecho-Slovakian Radio 1968, 1969.
Brick with sulphur paper cover
Approx. 5 7/8 x 8 2/3 x 2 3/4 in. (15 x 22 x 7 cm)
Collection of the artist

Tamás Szentjóby
Portable Trench for Three Persons (Háromszemélyes hordozható lövészárok) , 1969
Gauze, wood, reed, sulphur, aluminum
36 5/8 x 70 7/8 x 23 5/8 in. (93 x 180 x 60 cm)
Magyar Nemzeti Galéria (Hungarian National Gallery), Budapest

Tamás Szentjóby
7 dkg of Ground Objective, 1965
Porcelain mortar, pestle, broken glass
4 x 6 x 4 in. (10 x 14 x 10 cm); diameter 4 3/4 in. (12.6 cm)
Collection of the artist

Endre Tót
Zeropost, 1976
Postage stamps on paper
Approx. 9 x 12 9/16 in. (23 x 32 cm)
Collection of László Beke, Budapest

Goran Trbuljak
"From time to time I stuck my finger through a hole in the door of the Modern Art Gallery without the management's knowledge" ("Skozi luknjo v vratih Galerije Moderne Umetnosti sem vsake toliko pomolil prst, ne da bi vodstvo galerije vedelo, kaj počnem"), 1969
Black-and-white photograph
24 x 19 3/4 in. (61 x 50 cm)
Collection of the artist

Latin America

Artur Barrio
DEFL ... —situação ... +s+ ... ruas, April 1970
Documentation in slide projections
Dimensions variable
Collection of the artist

Artur Barrio
Situação ... ORHHHHHHHHHHHH ... 5,000 ... T.E. ... EM ... NY ... city ... 1969 ... Rio de Janeiro, November/December 1969
Documentation in slide projections
Dimensions variable
Collection of the artist

Artur Barrio
SITUAÇÃO T/T, 1 (1°/2°/3° PARTES), April 1970
Documentation in slide projections
Dimensions variable
Collection of the artist

Oscar Bony
La familia obrera (Proletarian Family), 1968
Documentary photograph of performance held at Experiencias 68 Instituto Torcuato di Tella, Buenos Aires
78 3/4 x 78 3/4 in. (200 x 200 cm)
Collection of the artist

Waltércio Caldas
Condutores de percepção (Conductors of Perception), 1969
Mixed media
15 3/4 x 5 7/8 x 2 3/8 in. (40 x 15 x 6 cm)
Private collection

Waltércio Caldas
Objeto (Object) [As 7 estrelas do silencio], 1970
Mixed media
11 13/16 x 3 15/16 in. (30 x 10 cm)
Gilberto Chateaubriand Collection, Museu de Arte Moderna, Rio De Janeiro

Antonio Caro
Colombia/Coca Cola, 1976
Enamel paint, tin
22 x 31 1/2 in. (56 x 80 cm)
Museu de Arte Moderno de Bogotá

Antonio Caro
Homenaje a Manuel Quintín Lame (Homage to Manuel Quintín Lame), 1979
Ink, cardboard
55 1/8 x 39 3/8 in. (140 x 100 cm)
Collection of the artist

Ricardo Carreira
Mancha de sangre (Bloodstain), 1966
Epoxy, pigment
Overall dimensions approx. 36 x 48 x 1/2 in. (91.44 x 121.92 x 1.9 cm)
Courtesy of family of the artist

Lygia Clark
Camisa de força (Straightjacket), 1968
Mesh object with weights (reconstruction)
Dimensions variable
Estate of Lygia Clark, Rio de Janeiro

Lygia Clark
Dialogo (Dialogue of Hands), 1966
Black-and-white photograph, elastic mobius strip (reconstruction)
3 x 8 in. (7.6 x 20.3 cm)
Estate of Lygia Clark, Rio de Janeiro

Lygia Clark
Máscara-Abismo (Mask-Abyss), 1968
Mesh mask with weights (reconstruction)
Dimensions variable
Estate of Lygia Clark, Rio de Janeiro

Eduardo Costa
Fashion Fiction I, 1966–69
Gold props, photographs, text, magazines
20 x 20 in. (50.8 x 50.8 cm)
Collection of the artist

Antonio Dias
Biografia Alfaômega (Alfaômega Biography), 1968
Acrylic, canvas
74 13/16 x 149 5/8 in. (190 x 380 cm)
Collection of the artist

Antonio Dias
Oppressor/Oppressed, 1968
Wood, Formica, synthetic grass, linoleum
3 1/8 x 12 9/16 x 12 9/16 in. (8 x 32 x 32 cm)
Collection of the artist

León Ferrari
"El arca de Noé" o "El árbol embarazador" 15/2/64, 1964
Manuscript, collage
16 9/16 x 12 9/16 in. (42 x 32 cm)
Collection of the artist

León Ferrari
Carta a un general, 1963
Ink, paper
9 7/16 x 5 1/2 in. (24 x 14 cm)
Collection of the artist

León Ferrari
Cuadro escrito 17/12/64 (Written Painting 17/12/64), 1964
Manuscript
26 x 19 in. (67 x 48 cm)
Collection of the artist

León Ferrari
Palabras ajenas (Others' Words), 1967
Book
7 1/2 x 7 1/4 x 3/4 in. (10.5 x 18.42 x 1.91 cm)
Private collection

León Ferrari
Swish and Swallow, 1964
Manuscript, collage
13 3/4 x 10 5/8 in. (35 x 27 cm)
Collection of the artist

Alberto Greco
Vivo dito, 1962
Documentary photographs
Each 8 x 6 in. (20 x 15 cm)
Courtesy of Lourdes Castro and the Greco Estate

Víctor Grippo
Analogía I (Analogy I), 1970–71
Potatoes, zinc, copper electrodes, electrical wires, instrument to measure low-voltage current, push-button, text, wood
19 x 61 x 4 1/3 in. (48.5 x 155 x 11 cm)
Ruth Benzacar Galería de Arte, Buenos Aires

Víctor Grippo
Construcción de un horno popular hacer pan (Construction of a Traditional Rural Oven for Making Bread), 1972
Each 11 x 14 in. (27.9 x 35.6 cm)
Collection of the artist

Roberto Jacoby
Mensaje en el di Tella (Message at the Tella), 1968
Documentary photographs
Dimensions variable
Collection of the artist

Roberto Jacoby with Raúl Escari and Eduardo Costa
Primer manifesto y obra de "arte de los medios" (First Manifesto and Work of "Arte de los medios"), 1966
Photocopies, folder
Closed folder: 12 x 9 x 3/4 in. (30.48 x 22.86 x 1.905 cm)
Collection of the artist

David Lamelas
Límite de una proyección (Limit of a Projection), 1967
Theater spotlight in darkened area
Dimensions variable
Collection of the artist

David Lamelas
Señalamiento de tres objetos (Signaling of Three Objects), 1966
Photograph
7 15/16 x 11 15/16 in (20.2 x 30.3 cm)
Collection of the artist

Antonio Manuel
Exposição de o a 24 horas (Exhibition from 0:00 to 24:00 Hours), 1973
Newspapers
21 7/8 x 14 3/4 in. (55.5 x 37.5 cm)
Collection of the artist

Antonio Manuel
O corpo é a obra (The Body Is the Work), 1970
Documentary photographs
10 x 8 in. (25.4 x 20.32 cm)
Collection of the artist

Antonio Manuel
Urnas quentes (Hot Ballot Boxes), 1968
Wood, sealing wax, tape, photographs
23 5/8 x 13 x 7 7/8 in. (60 x 33 x 20 cm)
Collection of the artist

Mariana Marchesi and Belén Gache
Tucumán Arde, 1999
Videotape, 25 min., color
Produced by Museo Nacional de Bellas Artes and Academia del Sur (Buenos Aires) and Queens Museum of Art, New York

Cildo Meireles
Arte física: Cordões / 30 km. de linha estendidos (Art Physics: 30 km of Extended Line), 1969
Rope, map, wooden box
3,000 meters
Collection of the artist

Cildo Meireles
Espaços virtuais: Cantos II (Virtual Spaces: Corners II), 1967–68
Wood, canvas, parquet floor
120 x 39 3/8 x 39 3/8 in. (305 x 100 x 100 cm)
Galería Luisa Strina, São Paolo

Cildo Meireles
Inserções em circuitos ideológicos: Proyecto cedula (Insertions into Ideological Circuits: Banknote Project [Who Killed Herzog?]), 1973
Stamped paper currency
Dimensions variable
Collection of the artist

Cildo Meireles
Inserções em circuitos ideológicos: Proyecto Coca-Cola (Insertions into Ideological Circuits: Coca-Cola Project), 1970
Silkscreen on Coca-Cola bottles
1 3/16 x 9 5/8 in.; 1 3/16 x 2 1/4 in. (3 x 24.5 cm; 3 x 5.8 cm)
Collection of the artist

Hélio Oiticica
Bólide vidro 1 (Glass Bolide 1), 1963
Glass container, earth, pigment
15 x 3 x 3 in. (38 x 8 x 8 cm)
Projeto Hélio Oiticica, Rio de Janeiro

Hélio Oiticica
Bólide vidro 3 (Glass Bolide 3), 1964
Glass container, earth, pigment
30 x 11 x 11 in. (75 x 28 x 28 cm)
Projeto Hélio Oiticica, Rio de Janeiro

Hélio Oiticica
Parangolé, Nildo of Mangueira with P-16 Cape 12, "On Adversity We Thrive," 1967
Acrylic on canvas, plastic, newspaper, burlap, pigment, oil on wood (reconstruction)
55 x 24 x 5 in. (140 x 60 x 12 cm)
Projeto Hélio Oiticica, Rio de Janeiro

Claudio Perna
El objeto como concepto (Object as Concept), 1960–70
Photograph
9 1/2 x 6 3/4 in. (25 x 19 cm)
Collection of Biblioteca Nacional de Venezuela, Caracas

Claudio Perna
El objeto como concepto (Object as Concept), 1960–70
Photograph
6 x 9 in. (15.5 x 25.5 cm)
Collection of Biblioteca Nacional de Venezuela, Caracas

Liliana Porter
Exhibition by Mail, Instituto Torcuato di Tella, Buenos Aires, 1969
Offset prints
Each 5 x 6 1/4 in. (12.7 x 15.8 cm)
Collection of the artist

Liliana Porter
Wrinkle, 1968
10 photoengraved etchings, interview by Emmett Williams, New York Graphic Workshop
Each 17 1/4 x 19 1/4 x 1 1/4 in. (43.8 x 48.8 x 3.1 cm); title page: 29 1/2 x 19 1/4 x 1 1/4 in. (74.93 x 48.8 x 3.1 cm)
Collection of the artist

North America

Eleanor Antin
Library Science, 1972
Photographs
Each 8 1/2 x 12 1/8 in. (21.59 x 30.79 cm)
Courtesy of Ronald Feldman Fine Arts, New York

Shusaku Arakawa and Madeline Gins
The Mechanism of Meaning, (1st ed.), 1962–71; (2d ed.), 1979; (3d ed.), 1988
Exhibition catalogues
Dimensions variable
Collection of the artists

John Baldessari
Baldessari Sings LeWitt, 1972
Videotape, 15 min.
Electronic Arts Intermix, New York

John Baldessari
Cremation Project, July 24, 1970, 1970
Mixed media
Affidavit: 8 x 10 in. (20.32 x 25.40 cm); bronze urn: 9 1/2 x 8 1/4 x 3/4 in. (24.1 x 20.9 x 1.9 cm); photos, graphic: dimensions variable
Collection of the artist, courtesy of Sonnabend Gallery, New York

Theresa Hak Kyung Cha
Mouth to Mouth, 1975
Videotape, 8 min.
University of California, Berkeley Art Museum, Gift of the Theresa Hak Kyung Cha Memorial Foundation

Carol Condé and Karl Beveridge
... It's Still Privileged Art, 1976, and *Red Women's Detachment*, 1966
2 comic books
Each 4 x 7 in. (10.16 x 17.78 cm)
Private collection

Hollis Frampton
Zorns Lemma, 1970
Film, 60 min., color, sound
Anthology Film Archives, New York

Harry Gamboa, Jr.
Decoy Gang War Victim. No Movie, 1976
Documentation of conceptual performance in slide projection
Dimensions variable
© 1975 Harry Gamboa, Jr.

Harry Gamboa, Jr.
Pistol Whippersnapper, 1976
Photos, layout boards
Dimensions variable
Collection of Stanford University Libraries, Stanford University Permanent Collection, Palo Alto

Hans Haacke
Milwaukee Visitors' Profile, 1971
Computer printouts
Questionnaire: 14 x 8 1/2 in. (35.56 x 21.59 cm); tabulated answers: 11 x 14 7/8 in. (37.62 x 27.94 cm)
Hans Haacke © VG Bild-Kunst

Douglas Huebler
Variable Piece 4: Secrets, 1973
Book
8 1/2 x 5 3/8 in. (21.25 x 13.33 cm)
Queens Museum of Art, 1999.3

Robert Huot
Robert Huot at Paula Cooper (Exhibition Catalogue), March–April 1969
Page spread from offset catalogue, printed in black
7 5/16 x 7 5/16 in. (20.1 x 20.1 cm); book closed: 7 15/16 x 7 15/16 in. (20.16 x 20.16 cm)
The Museum of Modern Art Library, New York

On Kawara
Postcards, I got up at... 1968
10 postcards
Each approx. 3 5/8 x 6 1/2 in. (9.20 x 16.51 cm)
LeWitt Collection, courtesy of the Wadsworth Atheneum, Hartford, Conn.

On Kawara
Telegram,"I am still alive" (From Hiroshima 1991 Jul 25)
Print on paper
8 1/2 x 11 in. (21.59 x 28 cm)
Collection of Andrea Rosen

On Kawara
Telegrams, "I am still alive" (stamped: 1970 Feb 5 pm 2:32 and Feb 11 pm 3:20)
Print on paper
5 3/4 x 8 in. (14.69 x 20.32 cm)
LeWitt Collection, courtesy of the Wadsworth Atheneum, Hartford, Conn.

Mary Kelly
Post-Partum Document Introduction, 1973
Perspex units, white card, wool vests, pencil, ink
4 units, each 8 x 10 in. (20 x 25.5 cm)
Collection of Eileen and Peter Norton, Santa Monica

Joseph Kosuth
Titled (Art as Idea as Idea) [meaning], 1967
Photostat on paper mounted on wood
47 x 47 in. (119 x 119 cm)
The Menil Collection, Houston

Christine Kozlov
Information: No Theory, 1970
Tape recorder, statement
Statement: 8 1/8 x 7 1/4 in. (20 x 18 cm); tape recorder: dimensions variable
Collection of the artist

Sol LeWitt
Four Basic Kinds of Lines and Colour, 1969
Book
7 3/4 x 7 3/4 in. (19.68 x 19.68 cm)
Queens Museum of Art, 1999.4

Sol LeWitt
"Sentences on Conceptual Art" (Art-Language 1, no. 1 [May 1969])
Printed journal
11 1/2 x 8 1/8 in. (28.18 x 20.62 cm)
Collection of Terry Smith

Lucy Lippard
C. 7,500, 1973
Exhibition catalogue: 30 printed index cards
Each 4 x 6 in. (10.16 x 15.24 cm)
Collection of Lesley Dick, Los Angeles

Lee Lozano
General Strike Piece, Feb. 8, 1969, 1969
Graphite, ink, paper
8 1/2 x 11 in. (21.59 x 27.94 cm)
Wadsworth Atheneum, Hartford, Conn., Alexander A. Goldfarb Contemporary Art Acquisition Fund

Yoko Ono and John Lennon
WAR IS OVER IF YOU WANT IT! Love and Peace from John & Yoko, 1969–1970
Offset on paper
29 7/8 x 20 in. (76 x 55.5 cm)
Collection of Yoko Ono

Adrian Piper
Hypothesis Situation #19, 1969–70
Text, chart, photocollage
Dimensions variable
Collection of the artist

Martha Rosler
Semiotics of the Kitchen, 1975
Videotape, 6:09 min. black and white, sound
Electronic Arts Intermix, New York

Seth Siegelaub (editor and publisher) and John W. Wendler
Carl Andre, Robert Barry, Douglas Huebler, Joseph Kosuth, Sol LeWitt, Robert Morris, Lawrence Weiner (a.k.a. *Xeroxbook*), December 1968
Book of photocopies
11 x 8 1/2 x 1 in. (27.9 x 21.5 x 2.5 cm)
Walker Art Center Library, Minneapolis

Michael Snow
Walking Woman, 1965
Page from *Village Voice*, February 4, 1965
Page size: 16 1/2 x 11 1/2 in. (41.91 x 29.21 cm)
Collection of the artist

Michael Snow
Wavelength, 1966–67
Film, 16mm, 45 min.
Anthology Film Archives, New York

Vincent Trasov (Mr. Peanut)
Campaign for Mayor of Vancouver, Off the Air Coverage; My Five Years in a Nutshell; The Rise and Fall of the Peanut Party, 1974–75
Videotapes, book
Book: 9 x 6 in. (22.86 x 15.24 cm)
Collection of Morris/Trasov Archives, Morris and Helen Belkin Art Gallery, University of British Columbia

Lawrence Weiner
Statement in Arts Magazine, April 1970
Print on paper
Approx. 5 5/8 x 7 in. (14.5 x 18 cm)
New Museum of Contemporary Art, New York

Joyce Wieland
True Patriot Love, Véritable amour patriotique, 1971
Exhibition catalogue
10 1/4 x 7 x 3/4 in. (26.3 x 17.78 x 1.9 cm)
Queens Museum of Art, 1999.5, gift of the National Gallery of Canada, Ottawa

Australia and New Zealand

Barrie Bates (Billy Apple)
Young Contemporaries 1962, 1961
Offset lithograph on canvas (printed by Roy Crossett, Royal College of Art)
20 x 30 in. (50.8 x 76.2 cm)
Collection of the artist

Art & Language
9 Gross and Conspicuous Errors, 1975
Videotape
Collection of Terry Smith

Gordon Bennett
Untitled (Dismay, Displace, Disperse, Dispirit, Display, Dismiss), 1989
Oil, synthetic polymer paint on 6 canvases
Each 11 13/16 x 11 13/16 in. (30 x 30 cm)
Museum of Contemporary Art, Sydney

Ian Burn and Mel Ramsden
Soft-Tape, 1966/90
Tape recorder, photostat
Photostat: 35 7/16 x 35 7/16 in. (90 x 90 cm)
Courtesy of Avril Burn and Mel Ramsden

Ian Burn, Mel Ramsden, and Terry Smith
"Draft for an Anti-Textbook" (Art-Language 3, no. 1 [September 1974], special issue)
11 1/2 x 8 1/8 in. (28.18 x 20.62 cm)
Collection of Terry Smith

Philip Dadson
Earthworks—Timezone Map of the World, Timezone Chart, 1971
Videotape, color map mounted on board
Map: 35 7/16 x 49 3/16 in. (90 x 125 cm)
Collection of the artist

Mike Parr and Peter Kennedy
Idea Demonstrations, 1972
Film, 16mm, 40 min., black and white and color, optical sound
Collection of Mike Parr

Soviet Union

Ilya Kabakov
Answers of the Experimental Group (Otvety eksperemental' noi gruppy), 1970–71
Mixed media, Masonite
59 x 122 in. (150 x 310 cm)
The John L. Stewart Collection, New York

Ilya Kabakov
Primakov Sitting in a Closet (Vskafusidiaschii Primakov), 1972/94
Album (facsimile, 1994)
21 x 14 x 5 in. (83.34 x 35.56 x 12.7 cm)
Collection of Ilya and Emilia Kabakov

Vitaly Komar and Aleksandr Melamid
Documents: Ideal Document (Dokumenty: Ideal' ny dokument), 1975
13 Plexiglas panels, text, 3 photographs
Overall: 48 x 60 in. (122 x 152 cm)
Collection of the artists

Vitaly Komar and Aleksandr Melamid
Hamburgers "Pravda" (Kotlety "Pravda"), 1975
3 mounted silver gelatin prints, ground newspaper in Plexiglas box on painted wooden pedestal
Overall: 50 1/2 x 11 3/8 x 11 1/4 in. (131 x 29 x 28.5 cm); prints: 15 3/4 x 15 3/4 x 1 1/4 in. (49 x 49 x 3 cm), 15 3/4 x 19 3/8 x 1 1/4 in. (40 x 49 x 3 cm)
Jane Voorhees Zimmerli Art Museum, Rutgers, the State University of New Jersey, Gift of Norton and Nancy Dodge

Boris Mikhailov
Unfinished Dissertation (Nezakonchennaia dissertatsiia), 1983–84
25 of a series of 180 photographs, paper, text
Each 8 1/4 x 11 13/16 in. (21 x 30 cm); installation dimensions variable
Collection of the artist

Andrei Monastyrskii and Collective Actions Group
Investigation of Documentation, 1976–83
Cardboard panels, each with 9 black-and-white photographs; videotape, table, chair
Panels: each 39 1/4 x 39 1/4 in. (99.6 x 99.6 cm)
Collection of the artists, courtesy of Victor and Margarita Tupitsyn

Irina Nakhova
Room (Komnata) No. 2, 1984
Photographic documentation, model of installation
Model: 40 x 40 x 30 in. (101.6 x 101.6 x 76.2 cm); photos: 11 x 14 in. (27.94 x 35.56 cm)
Collection of the artist

Africa

Willem Boshoff
Bangboek (The Book That Is Afraid), 1977–81
Ink, paper, Masonite
55 1/8 x 60 1/4 in. (140 x 153 cm); each column 13 7/16 x 4 13/16 in. (34.2 x 12.3 cm)
Billiton, Marshalltown, South Africa

Willem Boshoff
Kleinpen I (The Small Pen I), 1979
6 manuscript pages: ink, paper, microscopic writing
Each 8 1/2 x 6 7/16 in. (21.59 x 16.25 cm)
Ruth and Marvin Sackner Archive of Concrete and Visual Poetry, Miami

Willem Boshoff
Kykafrikaans, 1980
95-page book
14 11/16 x 11 in. (37.33 x 27.88 cm)
Ruth and Marvin Sackner Archive of Concrete and Visual Poetry, Miami

Willem Boshoff
Skynbord, 1979
Paint samples, Masonite, paper, pen, ink
48 x 71 13/16 in. (122 x 182.5 cm)
Collection of the artist

Frédéric Bruly Bouabré
Le musée du visage africain (The Museum of the African Face), 1975
39 pairs of drawings, colored pencil on cardboard
Each 5 15/16 x 4 3/16 in. (15 x 11 cm); framed pair: 8 5/8 x 11 13/16 in. (22 x 30 cm)
Galeria Jule Kewenig, Frechen

Frédéric Bruly Bouabré
Le musée du visage africain (The Museum of the African Face), 1975
Book with 172 original drawings and texts
11 13/16 x 8 1/2 x 1 3/16 in. (30 x 21 x 3 cm)
Contemporary African Art Collection (C.A.A.C), in collaboration with André Magnin, courtesy of Frédéric Bruly Bouabré

Frédéric Bruly Bouabré
West African Alphabet (The Bété), 1982
Manuscript
9 1/16 x 6 5/16 x 3/8 in. (23 x 16 x 1 cm)
Contemporary African Art Collection (C.A.A.C), in collaboration with André Magnin, courtesy of Frédéric Bruly Bouabré

Kendell Geers
Brick, 1988
Mixed media installation
4 x 8 3/4 x 3 in. (10.5 x 22 x 8 cm)
Private collection

Kendell Geers
Death Certificate, 1961–88
Found object
24 x 19 1/4 in. (35 x 23 cm)
Private collection

Kendell Geers
Untitled (ANC, AVF, AWB, CP, DP, IFP, NP, PAC, SACP), July 19, 1993–February 7, 1994
Printed ID cards, Plexiglas box
Cards: various dimensions; box: 4 3/8 x 5 7/8in. (11.11 x 14.92 cm)
Collection of the artist

Rachid Koraïchi
From *A Nation in Exile*, 1979–82
7 prints
Each 30 3/8 x 18 1/2 in. (77 x 47 cm)
Courtesy of Galerie Corinne Maeght, Paris

Malcolm Payne
Color Test, 1973–74
Screenprint
33 7/8 x 47 5/8 in. (86 x 121 cm)
Collection of Willem Strydom

Malcolm Payne
Good Mourning; Good Night, 1973
Slide projections
Dimensions variable
Collection of the artist

Courtesy of Galeria Corrine Maeght, Paris
Malcolm Payne
No title, 1974/99
Mirror, mosquito net, Braille on aluminum, screenprint (reconstruction)
Approx. 8 1/4 x 11 13/16 in. (21 x 30 cm)
Collection of the artist

Malcolm Payne
Rorschach Test, 1973–74/99
Screenprint on government geological maps (reconstruction)
63 x 86 5/8 in. (160 x 220 cm)
Collection of the artist

South Korea

Choi Byung-soo
Design of Funeral Procession for the Six Suicides, May 1991
Ballpoint drawing on paper, photographic documents
Variable dimensions
Collection of the artist

Choi Byung-soo
Funeral Procession for Lee Han-ryul, 1987
Ballpoint drawing on paper, photographic documents
Drawing: 2 9/16 x 3 15/16 in. (6.5 x 10 cm); number, dimensions of photographs variable
Collection of the artist

Kim Bong-joon and others
Catalogues for traveling exhibition for the labor unions, 1989
Books
Dimensions variable
Collection of the artist

Kim Dong-won
Sanggyedong Olympics, 1986
Videotape, 27 min.
Private collection

Kim Yong-min
Floor, 1975
Photographs, mixed media installation
Photos: each 9 13/16 x 14 3/4 in. (25 x 37.5 cm)
Collection of the artist

Kim Yong-tae
Pictures from the Dongduchon Photograph Salons, 1984
Found photographs
Each 5 x 7 in. (12.7 x 17.78 cm); overall dimensions variable
Collection of the artist

Labor Newsreel (Labor News Production)
Fired Workers, 1989/97
Video, VHS, 105 min.
Private collection

Labor Newsreel (Labor News Production)
Report on General Strike, 1 & 2, 1989/97
Video, VHS, 30 min.
Private collection

Park Bul-dong
Cohwacayomcolbyungla (Coca-Cola-Cocktail-Molotov), 1988
Mixed media
2 3/4 x 13 3/4 in. (7 x 35 cm)
Collection of the artist

Park Bul-dong
Nightmare No. 1, No. 2, No. 3 (Electoral Campaign Posters), 1985
Photo and text collages on paper
Each 15 3/4 x 21 2/3 in. (40 x 55 cm)
Collection of the artist

Sung Neung-kyung
Newspaper: After the 1st of June 1974, 1974
Wood, paint, newspaper, acrylic
24 13/16 x 34 1/4 x 2 3/16 in. (63 x 87 x 5.5 cm); boxes: 25 5/8 x 35 13/16 x 27 9/16 in. (65 x 91 x 70 cm)
Collection of the artist

Sung Neung-kyung
Performance: Reading Newspapers, 1976
Photographs on panels
Each 10 5/16 x 10 5/16 x 3/4 in. (26.2 x 26.2 x 2 cm)
Collection of the artist

Mainland China, Taiwan, Hong Kong

Chang Chaotang
Headless Self-Portrait (Wutou zihuaxiang), 1962
Photograph
42 1/8 x 41 1/8 in. (107 x 107 cm)
Collection of the artist

Geng Jianyi
Investigative Forms (Diao chabiao), 1988
Ink, type, photographs on 28 sheets of paper
Each 15 x 11 in. (38.7 x 26.9 cm)
Collection of Andreas Schmid, Berlin

Wenda Gu
pseudo characters of "still" written by three men and three women (san nan san nu shu xie de jing zi), 1986
Ink, acrylic on rice paper, mounted on silk scroll
150 1/2 x 78 in. (382.27 x 198.12 cm)
Collection of Zhen Guo, New York

Huang Huacheng
Washing Hands (Xishou), 1966
Wooden chair, steel washbasin (reconstruction)
Dimensions variable
Collection of the family of the artist

Huang Yong Ping
The Beard Was Easiest to Burn (Huzi zhiyi ranshao), 1986
4 photocopies
3: 11 3/4 x 8 3/8 in. (29.85 x 22.23 cm); 1: 11 3/4 x 8 3/8 in. (29.85 x 21.1 cm)
Collection of the artist

Huang Yong Ping
Drawing the National Art Gallery Away (Tozou zhongguo meishuguan), 1988
Color photographs on paper
11 5/8 x 8 1/4 in. (29.53 x 20.95 cm); 11 1/2 x 8 1/8 in. (28.58 x 20.64 cm)
Collection of the artist

Huang Yong Ping
Dust (Zhentu), 1987
Paper, wooden box
39 3/8 x 59 x 78 3/4 in. (100 x 150 x 200 cm)
Collection of the artist

Huang Yung-sung
Pawn (Dang), 1967
Clay seal, various found objects
Dimensions variable
Collection of the artist

Song Yongping and others
The Country Project (Xiangcun yishu huodong), 1987
Photographic and video documentation of performance
Collection of the artist

Wei Guangqing
Suicide Series (Zisha xilie), October 1988
18 documentary photographs
Each 20 7/16 x 18 7/8 in. (52 x 48 cm)
Collection of the artist

Wu Shan Zhuan
Red Humor (Hongse youmo): Big Characters (Dazibao), Swearing, 1987
Photographic documentation
Dimensions variable
Collection of the artist

Wu Shan Zhuan
Red Humor (Hongse youmo): Big Characters (Dazibao): (Sentence), (Red Seal), (Garbage and Nirvana), 1987
Photo documentation
Dimensions variable
Collection of the artist

Xiao Lu and Tang Song
Dialogue (Duihua), installation in "China/Avant-garde" exhibition (Zhongguo xiandai yishuzhan), Beijing, 1989, 1989
Video documentation
Collection of Wen Pulin

Xu Bing
Five Series of Repetition (Wuge fushu xilie), 1987
Woodcuts
387 x 380 1/2 in. (982.98 x 966.47 cm); images: each 29 1/8 x 13 in. (74 x 33 cm)
Collection of the artist

Danny Ning Tsun Yung
To Serve the People (Wei renmin fuwu), 1982
Videotape
Collection of the artist

Zhang Peili
Art Plan #2 (Yishujihua erhao), 1987
20-page book, print on paper
10 1/2 x 7 3/4 in. (26.67 x 19.69 cm)
Collection of Gao Minglu

Index

Lenders to the Exhibition

Artists in the exhibition and: Akasegawa Genpei, courtesy of Nagoya City Art Museum; Anthology Film Archives, New York; Archivio Opera Piero Manzoni, Milan; Auction Company SOGA, Bratislava; Avalanche Archives, Gilbert and Lila Silverman Collection, Detroit; Zuzana Bartošová; László Beke; Ruth Benzacar, Buenos Aires; Biblioteca Nacional de Venezuela, Caracas; Bijutsu Shuppan-sha, Ltd., Tokyo; Billiton, Marshalltown; Avril Burn and Mel Ramsden; Lourdes Castro; Centre National d'Art et de Culture Georges Pompidou, Paris; Col·lecció MACBA, Procedent del Fons d'Art de la Generalitat de Catalunya, Barcelona; Contemporary African Art Collection (C.A.A.C.), in collaboration with André Magnin, courtesy of Frédéric Bruly Bouabré; Cricoteka Collection, Cracow; Lesley Dick, Los Angeles; L. & M. Durand-Dessert, Paris; Electronic Arts Intermix, New York; Miklós Erdély Foundation, Budapest; Ildiko Erdes, Paris; Jennifer Bacon and Filippo Fossati—Esso Gallery, New York; Estate of Lygia Clark, Rio de Janeiro; Ronald Feldman Fine Arts, New York; Stano Filko; Fonds Régional d'Art Contemporain de Picardie, Amiens; Solomon R. Guggenheim Foundation; Gao Minglu; Generative Art Trust (P.N.); Gilberto Chateaubriand Collection, Museu de Arte Moderna, Rio de Janeiro; Zhen Guo; Tibor Hajas Estate, Budapest; Hikosaka Naoyoshi; Hirschl & Adler Modern, New York; Hori Kosai; Ilya and Emilia Kabakov; Sean Kelly Gallery, New York; Galerie Jule Kewenig, Frechen (Cologne); Suzanne Küper, Berlin; LeWitt Collection, courtesy of the Wadsworth Atheneum, Hartford, Conn.; Galerie Corinne Maeght, Paris; Magyar Nemzeti Galéria (Hungarian National Gallery), Budapest; The Menil Collection, Houston; Moderna Galerija, Ljubljana; Ghislain Mollet-Viéville, Paris; Morris/Trasov Archives, Morris and Helen Belkin Art Gallery, University of British Columbia, Vancouver; Musée Départemental d'Art Ancien et Contemporain, Épinal; Musée Départemental d'Art Contemporain de Rochechouart, France; Museo de Arte Moderno, Bogotá; Museum Haus Lange, Krefeld; Museum of Contemporary Art, Sydney; Museum of Modern Art Library, New York; Muzej Suvremene Umjetnosti (Museum of Contemporary Art), Zagreb; National Gallery of Canada, Ottawa; National Museum of Modern Art, Tokyo; Eileen and Peter Norton, Santa Monica; Yoko Ono; Panza Collection, Varese; Mike Parr; Projeto Hélio Oiticica, Rio de Janeiro; Robert Rehfeldt Estate, Berlin; Andrea Rosen; Jeff Rothstein and Reiko Tomii; Ruth and Marvin Sackner Archive of Concrete and Visual Poetry, Miami; Andreas Schmid; Gilbert and Lila Silverman Collection, Detroit; The Gilbert and Lila Silverman Fluxus Collection, Detroit; Terry Smith; Sonnabend Gallery, New York; Stadisches Museum Abteiberg Mönchengladbach; Stanford University Libraries, Stanford University Permanent Collection, Palo Alto; The John L. Stewart Collection, New York; Galería Luisa Strina, São Paolo; Willem Strydom; Victor and Margarita Tupitsyn; University of California, Berkeley Art Museum, The Theresa Hak Kyung Cha Memorial Foundation; Wadsworth Atheneum, Hartford, Conn., Alexander A. Goldfarb Contemporary Art Acquisition Fund; Walker Art Center Library, Minneapolis; John Weber Gallery, New York; Wen Pulin; Peter Wollen; Jane Voorhees Zimmerli Art Museum, Rutgers, the State University of New Jersey, Gift of Norton and Nancy Dodge

Queens Museum of Art

Photo Credits

p. 2: © 1998 The Museum of Modern Art, New York.
p. 7: (Tatlin) Courtesy of Annely Juda Fine Art, London. (Duchamp) © 1999 The Museum of Modern Art, New York.
p. 8: Photos by Jack Abraham
p. 10: Courtesy of Stephen Bann.
p. 11: Courtesy of Wenda Gu.
p. 14: Photo by Hanaga Mitsutoshi.
p. 19: Photo by Arnold Kanarvogel.
p. 21: (Tone) Photo by Arnold Kanarvogel. (Hi Red Center) Courtesy of Nagoya City Art Museum.
p. 22: Courtesy of Nagoya City Art Museum.
p. 24: Photos courtesy of Nomura Hitoshi.
p. 30: © Pierre Descargues.
p. 35: (*Un coup de dés jamais*) Photo: Marina Gilissen. (*Museum*) Private collection.
p. 36: Photo Saman.
p. 37: © Gianfranco Gorgoni, Estate of Robert Smithson, courtesy of John Weber Gallery, New York.
p. 38: Courtesy of John Weber Gallery, New York.
p. 40: Courtesy of Miklós Erdély Foundation, Budapest.
p. 43: Courtesy of Jozef Jankovič.
p. 44: (Meliš) Anna Mičnohová. (Štembera) Photo by Arnold Kanarvogel.
p. 45: (Koller, Bartoš) Courtesy of Slovak National Gallery, Bratislava.
p. 46: (Major) Courtesy of János Major. (Pauer) Courtesy of László Beke. (Hajas) Courtesy of Tibor Hajas Estate.
p. 47: (Tót, Szentjóby) Courtesy of László Beke.
p. 48: Courtesy of László Beke.
p. 49: Braco Dimitrijević Archive.
p. 50: Photo by Arnold Kanarvogel.
p. 53: Courtesy of León Ferrari.
p. 55: Photos courtesy of Graciela Carnevale, Rosario, Argentina.
p. 56: Photos by Wilton Montenegro.
p. 57: Photos by Mercedes Casanegra.
p. 59: Courtesy of Cildo Meireles.
p. 60: (Oiticica) Photo Carlos. (Morro de Mangueira) Photo by Desdémone Bardin.
p. 61: Courtesy of Greco Estate.
p. 62: Courtesy of the artist and Galerie Lelong, New York.
p. 63: Courtesy of the Estate of Lygia Clark.
p. 64: Courtesy of Liliana Porter.
p. 65: Oscar Monsalve.
p. 66: Photo by Oscar Bony.
p. 72: The Menil Collection, Houston.
p. 74: Fredrik Nilsen.
p. 76: Printed with permission of Lawrence Weiner.
p. 77: Courtesy of Barry Rosen and Jaap Van Liere Modern and Contemporary Art, New York.
p. 79: Courtesy of Adrian Piper.
p. 80: Courtesy of Electronic Arts Intermix, New York.
p. 81: (Wieland) Photo by Arnold Kanarvogel. (Snow) Courtesy of Anthology Film Archives, New York.
p. 82: Courtesy of Anthology Film Archives, New York.
p. 83: Courtesy of Art Museum, University of California, Berkeley, The Theresa Hak Kyung Cha Memorial Foundation.
p. 84: Photo by Arnold Kanarvogel.
p. 86: Courtesy of Mike Parr and Peter Kennedy.
p. 88: Courtesy of Terry Smith.
p. 89: Printed by Roy Crossett, Royal College of Art, London.
p. 90: Photo by Jenni Carter.
p. 91: Courtesy of Mike Parr.
p. 92: Govett-Brewster Gallery, New Plymouth, N.Z.
p. 93: Photo by Geoff Stevens.
pp. 98, 100, 101: Courtesy of Ilya Kabakov.
p. 102: Photos by Georgii Kizeval'ter.
p. 103: Courtesy of Vitaly Komar and Aleksandr Melamid.
p. 104: Courtesy of Boris Mikhailov.
p. 105: Photo by Georgii Kizeval'ter.
p. 108: Courtesy of Willem Boshoff.
p. 110: Courtesy of Contemporary African Art Collection (C.A.A.C.), in collaboration with André Magnin, courtesy of Frédéric Bruly Bouabré
p. 111: Courtesy of Malcolm Payne.
p. 112: Photo by E. Harvey, 1994.
p. 113: Photo by Arnold Kanarvogel.
p. 114: Courtesy of Willem Boshoff.
p. 115: Courtesy of Kendell Geers.
p. 116: Courtesy of Malcolm Payne.
p. 118: Photo by Park Bul-dong.
p. 120: Photo by Kim Yong-min.
p. 121: Photo by Park Bul-dong.
p. 122: Courtesy of Kim Bong-joon.
p. 123: Courtesy of Choi Byung-soo.
p. 126: Photo by Arnold Kanarvogel.
p. 128: Courtesy of family of Huang Huacheng.
p. 129: Courtesy of Chang Chaotang.
p. 130: Courtesy of Huang Yung-sung.
p. 131: Danny Ning Tsun Yung.
p. 133: (Wu) Courtesy of Red Humor International. (Xu) Photo by Arnold Kanarvogel.
p. 134: Photos by Arnold Kanarvogel.
p. 135: Courtesy of Huang Yong Ping.
p. 136: Courtesy of Xiao Lu and Tang Song.
p. 137: Courtesy of Song Haidong.
p. 142: Courtesy of Jim Supangkat.
p. 145: (Dono, Harsono) Courtesy of Cementi Gallery, Yogyakarta, Indonesia. (Bose) Photo by Apinan Poshyananda.
p. 146: Courtesy of Montien Boonma.
p. 147: Courtesy of Kamol Phaosavasdi.
p. 151: Photo by Arnold Kanarvogel.
p. 152: (*Painting in Three Stanzas*) Photo by George Maciunas, print by Oren Slor, courtesy of The Gilbert and Lila Silverman Fluxus Collection, Detroit. (Score) Courtesy of the artist and Jon Hendricks.
p. 153: Photo by D. James Dee, courtesy of Jon Hendricks.
p. 154: Photo by Arnold Kanarvogel, courtesy of Matsuzawa Yutaka.
p. 155: Courtesy of Nagoya City Art Museum.
p. 156: Photo by Arnold Kanarvogel.
p. 157: (*Exhibition*) Photo by Narita Hiromu, courtesy of Gallery 16, Kyoto. (*Rock*) Courtesy of Kashihara Etsutomu.
p. 158: Courtesy of Nomura Hitoshi.
p. 159: Courtesy of Gallery Te, Tokyo.
p. 160: Photo by Hikosaka Naoyoshi.
p. 161: Courtesy of Claude Gintz.
p. 162: Courtesy of Ildiko Erdes.
p. 163: Courtesy of The Gilbert and Lila Silverman Collection, Detroit.
p. 164: (Photo documentation) Courtesy of Gerhard Richter. (Program) Photo by Arnold Kanarvogel.
p. 165: Courtesy of L&M Durand-Dessert, Paris.
p. 166: Courtesy of Claude Gintz.
p. 167: Photo: Marina Gilissen.
p. 168: Courtesy of L&M Durand-Dessert, Paris.
p. 169: Courtesy of Giovanni Paolini.
p. 170: Courtesy of Daniel Buren.
p. 171: Conseil Général de la Haute-Vienne, Musée Départemental d'Art Contemporain de Rochechouart.
p. 172: Courtesy of John Weber Gallery, New York.
p. 173: Photo by D. James Dee.
p. 174: Museu d'Art Contemporani, Barcelona.
p. 175: Photo by Eustachy Kossakowski.
p. 176: Courtesy of László Beke.
p. 177: Braco Dimitrijević Archive.
p. 178: Courtesy of Goran Trbuljak.
p. 179: Courtesy of Moderna Galeria, Ljubljana; photo by Matija Pavlovec and Lado Mlekuz.
p. 180: Magyar Nemzeti Galéria (Hungarian National Gallery), Budapest.
p. 181: Courtesy of Marina Abramović Foundation.
p. 182: Courtesy of Ana Lupaş.
p. 183: Photos by Roberto Cecato.
p. 184: Photos by Cèsar Carneiro and Luis Alphonsus.
p. 185: Courtesy of Ruth Benzacar Galería de Arte, Buenos Aires.
p. 186: Photo by René Bèrtholo.
p. 187: Courtesy of Oscar Bony.
p. 188: Courtesy of the Estate of Lygia Clark.
p. 189: Photo by Claudio Oiticica.
p. 190: Courtesy of León Ferrari.
p. 191: Oscar Monsalve.
p. 192: © Richard Avedon, model Marissa Berenson.
p. 193: Courtesy of Antonio Manuel.
p. 194: Kelly Barrie.
p. 195: Courtesy of Sonnabend Gallery, New York.
p. 196: Printed with permission of Sol LeWitt.
p. 197: Photo by Arnold Kanarvogel; reproduced by permission of the Siegelaub Collection & Archives.
p. 198: Photo by D. James Dee.
p. 199: Photo by Arnold Kanarvogel.
p. 200: Courtesy of Hans Haacke © VG Bild-Kunst.
p. 201: Printed by Roy Crossett, Royal College of Art, London.
p. 202: Courtesy of Mike Parr and Peter Kennedy.
p. 203: Courtesy of Mel Ramsden.
p. 204: © Gordon Bennett.
p. 205: Courtesy of Ilya Kabakov.
p. 206: Courtesy of Vitaly Komar and Aleksandr Melamid.
p. 207: Photo by Georgii Kizeval'ter.
p. 208: Courtesy of Boris Mikhailov.
p. 209: Courtesy of Malcolm Payne.
p. 210: Courtesy of Willem Boshoff.
p. 211: Courtesy of Contemporary African Art Collection (C.A.A.C.), Jean Pigozzi Collection, Geneva.
p. 212: Courtesy of Sung Neung-kyung.
p. 213: Courtesy of Park Bul-dong.
pp. 214–15: Photos by Peter McClennan. Courtesy of Artists Space, New York.
pp. 216–17: Courtesy of Choi Byung-soo.
p. 218: Courtesy of Wenda Gu.
p. 219: Courtesy of Red Humor International.
p. 220: Photo by Arnold Kanarvogel.
p. 221: Video still, courtesy of Song Yongping.
p. 222: Courtesy of Wei Guangqing.
p. 223: Courtesy of Nagoya City Art Museum.
p. 224: Photo by Shunk-Kender.
p. 225: Photo by Bernard Prud'homme.
p. 226: Photo by György Czele.
p. 228: Photo by Sobre Billetes, courtesy of the artist and Galerie Lelong, New York.
p. 230: © 1969 Paula Cooper Gallery, courtesy of Museum of Modern Art, New York, 21.228.
p. 233: Courtesy of Józef Robakowski.
p. 238: Courtesy of Wei Guangqing.
p. 240: (Akasegawa) Courtesy of Nagoya City Art Museum. (Antin) Courtesy of Ronald Feldman Gallery, New York.
p. 241: (Baldessari) Courtesy of Electronic Arts Intermix, New York. (Barrio) Cèsar Carneiro and Artur Barrio.
p. 242: Courtesy of Willem Boshoff.
p. 243: Photo: Marina Gilissen.
p. 244: (Cadere) Photo Banco. (Cha) Courtesy of Art Museum, University of California, Berkeley, The Theresa Hak Kyung Cha Memorial Foundation.
p. 245: Courtesy of the Estate of Lygia Clark.
p. 246: (Dias) Photo by Roberto Cecato.
p. 247: (Filko) Courtesy of Stano Filko. (Gamboa) Courtesy of Harry Gamboa, Jr.
p. 248: Museu d'Art Contemporani, Barcelona.
p. 249: (Hikosaka) Photo by Yasunao Tone. (Hori) Photo by Hikosaka Naoyoshi.
p. 250: Photo by Arnold Kanarvogel.
p. 253: Photo: Juan Lepez.
p. 254: (Manuel) Photo Carlos. (Matsuzawa) Photo Win Riemens.
p. 255: Photo by Wilton Montenegro.
p. 256: (Nakhova) Photo by Georgii Kizeval'ter. (Oiticica) José Oiticica Filho. (1,000-Yen Note Incident Discussion Group) Courtesy of Nagoya City Art Museum.
p. 257: (Pauer) Courtesy of Gyula Pauer. (Perna) Courtesy of Claudio Perna.
p. 260: Courtesy of Morris/Trasov Archives, Morris and Helen Belkin Art Gallery, University of British Columbia.
p. 261: Courtesy of Red Humor International.

Contributors

Project Directors

Jane Farver is Director of Exhibitions, Queens Museum of Art, and former director of Lehman College Art Gallery, City University of New York, Bronx New York; assistant director/curator at the Alternative Museum, New York; and director of Spaces Gallery, Cleveland. She has curated numerous exhibitions of contemporary art, including *Out of India: Contemporary Art of the South Asian Diaspora*; *Cai Guo-Qiang, Projects for the 20th Century: Cultural Melting Bath*; *Across the Pacific: Contemporary Korean and Korean American Art*; *Yukinori Yanagi: Project Article Nine*; *Luis Camnitzer: Retrospective*; and *Adrian Piper: Reflections, 1967–1987*.

Luis Camnitzer, artist, critic, and professor of art at the State University of New York, Old Westbury, has authored numerous books and articles, including *New Art of Cuba* (1994), *Los San Patricios* (1993), "Art, Politics, and the Evil Eye," *Third Text* (1992), and "Cultural Identities Before and After the Exit of Bureau-Communism," *The Hybrid State* (1992). He edited a special issue of *Art Journal* (Winter 1992) entitled "Latin American Art" (College Art Association).

Rachel Weiss is Chair of the Program in Arts Administration and Director of Exhibition Studies at the School of the Art Institute of Chicago, and curator of *Cambio de Foco; Ante América: Regarding America*; *The Nearest Edge of the World: Art and Cuba Now*; *Imagining Antarctica*; *From a Moment of Truth: Works on Paper from Bulgaria*; and *Among Africas/In Americas*. Her book *Por América: La obra de Juan Francisco Elso* is forthcoming from the Instituto de Investigaciones Estéticas, Universidad Nacional Autónomo de México.

Curators/Essayists

Stephen Bann is professor of Modern Cultural Studies at the School of Drama, Film, and Visual Arts, University of Kent, Canterbury, and has held honorary appointments at the Australian National University, Canberra; Commonwealth Center for Literary and Cultural Change, University of Virginia; and Center for the Study of Modernism, University of Texas, Austin, among others. His publications include *Paul Delaroche: History Painted* (1997); *Romanticism and the Rise of History* (1995); and *The True Vine: On Visual Representation and the Western Tradition* (1989).

Japan. **Chiba Shigeo** is a curator at the National Museum of Modern Art, Tokyo. He is a specialist in postwar Japanese art and is the author of *Gendai bijutsu itsudatsu-shi, 1945–1985* (A History of Deviations in Contemporary Art; 1986) and *Bijutsu no genzai chiten* (The Present Place of Art; 1990). **Reiko Tomii** is currently working on a book-length study of Hikosaka Naoyoshi. She has been senior research associate at the Center for International Contemporary Arts, a lecturer in Japanese at major New York museums, a translator of numerous art texts, and an editor of Japanese-subject exhibition catalogues. She is a contributor to the catalogues for *Japanese Art After 1945: Scream Against the Sky* and *Cai Guo-Qiang, Projects for the 20th: Century Cultural Melting Bath*.

Western Europe. **Claude Gintz**, art critic and independent curator, organized *L'art conceptuel, une perspective* for the Musée d'Art Moderne de la Ville de Paris (1989). His publications include *Regards sur l'art americain des années soixante* (1979) and *Ailleurs et autrement* (1993).

Eastern Europe. **László Beke**, art critic and curator, was formerly chief curator at the Hungarian National Gallery in Budapest, and is now director of the Mücsarnok Palace of Art in Budapest. As a participant in various art movements of the 1960s, he amassed a large archive of materials which has been deposited at ArtPool. Beke is a contributor to *Art in Nature* (1996) and *Beyond Belief: Contemporary Art from East Central Europe* (1995), and the author of numerous books and articles on art theory and criticism.

Latin America. **Mari Carmen Ramírez** is Curator of Latin American Art at the Jack S. Blanton Museum of Art, University of Texas, Austin, and was formerly director of the Museum of Anthropology, History, and Art at the University of Puerto Rico. She was curator of *Cantos Paralelos: Visual Parody in Contemporary Argentinean Art* and *Re-Aligning Vision: Alternative Currents in South American Drawing*, both traveling exhibitions, and has written extensively on contemporary Latin American art and culture.

North America. PETER WOLLEN is professor of film studies and chair of the Department of Film and Television at University of California, Los Angeles. As a curator, he has organized *Frida Kahlo and Tina Modotti*; *Komar and Melamid*; *Nan Goldin: The Ballad of Sexual Dependency*; *On the Passage of a Few People Through a Rather Brief Moment in Time: The Situationist International, 1957–1972*; and *Addressing the Century: 100 Years of Art and Fashion*. His books include *Signs and Meaning in the Cinema* (1998), *Raiding the Icebox: Reflections on Twentieth-Century Culture* (1993), and *Singin' in the Rain* (1992). He co-edited *Visual Display* (1995) and *Howard Hawks, American Artist* (1996), and scripted Michelangelo Antonioni's film *The Passenger*. With Laura Mulvey, he wrote and directed *Penthesilea, Riddles of the Sphinx*, *AMY!*, *Crystal Gazing*, and *The Bad Sister*.

Australia and New Zealand. TERRY SMITH is an author and artist who exhibited with Art & Language in London and Australia in the 1970s. His publications include *Constructing Art & Language: Australia, 1975* (1976), *Australian Painting* (1990), *Making the Modern: Industry, Art, and Design in America* (1993); and *In Visible Touch: Modernism and Masculinity* (1997). Smith is professor of contemporary art at the Power Institute, Center for art and Visual Culture, University of Sydney.

Soviet Union. MARGARITA TUPITSYN is the author of numerous articles and books on 20th-century Soviet art, including *Margins of Soviet Art: Socialist Realism to the Present* (1989). She curated the groundbreaking *Sots Art* exhibition at the New Museum of Contemporary Art, New York (1986), as well as *The Green Show* (1990) and *Damaged Utopia* (1995). Her most recent books and exhibitions include *El Lissitzky: Beyond the Abstract Cabinet* and *Aleksandr Rodchenko: The New Moscow*.

Africa. OKWUI ENWEZOR is artistic director for Documenta XI, Kassel, and Adjunct Curator of Contemporary Art at the Art Institute of Chicago. From 1996–98 he was artistic director of the 2nd Johannesburg Biennale. He is the founder and editor of *Nka: Journal of Contemporary African Art* (Ithaca, N.Y.). Enwezor has curated a range of international exhibitions, including *In/sight: African Photographers, 1940–Present* in New York, and *Mirror's Edge* in Helsinki. He is the editor, with Olu Oguibe, of *Reading the Contemporary: African Art from Theory to the Marketplace* (1999).

South Korea. SUNG WAN-KYUNG is an art critic and professor of art theory at University of Inha. He has written numerous articles on modern art and visual culture, and curated many exhibitions, including *Min Joong Art: A New Cultural Movement from Korea* (New York, 1988). Sung has served as a commissioner for the last two Kwangju biennials, and his recent books include *Min Joong Art, Modernism, and Visual Culture: A Critical Reflection on the Context of Korean Modern Art* (1998) and *Photography and Society* (1999).

Mainland China, Taiwan, and Hong Kong. GAO MINGLU is a critic, art historian, and former editor of *Meishu* (Art) in Beijing. He has authored numerous publications, including *Zhongguo dangdai meishushi, 1985–86* (The History of Contemporary Art; 1991), and was chief curator of *China/Avant-garde* (Beijing, 1989), *Inside Out: New Chinese Art* (New York, 1998), and co-curator of *Fragmented Memory: The Chinese Avant-garde in Exile* (1993). He is currently a doctoral candidate in art history at Harvard University.

South and Southeast Asia. APINAN POSHYANANDA is associate professor and associate dean for research and foreign affairs on the Faculty of Fine and Applied Arts, Chulalongkorn University, Bangkok. He has been a curator and juror for international exhibitions in Sydney, Brisbane, Perth, Johannesburg, Osaka, Sapporo, Jakarta, and Istanbul, and has written extensively on the subject of South and Southeast Asian art. Poshyananda is the author of *Modern Art in Thailand: Nineteenth and Twentieth Centuries* (1992) and curator of *Contemporary Art in Asia: Traditions/Tensions* (1996).